THE **WEE GUIDE** TO
SCOTLAND

A CONCISE HISTORY WITH
1250 HERITAGE SITES TO VISIT

GOBLINSHEAD

Musselburgh

THE **WEE GUIDE** TO
SCOTLAND

First Published 2002
© Martin Coventry 2002

Published by GOBLINSHEAD
130B Inveresk Road
Musselburgh EH21 7AY Scotland
tel 0131 665 2894; *fax* 0131 653 6566
email goblinshead@sol.co.uk

British Library Cataloguing in Publication Data
A catalogue record for this book is available from the British Library.

ISBN 1 899874 28 3

Typeset by GOBLINSHEAD using Desktop Publishing
Printed by Polestar AUP in Aberdeen, Scotland

Written, printed and published in Scotland.

If you would like a colour catalogue of our publications please contact:
Goblinshead, 130B Inveresk Road,
Musselburgh EH21 7AY, Scotland, UK.

Disclaimer:

THE **WEE GUIDE** TO
SCOTLAND

Contents

Acknowledgements

Thanks to everyone who has been so kind and helped with the book, supplied illustrations or checked entries.

Particular thanks to Allan Devlin for Threave Castle (front cover) and Doug Houghton for (in the order they appear in the book) Brodgar, Eildon Hills, Clickimin, Ruthwell Cross, Jarlshof, Grey Cairns of Camster, Cuween Hill, Maes Howe, Knowe of Yarso, Taversoe Tuick, Corrimony, Stenness, Gurness, Midhowe, Nigg, Strathpeffer Eagle Stone, St Andrews Cathedral, Scalloway Castle, and Click Mill, Dounby. Also to Dilys Jones for Burns Cottage, Burns' Mausoleum, Canongate Cemetery, and Ellisland.

Thanks also to all those who provided illustrations for the following places (in the order they appear in the book): Dalmeny Parish Church; New Lanark; The Tall Ship at Glasgow Harbour; Andrew Carnegie Birthplace Museum; Queen's Cross Church; Highland Folk Museum; Summerlee Heritage Trust; Gordon Highlanders Museum; Scottish Crannog Centre; Tomb of the Eagles (Isbister); Groam House Museum; Abercorn Church and Museum; Netherton Cross; Pluscarden Abbey; Dunkeld Cathedral; Rosslyn Chapel; St Monans Parish Church; St John's Church, Edinburgh; Burntisland Parish Church; Kilmun Church; Stobo Kirk; Symington Parish Church; Thirlestane Castle; Blair Castle; Braemar Castle; Lauriston Castle; Storehouse of Foulis; Royal Yacht Britannia; Ayton Castle; Bowhill; Mellerstain; Dunninald; Fergusson Gallery, Perth; Scott Monument; Fordyce Joiner's Workshop; Northfield Farm Museum; Barony Mills, Birsay; Laidhay Croft Museum; Shetland Croft Museum; Glenlivet Distillery; Benromach Distillery; Edradour Distillery; Clydebuilt; Alford Valley Railway; Edinburgh Canal Centre; Shambellie House Museum of Costume; McManus Galleries, Dundee; Motherwell Heritage Centre; Inveraray Jail; Highland Museum of Childhood, Strathpeffer. Copyright remains with the above.

Thanks to Julie, Dorothy and Lindsay Miller for checking the maps (all mistakes please send for their attention), and to Dr Joyce Miller for reading over the manuscript. Thanks also to Hilary Horrocks at the NTS and those at the various area tourist boards who were so helpful, and to everyone who returned proofs.

Note

Historic Scotland (HS) and The National Trust for Scotland (NTS) manage many of Scotland's finest monuments. If you intend to visit many of these, you should consider joining both organisations, even if just on economic grounds – benefits include free or reduced admission, extending to properties managed by English Heritage and The National Trust. Contact information for both can be found on page 278 and opposite page 1.

Introduction

Scotland has hundreds of great places to visit, and some of the most impressive, diverse and picturesque monuments and buildings to be found anywhere in Europe. These range from the magnificent prehistoric sites of Skara Brae, Maes Howe, Brodgar and Callanish, through Iron Age brochs, Roman remains, enigmatic Pictish symbol stones, fine early Christian crosses, sprawling abbeys, mighty castles, rich palaces, elegant and stately mansions. There is also a wealth of folk, fishing and industrial museums, illustrating the lives of ordinary folk down the ages. Whisky is Scotland's most famous export, and there are many accessible distilleries, as well as excellent art galleries, gardens, churches, healing wells, grave slabs, hill forts and local museums – and dozens of sites associated with Macbeth, St Margaret, William Wallace, Robert the Bruce, Mary Queen of Scots, Bonnie Prince Charlie, Robert Burns and Sir Walter Scott.

In this book, all these places to visit have been brought together into one handy and practical guide, covering more than 1250 sites.

The book begins with a concise but detailed history, which highlights sites and puts them into a historical context. This is followed by themed sections, guiding the reader to places that they will find of interest. Full information on location, opening times, visitor facilities and contact details is provided, plus a full index and simple maps. This makes the book an invaluable guide for all those who wish to experience the diversity of Scotland's wonderful heritage at first hand.

Scotland has hundreds of great places to visit, and this book should ensure the reader gets the most from the nation's great history and heritage.

Martin Coventry
Musselburgh
June 2002

Written, printed and published in Scotland.

How to Use the Book

The Wee Guide to Scotland is easy to use, and is divided into four parts:
- **History**
- **Places to Visit**
- **Maps**
- **Index**

History (pages 1-50)

The first part is a concise history, covering all the main events and people who shaped Scotland. It is arranged chronologically, beginning with prehistoric times and ending with the present.

Places to visit are highlighted in bold, giving the name of the place and the 'place code'. These can then be looked up in the places to visit sections, which list further related sites, and on the maps. The place code is in the form of a letter and number in square brackets. The letter refers to the section which contains the place and the number to its order (For example, on page 5 – **Midhowe [D51]**: **D** is for Brochs, Forts and Duns; **51** is the 51st entry in this section).

People, battles, events and all places to visit in the history are listed in the index.

Places to Visit (pages 51-277)

The second part lists all the places to visit. These are arranged thematically into sections, such as ***D***: *Brochs, Forts and Duns*; ***S2***: *Gardens*; or ***X***: *Industry and Transport*. Each of these sections is given a letter (a full list follows on page viii) which forms the beginning part of the place code. Many places, however, fall into more than one section, and these are cross-referenced. For each place, there is a main entry, but there may also be several cross-references in other sections.

At the top of each page, in the running heads, are the codes for places on that page (ie on page 77 for **Midhowe [D51]** – Brochs, Forts and Duns **D48-D56**).

Measurements are given in feet (0.3 metres), yards (0.9 metres) and miles (1600m/1.6km).

The main entry consists of the:
- place code (such as D51, A9, S56 or X17)
- name of the place
- whether the place is managed by Historic Scotland (HS) or The National Trust for Scotland (NTS): contact details appear for these opposite page 1 and on page 278
- directions, including Wee Guide to Scotland map (such as Map 2) and grid box reference (of the form B2); location; and National Grid Reference and OS Landranger sheet number
- Description of the place
- Facilities, such as gift shop, tearoom, disabled access and indication of admission price – (£=under £3.50; ££= £3.50-£5.00; £££=£5.00+)
- Opening days and times
- Contact information, including telephone, fax, email and website (where available)

Cross-references refer to the main entry, which has full information on facilities, directions, opening and contact details. If not listed in the main entry, contact details for Historic Scotland (HS) and The National Trust for Scotland (NTS) sites appear opposite page 1 and on page 278.

Illustrations follow at the end of most places to visit sections (for Midhowe on page 80).

Maps (pages 278-296)

The third part starts with a list of, and contact information for, area tourist boards and Historic Scotland (HS) and The National Trust for Scotland (NTS).

Scotland is divided into nine maps. The place code is used on the map (D51, A9, S56 or X17). The maps are also divided into grids to find places. (Midhowe D51 is on map 2 grid box B2)

Locations on the maps are very approximate and are for guidance only. National grid references are given for most sites, and these should be used if a precise location is needed.

On the page facing each map is a list of all the places on that map. This list is sorted alphabetically and has the place code (for example, to find the place in the Places to Visit section use D51 for Midhowe), the name of the place, and its grid box reference on the map.

Index (pages 297-308)

The fourth part is a full index. All the places in the places to visit sections are in the index, as well as famous people, events and battles. Entries in bold refer to places which can be visited, and bold page numbers refer to the main entry for that place.

All the information on the places to visit in the text – including location, opening, facilities and contact information – have been checked (where possible) with the sites themselves, area tourist boards, Historic Scotland and The National Trust for Scotland. Information, however, is subject to change, and should only be used for guidance.

Summary

If you are interested in **brochs** in general, and **Midhowe Broch** in particular:

• Consult the index from page 297-308 for **brochs**: this is given as page 5
• Look this up. There is a brief description of **brochs** on page 5, followed by a list of some of the most accessible, including **Midhowe Broch [D51]**. The section also directs the reader to Section **D**: *Brochs, Forts and Duns* (which begins on page 72)
• Look up **D51** using the running heads at the top of the page: **Midhowe Broch** is on page 77
• Alternatively, consult section **D**, which begins on page 72, and concludes with illustrations of the places in that section on pages 79-80
or
• Using the contents page, go straight to **D**: *Brochs, Forts and Duns* (pages 72-80)
or
• Look up **Midhowe Broch** in the index. There are two references: page 5 and page **77**, the latter bold. A bold page number refers to the main entry for that place to visit

---

Warning

The majority of sites listed in the book are open as visitor attractions. A few places, however, such as ruined castles, duns, forts, cairns and churches, are in inaccessible and potentially dangerous locations. These should not be visited without assessing the risk – taking into account weather, footwear, footing, the state of the ruin, difficult access, fitness and any hazards. Particular care should always be taken with children. The inclusion of a site should not be taken as an indication that access is available. If there is any doubt, information should be checked locally with Tourist Information Centres or landowners.

Places to Visit Codes

The index includes a complete list of all the places to visit.

THE **WEE GUIDE** TO
SCOTLAND

Tourist Boards

VisitScotland
23 Ravelston Terrace, Edinburgh, EH4 3TP
Tel: 0131 332 2433   Fax: 0131 315 4545
Email: info@visitscotland.com
Web: www.visitscotland.com

Aberdeen & Grampian (Map 4, pages 286-7)
Aberdeen and Grampian Tourist Board
27 Albyn Place, Aberdeen AB10 1YL
Tel: 01224 288828   Fax: 01224 581367
Email: info@agtb.org   Web: www.castlesandwhisky.com

Angus & City of Dundee (Map 4, pages 286-7)
Angus & City of Dundee Tourist Board
21 Castle Street, Dundee DD1 3AA
Tel: 01382 527527   Fax: 01382 527551
Email: enquiries@angusanddundee.co.uk
Web: www.angusanddundee.co.uk

Argyll, the Isles, Loch Lomond, Stirling, Trossachs (Map 5, pages 288-91)
Argyll, the Isles, Loch Lomond, Stirling & Trossachs
Tourist Board
7 Alexandra Parade Dunoon PA23 8AB
Tel: 01369 703785   Fax: 01369 706085
Email: info@scottish.heartlands.org
Web: www.visitscottishheartlands.org

Ayrshire & Arran (Map 6, pages 292-6)
Ayrshire & Arran Tourist Board
Unit 2, 15 Skye Road, Prestwick KA9 2TA
Tel: 01292 678100   Fax: 01292 471832
Email: info@ayrshire-arran.com
Web: www.ayrshire-arran.com

Dumfries and Galloway (Map 6, pages 292-6)
Dumfries & Galloway Tourist Board
64 Whitesands, Dumfries DG1 2BR
Tel: 01387 253862   Fax: 01387 245555
Email: info@dgtb.ossian.net
Web: www.dumfriesandgalloway.co.uk

Edinburgh & Lothians (Map 6, pages 292-6)
Edinburgh & Lothians Tourist Board
3 Princes Street, Edinburgh EH2 2QP
Tel: 0131 473 3800   Fax: 0131 473 3881
Email: esic@eltb.org   Web: www.edinburgh.org

Greater Glasgow & Clyde Valley (Map 6, pp 292-6)
Greater Glasgow & Clyde Valley Tourist Board
11 George Square, GLASGOW G2 1DY
Tel: 0141 204 4400   Fax: 0141 221 3524
Email: enquiries@seeglasgow.com
Web: www.seeglasgow.com

Highlands of Scotland (Map 3, pages 282-5)
The Highlands of Scotland Tourist Board
Peffrey House, Strathpeffer IV14 9HA
Tel: 01997 421160   Fax: 01997 421168
Email: info@host.co.uk   Web:
www.highlandfreedom.com

Kingdom of Fife (Map 6, pages 292-6)
Kingdom of Fife Tourist Board
70 Market Street, St Andrews KY16 9NU
Tel: 01334 472021   Fax: 01334 478422
Email: fife.tourism@kftb.ossian.net
Web: www.standrews.com/fife

Orkney (Map 2, pages 280-1)
Orkney Tourist Board
6 Broad Street, Kirkwall, Orkney KW15 1NX
Tel: 01856 872856   Fax: 01856 875056
Email: info@otb.ossian.net   Web: www.visitorkney.com

Perthshire (Map 5, pages 288-91)
Perthshire Tourist Board
Lower City Mills, West Mill Street, PERTH PH1 5QP
Tel: 01738 627958   Fax: 01738 630416
Email: info@perthshire.co.uk
Web: www.perthshire.co.uk

Scottish Borders (Map 6, pages 292-6)
Scottish Borders Tourist Board
Murray's Green, Jedburgh, Roxburghshire TD8 6BE
Tel: 0870 863435   Fax: 01835 864099
Email: info@scot-borders.co.uk
Web: www.scot-borders.co.uk

Shetland Islands (Map 1, pages 280-1)
Shetland Islands Tourism
Market Cross, Lerwick, Shetland ZE1 0LU
Tel: 01595 693434   Fax: 01595 695807
Email: shetland.tourism@zetnet.co.uk
Web: www.visitshetland.com

Western Isles (Map 3, pages 282-6)
Western Isles Tourist Board
26 Cromwell Street, Stornoway, Isle of Lewis, HS1 2DD
Tel: 01851 703088   Fax: 01851 705244
Email: stornowaytic@witb.ossian.net
Web: www.witb.co.uk

The National Trust for Scotland
Wemyss House, 28 Charlotte Square, Edinburgh EH2 4ET
Tel: 0131 243 9300   Fax: 0131 243 9301
Email: information@nts.org.uk   Web: www.nts.org.uk

Historic Scotland
Longmore House, Salisbury Place, Edinburgh EH9 1SH
Tel: 0131 668 8800   Fax: 0131 668 8888
Email: hs.explorer@scotland.gsi.gov.uk
Web: www.historic-scotland.gov.uk

The First Peoples of Scotland

10,000 BC First people arrive (Middle Stone Age – Mesolithic)

Not much is known about the first settlers who came to Scotland after the last Ice Age. Evidence is restricted to tools, weapons and middens. These first incomers were nomads, who lived in caves (such as **Smoo Cave [A22]**) on the coast or rough shelters, and used tools of stone, flint, antler and bone. They ate what they could find or catch: deer, wild pigs, birds, eggs, berries, nuts and often shellfish – some of their middens contain millions of shells. Beyond the coast were forests covering much of the land, so they travelled by boat as journeys by foot would have been slow, difficult and possibly dangerous. Many wild animals, which are now extinct, roamed Scotland, such as bears and wolves. Places with Scottish wildlife and animals can be found in section **V2**.

A huge pit of hazelnut shells was found during excavations on Colonsay, one of the islands off the west coast of Scotland. This suggests that the people were managing groves of hazelnut trees rather than just depending on what they could find.

4000–2300 BC First people settle (New Stone Age – Neolithic)

About 4000 BC, settlers began to arrive and farm in Scotland, bringing with them domestic animals like dogs, cattle, sheep, goats and pigs; and cereal crops, such as wheat and barley. This new way of life involved forest clearance, although these settlers also depended on hunting and fishing. Stone and flint, antler and bone were used for tools and weapons including arrowheads, knives and axes; and they were skilled at making decorated pots, many of which have been found in their tombs.

Their settlements have left little or no trace – apart from a few caves – except in the Northern Isles, where there are remains of settlements at **Skara Brae [A21]**, **Barnhouse [A3]** and **Knap of Howar [A10]** on Orkney, and **Pettigarth's Field [A15]**, **Scord of Brouster [A19]**, **Jarlshof [D45]** and **Staneydale [A23]** on Shetland. These are built of fine dry-stone masonry.

These settlers created elaborate chambered tombs, finely built and engineered, covered by a cairn of stones, to bury their dead. These cairns take

Skara Brae – Neolithic village

many different forms, some having a single chamber, reached by a passageway, with smaller chambers off; some having a longer chamber, divided by stone slabs into stalls; and at least two have burial chambers one above the other.

An outstanding chambered cairn is at **Maes Howe [B31]**, and there are many other good chambered and stalled cairns in Orkney: **Blackhammer [B3]**, **Cuween Hill [B17]**, **Dwarfie Stane [B20]**, **Holm of Papa Westray [B24]**, **Isbister [B25]**, **Knowe of Yarso [B28]**, **Midhowe [B34]**, **Quoyness [B37]**, **Taversoe Tuick [B41]**, **Unstan [B46]**, **Vinquoy Hill [B48]** and **Wideford Hill [B50]**. Other fine cairns elsewhere include **Barpa Langass [B2]**, **Cairn o' Get [B7]**, **Cairnpapple Hill [B9]**, **Clava Cairns [B12]**, **Cnoc Freiceadain [B14]**, **Corrimony**

Clava Cairns – atmospheric burial cairns and stone circles

[B17], **Dun Bharpa [B18]**, and **Nether Largie Cairns** [B36] in Kilmartin Glen.

Practices in burying the dead seem to have varied with place and time: in some the remains were cremated before being buried; in others the body was simply interred; while in others thigh bones or skulls were collected together.

These tombs were used for hundreds of years, previous burials often being moved aside, and many had forecourts where it is assumed rituals took place. Pottery and grave goods were also buried with the bodies, and in some of the tombs in Orkney the remains of oxen, dogs or sea-eagles have also been found.

The settlers of this time also built henges and erected standing stones and stone circles, like those at **Ballymeanoch [C9], Balfarg [C4], Conon Bridge [C23], Machrie Moor [C42]**, and the **Stones of Stenness [C51]**. Henge monuments consist of an area enclosed by a ditch and bank, some of which have stone circles, such as the Stones of Stenness and **Ring of Brodgar [C47]**. Many sites are in spectacular prominent locations with excellent views.

In some cases, these stones were later decorated with cup and ring marks, which are found in many places throughout Scotland, although usually on natural rock faces. Collections of marks can be found at **Achnabreck [C2], Ballygowan [C8], Baluachraig [C10], Braids [C12], Cairn-baan [C13], Drumtroddan [C28], High Banks [C31], Kilmichael Glassary [C34]**, and **Loch Clachaig [C38]**.

Standing stones continued to have great significance thousands of years after they were erected. Holed standing stones were used for contracts, including handfasting. A couple could live as man and wife for a year and a day, and then marry or go their separate ways without any blame or complication, except that any child from their union should be provided for.

The **Kempock Stone [C33]** at Gourock was circled by newlyweds for good luck and by fishermen to ensure favourable winds.

2300-500 BC Copper and bronze come into use (Bronze Age)

Trade developed between the settlers in Scotland and the rest of the British Isles and the Continent, and there appears to have been a relatively large and increasing population.

By this time, copper or bronze weapons and implements had begun to be used, although many were still made of wood or bone. Gold was also used for decorative items, such as armlets, cloak pins and dress fasteners. Many artefacts survive from this period as copper, bronze and gold do not corrode as readily as iron from the later Iron Age.

These people lived in round houses, which now only survive as hut circles, or indentations, in the ground, such as those at **New and Old Kinord [A13]**. The walls were either of turf or stone, and a wooden post held up a thatched roof. A central hearth contained a fire for cooking and warmth. Remains of their field systems also survive, as do the heaps of stones which were removed to improve fields for ploughing.

Burials were now in a cist, or stone box, with a stone lid. The body was placed in the grave in a crouched position, usually with a food pot. Cremations replaced inhumations towards the end of the Bronze Age, the burnt bones being deposited in cinerary urns, many of which survive. This pottery is of a characteristic type, hard and thin, red in colour, and decorated with a tooth-like ornamentation. Some have distinguished these settlers as the Beaker People, suggesting they were incomers from the Continent.

Kilmartin Glen in Argyll has a fabulous group of prehistoric monuments, consisting of burial cairns, with cists inserted, and settings of standing stones in a progression down the valley, many within easy walk of each other. Sites include **Achnabreck [C2], Ballygowan [C8], Baluachraig [C10], Ballymeanoch [C9], Cairnbaan [C13], Dunadd [D38], Dunchraigaig [B19], Glebe [B21], Kilmartin [L12], Kilmichael Glassary [C34], Nether Largie [B36], Ri Cruin [B38]** and **Temple Wood [C55]**.

Many stone circles were built, or rebuilt at the same site, including the magnificent circle at the **Ring of Brodgar [C47]**, the stones at **Callanish [C15]**, and some of the circles at **Machrie Moor [C42]**. The stones at Callanish on Lewis have been interpreted as being a lunar observatory. The main site consists of a cross-shaped arrangement of stones, but there are many other outlying circles and settings, including **Ceann**

Ring of Brodgar – most impressive circle in Scotland

Hulavig **[C18]** and **Cnoc Fillibhir Bheag [C22]**.

There are other impressive circles at **Lochbuie [C39]** on Mull, **Lundin Links [C41]**, **Pobull Fhinn [C45]** on North Uist, **Torhouse [C58]** and **Twelve Apostles Circle [C60]**, this latter circle one of the largest in the UK with a diameter of 280 feet. A variation in design in the north-east of Scotland is to have a recumbent stone with two flanking stones in the circle, like **Easter Aquorthies [C29]**, **Loanhead of Daviot [C37]**, **Midmar [C61]**, **Sunhoney [C54]**, and **Tom-naverie [C57]** from which there are spectacular views.

Rows of stones at **Achavanich [C1]** and **Hill o' Many Stanes [C32]** are also thought to have been used for astronomical purposes. There are also stone settings and tall single stones well worth a visit – the full listing is in Section **C**.

Stone circles are associated with burials, cairns being built within or near the circles, such as at Callanish, **Clava Cairns [B12]** and **Cairnpapple Hill [B9]**. Clava Cairns, near Inverness, is one of the most atmospheric of settings for a prehistoric monument. There are round burial cairns and rings of standing stones, surrounded by trees and woods, giving the whole place a brooding feeling.

1000-400 BC Influx of Celtic peoples and the Iron Age

Around 1000 BC the climate seems to have deteriorated, and become colder and wetter. About this time, the first Celtic peoples (as they have become known) arrived in Scotland, people who may have shared a common language and religion. They built hill forts and lived in enclosed settlements with roundhouses, and their societies seem to have been divided into families or clans, led by a chief or king. **Archaeolink [A1]** features a reconstructed roundhouse and field system, although at least people in the Bronze or Iron Age did not have to contend with the scourge of rabbits. There is another reconstructed Iron Age roundhouse at **Bosta [A4]**.

There are many hill forts throughout Scotland. Often these consist of a series of ramparts surrounding a hill or cutting off a promontory; or alternatively dry-stone walls, without mortar, were built, some with a timber frame. This latter feature of the walls may have led to vitrification:

Eildon Hills – location of a large hill fort

it is assumed that the intense heat from burning the timber, either deliberately or during a siege, fused the stone.

Some of these enclosures are small, and could hold no more than one family; while others, such as those at **Castlelaw [D12]**, **Chesters [D13]**, **Dreva Craig Fort [D16]**, **Dunadd [D38]**, **Dun Nosebridge [D29]**, **Dunsinane Hill [D40]**, **Eildon Hill [D42]**, **Mither Tap o' Bennachie [D52]**, **Tap o' Noth [D60]**, **Traprain Law [D62] and Brown [D5]** and White [D65], could contain a whole town, with workshops as well as houses. Many other impressive hill forts are listed in Section **D**.

These forts were probably more to protect against a sudden onslaught or to make a striking impression, rather than a protracted siege, as many have no apparent water supplies. Others are in very poor defensive sites, although the defences themselves are very elaborate with several ramparts and walls.

Crannogs, small defensive settlements on islands in lochs, natural or man-made, were also used during this time. These often leave little trace except for a small islet, but a reconstruction has been made at the **Scottish Crannog Centre [A20]** in Perthshire.

The inhabitants were farmers as well as warriors, and had domesticated animals, including horses, cattle, pigs, sheep and goats. They also grew cereals, such as barley, and vegetables, like peas. Iron was smelted and forged into weapons and tools from about 500 BC, wool was spun and woven into cloth, and bone was still used for small items such as needles and combs.

As mentioned above, because iron corrodes readily, there are far fewer iron artefacts dating from this period than copper or bronze items from the Bronze Age.

400 BC-200 AD Duns and brochs

Hill forts were still built and occupied at this time, but other defensive structures, brochs and duns, were also developed.

Brochs were tall, round dry-stone towers. The walls had a gallery running up inside them, with a stair or storage area. There was only one low entrance, defended by a drawbar and guardroom. The sites were sometimes further strengthened by a series of ramparts, including a blockhouse, in front of the entrance. Like castles, brochs were permanently occupied and do not appear to have been built just for refuge. Many have wells or a water tanks, and they may have had a timber roof.

The best surviving example is that at **Mousa [D53]** in Shetland, although there are other well-preserved and accessible (although sometimes remote) brochs at **Clickimin [D14]**, **Dun Carloway [D23]**, **Dun Dornaigil [D24]**, **Dun Telve [D32]** and **Dun Troddan [D34]** at Glenelg, **Gurness [D44]** and **Midhowe [D51]**. Other good brochs and duns can be found in Section **D**, although again many are in remote locations.

Settlements built up around brochs, and were occupied and modified over many centuries, even after the broch has apparently fallen out of use. What is not clear is what brochs were built to defend against: rival families and clans, or invaders and pirates, or Roman slave ships.

Duns often resemble brochs in the method of construction, and were stone enclosures, surrounding a defensible rock, or cutting off a headland. Indeed the word dun simply means a hill or defensive site in Gaelic.

By about 100 BC, these tribes or clans were in two rough groups: the Picts, north of the Forth-Clyde valley; and the Britons to the south and into most of England. Their societies were complex, artistic and probably warlike, no longer purely farmers, with carpenters and masons, metalworkers and merchants, ruled over by a chief or dynasty. They were druids and pagans, although little is known of their beliefs except what was recorded by the Romans.

Clickimin – fine broch and settlement

79-84 AD The coming of the Romans and Battle of Mons Graupius

After successfully invading the south of England from 55 BC under Julius Caesar, the Romans moved north. In 79 AD Julius Agricola, Roman governor of Britain, advanced into Scotland, and built forts at strategic positions. He crushed any opposition, but the Caledonians – as the Romans called them – with a major fortress called Alcluyd at **Dumbarton [N88]** Rock, resisted him. Another invasion by the Romans in 82 AD was followed a year later by the reputed slaughter of the Ninth Roman Legion, probably in Galloway.

At the Battle of Mons Graupius in 84 AD the Caledonians suffered a terrible defeat, somewhere in the north-east, possibly near **Mither Tap o' Bennachie [D52]**. Their chief Calgacus, if the chronicler Tactius is to believed, is the first named Scot in history. Calgacus was slain at the battle, along with 10,000 of his men, while only 340 Roman soldiers were killed. Although this defeat was a major setback for the Caledonian tribes, the Romans found it difficult to consolidate their victory.

120-208 AD Hadrian's Wall and Antonine Wall

The northern Caledonian tribes continued to be so troublesome that the Emperor Hadrian had a wall built to keep them from attacking the Roman Province of Britain to the south. Hadrian's Wall stretched across the country, from Newcastle, on the east side of England, to Bowness, on the southern shore of the Solway Firth. The wall was built of stone, and many forts and outposts were constructed along its length. Many sites along the wall can be visited, although the wall never formed any part of the border of the kingdom of Scots.

The Romans invaded again in 139 AD under Lollius Ubricus. They built another wall, the **Antonine Wall [E1]**, between the Forth and the Clyde in an attempt to consolidate their hold on southern Scotland. However, they were soon pushed back to Hadrian's Wall, despite the efforts of the Second, Sixth and 20th Legions to provide the emperor with a victory, and it does not appear that their occupation was ever secure enough to facilitate the building of villas. In 208, the Romans, this time under Lucius Septimus Severus, attacked again after an uprising by the Caledonian tribes. But his force was harried relentlessly and soon forced to retreat.

Most of what survives from the Roman incursions are earthworks from the **Antonine Wall [E1]**, forts and camps such as **Ardoch [E2]**, **Birrens [E6]**, **Inchtuthil [E11]**; a likely amphitheatre near Melrose; and the courses of Roman roads such as **Dere Street [E10]** near Soutra, near **Durisdeer [K66]** in Clydesdale, and in Perthshire. The ruins of a bathhouse at **Bearsden [E5]** are probably the best surviving built remains. There are fine exhibitions of Roman finds in several museums, including the **Museum of Scotland [Y6]**, the **Hunterian Museum [Y4]**, and the **Trimontium [E14]** exhibition. There is a list of Roman sites in Section **E**.

296-360 AD Picts and Scots

The Picts were first mentioned by the Romans as the people who held the north and east of Scotland. Little is known of them or of their language – as with all those who came before them. The lasting remnant of their culture is restricted to carved symbol stones, place name elements, such as Aber- and Pit-, and souterrains.

Larger collections of Pictish carved stones and information about them can be found at **Groam House Museum [F18]**, **Meigle [F24]**, **Pictavia [F27]**, **St Vigeans [F30]**, **Tarbat Discovery Centre [F32]**, and the **Museum of Scotland [Y6]**, as well as outstanding examples at **Aberlemno [F3]**. Their stones are decorated with a range of motifs and symbols, some of which are representational such as the many bulls from **Burghead [D6]**, others are hard to interpret, such as the double disc and z-rod. There is a fuller list of Pictish carved stones and museums in Section **F**.

Pictish symbol stone, Aberlemno

Souterrains are underground passages associated with settlements, which date from the Iron Age, and are usually found in Scotland in places where the Picts settled. It remains a matter of some debate why they were built: stores, bolt holes, or some ritual purpose have all been suggested. There are good souterrains at **Ardestie [A2]**, **Carlungie [A5]**, **Culsh [A6]**, **Grain [A7]**, **Raitts Cave [A16]**, **Rennibister [A17]**, **Tealing [V81]** and **Tungadale [A24]**.

The Scots, from the north part of Ireland, were first mentioned about 360 AD by the Romans, although they did not use this name of themselves. After the withdrawal of the Roman legions from Britain, in 368 the Picts and Scots, along with the Saxons, attacked the south, ravaged the Roman province of Britain, and plundered London of its riches.

Little of Roman culture, learning or influence survived in Scotland.

The Building of the Kingdom of Scots

400 Picts and Britons

With the withdrawal of the Roman legions, the Picts controlled the east and north. The Picts had settlements in many places including at **Abernethy [K43]**, **Burghead [D6]**, **Dunkeld [K16]**, **Forteviot [K69]**, **Scone [S41]** and **Urquhart [N152]**. The Picts used matrilineal inheritance for their kings, where the line descended through the mother, so that a brother was as likely to be king as a son.

Strathclyde was held by the Britons, whose kingdom at one time stretched from Cornwall, through Wales and Cumbria, to **Dumbarton [N88]**. The Britons also spoke a language related to Welsh. These kingdoms, and the later realms of the Scots and Angles, spent much of their time, and vigour, fighting each other.

430 St Ninian and St Patrick

By 430, St Ninian, a Briton, had been active in Galloway, converting people to Christianity, probably to a Roman form of worship, and he also appears to have made missions up the Clyde estuary and into Angus. He founded a religious house, *Candida Casa* – so-called because the walls of his church were whitewashed – at **Whithorn [J33]**. Ninian died around 432. There is also a museum **Whithorn: Cradle of Christianity in Scotland [J34]**. **St Ninian's Cave [G14]**, south-west of Whithorn, is traditionally associated with the saint, and there are early Christian stones also at **Kirkmadrine [L16]**.

In the same year, St Patrick, said to have been born at Kilpatrick, near Dumbarton, converted many of the Irish to Christianity

Dunadd – fortress of the Scots

500 The coming of the Scots

It was in 503 that many Scots left Ireland and settled in Argyll – they had, however, apparently been doing so for years: Pictish influence never appears to have been strong here. The Scots had raided along the coasts of the south-west for many years. Their kingdom was known as Dalriada, and their king, Fergus MacErc, reputedly brought with him the Stone of Destiny. **Dunstaffnage [N93]**, later used as the site for a medieval castle, and **Dunadd [D38]**, an impressive hill fort, were two of their strongholds, along with **Dunollie [N91]**, **Tarbert [N149]** and Dunaverty. About this time the Scots became Christians.

547 Bernicia and the kingdom of the Angles

The Angles held much of the east of England by 547, and King Ida became the ruler of Bernicia, which included lands from the Firth of Forth to the River Tees, in the north of England. His capital was at Bamburgh – the site of which is occupied by a medieval castle – in Northumberland. The Angles were pagans.

563 St Columba and St Mungo

St Columba, a Scot from Ireland, settled at **Iona [J20]**, bringing with him the Celtic form of the Christian church. He converted the north Picts, ruled by King Brude from a stronghold at or near Inverness, and is said to have confronted a serpent in Loch Ness, the first mention of a monster there. Iona became the centre of Christianity in Scotland. The present restored abbey and the ruined nunnery date from medieval times, but early Scots, Irish and Norse kings are reputedly buried here. There is also the **St Columba Centre [G10]** at Fionnphort.

About the same time, St Mungo, who is also known as Kentigern, was active among the Britons of Strathclyde, and **Glasgow Cathedral [K19]** is dedicated to him. The Cathedral is mainly medieval, but is built over Mungo's tomb. **Culross [J10]**, **Govan [K71]** and **Inchinnan [L7]** are also associated with the early church. These early saints were as much holy warriors as holy men, and would perform many feats or miracles, such as confronting the Loch Ness monster, slaying dragons, taming wolves, bringing birds back to life, and plucking out their own eyes. After their death, miracles would be attributed to their bones and relics.

There are many Christian sites in Scotland

Ruthwell Cross – carved in the 7th c.

associated with early and native saints, including caves, such as **St Ninian' Cave [G14]** (mentioned above), **St Fillan's Cave [G13]** in Fife and **St Columba's Cave [G11]** in Argyll, old chapels in round enclosures including **St Blane's [K99]** near Kingarth on Bute, and holy and healing wells. These wells are often associated with a chapel or church, and these may have already been sacred places before the advent of Christianity. These wells were used for healing or good luck for hundreds of years, and some still are, such as **St Curitan's Well [M5] at** Munlochy, **St Triduana's [K128]** at Restalrig, **St Mary's Well [M6]** at Culloden, St Fergus Well and Pictish stone near **Glamis Church [F17]** and **St Queran's Well [M7]**, at Islesteps near Dumfries.

Another enduring legacy from this early period are magnificent carved crosses, such as the **Ruthwell Cross [L24]**, the **Kildalton Cross [L11]**, St Martin's Cross on **Iona [J20]** (which also has a fine museum housing many other carved stones) and the **Keills Cross [L8]**. The Ruthwell Cross was smashed to pieces after the Reformation, and had to be reassembled. Information about the restoration can be found at the **Savings Banks Museum [Y170]** at Ruthwell. Many Pictish cross-slabs are also excellent examples of carving, and there is a separate section on the Picts – section **F**.

600 Conversion of the Angles to Christianity

St Aidan, a missionary from Iona, converted the Angles of Bernicia to Christianity, the work being continued by St Cuthbert. Lindisfarne, in Northumberland, became a great religious centre, and the ruins of a later priory are in the care of English Heritage and open to the public.

663 The Celtic Church and the Synod of Whitby

The Synod of Whitby was held, in Yorkshire in England, at which the ritual and beliefs of the Roman Church, particularly the dating of Easter, were asserted over the practices of the Celtic Church. The Roman Church came to dominate the whole of Scotland.

685 Battle of Nechtansmere

The Angles of Bernicia tried to push their border far to the north, but were defeated by the Picts at the Battle of **Nechtansmere [G7]**, near Forfar. Their king, Egfrid, was slain with much of his army. The carved stones at **Aberlemno [F3]**, which are near Nechtansmere, probably commemorate this battle. The Picts extended their influence south again, and dominated the Scottish kingdom of Dalriada.

Aberlemno – commemorating Nechtansmere

733 St Andrew, Patron Saint of Scotland

Acca, Bishop of Hexham, brought the relics of St Andrew to Fife, where there was already a religious settlement, probably founded by St Rule, a disciple of Columba, about 590. **St Andrews Cathedral [K26]**, now a ruin, was founded on the site of this early community, although the tower of St Rule's older church survives. The flag of Scotland, the white saltire on a blue background, represents the crucifixion of St Andrew on an 'X' shaped cross. One story is that the cross appeared in the sky before a victory in 735 by the Picts over the Northumbrians at or near **Athelstaneford [Y26]**, and this was attributed to Andrew's intercession.

793-826 Lindisfarne and Iona attacked

The Norsemen sacked Lindisfarne in 793, and looted **Iona [J20]** in 795. These attacks forced Iona to be abandoned, and the monks moved to **Dunkeld [K16]** in 826, which was safer from Norse long ships. The partly ruined cathedral at Dunkeld is built on the site of an earlier church.

The Norsemen raided all along the coasts, and greatly weakened the northern kingdoms. They settled in Orkney and Shetland, and parts of the northern mainland and the western isles, forming a powerful Norse province.

843-59 Union of Scots and Picts – Kenneth MacAlpin

Kenneth MacAlpin united the crowns of the Scots and the Picts. What is unusual about this union is that at this time the Picts had the upper hand in the fighting between the two peoples. The union seems to have been peaceful, and the Picts and Scots had been intermarrying for generations. Kenneth had a claim to the throne of Picts through his mother, a Pictish princess, although he reputedly secured his position by slaughtering all his rivals at a drunken feast at **Forteviot [K69]**. Nearly all Pictish culture and language has been lost.

Kenneth moved from fortresses in the west to the former Pictish east.

859-900 Donald I, Constantine I, Aed, Eochaid and Giric, Donald II

Despite the union of the two kingdoms, fighting and kinstrife was unabated. Donald I, Kenneth's brother, succeeded to the throne, but died in 863. He was followed by Constantine I, who was slain in battle against the Norsemen in 877; and then Aed, who was killed by his cousin, Giric, in 878. Eochaid and Giric ruled as joint monarchs, but in 889 both kings were deposed, and Giric was killed in a siege at the fortress of Dundurn. They were succeeded by Donald II, but he was poisoned in 900.

900-943 Constantine II and the Battle of Brunanburgh

Constantine II came to the throne in 900 and ruled for 43 years, a very long reign indeed for the time. The kingdom of Strathclyde had become dependent on the Scots, and in 908 the throne passed to Constantine's brother. Constantine spent much of his reign fighting the Norse and driving them from his realm. However, in 937, Constantine and the Scots, and an army of Irish and Northumbrian Norsemen and Britons, were defeated by Athelstane, King of the Saxons, with great slaughter of the Scots and their allies. The southern borders of the kingdom of Scots were attacked, and in 943 Constantine resigned his throne to his cousin, Malcolm I.

943-1005 Malcolm I, Indulf, Duff, Culen, Kenneth II, Constantine III, Kenneth III

In return for land, Malcolm I apparently became a vassal of the English king, Athelstane. However, in 950 he captured Northumberland, but was killed in a battle with the men of Moray. He was followed by Indulf, who was probably killed about 962; then Duff, who was slain in Moray in 967; then Culen, who was put down by the Britons in Lothian in 971.

The reign of Kenneth II was relatively peaceful, until he was poisoned in 995 by Finella, whose son had been murdered by Kenneth. It is during his reign that the thistle traditionally became associated with Scotland. At a battle in 973 at Luncarty, sleeping Scottish forces were woken when the Norse enemy stumbled into a patch of thistles. The first recorded use of the thistle, however, is on coins in the reign of James III in 1470.

Constantine III came to the throne in 995, but was murdered in 997. He was followed by Kenneth III, who was slain in 1005 by Malcolm II.

Dynastic fighting, failed invasions, and Norse raids weakened the kingdom, and by 1005 the Scots had lost control of Lothian and Strathclyde, the north and west were held by the Norsemen, and Moray and other areas were in rebellion.

1005-34 Malcolm II and the Battle of Carham

Malcolm II came to the throne in 1005, and in 1010 he defeated a Norse army at Dufftown and secured his northern border, by a combination of fighting and marrying off his daughter to the Norse Jarl of Orkney. Turning his attention to the south, Malcolm and the Scots, aided by Owen the Bald of Strathclyde, defeated the Northumbrians, under King Uhtred, at the Battle of Carham, in 1018, occupying Lothian. Owen was killed at the battle and Strathclyde was absorbed into the kingdom of Scots – which more or less assumed its present southern border.

Malcolm II ensured Duncan's succession by slaughtering other claimants.

1034-58 Duncan and Macbeth

Duncan, a young man, came to the throne in 1034, but was, in his turn, slain in battle by Macbeth – not in his bed with a bloody dagger as described by Shakespeare. Macbeth ruled well, strengthening the kingdom sufficiently to make a pilgrimage to Rome in 1050. However, in 1053 he was defeated, probably at **Dunsinane [D40]**, and four years later he was killed at Lumphanan by the forces of Malcolm Canmore – Canmore meaning *big head* – son of Duncan, who was helped by Edward the Confessor of England. Malcolm Canmore – Malcolm III – was named king. Lulach the Fool, a distant relation of Macbeth, was set up as a rival claimant to the throne, but was slain by Malcolm in 1058.

There is an audiovisual presentation about Macbeth at the **Macbeth Experience [Y123]** at Bankhead, while **Dunsinane Hill [D40]** can be visited, as can various sites at Lumphanan (see **Peel Ring of Lumphanan [N136]**) which are associated with the king. **Glamis [N30]** and **Cawdor [N14]** both feature in Shakespeare's play, although there is no or only limited historical connection: Cawdor was not even built at the time, nor would it be until the 14th century .

Margaret's Sons

1066 Battle of Hastings

After William the Conqueror's defeat of King Harold and the English, at Hastings in the south of England, many Anglo-Saxons settled in the south of Scotland at Malcolm Canmore's invitation. Although Scotland was never conquered as England had been, the coming of the Normans had as profound an effect, reducing the Celtic influence, but strengthening the nation for the wars with the English in following centuries.

1068 Marriage of Malcolm Canmore to Margaret

In 1068 Malcolm Canmore married Margaret, sister of the Saxon heir to the throne of England, who had fled to Scotland with her brother. The marriage greatly angered William the Conqueror. Malcolm's first wife, Ingibiorg, by whom he had had several children including a son Duncan, had recently died.

Margaret, whose chapel survives in **Edinburgh Castle [N25]**, preferred English ways to those of her Celtic subjects. Her sons were given English names, she practised European customs and culture at court, she encouraged monastic foundations, such as that at **Dunfermline [J14]**, of which the church still survives, and revived the monastery on **Iona [J20]**. **St Margaret's Cave [K113]** in Dunfermline can also be visited. This led to discontent amongst some of Malcolm's

subjects. Margaret, however, appears to have been a very pious woman, doing good works – according to her devoted biographer Turgot – and was later made a saint, the only 'Scottish' saint now recognised by the Roman church.

1072 William the Conqueror invades Scotland

Malcolm Canmore attacked England and ravaged Northumberland. William the Conqueror, angered by the attack and Malcolm's marriage, invaded Scotland in 1072, forcing Canmore to pay homage to him. Malcolm responded with further raids into England, but in 1093 was treacherously murdered when accepting the surrender of Alnwick Castle, in Northumberland. Margaret died soon afterwards, at **Edinburgh Castle [N25]**, and she and Malcolm were buried in **Dunfermline Abbey [J14]**. Scotland was

Dunfermline Abbey – Margaret was buried here

again plunged into dynastic turmoil. Margaret's tomb became a place of pilgrimage, although her relics were taken abroad at the Reformation.

1093 Donald Bane (Donald III), Duncan II and Edmund

Trouble followed the deaths of Malcolm and Margaret. Donald III, Donald Bane – Bane meaning 'fair' – the 60-year-old brother of Malcolm Canmore, seized the throne and drove out Margaret's sons, partly because many resented the growing influence of the English and Normans. Donald was overthrown in turn in 1094 by Duncan II – Malcolm Canmore's eldest son by his first wife Ingibiorg – with English help. However, Duncan was not popular and was murdered. Donald III recovered the throne, this time aided by Edmund, son of Malcolm and Margaret. Edgar, another of their sons, defeated Donald and Edmund, again with an English army. Donald was blinded and was imprisoned on Iona, while Edmund retired to a monastery in England.

1097-1107 Edgar the Peaceable and Alexander the Fierce

A time of relative peace, Edgar the Peaceable ruled Scotland well, although he ceded the Western Isles to the Norwegians, including Iona. Edgar did not marry and his brother, Alexander, succeeded him. Alexander earned his nickname The Fierce by savagely putting down a rising in Moray. However, he encouraged monastic settlements in Scotland, and founded **Inchcolm Abbey [J18]**, after being washed up there following a shipwreck. He married Sibylla, an illegitimate daughter of Henry I of England. This match does not appear to have been happy, and Alexander died in 1124 without a son or daughter.

1124 David I

David I, brother of Alexander, came to the throne. He was married to Matilda, an English heiress, and David acquired the wealthy Earldom of Huntingdon in England, as well as other lands. He had spent many years in exile in England, and during this time had become friendly with many Nor-

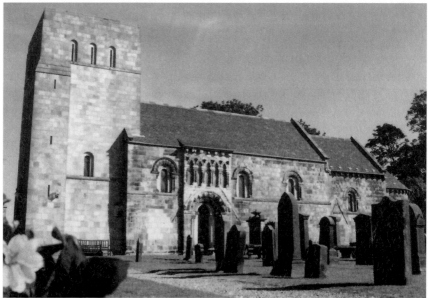

Dalmeny Parish Church – largely unaltered Norman church

St Margaret's Chapel, Edinburgh Castle

man families. He invited some of these men, with names such as Bruce, Comyn, and FitzAllan (Stewarts) to Scotland, and gave them land or married them to heiresses.

David also mostly ruled well, and burghs, with special trading privileges, were introduced. He founded abbeys at **Dryburgh [J12]**; **Holyrood [J17]**, Edinburgh; **Jedburgh [J22]**; **Kelso [J23]**; **Melrose [J26]**, and is usually credited with the building of St Margaret's Chapel at **Edinburgh Castle [N25]**. There is a list of abbeys and priories in Section **J**.

This increased the prosperity of the nation by encouraging trade and improving agriculture, although David had to put down rebellions in Moray in 1130, and in 1140.

The Norman influence extended to the building of churches, fine examples of which survive at **Birnie Kirk [K51]**, **Dalmeny Parish Church [K63]**, **St Athernase Church [K97]** at Leuchars, **St Fillan's Church [K107]** at Aberdour, **St Vigeans Church [K129]** near Arbroath, **Stobo Kirk [K131]**, and **Symington Parish Church [K132]**.

1138 Battle of the Standard

David became involved in the fighting in England between Stephen of Blois and his niece, the rightful heir, Maud or Matilda. He invaded England on her behalf, but at the Battle of the Standard, near Northallerton, the Scots suffered a crushing defeat. David, however, managed to acquire Northumberland and Cumberland from the English in 1139 when they were in disarray. The kingdom reached its furthest extent southwards. David died in 1153 at his prayers at Carlisle Castle.

Motte and bailey castles were built in Scotland around this time, although usually only where there was rebellion against the kings of Scots, such as in Galloway or unruly areas. Motte and bailey castles survive at **Coulter Motte [N75]**, **Druchtag Motte [N84]**, **Duffus Castle [N87]**, **Lanark Castle [H8]**, **Motte of Urr [N129]** and **Peel Ring of Lumphanan [N136]**. Early stone castles were built by Norsemen in parts of Scotland under their control, such as **Castle of Old Wick [N69]**, **Castle Sween [N68]**, **Cubbie Roo's Castle [N80]** and **Skipness Castle [N143]**.

Arbroath Abbey – founded by William the Lyon

1153 Malcolm the Maiden

Malcolm the Maiden, David's grandson, came to the throne in 1153 when he was 11 years old. He was called the Maiden because he took a vow of celibacy and never married. Malcolm lost the Earldom of Northumberland, exchanging it for the Earldom of Huntingdon with Henry II of England. He put down risings in 1160 by Fergus, Earl of Galloway, in the south-west, as well as by Somerled.

Somerled had pushed the Norsemen out of much of the Hebrides between 1156-8, making himself an independent prince. He was assassinated at Renfrew before a battle with Malcolm's forces. Somerled's sons divided his lands, and it was from him that the MacDonalds and MacDougalls originated. The MacDonalds were to become one of the strongest clans, controlling territory right down the western seaboard as Lords of the Isles.

Malcolm the Maiden died at the age of 23 without children.

1174-1214 William the Lyon

William the Lyon, brother of Malcolm, became King of Scots in 1174. After putting down a rebellion in Galloway, William tried to recover Northumberland in 1175 and invaded the north of England. He was captured by the English at Alnwick, and was held at Falaise in Normandy until he swore fealty to Henry II of England as his overlord.

In 1176 William had the abbey at **Arbroath [J2]** built, in memory of his friend, Thomas a Becket, who had been murdered in 1168. William brought the north of Scotland under his control during campaigns in 1179 and 1187, finally taking Caithness and Sutherland from Harald Maddadson, Earl of Orkney, who was blinded and castrated.

William restored Scotland's independence in 1189 by paying Richard the Lionheart 10,000 merks. During his reign the Scottish church was recognised by the Pope as being separate from that of England. He was married in 1186 to Ermengarde de Beaumont, and they had a son, Alexander, as well as three daughters. William died in 1214. Ermengarde and Alexander founded **Balmerino Abbey [J4]** in his memory. The lion rampant was used as a heraldic device by Scottish kings, and may have been introduced by William. It is still used on the Scottish Standard.

1214-49 Alexander II

Alexander II, son of William the Lyon, came to the throne in 1214. Again he had to put down rebellions in Argyll, Caithness and Galloway, building or strengthening castles at **Dunstaffnage [N93]**, Kirkcudbright, **Tarbert [N149]** and Wigtown. Alexander was known as a lawmaker, and a collection of laws, called *Regiam Majestatem*, was compiled at this time. Alexander tried to recover the Hebrides from Norway, but died (possibly at **Gylen [N108]**) on Kerrera, an island near Oban, and was succeeded by his young son, Alexander III.

1249-86 Alexander III

Alexander III, then only eight, came to the throne, and was married to Margaret, the 11-year-old daughter of Henry II, King of England, in 1251. This is often seen as a golden age in Scotland. Alexander managed to keep peace with England, and the nation prospered during his long reign. He further strengthened the mechanisms of government and justice, and built many royal castles to enforce his authority throughout the kingdom.

1263 Battle of Largs and Treaty of Perth

Alexander III attacked the island of Skye in an attempt to wrest the Hebrides from Hakon, King of Norway. Hakon responded by raising a large army and sailing south in an armada of long ships. A storm wrecked many of the ships, and a reduced force of Norwegians was engaged at the Battle of Largs. Hakon and his army retreated, and he died at the **Bishop's Palace [N54]**, in Kirkwall on Orkney. In 1266 in the Treaty of Perth, Magnus IV of Norway ceded the Hebrides and the Isle of Man to the Scots. Norse influence steadily waned in Scotland, although they held Orkney and Shetland until 1450. Sites associated with the Norsemen include **St Magnus Cathedral [K33]** and **[Y179]** in Kirkwall, **Jarlshof [D45]**, **Brough of Birsay [K54]**, **Orphir [K92]** and **St Magnus Church on Egilsay [K111]** and at **Birsay [K112]**. Information can also be found about the Norsemen at **Vikingar [G15]** at Largs, **Northlands Viking Centre [Y147]**, **Timespan Heritage Centre, Helmsdale [Y197]** and the **Orkneyinga Saga Centre [G8]** at Orphir on Orkney.

1286 Death of Alexander III

Margaret, Alexander's wife, died in 1275, and their elder son in 1284. Alexander had no other surviving children, and in 1285 married the young and beautiful Yolande de Dreux. On a stormy night on his way to meet her, hoping to give her an heir, he fell to his death off the cliffs at Kinghorn – the spot marked by the **Alexander III Monument [H1]** – and plunged Scotland into a war that nearly saw the country and its people absorbed into England.

> When Alexander our king wis deid
> That Scotland led in lauche and le[1]
> Away was sonse[2] of ale and breid
> Of wine and wax, of gamin and glee
> Our gold was changit into leid
> The fruit failet on every tree
> Christ succour Scotland and remeid
> That stade[3] us in perplexitie
>
> *Anonymous*   [1] law and peace [2] plenty [3] beset

The Wars of Independence

1289 Margaret, the Maid of Norway

Margaret, the Maid of Norway, was the next in line to the throne. She was the daughter of Margaret – daughter of Alexander II, who had died in 1283 – and the King of Norway.

It was agreed that Margaret, the Maid of Norway, should be brought to Scotland from Norway, and in the meantime the kingdom was to be ruled by six Guardians. In an attempt to avoid civil war, they asked Edward I of England – who had been friendly to the Scots – to help them. At the Treaty of Birgham, a marriage was arranged between Margaret and the son of Edward I of England, although this treaty stated that homage should not be paid to an English monarch, and all Scottish institutions should remain independent.

1290–96 Death of Maid of Norway and John Balliol becomes King

On her way to Scotland, Margaret died, reportedly from sea sickness, having only got as far as Orkney.

One of the Guardians, Bishop Fraser, fearing civil war, then unwisely asked Edward I of England to choose a king from 13 claimants, including John Balliol and Robert Bruce, the grandfather of the future king. Edward summoned the claimants to Norham Castle – now a substantial ruin in Northumberland – first getting them to swear allegiance to him. Edward then chose John Balliol, who accepted the English king as his overlord, Superior and Lord Paramount of Scotland.

1295 Treaty with France: the Auld Alliance

John Balliol married Isabel de Warenne, and they had a son, Edward. His father, another John, was married to Devorgilla of Galloway. They established Balliol College, and when he died, Devorgilla founded **Sweetheart Abbey [J32]** in his memory.

Balliol tried to restore royal authority, but was hampered by the interference of Edward of England, and the Bruces, who still had designs on the throne themselves. Edward I of England tried to provoke Balliol into defiance, and when in 1295 the Scots signed a treaty with France, England's enemy, so beginning the Auld Alliance, Edward had the excuse he needed to crush the Scots once and for all.

1296 Edward I invades Scotland and the Battle of Dunbar

Balliol's resistance against Edward I only stung the English king to act. An English army, said to number 35,000 men, invaded Scotland, and sacked Berwick – then a rich Scottish burgh – slaughtering 16,000 of its inhabitants: men, women and children.

A large but inexperienced Scottish army was heavily defeated by Edward at Dunbar, and the English occupied much of Scotland, advancing all the way to Elgin. Balliol surrendered at Brechin, earning his nickname Toom Tabard – empty coat – and was stripped of his office.

Edward took over control of Scotland, installing English garrisons in many castles. He eventually returned to the south, taking with him the Stone of Destiny and Coronation Chair, on which the kings of Scots had been inaugurated, and many other treasures.

The Stone of Destiny was kept beneath the Coronation Chair in Westminster Abbey in England, but has been returned to **Edinburgh Castle [N25]**, after 700 years. **Scone Palace [S41]** stands on the site of the abbey from which the stone was taken.

Edward forced over 2000 nobles, churchmen and landholders to swear allegiance to him. The list of their names became known as The Ragman Roll, after the ragged look of all the different seals and ribbons.

1297-1305 William Wallace: Battles of Stirling Bridge and Falkirk

The English occupation was harsh and the Scots rose, led by William Wallace and Sir Andrew Moray. Wallace was a son of the laird of Elderslie (which may have been at **Elderslie [H5]** in Renfrew, or near Kilmarnock in Ayrshire), and his wife had probably been murdered by the English sheriff of **Lanark [H8]**. Wallace was a successful guerrilla leader, and was greatly admired by the general population, although much of the nobility viewed him with suspicion. This included the Bruces, who still wished to assert their own claim to the throne – Wallace supported Balliol.

In 1297 Wallace and Moray defeated a large English army at **Stirling Old Bridge [H11]**, where Hugh de Cressingham, Edward's treasurer of Scotland, was skinned and turned into a saddle bag. Moray died soon afterwards, possibly from wounds received at the battle.

Wallace was knighted and became a Guardian, and ravaged the north of England. This prompted Edward into invading Scotland in 1298, and he crushed any Scottish resistance by defeating Wallace at the Battle of Falkirk. Many nobles fled the battle rather than fight on with Wallace.

Wallace left Scotland on a diplomatic mission to the continent, but when he returned was betrayed and captured by the English, then hanged, drawn and quartered in London in 1305. In killing Wallace so horribly, Edward I had only succeeded in creating a national hero.

The **National Wallace Monument [H10]** near Stirling celebrates William Wallace.

1305-08 Robert the Bruce and the Wars of Independence

Robert the Bruce had a claim to the throne as a descendant of David, Earl of Huntingdon, brother of both William the Lyon and Malcolm the Maiden. Bruce was first married to Isabella of Mar, and it was through their daughter Marjorie that the Stewarts became kings. By his second wife, Elizabeth de Burgh, he had a son, David.

In 1306 Bruce agreed to meet John Comyn of Badenoch, who had a more direct claim to the throne, and was related to John Balliol. The Comyns were one of the most powerful families in Scotland, supported by the MacDougalls of Lorne, MacDowalls of Galloway, and Earl of Ross.

Bruce and Comyn met in **Greyfriars Chapel [H6]** at Dumfries to resolve their differences, but

Stirling Old Bridge – site of William Wallace's triumph over the English

the two men argued and Comyn was stabbed to death by Bruce and his followers. Although Bruce was a hunted fugitive, and excommunicated, he declared himself King of Scots at **Scone [S41]** in 1306. His small army was defeated at Methven, and then scattered at Dalry, and he had to flee the country. He lost more than these battles: three of his brothers, Nigel, Thomas and Alexander, were executed by the English; his sister, Mary, was hung from a cage at **Roxburgh Castle [N140]**; his sister and daughter Christine and Marjorie, along with his second wife, Elizabeth de Burgh, were imprisoned after being captured by the Earl of Ross near Tain at **St Duthac's Chapel [K106]**.

Luckily for Bruce, however, Edward I of England died in July 1307 at Burgh by Sands, just on the English side of the Border. Edward died berating his son to ravage Scotland, but Edward II was not as ruthless or effective, and retreated to bury his father.

Bruce returned to Scotland and won battles at Loudoun Hill; **Loch Aweside [H9]**, where he defeated the MacDougalls; in Galloway, where the MacDowalls were crushed; and at Inverurie, where he destroyed the power of the Comyns, and their allies, and wasted Buchan. **Bruce's Stone [H4]** by Loch Trool celebrates a victory in 1307. The Earl of Ross submitted to Bruce. Other risings expelled the English garrisons from most Scottish castles, until only **Stirling Castle [N46]** was in the hands of the English. James Douglas, Neil Campbell, Angus Og MacDonald, and the High Stewards or Stewarts were among Bruce's loyal supporters, all later important families.

It was Bruce's policy to destroy castles so that they could not be held by the English. However, **Bothwell [N56]**, **Caerlaverock [N60]**, **Dirleton [N82]**, **Edinburgh [N25]**, **Kildrummy [N116]** and **Stirling [N46]** castles all survive – at least in part – from before the Wars of Independence. There is a listing of castles in Sections **N1** and **N2**.

1314 Bannockburn

By 1314, only **Stirling Castle [N46]** was held by the English, and was besieged by the Scots. Edward II and a large army marched north to relieve the castle. On the eve of the battle, Henry de Bohun challenged Bruce to single combat, but Bruce clove de Bohun's head with an axe. Although outnumbered three to one, the Scots won the Battle of **Bannockburn [H2]**, and many of the English were slaughtered or captured, although this was as much due to their bad tactics and poor

Dirleton Castle – besieged by Edward I of England

leadership. The battle site is open to the public, and there is a visitor centre. More information can also be found at the **Royal Burgh of Stirling Visitor Centre [Y168]**.

1320 Declaration of Arbroath

Battles continued and although the Scots had the best of it, notably by defeating the English deep into England at the Battle of Byland, Edward II would not recognise Scotland's independence – nor would the Pope. A Declaration, sealed by most of the nobles of Scotland, was drawn up at **Arbroath Abbey [J2]**, which urged the Pope to recognise Scotland as a free independent country, and to put pressure on the English to do the same.

Sites associated with the Wars of Independence can be found in Section **H**.

1329 Death of Robert the Bruce and Accession of David II

Edward III finally recognised Scotland's independence in 1328, the year before Bruce died, reportedly from leprosy, at Cardross, near Dumbarton. Bruce's heart was removed from his body, and taken on a crusade to Granada by James Douglas, although it was eventually interred at **Melrose Abbey [J26]**. This act is commemorated by the heart on the Douglas coat of arms, although James Douglas was himself slain in Spain and buried in **St Bride's Church, Douglas [K101]**. The rest of Bruce's body was buried at **Dunfermline Abbey [J14]**, while a fragment of bone is at the Bruce chapel in **St Conan's Kirk, Lochawe [K104]**.

David, his young son, was made king, but peace lasted for only a few years after Bruce's death.

1332-41 Edward Balliol and the Battle of Halidon Hill

Edward, son of John Balliol, invaded Scotland, with help from Edward III and the English, and was made king after defeating a Scottish army at Dupplin Moor. David II was sent to France for safety.

Edward III of England was a much more able king than Edward II, and besieged Berwick, crushing a Scottish army at the Battle of Halidon Hill, near Berwick upon Tweed, in 1333. Although Edward Balliol was initially successful, he was eventually defeated by Andrew Moray the Regent, son of the victor of the Battle of Stirling Bridge, and had to flee Scotland in 1341.

1346-71 Battle of Neville's Cross and the Treaty of Berwick

David II returned to Scotland, and led an invasion of England in support of the French, who were at war with the English – this was not the only time that the Auld Alliance would harm the Scots. The Scots were heavily defeated by the English at the Battle of Neville's Cross in the north of England, and David was taken prisoner. David fought bravely, but in vain, although Robert the High Steward fled the battle.

Edward ravaged the south of Scotland in 1356, known as the Burnt Candlemas. In 1357, however, David was released after a ransom of 100,000 merks was agreed, although the Scots never paid most of the money.

David died in 1371 at **Edinburgh Castle [N25]**, without an heir, although he was twice married: to Joan of England, who died in 1362; and to a former mistress, Margaret Logie. Although he hated the Stewarts, partly because of the cowardly action of Robert the High Steward, he could not prevent the succession to the throne of Robert II, son of Marjorie (she is buried in **Paisley Abbey [J28]**) – daughter of Robert the Bruce – and Walter the High Steward. David reportedly would have offered the English king the throne if he had been allowed. The Stewarts were so named because they were the High Stewards of the kingdom, their original family name having been FitzAllan.

The Stewarts

1371-88 Robert II

Robert II came to the throne when already 55 years of age, although as Guardian of the Realm, he had been involved in defending the country against the English. He became increasingly infirm, and control of the kingdom passed to his eldest son, John, Earl of Carrick; and then to his next son, Robert, later Duke of Albany. Robert II was married to Elizabeth Mure, and then to Euphemia Ross, by whom he had many children.

1388-90 The Battle of Otterburn and Death of Robert II

Fighting between England and Scotland continued. The English, under the Percy Earl of Northumberland, raided as far as Edinburgh in 1383, and again in 1385, although it was meant to be a time of truce.

The Scots got their revenge at the Battle of Otterburn in 1388, where they defeated a force led by Percy and captured him, although the Earl of Douglas, leader of the Scottish army, was killed at the battle.

In 1390 Robert II died at **Dundonald Castle [N89]** and was succeeded by his son, John. The name John, however, was not seen as a suitable name for a king of Scots, and he was crowned as Robert III.

1390-1406 Robert III and the Battle of Homildon Hill

Robert III had been left lame by a kick from a horse, and did not have the ruthlessness or vigour to rule well. He said of himself that his epitaph should be *Here lies the worst of kings and the most miserable of men.* During this time, the power of the MacDonald Lords of the Isles increased until

Tantallon Castle – stronghold of the Douglases

they ruled from **Finlaggan [N103]** a virtually independent kingdom in the north and west; in the Borders, the Douglas family was supremely powerful from its strongholds of **Threave [N150]** and **Tantallon [N148]**.

One brother of Robert III, Alexander Stewart, the Wolf of Badenoch, made himself Earl of Buchan by forcing the Countess of Buchan to marry him. When he was excommunicated by the Bishop of Moray, he sacked the town of Forres, and torched the town and cathedral of **Elgin [K17]**.

The kingdom was increasingly ruled by another brother, Robert, Duke of Albany. Robert III had a son, David, Duke of Rothesay, by his wife Anabella Drummond, as well as many other children. Uncle and nephew, Albany and David, Duke of Rothesay, competed with each other for power, until Albany had David imprisoned, and probably starved to death, at **Falkland Palace [N27]** in 1402.

The Scots raided deep into England the same year – but on their return, laden with plunder, were heavily defeated by the English, led by the Percys, at Homildon Hill, near Wooler, in Northumberland. The Earl of Douglas, leader of the army, was among those captured.

Partly to remove him from any possible harm by his uncle Albany, the young James, son of Robert III, and now heir to the throne, was sent to France. On his journey, however, he was captured by the English and imprisoned by Henry IV.

Robert III died at **Rothesay Castle [N139]** in 1406, a few days after hearing of his son's fate, and – there being none to oppose him, with James, the heir to the throne, imprisoned in the Tower of London – Albany ruled the kingdom. He may even have tipped off the English that James was being sent to France.

1410 Founding of St Andrews University
Teaching began at St Andrews in this year, and was formalised in 1413.

1411 The Battle of Harlaw
In pursuing his claim to the Earldom of Ross, Donald MacDonald, Lord of the Isles, descendant of Somerled, invaded the mainland of Scotland and marched on Aberdeen. He was met by an army, led by Alexander Stewart, illegitimate son of the Wolf of Badenoch, who had made himself Earl of Mar by forcing the Countess of Mar to marry him – like father, like son. The MacDonald forces were defeated at **Harlaw [Q13]** and retreated, although with such slaughter on both sides the battle is known as the Red Harlaw.

1424-37 James I
James I was released from imprisonment in England, after a ransom was paid by the Scots. During his captivity, he was married to Joan Beaufort, and they had a son James, born in 1430, as well as other children.

Although Albany was already dead, James I had Murdoch, his son, executed, traditionally at the **Beheading Stone, Stirling [Q3]**. James did not rule well, however, making himself unpopular by his uneven enforcement of order and high-handedness towards the nobles. In 1427 he imprisoned Donald, Lord of the Isles, and many other Highland chiefs, and had some of them executed – stinging Donald into ravaging Inverness and Lochaber.

James was murdered at Perth in 1437 by a party of disgruntled nobles. Joan, his wife, had the murderers captured and cruelly tortured before execution. James's heart was taken on a pilgrimage to the East, and later brought back from Rhodes by a Knight of St John.

1437-60 James II and the Destruction of the Black Douglases

James II, son of James I, came to the throne when he was only six. James had a red birthmark covering half of his face, which gave him his nickname James of the Fiery Face.

The families of Crichton and Livingston competed for power during his minority. They united briefly to murder the 6th Earl of Douglas, at the Black Dinner at **Edinburgh Castle [N25]** in 1440, as they both feared the power of the Douglases. Not unreasonably, the Douglases besieged Edinburgh Castle, and sacked **Crichton Castle [N78]** although the 7th Earl of Douglas, James the Gross, may have had a hand in the murder.

James II married Mary of Gueldres in 1449, when he finally assumed power, and they had a son, another James, in 1452. James II encouraged the arts and science, and Glasgow University was founded in 1450.

The Black Douglas family were very powerful in Scotland during his reign, having acquired much land and power through James Douglas, supporter and friend of Robert the Bruce. The Douglases were allied with the Lindsay Earls of Crawford and the MacDonald Lord of the Isles.

James II, fearing this alliance and detesting their pride, murdered William, 8th Earl of Douglas in **Stirling Castle [N46]**, despite having promised him safe conduct. James took, or destroyed, many Douglas strongholds, including the castle of **Threave [N150]**, and the Black Douglases were finally defeated and their power destroyed at the Battle of Arkinholm in 1455. James II then attempted to recover **Roxburgh Castle [N140]** and the town of Berwick from the English, but was killed by an exploding cannon at Roxburgh in 1460, at the age of 29. He was buried in **Holyrood Abbey [J17]**.

It was during his reign that, in 1446, **Rosslyn Chapel [K24]** was built. This is an outstanding example of ecclesiastical architecture with fabulous carving, although it was never completed, and has many legends associated with it. Many noblemen built collegiate churches, where prayers could be said for their souls: this was much less expensive than building an abbey or priory. Fine

Crichton Collegiate Church – the castle is nearby

collegiate churches include **Biggar [K1]**, **Bothwell [K2]**, **Corstorphine [K7]**, **Crail [K8]**, **Crichton [K10]**, **Cullen [K11]**, **Dunglass [K15]**, **Lincluden [K22]**, **Seton [K25]**, **St Duthac's Church [K29]** at Tain, and **St Nicholas Buccleuch Parish Church [K40]** in Dalkeith.

1460-88 James III and the Battle of Sauchieburn

James III was only eight when he became king, and during his minority the Boyd Earls of Kilmarnock were very powerful, having seized and imprisoned the young king.

James III married Margaret of Denmark in 1469, and so acquired Orkney and Shetland as part of the dowry. They had a son, another James. The king destroyed the power of the Boyds in retaliation for their earlier behaviour, but made himself very unpopular by acquiring much of the lands and property of the nobility. In 1482 James's favourite, Cochrane, and other friends of the king, were hanged by Archibald 'Bell the Cat' Douglas, Earl of Angus, from Lauder Bridge in front of the king. In 1482 and 1484 disgruntled nobles, such as the 9th Earl of Douglas, helped the English raid Scotland.

The Scottish nobles eventually decided to replace James with his 15-year-old son, the future James IV. James III raised an army, but was defeated at the Battle of Sauchieburn in 1488, and reputedly murdered after the battle by an assassin disguised as a priest. He was buried in **Cambuskenneth Abbey [J6]**, near Stirling.

The first recorded use of the thistle was in 1470, when it embellished one side of coins minted in Edinburgh.

1488-1513 James IV and the Battle of Flodden

James IV came to the throne when he was 15, and took control of the kingdom, although he reputedly wore a heavy iron chain for the rest of his life in penance for the death of his father. He ruled well, extending civil and criminal justice.

James destroyed the power of the Lord of the Isles in a campaign to the Hebrides in 1493, the final Lord of the Isles ending his days at **Paisley Abbey [J28]**.

James signed a treaty of perpetual peace with England at his marriage in 1502 to Margaret Tudor, sister of Henry VIII of England, although the couple do not seem to have liked each other. They did, however, have a son, James, born in 1512. He encouraged science and literature, and in 1507 printing was introduced to Scotland. He also remodelled the palaces at **Falkland [N27]**, **Holyrood [N31]** and **Linlithgow [N119]**; and he had the *Great Michael*, a huge warship, built at **Newhaven [Y143]**, near Edinburgh. Aberdeen University was founded, and whisky was drunk in the court by the end of his reign.

James also went on many pilgrimages to different sites around Scotland, as did both nobles, lairds and ordinary folk. This was to atone for sins, to find healing or even to help become pregnant (James also used them as an excuse to visit his many mistresses). Most places of pilgrimage were the shrines or relics of a saint or a holy well, such as **Dunfermline [J14]**, **Glasgow Cathedral [K19]**, **Iona [J20]**, **St Andrews [K26]**, **St Duthac's [K29]** at Tain, **St Magnus Cathedral [K33]**, **St Mary's Parish Church [K37]** at Whitekirk, **St Triduana's [K128]** at Restalrig and **Whithorn [J33]**.

James also founded **Ladykirk [K21]** near the English border, after he believed he had been saved from drowning by divine intervention. He was not to have a miraculous escape when it came to fighting the English.

The English and French, however, went to war, and in 1513, in support of France, James IV invaded England, although a peace had already been signed. At the Battle of Flodden, in Northumberland, despite holding a strong position, the Scottish army was disastrously defeated. James IV was slain, as were many Scottish nobles, lords, churchmen and soldiers, the worst defeat a Scottish army was ever to suffer. The story of the battle is told at Etal Castle in Northumberland.

1513-42 James V and the Battle of Solway Moss

James V was only one year old when he came to the throne. Margaret Tudor, widow of James IV, married the Douglas Earl of Angus, and the young king was kept a prisoner by Angus between 1526-8. Angus supported the English, but James wanted a French marriage, and eventually married Mary of Guise, by whom he had a daughter, Mary, in 1542 – after his first wife, Madeleine of France, had died. James also patronised the arts, and remodelled **Stirling Castle [N46]**. He, too, hated the Douglas family with a passion until he died – even pursuing his vendetta to Janet Douglas, Lady Glamis, whom he had burnt to death for witchcraft in 1537.

James made himself unpopular by his acquisitiveness from wealthy subjects and his reliance on disliked favourites. He enforced rule of law on the Border by dealing harshly with reivers such as the Armstrongs, further alienating many families. Johnnie Armstrong, head of the family, along with 50 of his men were summarily hanged, the site of the execution marked by the **Johnnie Armstrong of Gilnockie [Q14]** memorial.

James decided to invade England in 1542, but his army was divided by dislike of both James and his general and favourite, Oliver Sinclair. The Scottish army was soundly defeated by the English at the Battle of Solway Moss.

James died at **Falkland Palace [N27]** shortly after the battle, hearing of the birth of his daughter by Mary of Guise, at **Linlithgow Palace [N119]**. He reportedly said on his death bed *It cam wi' a lass and it'll gang wi' a lass*, meaning that the Stewarts had gained the throne through Marjorie Bruce and would lose it through his daughter, Mary, later Queen of Scots. He was wrong, however, as Mary married her cousin, Henry Stewart, Lord Darnley, from a close branch of the family, and it was Mary's son, James Stewart, who became king of both Scotland and England.

Falkland Palace – James V died here

Mary, James and Charles

1544-50 The Rough Wooing and Hertford's Invasions
Struggles followed the death of James V: between Mary of Guise, who supported the French, and the Hamilton Earl of Arran, Governor until 1554, who supported the English.

A treaty had been signed with the English that Mary, Queen of Scots, was to marry Edward, son of Henry VIII – but the Scots broke the agreement. In revenge, the south-east of Scotland was ravaged by the English, including the sacking of the abbeys; castles; and villages – 243 in all – by the Earl of Hertford. This became known as the Rough Wooing, a less than gentle attempt to encourage the Scots to change their mind.

A small English army was slaughtered at the Battle of Ancrum Moor in 1545, but the English invaded again and in 1547 the Scots, led by Hamilton, were heavily defeated at the Battle of Pinkie near Musselburgh. Much of southern Scotland was held by the English, who built a series of forts, including those at Haddington; Dunglass, south of Dunbar; and Eyemouth, north of Berwick.

The young Mary, Queen of Scots, who had been lodged at **Inchmahome Priory [J19]** and **Dumbarton Castle [N88]**, was sent to France for safety in 1548. By 1550, however, the Scots, with French help, had fought back. The English were forced to retreat from most of Scotland, abandoning the fort at Haddington after a long siege.

1550- The Reformation
The established Roman Catholic church was increasingly believed to be corrupt and overly wealthy – and its extensive lands were seen as a source of power and money by many Reforming nobles.

Henry VIII of England had renounced Papal authority, and had taken the church's wealth and lands for his own disposal. His dispute with the church was not only about doctrine – if at all: the church would not allow him to divorce his wife. Latterly, he took more direct action, and had several wives beheaded.

The teachings of Luther and Calvin had become popular in Scotland, particularly in the east, and some of those who advocated change were burnt as martyrs by the church. This had led, in part, to the murder of the Archbishop of St Andrews, Cardinal David Beaton, in 1546. He was slain at **St Andrews Castle [N146]**, and his dead body hung naked from one of the windows. The castle was then held by the Reformers, John Knox among them, until French aid broke their defence. Knox was captured after the battle and was made a slave on a French galley.

The Reformers continued to gain influence and power. In 1554 Mary of Guise, who supported the Roman Catholic church and the French, had herself made Regent, but in 1557 the First Bond was signed, in which several Reforming Earls and Lords declared their intent to overthrow the Roman Church.

This flared into open warfare in 1559, but peace was signed between the Lords and the Regent, allowing freedom of worship. The same year John Knox preached against idolatry, including at **St John's Kirk [K31]** in Perth. A mob then ransacked the church and destroyed the houses of friars in the town, and attacked **Scone [S41]** and **Coupar Angus [J7]** abbeys. Mary of Guise died in 1560, and Mary, Queen of Scots, returned from France in 1561 after Francis, her husband, had died. At a parliament the same year it was agreed to make Scotland a Protestant country, abolishing the Latin mass and introducing a reformed Confession of Faith.

Following the Reformation, all abbeys and priories were dissolved, ransacked and even destroyed, and many cathedrals were also abandoned or only part of the buildings were used, while others became ruinous.

Inchcolm Abbey [J18], although ruinous, has the best preserved set of monastic buildings, while **Dunfermline [J14]**, **Iona [J20]**, **Paisley [J28]**, and **Pluscarden [J29]** have been at least partly restored. There are fine ruins at **Arbroath [J2]**, **Beauly [J5]**, **Crossraguel [J9]**, **Dryburgh [J12]**, **Dundrennan [J13]**, **Glenluce [J16]**, **Holyrood [J17]**, **Jedburgh [J22]**, **Kelso [J23]**, **Melrose [J26]**, **Oronsay [J27]**, **Sweetheart [J32]** and **Whithorn [J33]**. Although the remains of **Inchmahome Priory [J19]** are very ruinous, it is located on an idyllic island in the Lake of Menteith. A list of abbeys can be found in Section **J**.

Only two cathedrals survived this period intact: **Glasgow [K19]** and **St Magnus [K33]**, Kirkwall. Others have since been restored to something of the former glory (**Brechin [K3]**, **Dornoch [K12]** and **Dunblane [K13]**) while **Cathedral of St Moluag [K4]** on Lismore, **Dunkeld [K16]** and **St Machar's [K32]** in Old Aberdeen are still used for worship, although part is ruinous. **Elgin Cathedral [K17]** and **St Andrews Cathedral [K26]** are fine ruins.

Unusually, **Fowlis Easter Church [K70]** survived the Reformation more or less intact, and still has original fittings and medieval board paintings.

Other good parish churches from before the Reformation include **Auld Kirk of Kilbirnie [K48]**, **Church of the Holy Rude [K6]**, **Kirk of St Nicholas [K20]**, **St Clement's Church [K28]** at Rodel, **St Giles Cathedral [K30]**, **St John's Kirk [K31]** in Perth, **St Mary's Church [K35]** in Haddington, **St Michael's Parish Church [K38]** with its unusual steeple in Linlithgow and **St Monans Parish Church [K39]**. Many other fine churches, both intact and ruinous, are listed in sections **K1** and **K2**. New churches were built after the Reformation, free from idolatrous images, such as **Burntisland Parish Church [K55]** and **Greyfriars Kirk [K72]** in Edinburgh.

1558-60 Mary, Queen of Scots

Mary had been taken to France in 1548 when she was only six years

Holyrood Abbey – the ruin stands by Holyroodhouse

old, and had been brought up in the French court. She was the legitimate heir to the throne of Scots; and the French believed she was the rightful Queen of England, as they considered Elizabeth of England to be illegitimate. Elizabeth was the daughter of Anne Boleyn, but Henry VIII had divorced his first wife to marry Anne, a divorce not recognised by the Catholic church.

Mary was married to Francis, the Dauphin of France in 1558 when she was 15, although it is not clear whether the marriage was ever consummated. The Dauphin, later Francis II of France, was a sickly young man, and after they had been married for only two years, he died in 1560 from an ear infection. Mary returned to Scotland in 1561, although she continued to use 'Stuart', a French misspelling of Stewart.

1561-87 Mary returns to Scotland

Mary began her personal reign sensibly, remaining a Catholic, but allowing the Scottish church to be Protestant: only Mary was allowed to hear Mass. She had trouble with the powerful Catholic Gordon Earl of Huntly in 1562, but her forces defeated the Earl at the Battle of Corrichie, and **Huntly Castle [N113]** was torched, while the Earl died, reputedly from apoplexy.

Her marriage in 1565 to Henry Stewart, Lord Darnley, however, precipitated a revolt. The murder of David Rizzio (who is buried in the **Canongate [K57]** Cemetery) – her secretary and favourite – by Darnley, and others, at **Holyroodhouse [N31]**, forced Mary and Darnley apart. Mary had to flee to the safety of **Craigmillar Castle [N76]**; it was also here that a plot was hatched to get rid of Darnley, although it is not clear if Mary knew of it. Knox, who returned from the Continent and England, further undermined her position by preaching against her, after they had had a series of heated meetings.

Mary gave birth to a son, the future James VI, at **Edinburgh Castle [N25]**; but Darnley was strangled at **Kirk o' Field [I1]** in Edinburgh in 1567 after the house in which he had been staying was blown up with gunpowder. Mary quickly married James Hepburn, Earl of Bothwell, who was suspected of being involved in the murder. Bothwell had apparently kidnapped the Queen, but she had previously visited him for several days at **Hermitage Castle [N110]** after riding the many miles from **Jedburgh [I2]**.

An army was raised against Mary and Bothwell, and they had to flee from **Borthwick Castle [N7]** in disguise. They were defeated at the Battle of Carberry Hill, and Mary surrendered while Bothwell fled Scotland. Mary was imprisoned in **Lochleven Castle [N121]**, where she was forced to abdicate in favour of her young son, James VI. Mary escaped from the castle in 1568, but – although supported by the Hamiltons, Kennedys and many other families – lost the Battle of Langside. She fled Scotland in 1568, spending her last night at **Dundrennan Abbey [J13]**, hoping for help from her cousin, Elizabeth of England, but was imprisoned when she arrived in England.

Many families still supported Mary and strongholds, such as **Edinburgh [N25]** and **Blackness [N55]** Castles, held out for her until support withered.

After having been imprisoned for many years, Mary was eventually found guilty of plotting against Elizabeth. Mary was beheaded in 1587 at Fotheringhay Castle in England.

Sites associated with Mary can be found in Section **I**.

Regents acted during the minority of James VI: the Stewart Earl of Moray, who was murdered at Linlithgow in 1570; the Stewart Earl of Lennox, father of Darnley, who was shot and killed at Stirling; the Erskine Earl of Mar, who died in 1572; and the Douglas Earl of Morton, who was Regent until 1578, but was executed in 1581 for his suspected part in the murder of Darnley.

The University of Edinburgh was founded in 1580.

1581-1602 James VI

James VI became king in his own right in 1581, but in 1582 was kidnapped by a group of Protestant nobles, led by the Ruthven Earl of Gowrie. This became known as the Ruthven Raid, and the king was held at Ruthven Castle, which is now known as **Huntingtower Castle [N112]**.

James escaped and by 1585 had assumed control of the kingdom. He attempted to bring about conciliation between the different factions of Scottish nobles, but dealt ruthlessly with those who kidnapped him. In 1600, James murdered the Earl of Gowrie and his brother, the Master of Ruthven, at Gowrie House in Perth, claiming that they had attacked him, in what was later known as the Gowrie Conspiracy.

James married Anne of Denmark, and had several children, including Charles, who was later king. James was also heir to the English throne while Elizabeth remained unmarried and without children. James attempted to force an Episcopal church – one where he could choose the bishops – onto the reformed Scottish church. He restored some of the prosperity of the country, but he was the first king to impose regular taxation in a time of peace. During this time, much of the former abbey and church lands were parcelled out to different families.

He extended royal authority in the more distant areas of the country, although there was a Catholic rising by the Gordon Earl of Huntly, in 1594, when royal forces were defeated at the Battle of Glenlivet. The rising failed and **Huntly Castle [N113]** was sacked again.

1603 Union of Crowns of Scots and England

Elizabeth I of England died, and James VI – James I of England – succeeded to the English throne. James, and his court, moved to London, from where he governed Scotland. He returned only once, although the countries maintained separate parliaments.

Many of the Scots nobility did well from the Union of Crowns with increased lands and wealth. Castles and houses became more elaborate and comfortable, and the need for defence was per-

Glamis Castle – one of the most impressive buildings in Scotland

ceived to have lessened. A few of the excellent examples of the grand castles of the nobility can be found at **Castle Fraser [N11]**, **Craigievar Castle [N15]**, **Crathes Castle [N16]**, **Dunrobin Castle [N23]**, **Fyvie Castle [N29]**, **Glamis Castle [N30]** and **Kellie Castle [N33]**. There is a full list of great castles to visit in Sections **N1** and **N2**.

Gardens were also an important feature, and **Aberdour Castle [N49]**, **Crathes Castle [N16]**, **Drummond Castle Gardens [N21]**, **Edzell Castle [N98]**, **Malleny House Gardens [S97]**, **Megginch Castle Gardens [N39]** and **Pitmedden Gardens [V62]** are all worth a visit. There is a full list in section **S2**.

Culross Palace [S15], **Argyll's Lodging [S3]** and **Mar's Wark [N126]** in Stirling, **Gladstone's Land [S23]** and **John Knox House [S31]** in Edinburgh, **Provost Ross's House [N43]** and **Provost Skene's House [N44]** in Aberdeen, **Skaill House [S42]**, and **Provand's Lordship [N42]** in Glasgow are all fine townhouses or dwellings.

The rest of the population meantime lived much as before, often facing periods of hunger, conflict and poverty, a gulf opening up between the richest of the nobles and the ordinary folk. The **Clansmen Centre [V20]** at Fort Augustus illustrates life of this period, as does the **Highland Folk Museum [V39/V40]**.

1610-18 Episcopal Church restored

James finally managed to reintroduce an Episcopal church, governed by bishops whom he could elect. He also tried to pacify the Highlands, where Catholic worship was still widespread, but without much success.

1625-40 Charles I

James VI died and was succeeded by his son, Charles I. Charles was married to Henrietta Maria, who was a Catholic, by whom he had two sons, Charles and James, as well as several other children.

Charles I did not rule well, angering many of his subjects, and his religious policy was even more Episcopalian than his father – some were worried that he would reintroduce Catholicism. The introduction of a new prayer book in 1637 caused outrage in Scotland, culminating in the signing at **Greyfriars [K72]** Kirkyard of the National Covenant of 1638, asserting the right of the people to keep the Reformed church and to introduce Presbyterianism. This was followed by the Bishop's Wars of 1639-41, and an army of Covenanters occupied Newcastle. Peace was signed in 1641.

1643-49 Civil War

The Scots, again angered by Charles's behaviour in trying to restore an Episcopal Church, agreed to an alliance with the English parliament – the Solemn League and Covenant – on the condition that England would adopt a Presbyterian church. Civil War broke out and Charles was defeated at the Battle of Marston Moor by an army of Scots, led by David Leslie, and English, by Cromwell, in 1644.

James Graham, Marquis of Montrose, although having signed the National Covenant, fought for Charles, leading a brilliant campaign, and winning a string of victories – battles at Tippermuir, Aberdeen, Inverlochy, **Auldearn [V10]**, Alford, and Kilsyth – against the Covenanters. He was eventually defeated, however, at the Battle of Philiphaugh, by Leslie in 1645 – although Montrose, himself, escaped. Atrocities on both sides, including the sacking of towns and castles, and the execution of prisoners and camp followers – including women and children – made the fighting particularly bitter.

Charles surrendered to the Scots at Newark in 1646, where he was turned over the English. Despite Scottish protests, Charles I was beheaded in 1649, and Cromwell assumed control.

Excise duty was first put on whisky at a parliament in 1644.

1650-54 The Battle of Dunbar and occupation by Cromwell

Montrose raised a small army for Charles II, but his men were slaughtered at Carbisdale. A few days later Montrose was captured and taken to Edinburgh, where he was hanged.

The Scots were angry at the beheading of Charles I, and rose against the Cromwellian administration. Cromwell invaded Scotland, and his army defeated Leslie and the Scots at the Battle of Dunbar, and went on to successfully invade Scotland. Many castles, such as **Dirleton [N82]**, **Neidpath [N132]** and **Tantallon [N148]** held out for the Scots, but these were quickly reduced. The Scots, in turn, marched into England, after Charles II was crowned at **Scone [S41]** in 1651, but were defeated at the Battle at Worcester the same year. Charles II only narrowly escaped and fled to the Continent. The last Scottish stronghold, **Dunnottar Castle [N90]**, fell in 1652, although the Scottish regalia was smuggled out and hidden in **Kinneff Old Parish Church [K83]** until the Restoration.

Although the Scots rose again in 1654, under the Cunningham Earl of Glencairn, resistance gradually fizzled out after a crushing defeat at Inverkeithing. Cromwell remained in power, holding Scotland as no foreign army had done before, and absorbing the country into his Commonwealth.

1660-85 Restoration of Charles II and Religious Wars

Charles II was restored in 1660, after the death of Cromwell and the collapse of his Commonwealth. Charles had spent many years in exile, and was married to Catherine of Braganza, although they had no children.

Charles re-established an Episcopal church in Scotland in 1661, and was intolerant of Covenanters, who wished to pursue a Presbyterian form of worship. Persecution of the Covenanters led to the Pentland Rising of 1666, which ended in their defeat at the Battle of Rullion Green.

In 1679, after further persecution and the murder of Archbishop Sharp, the Covenanters rose again and won a small battle at Drumclog against Bonnie Dundee. They quickly raised an army, but were crushed by a government force under the Duke of Monmouth at Bothwell Brig.

The struggle continued, led by Richard Cameron, but his supporters, the Cameronians – who denounced the King's authority – were defeated at the battle of Airds Moss in 1680. Cameron was slain and his hands and head were hacked off to be brought before Parliament.

The years 1681-85, known as the Killing Times, saw further atrocities committed against the Covenanters. Not least were those by Bonnie Dundee, John Graham of Claverhouse, also known as Bloody Clavers, from his base at the **Castle of St John [N70]** in Stranraer, although the actual number of deaths was about 100. The **Wigtown Martyrs [M8]**, two of whom were women tethered to a post to be drowned by the incoming tide, were some of Bonnie Dundee's victims. There is some debate as to whether they were actually rescued. There are many Covenanter memorials to those who lost their lives, and the **Greenhill Covenanter's House [V38]** illustrates life in the turbulent period. 167 men, women and children who had Covenanting sympathies were imprisoned at **Dunnottar Castle [N90]** and nine of them died. Others were imprisoned on the **Bass Rock [G1]**.

It was during this time, in 1680, that Scotland's first free lending library was established at **In-**

Dunnottar Castle – an imposing stronghold perched on cliffs above the sea

nerpeffray [K76] by David, Lord Madderty. Fashions were also changing with the construction of symmetrical mansions with Palladian influences, such as **Drumlanrig Castle [N20]**, the re-modelling of **Holyroodhouse [N31]**, **Kinross House [S94]**, **Newhailes [S36]**, **The Binns [S43]** and **Winton House [S47]**.

1685-89 James VII

In 1685 Charles II died, and James VII, his younger brother, came to the throne at the age of 52. He was married twice: firstly to his mistress, Anne Hyde, by whom he had several children: including Mary and Anne, who both later came to the throne.

When Anne Hyde died, he married the young Mary of Modena, and their children included James Francis, who became James VIII, the Old Pretender.

James converted to Catholicism in the 1660s, and made himself unpopular during his short reign by trying to remove any penalties for Catholic worship.

The Duke of Monmouth, Charles II's illegitimate son, rebelled against James, supported in Scotland by the Campbell Earl of Argyll, but the rebellion failed and both were executed. In 1688, however, James's English subjects rose against him and he fled abroad. William of Orange – husband of Mary, James's daughter – was invited to become king. This was confirmed in 1689 by a Scottish Convention, which had dubious legality.

The stage was set for years of strife and rebellions.

The Jacobite Risings

1689-90 Revolution

William and Mary were confirmed as joint rulers of Scotland in 1689.

John Graham of Claverhouse, Bonnie Dundee, raised a Jacobite army in support of James VII and II, and defeated a government army at the Battle of **Killiecrankie [O8]**. Graham, however, was mortally wounded during the fighting, and the Jacobites were frustrated besieging Dunkeld, and eventually mostly dispersed. A small force was defeated at the Battle of Cromdale in 1690.

James landed in Ireland, but his army was defeated at the Battle of the Boyne in 1690, and he fled back to France.

1692 The Massacre of Glencoe

William offered to pardon Jacobite chiefs if they swore allegiance to him by 31 December 1691. Most chiefs took the oath by the deadline, but the chief of the MacDonalds of Glencoe was a few days late in signing, having been delayed by the weather. Deciding to make an example of the clan, William ordered fire and sword against the MacDonalds. The massacre took place in **Glencoe [O4]** on 13 February 1692, carried out by troops, commanded by Campbell of Glenlyon, who were billeted on the MacDonalds and received their hospitality. About 40 of the clan were killed, many dying in the snow as they fled from the Campbells. This was by no means the only or even worst atrocity, but a storm of protest grew from an act which had government sanction and had been approved by William.

1695 Founding of the Bank of Scotland and the Darien Scheme

The Bank of Scotland was founded in this year, as was the Company of Scotland Trading to Africa and the Indies. The Scots tried to set up a colony on the isthmus of Panama in 1698. The scheme was a disaster because of disease, attacks by the Spanish, and hostility and lack of support from the English. It was also poorly planned and organised by the Scots, and a huge amount of the nation's capital was lost in the venture.

1694-1707 Deaths of Mary and William

Mary died in 1694 and William in 1702, after his horse stumbled on a molehill, the Jacobites thereafter toasting *the little gentleman in the velvet jacket*. As they had no children, Anne, second daughter of James VII by Anne Hyde, came to the throne. Anne was married to Prince George of Denmark, and although they had 18 children, all of them and her husband predeceased her.

1707 Union of Parliaments of Scotland & England

Despite fierce opposition in Scotland and rioting in Edinburgh, the parliaments of England and Scotland were united under the direction of Anne. This union was achieved more by bribery and coercion than by any wish of the Scots to join with the English – although some saw considerable economic advantages in sharing the wealth of England's growing empire. The last Scottish parliament did vote to keep its own church, courts and legal system. The separate kingdom of Scots ceased to exist, and was incorporated into the United Kingdom of Great Britain.

1714 Death of Queen Anne and Accession of George I

Anne died, and there being no other close Protestant heirs, George, Elector of Hanover, was asked to be king. Anne was the last Stewart monarch, although since the Union of the Crowns in 1603, the Stewarts had seldom visited Scotland, except in times of need or war. Few of them ruled well, many were motivated by greed and lust, and latterly they had shown little concern for their Scottish subjects.

George I, first of the Hanoverian monarchs, was crowned king, although he could not speak English, and had even less interest in the northern part of his kingdom. There was much discontent in Scotland, and to a lesser extent in England.

1715 Jacobite Rising

The Erskine Earl of Mar raised the standard for James VIII, son of James VII and Mary of Modena, at Braemar; but the Jacobite army was poorly led. The Jacobites were brought to battle at **Sheriffmuir [O12]**, after which, although indecisive, the Jacobites withdrew and disbanded. Another small army was also defeated at Preston in England.

James VIII landed at Peterhead after the battle, and although he stayed in Scotland until 1716, it was too late to make any difference, and he retreated back to France. Some of his supporters were forfeited, and lost their titles and lands, a few lost their heads.

1719 Jacobite Rising

A small army of Spaniards, numbering about 300, landed at **Eilean Donan Castle [N26]**, but they were soon defeated by Hanoverian forces at the Battle of **Glenshiel [O6]**.

1724 Building of roads

General Wade began a programme of building military roads and barracks throughout the Highlands of Scotland to enable the Hanoverian government deal effectively with any rising by the clans. They also aided the passage of Jacobite forces. Many stretches of these military ways remain,

Eilean Donan Castle – scene of the 1719 Jacobite Rising

and also worth a mention are **Garva Bridge [O3]**, near Laggan and **Wade's Bridge [O13]** at Aberfeldy.

1727 Death of George I and burning of the Last Witch

George I died in 1727 at Hanover, and was succeeded by his son, George II.

This year also saw the founding of the Royal Bank of Scotland, and reputedly the burning, at Dornoch, of the last person found guilty of witchcraft. The **Witch's Stone [M9]** at Dornoch commemorates the event. Witchcraft accusations were relatively numerous in Scotland after James VI had become obsessed with the subject following the North Berwick Witch Trials. Hundreds of people were accused in the 17th century, although by the beginning of the 18th century this had reduced to very few. **Maggie Walls Monument [M3]** commemorates one of the alleged victims.

1728 Birth of Robert Adam

Robert Adam was born in 1728 at Kirkcaldy into a famous family of architects, which included his father, William, and his brothers. William was responsible for work at **Fort George [P6]**, and later at **Chatelherault [S13]**, **Duff House [S18]**, **Floors Castle [S21]**, **Haddo House [S25]**, **Hopetoun House [S28]** and **House of Dun [S29]** – and many others. Robert, and his brothers James and John, founded an architectural style based on classical designs. Robert was responsible for designing **Culzean Castle [S16]**, the **Georgian House [S22]** and **No 28 Charlotte Square [S37]** Edinburgh, and part of **Mellerstain [S34]**, and there are many examples of their work throughout Scotland. For a full list of mansions see Section **S1**.

1733 Allan Ramsay

Ramsay, who was born in Edinburgh in 1713, returned to Edinburgh in 1733 after studying abroad. He became one of the major portrait painters of the 18th century, moving to London, and was a friend of David Hume, Adam Smith, Robert Adam and other influential people of the Enlightenment. Some of his many portraits are exhibited in the **Scottish National Portrait Gallery [Y12]** and the **National Gallery of Scotland [U13]**.

1734 Death of Rob Roy MacGregor

Rob Roy MacGregor died, and was buried at **Balquhidder [K50]**. He was a farmer and cattle dealer, but took part in thievery and blackmail, and was involved in the Jacobite Risings of 1689, 1715 and 1719. He became a legend in his own lifetime, although he died peacefully at the ripe old age of 74. There is information about MacGregor at the **Rob Roy and the Trossachs Visitor Centre [Y165]**.

1736 Birth of James Watt

James Watt, the pioneer of steam engines, was born in 1736 at Greenock. There is information about him at **McLean Museum [Y126]** in Greenock and the **Kinneil Museum [Y111]** near Bo'ness.

1744 Golf

Although a form of golf had been played in Scotland from the 15th century, it was in 1744 that the first golf club, the Honourable Company of Edinburgh Golfers, was founded. The **British Golf Museum [Y1]** is in St Andrews.

1745-46 Jacobite Rising

Bonnie Prince Charlie, the Young Pretender, son of James VIII and Princess Maria Clementina Sobieska, landed in Scotland and raised an army at **Glenfinnan [O5]**, most of it from the Highlands. His army advanced south and defeated a Hanoverian force at the Battle of **Prestonpans [O11]**: a cairn commemorates the event. The Jacobites then marched into England, and got as far south as Derby, but eventually had to retreat, although in good order. The Prince was disappointed by lack of support in England and the Scottish lowlands, and argued with his generals.

After winning the Battle of Falkirk in 1746, the Jacobites were brought to battle at **Culloden Moor [O2]** by the Duke of Cumberland. The Jacobites were defeated and slaughtered, and atrocities committed after the battle well earned Cumberland the title Butcher.

After many adventures, including a dramatic escape with help from Flora MacDonald, Charles eventually fled to France, but many of his supporters were executed and their property forfeited. The wearing of tartan and Highland dress and the playing of bagpipes were proscribed, and the carrying of arms forbidden. Forts were also built, such as **Fort George [P6]**, to accommodate garrisons for quelling any further risings.

Charlie returned to the continent a folk hero, but little in the rest of his life inspired any admiration. He began to drink and in 1760 his wife deserted him. He was forced to move to Rome, and there died at the age of 67, in 1788.

Many sites which are open to the public are associated with Bonnie Prince Charlie and the Jacobites. There is a visitor centre at **Culloden [O2]**, and the battlefield can be visited. Various barracks and forts were built around the Highlands including **Fort George [P6]**, **Fort Augustus [Y80]**, Fort William, **Bernera Barracks [O1]** and **Inversnaid Barracks [O7]**. A list of Jacobite sites can be found in Section **O**.

Culloden Moor – site of the last pitched battle on British soil in 1746

Modern Scotland

1753 Opening of Bonawe Iron Furnace
Bonawe Iron Furnace [X5] was established in this year, and was in operation until 1876. Parts of Scotland became increasingly industrialised, especially the central belt around Glasgow and Edinburgh, but also other parts of the country which are now considered rural such as Bonawe and **Easdale [X16]**, a centre of slate extraction.

1754 Founding of the Royal and Ancient Golf Club
The Royal and Ancient Golf Club was founded at St Andrews in 1754.

1756 Birth of Sir Henry Raeburn
Raeburn was born in 1757 in Edinburgh, and became a leading portrait painter, following in the footsteps of Allan Ramsay. He produced about 600 portraits, including the famous portrait of Walter Scott, some of which are on display at the **Scottish National Portrait Gallery [Y12]** and the **National Gallery of Scotland [U13]** in Edinburgh, and was knighted in 1822. He died in 1823.

1757 Birth of Thomas Telford
Thomas Telford, the famous and prolific civil engineer, was born at Westerkirk in Dumfries in 1757. He was the chief engineer involved in the building of the **Caledonian Canal [X7]**, begun in 1804; and he built the Telford Bridge in Edinburgh, as well as harbours at Aberdeen and Wick. He died in 1834 and is buried in Westminster Abbey.

1759 Birth of Robert Burns
Robert Burns, Scotland's most popular poet, was born in Alloway, Ayrshire, in 1759. He was a farmer, both in Ayrshire and Dumfries, and an excise man. His poetry in Scots and English won him renown, and among his best-known poems are *For Auld Lang Syne*, *Scots Wha Hae* and *Tam o' Shanter*. He died in 1796 at Dumfries, when only 37 years old. Many sites and museums associated with poet are open to the public, including **Burns Cottage [T6]** in Alloway, **Burns House Museum [T7]** in Mauchline, **Ellisland [T12]**, and **Burns House [T8]** in Dumfries. There is a full list in Section **T**.

Burns Cottage – the poet was born here in 1759

1760 Death of George II and Accession of George III
George II, the last British monarch to lead an army into battle, died in 1760, and was succeeded by his son, George III.

1776 Edinburgh's New Town started
Edinburgh became very cramped, confined within the city walls and by Castle Hill. In 1776, land to the north of the castle was drained and cleared, and broad well-planned streets laid out, including Princes Street, George Street and Queen Street. It was to a design by James Craig. Building continued in different phases until 1840. Fine examples of buildings include the **Georgian House [S22]** and **No 28 Charlotte Square [S37]**.

1770 Founding of the Clyde Trust
The Clyde Trust was founded in 1770, and was responsible for a massive programme of excavation and dredging which eventually made the River Clyde navigable as far as Glasgow. This made Glasgow a centre of trade to rival Liverpool or London.

1771 Birth of Sir Walter Scott
Walter Scott was born in 1771 in Edinburgh. He revived interest in Scottish history, encouraging George IV to come to Scotland in 1822 after the rediscovery of the Scottish regalia in 1818. Scott moved to **Abbotsford [S1]** in 1812, which now houses a collection of historic artefacts. Scott wrote a number of novels and poems including *Ivanhoe* and *Waverley*. He died at Abbotsford in 1832, and is buried at **Dryburgh Abbey [J12]**.

1776 Publication of *Wealth of Nations* and death of David Hume
Adam Smith, born in Kirkcaldy in 1723, published the influential work, the *Wealth of Nations*. David Hume, the well-known philosopher, who was born in 1711, died this year.

1785 Founding of New Lanark
New Lanark was planned in 1785, and became one of the largest and important water-powered spinning mills and a model industrial complex. Robert Owen took over as manager in 1800, and introduced many enlightened social reforms, such as schools and sub-sidised shops. **New**

New Lanark – a World Heritage Site

Lanark [X39], a World Heritage Site, is open to the public.

1782
The Act proscribing Highland dress was repealed. Despite this, few folk ordinary went back to

wearing it, and increasingly it was the nobility who liked to be decked in tartan and plaid.

1790 Death of Flora MacDonald and opening of Forth and Clyde Canal

Although she had spent much of her life in North America, Flora MacDonald returned to her native Skye, where she died in 1790. Flora was born at **Milton [O10]** on South Uist, and is buried at Kilmuir by the **Skye Museum of Island Life [V73]**.

The **Forth and Clyde Canal [X19]**, between the two rivers, also opened this year.

1790- The Clearances

Many Highland estates were reorganised for the farming of sheep (then shooting) rather than farming, and landless tenants were thrown off land they had held for generations. They left for the industries of the lowlands or went abroad, although those who left fared better than those that stayed. Lowland areas were also cleared of people to make way for improved agricultural techniques. One particularly bitter episode was in Sutherland, and there are displays at the **Strathnaver Museum [Y185]** at Bettyhill and **Timespan Heritage Centre [Y197]** at Helmsdale.

1792 Death of John Paul Jones

John Paul Jones, born near Kirkbean in 1747, is generally credited with the founding of the American Navy. He supported American independence. His daring exploits won him recognition from America, including monuments at the Annapolis Naval Academy and in Washington DC, and a reputation as a feared pirate from the British. There is a information about him at the **John Paul Jones Birthplace Museum [Y106]** at Kirkbean.

1801 Opening of Crinan Canal

The **Crinan Canal [X11]** was opened, allowing shipping to avoid sailing around the Mull of Kintyre.

1811 Birth of Sir James Young Simpson

Simpson, who was born at Bathgate in 1811, pioneered the use of anaesthesia in childbirth in 1847, while professor of Midwifery at Edinburgh. He died in 1870.

1812 Launching of *The Comet* and ship building on the Clyde

The Comet, the first steamboat used on a navigable river, was launched on the Clyde. The Clyde became famous for shipbuilding, after the *Vulcan* (1818), an early iron ship, and *Faerie Queen* (1831), an iron steamer, were launched here. By the 1850s, it had become the major shipbuilding centre. The *Queen Mary* (1934) and *Queen Elizabeth* (1939) were also built here. By the 1960s, however, shipbuilding was in decline. **Clydebuilt [X10]** and **The Tall Ship at Glasgow Harbour [X51]** explore Glasgow's maritime heritage. Cruises are available on the **Waverley [X55]**, the last sea-going paddle steamer in the world

1813 Birth of David Livingstone

David Livingstone was born at Blantyre in 1813, and later achieved fame as an African explorer. In 1834 he became a medical missionary, and travelled extensively through Africa. Livingstone disappeared and after some years' silence, Stanley went to look for him. He found him in 1871, although Livingstone went on exploring until his death two years later. The **David Livingstone Centre [Y65]** is located in Blantyre.

1820 The Radical War

Following years of deep economic depression, a series of riots and unrest culminated in the Radical War, led by radical weavers. This war was in fact two small uprisings, one to seize the Carron Iron Works, near Falkirk, and another in Strathaven. Both were crushed by government forces, and the leaders were executed, while others were transported. The **John Hastie Museum [Y103]** at Strathaven, has information on radical revolts.

1820s- Whisky

Whisky had been distilled in Scotland probably from the earliest times, and had reached the Lowlands by 1500. It was first taxed in 1644, and it was henceforth illegal to produce whisky for sale. There were, however, many hundreds of illicit stills. This was seen as a problem by the government, and steps were taken to prevent whisky being produced.

The Tall Ship at Glasgow Harbour

The whisky of the time was of varied quality, and turned cloudy when water was added to it. When vineyards were hit by disease, whisky began to be produced commercially after problems with consistency and colour had been overcome. Whisky is now one of Scotland's major exports, and distilleries – some 40 of which are open to the public – throughout Scotland, produce both malt and blended whiskies – see section **W** for a full list.

1822 George IV visits Scotland and opening of the Union and the Caledonian Canals

George IV visited Edinburgh this year, the first monarch to do so since Charles II in the 17th century.

This year saw the opening of the Union Canal, which linked Edinburgh to the **Forth and Clyde Canal [X19]** at Falkirk. The canals have recently been renovated and joined by the Falkirk Wheel. The **Edinburgh Canal Centre [X17]** and **Linlithgow Canal Centre [X28]** are on the Union Canal.

The **Caledonian Canal [X7]** was also opened this year, designed by Thomas Telford, running from Fort William to near Inverness. There is a heritage centre in **Fort Augustus [Y80]**.

1823 Royal Botanic Garden

The **Royal Botanic Garden [S102]** was moved to Inverleith from Holyrood, where it had been founded in 1670. **Benmore Botanic Garden [S65], Botanic Gardens [S68]** in Glasgow, **Cruickshank Botanic Garden [S77], Dawyck Botanic Garden [S78], Linn Botanic Garden [S95], Logan Botanic Garden [S96], St Andrews Botanic Garden [S105]** and **University Botanic Garden [S109]** in Dundee are also open to the public. Gardens are listed in Section **S2**.

1824 James Hogg and *The Private Memoirs and Confessions of a Justified Sinner*

James Hogg was born at Ettrick in the Borders, and is known as the 'Ettrick Shepherd'. He is best known for *The Private Memoirs and Confessions of a Justified Sinner* but was also a poet and biographer of Sir Walter Scott. There is an exhibition about Hogg at **Aikwood Tower [N1]**, and the **James Hogg Monument [T19]** is at Ettrick.

1826 Marriage of Thomas Carlyle and Jane Baillie Welsh

Thomas Carlyle, who was born at Ecclefechan in 1795, was a fine essayist, historian and social reformer, while Jane Baillie Welsh, born in Haddington in 1801, is best known for her collections of letters. They married in 1826. **Thomas Carlyle's Birthplace [T31]** is open to the public, as is the **Jane Welsh Carlyle Museum [T20]**.

1827 Birth of Joseph Lister

Joseph Lister, who was born in 1827, pioneered the use of antiseptic surgery during the 1860s, while at Glasgow Royal Infirmary.

1829 Burke and Hare and bodysnatching

By the 1820s, Edinburgh had become a centre of excellence for medicine and anatomy. To supply the demand for new corpses to dissect, some took to digging up newly buried bodies, and sold them to the medical school. This gruesome practice became widespread, and families took steps to protect their dead. Mort safes and watchtowers were introduced to protect burial grounds.

Burke and Hare (Irishmen who had come to Scotland to build the Union Canal) decided it was easier to murder acquaintances and even family to provide fresh corpses. They were eventually caught after killing some 18 individuals. Although Hare turned King's evidence, Burke was hanged in 1829 and his corpse was dissected: his skeleton is retained in the University of Edinburgh.

1838 Accession of Queen Victoria

Queen Victoria came to the throne, and she and Prince Albert first visited Scotland in 1842, and every year thereafter.

1842 Railway line between Edinburgh and Glasgow opened

The first railway line between Edinburgh and Glasgow was opened in 1842, followed by a great expansion in railways in Scotland, greatly improving transport and communications. The railways flourished, but gradually road transport improved, and much of the once good rail network was dismantled. Sites of interest include **Bo'ness and Kinneil Railway [X6], Caledonian Railway [X8], Keith and Dufftown Railway [X25], Scottish Industrial Railway Centre [X42]**, and the **Strathspey Steam Railway [X49]**. There are also museums such as the **Museum of Scotland [Y6], Springburn Museum [X48], Museum of Transport [X37]** in Glasgow, **Glenfinnan Station Museum [X21], Maud Railway Museum [X29], Scottish Railway Exhibition**

[X6] at Bo'ness, and the **Old Royal Station [R3]** at Ballater.

There is a full list of transport and industrial sites in Section **X**.

1843 The Disruption and forming of the Free Church

After a long-running dispute within the Church of Scotland, a large number of ministers broke away from the established church and formed the Free Church of Scotland. The Free Church is still popular in the Highlands and Islands.

1847 Birth of Alexander Graham Bell

Bell, born in Edinburgh in 1847, invented the telephone in 1876 in the USA. He died in 1922.

1847 Andrew Carnegie

Carnegie, who was born in Dunfermline in 1835, emigrated with his family to the USA. Carnegie was a successful entrepreneur, investing in iron and steel, and the railways, and became one of the richest men in the world. He often holidayed in Scotland, and became a noted philanthropist, his generosity extending to Dunfermline. There is the **Andrew Carnegie Birthplace Museum [Y22]**, and **Pittencrieff House [Y161]** in Dunfermline, the latter purchased for the burgh after he had not been allowed to play in the grounds when a child.

Andrew Carnegie Birthplace Museum

1850 Birth of Robert Louis Stevenson

Robert Louis Stevenson, the author who wrote *Treasure Island*, *The Strange Case of Dr Jekyll and Mr Hyde* and *Kidnapped*, was born in Edinburgh in 1850. The **Writer's Museum [T33]** in Edinburgh has displays on Stevenson, as well as on Robert Burns and Walter Scott.

Stevenson's grandfather designed lighthouses, including the outbuildings around **Kinnaird Head Castle [X26]**, which now forms part of a lighthouse museum.

1855 Balmoral Castle

Queen Victoria and Prince Albert purchased the Balmoral Estate and built a new castle. Queen Victoria rehabilitated (or even invented) the Highlands and all things tartan, a process that Walter Scott had started.

The royal family still holiday at **Balmoral [R1]**, and **Crathie Parish Church [R2]** is used by the family when at the castle. **Old Royal Station [R3]** at Ballater was built for Queen Victoria.

1855- Clans and tartans

While it is true that clans and tartans were part of Highland life, the romanticised nature of the connection has now been extended to all parts of Scotland. Many people like to trace their Scottish ancestry. There is a list of museums, castles and other sites associated with different families and clans, tartan and bagpipes in Section **Q**.

1858 Greyfriars Bobby

When John Gray, a Midlothian farmer, died in 1858 and was buried in Greyfriars Kirkyard in Edinburgh, his terrier Bobby stayed by his master's grave until the dog died in 1872. There is a statue of **Greyfriars Bobby [Z7]** near the kirkyard, and information and mementoes in **Greyfriars Kirk [K72]**.

1868 Charles Rennie Mackintosh

Mackintosh was born in Glasgow, and won a competition to design the new **Glasgow School of Art [U6]** in 1894, and his designs won him much renown. He died in 1928. **The Hill House [U19]** at Helensburgh is an outstanding example of his work, and in Glasgow are the **House for an Art Lover [U8]**, **Queen's Cross Church [U15]**, **Scotland Street School [Y10]**, **The Lighthouse [Y17]** and **Willow Tearooms [U22]**, all designed by Mackintosh.

1873 Scottish Football Association founded

The Scottish Football Association was founded after a meeting of the representatives of eight clubs. Glasgow Rangers football club was also founded. There **Scottish Football Museum [Y11]** is housed at Hampden Park in Glasgow.

Queen's Cross Church – Mackintosh's masterpiece

1875 Death of Alexander 'Greek' Thomson

Alexander Thomson, the famous architect, was born at Balfron in 1817, and developed Gothic and Grecian styles in his buildings. He is particularly associated with Glasgow, and **Holmwood House [S27]** is a good example of his work.

1879 Tay Bridge Disaster

The Tay Bridge, linking Dundee to Fife, collapsed as a train crossed it, killing all those aboard, reportedly around 150 people. **McManus Galleries [Y127]** has information about the disaster.

1880- Crofters' Rights

By the 1880s there was general discontent with the way that crofters were treated by their landlords. In 1882 this came to a head at the Battle of the Braes on Skye, when crofters defied their landlords over the introduction of sheep, and policemen from Glasgow were brought in. This forced the government to review the situation and set up a commission of inquiry. The Crofters' Holding Act was passed by parliament in 1886, giving crofters new rights and security of tenure.

Although Scots from the Highlands moved to the industrial areas of Scotland, or abroad, many continued to pursue life in the country. Museums which illustrate life in farming and crofting communities include (see Section **V** for a full listing) the **Angus Folk Museum [V4]**, **Arnol Blackhouse Museum [V6]**, **Auchindrain Township Open Air Museum [V9]**, Dubharaidh (**Barra Heritage and Cultural Centre [Y34]**), **Corrigall Farm Museum [V23]**, **Cruck Cottage [V26]** (Torthorwald), **Fife Folk Museum [V28]**, **Kirbuster Museum [V46]**, **Laidhay Croft Museum [V47]**, **Moirlanich Longhouse [V55]**, **Museum of Scottish Country Life [V56]**, Museum of Farming Life (**Pitmedden Garden [V62]**), **Shetland Croft House Museum [V71]**, **Skye Museum of Island Life [V73]** and **Tingwall Agricultural Museum [V82]**.

A special mention is needed for the **Highland Folk Museum [V39/V40]**, with sites at Kingussie and Newtonmore.

There is a list of folk, agricultural and fishing museums in Section **V**.

Highland Folk Museum – there are sites at Kingussie and Newtonmore

1881 Birth of Sir Alexander Fleming, the Great Fishing Disaster, and the devastation of slate quarries on Easdale

Sir Alexander Fleming was born at Lochfield in Ayrshire in 1881, and in 1928 discovered penicillin. His discovery was not used fully until the Second World War, and he received the Nobel Prize in 1945. He died in 1955.

189 men lost their lives in the Great Fishing Disaster when the herring fleet was caught in storms off Eyemouth. The town is still a major fishing centre, and the **Eyemouth Museum [Y75]**

is open to the public. There are many other fine museums concerning fishing in Scotland, including the **Scottish Fisheries Museum [V67]** at Anstruther, Aberdeen Maritime Museum (**Provost Ross's House [N43]**), **Buckie Drifter [V16]**, **Fraserburgh Heritage Centre [V33]**, **Nairn Fishertown Museum [V57]**, **Peterhead Maritime Heritage [V61]** and **Wick Heritage Centre [Y208]**. **Maggie's Hoosie [V52]** is a typical fisher cottage.

There is a list of folk, agricultural and fishing museums in Section **V**.

The sea defences of the deep slate quarries on the island of Easdale were also breached, and the quarries flooded. Easdale was a famous site for the extraction of slate. The excellent **Easdale Island Folk Museum [X16]** and **Scottish Slate Islands Heritage Trust [X45]** at Ellenabeich on Seil tell the story of slate quarrying. Slate was also extracted at Ballachulish, and there are displays at the **Glencoe and North Lorn Folk Museum [V36]**. Flagstones, which used for pavements all over Britain, were quarried in Caithness and there is the **Castletown Flagstone Trail [X9]**.

1886 Launching of the *Cutty Sark*
The *Cutty Sark*, the famous tea clipper, was launched at Dumbarton.

1887 Scottish Office established
The Scottish Office, which administered most of Scottish government, was established at Whitehall in London in 1887.

1888 Birth of John Logie Baird
Baird was born in Helensburgh in 1888, and built the first working television in 1929 after studying at the University of Glasgow. Baird was associated with many of the outside broadcasting advances of the 1930s. He died in 1946.

Glasgow Celtic football club was founded this year.

1890 Forth Bridge Opened and Glasgow Boys
The Forth Bridge, a spectacular cantilever railway bridge, which connects Fife to Edinburgh, was opened by the Prince of Wales. It took six years to build, and was over-engineered to prevent another disaster. There is information about the bridge (and the later Road Bridge) at the **Queensferry Museum [Y163]** and the **Forth Bridges Exhibition [X18]**.

The Glasgow Boys were an association of painters, including Hornel, Paterson, Lavery, Guthrie and Henry. They went against the establishment in the shape of Royal Scottish Academy, and were more concerned with French and European influences. There is an exhibition of the 'Glasgow Style' at **Kelvingrove Art Gallery and Museum [U11]**, **Broughton House [S10]** in Kirkcudbright was used as a studio by Hornel, and the **James Paterson Museum [U10]** is in Moniaive.

1896 Glasgow underground opened
The only underground railway in Scotland, serving Glasgow, was opened in 1896, although it was not electrified until 1935. The **Museum of Transport [X37]** features a Glasgow subway station.

1900 Scottish industries
By this time heavy industry had developed in many parts of Scotland, including coal mining, textiles, iron and steel works and ship building. These flourished, although the working conditions were often appalling, and even by World War I many businesses were in decline. There are many

Summerlee Heritage Trust – Scotland's last operating tram

museums and sites devoted to industry in Scotland, including the **Clydebank Museum [Y59]**, **Dunaskin Experience [X15]**, **Grangemouth Museum [Y88]**, **Mill Trail Visitor Centre [X30]**, **Motherwell Heritage Centre [Y134]**, **Museum of Lead Mining [X36]**, **New Lanark [X39]**, **Prestongrange Museum [X40]**, **Scottish Mining Museum [X44]**, **Summerlee Heritage Trust [X50]** and **Verdant Works [X53]**.

There is a full list of transport and industrial sites in Section **X**.

The **People's Story Museum [Y159]** in Edinburgh and the **People's Palace [Y158]** in Glasgow cover the lives of ordinary folk, and the **Tenement House [Y191]**, also in Glasgow, is a typical tenement of the early 20th century.

1902 Arthur Conan Doyle and the publication of the *Hound of the Baskervilles*

Arthur Conan Doyle was born in Edinburgh in 1859, and he studied medicine. Doyle's best-known character is Sherlock Holmes, who first appeared in *A Study in Scarlet* in 1887, then in several adventures including *The Hound of the Baskervilles* (1902). Doyle also wrote *The Lost World* in 1912.

1904 Scottish Colourists

The Scottish Colourists – Cadell, Fergusson, Hunter and Peploe – were a fine group of painters, who concentrated on colour and light. There are collections of their work, including at **Blairquhan [S8]**, **City Art Centre [U2]**, **Kirkcaldy Museum and Art Gallery [Y112]**, **Scottish National Gallery of Modern Art [U18]** and **Fergusson Gallery, Perth [U4]**.

1906 First performance of 'Peter Pan'.

'Peter Pan', written by J(ames) M(atthew) Barrie, was first performed. Barrie was born in 1860 at Kirriemuir, the son of a handloom weaver, and wrote stories and plays. **J. M. Barrie's Birthplace [T18]** features the author.

1906 Founding of the Scottish Labour Party

The Scottish Labour Party was founded by Keir Hardie and others in 1906. In 1909 it was amalgamated into the British Labour Party. There is a room dedicated to Keir Hardie in the **Baird Institute, Cumnock [Y30]**.

1915 Gretna Green rail disaster and publication of *The Thirty-Nine Steps*

Three trains collided just outside Gretna Green, and burst into flames, killing over 200 people.

The Thirty Nine Steps was also published this year, featuring the character Richard Hannay, and written by John Buchan. Buchan was born in Perth in 1875, and wrote prolifically – both fiction and biographies, including Sir Walter Scott and the Marquis of Montrose. The **John Buchan Centre [T21]** is at Broughton in the Borders.

1917 Sinking of the HMS *Vanguard*

HMS *Vanguard*, a British warship, blew up in Scapa Flow, with the loss of 800 lives.

1919 Red Clydeside and scuttling of German fleet in Scapa Flow

Many years of conflict with employers and the authorities led to a period of major unrest in the shipyards of the Clyde. The workers were led by men such as Mannie Shinwell, and other socialists and communists. The unrest culminated in a riot in George Square, which took tanks to quell.

The German fleet, which surrendered after World War I, was scuttled in Scapa Flow. There is information about this at the **Stromness Museum [Y187]** and the **Scapa Flow Visitor Centre [P14]**.

1924 Labour Prime Minister

Ramsay MacDonald, born in Lossiemouth in 1866, was named Prime Minister in 1924 and 1929-35. He was a member of the Labour Party, and an MP from 1906. He died in 1937. There is information about MacDonald at the **Lossiemouth Fisheries and Community Museum [V49]**.

1926 Post of Secretary of State for Scotland created

In the same year as the General Strike, the cabinet post of Secretary of State for Scotland was created.

1927 Scottish National War Memorial

The memorial, located in **Edinburgh Castle [N25]**, was designed by Sir Robert Lorimer and lists all the Scots who lost their lives in various wars. The National War Museum of Scotland is also here.

Many Scottish regiments in the British army have distinguished service, and more information can be found at

Gordon Highlanders Museum, Aberdeen

the **Argyll and Sutherland Highlanders Museum [P1]** in **Stirling Castle [N46]**, **Balhousie Castle [P2]** (Black Watch), **Clan Cameron Museum [Q6]** (Queen's Own Cameron Highlanders), **Coldstream Museum [Y60]** (Coldstream Guards), **Fort George [P6]** (Queen's Own Highlanders), **Gordon Highlanders Museum [P7]**, **Low Parks Museum [Y122]** (Cameronians Regimental Museum), Regimental Museum of the Royal Scots (**Edinburgh Castle [N25]**) and the **Royal Highland Fusiliers Regimental Museum [P12]**.

Places and museums associated with military heritage are listed in Section **P**.

1929 Death of Sir Robert Lorimer

The famous architect was born in 1864 in Edinburgh, but spent many of his early years at **Kellie Castle [N33]**, which his father restored. He was apprenticed to Robert Rowand Anderson (who designed **Mount Stuart House [S35]**), and went on to remodel or restore many famous Scottish buildings, including **Dunrobin Castle [N23]**, **Paisley Abbey [J28]**, **St John's Kirk [K31]** in Perth, **Dunblane Cathedral [K13]** and **Hill of Tarvit [S26]**. He was also responsible for the Scottish National War Memorial at **Edinburgh Castle [N25]** and the Thistle Chapel in **St Giles Cathedral [K30]**.

1932 Publication of *Sunset Song*, founding of the Scottish National Party, and the Loch Ness Monster resurfaces

Sunset Song, the first of the trilogy *A Scots Quair*, was published this year, written by James Leslie Mitchell under the pen-name of Lewis Grassic Gibbon. Mitchell was born in 1901 near Auchterless in Aberdeenshire, then moved to the Howe of the Mearns and was educated at Arbuthnott. He died young in 1935. He is buried in **St Ternan's [K127]** and there is a centre devoted to him, the **Grassic Gibbon Centre [T14]** at Arbuthnott.

The Scottish National Party was founded in 1932, and although initially it had little success, by the 1990s was a major player in politics.

Many sightings of the Loch Ness Monster were reported from the 1930s until the present day. St Columba had confronted a beast in the loch in the 6th century, but the Loch Ness Monster appears to have been quiet until the 20th century. It has proved very difficult to prove its existence one way or another. There are two exhibition centres about Nessie at Drumnadrochit (**[Y120]** and **[Y154]**).

1939 Sinking of the *Royal Oak*

The *Royal Oak*, a British warship, was sunk by a German U-boat in Scapa Flow in Orkney, with the loss of 803 lives. There is information about Scapa Flow at the **Stromness Museum [Y187]**, **Scapa Flow Visitor Centre [P14]** and the **Orkney Wireless Museum [P11]**.

1941 Clydebank blitz

Clydebank, near Glasgow, was bombed in 1941, reducing most of the town to rubble, and killing around 1000 people. Glasgow, Greenock, Gourock and Dumbarton were also badly hit.

1949 Scottish Covenant

A Scottish Covenant, supporting devolution, was signed by over 2.5 million Scots.

1950 Stone of Destiny taken from Westminster Abbey

The Stone of Destiny, which had been taken from Scone by Edward I, was returned to Scotland from Westminster Abbey by Scottish nationalists. It was found at **Arbroath Abbey [J2]**, and then returned to Westminster Abbey. The Stone has been returned to Scotland, and is now at **Edinburgh Castle [N25]**.

1961 Opening of the Forth Road Bridge
The Forth Road Bridge, linking Edinburgh to Fife, then the longest suspension bridge in Europe, was opened.

1974 Scottish National Party
In an election this year, the Scottish National Party won 11 seats.

1975 Oil
Oil was first pumped ashore from the North Sea, the industry becoming one of Britain's biggest exports, along with Scotch whisky. There is information about the oil industry at the Aberdeen Maritime Museum (**Provost Ross's House [N43]**) and **Peterhead Maritime Heritage [V61]**.

1979 Referendum on a Scottish Parliament
A referendum on the setting up of a Scottish parliament was held this year. Although there was a small majority in favour, a clause meant that 40% of the total electorate, including those who did not vote, should be in favour. As only 51% of those who voted in the referendum voted for a parliament, this was well below the 40% minimum required by the clause, so this was seen as a rejection.

1989 Lockerbie Disaster
A Pan-Am Jumbo jet was blown up by a terrorist bomb, killing all those on board, and showering the town of Lockerbie with wreckage. In total, 270 people died, including inhabitants of the town.

1998 Museum of Scotland
The magnificent **Museum of Scotland [Y6]** opened, with displays and exhibits covering Scotland from earliest times, beginnings, early people, the kingdom of Scots, Scotland transformed, industry and empire, and the 20th century.

1999 Scottish Parliament established
Following an overwhelming yes vote in a referendum, the first Scottish parliament in nearly 300 years was established. The parliament can be visited, and the **Scottish Parliament Visitor Centre [Y13]** is in Edinburgh.

A: Prehistoric Museums and Settlements

This section consists of museums dedicated to the prehistoric period, and prehistoric settlements. This latter group covers sites from the Stone Age to Iron Age souterrains. See also the sections on *Υ: Local Museums*, and *D: Brochs, Forts and Duns*.

A1 Archaeolink

[Map: 4, F5] On B9002, 5 miles NW of Inverurie, Berryhill, Oyne, Aberdeenshire. (NGR: NJ 665257 LR: 38)

The park and centre interpret Scotland's prehistoric past and early times with an interesting audio-visual presentation, interactive exhibits, and reconstructions. Ancient traditions are explored along with legends of kelpies, giants and stones. Other features are an Iron Age farm, a prehistory play corner, and landscaped paths up to the remains of an ancient fort.

Guided tours by arrangement. Explanatory displays. Gift shop. Restaurant. WC. Baby-changing facilities. Disabled access. Car and coach parking. Group concessions. ££.

Open end May-Oct, daily 9.30-17.00; Nov-Dec 11.00-16.00, wknds 10.00-16.00.

Tel: 01464 851500 Fax: 01464 851544 Web: www.archaeolink.co.uk

A2 Ardestie Souterrain (HS)

[Map: 4, J4] Off B962, 1.25 miles N of Monifieth, Ardestie, Angus. (NGR: NO 502344 LR: 54)

The site consists of the outlines of four huts, one of which had one of the two entrances into a souterrain, which is some 80 feet long. The site was in use between 150 AD and 450 AD. There is another souterrain at **Carlungie [A5]**.

Parking nearby.
Access at all reasonable times.

A3 Barnhouse Prehistoric Settlement

[Map: 2, C2] On A9055, 3.5 miles NE of Stromness, Barnhill, Orkney. (NGR: HY 306126 LR: 6)

The site at Barnhouse, which is similar to **Skara Brae [A21]**, displays the reconstructed remains of a Neolithic village. The excavations uncovered at least 15 houses with the remains of box-beds, dressers and hearths. It is believed that the people who built **Maes Howe [B31]** and the **Ring of Brodgar [C47]** and

Stones of Stenness [C51] lived here.

Explanatory boards. Disabled access. Parking (Stenness Stones car park).
Access at all reasonable times.

Tel: 01856 873535 Web: www.orkneyheritage.com
Fax: 01856 875846 Email: steve.callaghan@orkney.gov.uk

A4 Bosta Prehistoric Settlement

[Map: 3A, B3] Off B8059, 2.5 miles N of Breaclete, Bosta, Great Bernera. (NGR: NB 138401 LR: 13)

The remains of a prehistoric settlement were uncovered with the erosion of sand dunes. The site consists of several ruinous roundhouses, dating from about 400 AD, with later settlement until Viking times. There is the reconstruction of an Iron Age house near the archaeological site. For further information contact **Bernera Centre [Y39]** on 01851 612331.

Bernera Centre: Guided tours. Explanatory displays. Refreshments available in community centre. WC. Disabled WC. Car and coach parking. Group concessions. £.

Tel: 01851 612331/285 Fax: 01851 612331 Email: cesb@zoom.co.uk

Y125 Bute Museum

See main entry Y125

A5 Carlungie Souterrain (HS)

[Map: 4, J4] Off B962, 2.5 miles N of Monifieth, Ardestie, Angus. (NGR: NO 511359 LR: 54)

There are the foundations of eight huts, seven of which are arranged around a paved courtyard. Four entrances led into the souterrain, one of which was off the courtyard. The souterrain was some 150 feet long and there is a complex of galleries. There is another souterrain at **Ardestie [A2]**.

Parking nearby.
Access at all reasonable times.

Y54 Campbeltown Museum

The museum houses the famous Campbeltown Jet Necklace, found in a Bronze Age burial cist and made of Whitby jet.

See main entry Y54

D12 Castlelaw Hill Fort (HS)

A 75 foot souterrain was built into one of the ditches of the fort. Along the passage is a corbelled cell.

See main entry D12

A6 Culsh Souterrain (HS)

[Map: 4, G4] On B9119, 1 mile E of Tarland, Culsh, Aberdeenshire. (NGR: NJ 504054 LR: 37)

A well-preserved souterrain, consisting of a curving passage about 45 feet long and up to seven feet wide and high. The roof is intact.

Access at all reasonable times: torch required, and may be muddy

Tel: 01466 793191

Y70 Dumfries Museum
See main entry Y70

A7 Grain Souterrain (HS)
[Map: 2, C2] Off A965, 0.5 miles NW of Kirkwall, industrial estate, Orkney. (NGR: HY 441116 LR: 6)
The souterrain is almost six feet below ground surface and very well preserved. A flight of steps led down to a curving, sloping passage, roofed by slabs, by which entry was gained to the kidney-shaped chamber. The chamber roof, also roofed by slabs, is supported by four stone pillars.
Access at all reasonable times.
Tel: 01856 841815

A8 Holyrood Park (HS)
[Map: 6B, E9] Off A1, 1 mile E of Edinburgh Castle, Holyrood Park, Edinburgh. (NGR: NT 274734 LR: 66)
The picturesque park is in the centre of Edinburgh, and can be reached from various points in the city including a gate beside Holyroodhouse. There are several small lochs with many birds, as well as fine views over Edinburgh and pleasant walks. The hills of Holyrood Park have evidence of fortifications, settlements and traces of ancient farming. There is a large fort on Arthur's Seat, enclosed by two stone ramparts. Above Samson's Ribs and on the hillside by Dunsapie Loch are two more forts. Hut circle remains include some on the hillside east of Hunter's Bog.
Within the park are the remains of St Anthony's Chapel, and St Anthony's Well [NT 275736], and **Holyroodhouse [N31]** is nearby.
Car parking.
Access at all reasonable times.
Tel: 0131 556 1761

Y4 Hunterian Museum
See main entry Y4

Y100 Inverness Museum
See main entry Y100

D45 Jarlshof (HS)
One of the most remarkable archaeological sites in Europe, dating from Neolithic times. There are also remains from the Bronze Age, Iron Age, Pictish and Viking settlements, as well as a medieval farm. There is also a 16th-century Laird's House, once home of the Earls Robert and Patrick Stewart. There is a small visitors' centre with artefacts from the excavations.
See main entry D45

U11 Kelvingrove Art Gallery and Museum
See main entry U11

A9 Kilmartin House Museum of Ancient Culture
[Map: 5A, D4] On A816, 9 miles N of Lochgilphead, Kilmartin, Argyll. (NGR: NR 834980 LR: 55)
Award-winning archaeological museum exploring man's relationship with the natural environment and ancient monuments over 5000 years. There are artefacts and interactive exhibits, as well as an outstanding audio-visual presentation. Kilmartin Glen has many outstanding prehistoric sites.
STB four star museum dedicated to the Kilmartin valley: a rich prehistoric landscape. Guided tours by appt. Audio-visual presentation. Book shop. Wildfood cafe. WC. Full disabled access. Concessions available. ££.
Open all year, daily 10.00-17.30.
Tel: 01546 510278   Fax: 01546 510330
Web: www.kilmartin.org Email: museum@kilmartin.org

A10 Knap of Howar (HS)
[Map: 2, A3] W side of island of Papa Westray, Orkney. (NGR: HY 483519 LR: 5)
The settlement consists of two stone-built structures, connected by a doorway. The entrance to the larger building led into a room with a bench along one wall. Stone slabs partition off a smaller room which, from its hearth and quern may have been used for the preparation and cooking of food. The smaller building, possibly a store, is divided into three, again by stone slabs. The building is about 5,500 years old.
Access at all reasonable times – sign-posted track.
Tel: 01856 841815

A11 Liddle Burnt Mound
[Map: 2, D3] Off B9041, 5 miles S of St Margaret's Hope, Liddle, South Ronaldsay, Orkney. (NGR: ND 464841 LR: 7)
Over 400 burnt mounds are known in Orkney and Shetland, and probably date from the Bronze Age. Excavation of the burnt mound here revealed a central stone-built trough surrounded by paving and a stone wall, possibly a windbreak. A hearth was set in an alcove. One theory is that stones were heated in the fire and dropped into water in the trough, heating the water to boiling when food was then added for cooking.
See Isbister Chambered Cairn [B25].
Tel: 01856 831339

A12 Mine Howe, Tankerness
[Map: 2, C3] Off A960, 5 miles SE of Kirkwall, Veltigar Farm, Tankerness, Orkney. (NGR: HY 511060 LR: 6)
Built into a massive earthen mound is a subterranean structure, which may have been a well. There are two flights of stone stairs, leading from the summit of the mound, dropping down some 29 steps into the earth. At a landing between the flight are two galleries, and at the bottom is a corbelled chamber. The structure

appears to date from the Iron Age, but its purpose remains a mystery despite being excavated by Time Team.

Parking nearby. £.
Open: tel to confirm.
Tel: 01856 861209

Y127 McManus Galleries
See main entry Y127

Y137 Museum nan Eilean
See main entry Y137

Y138 Museum of Edinburgh
See main entry Y138

Y6 Museum of Scotland
See main entry Y6

A13 New and Old Kinord
[Map: 4, G4] Off A97, 4.5 miles E of Ballater, New Kinord, Muir of Dinnet National Nature Reserve, Kincardine and Deeside. (NGR: NJ 449001 LR: 37)
The hut circles known as New Kinord are set within a triangular enclosure. The largest of the hut circles is 60 feet in diameter. There are also souterrains associated with the huts, and there are also the remains of field systems, with banks, clearance heaps, and the courses of tracks. A little to the west is a further enclosed group of hut circles. Although there has been some excavation at these sites, it has not been possible to date them closer than the later part of the first millennium BC. The small island in Loch Kinord, east of the largest island, is what remains of a crannog, and there is a fine 9th-century cross-slab (**Kinord Cross-Slab [L15]**) by the track on the northern shore.

There was a castle, on the western-most island, a property of the Gordons of Huntly in the 16th century. It was besieged in 1335, and again by the Covenanter General David Leslie in 1647.
Access at all reasonable times: in the National Nature Reserve.

A14 Ord Archaeological Trail
[Map: 3B, C9] Off A839, The Ord, Lairg, Ferrycroft Countryside Centre, Sutherland, Highland. (NGR: NC 575055 LR: 16)
Near the summit of The Ord, a low hill overlooking Loch Shin, are two chambered tombs and several later cairns as well as hut-circles. Leaflets for the archaeological trail, which winds across the hillside, can be obtained from the **Ferrycroft Countryside Centre [Y77]**. There is another archaeological trail at **Yarrows [D66]**, between Lybster and Thrumster.
Access at all reasonable times.
Tel: 01463 702502 Web: www.higharch.demon.co.uk
Fax: 01463 702280 Email: archaeology@higharch.demon.co.uk

Y156 Orkney Museum
See main entry Y156

Y160 Perth Museum
See main entry Y160

A15 Pettigarth's Field
[Map: 1, C3] Pettigarth's Field, island of Whalsay, Shetland. (NGR: HU 587652 LR: 2)
Two Neolithic houses, known locally as the 'Standing Stones of Yoxie' and the 'Benie House', stand in Pettigarth's Field. Both are of a similar plan, comprising an outer court linked by an entrance passageway to the main house. The island can be reached by ferry from Laxo Voe on the mainland of Shetland to Symbister on Whalsay.

A16 Raitts Cave Souterrain
[Map: 3B, G9] Off B9152, 1.5 miles NE of Kingussie, Lynchat, Badenoch and Strathspey, Highland. (NGR: NH 777019 LR: 35)
The remains of a large souterrain, which may date to the late Iron Age, but is also said to have been used as a refuge by the MacNivens.
Park in Lynchat.
Access at all reasonable times: via tunnel under A9 then track.

A17 Rennibister Souterrain (HS)
[Map: 2, C2] Off A965, 4 miles W of Kirkwall, Rennibister, Orkney. (NGR: HY 397125 LR: 6)
The souterrain was discovered in 1926 when its roof gave way. Entry into the oval chamber is now by a hatch in the roof. When the chamber was cleared, the remains of at least 18 individuals were found – it is rare for human bones to be found in a souterrain.
Parking nearby.
Access at all reasonable times.
Tel: 01856 841815

A18 Rispain Camp (HS)
[Map: 6A, I6] On A746, 1 mile W of Whithorn, Rispain Farm, Dumfries and Galloway. (NGR: NX 429399 LR: 83)
A settlement, dating from the 1st or 2nd century AD, with a bank and ditch.
Parking nearby.
Access at all reasonable times.

A19 Scord of Brouster
[Map: 1, D2] Off A971, 1.5 miles NW of Bridge of Walls, Scord of Brouster, Shetland. (NGR: HU 255516 LR: 3)
The stone walls of the settlement at Scord of Brouster stand out clearly from the hillside. Material recovered from excavations give the period of use to 3000 to 2500 BC. The house has an oval central area, in the middle of which was a hearth and partitions dividing the area around the walls into six.
Access at all reasonable times.

A20 Scottish Crannog Centre

[Map: 5B, B8] Off A827, 6 miles W of Aberfeldy, Kenmore, Perthshire. (NGR: NN 772453 LR: 51)

The reconstructed crannog shows what a loch dwelling would have looked like when it was occupied in 500 BC. The Crannog Centre, on the shore, features an exhibition exploring the way of life of the people who lived in the crannogs, and videos explaining how the crannog was built and archaeologists research underwater sites. There are guided tours and ancient craft demonstrations which bring the past back to life.
Guided tours. Audio-visual presentation. Explanatory displays. Gift shop. Refreshments. WC. Disabled access. Group bookings and school parties welcome. Parking nearby. Group concessions. ££.
Open mid March-Nov, daily 10.00-17.30; Nov and Mar, daily 10.00-16.00; last entry 1 hour before closing.
Tel: 01887 830583/0131 650 2368   Fax: 01887 830876
Web: www.crannog.co.uk   Email: info@crannog.co.uk

Y173 Shetland Museum

See main entry Y173

A21 Skara Brae Prehistoric Settlement (HS)

[Map: 2, C2] Off B9056, 6 miles N of Stromness, Skara Brae, Orkney. (NGR: HY 231188 LR: 6)

This is one of the best preserved groups of prehistoric houses in Europe, and dates from the Neolithic period. The complex of houses, joined by lanes and once buried in sand, contains stone furniture and fittings, hearths, and an advanced system of drainage. The visitor centre features interactive displays, original artefacts and an audio-visual presentation telling the story of the village and its people. There is also a replica house, which can be entered. Near to **Skaill House [S42]**.
Visitor centre. Sales area. Restaurant. WC. Partial disabled access and WC. Parking. ££. Joint ticket with Skaill House (in summer) and a joint ticket for entry to Orkney monuments (HS) is also available.
Open all year: Apr-Sep, daily 9.30-18.30; Oct-Mar, Mon-Sat 9.30-16.30, Sun 14.00-16.30; closed 25/26 Dec and 1/2 Jan.
Tel: 01856 841815   Fax: 01856 841885

A22 Smoo Cave

[Map: 3B, A8] Off A838, 1 mile E of Durness, Smoo, Sutherland, Highland. (NGR: NC 419671 LR: 9)

A large cave, created by the action of a burn and the sea. Middens, mostly shells and bone, have been excavated around the cave and surrounding area which date from the Mesolithic period. The cave was also used by Norsemen.
Parking nearby.
Access at all reasonable times: steep descent down to cave. Great care should be taken as may be dangerous.

A23 Staneydale (HS)

[Map: 1, D2] Off A971, 2 miles SE of Bridge of Walls, Staneydale, Shetland. (NGR: HU 285502 LR: 3)

The walk (the path to the site from the road is marked by posts) to the so-called Staneydale Temple passes an excavated and partially reconstructed house which puts the scale of the former building into perspective. The 'temple' has a crescent-shaped facade with an entrance through two doors (their positions marked by checks) leading into an oval room much larger than that of the house. This may have been a meeting place for the community.
Access at all reasonable times – may be wet underfoot.
Tel: 01466 793191

B40 Steinacleit (HS)

See main entry B40

V81 Tealing Souterrain (HS)

There are the remains of an Iron Age souterrain – consisting of an underground passage, long curved gallery and small inner chambers – which has been uncovered.
See main entry V81

Y196 Thurso Heritage Museum

See main entry Y196

A24 Tungadale Souterrain

[Map: 3A, F4] Off B885, 5 miles W of Portree, Glen Tungadale, Skye. (NGR: NG 408401 LR: 23)

The remains of a souterrain, consisting of a long underground passageway, stand in a forestry plantation, east of Loch Duagrich. It was associated with a house above ground, and this has recently been excavated.
Long walk to site.

D66 Yarrows Archaeological Trail

See main entry D66

Top *Culsh Souterrain*
Right *Jarlshof*
Bottom *Scottish Crannog
Centre*

B: Burial and Chambered Cairns

These were in use from the Neolithic period through to the Iron Age. Also see the section on *C: Stones*.

B1 Auchagallon Cairn (HS)

[Map: 6A, F4] Off A841, 4 miles N of Blackwaterfoot, Auchagallon, Arran. (NGR: NR 893346 LR: 69)

The remains of a Bronze Age burial cairn, 50 feet in diameter, surrounded by a circle or kerb of 15 standing stones. The tallest stone is over seven feet high.
Parking Nearby
Access at all reasonable times.

C7 Ballochroy Stone Setting
See main entry C7

B2 Barpa Langass

[Map: 3A, E2] Off A867, 5 miles W of Lochmaddy, Ben Langass, North Uist. (NGR: NF 837657 LR: 18)

The impressive chambered cairn, dating from the Neolithic period, rises to 13 feet or so above the moorland. The entrance passage is 15 feet long and leads into an oval burial chamber, with the roof corbelled over. The passage and the chamber are still covered. Nearby is **Pobull Fhinn [C45]**.
Parking.
Access at all reasonable times.

C11 Beacharr
See main entry C11

B3 Blackhammer Chambered Cairn (HS)

[Map: 2, B2] On B9065, S of island of Rousay, Orkney. (NGR: HY 414276 LR: 6)

This chambered tomb has been excavated and is now entered down a ladder through a modern concrete roof. The original entrance opened from the middle of the cairn. The chamber has seven burial compartments. The slabs on the exterior of the cairn were arranged in a triangular pattern, some of which is visible near the entrance.
Access at all reasonable times – access to chamber.
Tel: 01856 841815

B4 Boath Chambered Cairns

[Map: 3B, D9] Off A836, 5 miles NW of Alness, Boath, Ross and Cromarty. (NGR: NH 582748 LR: 21)

Two large chambered burial cairns, although the chambers are roofless. A third cairn lies to the south but has been mostly robbed.
Access at all reasonable times.

B5 Bucharn Cairn

[Map: 4, G5] Off B976, 3 miles SW of Banchory, Bucharn, Aberdeenshire. (NGR: NO 659929 LR: 45)

Large cairn, some 60 feet in diameter and 15 feet high, in a fine location with spectacular views.
Access at all reasonable times: access via farm track and field margins.

B6 Cairn Holy Cairns (HS)

[Map: 6B, I7] Off A75, 5 miles SW of Gatehouse of Fleet, Dumfries and Galloway. (NGR: NX 518540 LR: 83)

The remains of two chambered tombs, dating from about 2000 BC, consisting of the larger stones of the passage and chamber: most of the cairn material has been removed. There are fine views to Wigtown Bay.
Car parking.
Access at all reasonable times.

B7 Cairn o' Get, Ulbster (HS)

[Map: 3B, B11] Off A9, 5 miles NE of Lybster, Ulbster, Caithness. (NGR: ND 313411 LR: 12)

A horned and chambered burial cairn, which still stands to a height of about eight feet. The chamber is uncovered and divided into three, and can be viewed along with the passage. Nearby [ND 312414] is Garrywhin Fort, which is defended by a ruinous wall with at least three entrances.
Parking nearby.
Access at all reasonable times – may be wet underfoot.
Tel: 01667 460232

B8 Cairn o' Mount

[Map: 4, H5] On B974, 9 miles S of Banchory, Cairn o' Mount, Kincardine and Deeside. (NGR: NO 649806 LR: 45)

The cairn is about 50 feet across and some 11 feet high, and there are fine views from here, at least when the weather is fine, as it stands in a commanding position. There was a Pictish carved cross here, but this has gone, and the cairn stands on an important route to the north and south.
Parking.
Access at all reasonable times.

B9 Cairnpapple Hill (HS)

[Map: 6B, E8] Off B792, 3 miles S of Linlithgow, Cairnpapple, West Lothian. (NGR: NS 987717 LR: 65)

Cairnpapple, from where there are fabulous views, was a ceremonial site for at least 1500 years. Around 2500 BC a henge was constructed, within which was a circle of 24 standing stones. Burials were inserted within the circle, which was probably dismantled. The cairn was later enlarged with a boulder kerb. Burials continued to be added until at least the Iron Age.
Explanatory display. Shop. Short walk to monument. Car parking. Group concessions. £.
Open Apr-Sep, daily 9.00-18.30.
Tel: 01506 634622

B10 Capo Long Barrow

[Map: 4, H4] Off A92, 4 miles NE of Brechin, Capo, Kincardine and Deeside. (NGR: NO 633664 LR: 45)

Capo is a Neolithic earthen long mound 250 feet long, 65 feet wide at the east end, and is about eight feet high. From excavated examples, the wider eastern end would be expected to cover burials and timber mortuary structures. While stone-built tombs are more common in Scotland, there are many examples of mounds of earth and turf in the south and east. The mound is situated in a clearing in Inglismaldie forest, on a natural terrace above the River Esk.

Access at all reasonable times.

B11 Carn Ban, Arran (HS)

[Map: 6A, F5] Off A841, 7 miles S of Brodick, Carn Ban, Arran. (NGR: NR 991262 LR: 69)

In a clearing in a forestry plantation are the remains of a Neolithic burial cairn, about 100 feet by 60 feet with a forecourt. The cairn rises to 15 feet in height, and several upright stones can be seen forming the kerb and court. The chamber was divided into four compartments, but is full of debris.

Parking nearby
Access at all reasonable times.

B12 Clava Cairns (HS)

[Map: 3B, F9] Off B9006 or B851, 6 miles E of Inverness, Highlands. (NGR: NH 757445 LR: 27)

Located in an atmospheric wooded setting is an impressive group of circular burial cairns and rings of standing stones. They date from around 1600 BC — late Neolithic or early Bronze Age, and both cremations and inhumations have been recovered.

Parking.
Access at all reasonable times.
Tel: 01667 460232

B13 Clettraval Chambered Cairn

[Map: 3A, E2] Off A865, 11 miles W of Lochmaddy, South Clettraval, North Uist. (NGR: NF 749713 LR: 18)

A Neolithic cairn which has been much reduced by robbing of stone. The slabs of the burial chamber and its entrance passageway can be traced, and the cairn had a forecourt. Three kerb stones can be seen. The site was reused in the Iron Age, and there are remains of a wheel- or aisled house.

Walk along track from Taigh a Ghearraidh.

B14 Cnoc Freiceadain Long Cairns (HS)

[Map: 3B, A10] Off A836, 6 miles SW of Thurso, Cnoc Freicadain, Caithness, Highland. (NGR: ND 012653 LR: 12)

The remains of two long cairns, now grass-covered, the southern-most of which is 250 feet long and one of the largest in Scotland. One cairn has horns at one

end, the other has horns at both ends. There are fine views from here in good weather.

Access at all reasonable times.
Tel: 01667 460232

B15 Correchrevie Cairn

[Map: 5A, E4] Off A83, 7 miles N of Tayinloan, Correchrevie, Kintyre, Argyll. (NGR: NR 738540 LR: 62)

The remains of a large burial cairn, some 90 feet in diameter and standing 16 feet high. It may be seen from the main Campbeltown road.

B16 Corrimony Chambered Cairn (HS)

[Map: 3B, F8] Off A831, 8.5 miles W of Drumnadrochit, Corrimony, Glen Urquhart, Highlands (NGR: NH 383303 LR: 26)

The remains of a Clava-type cairn, having a circular cairn with a kerb retaining the cairn material and a central circular chamber reached by a passage. Surrounding the cairn is a ring of 11 standing stones.

Parking nearby.
Access at all reasonable times.
Tel: 01667 460232

B17 Cuween Hill Chambered Cairn (HS)

[Map: 2, C2] Off A965, 7 miles NW of Kirkwall, 0.5 miles SE of Finstown, Cuween Hill, Orkney. (NGR: HY 364128 LR: 6)

The chambered tomb at Cuween is notable for having contained the skulls of 24 dogs, as well as the remains of at least eight humans. The tomb has a rectangular main chamber with a cell leading off each side, one of which is divided into two. The walls are well built, using thin flagstones. The roof is modern.

Car Parking.
Access at all reasonable times – a torch will be needed and the Key should be collected at the farm – access may be muddy.
Tel: 01856 841815

B18 Dun Bharpa

[Map: 3A, G2] Off A888, 2.5 miles N of Castlebay, Craigston, Barra. (NGR: NF 671019 LR: 31)

A well-preserved Neolithic chambered cairn, with a number of large slabs of the kerb still in position. The cairn survives to a height of 17 feet, and measures 85 feet in diameter.

B19 Dunchraigaig Cairn (HS)

[Map: 5A, D4] On A816, 1.25 miles S of Kilmartin, Kilmartin Glen, Argyll. (NGR: NR 833968 LR: 55)

One of the many fine monuments in Kilmartin Glen, the Bronze Age burial cairn consists of a large mound of stones with cists visible. Near **Baluachraig Cup and Rings [C10]** marked stone.

Picnic area. Car parking.
Access at all reasonable times.

B20 Dwarfie Stane, Hoy (HS)

[Map: 2, D2] Off B9047, N of island of Hoy, off road to Rackwick, near foot of Ward Hill, Orkney. (NGR: HY 244005 LR: 7)

Named 'Dvergasteinn' and thought by the Vikings to be the home of dwarves, the Dwarfie Stane is probably a Neolithic tomb. Hollowed out of the stone are a pair of rounded cells, one on each side of a passage, and divided from the passage by a kerb. The cell on the right has a low step or pillow within it.

Parking nearby.

Access at all reasonable times – access to chambers.
Tel: 01856 841815

B21 Glebe Cairn (HS)

[Map: 5A, D4] Off A816, Kilmartin Glebe, Kilmartin, Argyll. (NGR: NR 832989 LR: 55)

The remains of a Bronze Age burial cairn, with two cists, survive in a field behind **Kilmartin House Museum [A9]**. The monument consists of a large mound of stones.

Parking nearby.

Access at all reasonable times.

B22 Gort na h'Uilidhe

[Map: 5A, F4] Off B842, 4 miles N of Campbeltown, 2 miles SW of Kildonan (track), Kintyre, Argyll. (NGR: NR 745268 LR: 68)

Large well-preserved chambered cairn, some 100 feet long with the remains of the main and side chambers. The name means 'cairn of the treasure', and there are fine views.

Signposted. Information Board.

Access at all reasonable times.

B23 Grey Cairns of Camster (HS)

[Map: 3B, B11] Off A9, 5 miles N of Lybster, Camster, Watten, Caithness, Highland. (NGR: ND 260442 LR: 12)

The massive cairns at Camster stand some 250 yards apart. The round cairn is at least 50 feet in diameter, and the entrance to the chamber is set midway along a straight facade. Entry to an antechamber is marked by a couple of portal stones and a further pair of stones mark the entry to the chamber. The long cairn is 230 feet long and completely covered two separate round cairns along one side of the cairn. One of the cairns has a simple chamber and the other has a passage, antechamber, main chamber and side cell. Both the cairns have been restored.

Parking.

Access at all reasonable times.
Tel: 01667 460232

B24 Holm of Papa Westray Chambered Cairns (HS)

[Map: 2, A3] Island and Holm of Papa Westray, Orkney. (NGR: HY 509518 LR: 5)

There are two impressive chambered cairns on the island. The one at the north of the island has a chamber divided into four by upright slabs and there is a cell off the end compartment. The latter was part of an earlier tomb. At the south of the island is another cairn, this time with 12 side cells, including two double cells. Entry to the chamber is down a ladder through the modern concrete roof.

Access at all reasonable times – access to chamber.
Tel: 01856 841815

B25 Isbister Chambered Cairn

[Map: 2, D3] Off B9041, 5 miles S of St Margaret's Hope, SE side of South Ronaldsay, Liddle Farm, Orkney. (NGR: ND 470845 LR: 7)

Isbister, also known as Tomb of the Eagles, is a Neolithic stalled cairn with the main chamber divided into three by stone slabs. At each end is a partitioned area, originally shelved. Three side cells lead off the chamber. The remains of about 340 people were recovered during the excavations as well as bones and talons from white-tailed sea eagles, giving the tomb its more popular name, 'Tomb of the Eagles'. The tour includes interpretation and a visit to **Liddle Burnt Mound [A11]**.

Guided tours. Museum interpretation includes hands-on talk. Shop. Refreshments. WC. Disabled access to museum; partial access to sites. Car and coach parking. Group concessions. £.

Open Apr-Oct, daily 10.00-18.00, Nov-Mar, welcome by arrangement or check with Orkney Tourist Board (01856 872856)
Tel: 01856 831339

B26 Kensalyre Cairns

[Map: 3A, E4] On A856, 5 miles NW of Portree, Kensalyre, Skye. (NGR: NG 426506 LR: 23)

There are the remains of a burial cairn by the side of the main road, robbed in places but seven feet in height, and about 60 feet long and 40 wide. There is a much smaller cairn to the north-east.

B27 Kintraw Cairns and Standing Stone

[Map: 5A, C4] On A816, 4 miles N of Kilmartin, Kintraw, Argyll. (NGR: NM 830050 LR: 55)

The site consists of a large cairn, a small cairn and a standing stone. The larger of the cairns was surrounded by a kerb and had a cist. The site has been interpreted as marking the sunset at the mid-winter solstice through a notch in the Paps of Jura. The stone was re-erected on a slightly different alignment after falling over.

B28 Knowe of Yarso Chambered Cairn (HS)

[Map: 2, B2] Off B9064, S side of island of Rousay, Orkney. (NGR: HY 404279 LR: 6)

The Neolithic chambered cairn has concentric walls

enclosing a rectangular chamber, which is divided into three compartments and entered by a passageway. The cairn had the remains of some 29 people as well as reindeer, sheep and a dog, and flint items and sherds of pottery were also found.

Parking nearby.
Access at all reasonable times – access to chamber.
Tel: 01856 841815

B29 Lews Castle

[Map: 3A, B4] Off A866, W of Stornoway, Lews Castle, Lewis. (NGR: NB 419335 LR: 8)
The park is set in the pleasant wooded grounds and gardens of Lews Castle, built by the Mathesons in the 19th century, on the west side of Stornoway Harbour. Cnoc na Croich [NB 417323] – 'Gallows Hill' is traditionally the site where criminals were executed, and nearby are the remains of a chambered cairn. The park has shore, woodland, river walks and moorland.
Castle not open; park open all year.

B30 Logie Newton Cairns

[Map: 4, F5] Off B9001, B992 or A96, 7 miles E of Huntly, 5 miles NW of Rothienorman, Aberdeenshire. (NGR: NJ 659391 LR: 29)
A group of three small cairns, made from quartzite stones, which can sparkle in the sun. They are located on a ridge of Kirk Hill, north-west of Logie Newton.

B31 Maes Howe Chambered Cairn (HS)

[Map: 2, C2] On A965, 9 miles W of Kirkwall, Tormiston, Orkney. (NGR: HY 318128 LR: 6)
One of the finest prehistoric sites in Europe. The chambered cairn is set on a low platform which is surrounded by a ditch and bank. Entry to the chamber is through a low narrow passage, and just inside the entrance is a recess containing a block of stone which would have sealed the entrance. The passage enters the square chamber midway along one wall, and midway along each of the other walls is an entrance to a side chamber. Norsemen entered the tomb in the 12th century and left the largest collection of runic graffiti to be found in one place.

The tomb is said to have been protected by hogboy, a supernatural guardian. The passage to the chamber is aligned so that when the sun sets over the Hoy Hills on the winter solstice it shone up the passageway and onto the back wall of the tomb.

Exhibition. Tormiston Mill: Gift shop. Tearoom. WC. Car and coach parking. Group concessions. £. Joint entry ticket for all Orkney monuments.
Open all year: Apr-Sep, daily 9.30-18.30; Oct-Mar, daily 9.30-17.00; last ticket 30 mins before closing; closed 25/26 Dec & 1/2 Jan.
Tel: 01856 761606

B32 Marionburgh Cairn

[Map: 4, F3] Off A95, 7.5 miles SW of Aberlour, Marionburgh, Moray. (NGR: NJ 183364 LR: 28)
The remains of a chambered cairn and the surrounding stone circle. The cairn is about 40 feet in diameter and the central chamber can be traced. Six stones of the circle are upright, while others have fallen. The tallest stone is about nine feet tall.
Access at all reasonable times.

B33 Memsie Cairn (HS)

[Map: 4, E5] On A981, 3.5 miles S of Fraserburgh, Memsie, Aberdeenshire. (NGR: NJ 976620 LR: 30)
The remains of a large cairn, built of stones, probably dating from the Bronze Age. The cairn has been enlarged by field clearance.
Parking nearby.
Access at all reasonable times.
Tel: 01466 793191

B34 Midhowe Chambered Cairn (HS)

[Map: 2, B2] Off B9064, SW side of island of Rousay, Orkney. (NGR: HY 373306 LR: 6)
The remains of a stalled cairn, now encased in a modern shed for protection. The chamber is some 75 feet long, and divided into 12 compartments. The first few compartments have no shelves, but most of the others are shelved, along their east wall. The remains of 25 individuals were found in the tomb, nine of which were laid on the benches. **Midhowe Broch [D51]** is nearby.
Parking nearby
Access at all reasonable times – steep descent down to cairn.
Tel: 01856 841815

B35 Moss Farm Road Cairn (HS)

[Map: 6A, F4] Off A841, 3 miles N of Blackwaterfoot, Tormore, Arran. (NGR: NR 901326 LR: 69)
The remains of a Bronze Age cairn, about 75 feet in diameter, surrounded by a kerb of several upright stones. The tallest of these is just over four feet high.
Parking nearby.
Access at all reasonable times.

B36 Nether Largie Cairns (HS)

[Map: 5A, D4] Off A816, 0.5 miles SW of Kilmartin, Nether Largie, Argyll. (NGR: NR 828979 LR: 55)
Three splendid cairns, known as Nether Largie North, Mid and South, are part of a large complex of stones and tombs in Kilmartin Valley.

Nether Largie South is a chambered cairn. It is the earliest and has an oblong central chamber built with slabs and walling. Three slabs divide the interior into four compartments. Two cists had been inserted into the cairn. Only one is now visible.

The two other cairns covered only cists, two in the case of Nether Largie Mid and one in the case of Nether Largie North. These cairns may be reached along the track by the school.

Other cairns in Kilmartin include the **Glebe Cairn [B21]** at Kilmartin, **Ri Cruin [B38]**, 1 mile SW of Kilmartin, and **Dunchraigaig Cairn [B19]**, 1.25 miles south of Kilmartin.

Explanatory boards. Parking nearby.
Access at all reasonable times.

A14 Ord Archaeological Trail

See main entry A14

B37 Quoyness Chambered Cairn (HS)

[Map: 2, B3] Off B9069, S side of island of Sanday, Orkney. (NGR: HY 677378 LR: 5)

Quoyness is a **Maes Howe [B31]** tomb. The entrance passage was originally 30 feet long but is now roofed for only about 10 feet as the exterior around the entrance has been reconstructed to show the construction of the cairn. The chamber is rectangular and has six cells leading off it. During excavations human bones were found in four of the cells and in a cist dug into the chamber floor.

Access at all reasonable times – along a footpath and torch required: access to chamber.
Tel: 01856 841815

B38 Ri Cruin Cairn (HS)

[Map: 5A, D4] Off A816, 1 mile SW of Kilmartin, Argyll. (NGR: NR 825971 LR: 55)

The large burial cairn in Kilmartin Glen, which dates from the Bronze Age, has three cists, one of which has an axe head carved on one of the cist slabs.
Parking nearby.
Access at all reasonable times.

B39 Rubh' an Dunain Chambered Cairn

[Map: 3A, G4] Off B8009, 4 miles S of Glenbrittle, Rubh' an Dunain, Skye. (NGR: NG 393163 LR: 32)

A Neolithic chambered cairn, reused in the Bronze Age, consists of a round mound and concave forecourt. The entrance passage, from the forecourt, is still roofed with stone lintels, but the burial chamber is roofless. Remains of six adults were found .

Nearby [NG 396160] are the ruins of a dun on a promontory. The wall rises to nine feet, and there are the remains of the entrance and galleries within the walls.
Long walk.

B40 Steinacleit (HS)

[Map: 3A, B4] Off A857, 12.5 miles N of Stornoway, S of Loch an Duin, Shader, Lewis. (NGR: NB 393541 LR: 8)

The remains of an enigmatic building of early prehistoric date, variously described as a stone circle and denuded cairn or a defensible homestead. The site was in use from around 3000 to 1500 BC.
Parking nearby.
Access at all times.

C53 Strontoiller

See main entry C53

B41 Taversoe Tuick Chambered Cairn (HS)

[Map: 2, B2] On B9065, SE side of island of Rousay, Orkney. (NGR: HY 426276 LR: 6)

An unusual two-level chambered cairn, the storeys of which were not linked and had separate entrances. The lower chamber is cut into rock, and divided by upright slabs into four compartments with flagstone shelves. Bones were found here. The upper chamber is divided in two, and contained cremated remains in three stone cists. Near the cairn is a smaller chamber dug into the ground, five feet long, and divided by slabs into five. Pottery bowls were found, but no skeletal remains.

Access at all reasonable times – access to chambers.
Tel: 01856 841815

C55 Temple Wood Stone Circles (HS)

See main entry C55

B42 Tinto Hill Cairn

[Map: 6B, F8] Off A73, 5.5 miles SW of Biggar, Tinto Hill, Lanarkshire. (NGR: NS 953343 LR: 72)

The cairn on the summit of Tinto Hill is one of the largest Bronze Age round cairns in Scotland. It measures 160 feet in diameter and is nearly 20 feet high. There are extensive views of the Clyde Valley and the Southern Uplands from the summit of the hill .

There is a public footpath from Fallburn to the summit.

V83 Tormiston Mill

The visitor centre for the impressive tomb of **Maes Howe [B31]** is located in the mill.
See main entry V83

B43 Torrylinn Chambered Cairn (HS)

[Map: 6A, F4] Off A841, 5 miles SE of Blackwaterfoot, Lagg, Arran. (NGR: NR 955211 LR: 69)

The Neolithic chambered burial cairn survives to a

height of six feet and about 65 feet in diameter. The cairn has been robbed, and the chamber, with its compartments, can be seen.

Parking nearby.
Access at all reasonable times.

B44 Toum Cairn

[Map: 3B, F10] Off A95, 5 miles SW of Grantown on Spey, Ouchnoire, Badenoch and Strathspey, Highland. (NGR: NH 960217 LR: 36)
Large burial cairn, some ten feet high and about 70 feet in diameter. There are fine views to the south.
Parking nearby: ensure farm traffic is not obstructed.
Access at all reasonable times: short walk.

B45 Uneval Chambered Cairn

[Map: 3A, E2] Off A865, 7.5 miles W of Lochmaddy, S of Uneval, North Uist. (NGR: NF 800667 LR: 18)
The remains of a Neolithic chambered cairn and Iron Age house. Upright slabs survive from the cairn, although much of the stone has been robbed. Some fragments of burnt bone, from an adult woman, were found here during excavations, as well as pottery. A visit involves a long walk.

B46 Unstan Chambered Cairn (HS)

[Map: 2, C2] Off A965, 3 miles NE of Stromness, Unstan, Orkney. (NGR: HY 283117 LR: 6)
The chambered cairn, situated on a promontory in the Loch of Stenness, is now capped by a modern concrete dome. A long passage leads into the chamber, which is divided by slabs into stalls. A side cell leads off the central chamber. Skeletal remains of humans, animals and birds were found, as well as sherds from shallow bowls with wide collars, a style of pottery now known as 'Unstan Ware'.
Parking nearby.
Access at all reasonable times – access to chamber.
Tel: 01856 841815

B47 Vatten Chambered Cairns

[Map: 3A, F4] On A863, 3.5 miles SE of Dunvegan, Glen Heysdale, Skye. (NGR: NG 298441 LR: 23)
Two impressive, little-disturbed and well-preserved burial cairns. The more northerly is 100 feet in diameter and 16 feet high, and the kerb can be traced; while the southerly cairn is 110 feet in diameter and 11 feet high, and has been robbed of stones. The kerb can also be seen.

B48 Vinquoy Hill Chambered Cairn, Eday

[Map: 2, B3] Off B9063, 0.25 miles SW of Carrick House, Eday, Orkney. (NGR: HY 560381 LR: 5)
The remains of a chambered cairn, located in a scenic spot with magnificent views in all directions. The cairn had an entrance passageway leading to a central chamber with four small side cells (rather than the three at **Maes Howe [B31]**). The cairn stands by a heritage walk with fine views, and there are further chambered cairns and the impressive **Stone of Setter [C50]**.
Access at all reasonable times.

B49 White Cow Wood Cairn

[Map: 4, E5] Off A981 or A950, 9 miles S of Fraserburgh, 2 miles S of Strichen, Aberdeenshire. (NGR: NJ 947519 LR: 30)
The remains of a chambered cairn, consisting of the kerb and part of the burial chamber, although most of the stones of the cairn have been removed.
Picnic area nearby. Forest walk. Parking in Forestry Commission car park.
Access at all reasonable times: long walk.

B50 Wideford Hill Chambered Cairn (HS)

[Map: 2, C2] Off A965, 3 miles W of Kirkwall, Wideford Hill, Orkney. (NGR: HY 409122 LR: 6)
The cairn is similar in layout to the chambered cairns at **Maes Howe [B31]** and **Quoyness [B37]**, having a rectangular chamber with three side-cells leading from it, one of which is cut into the bedrock. Entry to the chamber was originally through a long low passage, but is now through a trapdoor in the roof and down a ladder.
Parking nearby.
Access at all reasonable times – involves a long walk: access to chamber.
Tel: 01856 841815

D66 Yarrows Archaeological Trail
See main entry D66

Top Left *Nether Largie South*
Top Right *Isbister*
Above *Barpa Langass*
Left *Grey Cairns of Camster*
Bottom *Cuween Hill*

Top *Maes Howe*
Right *Knowe of Yarso*
Bottom left *Taversoe Tuick*
Bottom right *Corrimony*

C: Stones

Standing stones, stone circles and henges (monuments enclosed by a ditch and bank) are found in all parts of Scotland. There are a huge number of these monuments, many of them very impressive or atmospheric. Cup and ring marked stones date from the Bronze Age.

C1 Achavanich Stone Setting

[Map: 3B, B11] Off A895, 12 miles SW of Wick, Achavanich, Caithness, Highland. (NGR: ND 187417 LR: 12)

This is a horseshoe-shaped arrangement of 36 small standing stones – it is probable that there were originally 54 stones. The stones are short – the tallest is only 7 feet high – and seem to have been set into a low mound. Nearby is a round cairn, probably dating from the Neolithic period – some of the stones of the chamber protrude through the stones of the mound.

Access at all reasonable times: view from roadside – do not enter the site.

C2 Achnabreck Cup & Ring Marks (HS)

[Map: 5A, D4] Off A816, 1.5 miles NW of Lochgilphead, Kilmartin Glen, Argyll. (NGR: NR 856907 LR: 55)

The cup-and-ring markings at Achnabreck are among the most impressive groups in Scotland. The site comprises two groups about 100 feet apart. The lower group comprises three areas many with multi-ringed cups. The upper site has some of the largest ring-marks in Scotland, some almost 3.5 feet in diameter, and includes double-ended spirals and a triple spiral.

Parking nearby – walk to site.
Access at all reasonable times.

C3 Aikey Brae Stone Circle

[Map: 4, G5] Off A947 or A96, 6.5 miles NW of Aberdeen, Aikey Brae, Aberdeenshire. (NGR: NJ 859132 LR: 38)

The remains of a recumbent stone circle, dating to 3000-2000 BC, stand in a fenced enclosure with fine views to the south.

Access at all reasonable times.

C4 Balfarg Henge

[Map: 6B, C10] Off B969, 6.5 miles N of Kirkcaldy, Balfarg, Fife. (NGR: NO 281031 LR: 59)

The henge is about 200 feet across, and within it were various settings, including a timber circle built around 3000 BC (marked by wooden posts) and a stone circle, of which two stones remain. The flat slab in the centre is the capstone from a later burial. An archaeological trail leads past another excavated site, marked by a setting of posts, and the stone circle of Balbirnie, moved after excavation.

C5 Ballinaby Standing Stones

[Map: 5A, E2] Off B8018, 4.5 miles NW of Bruichladdich, Ballinaby, Islay. (NGR: NR 219672 LR: 60)

One of the most impressive standing stones in western Scotland. The stone is in a prominent position and, despite its thinness, can be seen from considerable distances. The stone is about 16 feet tall. A second stone, 200 yards to the north, is six feet high and has been damaged – originally there were a group of three stones here.

C6 Ballochmyle Cup & Ring Marks

[Map: 6A, F6] Off A76, 1 mile SE of Mauchline, Ballochmyle, Ayrshire. (NGR: NS 511255 LR: 70)

The set of carvings at Ballochmyle, which were only discovered in 1986, comprise a variety of motifs including cups, and cup-and-rings, and more geometric compositions. This is one of the largest group of such markings in Britain, and is also unusual in having been executed on a vertical face – horizontal faces were more often decorated in this way (such as **Achnabreck [C2]** in Argyll).

C7 Ballochroy Stone Setting

[Map: 5A, E4] Off A83, 4 miles N of Tayinloan, Ballochroy, Kintyre, Argyll. (NGR: NR 731524 LR: 62)

Setting of three standing stones, the tallest of which is 11 feet high. There are also the remains of a burial cist with a large capstone.

C8 Ballygowan Cup & Ring Marks (HS)

[Map: 5A, D4] Off A816, 1 mile SW of Kilmartin, near Poltalloch, Kilmartin Glen, Argyll. (NGR: NR 816978 LR: 55)

Natural rock faces are carved with cup and ring marks, which date from the Bronze Age.

Parking Nearby
Access at all reasonable times.

C9 Ballymeanoch

[Map: 5A, D4] Off A816, 2 miles S of Kilmartin, Ballymeanoch, Argyll. (NGR: NR 833965 LR: 55)

A henge stands near a setting of four impressive stones and, parallel to this, two further stones, with the remains of a burial cairn a short distance away. Some of the stones are carved with cup and ring marks. **Dunchraigaig Cairn [B19]** is nearby, as are **Baluachraig Cup and Ring** marks **[C10]**.

Parking nearby (Dunchraigaig).
Access at all reasonable times.

C10 Baluachraig Cup & Ring Marks (HS)

[Map: 5A, D4] Off A816, 1 mile SE of Kilmartin, Baluachraig, Argyll. (NGR: NR 831969 LR: 55)
Several groups of Bronze Age cup and ring marks have been carved on natural rock faces. Near **Dunchraigaig Cairn [B19]**.
Parking nearby.
Access at all reasonable times.

C11 Beacharr Stone and Cairn

[Map: 5A, F4] Off A83, 2 miles S of Tayinloan, Beacharr, Kintyre, Argyll. (NGR: NR 693433 LR: 62)
Tall and impressive standing stone, some 16 feet high. To the north and east are the remains of a chambered cairn.

C12 Braids Cup & Ring Marks

[Map: 5A, E4] Off A83, 1.5 miles NE of Tayinloan, S of Braids, Kintyre, Argyll. (NGR: NR 718444 LR: 62)
The carved stone has many cup marks in the stone, four of them with rings around them. There is also a carving resembling a wheel, and another like a star with rays.

C13 Cairnbaan Cup & Ring Marks (HS)

[Map: 5A, D4] On A841, 2.5 miles NW of Lochgilphead, near Cairnbaan Hotel, Argyll. (NGR: NR 838910 LR: 55)
Two outcrops of rock are decorated with cups, and cups and rings, some having grooves across the rings.
Parking nearby.
Access at all reasonable times.

C14 Caiy Stone (NTS)

[Map: 6B, E9] Off B701, Oxgangs Road, Caiystane View, Fairmilehead, Edinburgh. (NGR: NT 242684 LR: 66)
The Caiy Stone is an imposing standing stone, some nine feet tall. It is traditionally said to commemorate a battle between the Picts and the Romans. On one side are six weathered cup marks.
Access at all reasonable times.

C15 Callanish (HS)

[Map: 3A, B4] Off A858, 14 miles W of Stornoway, Callanish, Lewis. (NGR: NB 213330 LR: 8)
Probably constructed between 3000 and 1500 BC, this is one of the most important and unique sites in Scotland, and even in Britain. It forms only part of a much larger complex of single stones, groups of stones and circles, believed to cover some 20 sites in all.

The main setting consists of an avenue of 19 upright stones, leading north from a circle of 13 stones, with rows of more stones fanning out to the south, east and west.

The tallest stone is over 15 feet tall, and inside the central circle is a small burial cairn.

The stones seem to have been aligned to mirror, with outlying settings, the position of the moon at the summer and winter solstices, and at the equinoxes.

The visitor centre, which is not visible from the stones, has an exhibition 'The Story of the Stones' and interpretive information about Callanish.
Visitor Centre: Explanatory displays. Gift shop. Tearoom. WC. Disabled access. Disabled WC. Car and coach parking. £ (visitor centre)
Sites open all year; visitor centre open Apr-Oct, Mon-Sat 10.00-19.00; Oct-Mar, Mon-Sat 10.00-16.00.
Tel: 01851 621422   Fax: 01851 621446

C16 Candle Stone

[Map: 4, F5] Off A948 or B9005, 3.5 miles NW of Ellon, 0.5 miles N of Inverebrie, Aberdeenshire. (NGR: NJ 921348 LR: 30)
Fine standing stone, some ten feet tall.
Parking at school.
Access at all reasonable times.

C17 Carinish Stone Circle

[Map: 3A, E2] On A865, 5 miles NE of Balivanich, Carinish, North Uist. (NGR: NF 832602 LR: 22)
The main road has been built through the middle of this stone circle. Seven stones survive on the north side of the road, with another two on the south.
Access at all reasonable times.

C18 Ceann Hulavig Circle

[Map: 3A, B4] Off B8011, 12 miles W of Stornoway, Ceann Hulavig, Lewis. (NGR: NB 230304 LR: 13)
A stone circle, just west of the main road, now consists of five upright stones, varying in height from seven to nine feet. There are traces of a burial cairn within the stones. This circle is probably associated with the main site at **Callanish [C15]**, and is also known as Callanish IV.

C19 Clach Mhic Leoid

[Map: 3A, D3] Off A859, 6 miles N of Leverburgh, Nisabost, Harris. (NGR: NG 041973 LR: 18)
A tall and impressive standing stone, over ten feet high, in a striking location.
0.5 miles walk across the beach.

C20 Clach an Trushal

[Map: 3A, B4] Off A857, 12.5 miles N of Stornoway, Ballantrushal, Lewis. (NGR: NB 375538 LR: 8)
This is an impressive standing stone, at a slight angle, some 20 feet or so high. It is said to mark the site of a battle, and to be one of the tallest standing stones in Scotland.

B12 Clava Cairns (HS)

See main entry B12

C21 Clune Hill Stone Circle

[Map: 4, G5] Off B9077, 7 miles E of Banchory, Clune Hill, Kincardine and Deeside. (NGR: NO 794949 LR: 38)
The remains of a recumbent stone circle with six upright stones and three fallen. There are also two cairns.
Access at all reasonable times.

C22 Cnoc Fillibhir Bheag Circle

[Map: 3A, B4] Off A858, 13 miles W of Stornoway, Cnoc Fillibhir Bheag, Lewis. (NGR: NB 225327 LR: 8)
The remains of two concentric stone circles. The outer ring consists of 13 stones, eight of which are still upright and vary in height from six to three feet. The inner ring has four upright stones, the tallest of which is over seven feet high. Also known as Callanish III.

C23 Conon Bridge Henge

[Map: 3B, E9] On A862, 3 miles S of Dingwall, SW side of Conon Bridge, Ross and Cromarty, Highland. (NGR: NH 542551 LR: 26)
The remains of a henge monument, an enclosure with a ditch and bank, some 5000 years old.
Park in Station Road.
Access at all reasonable times.

C24 Coultoon Stone Circle

[Map: 5A, E2] Off A847, 4 miles NE of Portnahaven, Coultoon, Islay. (NGR: NR 196570 LR: 60)
Remains of a small stone circle, in a fine location, dating from around 1000 BC. The circle was never apparently completed, and although there are sockets for the upright stones, many were never put in place.
Access at all reasonable times.

C25 Cullerlie Stone Circle (HS)

[Map: 4, G5] Off B9215, 9.5 miles W of Aberdeen, 3 miles SW of Westhill, Cullerlie, Aberdeenshire. (NGR: NJ 786042 LR: 38)
The stone circle at Cullerlie comprises eight unshaped boulders, enclosing eight small kerb cairns. When the site was excavated, only one of the outer cairns was found to be undisturbed, and cremated human bone and charcoal were found.
Parking.
Access at all reasonable times.
Tel: 01466 793191

C26 Deer Park Stones

[Map: 6A, F5] Off A841, 1 mile NW of Brodick, Deerpark, Arran. (NGR: NS 006374 LR: 69)
A group of three standing stones, located across the road from **Brodick Castle [N9]**. The tallest is over 11 feet high, while the other two stones are about eight feet.

C27 Dervaig Standing Stones

[Map: 5A, B3] Off B8073, E of Dervaig, Mull. (NGR: NM 438517 LR: 47)
Three settings of standing stones. The first [NM

438517] is just beyond the burial ground at Kilmore: three small upright stones survive, while a fourth forms side of a gateway. Another group, Cnoc Fada, survive just within the forestry plantation [NM 439521], and consists of two taller upright stones. The third group of stones, two of which are upright and about seven feet tall, is deep in the plantation at Maol Mor [NM 436531] and involves a long walk.

C28 Drumtroddan Cup & Ring Marks (HS)

[Map: 6A, I6] Off A714, 10 miles SW of Whithorn, Drumtroddan, Galloway, Dumfries and Galloway. (NGR: NX 364447 LR: 83)
Three slabs of bedrock are decorated with groups of cup and ring marks, which probably date from the Bronze Age. There is an alignment of three standing stones, one of which has fallen, located 400 yards to the south [NX 364443].
Access at all reasonable times.

C29 Easter Aquorthies Stone Circle (HS)

[Map: 4, G5] Off A96, 3 miles W of Inverurie, Easter Aquorthies, Aberdeenshire. (NGR: NJ 732209 LR: 38)
Easter Aquorthies (pronounced 'Ah-whawrthies') is almost 70 feet in diameter and has nine stones graded in height and set in a bank, as well as a recumbent and two flanking stones. There are a further two stones in front of the recumbent. The raised area in the circle is the remains of a burial cairn.
Parking nearby.
Access at all reasonable times – short walk to site.
Tel: 01466 793191

F15 Edderton Pictish Stone
See main entry F15

C30 Gathering Stone

[Map: 5B, D8] Off B8033 or A8, 1.5 miles E of Dunblane, Sheriffmuir, Stirlingshire. (NGR: NN 810021 LR: 57)
The stone, which is about seven feet long and split into three parts, is believed to be where the Jacobite forces gathered before the Battle of **Sheriffmuir [O12]** in 1715. It was also known as the Battle Stone, but had previously been called the Beltane Stone.

C31 High Banks Cup & Ring Marks

[Map: 6B, I7] Off A711, 2 miles SE of Kirkcudbright, High Banks, Dumfries and Galloway. (NGR: NX 709489 LR: 83)
The site at High Banks has some of south-west Scotland's most impressive cup-and-ring carvings. At the south of the outcrop are over 350 cup marks, some grouped together to form designs and many examples of cup and rings, some with multiple rings.

C32 Hill o' Many Stanes (HS)

[Map: 3B, B11] Off A9, 4 miles NE of Lybster, Mid Clyth, Caithness, Highland. (NGR: ND 295384 LR: 11)

This stone setting is a fan-shaped arrangement of over 200 standing stones set in 22 rows down the side of the hill. It is estimated that if the rows were complete the arrangement would originally have comprised over 600 stones. The function of the site is not known, but it may have been an astronomical observatory. This type of site is only found in northern Scotland and in Brittany in northern France.

Access at all reasonable times.
Tel: 01667 460232

C33 Kempock Stone, Gourock

[Map: 6A, D5] Off A770, 2.5 miles W of Greenock, Kempock Point, Gourock, Renfrewshire. (NGR: NS 243780 LR: 63)

The stone, which is about six feet high, is known as Granny Kempock's Stone, and was used by fishermen in rituals to try to ensure good weather and fair winds, as well as a good catch of fish. Fisherman and others would walk around the stone seven times, carrying a basket of sand. The same ritual was used by betrothed and newly married couples to get Granny's blessing.

Parking nearby.
Access at all reasonable times.

C34 Kilmichael Glassary Cup and Ring Marks (HS)

[Map: 5A, D4] Off A816, 5 miles N of Lochgilphead, near the schoolhouse, Kilmichael Glassary, Kilmartin Glen, Argyll. (NGR: NR 857934 LR: 55)

There are many cup and ring marks, which date from the Bronze Age, on a natural outcrop of rock.

Parking nearby.
Access at all reasonable times.

B27 Kintraw Cairns and Stone

See main entry B27

C35 Laggangairn Stones (HS)

[Map: 6A, H5] Off A75, 7 miles N of Glenluce, Southern Upland Way, Killgallioch, Dumfries and Galloway. (NGR: NX 222716 LR: 76)

The two standing stones are carved with early Christian crosses.

Access at all reasonable times – difficult access signposted through Forest Enterprise land.

C36 Lang Stane o' Craigearn

[Map: 4, G5] Off B993, 4.5 miles SW of Inverurie, 1 mile SW of Kemnay, Aberdeenshire. (NGR: NJ 723149 LR: 38)

Prominent standing stone, some 11 feet tall.

Access at all reasonable times.

C37 Loanhead of Daviot Stone Circle (HS)

[Map: 4, F5] Off A920, 5 miles NW of Inverurie, Aberdeenshire (NGR: NJ 747288 LR: 38)

A recumbent stone circle with eight upright stones, as well as the recumbent stone and its flanking stones. The stones are graded, with the lower stones opposite the recumbent. The stone beside the east flanking stone is decorated with cup marks. A ring-cairn was later constructed within the circle. Nearby is a Bronze Age site, enclosed by a bank and ditch, which contained the cremated remains of over 30 individuals, placed in urns or small pits.

Car parking.
Access at all reasonable times.
Tel: 01466 793191

C38 Loch Clachaig Cup & Ring Marks

[Map: 5A, F4] Off A83, 3.5 miles S of Tayinloan, E of Low Clachaig, Kintyre, Argyll. (NGR: NR 704403 LR: 62)

In Forestry Commission land, the cup and ring marked stone has been reassembled. It is carved with cups and rings, some of them double rings.

C39 Lochbuie Stone Circle

[Map: 5A, C3] Off A849, Lochbuie, 300 yards N of Lochbuie House, Mull. (NGR: NM 618251 LR: 49)

An impressive stone circle in a pleasant location. Eight upright stones remain to a height of six feet. There are four outliers outside the circle. The first is some 15 feet from the circle; another, ten feet tall, is 30 yards to the SW [NM 617251]; another is 400 yards to the N [NM 616254], and is six feet tall; another is 350 yards to the SW [NM 619251], but the top has been broken off. These 'outliers' may have been used in astronomical observations. Lochbuie is a magnificent location, and Moy Castle, the stronghold of the MacLaines of Lochbuie, stands along the shore.

C40 Loudon Hill Stone Circle

[Map: 4, E5] Off A950, 10 miles W of Peterhead, 2 miles NW of Old Deer, Loudon Wood, Banff and Buchan. (NGR: NJ 961497 LR: 30)

Located in a wood are the remains of a recumbent stone circle. Three stones are still upright, while others have fallen.

Access at all reasonable times.

C41 Lundin Links Stones

[Map: 6B, C10] Off A915, 3 miles NE of Methil, Lundin Links, golf course, Fife. (NGR: NO 404027 LR: 59)

The remains of a stone circle, of which only three upright although spectacular stones survive. The tallest is 18 feet high, while the others are 17 feet and 13 feet. According to folk tradition these are the gravestones of Viking warriors defeated by Macbeth.

C42 Machrie Moor Circles (HS)

[Map: 6A, F4] Off A841, 3 miles N of Blackwaterfoot, Machrie Moor, Arran. (NGR: NR 910324 LR: 69)

This is a very important and impressive complex of stone circles and cairns.

One circle [NR 912324] is made up of 11 stones, six granite boulders and five slabs, set alternately.

The stones of another circle [NR 911324] are the most memorable. Only three upright stones survive, but the tallest is over 16 feet tall, while the lowest is still over 12 feet.

Of another circle [NR 910324] only one erect stone remains, although this stone is 14 feet high.

The fourth [910323] is a setting of four low boulders on the arc of an ellipse.

The fifth [NR 909323], and probably the most interesting is known as Suidhe Coire Fhionn ('Fingal's cauldron seat'). It consists of two rings of boulders. The inner is made up of eight stones, about three to four feet high. The outer consists of 15 slightly smaller stones.

Parking nearby.
Access at all reasonable times – involves 1.5 mile walk.

B32 Marionburgh Cairn

See main entry B32

C61 Midmar Stone Circle

[Map: 4, G5] Off B9119, 6 miles N of Banchory, Midmar Church, Aberdeenshire. (NGR: NJ 699065 LR: 38)

An impressive recumbent stone circle stands in the burial ground of the church.

Parking.
Stone circle: access at all reasonable times.

C43 Nine Stanes Mulloch

[Map: 4, G5] Off B974 or A957, 2.5 miles S of Banchory, West Mulloch, Aberdeenshire. (NGR: NO 723912 LR: 45)

The remains of a recumbent stone circle, which was built about 2000 to 1000 BC. The circle was used for burials and there is a low ring cairn. A pit here was found to contain cremated bone.

There is another recumbent stone circle nearby [NO 717916], and another circle in woodland to the south [NO 723912].

Park in the Forestry Commission car park in old quarry.
Access at all reasonable times.

C44 Nine Stones Stone Circle

[Map: 6B, E11] Off B6355, 9 miles SW of Dunbar, 3.5 miles S of Garvald, Mayshiel, East Lothian. (NGR: NT 625655 LR: 67)

The remains of a stone circle, of which three stones remain upright, while others have fallen. There is another circle, or possibly the remains of a cairn, by the path [NT 627648].

Access at all reasonable times – park by cattle grid at E end of Mayshiel Wood.

C45 Pobull Fhinn Stone Circle

[Map: 3A, E2] Off A867, 5 miles W of Lochmaddy, Langass, North Uist. (NGR: NF 843650 LR: 18)

The name of this stone circle refers to the warriors who followed Fionn mac Cumhaill – Finn MacCool. The circle, which is actually oval, is cut into the side of the hill, and consisted of about 48 stones, around 30 of which still remain, although some have fallen. The tallest stone is over seven feet high. The circle dates from between 3000 BC to about 1500 BC. **Barpa Langass [B2]** cairn is close by.

Parking nearby.
Access at all reasonable times.

C46 Pollachar Standing Stone

[Map: 3A, G2] On B888, 6 miles SW of Lochboisdale, Pollachar, South Uist. (NGR: NF 746145 LR: 31)

A standing stone, about six feet tall, from where there are fine views across to Barra and Eriskay.

C47 Ring of Brodgar (HS)

[Map: 2, C2] On B9055, 5 miles NE of Stromness, Orkney. (NGR: HY 294134 LR: 6)

The Ring of Brodgar is the most impressive stone circle in Scotland: 36 stones out of an original total of 60 remain, some up to 15 feet high. The site is surrounded by a ditch, making this a henge monument, which was originally up to ten feet deep and 30 feet across. It is crossed by two causeways. On one of the broken stones in the northern section of the circle, a Norse visitor to the site has carved runes and a cross.

Car and coach parking.
Access at all reasonable times.
Tel: 01856 841815

C48 Stone, North Ronaldsay

[Map: 2, A4] Off unlisted road, Holland, SW side of North Ronaldsay, Orkney. (NGR: HY 752529 LR: 5)

The standing stone, which is over 13 feet high, has a small hole through it some six feet above the ground. The stone was a meeting place on New Year's Day.

C49 Standing Stones of Urquhart

[Map: 4, E3] Off A96, 4 miles E of Elgin, 1 mile N of Urquhart, Moray. (NGR: NJ 290641 LR: 28)

The remains of a stone circle, five stones of which survive upright, while two others have fallen. The tallest stone rises to about six feet. Others stones appear to have been removed, as the circle was known as 'the Nine Stones'. It has also been called the Devil's Stanes.

Access at all reasonable times.

B40 Steinacleit (HS)

See main entry B40

C50 Stone of Setter, Eday

[Map: 2, B3] Off B9063, 0.5 miles S of Carrick House, Eday, Orkney. (NGR: HY 565372 LR: 5)

A prominent and impressive standing stone, more than 15 feet high. It stands by a heritage walk which passes this stone and the remains of several chambered cairns, including the cairn at Vinquoy Hill [B48].

Access at all reasonable times.

C51 Stones of Stenness (HS)

[Map: 2, C2] On B9055, 5 miles NE of Stromness, Stenness, Orkney. (NGR: HY 306126 LR: 6)

Only four stones of this impressive circle remain out of 12. A ditch, originally over seven feet deep, surrounds the stone circle and was crossed by a causeway. A stone setting was uncovered in the centre of the circle. Animal bones found in the ditch were interpreted as the remains of feasting or sacrifice at the henge. The circle is of a similar date to the nearby settlement at Barnhouse [A3].

Car and coach parking.

Access at all reasonable times.

Tel: 01856 841815

C52 Strichen Stone Circle

[Map: 4, E5] Off A981, 7 miles S of Fraserburgh, 0.5 miles SW of Strichen, Aberdeenshire. (NGR: NJ 937545 LR: 30)

Built on a site with fine views, Strichen consists of the remains of a stone circle with a recumbent stone and its flanking stones

Parking nearby.

Access at all reasonable times.

C53 Strontoiller Cairn and Standing Stones

[Map: 5A, B4] Off A816, 3 miles E of Oban, S of Strontoiller, Argyll. (NGR: NM 907289 LR: 49)

The impressive standing stone at Strontoiller is a rough-cut pillar, standing some 13 feet high. It is said to mark the grave of Diarmid, the mythical hero. The adjacent cairn was excavated, and some cremated bone was found. Quartz chips and pebbles were found under the kerbstones: quartz is often associated with burial sites in the west.

C54 Sunhoney Stone Circle

[Map: 4, G5] Off B9119, 5.5 miles N of Banchory, Sunhoney, Aberdeenshire. (NGR: NJ 715056 LR: 38)

The circle at Sunhoney, now surrounded by trees, has 11 standing stones and a recumbent stone. The recumbent is of grey granite and the uprights are of red granite. The recumbent has probably fallen over and the face, which is now its upper face, is decorated with 30 cup marks. There is a ring cairn within the circle, and deposits of burnt bone were found here.

Parking nearby: do not block farm access.

Access at all reasonable times: short walk past house and along field boundary.

C55 Temple Wood Circles (HS)

[Map: 5A, D4] Off A816, 1 mile S of Kilmartin, Temple Wood, Argyll. (NGR: NR 826978 LR: 55)

A circle of stones, some 40 feet in diameter. Two of the stones are decorated: one with two concentric circles, the other with a double spiral. There were several burials in small cairns and cists, and the circle was eventually engulfed in a large cairn. There was another smaller circle nearby, and is a setting of standing stones [NR 827977] where several stones are in a row, past which the footpath to Temple Wood passes.

Parking nearby.

Access at all reasonable times.

C56 Templestone

[Map: 4, E2] Off B9010, 2 miles SE of Forres, Templestone, Moray. (NGR: NJ 069569 LR: 27)

The site consists of a setting of four upright standing stones, in the shape of a rectangle.

Access at all reasonable times.

C57 Tomnaverie Circle (HS)

[Map: 4, G4] On B9094, 3.5 miles NW of Aboyne, Aberdeenshire. (NGR: NJ 487035 LR: 37)

The circle is 60 feet in diameter: four of the stones and the recumbent remain in place. Within the circle is a circle of smaller stones, the kerb of a ring cairn. There are extensive views to Lochnagar and the Cairngorms, and the site is to be landscaped.

Parking nearby.

Access at all reasonable times – short walk.

Tel: 01466 793191

C58 Torhouse Circle (HS)

[Map: 6A, I6] Off B733, 3.5 miles W of Wigtown, Torhouse, Dumfries and Galloway. (NGR: NX 382565 LR: 83)

The circle has 19 granite boulders, graded in height with the largest boulder, weighing some six tons, situated in the south-east. In the middle of the circle are three stones, two large ones with a smaller one between, which may indicate a link with the recumbent stone circles of the north-east. Nearby are further standing stones and burial cairns.

Parking nearby.

Access at all reasonable times.

C59 Twelve Apostles Circle

[Map: 6B, H8] Off A76 or B729, 3 miles NW of Dumfries, Newbridge, Dumfries and Galloway. (NGR: NX 947794 LR: 84)

Eleven stones survive of the stone circle, although it is thought that there were originally 18 stones. The circle is the largest in Scotland (although not the most impressive) and one of the largest in Britain, measuring almost 280 feet at its widest point. Four of the stones are boulders, while the remainder were quarried.

Access at all reasonable times: park beside first road on left and walk 100 yards to waymarker and site.

C60 Whitehill Stone Circle

[Map: 4, G4] Off A944 or B993, 4 miles E of Alford, N of Tillyfourie, Aberdeenshire. (NGR: NJ 643134 LR: 37)

Standing within a forestry plantation are the remains of a recumbent stone circle. It consists of three upright stones, the recumbent, and several fallen stones, encircling a smaller cairn with an outer kerb.

Access at all reasonable times.

Top *Machrie Moor*
Right *Strontoiller*
Bottom *Tomnaverie*

Top *Callanish*
Right *Stones of Stenness*
Bottom *Kilmichael Glassary
Cup and Ring Marks*

D: Brochs, Forts and Duns

D1 Arbory Hill Fort

[Map: 6B, F8] Off M74, 0.5 miles NE of Abington, Arbory Hill, Lanarkshire. (NGR: NS 944238 LR: 72)

Three lines of defences representing two phases of fort building surround the summit of Arbory Hill. The earlier fort had two ditches and ramparts which were cut by five entrances. A circular stone-walled enclosure was later added. Hut circles can be traced inside the inner rampart and inside the stone enclosure.

E4 Bar Hill Fort (HS)

See main entry E4

D2 Barsalloch Fort (HS)

[Map: 6A, J6] Off A747, 7.5 miles NW of Whithorn, Barsalloch Point, Dumfries and Galloway. (NGR: NX 347412 LR: 82)

The remains of an Iron Age hill fort on the edge of a raised beach ridge. It was defended by a deep ditch shaped like a horse shoe.

Car parking.

Access at all reasonable times – steep climb.

D3 Black Hill (NTS)

[Map: 6B, F8] Off B7018 or A744, 3 miles W of Lanark, Blackhill, Stonebyres, Lanarkshire. (NGR: NS 832435 LR: 72)

The remains of an Iron Age fort, and the site of a Bronze Age burial cairn. There are fine views over the Clyde valley.

Explanatory board. Parking nearby.

Access at all reasonable times.

D4 Borgadel Dun

[Map: 5A, G3] Off B842, 10.5 miles SW of Campbeltown, 4 miles W of Southend, Borgadel, Kintyre, Argyll. (NGR: NR 625061 LR: 68)

In a remote location are the well-preserved ruins of a dun. The walls stands to a height of six feet, and the entrance passage survives.

Great care must be taken.

D5 Brown Caterthun (HS)

[Map: 4, H4] Off A94, near Menmuir, 5 miles NW of Brechin, Angus. (NGR: NO 555668 LR: 44)

The fort has several ramparts around the summit and, further down the hill, a wall (cut by nine entrances) surrounded by double ramparts and ditch. Still further down slope are two more ramparts with an external ditch. Recent excavations indicate a date of 700 BC for the inner rampart, and 500-300 BC for the middle group. **White Caterthun [D65]** is nearby.

Parking nearby

Access at all reasonable times.

D6 Burghead

[Map: 4, E2] Off B9089, 8 miles NW of Elgin, Burghead, Moray. (NGR: NJ 110690 LR: 28)

Burghead was one of the major fortresses of the Picts, although it had been used since prehistoric times. Many fine Pictish carvings of bulls were found here, which can now be seen on display in the Burghead Library, **Elgin Museum [Y74]**, the **Museum of Scotland [Y6]** in Edinburgh and the British Museum in London. The fort was used by Thorfinn the Mighty, Earl of Orkney, as a base, and it was nearby that Duncan (of Macbeth fame) was defeated by Thorfinn in 1040. Duncan was also defeated by Macbeth in battle, and died of his wounds at Spynie. The fort was mostly destroyed when the village was built.

The Well, rediscovered in 1809, consists of a rock-hewn chamber, reached down stone steps. It has been identified by some as being associated with St Ethan, a disciple of St Columba, and has a deep tank of water surrounded by a platform, with a basin and pedestal. Burghead is also well known for the 'Burning of the Clavie', an old fire festival when a burning barrel of tar is taken around the streets on 12 January.

Parking nearby.

Well: access at all reasonable times.

Tel: 01667 460232

D7 Burnswark Hill

[Map: 6B, H9] Off B725, 3 miles SE of Lockerbie, Burnswark, Dumfries and Galloway. (NGR: NY 185787 LR: 85)

The hill fort, with extensive earthworks, dates from around 600 BC. It is flanked by a Roman artillery range, best seen from the hilltop.

Parking nearby.

Access at all reasonable times.

D8 Burroughston Broch

[Map: 2, C3] Off B9058, Burroughston, NE side of Shapinsay, Orkney. (NGR: HY 541210 LR: 6)

The impressive remains of a broch, which was defended by a ditch. The walls stand to about 12 feet high in one place, and there is the roofless entrance passage and guard chamber, and a well.

D9 Caisteal Grugaig

[Map: 3A, F6] Off A87, 7 miles E of Kyle of Lochalsh, 6 miles NW of Shiel Bridge, Totaig, Highland. (NGR: NG 867251 LR: 33)

Set in a picturesque but remote location, Caisteal Grugaig consists of the impressive remains of a broch. The wall survives to a height of 13 feet, and there are mural chambers, a door check and the remains of a stair. A massive triangular lintel is still in place above the entrance passageway.

D10 Carn Liath, Golspie (HS)

[Map: 3B, C10] On A9, 3 miles E of Golspie, Sutherland. (NGR: NC 870013 LR: 17)
The fine remains of a broch and surrounding settlement. A silver brooch was found here, dating from the 4th or 5th century, suggesting the settlement was used by the Picts. The brooch is now held at the **Museum of Scotland [Y6]** in Edinburgh.
Explanatory board. Disabled access. Parking.
Access at all reasonable times.
Tel: 01667 460232

D11 Castle Haven

[Map: 6B, I7] Off B727, 5 miles S of Gatehouse of Fleet, Kirkandrews, Dumfries and Galloway. (NGR: NX 594483 LR: 83)
This is a D-shaped galleried dun with the straight part of the wall along the cliff edge. The dun has two entrances, a main entrance at the north and a smaller one leading to the shore. Six entrances lead off the central courtyard into the galleries. It is not certain if the surrounding walk was contemporary with the dun. Earlier this century the dun was cleared out and restored by the landowner. The dun was occupied into medieval times.

N71 Castle of Troup

See main entry N71

D12 Castlelaw Hill Fort (HS)

[Map: 6B, E9] Off A702, 6 miles S of Edinburgh, near Glencorse, Castlelaw, Midlothian. (NGR: NT 229638 LR: 66)
Excavations at Castlelaw in the 1930s and 1940s revealed that, prior to the fort defined by the multiple ramparts, there was a palisaded enclosure dating to the first millennium BC and a fort with a single rampart. The 75 foot souterrain was built into one of the ditches once the defences were no longer being maintained. Midway along the passage is a corbelled cell.
Car and coach parking.
Access at all reasonable times.

D13 Chesters Hill Fort (HS)

[Map: 6B, D10] Off B1377, 3 miles N of Haddington, 1 mile S of Drem, The Chesters, East Lothian. (NGR: NT 507782 LR: 66)
An oval fort with a series of seven ramparts, unusually sited on a low ridge, suggesting that it was built more for show than defence. Within the hill fort are over 20 hut-circle platforms.
Parking nearby.
Access at all reasonable times – visit involves walk.

D14 Clickimin Broch (HS)

[Map: 1, D3] Off A970, 1 mile SW of Lerwick, Clickimin, Shetland. (NGR: HU 464408 LR: 4)
The settlement at Clickimin was originally on an island, joined to the shore by a causeway. The islet was surrounded by a stone wall with a massive blockhouse and a broch, which survives to a height of 17 feet. At the end of the causeway is a stone with two footprints carved into it, which has been linked with inauguration rites of early kings. It was occupied by the Picts.
Parking nearby.
Access at all reasonable times.
Tel: 01466 793191

D15 Doune Broch Centre

[Map: 3A, B3] Off A858, 15 miles NW of Stornoway, Carloway, Lewis. (NGR: NB 190412 LR: 8)
The centre houses an interpretive chamber, called 'Scenes from the Broch', and a graphics display, which recreates views of nearby **Dun Carloway [D23]** broch, illustrating the life of the inhabitants.
Explanatory displays. Gift shop. WC. Car and coach parking.
Open May-Sep, Mon-Sat 10.00-17.00.
Tel: 01851 643338/01851 621422   Fax: 01851 621446
Email: calanais.centre@btinternet.com

D16 Dreva Craig Fort

[Map: 6B, F9] Off A701, 5.5 miles E of Biggar, Dreva Craig, Borders. (NGR: NT 126353 LR: 72)
The fort has two stone ramparts, with the entrance to the east, as well as a defensive outwork, down slope to the south: over 100 upright stones to break up an attack. There are traces of Iron Age round houses inside the fort, some of which are later than the fort as they are built into the walls. On the way to the fort are further hut-circles and field systems.

D17 Dun Ardtreck

[Map: 3A, F4] Off B8009, 3.5 miles NW of Corbost, Portnalong, Skye. (NGR: NG 335358 LR: 32)
Standing on a rocky crag above the sea is a dun with the remains of a wall, on the landward side, surviving to a height of eight feet. The entrance is in the middle of the wall, and has a guard chamber. The dun was burnt out at some time, but was later reoccupied, and finds from here included pottery, iron tools, and bronze and glass ornaments.

D18 Dun Baravat

[Map: 3A, B3] Off B8059, 1 mile S of Breaclete, Loch Baravat, Great Bernera. (NGR: NB 156356 LR: 13)
Standing on a small island on the east side of Loch Baravat are the remains of a dun or broch, the walls of which survive to a height of 11 feet
Long walk, then ford the causeway: care must be taken.

D19 Dun Beag (HS)

[Map: 3A, F4] On A863, 8 miles SE of Dunvegan, Struanmore, Skye. (NGR: NG 339386 LR: 23)
Dun Beag ('small dun') is a well-preserved ruined broch on a small knoll. The entrance passage, an adjoining cell and mural stair rising about 20 steps all

survive. The broch was still apparently occupied in the 18th century.

Parking.
Access at all reasonable times.
Tel: 01667 460232

D20 Dun Borranish

[Map: 3A, B3] Off B8011, 24 miles W of Stornoway, Uig Sands, Lewis. (NGR: NB 050332 LR: 13)

A ruinous dun is located on a rocky crag at the edge of the splendid Uig sands. The dun is connected to the mainland by a causeway. This is said to be the place where a giant known as Cuithach, who was terrorising the area, was slain.

Long walk and may be wet.

D21 Dun Bragar

[Map: 3A, B4] Off A858, 12 miles NW of Stornoway, Loch an Duna, Lewis. (NGR: NB 285474 LR: 8)

Standing on an island in a small lochan, Dun Bragar is a ruinous broch, the walls of which survive to a height of 14 feet on the south side.

Access via causeway – care must be taken.

D22 Dun Canna

[Map: 3B, D7] Off A835, 7 miles N of Ullapool, Blughasary, Ross and Cromarty, Highland. (NGR: NC 112008 LR: 15)

The remains of a small fort, built on a promontory, rectangular in shape and defended by a wall. The wall is ruinous but impressive.

Parking.
Access at all reasonable times: long and picturesque walk from car park.

D23 Dun Carloway (HS)

[Map: 3A, B3] Off A858, 15 miles NW of Stornoway, Carloway, Lewis. (NGR: NB 190412 LR: 8)

A well-preserved broch, which stands to about 30 feet high, although one half of the building has fallen away to the lintel of the entrance passageway. A covered gallery within the wall can be seen, as can an entrance passage and guard cell. In the 17th century the Morrisons of Ness used the broch as their stronghold against the MacAulays of Uig. The **Doune Broch Centre [D15]** is located nearby.

Car and coach parking. The Doune Broch Centre is nearby.
Access at all reasonable times – short walk.

D24 Dun Dornaigil (HS)

[Map: 3B, B8] Off A838, 17 miles S of Durness, 3.5 miles S of end of Loch Hope, Sutherland, Highland. (NGR: NC 457450 LR: 9)

Dun Dornaigil (also known as Dun Dornadilla) survives to almost 25 feet in one section (now supported by a modern buttress) which places it among the best preserved examples in Scotland. The entrance is crowned with a huge triangular lintel. The broch has

not been excavated and the interior is full of rubble.

Parking.
Access at all reasonable times: walk to broch.
Tel: 01667 460232

D25 Dun Fiadhairt

[Map: 3A, E4] Off A850, 2.5 miles NW of Dunvegan, Fiadhairt, Skye. (NGR: NG 231504 LR: 23)

Built on a rocky outcrop are the ruins of an Iron Age broch. The wall survives to a height of five feet, and there are two entrances, the main one between two walls with openings into guard cells. Galleries within the walls can be traced.

D26 Dun Grugaig, Glenelg

[Map: 3A, G6] Off A87, 9 miles SE of Kyle of Lochalsh, 3.5 miles SE of Glenelg, N of river, in Gleann Beag. (NGR: NG 852159 LR: 33)

The remains of a D-plan dun stands above a steep gorge. The walls stand to a maximum height of about 16 feet, and mural chambers and a blocked entrance passage can be traced. This stands further up the glen from **Dun Telve [D32]** and **Dun Troddan [D34]**.

D27 Dun Grugaig, Elgol

[Map: 3A, G5] Off A881, 1.5 miles SE of Elgol, Glasnakille, Skye. (NGR: NG 535124 LR: 32)

Standing on a small rocky outcrop above the sea is a strong wall, which cuts off the promontory on the landward side. The wall, which survives to a height of 13 feet above the inside level, has mural galleries and there are the treads of a stair. A massive lintel survives above the entrance, and the passageway is still roofed over.

D28 Dun Mor, Vaul

[Map: 5A, B1] Off B8069, 2.5 miles N of Scarinish, Vaul, Tiree. (NGR: NM 042492 LR: 46)

A well-preserved broch and outworks, the walls of which survive to a height of about seven feet. A gallery ran up inside the wall, and a doorway gave access to a stair, which led up to the upper parts of the broch. The entrance has a small guard chamber, and there was a water tank in the floor. The skeleton of man was found in the broch, dating from Norse times.

D29 Dun Nosebridge

[Map: 5A, E2] Off A846, 2.5 miles SE of Bridgend, Cluanach, Islay. (NGR: NR 372603 LR: 60)

The large and impressive fort dates from the Iron Age. It is protected by a series of well-preserved ramparts and a wall, tiered one above the next, and by a cliff on one side. The fort is roughly rectangular in shape, and the entrances through the ramparts can be traced.

Landrover trips to the fort can be arranged – tel: 01496 810274

D30 Dun Ringill

[Map: 3A, G5] Off A881, 11 miles SW of Broadford, Kilmarie, Skye. (NGR: NG 562171 LR: 32)

An Iron Age dun, defended by the steepness of the cliffs above the shore and a strong wall and ditch on the landward side. The wall has had a mural gallery, a cell, and an altered entrance. Within the dun are the foundations of two small medieval rectangular buildings, used by Clan MacKinnon before they moved to Castle Maol in the late 16th century, although the family eventually moved back to Kilmarie.

D31 Dun Skeig, Clachan

[Map: 5A, E4] Off A83, 9.5 miles SW of Tarbert, 1 mile NW of Clachan, Kintyre, Argyll. (NGR: NR 758572 LR: 62)

The remains of a wall enclose the ruin of two duns, one of which has a vitrified wall, while the other is smaller but better preserved. The entrance of this dun can be traced, and there are spectacular views.

D32 Dun Telve (HS)

[Map: 3A, G6] Off A87, 8 miles SE of Kyle of Lochalsh, 2 miles SE of Glenelg, Gleann Beag, Highland. (NGR: NG 829172 LR: 33)

A large part of the wall of Dun Telve is missing, but within the remaining parts of wall are scarcements to support upper floors, and voids above the interior doors. The entrance has a bar-hole and door checks. There are various outbuildings around the broch, although they may be later in date. **Dun Troddan [D34]** is close by.

Parking nearby.
Access at all reasonable times.
Tel: 01667 460232

D33 Dun Torcuill

[Map: 3A, E2] Off A865, 4 miles NW of Lochmaddy, Loch an Duin, North Uist. (NGR: NF 888737 LR: 18)

On a small island in the loch, connected to the mainland by a short causeway, is a dun or possible broch. The entrance, cells and gallery can be traced, and the walls survive to a height of about ten feet, although the inside of the building is choked with rubble and undergrowth.

Long walk.

D34 Dun Troddan (HS)

[Map: 3A, G6] Off A87, 8 miles SE of Kyle of Lochalsh, 2.5 miles SE of Glenelg, Corrary, Gleann Beag, Highland. (NGR: NG 833172 LR: 33)

Dun Troddan is the neighbour of **Dun Telve [D32]**, located 0.3 miles further along the glen. As with Dun Telve, a section of the wall survives and the structure of the building – two skins held together with horizontal slabs – can be seen. It is possible to go up a section of the staircase within the gallery. Off the entrance is a corbelled guard cell.

Parking nearby.
Access at all reasonable times.
Tel: 01667 460232

D35 Dun Vulan

[Map: 3A, F2] Off A865, 8.5 miles NW of Lochboisdale, Rubha Ardvule, South Uist. (NGR: NF 713297 LR: 22)

A broch or dun with walls surviving to a height of about 14 feet. There is a wall chamber and a stairway to a first-floor gallery, and the entrance can be identified. The site was occupied from the Bronze Age until at least 300 AD, and there is apparently a medieval building outside the broch wall.

At the end of the Bornais Road.

D36 Dun an Sticar

[Map: 3A, D2] On B893, 6 miles N of Lochmaddy, Newton Ferry, North Uist. (NGR: NF 898778 LR: 18)

An altered Iron Age dun, the walls of which survive to a height of over ten feet. A gallery in the wall can be seen, and the entrance can be traced. There are two splendid causeways out to a neighbouring islet, then another causeway out to the dun. Dun an Sticar was used by Hugh MacDonald, one of the MacDonalds of Sleat, in 1602. He sheltered here after plotting to slaughter his kin, but was eventually captured to be starved to death in **Duntulm Castle [N94]**.

Parking nearby.
View from exterior – care should be taken.

D37 Dun da Lamh Fort

[Map: 3B, G9] Off A86, 8 miles SW of Newtonmore, 2.5 miles W of Laggan, Highland. (NGR: NN 582929 LR: 35)

Set on a rock are the remains of an impressive fort. It was defended by a strong wall, which survives to a height of about 12 feet. The fort dates from the Iron Age, but may have been used by the Picts.

Parking nearby.
Access at all reasonable times: long and steep climb.

D38 Dunadd (HS)

[Map: 5A, D4] Off A816, 3.5 miles S of Kilmartin, Dunadd, Argyll. (NGR: NR 836936 LR: 55)

Dunadd stands on a steep-sided hill, and consists of lines of fortifications, some well preserved, dating from the 1st century AD. There is also an impressive entrance, and fine views from the windswept top. Dunadd was a stronghold of the Scots, and inaugurations of their kings were held here, with a basin, footprint and carving of a Pictish boar in the rock. The Stone of Destiny was kept here. It is recorded that Dunadd was besieged by the Picts in 683 and 736.

Information board. Parking.
Access at all reasonable times: ascent is short but steep and may be slippy in wet weather.

D39 Dunnideer

[Map: 4, F4] Off B992, 1 mile W of Insch, 0.5 miles S of Dunnideer, in ramparts of fort and settlement, at Dunnideer. (NGR: NJ 613282 LR: 37)

The earthworks of an Iron Age fort, parts of which are vitrified, and said to be where King Arthur held court with Giric, King of Scots, in the 9th century. A later castle was built in the fort around 1260 by John Balliol, father of John I, King of Scots, 'Toom Tabard'. The Tyrie family occupied the castle until 1724.

Access at all reasonable times: sign-posted footpath and steep ascent.

D40 Dunsinane Hill

[Map: 5B, B9] Off B953, 7 miles NE of Perth, Dunsinane, Perthshire. (NGR: NO 214316 LR: 53)

The summit of Dunsinane Hill is surrounded by lines of defences, and is known as 'Macbeth's Castle'. Traditionally it is where Macbeth awaited the forces of Malcolm Canmore and most of Birnam Wood (which, although some 12 miles away, can be seen from the summit). According to the play, Macbeth was killed at the battle – but although it is likely Macbeth was defeated here in 1054, it was not until 1057 that he was slain, and at Lumphanan.

The hill is reached by a steep footpath on the N side.

D41 Edin's Hall Broch (HS)

[Map: 6B, E12] Off A6112, 5 miles N of Duns, Cockburns Law, Borders. (NGR: NT 772603 LR: 67)

A fort, with a double rampart and ditches, has a broch in one corner. The broch is very large, having an internal diameter of 60 feet and walls up to 20 feet thick. The broch is said to have been the stronghold of a three-headed giant, known as Etin or Edin.

Parking (nearby).

Access at all reasonable times – 1.5 miles walk.

D42 Eildon Hill

[Map: 6B, F10] Off A6091, 1 mile SE of Melrose, Eildon, Borders. (NGR: NT 555238 LR: 73)

The summit of Eildon Hill North, the largest of three peaks above Melrose and the Tweed, was occupied from at least the Bronze Age. Some of the 300 or so houses (represented by house-platforms) date to the late Bronze Age, but others will be of Iron Age date. On the west end of the summit are traces of a Roman signal station.

D43 Finavon Fort

[Map: 4, I4] Off B9134, 4 miles NE of Forfar, Hill of Finavon, Angus. (NGR: NO 506556 LR: 54)

The ramparts of the fort on Finavon Hill are massive, over 20 feet thick, and straight rather than following the contours of the hilltop. The fort was destroyed by fire – the heat was so intense that the core of the rampart vitrified. In the interior of the fort to the east is a rock-cut tank.

D44 Gurness Broch (HS)

[Map: 2, B2] Off A966, 10.5 miles N of Kirkwall, 1 mile NE of Evie, Gurness, Orkney. (NGR: HY 381268 LR: 6)

The broch has a solid wall base with a guard cell on each side of the entrance passage, and the walls survive to a height of 10 feet. The surrounding settlement is defended by ramparts and ditches. Some of the houses date to the later Iron Age, including one with five cells and a hearth, which has been reconstructed beside the visitor centre. The settlement was occupied by the Picts, and the museum has prehistoric and some Pictish artefacts.

Explanatory displays. Disabled access. Car and limited coach parking. Group concession. £. Joint entry ticket for all Orkney monuments available.

Open Apr-Sep, daily 9.30-18.30; last ticket 30 mins before closing – combined ticket available for Orkney monuments. Walk to broch.

Tel: 01856 751414

D45 Jarlshof (HS)

[Map: 1, E3] Off A970, 22 miles S of Lerwick, Sumburgh, Shetland. (NGR: HU 398095 LR: 4)

One of the most remarkable archaeological sites in Europe, dating from Neolithic times. There are also remains from the Bronze Age, Iron Age, Pictish and Viking settlements, as well as a medieval farm. There is also a 16th-century Laird's House, once home of the Earls Robert and Patrick Stewart, and the basis of Jarlshof in Walter Scot's novel *The Pirate*. There is a small visitors' centre with artefacts from the excavations.

Visitor centre with exhibition. Gift shop. Car and coach parking. £.

Open Apr-Sep, daily 9.30-18.30; last ticket 18.00.

Tel: 01950 460112

D46 Kemp's Walk Fort

[Map: 6A, I5] Off B738, 4.5 miles W of Stranraer, Larbrax, Dumfries and Galloway. (NGR: NW 975598 LR: 82)

Kemp's Walk is a large promontory fort, measuring 300 feet by 150 feet, overlooking Broadsea Bay. It has three large ramparts and ditches crossing the northern approach. The other sides of the promontory have steeper slopes and would have been easier to defend.

D47 Kildonan Dun

[Map: 5A, F4] On B842, 5 miles NE of Campbeltown, Kildonan, Kintyre. (NGR: NR 780277 LR: 68)

Excavations at this drystone-walled D-shaped dun indicate that it was built in the first or second century AD, and then reoccupied later in the 9th to 12th centuries. The wall is seven feet thick and the door check and bar holes can still be seen. Also visible are the double stairway to the wall-head and a mural cell.

D48 Kilphedir Broch

[Map: 3B, C10] Off A897, 3 miles NW of Helmsdale, Kilphedir, Sutherland, Highland. (NGR: NC 995189 LR: 17)
The broch, which is rubble-filled, is situated on a hilltop, and defended by a series of ramparts and ditches around the broch. Down slope from the broch are a number of hut-circles, including a group of five which have been excavated and were contemporary with the broch.

D49 Knockfarrel Fort

[Map: 3B, E9] Off A834, 3 miles W of Dingwall, 1.5 miles E of Strathpeffer, Ross and Cromarty, Highland (NGR: NH 504585 LR: 26)
The Iron Age fort is enclosed by the ruins of a large wall and outworks, which are vitrified in many places.
Parking nearby.
Access at all reasonable times: shortest path from Knockfarrel Crofts, although also walks from Strathpeffer, Fodderty and Blackmuir Wood.

D50 Lamb Ness Broch

[Map: 2, C3] Off B9060, Lamb Ness, Lamb Head, SE side of Stronsay, Orkney. (NGR: HY 690215 LR: 5)
The remains of a broch have been excavated revealing two side or guard chambers off the entrance passageway – which is blocked at both ends.

D51 Midhowe Broch (HS)

[Map: 2, B2] Off B9064, SW side of island of Rousay, Orkney. (NGR: HY 371306 LR: 6)
Two ditches, with a wall between them, cut off the promontory. The broch is different from the majority of northern brochs as it has a gallery at ground level, rather than a solid base. This meant that it was not strong enough to take the weight of the building, and the outside wall had to be buttressed with vertical slabs. The chambered tomb of **Midhowe [B34]** is close by.
Parking nearby.
Access at all reasonable times – steep descent down to broch.
Tel: 01856 841815

D52 Mither Tap o' Bennachie

[Map: 4, G5] Off A96, 5 miles W of Inverurie, 2.5 miles S of Oyne, Bennachie, Aberdeenshire. (NGR: NJ 683224 LR: 38)
An impressive hill fort, dating from the Iron Age or Pictish period, enclosed by the remains of two massive stone walls near the summit. Entrances can be traced, and there are also remains of a causeway, the Maiden Causeway, which is said to have run from this fort to Maiden Castle [NJ 694244], another fort. There is a visitor centre at **Bennachie [Y37]**.
Parking at Rowantree car park.
Access at all reasonable times.

D53 Mousa Broch (HS)

[Map: 1, E3] Off A970, 14 miles S of Lerwick, W side of island of Mousa, Shetland. (NGR: HU 457236 LR: 4)
The best preserved of all brochs in Scotland, and one of the foremost Iron Age monuments in Britain, the broch at Mousa consists of a dry-stone tower rising to about 35 feet in height. The solid base of the tower has three small cells, but above this the walls are hollow and contain galleries. A narrow stair climbs through the galleries to the wallhead. There may have been a wooden roof, and floors within the tower.

An eloping couple took shelter in the broch when their ship was wrecked about 900, as recounted in *Egil's Saga*. The *Orkneyinga Saga* tells the story of the abduction of Margaret by Erlend in 1153. Erlend and Margaret, mother of Earl Harald Maddadson, were eventually married.
Open all year – accessible by boat from Sandwick: weather permitting.
(tel/fax 01950 431367; email info@mousaboattrips.co.uk; web www.mousaboattrips.co.uk).
Tel: 01466 793191

D54 Ness of Burgi Fort (HS)

[Map: 1, E3] Off A970, 1 mile SW of Sumburgh, Ness of Burgi, Scatness, Shetland. (NGR: HU 386085 LR: 4)
Positioned across the neck of the promontory is a blockhouse similar to that found in association with the broch at **Clickimin [D14]**. The blockhouse is a rectangular block of walling with an entrance passage running through it, which has door checks and bar holes part of the way along it. The blockhouse is protected by a rampart with a ditch on either side (the pile of stones is excavation debris).
Access at all reasonable times – access is difficult, especially in bad weather.
Tel: 01466 793191

D55 Nybster Broch

[Map: 3B, A12] Off A9, 10 miles N of Wick, Nybster, Caithness, Highland. (NGR: ND 370631 LR: 12)
The ruins of a broch, outlying buildings and defences on a promontory above the sea. **Northlands Viking Centre [Y147]** is close by.
Parking nearby.
Access at all reasonable times: walk to broch.

D56 Old Scatness Broch and Settlement

[Map: 1, E3] On A970, 0.5 miles NW of Sumburgh, Old Scatness, Scord, Shetland. (NGR: HU 390106 LR: 4)
The site at Scatness consists of a broch, of which up to 17 feet of the wall appears to be standing, and its surrounding settlement, some of which postdate the broch. The site was later used by Norsemen. One of

the buildings was reused as a smithy, and has been reconstructed near to the site.

Exhibition. Guided tours. Living history demonstrations illustrate past life and Iron Age crafts.
Open Jul-early Aug, Sat-Thu 10.00-17.30.
Tel: 01595 694688   Fax: 01595 693956
Web: www.shetland.news.co.uk/website/amenity

Y164 Queen's View Visitor Centre
See main entry Y164

D57 Rockcliffe (NTS)
[Map: 6B, I8] Off A710, 7 miles S of Dalbeattie, Rockcliffe, Dumfries and Galloway. (NGR: NX 845540 LR: 84)

Within Rockcliffe is the Mote of Mark, an Iron Age hill fort covering some 20 acres, while Rough Island is a bird sanctuary. Muckle Lands and Jubilee Path cover a fine stretch of coastline between Kippford and Rockcliffe. Programme of guided walks in summer.

Explanatory display. Restaurant and tearoom in village. WC. Disabled access. Car and coach parking.
Access at all reasonable times; Rough Island should not be visited May-Jun.
Tel: 01556 502575

B39 Rubh' an Dunain
See main entry B39

D58 Sallachy Broch, Lairg
[Map: 3B, C9] Off A839, 2.5 miles NW of Lairg, Sallachy, Sutherland, Highland. (NGR: NC 549092 LR: 16)

The substantial ruin of a broch, in a picturesque location by the banks of Loch Shin. The walls stand to a height of 12 feet, and the entrance with guard chambers can be seen.

Parking.
Access at all reasonable times: walk from car park.

D59 Sron Uamha Fort
[Map: 5A, G3] Off B842, 10 miles SW of Campbeltown, 5 miles W of Southend, Sron Uamha, Kintyre, Argyll. (NGR: NR 612060 LR: 68)

Situated in a remote location on the southern-most tip of Kintyre are the remains of a fort on cliffs above the sea, defended on the landward side by the ruins of three walls.
Care should be taken.

D60 Tap o' Noth Fort
[Map: 4, F4] Off A941, 8 miles S of Huntly, 1.5 miles NW of Rhynie, Aberdeenshire. (NGR: NJ 484293 LR: 37)

Perched over 1800 feet high, overlooking the countryside around Gordon, this is the second highest hill fort in Scotland. A massive timber-laced stone rampart, originally up to 30 feet thick, surrounds the summit and there is a further rampart lower down the hill. Up to 150 hut platforms pepper the fort.
Parking on A941.
Access at all reasonable times – 3 mile walk from Brae of Scurdargue.

D61 Tirefour Broch
[Map: 5A, B4] Off B8045, 2 miles NE of Achnacroish, Lismore. (NGR: NM 867429 LR: 49)

Standing on a rocky outcrop is a well-preserved broch. The wall rises to over ten feet for most of its length, and in one place to 16 feet. The inside is partly filled with debris, but a doorway in one interior face survives. The entrance and the remains of an intramural gallery can be seen, and outside the broch are two ruinous outworks defending the approach.

D62 Traprain Law Fort
[Map: 6B, E11] Off A1, 4 miles E of Haddington, 2 miles SE of East Linton, Traprain Law, East Lothian. (NGR: NT 581746 LR: 67)

The summit of Traprain Law has two main ramparts, clearest along the north and west of the hill – a large part of the north-east of the hill has been removed by quarrying. A hoard of late Roman, Christian and pagan silver (now in the **Museum of Scotland [Y6]**, Edinburgh) was found in 1919 under the floor of one of the huts around the summit. The hoard included bowls, flagons, cups, plates and spoons, many of which had been deliberately cut up and crushed.
Parking nearby.
Access at all reasonable times.

D63 Tynron Doon
[Map: 6B, G7] Off A702, 4 miles W of Thornhill, Tynron Doon, Dumfries and Galloway. (NGR: NX 819939 LR: 78)

Site of castle, within the ramparts of an Iron Age fort. Robert the Bruce is said to have sheltered here, with Kirkpatrick of Closeburn, in 1306 after stabbing the Red Comyn at Dumfries.

The ramparts of Tynron Doon, which defend the western slopes, can be seen clearly from the approach to the hill. There are three ramparts separated by deep ditches and a drystone wall around the summit. The outlines of a number of hut circles can be identified within the enclosure.

D64 Wag of Forse Broch and Settlement
[Map: 3B, B11] Off A9 or A895, 2 miles W of Lybster, Forse, Caithness, Highland. (NGR: ND 204352 LR: 11)

The site at Forse was excavated in the 1930s and 1940s, uncovering a turf-walled enclosure with the remains of a succession of houses of different styles. The first houses on the site were small roundhouses. The next building on the site was a large circular building which has features similar to brochs, including a cell and stretch of gallery with a stair. The 'broch' was succeeded by rectangular buildings with stone pillars inside, which would presumably have supported lintel stones. One wag, to the west of the broch, is 42 feet long and has the remains of two rows of stone pillars.

D65 White Caterthun (HS)

[Map: 4, H4] Off A94, near Menmuir, 5 miles NW of Brechin, Angus. (NGR: NO 547660 LR: 44)

The forts of **Brown Caterthun [D5]** and White Caterthun sit atop neighbouring hills just over 1.5 miles apart. The higher of the two is the White Caterthun which has a double rampart defending the fort, one of them stone.

Parking nearby

Access at all reasonable times.

D66 Yarrows Archaeological Trail

[Map: 3B, B11] Off A9, 5 miles SW of Wick, 2 miles W of Thrumster, Caithness, Highland. (NGR: ND 305434 LR: 12)

The trail passes an excavated broch, round houses and burial cairns. The complete trail is about two miles long, and may take two hours or more. There is another archaeological trail at the **Ord [A14]**, based at the **Ferrycroft Countryside Centre [Y77]**.

Leaflet available. Parking.

Access at all reasonable times – track may be muddy.

Tel: 01463 711176   Web: www.higharch.demon.co.uk

Fax: 01462 711455   Email: archaeology@higharch.demon.co.uk

Right *Dun Beag*
Bottom *Dun Carloway*

Top *Gurness* Left *Dun an Sticar*
Above *Dunadd* Bottom *Midhowe*

E: Romans

The lands now known as Scotland were only intermittently held by the Romans. This occupation was restricted to the south, and did not last long.

E1 Antonine Wall (HS)

[Map: 5B, D8] Off A803, E of Bonnybridge, Falkirk. (NGR: NS 835798 LR: 65)
This Roman fortification stretched from Bo'ness on the Forth to Old Kilpatrick on the Clyde. Built about 142-3 AD, it consisted of a turf rampart behind a ditch, with forts about every two miles. It was probably abandoned around 163. Remains are best preserved in the Falkirk/Bonnybridge area. There are sites at **Bar Hill Fort [E4]**, **Bearsden Bathhouse [E5]**, **Castlecary [E8]**, **Croy Hill [E9]**, Dullater, **Rough Castle [E12]**, **Seabegs Wood [E13]**, Tollpark and Garnhall, and **Watling Lodge [E15]**.
Explanatory board. Limited car parking.
Access at all reasonable times.

E2 Ardoch Fort

[Map: 5B, C8] Off A822, 14 miles S of Crieff, NE of Braco, Ardoch, Perthshire. (NGR: NN 839099 LR: 57)
The camp is one of the largest Roman stations in Britain, and there are substantial earthworks dating from the 2nd century.
Access at all reasonable times.

E3 Ardunie Signal Station (HS)

[Map: 5B, C8] Off B8062, 4 miles N of Auchterarder, Ardunie, Trinity Gask, Perthshire. (NGR: NN 946187 LR: 58)
The site of a Roman watchtower, one of a series running between **Ardoch [E2]** and the River Tay. It dates from 1st century AD, and stands near the course of a Roman road.
Parking nearby.
Access at all reasonable times.

E4 Bar Hill Fort (HS)

[Map: 6B, D7] Off B802 or B8023, 3.5 miles NW of Cumbernauld, Lanarkshire. (NGR: NS 707759 LR: 64)
The highest on the line of the **Antonine Wall [E1]**, containing the foundations of the headquarters building and bathhouse. A small Iron Age fort lies to the east. There are fine views of the Kelvin Valley.
Car parking nearby.
Access at all reasonable times.

E5 Bearsden Bathhouse (HS)

[Map: 6A, D6] Off A890, NW of Glasgow, Roman Road, Bearsden. (NGR: NS 546720 LR: 64)
Probably the best surviving Roman remains in Scotland, the ruined bathhouse was discovered in 1973 during excavations for a construction site. It was originally built around 142 AD for the Roman garrison at nearby Bearsden Fort, which was part of the **Antonine Wall [E1]** defences. It was not in use long, and had probably been abandoned by 158. Finds from here are in the **Hunterian Museum [Y4]**.
Disabled access. Parking nearby.
Access at all reasonable times.

E6 Birrens Roman Fort

[Map: 6B, H9] Off B725 or B722, 6 miles SE of Lockerbie, Birrens, Dumfries and Galloway. (NGR: NY 219751 LR: 85)
The well-preserved earthworks of a Roman fort, known as Blatobulgium. Many finds have been recovered from the site and are in **Dumfries Museum [Y70]**. Within the earthworks was a small tower house of the Carlyles, little of which survives.

E7 Blackhill Camps (HS)

[Map: 5B, C8] Off A822, 6.5 miles W of Auchterarder, 0.5 miles N of Braco, Ardoch, Perthshire. (NGR: NN 840109 LR: 58)
Parts of the defences of two Roman marching camps, probably dating from about the 3rd century AD.
Parking nearby.
Access at all reasonable times.

D7 Burnswark Hill

The hill fort, with extensive earthworks, dates from around 600 BC. It is flanked by a Roman artillery range, best seen from the hilltop.
See main entry D7

E8 Castlecary (HS)

[Map: 5B, D8] Off B816, 2 miles NE of Cumbernauld, E of Castlecary village, Stirlingshire. (NGR: NS 790783 LR: 64)
The much-reduced earthworks of a Roman fort on the **Antonine Wall [E1]**.
Parking nearby.
Access at all reasonable times.

K9 Cramond Kirk

A Roman fort stood behind the church.
See main entry K9

E9 Croy Hill (HS)

[Map: 6B, D7] Off B802, 2 miles NW of Cumbernauld, between Croy and Dullatur, North Lanarkshire. (NGR: NS 730765 LR: 64)
The site of a Roman fort on the **Antonine Wall [E1]**. The ditch for the wall can be seen, beside two beacon platforms on the west side of the hill.
Access at all reasonable times.

E10 Dere Street (HS)

[Map: 6B, E10] On B6368, 8 miles SE of Gorebridge, Soutra, Fala, Lothian. (NGR: NT 452580 LR: 66)

A fine stretch of Dere Street, a Roman road which ran from the south of England to Corbridge, near Hadrian's Wall, to **Cramond [K9]**. The stretch of road is near **Soutra Aisle [K96]**.

Access at all reasonable times.

Y70 Dumfries Museum

Dumfries Museum has Roman finds from **Birrens [E6]**, **Burnswark [D7]** and other Roman sites.

See main entry Y70

K66 Durisdeer

The Well Path runs through the village, a Roman road which was used as a pilgrimage route to **Whithorn [J34]** in medieval times.

About 1 mile to the north-east [NS 903049] are the well-preserved earthworks of a Roman fortlet. **Drumlanrig Castle [N20]** is nearby.

See main entry K66

D42 Eildon Hill

On the west end of the summit are traces of a Roman signal station.

See main entry D42

Y4 Hunterian Museum

The museum has a major exhibition on the Romans, including distance slabs and Roman coins.

See main entry Y4

E11 Inchtuthil Fort

[Map: 5B, B9] Off A984, 7 miles E of Dunkeld, 2.5 miles E of Caputh, Inchtuthil, Perthshire. (NGR: NO 125397 LR: 53)

The impressive earthworks and ramparts of a large Roman fort, known as Pinnata Castra. It was built around 83 AD on the orders of Agricola, but was completely demolished by the Romans only a few years later

Please contact Mr D Gemmel prior to a visit.
Tel: 01738 710485

Y111 Kinneil Museum and Roman Fortlet

There are the remains of the Roman fortlet nearby, and displays of finds in the museum.

See main entry Y111

Y131 Moat Park Heritage Centre

The centre has a display on the Romans.

See main entry Y131

Y134 Motherwell Heritage Centre

The centre has displays on the Romans.

See main entry Y134

Y6 Museum of Scotland

There is also a major display of Roman finds, including commemorative slabs, altars and the 'Traprain Treasure' from **Traprain Law [D62]**.

See main entry Y6

E12 Rough Castle (HS)

[Map: 5B, D8] Off B816, 3 miles W of Falkirk, 1.5 miles E of Bonnybridge, West Lothian. (NGR: NS 855803 LR: 65)

The earthworks of a large Roman fort on the **Antonine Wall [E1]**. The buildings have gone, but the mounds and terraces mark the sites of barracks, granary and bath buildings. The military road, which linked all the forts on the wall, is still well defined, and a fine length of rampart and ditch survives.

Parking.
Access at all reasonable times.

E13 Seabegs Wood (HS)

[Map: 5B, D8] Off B816, 1 mile W of Bonnybridge, Falkirk. (NGR: NS 811792 LR: 65)

A stretch of Roman rampart and ditch, part of the **Antonine Wall [E1]**, with a military way.

Parking nearby.
Access at all reasonable times.

E14 Trimontium Roman Heritage Centre, Melrose

[Map: 6B, F10] Off A6091, The Ormiston, The Square, Melrose, Borders. (NGR: NT 545343 LR: 73)

Trimontium, the 'Three Peaks' Roman fort, was built by the Roman general Agricola in the 1st century AD. The exhibition 'Daily Life on the Roman Frontier' has an audio guide, models, aerial photography and other artefacts. Other features include an amphitheatre, blacksmith's, kitchen and pottery shops, the mystery of Walter's well, and a Roman chamfron and parade helmet.

Explanatory displays. Audio guide. Gift shop. WC. Disabled access. Parking nearby. £. Thu PM walk to site (and tea) £.
Open Apr-Oct, daily 10.30-16.30; closed for lunch Sat and Sun 13.00-14.00; Nov-Mar, open by appt..

Tel: 01896 822651/463 Email: secretary@trimontium.fsworld.co.uk
Fax: 01896 823233 Web: www.trimontium.net

E15 Watling Lodge (HS)

[Map: 5B, D8] Off B816 (signposted), Watling Lodge, to W of Falkirk. (NGR: NT 866798 LR: 65)

The best section of ditch on the **Antonine Wall [E1]**.

Parking nearby.
Access at all reasonable times.

F: Picts

Little remains of the Picts, except for their fabulous symbol stones and magnificent jewellery. Class 1 stones have Pictish but no Christian symbols, Class 2 stones have both, while Class 3 stones have only Christian symbols. See also the section on Early Scotland.

F1 Abdie Church

[Map: 6B, C9] Off B937, 6 miles NW of Cupar, Abdie, Fife. (NGR: NO 259163 LR: 59)

Originally located on the crest of nearby Kaim Hill, the stone, sometimes known as the Lindores Stone, bears a cauldron above a fine crescent and v-rod. When it was moved to Abdie Church, a mirror symbol was found on one side. The ruinous church, dedicated to St Magridin, dates from the 13th century but was much altered with the addition of a new aisle in the 17th century. There are several 17th-century burial monuments.

Parking nearby.
Open all year.

F2 Aberdeenshire Council Offices

[Map: 4, G5] Woodhill House, Westburn Road, Aberdeen. (NGR: NJ 940060 LR: 38)

The council offices hold a fine Pictish Class 1 carved stone found near Rhynie, known as Rhynie Man, a ferocious axe-wielding giant with sharpened teeth. Also see **Craw Stane, Rhynie [F9]**.

Parking nearby.
Open all year during council hours.
Tel: 01467 620981   Fax: 01224 665204

F3 Aberlemno Sculpted Stones (HS)

[Map: 4, I4] Off B9134, 6 miles NE of Forfar, Angus. (NGR: NO 523557 LR: 54)

A renowned group of Pictish stones, the most impressive and elaborate of which is the double-sided cross-slab in Aberlemno churchyard. The front carries a full-length cross, while the reverse is framed by two serpents surrounding battle scenes, believed to be **Nechtansmere [G7]** in 685 when the Picts routed a Northumbrian army.

Three other stones stand by the B9134, a little north of Aberlemno.

One is a double-sided cross-slab with Pictish carvings on the reverse.

A fine Class 1 stone has a carved serpent above a double-disc and z-rod and a mirror and comb. The last is an unadorned standing stone.

Parking nearby, but may be problematic for the three stones by B9134.
Accessible all year – stones enclosed for protection from Oct-Apr and cannot be viewed during this time.

K43 Abernethy (HS)

A fine Class 1 Pictish carved stone is located at the base of the round tower.
See main entry K43

Y21 Alyth

There is a Pictish cross-slab, rediscovered in the late 19th century, in the vestibule of the church in Alyth village [NO 243488].
See main entry Y21

K51 Birnie Kirk

A Pictish carved stone stands in the burial ground, carved with an eagle and notched rectangle and z-rod. In the church are fragments of a cross-slab.
See main entry K51

F4 Brandsbutt Stone (HS)

[Map: 4, G5] Off A96, Brandsbutt, N of Inverurie, Aberdeenshire. (NGR: NJ 760224 LR: 38)

A Class 1 Pictish carved stone bearing a crescent and v-rod, and a snake and z-rod. The stone also carries an Ogham inscription, reading IRATADDOARENS. The stone had been smashed and built into a nearby dyke, and not all of it was found when reassembled.
Parking nearby.
Access at all reasonable times.
Tel: 01466 793191

K3 Brechin Cathedral

There is a fine Pictish cross-slab in the cathedral, and other fragments, including the 9th-century St Mary's Stone.
See main entry K3

N10 Brodie Castle (NTS)

A fine Pictish cross-slab stands in the avenue up to the castle.
See main entry N10

K54 Brough of Birsay (HS)

A fine Pictish sculptured stone decorated with figures was found here, now in the **Museum of Scotland [Y6]**, while there is a replica on the islet; there is also a Pictish well.
See main entry K54

D6 Burghead

Burghead was one of the major fortresses of the Picts, although it had been used since prehistoric times.

Many fine Pictish carvings of bulls were found here, which can now been seen on display in the Burghead Library, **Elgin Museum [Y74]**, the **Museum of Scotland [Y6]** in Edinburgh and the British Museum.
See main entry D6

Y55 Carnegie Museum

The museum houses the Formaston Stone, a Pictish cross-slab with both symbols and Ogham.
See main entry Y55

F5 Clach Ard

[Map: 3A, E4] Off B8036, 4.5 miles NW of Portree, Tote, Skye. (NGR: NG 421491 LR: 23)
Set within railings, this is probably a standing stone which was reused by the Picts. The stone, which is about five feet high, is carved with a crescent and v-rod, double-disc and z-rod, and mirror and comb. It is one of the few Pictish stones in the Hebrides.
Parking nearby.
Access at all reasonable times.

F6 Collessie Carved Stone

[Map: 6B, C9] Off B937, 4 miles W of Cupar, 0.25 miles E of Collessie, Fife. (NGR: NO 293133 LR: 59)
The stone, some ten feet high, carries an incised figure of a naked warrior. Armed with a large rectangular shield and a long spear with a leaf-shaped blade, he marches from right to left across the top third of the monolith. Two other faint symbols have been identified as an arch and a Pictish beast.

F7 Congash Pictish Stones

[Map: 3B, F10] On A95, 3 miles SE of Grantown on Spey, Congash, Highland. (NGR: NJ 058262 LR: 36)
Located on Congash Farm, these two stones form the gateposts to a former burial ground. Both stones have sunk into the ground, and only the upper halves are visible. One carries a Pictish beast below an arch; the other bears a double disc and z-rod over a unique 'bow and arrow' symbol.
Parking in quarry: can be reached through gate at back of quarry.
Access at all reasonable times.

F8 Covesea Caves

[Map: 4, E3] Off B9040, between Lossiemouth Lighthouse and Hopeman, Covesea, Moray. (NGR: NJ 175707 LR: 28)
Also known as Sculptor's Cave, these large dry caves on the coast, contain a variety of Pictish symbols incised into their walls. There may have been a connection to the major Pictish fort at Burghead.
Access to caves at all reasonable times – care should be taken.

F9 Craw Stane, Rhynie

[Map: 4, F4] On A97, 10 miles S of Huntly, just S of Rhynie, Aberdeenshire. (NGR: NJ 497263 LR: 37)
This large standing stone, known as the Craw Stane, is carved with a salmon above a Pictish beast. Other carved stones have been found in the area. Two are now located on the village green; two more have been set up at the entrance to the burial ground; while another, Rhynie Man, can be seen in the **Aberdeenshire Council Offices [F2]**.

F10 Dingwall Pictish Stone

[Map: 3B, E9] Off A826, St Clement's churchyard, Dingwall, Ross-shire, Highland. (NGR: NH 549589 LR: 26)
Probably a prehistoric standing stone reused by the Picts, this carved stone has a double-disc and v-rods on one side; on the other are three discs above a crescent and v-rod, and a collection of much older cup and ring marks.
Access at all reasonable times.

F11 Dunfallandy Stone (HS)

[Map: 5B, B9] Off A9, 1 mile S of Pitlochry, Dunfallandy, Perthshire. (NGR: NN 944564 LR: 52)
This intriguing Class 2 Pictish cross-slab has a beautifully carved full-length cross, although the central panel is blank. Surrounding the cross are two four-winged angels and a sea monster with a pair of human legs emerging from its jaws. The back is framed by two fish-tailed serpents, holding a human head between their jaws, as well as much other carving.
Not signposted.
Access at all reasonable times – stone is enclosed in a glass case for protection – viewing may be difficult in wet weather.

N23 Dunrobin Museum

The museum, in the grounds of **Dunrobin Castle [N23]**, has a fine collection of 20 carved Pictish stones from Sutherland, including a cross-slab from St Andrews kirkyard with Pictish devices and an Ogham inscription.
See main entry N23

F12 Dyce Symbol Stones (HS)

[Map: 4, G5] Off A947, 7 miles NW of Aberdeen, Dyce Church, Aberdeenshire. (NGR: NJ 875154 LR: 38)
There are two Pictish carved stones here at the ruined parish church. The first, a Class 1 stone showing a Pictish beast above a double disc and z-rod, is built into the east wall of the church. The second is a Class 2 cross-slab, with a decorated cross on the front, and Pictish symbols on the back.
Car parking.
Access at all reasonable times.
Tel: 01466 793191

F13 Eassie Stone (HS)

[Map: 4, I3] Off A94, 6 miles W of Forfar, Eassie Church, Angus. (NGR: NO 353474 LR: 54)
Standing in the ruins of Eassie Church, this early Class

2 cross-slab displays a full-length cross decorated with intricate interlaced designs and other Pictish carving. The stone has recently been cleaned, and is now encased in glass for protection, although this does not make it very easy to see. The ruinous church stands in an irregular shaped burial ground, indicating an old site.

Parking nearby.
Access at all reasonable times.

F14 East Wemyss Caves

[Map: 6B, D10] Off A955, 4.5 miles NE of Kirkcaldy, East Wemyss, Fife. (NGR: NT 344972 LR: 59)
There are five caves on the coast at East Wemyss, four of which have incised Pictish symbols, including double discs, crescents and v-rods, a mirror and animal heads, as well as a figure with a spear and a boat with oars. Access to the caves is not always easy.
Access at all reasonable times – care should be taken.

F15 Edderton Pictish Stone

[Map: 3B, D9] Off A836, 5 miles NW of Tain, Edderton, Ross, Highland. (NGR: NH 708851 LR: 21)
This massive prehistoric standing stone, over 10 feet high, is associated with the nearby stone circle. The Picts later carved a salmon and double disc and z-rod into it. It is known as Clach Biorach, the 'sharp-pointed stone'.
Access at all reasonable times: view from roadside.

K17 Elgin Cathedral (HS)

In the remains of the cathedral is an impressive Class 2 Pictish cross-slab, with a decorated cross and other carvings.
See main entry K17

Y74 Elgin Museum

The award-winning museum houses carved Pictish stones from **Burghead [D6]** and Kinneddar.
See main entry Y74

Y76 Falconer Museum, Forres

The museum has information and displays on the Picts.
See main entry Y76

N27 Falkland Palace (NTS)

There are two Pictish Class 1 carved stones here on display in the museum.
See main entry N27

F16 Fowlis Wester Stone (HS)

[Map: 5B, C8] Off A85, 5 miles E of Crieff, Fowlis Wester, Perthshire. (NGR: NN 928240 LR: 52)
This Class 2 Pictish cross-slab, the Cross of Fowlis, over ten feet tall, is now inside Fowlis Wester parish

church (see **St Bean's Church, Fowlis Wester [K98]**), with a replica at the original site in the village. The front of the stone has a tall cross, with carved decoration inside the arms, while on the reverse are Pictish symbols and other carving. The iron chain attached to the stone is probably the remains of jougs, an iron collar to which petty criminals would be attached for public ridicule.

The church also holds a second Pictish carved stone with a large ringed cross, filled with interlaced decoration, sitting on a square base, as well as biblical scenes.
Access at all reasonable times.

F17 Glamis Church, Pictish Stone and Well

[Map: 4, 13] Off A928, 5.5 miles SW of Forfar, Glamis, Angus. (NGR: NO 386468 LR: 54)
In the garden of Glamis Manse (across the road from the church) is a fine carved Pictish stone. Fragments of other Pictish carved stones are housed in the modern church. A healing well lies below the church, and is reached by a landscaped trail. Glamis is also home to the **Angus Folk Museum [V4]** and **Glamis Castle [N30]**.
Parking nearby. Sales area nearby.
Church, carved stone and healing well open at all reasonable times.

F18 Groam House Museum and Pictish Centre

[Map: 3B, E9] On A832, 7 miles NE of Inverness, 1 mile NE of Fortrose, High Street, Rosemarkie, Highland. (NGR: NH 738575 LR: 27)
This award-winning museum holds 15 Class 2 and Class 3 Pictish stones, all found within the village, as well as the beautiful Rosemarkie Cross-slab. The museum also has a fine collection of audio-visual and static displays, activities and temporary exhibitions.
Guided tours on request. Exhibitions. Gift Shop. Disabled limited access and WC. Car and coach parking. Group concessions. £.
Open Easter week, then May-Sep, Mon-Sat 10.00-17.00, Sun 14.00-16.30; Oct-Apr Sat & Sun 14.00-16.00.
Tel: 01381 620961 (museum) 01381 621730 (office)   Fax: 01381 621730 Email: groamhouse@ecosse.net

D44 Gurness Broch (HS)

The settlement was occupied by the Picts, and the museum has prehistoric and some Pictish finds.
See main entry D44

F19 Inverallan

[Map: 3B, F10] Off A95, 0.5 miles S of Grantown on Spey, Inverallan Burial Ground, Highland. (NGR: NJ 027269 LR: 36)
Inverallan was an early Christian site, and there was a church here, dedicated to St Futach or Fiacre, a 7th-

century Irish saint. In the burial ground is a weathered Class 1 Pictish carved stone, as well as Figgat's or Futach's Cross.

Access at all reasonable times.

F20 Inveravon Church

[Map: 4, F3] Off A95, 605 miles SW of Aberlour, Bridge of Avon, St Peters (Inveravon Church), Moray. (NGR: NJ 183376 LR: 36)

Four Class 1 Pictish carved stones are displayed against the south wall of the 19th-century church, dedicated to St Peter, although the site is much older. The church was built in 1808, and the four stones are on the south wall of the building. The gothic mausoleum in the burial ground was built for the Macpherson-Grants in 1829.

Y100 Inverness Museum

The museum houses an excellent collection of Pictish finds and exhibitions, including the beautiful Ardross Wolf and Deer, and other Class 1 Pictish stones.

See main entry Y100

F21 Kintore Carved Stone

[Map: 4, G5] Off A96, 3 miles S of Inverurie, Kintore, Aberdeenshire. (NGR: NJ 793163 LR: 38)

In the burial ground is a Class 1 Pictish carved stone, with a crescent and v-rod and Pictish beast on one side, and salmon and cauldron on the other. It had been reused as a burial marker. The present church dates from early in the 19th century, and replaced an older building, dedicated to St Mary. It was originally the chapel for the nearby castle, although there are no remains.

Access at all reasonable times.

F22 Knocknagael Boar Stone (HS)

[Map: 3B, F9] Off A82, Highland Council Chambers, Glenurquhart Road, Inverness, Highland. (NGR: NH 662447 LR: 26)

The Knocknagael Boar Stone, which was moved to Highland Council Chambers in 1991 for conservation from Essich [NH 656413], has a fine incised carving of a boar beneath a disc and rectangle.

Parking nearby.

Open all year, Mon-Fri 9.00-17.00; closed pub hols; can be viewed through window at all times.

Tel: 01463 702000

F23 Maiden Stone (HS)

[Map: 4, G5] Off A96, 1 mile NW of Chapel of Garioch, 5 miles NW of Inverurie, Aberdeenshire. (NGR: NJ 704247 LR: 38)

Known as the Maiden Stone, this is a highly decorated Class 2 Pictish carved cross-slab, although much of the carving has been lost or defaced, and the stone is weathered. One side has a ringed cross, with traces

of interlaced decoration and other carving. The back of the stone is less weathered and shows several beasts and Pictish symbols. It is likely that the stone was deliberately defaced during the Reformation.

Parking nearby.

Access at all reasonable times.

Tel: 01466 793191

Y125 Marischal Museum

The museum exhibits several Pictish stones and artefacts from across Scotland, including the Goose, Collace and Fairy Green Pictish carved stones.

See main entry Y125

Y127 McManus Galleries

There are carved stones and exhibits on the Picts, including the Dunnichen Stone found near the site of the Battle of **Nechtansmere [G7]**, as well as an ancient burial site.

See main entry Y127

F24 Meigle Museum (HS)

[Map: 5B, B10] On A94, 12 miles SW of Forfar, Meigle, Angus. (NGR: NO 287447 LR: 53)

A collection of Pictish and early sculpted stones, one of the best collections of Dark Age sculpture in Western Europe. The stones were found at or near the old churchyard, and include the beautiful and remarkable Daniel Stone. A church is said to have first been established here by monks from Iona in 606, and Meigle is said to be the burial place of Guinevere, wife of Arthur.

Exhibition. Sales area. WC. Disabled access and WC. Parking nearby. £.

Museum open Apr-Sep, daily 9.30-18.30; Oct-Nov, Mon-Sat 9.30-16.30, Sun 14.00-16.30; last ticket 30 mins before closing.

Tel: 01828 640612

D52 Mither Tap o' Bennachie

An impressive hill fort, dating from the Iron Age or Pictish period, enclosed by the remains of two massive stone walls near the summit. Entrances can be traced, and there are also remains of a causeway, the Maiden Causeway, which is said to have run from this fort to Maiden Castle [NJ 694244], another fort. There is a visitor centre at **Bennachie**.

See main entry D52

N40 Moniack Castle

In the grounds of the castle is a carved Pictish stone, bearing a bird-headed man carrying a club, as well as prehistoric cup and ring marks.

See main entry N40

Y133 Montrose Museum

There is a small collection of Pictish sculpted stones, including the striking Samson Stone.
See main entry Y133

K89 Mortlach Parish Church

The Battle Stone, a Pictish symbol stone, survives in the interesting graveyard, along with another stone built into the church.
See main entry K89

Y6 Museum of Scotland

The magnificent museum houses many fine carved Pictish stones and jewellery.
See main entry Y6

G7 Nechtansmere Memorial

[Map: 4, 14] Off B9128 or A932, 3 miles SE of Forfar, 1.5 miles W of Letham, Dunnichen, Angus. (NGR: NO 509488 LR: 54)
The monument here commemorates the Battle of Nechtansmere in 685, when the Picts under Brude defeated the Northumbrians. The stones at **Aberlemno [F3]** probably commemorate the battle.
Access at all reasonable times.

F25 Nigg Cross-Slab (HS)

[Map: 3B, E10] Off B9175, 7 miles S of Tain, Nigg, Ross and Cromarty. (NGR: NH 804717 LR: 21)
Housed inside Nigg Old Parish Church is the fine carved Pictish cross-slab, broken and with a section missing, which dates from the 8th or 9th century. One side is decorated with a large cross, filled with interlaced patterns, and other decoration. The other side has been badly damaged, but there are traces of figures and animals.
Parking nearby.
Open Apr-Oct, daily 10.00-17.00: key available from the manse opposite.
Tel: 01862 832214 (Nigg Old Trust)

Y156 Orkney Museum

The museum has several stones and items from Pictish times.
See main entry Y156

Y160 Perth Museum

This museum houses some Pictish stones including the St Madoe's cross-slab.
See main entry Y160

F26 Picardy Stone (HS)

[Map: 4, F4] Off A96, 11 miles SE of Huntly, Myreton, Insch, Aberdeenshire. (NGR: NJ 610303 LR: 37)
A seven-foot-high Pictish carved stone decorated with a double disc and z-rod, a snake and z-rod, and a mirror. It may date from the 7th century or earlier, and a path to the stone is always kept clear, even when crops are present. The stone is thought to mark a burial.
Parking nearby.
Access at all reasonable times.
Tel: 01466 793191

F27 Pictavia

[Map: 4, 14] Off A90, Brechin Castle Centre, Brechin, Angus. (NGR: NO 597599 LR: 54)
The fine attraction of Pictavia features information about the Picts and their enduring legacy, their carved stones. There is a film about the Picts, information about the Battle of **Nechtansmere [G7]**, as well as carved stones, Pictish jewellery and music.
Guided tours by prior arrangement. Gift shop. Restaurant. Picnic area. Play area for under fives and main play area in country park. Garden Centre. Tourist Information Centre. WC. Car and coach parking. Group concessions. £.
Open all year: summer, Mon-Sat 9.00-18.00, Sun 10.00-18.00; winter, Mon-Sat 9.00-17.00, Sun 10.00-17.00.
Tel: 01356 626241   Fax: 01356 626814
Web: www.pictavia.org.uk

F28 Raven Stone, Tyrie

[Map: 4, E5] Off A98, 5 miles SW of Fraserburgh, Tyrie Church, Buchan, Aberdeenshire. (NGR: NJ 930631 LR: 30)
The Class 1 Pictish carved stone, known as the Raven Stone, is decorated with an eagle (or raven) above a notched rectangle and z-rod. There are several interesting grave stones in the burial ground.
Parking nearby.
Access at all reasonable times.

Y173 Shetland Museum

Exhibits include replicas of the St Ninian's Isle treasure (in the **Museum of Scotland [Y6]**), as well as sculpted stones such as the Mail figure with a wolf-headed man and the Monk's Stone, an early cross-slab.
See main entry Y173

K98 St Bean's Church, Fowlis Wester

The church, which dates from the 13th century, was dedicated to St Bean. It has been rebuilt several times down the centuries, and now house houses **Fowlis Wester Carved Stone [F16]**, as well as a Class 2 Pictish carved stone.
See main entry K98

K118 St Mary's Church, Monymusk

Housed in the church is the Monymusk Stone, a Pictish symbol stone, as well as other stones dating from the 7th-9th centuries.
See main entry K118

F29 St Orland's Stone, Cossans (HS)

[Map: 4, 13] Off A928, 3.5 miles W of Forfar, Cossans, Angus. (NGR: NO 401500 LR: 54)

Known as St Orland's Stone, this Class 2 Pictish cross-slab probably marks the position of an early Christian site. The front carries a full-length ringed cross, decorated with ornate interlaced patterns. The back of the stone has various Pictish symbols and other carvings.
Parking nearby.
Access at all reasonable times.

F30 St Vigeans Museum (HS)

[Map: 4, 14] Off A933, 0.5 miles N of Arbroath, St Vigeans, Angus. (NGR: NO 637430 LR: 83)

The museum has a fine collection of 30 early Christian and Pictish stones housed in cottages, including the St Drostan Stone. The stone has an Ogham inscription, as well as other carvings of beasts, men and symbols. This is a fine collection but has very limited opening. Nearby, standing on a hillock, is **St Vigeans Church [K129]**.
Parking nearby.
Key available locally: check before setting out.

L27 Stones, Stocks and Stories

The exhibition features Crieff Town Stocks, which are unique in design and one of the few sets remaining; the Drummond or Market Cross; and the 1000-year-old Burgh Cross, a Pictish cross-slab.
See main entry L27

F31 Strathpeffer Eagle Stone

[Map: 3B, E9] On A834, 5 miles W of Dingwall, Strathpeffer, Ross-shire, Highland. (NGR: NH 485585 LR: 26)

The Pictish carved stone, which is located in a field, is decorated with a fine carved eagle, and dates from the 7th or 8th century. The Brahan Seer predicted that if the stone fell over three times the Strathpeffer area would be flooded. To date it has fallen twice, and is now – as a precaution – fixed into place.
Access at all reasonable times: short walk from road.

L28 Sueno's Stone, Forres (HS)

The magnificent sculpted stone, which dates from around the 9th century, is some 22 foot in height. One face is carved with a large ring-headed cross filled with interlaced knotwork. The other side is divided into four panels relating the events of a battle. It has been suggested that this stone marks the end of the Pictish period, the final triumph of the Scots. This seems unlikely, and it probably commemorates a battle against the Norsemen.
See main entry L28

Y189 Tain Through Time

There are Pictish carved stones here, including from **Edderton [L5/F15]**.
See main entry Y189

F32 Tarbat Discovery Centre

[Map: 3B, D10] Off B9165, 8 miles E of Tain, Tarbatness Road, Portmahomack, Ross and Cromarty, Highland. (NGR: NH 915845 LR: 21)

The centre, which is housed in a historic church, has displays on one of the largest ongoing archaeological digs in Europe and information on the Picts. Carvings from here include cattle licking their new-born calf, a wild boar, and a dragon with a serpent head on its tail. The centre features a video on the Picts of Easter Ross. Guided tours of the dig are available when a dig is in progress.
Explanatory displays. Audiovisual presentation. Gift shop. Disabled access. Parking. £.
Open Mar-Dec: 1st Sat Mar-1st Sat May, daily 14.00-17.00; 1st Sun May-last Sat Sep, daily 10.00-17.00; last Sun Sep-23 Dec, daily 14.00-17.00; closed 24 Dec-1st Sat Mar.
Tel: 01862 871351 Fax: 01862 871361
Web: www.tarbat-discovery.co.uk Email: tarbat@globalnet.co.uk

Y194 The Meffan, Forfar

The museum holds a collection of Pictish carved stones, all from Kirriemuir, and there is an excellent interactive guide to the stones. Other displays chart the story of Forfar, including witch trials, and there are two galleries with changing exhibitions.
See main entry Y194

F33 Thief's Stone, Rosskeen

[Map: 3B, E9] Off A9, 9 miles S of Tain, Rosskeen, Ross and Cromarty, Highland. (NGR: NH 681690 LR: 21)

This Class 1 Pictish carved stone, known as the Thief's Stone (Clach a' Mheorlich), has a stepped rectangle with a faint crescent and tongs on one side.
Parking nearby.
Accessible at all reasonable times: view from roadside.

Y196 Thurso Heritage Museum

The museum features a varied collection of carved stones, including two fine Class 2 Pictish stones.
See main entry Y196

Top *Abernethy* Right *Groam House*
Below *Nigg* Bottom Right *Strathpeffer*

G: Early Scotland

Sites and museums which are associated with the development of Scotland during what has been called the Dark Ages, including the early kingdoms and church, saints such as Ninian and Columba, the Norsemen, and Macbeth. See also the section on the Picts and Carved Crossed and Monuments.

K41 Abercorn Church and Museum

Abercorn was one of the first bishoprics in Scotland, dating from 670 AD, and founded as part of the Anglian church of Northumbria, which included Hexham, York and Lindisfarne. The present church, dedicated to St Serf, mostly dates from the Reformation until the present day, although part may be from the 11th century, and it is built on an older site. There are two Norse burial stones, a wheel cross-stone, and a cross-shaft dating from the 8th century.
See main entry K41

Y21 Alyth

Not much remains of a castle near Alyth, said to be where Guinevere, wife of King Arthur, was reputedly imprisoned by Mordred.
See main entry Y21

K46 Applecross

The site of a monastery, founded by St Maelrubha in 673. It became a place of pilgrimage, and earth taken from the saint's grave was said to ensure a safe return from any journey. An 8th-century cross-slab stands by the gate, and inside the modern church are other fragments. The nearby 15th-century ruinous chapel is roofed over by greenery. A spring [NG 717450] issuing from near the road, west of Applecross House, is said to be a holy well. A heritage centre is being set up at Clachan in Applecross.
See main entry K46

Y26 Athelstaneford Heritage Centre

The 16th-century doocot has been restored to house an unmanned audio-visual display which describes the battle in 832 at which the Picts and Scots defeated the Northumbrian king Athelstane. It was before the battle that a white cross of clouds floated over the deep blue sky. This gave the Picts and Scots the inspiration to defeat the larger Northumbrian army. Since that time, the St Andrews Cross or saltire has been the national flag of Scotland – or so the story goes. Athelstaneford Parish Church, which dates from 1780, is also open to the public.
See main entry Y26

G1 Bass Rock

[Map: 6B, D11] A rock in the Firth of Forth, 3 miles NE of North Berwick, East Lothian. (NGR: NT 602873 LR: 67)
The Bass, a huge rock in the Firth of Forth, was the hermitage of St Baldred of Tyninghame, who died here in 756. There are some remains of a chapel. A castle and prison was later built, used for holding both Covenanters and Jacobites, then a lighthouse. The island is home to thousands of seabirds, and is the third largest gannetry in the world. Also see **Scottish Seabird Centre [V109]**.
Car parking in North Berwick.
Boat trips from North Berwick go around Bass Rock – tel 01620 892838 (boat trips) or 01620 892197 (tourist information office).
Tel: 01620 892838

Y44 Breadalbane Folklore Centre

The folklore centre has displays on St Fillan, an early saint, who also has dedications in Fife.
See main entry Y44

K54 Brough of Birsay (HS)

On a tidal island is the Brough of Birsay, an early Christian settlement, which was later used by Norsemen, and became an important centre. Earl Thorfinn of Orkney had a house here, and there was a substantial 12th-century church. A fine Pictish sculptured stone decorated with figures was found here, now in the **Museum of Scotland [Y6]**, while there is a replica on the islet; there is also a Pictish well.
See main entry K54

D6 Burghead

Burghead was one of the major fortresses of the Picts, although it had been used since prehistoric times. Many fine Pictish carvings of bulls were found here, which can now been seen on display in the Burghead Library, **Elgin Museum [Y74]**, the **Museum of Scotland [Y6]** in Edinburgh and the British Museum in London. The fort was used by Thorfinn the Mighty, Earl of Orkney, as a base, and it was nearby that Duncan (of Macbeth fame) was defeated by Thorfinn in 1040. Duncan was also defeated by Macbeth in battle, and died of his wounds at Spynie. The fort was mostly destroyed when the village was built.
The Well, rediscovered in 1809, consists of a rock-

hewn chamber, reached down stone steps. It has been identified as being associated with St Ethan, a disciple of St Columba, and has a deep tank of water surrounded by a platform, with a basin and pedestal.

Burghead is well known for the 'Burning of the Clavie', an old fire festival when a burning barrel of tar is taken around the streets on 12 January.

See main entry D6

N14 Cawdor Castle

One of the most magnificent strongholds in Scotland, Cawdor Castle's association with the slaying of Duncan by Macbeth is wholly from Shakespeare's play – the castle was not built at the time.

See main entry N14

K60 Chapel Finian (HS)

The foundations of a small rectangular chapel survive, dating from the 10th or 11th century, standing in a 50-foot-wide enclosure. It was dedicated to St Finian of Moville, who was educated at Findhorn and died around 579, and was used by pilgrims on their way to **Whithorn [J33]**.

See main entry K60

K61 Cille Bharra

The ruinous medieval church was built about the 12th century and dedicated to St Barr. Two chapels also survive, one of which has been reroofed to shelter carved burial slabs, some used to mark the burials of the MacNeils of Barr. Other interesting slabs lie in the yard, while a fine 10th-century carved stone – with a cross and runic inscription – is kept in the **Museum of Scotland [Y6]**: a cast is displayed at Cille Bharra.

See main entry K61

J10 Culross Abbey (HS)

It was to Culross that St Enoch or Thenew, who was a daughter of the king or ruler of Lothian, came in the 6th century. Enoch was pregnant, although unmarried, and eventually had a son, St Mungo or Kentigern. Mungo was educated here by St Serf, and was active among the Britons of Strathclyde. He founded a church on the site of **Glasgow Cathedral [K19]** in 573, where he is buried.

See main entry J10

G2 Dim Riv Norse Longship Boat Trips, Lerwick

[Map: 1, D3] Off A970, Lerwick, Shetland. (NGR: HU 477419 LR: 4)
Boat trips can be taken in a working replica of a Norse longboat.

Car and coach parking. ££.
Open Jun-Aug, Wed only: tel to check.
Tel: 01595 693097

G3 Doonhill Homestead (HS)

[Map: 6B, D11] Off A1, 2 miles S of Dunbar, Doonhill, East Lothian. (NGR: NT 686755 LR: 67)
The site of a hall house of a British chief, dating from the 6th century, and then of an Anglian chief's hall, which superseded it in the 7th century when the area was controlled by Northumbria. The site is marked out in the grass.

Car parking.
Access at all reasonable times.

N88 Dumbarton Castle (HS)

Meaning 'fortress of the Britons', Dumbarton is mentioned around 450 as the stronghold of the kings of Strathclyde. In 756 it was captured by Picts and Northumbrians, and in 870 was besieged by Irish raiders. Owen the Bald, the last King of Strathclyde, died at the Battle of Carham in 1018, and Strathclyde was absorbed into the kingdom of Scots.

See main entry N88

D38 Dunadd (HS)

Dunadd stands on a steep-sided hill, and consists of lines of fortifications, some better preserved than others, dating from the 1st century AD. There is also an impressive entrance, and fine views from the windswept top.

Dunadd was a stronghold of the Scots, and inaugurations of their kings were held here, with a basin, footprint and carving of a Pictish boar in the rock. The Stone of Destiny was kept here. It is recorded that Dunadd was besieged by the Picts in 683 and 736.

See main entry D38

K13 Dunblane Cathedral (HS)

In the picturesque town by the banks of the Allen River is the fine cathedral, which is dedicated to St Blane and still used as a parish church. The cathedral dates substantially from the 13th century, except for the bell-tower which is probably 11th century. There is fine carving within the church, medieval stalls, and a 9th-century ringed cross-slab with two serpent heads. On the back are several more carvings with animals, figures and a disc and cross. There is a second carved stone.

See main entry K13

N90 Dunnottar Castle

There was a stronghold here from early times, and it was besieged by the Picts, and then in 900 by Vikings when Donald King of Scots was slain.

See main entry N90

D40 Dunsinane Hill

The summit of Dunsinane Hill is surrounded by lines of defences, and is known as 'Macbeth's Castle'. It is traditionally where Macbeth awaited the forces of Malcolm Canmore and most of Birnam Wood (which, although some 12 miles away, can be seen from the summit). According to the play, Macbeth was killed at the battle – but although it is likely Macbeth was defeated here in 1054, it was not until 1057 that he was slain: see **Peel Ring of Lumphanan [N136]**.
See main entry D40

G4 Eileach an Naoimh (HS)

[Map: 5A, C3] N of Jura, one of the Garvellach islands. (NGR: NM 640097 LR: 55)
On the picturesque island are the ruins of beehive cells from a monastery, first founded by St Brendan of Clonfert in 542. There are also the ruins of two churches within an enclosure and two burial grounds, as well as other buildings. Other features include a small underground cell and the traditional burial place of Eithne, St Columba's mother. The island can be reached by boat, weather permitting – contact Oban TIC for details.
Access at all reasonable times – subject to weather.

G5 Eilean Mor

[Map: 5A, D3] E of Jura, 2 miles W of the mainland at Kilmory, Eilean Mor, South Knapdale. (NGR: NR 665755 LR: 61)
Standing on an island are several sites associated with St Cormac. The remains of a chapel [NR 666752] with a barrel-vaulted chancel survive. There is a stone effigy of a priest preserved in the chapel, possibly dating from the 12th century. St Cormac is reputedly buried on the island, a broken and weathered cross marking the spot [NR 667753]. A cave Uamh nam Fear [NR 666750] is also associated with the saint.

K69 Forteviot

Forteviot was the site of a palace of the Pictish kings, traditionally at Halyhill, to the west of the village. Kenneth MacAlpin slaughtered his rivals here at a drunken feast to secure his position as ruler of Dalriada and Pictland. A bronze bell, dated 900, is kept at Forteviot Parish Church is preserved a bronze bell, dated 900, and there are medieval carved stones, including the remains of the Dronachy Cross, which formerly stood at Invermay.
See main entry K69

G6 Fortingall

[Map: 5B, B8] Off B846, 5 miles W of Aberfeldy, Perthshire. (NGR: NN 736470 LR: 52)
Fortingall is reputed to be the birthplace of Pontius

Pilate, the son of a Roman emissary and a local girl. In the churchyard is a 3000-year-old yew tree, and in the church itself a bell said to have been used by St Adamnan, biographer of St Columba, and a 7th-century font. Fortingall, a picturesque village with thatched cottages, was a religious centre from the 6th century. *Car parking.*
Access to churchyard at all reasonable times.

N30 Glamis Castle

Glamis is associated with Shakespeare's play *Macbeth*, although there does not appear to be any historical connection.
See main entry N30

K19 Glasgow Cathedral (HS)

Dedicated to St Mungo, Glasgow's patron saint, the present cruciform church with a central tower is the only medieval cathedral on mainland Scotland to survive the Reformation more or less intact. St Mungo was active among the Britons of Strathclyde and founded a church here in 573. Glasgow is also associated with St Enoch or Thenew, Mungo's mother, and was a major centre of pilgrimage in medieval times.
See main entry K19

J20 Iona Abbey (HS)

Situated on the beautiful and peaceful island of Iona, this is where St Columba came from Ireland to form a monastic community. Columba's shrine, within the Abbey buildings, dates from the 9th century. The abbey was abandoned after raids by Norsemen, but was re-established by Queen Margaret, wife of Malcolm Canmore, in the 11th century. The church was restored from 1899-1910, and the cloister in 1936. It is possible to stay at the Abbey.

Many of the early Kings of Scots are buried in 'Reilig Odhrain' Oran's cemetery by the 'Street of the Dead' – as well as kings of Ireland, France and Norway: 48 Scottish, eight Norwegian and four Irish kings according to one 16th-century source.

The 11th-century chapel of St Oran also survives, and may have been built on the orders of St Margaret. Among the kings buried here are reputedly both Duncan and Macbeth.
See main entry J20

J21 Isle of May

The island is believed to have been where St Adrian was murdered by Vikings around 875, and became a place of pilgrimage: St Adrian's shrine and spring were visited by many folk.
See main entry J21

L8 Keills Chapel (HS)

In the old chapel, which has been reroofed, is the Keills Cross, which is believed to date from the second half of the 8th century. The cross is carved with a central boss, panels of interlace, as well as figures. It formerly stood just behind the chapel. Keills was an important ecclesiastical centre, and there is also a fine collection of carved grave slabs, most medieval.
See main entry L8

L11 Kildalton Cross and Chapel (HS)

The finest surviving intact cross in Scotland, dating from the 8th century, and carved from a single slab. The ringed cross has a representation of the Virgin and Child flanked by angels on one side, while the other has serpent and boss patterns with four lions around the central boss. Other representations illustrate biblical scenes. The remains of a Viking ritual killing are said to have been found beneath the cross when it was excavated in 1890; and there may have been an early Christian community here.
See main entry L11

L16 Kirkmadrine Stones (HS)

Displayed in the porch of the former 19th-century chapel are some of the oldest Christian monuments in Britain. A pillar stone, dating from the 5th century, is carved with a circled cross and Latin inscription 'Here lie the holy and chief priests, Ides, Viventius and Mavorius'. Two other 5th- or early 6th-century stones are also inscribed.
See main entry L16

Y123 Macbeth Experience – Perthshire Visitor Centre

The 'Macbeth Experience' is a multi-media audio-visual presentation showing the comparison between Shakespeare's play and the real king of Scots. There is also information for visitors to Perthshire.
See main entry Y123

F24 Meigle Museum (HS)

A collection of Pictish and early sculptured stones, one of the best collections of Dark Age sculpture in Western Europe. The stones were found at, or near, the old churchyard, and include the beautiful and remarkable Daniel Stone. A church is first said to have been established here by monks from Iona in 606, and Meigle is said to be the burial place of Guinevere, wife of Arthur.
See main entry F24

K89 Mortlach Parish Church

The present church, dedicated to St Moluag, dates from the 11th or 12th century, but stands on the site of an early Christian site, said to date from 566. In 1016 the church was lengthened by three spears' length on the command of Malcolm II after his victory over the Norsemen. The Battle Stone, a Pictish symbol stone, survives in the interesting graveyard, along with another stone built into the church.
See main entry K89

Y6 Museum of Scotland

This magnificent museum houses extensive collections. Items of particular interest include the Monymusk Reliquary, the crosier of St Fillan, and many fine carved Pictish stones and jewellery.
See main entry Y6

G7 Nechtansmere Memorial

[Map: 4, 14] Off B9128 or A932, 3 miles SE of Forfar, 1.5 miles W of Letham, Dunnichen, Angus. (NGR: NO 509488 LR: 54)
The monument here commemorates the Battle of Nechtansmere in 685, when the Picts under Brude defeated the Northumbrians.
Access at all reasonable times.

L20 Netherton Cross

Standing in the burial ground of Hamilton Old Parish Church is the Netherton Cross, a 10th-century sculpted cross, decorated with figures, animals and cross-weave.
See main entry L20

L21 Nith Bridge Cross-Slab

The most complete Anglian Cross apart from Ruthwell, the Nith Bridge Cross stands to about a height of nine feet, and carvings include animals and winged beasts.
See main entry L21

Y147 Northlands Viking Centre

The centre has displays on the heritage of Caithness, explaining the pre-Viking province of the Catti and Norse settlers. There are models of the Viking settlement at Freswick, a Viking longship and currency. There is a broch nearby at **Nybster [D55]**.
See main entry Y147

G8 Orkneyinga Saga Centre

[Map: 2, C2] Off A964, 8 miles SW of Kirkwall, Orphir, Orkney. (NGR: HY 335044 LR: 6)
An interpretation and orientation centre with an audio-visual presentation. Nearby are the remains of a Norse drinking hall and the remains of the only round

medieval church in Scotland (**Orphir Church [K92]**). One of the passages from the *Orkneyinga Saga* relates to Orphir.

Open all year, daily dawn to dusk.
Tel: 01856 873191/811319 Email: steve.callaghan@orkney.gov.uk
Fax: 01856 875846 Web: www.orkneyheritage.com

J28 Paisley Abbey

The striking **Barochan Cross [L1]**, dating from as early as the 8th century, is housed here.
See main entry J28

N136 Peel Ring of Lumphanan

It was at Lumphanan that Macbeth was slain in battle with the forces of Malcolm Canmore in 1057. There is a large boulder – Macbeth's Stone – at which he is said to have died [NJ 575034] and spring – Macbeth's Well – where he drank before the battle [NJ 580039]. Macbeth's Cairn [NJ 578053] is where he is believed to have been buried before his body was taken to Iona – although the robbed and disturbed mound is probably a prehistoric burial cairn.
See main entry N136

G9 Rona

[Map: 3A, A5] 44 miles NE of Butt of Lewis, Rona. (NGR: HW 809323 LR: 8)
Rona is a small triangular-shaped island, and there was a cell or hermitage here, dedicated to St Ronan, and consisting of a small oratory, dating from the 7th or 8th century, and cashel. The complex forms one of the most complete groups of buildings from the early Celtic church in Scotland. There are several cross-incised burial markers, dating from the 7th to 12th centuries. The island is accessible from Ness (in calm weather). It is a National Nature Reserve, in the care of Scottish National Heritage, from whom permission should be sought before visiting.
Boats can be hired from Lewis but require booking well in advance.
Tel: 01851 705258

L24 Ruthwell Cross (HS)

A magnificent Anglian sculpted cross, dating from the 7th century, standing about 17 feet high.
See main entry L24

S41 Scone Palace

The Kings of Scots were inaugurated at the Moot Hill, near the present palace. The last king to be so was Charles I in 1651. The Stone of Destiny, also called the Stone of Scone, was kept here, until taken to Westminster Abbey by Edward I in 1296 – although it was returned to **Edinburgh Castle [N25]** in 1996.
See main entry S41

K26 St Andrews Cathedral (HS)

St Regulus, or Rule, is said to have founded a monastery here in the 6th century. The relics of St Andrew were brought here, and the Bishopric was transferred from Abernethy in 908. The church of the time – the tower of which, St Rule's Tower, still survives and dates from as early as 1070. The museum houses a large and magnificent collection of Christian and early medieval sculpture, including the magnificent St Andrews Sarcophagus.
See main entry K26

K99 St Blane's Church (HS)

In a peaceful and pleasant location on the island of Bute is the site of a 6th-century Christian community, founded by St Blane, who was born on Bute. The site is surrounded by an enclosure wall, and there are several ruinous buildings, including a 12th-century chapel. There is a holy well nearby.
See main entry K99

G10 St Columba Centre (HS)

[Map: 5A, C2] On A849, Fionnphort, Mull. (NGR: NM 305235 LR: 48)
The centre features an exhibition about the Celtic church, Iona and St Columba, the 6th-century saint, who founded a monastery on Iona and converted the Picts of the northern mainland. Displays include photographs, calligraphy, Chiro Stone, recreation of ancient landscape, and a model of a curragh. The centre also provides information on the local area.
Explanatory displays. Gift shop. Refreshments. WC. Disabled access. Car and coach parking. Group concessions. ££. Groups by appt.
Open Apr-Sep, daily 11.00-17.00; other times by prior arrangement with abbey.
Tel: 01681 700660 Fax: 01898 840270

G11 St Columba's Cave

[Map: 5A, D4] Off B8024, 12 miles SW of Lochgilphead, 1 mile N of Ellary, Knapdale, Argyll. (NGR: NR 751768 LR: 62)
The cave, which is associated with St Columba's arrival in Scotland, has a rock-cut shelf with an altar, above which are crosses carved in the wall. A basin may have been used as a font. A ruined chapel, possibly dating from the 13th century, stands nearby, and there is another cave.
Parking nearby.
Access at all reasonable times.

G12 St Columba's Footprint

[Map: 5A, G4] Off B842, 8 miles S of Campbeltown, W of Sithern, Keil, Southend, Kintyre, Argyll. (NGR: NR 670077 LR: 68)
It is believed that this is the first place St Columba put ashore in Scotland. Two 'feet' have been carved in a flat-topped rock on a knoll near the ruin of the

old chapel, one of them modern, although the original footprint may be associated with an inauguration rite for holding the lands rather than the saint. There is an old ruinous church. There are also several caves.
Parking. Signposted.
Access at all reasonable times.

G13 St Fillan's Cave

[Map: 6B, C11] Off A917, 1 mile W of Anstruther, Cove Wynd, Pittenweem, Fife. (NGR: NO 550024 LR: 59)
The cave, which was renovated in 1935 and rededicated for worship, is associated with St Fillan, a 7th-century saint.

St Fillan was apparently a hermit here for many years, but was eventually made abbot of a monastery on the Holy Loch. Many miracles were associated with him, including taming a wolf using only the power of prayer.

His relics were also believed to be very powerful, and Robert the Bruce carried them at the Battle of Bannockburn in 1314.
Car parking. £.
Open all year: Easter-Oct, Mon-Sat 9.00-17.30; Nov-Easter, Tue-Sat 9.00-17.30, Sun 12.00-17.00. Collect key from The Gingerbread Horse, 9 High Street, Pittenweem.
Tel: 01333 311495 Fax: 01333 312212

K113 St Margaret's Cave

The cave is associated with St Margaret, wife of Malcolm Canmore in the 11th century, and was a place of pilgrimage.
See main entry K113

K118 St Mary's Church, Monymusk

Part of the fine church may date from 12th century, and a priory of Augustinian canons was founded here. Housed in the church is the Monymusk Stone, a Pictish symbol stone, as well as other stones dating from the 7th-9th centuries. The Monymusk Reliquary, which once held the relics of St Columba, was also sometimes displayed here. It was carried before Bruce's army at Bannockburn, and is now kept in the **Museum of Scotland [Y6]** in Edinburgh. There are fine modern stained-glass windows.
See main entry K118

K39 St Monans Parish Church

St Monans is associated with St Monan and St Adrian. St Monan was slain by Norsemen here about 870, while St Adrian sought refuge on the **Isle of May [J21]**, where he was also killed. St Monans became a place of pilgrimage, as was the Isle of May.
See main entry K39

G14 St Ninian's Cave (HS)

[Map: 6A, J6] Off A747, 4 miles SW of Whithorn, Physgill, Dumfries and Galloway. (NGR: NX 421359 LR: 83)
This cave is traditionally believed to have been the retreat of St Ninian from **Whithorn [J33]** – although the cave has partially collapsed. Crosses were carved on the walls, probably by pilgrims, and carved stones have also been found during excavations. Eleven stones, dating from the 11th century or earlier, which were found here are now at **Whithorn: Cradle of Christianity in Scotland [J34]**. The cave is still a place of pilgrimage.
Car and coach parking nearby.
Access at all times – involves walk from car park.

K128 St Triduana's Chapel (HS)

There is an extremely unusual hexagonal vaulted chamber, known as St Triduana's Chapel or Well, the remains of a two-storey building. Water still flows from a spring here. Visiting Triduana's shrines were supposed to help blindness and other conditions of the eye. Triduana had blinded herself by plucking out her own eyes and sending them to an unwanted admirer.
See main entry K128

Y205 Up Helly Aa Exhibition

The exhibition features displays including artefacts, photographs, costumes and a replica ship from the annual fire festival 'Up Helly Aa'.
See main entry Y205

G15 Vikingar, Largs

[Map: 6A, E5] Off A78, Greenock Road, Largs, Ayrshire. (NGR: NS 203603 LR: 63)
Vikingar charts the history of the Norsemen in Scotland, from the first raids in Scotland to the battle of Largs in 1263. Displays use multimedia techniques, including sight, sounds and smells.
Guided tours. Multimedia exhibition. Gift shop. Cafe and bar. Swimming pool and play area. WC. Full disabled access. Car and coach parking. Group concessions. ££.
Open all year: Apr-Sep, 10.30-18.00; Oct-Mar, 10.30-16.00.
Tel: 01475 689777 Fax: 01475 689444
Web: www.vikingar.co.uk Email: anyone@vikingar.co.uk

J33 Whithorn Priory (HS)

The site of the 5th-century Christian community of St Ninian, who built a stone church here known as 'Candida Casa'. Whithorn was a Northumbrian bishopric but is last mentioned in 803. Later it became a popular place of pilgrimage. The arm bone of St Ninian was taken to the Scottish seminary at Douai, where it was kept until the French Revolution.

The existing ruins are of a 12th-century Premonstrat-

ensian priory and cathedral: the nave of the Romanesque church survives, although it is unroofed. The
vaulted chambers under the former nave also survive,
and probably housed the shrine and relics of St Ninian.

A fine collection of early Christian sculpture is
housed in the nearby museum, including the 'Latinus Stone', the earliest Christian memorial in Scotland; the 'St Peter's Stone'; and the 10th-century
Monreith Cross. Also see **Whithorn: Cradle of
Christianity in Scotland [J34]**.
See main entry J33

Above *Whithorn*
Left *St Mary's
Church, Monymusk*
Below *Abercorn*

Left *Netherton Cross*
Above *Keills*
Right *St Martin's
Cross, Iona*
Below left *St Blane's*
Below right *Kildalton*
Bottom left *Dunadd*

H: Wars of Independence

Sites which are associated with the Wars of Independence, William Wallace and Robert the Bruce.

H1 Alexander III Monument

[Map: 6B, D10] On A921, 3 miles S of Kirkcaldy, E of Kinghorn, Fife. (NGR: NT 254864 LR: 66)

The monument, standing on King's Crag, marks the spot where Alexander III fell from his horse and was killed on the night of 18 March 1286. Alexander was on his way to Kinghorn to see his new bride, and his death threw Scotland into dynastic troubles.

Car parking.

Access at all reasonable times.

J2 Arbroath Abbey (HS)

The Declaration of Arbroath was signed here in 1320.

See main entry J2

H2 Bannockburn Battlefield and Heritage Centre (NTS)

[Map: 5B, D8] 2 miles S of M80/M9 at Junction 9, 2 miles S of Stirling, Glasgow Road, Bannockburn. (NGR: NS 814917 LR: 57)

Site of the battle of Bannockburn, where in 1314 the large army of Edward II of England was crushed by the Scots under Robert the Bruce. The Heritage Centre stands close to the Borestone site, which by tradition was Bruce's command post. Bruce is commemorated by a bronze equestrian statue, unveiled in 1964. The site is enclosed by the Rotunda. The centre has an exhibition 'The Kingdom of Scots', and an audiovisual display on the battle.

Audio-visual programme. Explanatory displays. Gift shop. WC. Disabled access. Induction loop. Car and coach parking. £.

Rotunda and site open all year; heritage centre, shop and cafe open (2002): 20 Jan-24 Mar and 28 Oct-24 Dec, daily 10.30-16.00; 25 Mar-27 Oct, daily 10.00-18.00; last audiovisual show 30 mins before closing.

Tel: 01786 812664 Fax: 01786 810892

N56 Bothwell Castle (HS)

The castle was important during the Wars of Independence, and was besieged and changed hands several times.

See main entry N56

H3 Bruce's Cave

[Map: 6B, H9] Off B6357, 4 miles NW of Gretna, Kirkpatrick Fleming, Dumfries and Galloway. (NGR: NY 265705 LR: 85)

The beauty spot is associated with Robert the Bruce,

and there are 80 acres of wooded and secluded grounds.

WC. Play area. Disabled access with assistance and WC. Car and coach parking. £.

Open all year: summer, daily 9.00-21.00; winter, daily 9.00-17.00.

H4 Bruce's Stone (NTS)

[Map: 6A, H6] Off A714, 10.5 miles N of Newton Stewart, Loch Trool, Dumfries and Galloway. (NGR: NX 423798 LR: 77)

The inscribed granite boulder commemorates Robert the Bruce's victory over the English in 1307 and is said to be where he rested after the battle. There are fine views of Loch Trool and the hills of Galloway, including Merrick, the highest hill in southern Scotland at 2764 feet.

Parking nearby.

Access at all reasonable times.

N60 Caerlaverock Castle (HS)

The castle was captured by Edward I of England in 1300 after a difficult siege. It was eventually retaken by the Scots.

See main entry N60

N82 Dirleton Castle (HS)

The castle was held by the De Vaux family, but was captured by the English after a hard siege in 1298.

See main entry N82

J14 Dunfermline Abbey (HS)

Robert the Bruce's body (apart from his heart) is buried here.

See main entry J14

N90 Dunnottar Castle

Dunnottar was captured by Wallace in 1296, one story being he burnt 4000 Englishmen here.

See main entry N90

N91 Dunollie Castle

The castle was built by the MacDougalls, who were bitter enemies of Robert the Bruce. A MacDougall force defeated Bruce at Dalry, nearly killing him and wrenching a brooch from his cloak. This was known as the Brooch of Lorne and kept at the castle, then at **Gylen [N108]**. Bruce returned and ravaged MacDougall lands in 1309 after defeating them at **Loch Aweside [H9]**.

See main entry N91

N25 Edinburgh Castle (HS)

The castle had an English garrison from 1296 until 1313, when the Scots, led by Thomas Randolph, climbed the rock, and retook it.

See main entry N25

H5 Elderslie Wallace Monument

[Map: 6A, E6] On A737, 2 miles SW of Paisley, Johnstone Road, Elderslie, Renfrewshire. (NGR: NS 442630 LR: 63)

This memorial stands in the centre of Elderslie, believed by many to be the birthplace of William Wallace. Grassy mounds remain of the site.

Monument: access at all reasonable times.

H6 Greyfriars Chapel, Dumfries

[Map: 6B, H8] On A701, Dumfries. (NGR: NX 971763 LR: 84)

Nothing remains of Greyfriars, a Franciscan friary founded in 1266, probably by Devorgilla of Galloway. It was in the church of the Friary that John Comyn was stabbed to death by Robert the Bruce and his men. A plaque on a wall in Castle Street commemorates the event.

Parking nearby.

Site only; access to plaque at all reasonable times.

N116 Kildrummy Castle (HS)

The castle was captured by the English in 1306 from a garrison led by Nigel Bruce, younger brother of Robert the Bruce. Nigel was executed.

See main entry N116

H7 King's Cave, Drumadroon

[Map: 6A, F4] Off A841, 2 miles N of Blackwaterfoot, Torr Righ Mor, Arran. (NGR: NR 884309 LR: 69)

The cliffs here have several caves, one of which is known as 'King's Cave' from the tradition that Robert the Bruce sheltered here after being crowned king in 1306 – one story is that it was here that he saw the famous spider. It was, however, apparently known as Fingal's Cave as late as the 18th century, and may have been used as a Christian retreat or hermitage.

The cave has numerous carvings, including crosses, as well as a seat carved into the rock. A grille has been fitted across the mouth of the cave.

H8 Lanark Castle

[Map: 6B, F8] Off A73, Castlebank, Lanark. (NGR: NS 875435 LR: 72)

Site of 12th-century castle, which stood on Castle Hill, a prominent knoll. It was visited by 12th-century kings of Scots, but occupied by the English, during the Wars of Independence, until recovered by Robert the Bruce in 1310. William Wallace had massacred the garrison here, and murdered Hazelrigg, the English governor, after his wife, Marion Braidfute, had been killed by Hazelrigg.

H9 Loch Aweside Battle Monument

[Map: 5A, B5] On A85, 3 miles E of Dalmally, railway station, Loch Awe, Argyll. (NGR: NN 124274 LR: 50)

The monument commemorates the battle here in 1308, when Robert the Bruce defeated the MacDougalls and John of Lorne.

Access at all reasonable times.

J26 Melrose Abbey (HS)

The heart of Robert the Bruce is buried in the nave.

See main entry J26

H10 National Wallace Monument

[Map: 5B, D8] Off B998, 1 mile NE of Stirling Castle, Abbey Craig, Stirlingshire. (NGR: NS 808956 LR: 57)

The 200 foot tower, with 246 steps, was built in 1869 to commemorate William Wallace, the freedom-fighter, hero, and victor at the Battle of **Stirling Bridge [H11]** in 1297. There are fine views towards the Highlands, and from the Forth Bridges to Ben Lomond. Wallace's two-handed sword is preserved inside. Displays include a Hall of Heroes, with great Scots such as Robert the Bruce, Robert Burns and Sir Walter Scott, and an audio-visual show on the life of Wallace.

Explanatory displays. Gift shop. Tearoom. WC. Nature trails. Parking. ££.

Open Mar-Oct, daily 10.00-17.00; Jul and Aug, 9.30-18.30; Nov and Dec, 10.00-16.00; Jan and Feb, Sat and Sun only 10.00-16.00.

Tel: 01786 472140 Fax: 01786 461322

Y168 Royal Burgh of Stirling Visitor Centre

The visitor centre charts the history of Stirling from the Wars of Independence, through life in the medieval burgh, to the present day. There is a sound and light exhibition and audio-visual show.

See main entry Y168

K101 St Bride's Church (HS)

Although there was probably a church here in earlier times, the present ruin dates from 1330 and later. The remains consist of the chancel, and the south transept. The church houses the stone effigy of the Good Sir James Douglas, who died in 1331 in Spain.

See main entry K101

K104 St Conan's Kirk

The Bruce Chapel has a fragment of bone reputed to be from Robert the Bruce.

See main entry K104.

N46 Stirling Castle (HS)

Edward I of England captured the castle in 1304 when he used – although after the garrison had surrendered – a siege engine called the 'War Wolf'. William Wallace took the castle for the Scots, but it was retaken

by the English until the Battle of Bannockburn in 1314.
See main entry N46

H11 Stirling Old Bridge (HS)

[Map: 5B, D8] Off A9, N of Stirling Castle, beside Customs Roundabout, off Drip Road, Stirling. (NGR: NS 797945 LR: 57)
Although this bridge was built in the early 15th century, it stands on or very near the site of William Wallace's crushing victory of Stirling Bridge in 1297. The road leading north from the bridge is still called Causewayhead Road. Part of the bridge was blown up in 1746 during the Jacobite Rising.
Parking nearby
Access at all reasonable times.

H12 Turnberry Castle

[Map: 6A, G5] Off A716, 6 miles N of Girvan, Turnberry, Ayrshire. (NGR: NS 196073 LR: 70)
Standing on a promontory, not much remains of a 13th-century castle of the Earls of Carrick, which may be the birthplace of Robert the Bruce, Robert I, King of Scots. His mother, Marjorie, the widowed Countess of Carrick, kidnapped Robert Bruce of Annandale, and forced him to marry her in 1271. The castle was dismantled on the orders of Robert the Bruce in 1310, and probably never rebuilt.
Parking nearby.
Access at all reasonable times.

D63 Tynron Doon

Site of castle, within the ramparts of an Iron Age fort. Robert the Bruce is said to have sheltered here, with Kirkpatrick of Closeburn, in 1306 after stabbing the Red Comyn at **Greyfriars Chapel, Dumfries [H6]**.
See main entry D63

Above left *Kildrummy Castle*   Above right *Melrose Abbey*
Below left *Bothwell Castle*   Below right *Dirleton Castle*

I: Mary, Queen of Scotland

Some sites which are associated with Mary and her life and times.

N2 Alloa Tower (NTS)

Mary was reconciled with Darnley here in 1565.
See main entry N2

N7 Borthwick Castle

Mary and Bothwell visited the castle in 1567 after their marriage, but were besieged here, Mary only escaping disguised as a man. She went on to surrender at Carberry Hill.
See main entry N7

N76 Craigmillar Castle (HS)

Mary used Craigmillar often, and fled here after the murder of Rizzio. It was also here that the Earl of Moray, Bothwell and William Maitland of Lethington plotted Darnley's murder.
See main entry N76

N88 Dumbarton Castle (HS)

The infant Mary was kept at Dumbarton before being taken to France.
See main entry N88

J13 Dundrennan Abbey (HS)

After defeat at Langside, Mary is said to have spent her last night here (15-16 May 1568) before fleeing to England.
See main entry J13

N25 Edinburgh Castle (HS)

In 1566 Mary, Queen of Scots, gave birth to the future James VI in the castle.
See main entry N25

N27 Falkland Palace (NTS)

Mary, James VI, Charles I and Charles II stayed here.
See main entry N27

N109 Hailes Castle (HS)

Bothwell brought Mary here after abducting her in 1567, and they married soon afterwards.
See main entry N109

N110 Hermitage Castle (HS)

In 1566 Bothwell was badly wounded in a skirmish with the Border reiver 'Little Jock' Elliot of Park, and was paid a visit on his sick bed by Mary, who had been staying in Jedburgh at what is now the **Mary Queen of Scots Visitor Centre [I2]**.
See main entry N110

N31 Holyroodhouse

David Rizzio, favourite of Mary, was murdered here in 1566 in front of the pregnant queen. He is buried in **Canongate [K57]** kirkyard.
See main entry N31

J19 Inchmahome Priory (HS)

The young Mary was sent here for safety in 1547 before leaving for France.
See main entry J19

I1 Kirk o' Field, Edinburgh

[Map: 6B, E9] Old College, University of Edinburgh, Edinburgh. (NGR: NT 260735 LR: 66)
Site of the house where Darnley and his servant were strangled in 1567. The building was blown up using gunpowder.
Site only.

N37 Lennoxlove

It was a property of the Maitlands, one of whom was secretary to Mary. Among the treasures it contains are the death mask of Mary, a sapphire ring given to her by Lord John Hamilton, and the casket which may have contained the 'Casket Letters'.
See main entry N37

N119 Linlithgow Palace (HS)

James V was born here in 1512, as was Mary in 1542.
See main entry N119

N121 Lochleven Castle (HS)

Mary was held here from 1567 following Carberry Hill until she escaped in 1568, during which time she signed her abdication in favour of the infant James VI. Mary when on to defeat at Langside.
See main entry N121

I2 Mary Queen of Scots Visitor Centre, Jedburgh

[Map: 6B, F11] Off A68, in Jedburgh, Borders. (NGR: NT 651206 LR: 74)
Situated in a public park, the building is an altered 16th-century tower house, and belonged to the Kerrs. Mary stayed in a chamber on the second floor. She was ill and lay near death for many days after her visit to Bothwell at **Hermitage Castle [N110]** in 1566. The building houses a museum displaying exhibits relating to the visit by Mary to Jedburgh. Scottish Borders Council Museum. The fine ruins of **Jedburgh**

Abbey [J22] are nearby, as is the **Jedburgh Castle Jail and Museum [Y102]**.

Award-winning 16th-century house. Explanatory displays. Gift shop. Formal garden. WC. Disabled access to ground floor only. Parking nearby. £.

Open Mar-Nov, Mon-Sat 10.00-16.30, Sun 11.00-16.30.
Tel: 01835 863331 Fax: 01450 378506

N46 Stirling Castle (HS)

Mary was crowned in the old chapel in 1543, and the future James VI was baptised here in 1566.
See main entry N46

N48 Traquair House

The house has a collection of mementoes associated with Mary who stayed here with Darnley.
See main entry N48

Top right *Holyroodhouse*
Right *Linlithgow Palace*
Bottom right *Lennoxlove*
Bottom left *Mary Queen of Scots Visitor Centre*

J: Abbeys and Priories

Although there were monasteries of the Celtic church before this (see the section on Early Scotland), from the 11th and 12th centuries the Kings and nobles of Scots established many religious houses throughout Scotland.

J1 Abbey St Bathans

[Map: 6B, E11] Off A6112 or B6355, 5.5 miles N of Duns, Abbey St Bathans, Berwickshire, Borders. (NGR: NT 758623 LR: 67)

Little remains except part of the church, built into the present parish church, of a Cistercian nunnery, founded in the 13th century by Ada Countess of Dunbar and dedicated to St Mary the Virgin. Nearby is a spring [NT 761620] which is believed to have healing powers, and was dedicated to St Bathan. It is said that the water would never freeze no matter how cold the weather.

J2 Arbroath Abbey (HS)

[Map: 4, I4] Off A92, Arbroath, Angus. (NGR: NO 643413 LR: 54)

The substantial ruins of a Tironsenian abbey survive, founded in 1178 by William the Lyon, in memory of his friend Thomas a Becket. Part of the church remains, including the fine west end, the gatehouse, sacristy and Abbot's House, which houses a museum. The Declaration of Arbroath was signed here in 1320. New visitor centre.

Explanatory displays in visitor centre and Abbot's House. Audiovisual presentations. Gift shop. WC. Explanatory boards. Parking nearby. £.

Open all year: Apr-Sep, daily 9.30-18.30; Oct-Mar, Mon-Sat 9.00-16.30, Sun 14.00-16.30; closed 25/26 Dec & 1/2 Jan.
Tel: 01241 878756

J3 Ardchattan Priory (HS)

[Map: 5A, B5] Off A828, 6.5 miles NE of Oban, Argyll. (NGR: NM 971349 LR: 49)

Set in a peaceful location, this was a Valliscaulian priory dedicated to St Modan, founded in 1231 by Duncan MacDougall.

Part of the ruinous church, houses carved grave slabs and an early Christian carved wheel cross. Other priory buildings were incorporated into a mansion, and there are fine gardens.

Colin Campbell of Glenure, murdered in 1752, is buried here – the events feature in *Kidnapped* by Robert Louis Stevenson.

Facilities are for gardens. Guidebook. WC. Disabled access. Car and limited coach parking. £ (gardens)/priory ruins free.
Ruins of priory (Historic Scotland) open all reasonable times; house NOT open; gardens (privately owned) open Apr-Oct, daily 9.00-18.00.
Tel: 01631 750274/0131 668 8800 (HS)
Fax: 01631 750238/0131 668 8888 (HS)

J4 Balmerino Abbey (NTS)

[Map: 6B, C10] Off A914, 4.5 miles SW of Newport on Tay, Balmerino, Fife. (NGR: NO 358246 LR: 59)

The remains of a 13th-century Cistercian abbey in a peaceful setting by the sea, founded in 1229 by Ermengarde, widow of William the Lyon, and their son Alexander II. Little remains except the basement of the chapter house and adjoining buildings. An interesting old chestnut tree is said to have been planted by the monks.

Parking nearby.
Access at all reasonable times.
Tel: 0131 243 9300   Fax: 0131 243 9301

J5 Beauly Priory (HS)

[Map: 3B, E9] On A862, 10 miles W of Inverness, Beauly, Invernessshire, Highland. (NGR: NH 527465 LR: 26)

The fine ruined cruciform church of a Valliscaulian priory, dedicated to St Mary and St John the Baptist and founded in 1230 by John Bisset and Alexander II. The priory was plundered in 1506, and became a Cistercian house around 1510. There are fine windows and window-arcading, and several old burial slabs and tombs. The north transept was used as the burial aisle for the Mackenzies of Kintail.

Parking.
Access at all reasonable times.

J6 Cambuskenneth Abbey (HS)

[Map: 5B, D8] Off A907, 1 mile E of Stirling, Cambuskenneth, Stirlingshire. (NGR: NS 809939 LR: 57)

The ruins of an abbey founded in 1147 as a house of Augustinian canons. Robert the Bruce held a parliament in 1326. James III is buried here, after being murdered following the battle of Sauchieburn in 1488, as well as his queen. The fine detached bell-tower is the only substantial part remaining, although extensive foundations survive of the rest.

Parking nearby.
Open Apr-Sep, daily 9.00-18.30 – view exterior only: keys available locally.

J7 Coupar Angus Abbey

[Map: 5B, B9] On A923, 12 miles NE of Perth, just S of Coupar Angus, Perthshire. (NGR: NO 223397 LR: 53)

Little remains of the abbey, except a ruined gatehouse and some architectural fragments. It was founded in 1164 by Malcolm the Maiden, King of Scots, and was a Cistercian establishment dedicated to the Blessed

Virgin Mary. The buildings were burned by a mob in 1559. The existing church is probably built on the site of the abbey church. There are carved fragments in the church, including the stone effigy of an abbot, and another of a knight.

Access at all reasonable times.

J8 Cross Kirk, Peebles (HS)

[Map: 6B, F9] On A703, Cross Road, Peebles, Borders. (NGR: NS 250407 LR: 73)

The ruins of a Trinitarian friary, founded about 1474, and named after the discovery of a large cross on the site in 1261. It was dedicated to St Nicholas, and a place of pilgrimage. The church was taken over by the parish in 1561, but became ruinous. Much of the late 13th-century church survives, with later burial aisles.

Parking nearby. Disabled access.
Access at all reasonable times.

J9 Crossraguel Abbey (HS)

[Map: 6A, G6] Off A77, 2 miles SW of Maybole, Crossraguel, Ayrshire. (NGR: NS 275084 LR: 70)

The well-preserved ruin of a Cluniac abbey, founded by Duncan, Earl of Carrick, in 1216. Substantial remains survive of the church, cloister, chapter house and some of the domestic buildings. Allan Stewart, Commendator (lay administrator) of the abbey, was roasted 'in sop' in Dunure Castle by the Kennedys until he signed over the lands of the dissolved abbey.

Exhibition on medieval building techniques. Sales area. WC. Picnic area. Car and coach parking. £.
Open Apr-Sep, daily 9.30-18.30; last ticket sold 18.00.
Tel: 01655 883113

J10 Culross Abbey (HS)

[Map: 6B, D8] Off B9037, 6.5 miles W of Dunfermline, Kirk Street, Culross, Fife. (NGR: NS 989863 LR: 65)

Situated in the pretty town of Culross with its white-washed houses, the Cistercian Abbey was dedicated to St Serf and St Mary, and founded in 1217 by Malcolm, Earl of Fife. Most of the buildings are ruinous, except the monk's choir, which is used as the parish church. There are fragments of three cross shafts near the church, dating from the 8th or 9th century.

St Enoch or Thenew came to Culross in the 6th century. Enoch was pregnant, although unmarried, and had a son, St Mungo or Kentigern. Mungo was educated here by St Serf, and was active among the Britons of Strathclyde. He founded a church on the site of **Glasgow Cathedral [K19]** in 573.

WC. Sales area. Disabled access. Parking Nearby.
Open all year at reasonable times; parish church open summer, daily 10.00-dusk; winter daily 10.00-16.00.

J11 Deer Abbey (HS)

[Map: 4, E5] Off A950, 9 miles W of Peterhead, 2 miles W of Mintlaw, Aberdeenshire. (NGR: NJ 968482 LR: 30)

Deer Abbey, a Cistercian house, was founded in 1219 by William Comyn, Earl of Buchan, and dedicated to the Blessed Virgin Mary. Not much of the church remains except foundations, although the infirmary, Abbot's House and the southern cloister range are better preserved. The beautifully illustrated Book of Deer is now in the University Library at Cambridge. The original monastery was probably founded by St Drostan, Columba's nephew.

Parking.
Access at all reasonable times.
Tel: 01466 793191

J12 Dryburgh Abbey (HS)

[Map: 6B, F11] Off B6356 or B6404, 8 miles SE of Melrose, Dryburgh, Borders. (NGR: NT 591317 LR: 73)

A picturesque and substantial ruin in a fine situation by the Tweed, the Abbey was founded by David I as a Premonstratensian establishment, dedicated to St Mary. Most of the buildings date from the 12th and 13th centuries, and part of the church survives, as do substantial portions of the cloister, including the fine chapter house, parlour and vestry. The Abbey was burnt by the English in 1322, 1385 and 1544. Sir Walter Scott and Earl Haig are both buried here.

Gift shop. WC. Picnic area. Disabled access. Car and coach parking. WC. Group concessions. £.
Open all year: Apr-Sep, daily 9.30-18.30; Oct-Mar, Mon-Sat 9.30-16.30, Sun 14.00-16.30, last ticket 30 mins before closing; closed 25/26 Dec and 1/2 Jan.
Tel: 01835 822381

J13 Dundrennan Abbey (HS)

[Map: 6B, I7] On A711, 6 miles SE of Kirkcudbright, Dundrennan, Dumfries and Galloway. (NGR: NX 749475 LR: 83)

The fine ruins of a Cistercian abbey, founded in 1142 by David I and dedicated to the Blessed Virgin Mary. Substantial parts of the church, chapter house and cloister survive. Mary, Queen of Scots, is said to have spent her last night (15-16 May 1568) on Scottish soil here before fleeing to England.

Sales area. Disabled access. Car and coach parking. Group concessions. £.
Open Apr-Sep, daily 9.30-18.30; Oct-Mar wknds only, Sat 9.30-16.30, Sun 14.00-16.30; last ticket 30 mins before closing; closed 25-26 Dec and 1-2 Jan.
Tel: 01557 500262

J14 Dunfermline Abbey and Palace (HS)

[Map: 6B, D9] Off A994, Monastery Street, Dunfermline, Fife. (NGR: NT 089872 LR: 65)

Dunfermline Abbey was founded about 1070 by

Queen Margaret, wife of Malcolm Canmore, as a Benedictine house on the site of an older Christian site. Margaret was made a saint, and she and Malcolm were buried here. Dunfermline became a major centre of pilgrimage in medieval times, and **St Margaret's Cave [K113]** is nearby. Abbot George Durie, the last abbot, was responsible for removing their remains to the continent at the Reformation, where the Jesuits of Douai in Spain secured her head. Robert the Bruce's body (apart from his heart) is buried here. Part of the church continued to be used after the abbey was dissolved, and it was restored and rebuilt in modern times. The church, domestic buildings of the abbey, and the remains of the Royal Palace are open to the public. **Abbot House [Y18]** is nearby.

There appears to have been a Royal Palace from the 14th century, substantial ruins of which remain. David II was born here in 1323, as was James I in 1394. James IV, James V, and Mary, Queen of Scots, visited. The Palace was remodelled in 1587 by Queen Anne, wife of James VI, and Charles I was born here in 1600.

Explanatory displays. Gift shop. Parking nearby. Group concessions. £.

Open Apr-Sep, daily 9.30-18.30; Oct-Mar, Mon-Wed and Sat 9.30-16.30, Thu 9.30-12.00, Sun 14.00-16.30, closed Fri; last ticket 30 mins before closing; choir of abbey church open Mon-Sat 10.00-16.30, Sun 14.00-16.30.

Tel: 01383 739026 Fax: 01383 739026

J15 Fearn Abbey

[Map: 3B, D10] Off B9166, 5 miles SE of Tain, Fearn, Highland. (NGR: NH 837773 LR: 21)

Known as the 'Lamp of the North', this 14th-century church is one of the oldest pre-Reformation Scottish churches still used for worship as the parish church. The abbey was a Premonstratensian establishment of the order of St Augustine, founded by Ferquhard MacTaggart, Earl of Ross, around 1227. The abbey church was rebuilt in 1772 – after the nave roof had collapsed in 1742, killing 44 people – and again in 1972, but little remains of the other abbey buildings. Patrick Hamilton, Commendator of the abbey from 1517, was burnt for heresy at St Andrews in 1528.

Sales area. WC. Disabled access. Parking.

Open May-Sep, Sat and Sun 10.00-16.30; other times tel for appt.

Tel: 01862 871247

J16 Glenluce Abbey (HS)

[Map: 6A, I5] Off A75, 1.5 miles N of Glenluce village, Dumfries and Galloway. (NGR: NX 185586 LR: 82)

In a peaceful setting are the ruins of a Cistercian abbey, dedicated to the Blessed Virgin Mary. It was founded about 1192 by Roland, Lord of Galloway. Mary, Queen of Scots, stayed here in 1563 during a Progress. Not much remains of the church, but the fine 16th-century chapter house is still roofed and decorated with Green Men. Parts of the cloister and domestic buildings survive.

Explanatory panels. Exhibition of finds. Shop. Refreshments. Disabled access. Car and coach parking. £.

Open Apr-Sep, daily 9.30-18.30; last ticket 18.00; Oct-Mar wknds only, Sat 9.30-16.30, Sun 14.30-16.30; last ticket sold at 16.00.

Tel: 01581 300541

J17 Holyrood Abbey (HS)

[Map: 6B, E9] Edinburgh, adjacent to Holyrood Palace. (NGR: NT 269740 LR: 66)

The fine ruined church of an Augustinian abbey, founded by David I in 1128, survives beside the palace.

See Holyroodhouse.

J18 Inchcolm Abbey (HS)

[Map: 6B, D9] Inchcolm, 6.5 miles SE of Kirkcaldy, island in the Firth of Forth, Fife. (NGR: NT 191827 LR: 66)

The best preserved monastic complex in Scotland, the cloister and chapter house being complete. The abbey was dedicated to St Columba, and founded in 1123 by Alexander I, King of Scots, after he had been rescued from the sea. He was washed up on Inchcolm and given refuge by a hermit. Much later the island was used as a naval quarantine station, fort, and Russian naval hospital, and had gun emplacements built to defend the Forth Bridge in World War II. There are also many seals.

Exhibition. Explanatory boards. Gift shop. Picnic area. WC. Disabled access. £ + ferry.

Open Apr-Sep, daily 9.30-18.30; ferry (&) (30 mins) from South or North Queensferry (phone 0131 331 4857).

Tel: 0131 331 4857

J19 Inchmahome Priory (HS)

[Map: 5B, D7] Off A91, 4 miles E of Aberfoyle, Lake of Menteith, Stirlingshire. (NGR: NN 574005 LR: 57)

Set on an idyllic wooded island in a picturesque loch are the ruins of a small Augustinian priory, dedicated to St Colman. The priory was founded in 1238 by Walter Comyn, 4th Earl of Menteith, although there may have been an earlier Christian community on the island. Robert the Bruce visited the priory, and David II was married here. Mary, Queen of Scots was sent here for safety in 1547 before leaving for France. The chapter house is still roofed, and a substantial part of the church also survives. Ferry out to island from Port of Menteith.

Gift shop. Picnic area. WC. Parking (ferry). £.

Open Apr-Sep, daily 9.30-18.30; last ticket 18.00; ferry subject to cancellation during bad weather.

Tel: 01877 385294 Fax: 01877 385294

Y99 Inverkeithing Museum

The friary was a Franciscan establishment which was founded around 1268 by Philip Mowbray. The site is now a public garden, although the former guest house, dating from the 14th century, survives. A museum is located on the upper floor of the building via an external stair, and there are displays and information on Inverkeithing and Rosyth, and on Admiral Greig, who founded the Russian Navy.

See main entry Y99

J20 Iona Abbey (HS)

[Map: 5A, C2] Off unlisted road, Iona, Argyll. (NGR: NM 287245 LR: 48)

Situated on the beautiful and peaceful island of Iona, this is where St Columba came from Ireland to form a monastic community. Columba's shrine, within the Abbey buildings, dates from the 9th century. The abbey was abandoned after raids by the Vikings, but was re-established by Queen Margaret, wife of Malcolm Canmore, in the 11th century.

Some of the surviving abbey buildings date from the early 13th century after it had been refounded as a Benedictine establishment in 1203 by Reginald, son of Somerled, Lord of the Isles, and it was dedicated to the Virgin Mary. The Abbey was used as a cathedral by the protestant Bishop of the Isles in the 17th century. Although the buildings became ruinous after the Reformation, the abbey church was rebuilt from 1899-1910, and the cloister was restored in 1936 for the Iona Community. It is possible to stay at the Abbey.

The magnificent St Martin's Cross and St John's Cross – the latter a replica: the original is reconstructed and displayed in the Infirmary Museum – stand just outside the church, and the Infirmary Museum houses a splendid collection of sculpted stones and crosses, one of the largest collections of early Christian carved stones in Europe. The Black Stones of Iona were kept by St Martin's Cross and would reputedly turn black when somebody was lying. Between the abbey and the nunnery is MacLean's Cross, a fine 15th-century carved stone cross.

Many of the early Kings of Scots are buried in 'Reilig Odhrain' Oran's cemetery by the 'Street of the Dead' – as well as kings of Ireland, France and Norway: 48 Scottish, eight Norwegian and four Irish kings according to one 16th-century source. The 11th-century chapel of St Oran also survives, and may have been built on the orders of St Margaret. Among the kings buried here are reputedly both Duncan and Macbeth.

The nearby Augustinian nunnery of St Mary was founded in 1208, also by Reginald, and is a fine consolidated ruin. There is a sexually explicit Sheila na Gig, much weathered, on one wall.

Day tours from Oban in summer. Explanatory displays. Gift shop. Tearoom. WC. Picnic area. Car and coach parking at Fionnphort. £ (ferry). £ (admission).

Open all year: Apr-Sep, daily 9.30-18.30; Oct-Mar, daily 9.30-16.30; last ticket 30 mins before closing – ferry from Fionnphort (&), no cars on Iona. Walk to abbey.

J21 Isle of May

[Map: 6B, D11] Island in the Firth of Forth, 6.5 miles S of Fife Ness; boat leaves from The Harbour, Anstruther, Fife. (NGR: NT 655995 LR: 59)

The island is believed to have been where St Adrian was murdered by Vikings around 875, and became a place of pilgrimage: St Adrian's shrine and spring were visited by many folk. David I founded the priory in the 12th century, but little of it survives. In 1636 a lighthouse was built, the first in Scotland.

There are daily boat trips to the Isle of May nature reserve, and there are a large numbers of sea birds, as well as a colony of grey seals. The trip takes five hours, including three hours ashore and a cruise around the island. The boat carries 100 passengers.

Explanatory displays. Snack bar on board. Visitor centre and picnic area on Isle of May. WC. Well-marked paths. Car and coach parking at harbour. £££.

Open May-Sep: telephone for sailing times.

Tel: 01333 310103/01333 451152

J22 Jedburgh Abbey (HS)

[Map: 6B, F11] On A68, Jedburgh, Borders. (NGR: NT 650204 LR: 74)

The abbey, which was founded by David I about 1138 as an Augustinian establishment, is now ruinous, but much of the impressive Romanesque and early Gothic church survives, as do some remains of the domestic buildings. The Abbey was sacked numerous times by the English.

Visitor centre. Exhibition. Explanatory panels. Gift shop. Tearoom. Picnic area. Limited disabled access and WC. Parking. £.

Open all year: Apr-Sep, daily 9.30-18.30; Oct-Mar, Mon-Sat 9.30-16.30, Sun 14.00-16.30; last ticket 30 mins before closing; closed 25/26 Dec and 1/2 Jan.

Tel: 01835 863925

J23 Kelso Abbey (HS)

[Map: 6B, F11] Off A698, Kelso, Borders. (NGR: NT 729338 LR: 74)

This was one of the richest and largest monastic establishments in Scotland, yet it is much more ruinous than the other Border abbeys. It was originally founded as a Tironensian abbey of the Blessed Virgin and St John in 1113 at Selkirk, but was moved here in 1138. Much of the church and abbey were destroyed

by the English in 1544-5. The west transept was used as the parish church, and little else now remains.
Limited disabled access. Parking nearby.
Access at all reasonable times.

J24 Kilwinning Abbey (HS)

[Map: 6A, F6] Off A737, 3 miles N of Irvine, Kilwinning, Ayrshire. (NGR: NS 303433 LR: 63)

Not much remains of the abbey, which was a Tironensian establishment and dedicated to St Mary and St Wynnyn. St Wynnyn or Winning (and hence the name of the town), who was from Ireland, is said to have had a church here in 715, but the abbey was founded in 1162 by Hugh de Morville, Lord High Constable of Scotland. Kilwinning was a place of pilgrimage, and most of the surviving remains date from the 13th century. A church, built in 1774, stands on much of the site.
Parking.
Abbey ruins: access at all reasonable times; Abbey Church open by appt (tel: 01294 552929).

J25 Lesmahagow Priory

[Map: 6B, F8] Off M74, 4.5 miles SW of Lanark, Lesmahagow. (NGR: NS 814398 LR: 72)

Little remains of the priory, but the plan can be traced. The church was demolished in 1803, and replaced by the current building. St Maclou or Machute was a follower of St Brendan, and Lesmahagow is said to have had some of his relics. The priory was founded in 1144 by David I as a Tironensian priory, and four crosses marked the sanctuary for anyone 'in peril of life or limb'. There is a display in the chapter house of the church, and a bell dated 1625.
Explanatory displays. Sales area. Refreshments. Parking nearby.
Church: open by appt; excavated site: open at all reasonable times.
Tel: 01555 892425

J26 Melrose Abbey (HS)

[Map: 6B, F10] Off A7 or A68, in Melrose, Borders. (NGR: NT 550344 LR: 73)

An elegant and picturesque ruin, Melrose Abbey was founded as a Cistercian house by David I about 1136, and dedicated to the Blessed Virgin Mary. The church is particularly well preserved, while the domestic buildings and the cloister are very ruinous. The heart of Robert the Bruce is buried in the nave, and many of the powerful Douglas family are also interred here.
Visitor centre. Museum in former Commendator's House. Gift shop. Refreshments. WC. Disabled WC. Picnic area. Car and coach parking (£). Group concessions. £.
Open all year, daily 9.30-18.30; last ticket sold 18.00; closed 25/26 Dec and 1/2 Jan.
Tel: 01896 822562

J27 Oronsay Priory

[Map: 5A, D2] Off unlisted road, W side of Oronsay. (NGR: NR 349889 LR: 61)

Founded in the 14th century by John, Lord of the Isles, this was a house of Augustinian canons. Substantial parts of the church, cloister and domestic buildings survive. The Oronsay Cross is a fine late-medieval carved cross. On one side is the figure of Christ being crucified, a pattern of foliage on both sides, as well as: 'this is the cross of Colinus, son of Cristinus MacDuffie'. More than 30 fine carved grave slabs are in the Prior's House.
Open all year – on tidal island: access by foot or post-bus is regulated by tides.

J28 Paisley Abbey

[Map: 6A, E6] Off A726 or A737, Paisley, Renfrewshire. (NGR: NS 486640 LR: 64)

Founded in 1163 by Walter, son of Alan, Steward of Scotland, a Cluniac Priory replaced an earlier Christian establishment, and was dedicated to St Mirren. The priory was elevated to an abbey in 1219, but the present church dates mostly from the 14th century, although it was rebuilt and restored in the 20th century. The church houses the stone effigy of Marjorie, daughter of Robert the Bruce; and the tomb of Robert III. The striking Barochan Cross, dating from as early as the 8th century, is also housed here. The abbey is now used as the parish church.
Refreshments. Sales area. WC. Limited disabled access. Parking nearby.
Open all year: Mon-Sat 10.00-15.30.
Tel: 0141 889 7654   Fax: 0141 887 3929

J29 Pluscarden Abbey

[Map: 4, E3] Off B9010, 6 miles SW of Elgin, Pluscarden, Moray. (NGR: NJ 142576 LR: 28)

Originally founded by Alexander II in 1230, the abbey was one of only three Valliscaulian priories in Scotland, and was dedicated to St Mary, St John the Baptist, and St Andrew. In 1390 it may have been torched by Alexander Stewart, the Wolf of Badenoch, along with **Elgin Cathedral [K17]**. In 1454 it became a Benedictine house, but the church and domestic buildings became ruinous after the Reformation. The abbey was refounded, and almost completely rebuilt, in 1948 as a Benedictine monastery, and there are now about 30 monks, priests and novices. Retreat facilities are available for men and women.
Guided tours by arrangement. Gift shop. WC. Disabled facilities. Parking nearby. Retreats (accommodation available).
Open all year – short walk: daily 4.45-20.30; shop 8.30-17.00.
Tel: 01343 890257   Web: monks@pluscardenabbey.org
Fax: 01343 890258   Email: www.pluscardenabbey.org

J30 Restenneth Priory (HS)

[Map: 4, 14] Off B9113, 1.5 miles NE of Forfar, Angus. (NGR: NO 482516 LR: 54)

The ruins of an Augustinian priory consist of the chancel and tower of the priory church with some remains of the other buildings and cloister. The tower may date from the 8th century, and this is said to be where St Boniface baptised Nechtan, King of Picts. The priory, dedicated to St Peter, was established about 1153 by Malcolm IV. The church was used by the parish until 1590, and then as a burial place for the Dempster and Hunter families.

Parking.
Access at all reasonable times.

J31 Saddell Abbey

[Map: 5A, F4] On B842, 6 miles N of Campbeltown, Saddell, Argyll. (NGR: NR 785321 LR: 68)

Not much remains of a small abbey except scant ruins of part of the church and cloister. There are 11 medieval grave slabs, including three men in armour, a priest and a (now) headless monk, protected in a modern building. There is also a reconstructed 15th-century standing cross. The abbey was built by Somerled Lord of the Isles, or Reginald his son, around 1160. It was Cistercian establishment, and was dedicated to the Blessed Virgin Mary.

Parking.
Access at all reasonable times.

G10 St Columba Centre, Fionnphort (HS)

The centre features an exhibition about the Celtic church, Iona and St Columba, the 6th-century saint, who founded a monastery on **Iona [J20]**.

See main entry G10

J32 Sweetheart Abbey (HS)

[Map: 6B, 18] On A710, 6 miles S of Dumfries, New Abbey, Dumfries and Galloway. (NGR: NX 964663 LR: 84)

The fine picturesque ruins of a Cistercian abbey, dedicated to the Blessed Virgin Mary, the church of which is well preserved. Much of the massive precinct wall survives, enclosing an area of some 30 acres. The abbey was founded in 1273 by Devorgilla of Galloway in memory of her husband, John Balliol – they are both buried here. She kept the embalmed heart of Balliol in a casket after his death in 1268, and was the mother of John Balliol, King of Scots. Her headless effigy survives within the abbey. **New Abbey Corn Mill [V59]** and **Shambellie House [Y14]** are nearby.

Sales area. Disabled access. Joint entry ticket with New Abbey Corn Mill. Parking. £. Combined ticket with New Abbey Corn Mill

available (££).

Open Apr-Sep, daily 9.30-18.30; Oct-Mar, Mon-Wed and Sat 9.30-16.30, Thu 9.30-12.00, Sun 14.00-16.30, Fri closed; last entry 30 mins before closing; closed 25/26 Dec and 1/2 Jan.
Tel: 01387 850397

K135 Temple Preceptory

See main entry K135

K136 Torphichen Preceptory (HS)

A rather unusual and eerie place, the preceptory has been reduced to the crossing and transepts of the church, and traces of other buildings. It dates from the 12th century, and the parish church was built on the nave. This was the main seat of the Knights Hospitallers from the 12th century. William Wallace held a convention of barons here in 1298.

See main entry K136

J33 Whithorn Priory (HS)

[Map: 6A, 16] On A746, Whithorn, Dumfries and Galloway. Joint ticket with Whithorn Priory and Museum. (NGR: NX 444403 LR: 83)

The site of the 5th-century Christian community of St Ninian, who built a stone church here known as 'Candida Casa'. Whithorn was a Northumbrian bishopric but is last mentioned in 803. Later it became a popular place of pilgrimage. The arm bone of St Ninian was taken to the Scottish seminary at Douai, where it was kept until the French Revolution.

The existing ruins are of a 12th-century Premonstratensian priory and cathedral: the nave of the Romanesque church survives although it is unroofed. The vaulted chambers under the former nave also survive, and probably housed the shrine and relics of St Ninian.

A fine collection of early Christian sculpture is housed in the nearby museum, including the 'Latinus Stone', the earliest Christian memorial in Scotland; the 'St Peter's Stone'; and the 10th-century Monreith Cross. Also see **Whithorn: Cradle of Christianity in Scotland [J34]**.

Explanatory boards. Disabled access. Parking nearby. £ (priory, priory museum and archaeological dig).
Open Easter-Oct, daily 10.30-17.00 – tel to confirm.
Tel: 01988 500508

J34 Whithorn: Cradle of Christianity in Scotland

[Map: 6A, 16] Off A75, 45-47 George Street, Whithorn, Dumfries and Galloway. (NGR: NX 443403 LR: 83)

The discovery centre features guided tours of the excavations near the church of an abandoned town, the priory itself, the museum and crypts. The discovery centre features an audio-visual presentation, exhibition and an archaeology puzzle. St Ninian founded a church at Whithorn in the 5th century. Also see **Whithorn Priory [J33]**.

Explanatory displays. Gift shop. Picnic area. WC. Disabled access. Car and coach parking. Group concessions. Joint ticket with Whithorn Priory and Museum.
Open Apr-Oct, daily 10.30-17.00.
Tel: 01988 500508   Fax: 01988 500700

Top right
Beauly Priory
Right
Kelso Abbey
Left
Saddell Abbey
Bottom
Iona Abbey

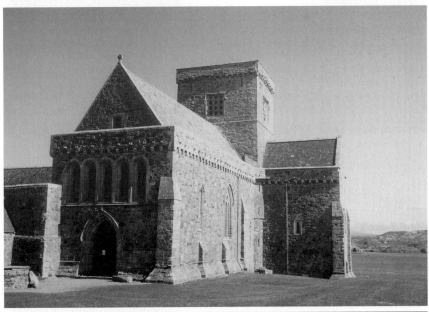

Above *Pluscarden Abbey*
Left *Dryburgh Abbey*
Bottom left *Jedburgh Abbey*
Below *Holyrood Abbey*

K1: Cathedrals and Larger Churches

Cathedrals were originally the seats of bishops, and many were and are very impressive buildings, while others are now ruinous.

K1 Biggar Kirk

[Map: 6B, F9] Off A72 or A702, Manse, High Street, Biggar, Lanarkshire. (NGR: NT 042378 LR: 72)

The impressive 16th-century church, dedicated to St Mary, has a crenellated tower and is still used as a parish church. The kirk was a collegiate establishment, founded by Malcolm Lord Fleming in 1545, although it probably incorporates older work. The tower has gunloops for muskets. It was restored in the 1870s and again in the 1930s, and there are good examples of modern stained glass. **Moat Park Heritage Centre [Y131]** is nearby

Explanatory displays. Sales area. Induction loop for church services. Car parking.

Open during summer months, daily 9.00-1700; other times key from Moat Park Heritage Centre.

Tel: 01899 211050

K2 Bothwell Parish Church

[Map: 6B, E7] Off A725, 2 miles N of Hamilton, Main Street, Bothwell, Lanarkshire. (NGR: NS 705586 LR: 64)

Occupying the site of a 6th-century church, the present building has a medieval choir, although the tower and nave date from 1833. The church was a collegiate establishment, and was founded by Archibald the Grim, 3rd Earl of Douglas, in 1398. It was dedicated to St Bride. The church houses 17th- and 18th-century monuments, fine stained glass, 'The Bothwell Embroideries', and there is an interesting burial ground.

Guided tours available 10.30-16.00. Sales area. WC. Disabled access. Parking nearby.

Open Easter-Sep, daily.

Tel: 01698 853189 Fax: 01698 853229 Email: bothwell@presbyteryofhamilton.co.uk

K3 Brechin Cathedral

[Map: 4, 14] Off A90, Brechin, Angus. (NGR: NO 596601 LR: 44)

A fine atmospheric building, which is still used as a parish church, with splendid modern stained-glass windows. There is a fine Pictish cross-slab, and other fragments, including the 9th-century St Mary's Stone.

Adjacent to the church is an unusual 11th-century round tower, which was probably used to store precious relics. Only two of these towers survive in Scotland, the other being at **Abernethy [K43]**. There are some interesting markers in the burial ground.

Parking nearby. Sales area.

Open all year, daily 9.00-17.00.

Tel: 01356 629360

K4 Cathedral of St Moluag and Parish Church, Lismore

[Map: 5A, B4] Off B8045, 1.5 miles N of Achnacroish, Lismore. (NGR: NM 860434 LR: 49)

The church, much reduced in size and now the parish church, was once used as the Cathedral of Argyll and the Isles. Only the 14th-century choir of the original building still stands, although foundations remain of the nave and tower – the original building was 125 feet long. The church was dedicated to St Moluag, who died in 592 at Rosemarkie, but it is said that his relics were brought back here: his crozier is still kept on the island at Bachuil. Several carved slabs, dating from medieval times, survive in the burial ground. There is a traditional baptismal font, as well as an exhibition on 800 years of Christianity on Lismore.

Parking nearby. Donations welcome.

Access at all reasonable times.

K5 Cathedral of the Isles, Millport

[Map: 6A, E5] Off A860, College Street, Millport, Great Cumbrae. (NGR: NS 166553 LR: 63)

Britain's smallest cathedral, dating from 1851 and designed by William Butterfield. The cathedral has fine stained glass, and there is a collection of carved stones from Mid Kirkton.

Parking. Sales area. Picnic area. WC. Retreat House: accommodation available.

Open all year, daily.

Tel: 01475 530353 Web: www.scotland.anglican.org/retreats
Fax: 01475 530204 Email: tccumbrae@argyll.anglican.org

K6 Church of the Holy Rude

[Map: 5B, D8] Off A9, St John Street (near Stirling Castle), Stirling. (NGR: NS 793937 LR: 57)

This fine church, built in the 16th and 17th centuries, was used for the Coronation of James VI in 1567, at which John Knox preached. Other Scottish Kings and Queen worshipped here, including Mary, Queen of Scots. The church has a medieval nave, and the choir and apse were added in 1555. Still used as a parish church, the building has a magnificent pipe organ, fine stained glass windows, and a historic churchyard.

Explanatory displays. Sales area. WC. Disabled access. Car parking.

Open May-Sep, Mon-Sat 10.00-17.00.

Tel: 01786 471848 Fax: 01786 471088 Email: tfgmacdoug@aol.com

K7 Corstorphine Old Parish Church

[Map: 6B, E9] Off A8, Kirk Loan, Corstorphine, Edinburgh. (NGR: NT 201728 LR: 66)

Dating from the 14th century, the Old Parish Church has a stone-slabbed roof and a 15th-century tower, and was used as a collegiate church. Tombs within the church include that of the founder of the collegiate church: Sir Adam Forrester, Lord Provost of Edinburgh (who died in 1405), and Sir John Forrester, Lord Chamberlain in the reign of James I. The collegiate establishment was dedicated to St John the Baptist. There is an interesting burial ground, although nothing survives of the nearby castle. **Corstorphine Doocot [V24]** (off Saughton Road North) is close by.

Sales area. Limited disabled access. Parking nearby.
Open Feb-Nov, Wed 10.30-12.00.

K8 Crail Parish Church

[Map: 6B, C11] On A917, Marketgate, Crail, Fife. (NGR: NO 614080 LR: 59)

Built in 1243, this large aisled church was altered in 1517, when it was raised to collegiate status by William Myrton. Dedicated to St Maelrubha or St Mary, the church was further altered in later centuries. Standing in the south entrance to the church is a very worn Class 3 Pictish stone. It shows a man holding a tall cross and other scenes. A coat-of-arms has been added at a later date at the bottom of the shaft. There is an interesting burial ground.

Sales area. WC. Disabled access. Parking nearby.
Open Jun-mid Sep, 14.00-16.00.

K9 Cramond Kirk

[Map: 6B, D9] Off A90, Cramond Glebe Road, Cramond, Edinburgh. (NGR: NT 190709 LR: 66)

Set in the picturesque village of Cramond, the tower of the church dates from the 15th century, although most of the rest of the cruciform kirk was built in 1656 and altered in following centuries. There is a fine roof and interesting burial ground – the remains of the Roman fort are behind the kirk.

WC. Disabled access. Parking nearby.
Open during Edinburgh Festival, daily 14.00-17.00; services Sun 9.30 and 1100.
Tel: 0131 336 2036 Web: www.cramondkirk.org.uk
Fax: 0131 336 2036 Email: cramond.kirk@cwcom.net

K10 Crichton Collegiate Church

[Map: 6B, E10] Off B6367, 2 miles E of Gorebridge, Crichton, Midlothian. (NGR: NT 381616 LR: 66)

A substantial impressive collegiate church with a square tower, dedicated to St Mary and St Kentigern and dating from 1449. There are fine pointed barrel vaults, but it would appear the nave was never built. The collegiate establishment was founded by William Crichton, Lord Chancellor of Scotland, who also built the magnificent **Crichton Castle [N78]**, a short walk away.

WC. Disabled access. Parking.
Open May-Sep, Sun afternoons or by appt.
Tel: 01875 320364 Fax: 01875 320508

K11 Cullen Collegiate Church

[Map: 4, E4] Off A98, 0.75 miles SW of Cullen town centre, Aberdeenshire. (NGR: NJ 507663 LR: 29)

A fine well-preserved collegiate church, founded in 1543 by Alexander Ogilvie, and dedicated to St Mary. Still used as a parish church, the building is cruciform in plan: the nave dates from the 13th century, the south transept from 1536, and the north transept from the 18th century. The church houses a 16th-century carved grave slab and a stone effigy of Alexander Ogilvie of Deskford, who died in 1554. The 'interior parts' of Elizabeth de Burgh, wife of Robert the Bruce, are said to be buried here, and Robert founded a chaplaincy in 1327.

Parking.
Open summer, Tue and Thu 14.00-16.00, or by appt.
Tel: 01542 841851

K12 Dornoch Cathedral

[Map: 3B, D10] Off A949, Castle Street, Dornoch, Sutherland, Highland. (NGR: NH 797896 LR: 21)

Although restored in the 19th century, much of the 13th-century cruciform-plan cathedral survives, including the chancel and crossing piers. There may have been a monastery here, founded by St Finnbarr in the 7th century, but the cathedral was first built in 1224 by Gilbert de Moravia, Bishop of Caithness. The nave was destroyed by fire in 1570 after being torched, and the transepts and choir were not reroofed until 1616. The nave was rebuilt and the rest of the building restored in the 19th century. The former Bishop's Palace is now the Dornoch Castle Hotel.

Explanatory boards. Gift shop (summer only). WC. Disabled access. Car and coach parking.
Open all year, 9.00-dusk; gift shop summer, Mon-Fri 10.00-16.00.
Tel: 01862 810357/296

K13 Dunblane Cathedral (HS)

[Map: 5B, D8] Off B8033, 5.5 miles N of Stirling, Dunblane, Stirlingshire. (NGR: NN 782015 LR: 57)

In the picturesque town by the banks of the Allen River is the fine cathedral, which is dedicated to St Blane and still used as a parish church. The cathedral dates substantially from the 13th century, except for the bell-tower which is probably 11th century. There is fine carving within the church, medieval stalls, and a 9th-century ringed cross-slab with two serpent heads. On the back are several more carvings with animals, figures and a disc and cross. There is a second carved stone.

Sales area. WC. Disabled access. Parking nearby.
Open all year.
Tel: 01786 823338

K14 Dunblane Cathedral Museum

[Map: 5B, D8] Off B8033, 5.5 miles N of Stirling, The Cross, Dunblane, Stirlingshire. (NGR: NN 782015 LR: 57)

The museum is housed in barrel-vaulted chambers dating from the 17th century, and displays include paintings, artefacts and books that chart the history of the nearby Cathedral from St Blane in the 6th century through to the restoration of 1893. There is also a large collection of communion tokens.

Explanatory displays and video. Gift shop. WC. Disabled access. Limited car and coach parking.
Open May-Oct, Mon-Sat 10.30-13.00 and 14.00-16.30.
Tel: 01786 823440

K15 Dunglass Collegiate Church (HS)

[Map: 6B, D11] Off A1, 6.5 miles SE of Dunbar, Dunglass, Berwickshire, Borders. (NGR: NT 766718 LR: 67)

The fine ruined cruciform church of St Mary, was founded about 1450 as a college of canons by Sir Alexander Home. It has a stone vaulted ceiling, central tower, and stone-slabbed roof. The church was held against English raiders in 1544, but by the 18th century was being used as a barn.

Parking nearby.
Access at all reasonable times.

K16 Dunkeld Cathedral (HS)

[Map: 5B, B9] Off A9, Dunkeld, Perthshire. (NGR: NO 025426 LR: 52)

Standing in the picturesque village of Dunkeld on the banks of the Tay is the imposing cathedral: the 14th-century choir is still used as the parish church, while the nave is now ruinous.

Alexander Stewart, the 'Wolf of Badenoch', is buried here and has a splendid tomb with a stone effigy; and the 15th-century chapter house has a small museum. In the cathedral is a large Class 3 Pictish carved stone, badly weathered but with biblical scenes. Relics of St Columba were brought to Dunkeld after **Iona [J20]** was abandoned in the 9th century, and it became a major religious centre.

To the east of Dunkeld is Birnam, from where – in Shakespeare's play 'Macbeth' – the wood is said to have travelled the 12 miles to **Dunsinane Hill [D40]**.

Explanatory displays. Cathedral shop. Picnic area. Disabled access. WC and Parking nearby. Donations welcome.
Ruined nave and tower open all year; choir used as parish church: open Apr-Sep, Mon-Sat 9.00-18.30, Sun 14.00-18.30; Oct-Mar, Mon-Sat 9.30-16.00, Sun 14.00-16.00; closed New Year's Day.
Tel: 01350 727688   Fax: 01350 727688

K17 Elgin Cathedral (HS)

[Map: 4, E3] Off A96, North College Street, Elgin. (NGR: NJ 222632 LR: 28)

Once one of the most impressive churches in Scotland, Elgin Cathedral is now a substantial and picturesque ruin. The cathedral was founded in 1224 as the seat of the Bishops of Moray, after they removed from Spynie. It was torched by the 'Wolf of Badenoch' in 1390. There is a fine octagonal roofed chapter house, as well as a large stone effigy of a bishop and an impressive Class 2 Pictish cross-slab, with a decorated cross and other carvings. Table tombs survive in the interesting graveyard. The Bishop's Palace at **Spynie [N145]** is also open to the public.

Explanatory displays. Gift shop. Disabled access. Parking nearby. £. Joint entry ticket for Spynie Palace available (£).
Open all year: Apr-Sep, daily 9.30-18.30; Oct-Mar, Mon-Wed and Sat 9.30-16.30, Thu 9.30-12.00, Sun 14.00-16.30, closed Fri; last ticket 30 mins before closing; closed 25/26 Dec and 1/2 Jan.
Tel: 01343 547171

K18 Fortrose Cathedral (HS)

[Map: 3B, E9] On A832, 6 miles NE of Inverness, Fortrose, Highland. (NGR: NH 727565 LR: 27)

Only the south aisle and the north choir range, housing the chapter house and sacristy, survive from the medieval cathedral church of Ross, but the plan of the buildings are laid out in the grass. Within the aisles are three arched tombs: Euphemia, Countess of Ross, who was forced to marry Alexander Stewart, the 'Wolf of Badenoch'; Bishop Cairncross, who died in 1545; and Bishop Fraser, who died in 1507.

Parking.
Keys available locally at reasonable times.

K19 Glasgow Cathedral (HS)

[Map: 6B, E7] Off A8, Castle Street, centre of Glasgow. (NGR: NS 602655 LR: 64)

Dedicated to St Mungo, Glasgow's patron saint, the present cruciform church with a central tower is the only medieval cathedral on mainland Scotland to survive the Reformation more or less intact. Bishop Blackadder started the incomplete Blackadder Aisle on the south side of the church in the 15th century, and the west end of the church was flanked by two towers, which were demolished in 1846. The building has a fine crypt, a 15th-century stone screen, and a collection of carved stones. St Mungo was active among the Britons of Strathclyde and founded a church here in 573. Glasgow is also associated with St Enoch or Thenew, Mungo's mother, and was a major centre of pilgrimage in medieval times.

Gift shop. Parking nearby.
Open all year: Apr-Sep, Mon-Sat 9.30-18.30, Sun 12.00-18.30; Oct-Mar Mon-Sat 9.30-16.30, Sun 14.00-16.30; closed 25/26 Dec & 1-2 Jan.
Tel: 0141 552 6891

K20 Kirk of St Nicholas

[Map: 4, G5] Off A956, Back Wynd off Union Street, Aberdeen. (NGR: NJ 940062 LR: 38)

There has been a church here from early times, and the crossing and transepts may date from the 12th century. The church was divided into two after the Reformation, then largely rebuilt. The congregations were united in 1980. St Mary's Chapel, in the crypt, dates from the 15th-century church, and Sir John Gordon, executed after the Battle of Corrichie in 1562, is interred here. There is also fine 17th-century embroidery. The adjoining burial ground has many table-tombs and memorials, dating from as early as the 17th century.

Guided tours. Explanatory displays. WC. Disabled access and bearing induction loop for the deaf. Car parking nearby.
Open May-Sep, Mon-Fri 12.00-16.00, Sat 13.00-15.00, except closed local holidays; other times by appt.
Tel: 01224 643494

K21 Ladykirk

[Map: 6B, E12] Off B6470, 5.5 miles NE of Coldstream, Ladykirk, Borders. (NGR: NT 889477 LR: 74)

The substantial vaulted church, cruciform in plan and with a small tower at one end, was built by James IV around 1500, and is only about 300 yards from the English border. The church was vaulted in stone so that it could withstand fire. The church is dedicated to Our Lady, who James IV believed had saved him from drowning (although not, as it turned out, death in battle).

Car parking.
Access at all reasonable times.

K22 Lincluden Collegiate Church (HS)

[Map: 6B, H8] Off A76, 1.25 miles N of Dumfries, Lincluden, Dumfries and Galloway. (NGR: NX 967779 LR: 84)

A nunnery here was founded by Uchtred, son of Fergus, Lord of Galloway, but was converted to a collegiate establishment in 1389 by Archibald the Grim, 3rd Earl of Douglas, as he considered it had fallen into a state of disrepute, disgrace and disrepair. There

is a fine stone effigy in a recessed tomb of Margaret, daughter of Robert III. Much of the chancel and south transept survive, as does the north range.

Disabled access. Parking nearby.
Access at all reasonable times.

K23 Parish Church of St Cuthbert, Edinburgh

[Map: 6B, E9] W end of Princes Street, 5 Lothian Road, Edinburgh. (NGR: NT 247735 LR: 66)

It is said that St Cuthbert built a church here in the 7th century, and the present building is the seventh on the site. It was begun in 1894 although it incorporates a tower of 1790, and features stained glass, Renaissance-type stalls, and a marble communion table. Many well-known people are buried in the kirkyard.

Explanatory displays. Burial ground. Cafe nearby. Gift shop nearby. WC. Disabled access. Parking nearby.
Open May-Sep, Mon-Sat 10.00-16.00, Sun for worship.
Tel: 0131 229 1142

K24 Rosslyn Chapel, Roslin

[Map: 6B, E10] Off A701, 6 miles S of Edinburgh, Roslin, Midlothian. (NGR: NT 275630 LR: 66)

Overlooking the River Esk, Rosslyn Chapel, dedicated to St Matthew and intended to be a Collegiate Church, was founded by William Sinclair, Earl of Caithness and Orkney, in 1446. It was never completed: only the choir and parts of the transepts were built. The chapel is richly carved with Biblical stories, and has the largest number of 'Green Men' found in any medieval building. In the burial vault are interred ten of the Sinclairs of Rosslyn and their kin, said to be laid out in their armour without coffins. The chapel is also home to the famous Apprentice Pillar with magnificent carving and ornament.

Guided tours available. Explanatory displays. Gift shop. Tearoom. WC. Disabled access. Car and coach parking. £.
Open all year, Mon-Sat 10.00-17.00, Sun 12.00-16.45.
Tel: 0131 440 2159 Fax: 0131 440 1979
Web: www.rosslyn-chapel.com Email: rosslynch@aol.com

K25 Seton Collegiate Church (HS)

[Map: 6B, D10] On A198, 5.5 miles W of Haddington, Seton, East Lothian. (NGR: NT 418751 LR: 66)

A fine collegiate church, founded in 1492 by the 4th Lord Seton. The roof is vaulted, and transepts were added in the 16th century, as was a square, rib-vaulted tower. There are several stone tombs within the church, and the remains of other buildings nearby.

Explanatory displays. Sales area. Car and coach parking. £.
Open Apr-Sep, daily 9.00-18.30, last ticket 18.00.
Tel: 01875 813334

K26 St Andrews Cathedral (HS)

[Map: 6B, C10] Off A91, St Andrews, Fife. (NGR: NO 516166 LR: 59)
The very ruinous remains of formerly the largest cathedral in Scotland. The adjoining Augustinian priory was founded in 1144 by Robert, Bishop of St Andrews, but not much remains. The priory wall is well preserved. St Regulus, or Rule, is said to have founded a monastery here in the 6th century. The relics of St Andrew were brought here, and the Bishopric was transferred from **Abernethy [K43]** in 908. The church of the time – the tower of which, St Rule's Tower, still survives and dates from as early as 1070 – was too small so a large new cathedral was begun and completed in 1380. St Andrews was a major pilgrimage site in medieval times. After the Reformation, the buildings fell into disuse and were demolished. The museum houses a large and magnificent collection of Christian and early medieval sculpture, including the magnificent St Andrews Sarcophagus. St Rule's Tower is open to the public – magnificent views from the top. **St Andrews Castle [N146]**, the bishops' place, is nearby.
Visitor centre with fine collection of Christian and early medieval sculpture, including cross-slabs, effigies, and other relics. Explanatory boards. Gift shop. Car parking nearby. Group concessions. £. Combined ticket for cathedral & castle is available (££).
[Museum and St Rule's Tower] Open all year: Apr-Sep, daily 9.30-18.30; Oct-Mar, daily 9.30-16.30; last ticket sold 30 mins before closing; closed 25/26 Dec and 1/2 Jan.
Tel: 01334 472563

K27 St Andrews Cathedral, Inverness

[Map: 3B, F9] Off A82, Ardross Street, W bank of River Ness, Inverness, Highlands. (NGR: NH 665449 LR: 26)
Standing in a pleasant setting on the bank of the River Ness, the cathedral was built in 1886-9 in the Gothic style by the architect Alexander Ross. The twin-towered church has an octagonal chapter house, pillars of granite, stained glass, sculpture and a fine font.
Explanatory displays. Gift shop. Tearoom. WC. Parking nearby.
Cathedral open daily, 8.30-18.00 (later in summer); tearoom open May-Sep, 10.30-15.30.
Tel: 01463 233535

K28 St Clement's Church (HS)

[Map: 3A, D3] On A859, 2.5 miles SE of Leverburgh, Rodel, S of Harris. (NGR: NG 047833 LR: 18)
The fine 16th-century cruciform church has a strong square tower at one end. The church was dedicated to St Clement, a Bishop of Dunblane in the 13th century. In the church is the splendid carved tomb of Alasdair Crotach MacLeod, who built the 'Fairy Tower' of **Dunvegan Castle [N24]**. There is another tomb, as well as several carved grave slabs, and a disc-headed cross. There is also a Sheila na Gig on the outside of the south wall of the tower, which is quite interesting.
Parking nearby.
Access at all reasonable times.

K29 St Duthac's Church, Tain

[Map: 3B, D9] On B9174, High Street, Tain, Ross-shire. (NGR: NH 780821 LR: 21)
A well-preserved medieval church, dating from the 14th and 15th centuries and dedicated to St Duthac or Duthus, a saint said to have been born in Tain about 1000. Duthac died in Ireland about 1065, but his bones were returned to Tain. Thousands of pilgrims visited his shrine, including James IV and James V who walked here barefoot. The church has large windows with restored tracery. A statue on the outside of the west wall is thought to be that of St Duthac, which unusually survived the Reformation. The church became a collegiate establishment in 1487, founded by Thomas Hay, Bishop of Ross – who used the choir of the building, while the townsfolk used the nave. There is a nearby visitor centre **Tain Through Time [Y189]** associated with the story of St Duthac and Tain. Also see **Duthac's Chapel, Tain [K106]**.
Visitor centre (£). Parking nearby.
Open all year.

K30 St Giles Cathedral

[Map: 6B, E9] Off A1, High Street (Royal Mile), Edinburgh. (NGR: NT 257735 LR: 66)
Although there has been a church here since 854 or earlier, the present building dates substantially from the 14th and 15th century. It has an unusual crown steeple, added in 1495. There are several aisles which house separate chapels and numerous memorials, including to the Marquis of Montrose and Earl of Argyll, Robert Louis Stevenson and Robert Burns. There is also fine stained glass, a magnificent organ and the Thistle Chapel, designed by Sir Robert Lorimer.
Explanatory displays. Guides on duty at all times. Gift shop. Restaurant. WC. Limited disabled access. Parking nearby (but often difficult).
Open all year: Easter-mid Sep, Mon-Fri 9.00-19.00, Sat 9.00-17.00, Sun 13.00-17.00; mid-Sep-Easter, Mon-Sat 9.00-17.00, Sun 13.00-17.00.
Tel: 0131 225 9442 Fax: 0131 225 9576
Web: www.stgiles.net Email: stgiles@hotmail.com

K31 St John's Kirk, Perth

[Map: 5B, C9] Off A912, St John Street, centre of Perth. (NGR: NO 121233 LR: 58)
The church, parts of which may date from the 12th century, was consecrated in 1242 and dedicated to St

John the Baptist. It was probably built on the site of a much older building, and was largely rebuilt in the 15th century, then restored in the 1920s. It was here that John Knox preached against idolatry in 1559, and his congregation then 'purged' the church, which then had many altars. They went on to sack the houses of the Blackfriars, Greyfriars and Charterhouse monks in the town, as well as nearby monastic houses such as **Scone [S41]** and **Coupar Angus [J7]**.

Guided tours by arrangement. Disabled access. Induction loop. Parking nearby.
Open Easter-Sep, Mon-Sat 10.00-16.00, Sun 12.00-14.00; Oct-Apr tel to confirm.
Tel: 01738 626520

K32 St Machar's Cathedral

[Map: 4, G5] Off A956, The Chanonry, Old Aberdeen, N of Aberdeen. (NGR: NJ 939088 LR: 38)

There was a Christian community here from 580, and it became the cathedral of the bishops of Aberdeen in 1140.

St Machar is the patron saint of Aberdeen, and was a follower of St Columba. He is believed to have been Bishop of Tours, and died in France. The present building dates mostly from 1350-1520, and replaced an earlier church on the site. The nave and twin towers remain in use, while the transepts are ruinous – the central tower collapsed in 1688.

There is an impressive heraldic ceiling of panelled oak dating from 1520, which is decorated with the coats of arms of many noble families; and impressive stained-glass windows. A collection of medieval charters is housed in the Charter Room. There are several interesting tombs as well as the burial ground.

Guided tours by arrangement. Gift shop. WC. Disabled access and induction loop. Coach parking.
Open all year, daily 9.00-17.00 (except because of weddings, funerals and unscheduled special events).
Tel: 01224 485988

K33 St Magnus Cathedral

[Map: 2, C3] Town centre, Broad Street, Kirkwall, Orkney. (NGR: HY 449112 LR: 6)

Founded in 1137, the cathedral is one of the finest churches in Scotland. It dates substantially from 1137-1200, was founded by Earl Rognvald Kolson, and completed about 1500. It is dedicated to St Magnus the Martyr, grandson to Thorfinn the Mighty, whose bones are interred within the church in the massive east choir pillar. The cathedral survived the Reformation, and there are fine stained-glass windows. There is also an interesting burial ground.

Explanatory displays. Disabled access to half of the building. Car

and coach parking nearby.
Open Apr-Sep, Mon-Sat 9.00-18.00, Sun 14.00-18.00; Oct-Mar, Mon-Sat 9.00-13.00 and 14.00-17.00.
Tel: 01856 874894   Web: www.orkneyheritage.com
Fax: 01856 875846   Email: steve.callaghan@orkney.gov.uk

Y179 St Magnus Centre

The centre features a multilingual video, lasting for 15 minutes, on the nearby **St Magnus Cathedral [K33]**.
See main entry Y179

K34 St Mary's Cathedral, Glasgow

[Map: 6B, E7] Off A82 from M8, 300 Great Western Road, Glasgow. (NGR: NS 578669 LR: 64)

The fine Gothic Revival church was designed by Sir George Gilbert Scott, and there are contemporary murals by Gwyneth Leech.

Bookshop. Partial disabled access. Limited parking.
Open all year, daily Mon-Fri 9.30-17.45, Sat 9.30-12.00; tel for services; bookshop Mon-Fri, 10.00-16.00.
Tel: 0141 339 6691   Fax: 0141 339 6691

K35 St Mary's Church, Haddington

[Map: 6B, E10] Off A6093, Sidegate, Haddington, East Lothian. (NGR: NT 518736 LR: 66)

In a pleasant and peaceful location beside the River Tyne, St Mary's is a substantial cross-shaped church with an aisled nave and choir, which dates from the 14th century. It was partially destroyed in the 16th century, but fully restored in the 1970s. There are interesting medieval carvings, including 'Green Men' and a scallop shell.

It houses a marble monument to John Maitland, Chancellor of Scotland, of **Thirlestane Castle [N47]**, who died in 1595, his wife and son, now known as 'The Chapel of the Three Kings'. Beneath is the Lauderdale family vault.

Guided tours available. Explanatory displays. Printed guides in several languages. Gift and book shop. Tearoom. WC. Picnic area by river. Children's activity area. Brass rubbing by arrangement. Disabled access. Car and coach access.
Open Apr-Sep, Mon-Sat 11.00-16.00, Sun 14.00-16.30.
Tel: 01620 823109   Web: www.kylemore.btinternet.co.uk/stmarys.htm   Email: chrystals@btinternet.com

K36 St Mary's Episcopal Cathedral, Edinburgh

[Map: 6B, E9] 0.5 miles W of city centre, Palmerston Place, Edinburgh. (NGR: NT 241735 LR: 66)

The Gothic Episcopal Cathedral was built in 1879, while the western towers were added in 1917. The central spire is 276 feet high, and the church has an impressive interior.

Explanatory displays. Gift stall. Creche. WC. Disabled access, WCs and induction loop. Parking nearby.

Open all year, Mon-Fri 7.30-18.00, Sat-Sun 7.30-17.00
Tel: 0131 225 6293 Fax: 0131 225 3181
Web: www.cathedral.net Email: office@cathedral.net

K37 St Mary's Parish Church, Whitekirk

[Map: 6B, D11] On A198, 3.5 miles SE of North Berwick, Whitekirk, East Lothian. (NGR: NT 596815 LR: 67)

Dating from the 12th century with a 16th-century tower, the fine cruciform church stands in an interesting burial ground. It was burned in 1914 by suffragettes, but was restored. Whitekirk was a place of pilgrimage from around 1295 after Agnes, Countess of Dunbar, was healed at a nearby well [NT 598817?]. The number of miracles which occurred at the well was so great that a shrine was built in 1309 and dedicated to St Mary. It was visited by Aeneas Sylvius Piccolomini (later Pope Pious II) in 1435 who, after being saved from a storm, walked barefoot to Whitekirk from Dunbar. A fresco in the chapter house of Siena Cathedral records his visit. This well apparently dried up around 1830, and its location is not certain.

Sales area. WC. Parking nearby.

Church: open at all reasonable times.
Tel: 01620 880378

K38 St Michael's Parish Church, Linlithgow

[Map: 6B, D8] Off M9, Kirkgate, Linlithgow, West Lothian. (NGR: NT 003773 LR: 65)

Founded in 1242 on the site of an earlier church, St Michael's dates mostly from the 15th century, although it now has a modern steeple. It has associations with the Stewart monarchs, particularly James IV and V. There are interesting 15th-century relief slabs in the vestry. Nearby [NT 004771] is St Michael's Well, housed in a stone building, with a rough stone depicting the saint and 'St Michael is Kinde to Strangers'. By **Linlithgow Palace [N119]**.

Guided tours by arrangement. Explanatory displays. Gift shop. Picnic area. Car and coach parking.

Open May-Sep, daily 10.00-16.30; Oct-Apr, Mon-Fri 10.00-15.00.
Tel: 01506 842188 Web: www.stmichaels-parish.org.uk Email: stmichael@connectfree.co.uk

K39 St Monans Parish Church

[Map: 6B, D10] Off A917, 2.5 miles W of Anstruther, St Monans, Fife. (NGR: NO 523014 LR: 59)

Located on an impressive cliff-top location, the church dates from 1370 and is of cruciform plan with a rib-vaulted roof and central tower. The church houses

14th-century sedilia, piscinas and aumbries, as well as medieval consecration crosses. St Monans is associated with St Monan and St Adrian. St Monan was slain by Norsemen here in about 870, while St Adrian sought refuge on the **Isle of May, [J21]** where he was also killed. St Monans became a place of pilgrimage, as was the Isle of May.

Welcomers on duty. Leaflet. Parking.

Open Apr-Oct.

K40 St Nicholas Buccleuch Parish Church, Dalkeith

[Map: 6B, E10] Off A68/A6094 junction, 6.5 miles SE of Edinburgh, High Street, Dalkeith, Midlothian. (NGR: NT 330670 LR: 66)

Dedicated to St Nicholas, this medieval church became a collegiate establishment in 1406 and was founded by Sir James Douglas. The inside of the church was greatly altered in 1851. The chancel was abandoned in 1590, walled off from the rest of the church, and is now ruinous. Sir James Douglas, 1st Earl of Morton, and his wife Joanna, daughter of James I, are buried in the choir, their tomb marked by stone effigies.

Refreshments. WC. Disabled access. Parking nearby.

Open Easter Sun-end Sep, Mon-Fri 10.00—16.00, Sun 10.00-11.00.

Web: www.btinternet.com~stnicholasbuccleuch
Email: edward.andrews@btinternet.com

J33 Whithorn Priory (HS)

The site of the 5th-century Christian community of St Ninian, who built a stone church here known as 'Candida Casa'. Whithorn was a Northumbrian bishopric but is last mentioned in 803. Later it became a popular place of pilgrimage. The arm bone of St Ninian was taken to the Scottish seminary at Douai, where it was kept until the French Revolution.

The existing ruins are of a 12th-century Premonstratensian priory and cathedral: the nave of the Romanesque church survives although it is unroofed. The vaulted chambers under the former nave also survive, and probably housed the shrine and relics of St Ninian. The church was not abandoned until 1822.

A fine collection of early Christian sculpture is housed in the nearby museum, including the 'Latinus Stone', the earliest Christian memorial in Scotland; the 'St Peter's Stone'; and the 10th-century Monreith Cross. Also see **Whithorn: Cradle of Christianity in Scotland [J34]**.

See main entry J33

Top left *Brechin Cathedral*
Above left *Dunkeld Cathedral*
Left *St Machar's Cathedral*
Above right *St Andrews Cathedral*
Below *Dunglass Collegiate Church*

Top *Elgin Cathedral* Above left *Glasgow Cathedral* Above centre *Rosslyn Chapel* Above right *Dunblane Cathedral* Right *St Monans Parish Church*

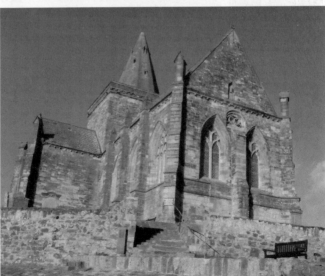

K2: Churches and Chapels

These are mainly parish churches and chapels, some of which are complete, some ruinous.

F1 Abdie Church

See main entry F1

K41 Abercorn Church and Museum

[Map: 6B, D9] Off A904, 5 miles E of Linlithgow, Abercorn, Hopetoun Estate. (NGR: NT 083792 LR: 65)

Abercorn was one of the first bishoprics in Scotland, dating from 670 AD, and founded as part of the Anglian church of Northumbria which included Hexham, York and Lindisfarne. The present church, dedicated to St Serf, mostly dates from the Reformation until the present day, although part may be from the 11th century, and it is built on an older site. There are two Norse burial stones, a wheel cross-stone, and a cross-shaft dating from the 8th century.

Explanatory displays. Disabled access. Car Parking.
Open all year, daily.
Tel: 01506 834331

K42 Aberlady Parish Church

[Map: 6B, D10] Off A198, 3.5 miles NW of Haddington, Main Street, Aberlady, East Lothian. (NGR: NT 462798 LR: 66)

The body of the church was remodelled in 1886, but the tower dates from the 16th century. The church houses an 8th-century cross, and marble monuments.

Sales area. Disabled access. Parking nearby.
Open May-Sep, 8.00-dusk.
Tel: 01875 853137/870237

K43 Abernethy (HS)

[Map: 5B, C9] On A913, 6 miles SE of Perth, Abernethy, Perthshire. (NGR: NO 190165 LR: 58)

The imposing 11th-century round tower, 74 feet high and all that remains of an important monastic centre which is said to have been founded by nuns from Kildare around 625. The tower is one of only two such Irish-style towers remaining in Scotland – the other is at **Brechin Cathedral [K3]**. There are fine views from the top. A Class 1 Pictish carved stone is located at the base of the tower. There is also a small museum at School Wynd in Abernethy.

Parking nearby.
Open Apr-Sep – for access apply to key holder.
Tel: 0131 668 8800 (tower)/01738 850889 (museum)

K44 Alloway Old Kirk

[Map: 6A, F6] Off B7024, 2 miles S of Ayr, Alloway, Ayrshire. (NGR: NS 330180 LR: 70)

The ruin of this old church is where Tam – from Robert Burns's poem 'Tam o' Shanter' – saw the dancing witches. It was already a ruin in Burns's day, and William Burnes, Burns's father, is buried here.

Car and coach parking.
Access at all reasonable times.

K45 Amulree Church

[Map: 5B, B8] Off A822, 14 miles N of Crieff, Amulree, Perthshire. (NGR: NN 899366 LR: 52)

The church, from the 18th century, has a bell cast in 1519, and houses a display of local information.
Open all year, daily.

K46 Applecross

[Map: 3A, F5] Off A896, Applecross, 1 mile N of village, Ross-shire. (NGR: NG 713458 LR: 24)

The site of a monastery, founded by St Maelrubha in 673. It became a place of pilgrimage, and earth taken from the saint's grave was said to ensure a safe return from any journey. An 8th-century cross-slab stands by the gate, and inside the modern church are other fragments. The nearby 15th-century ruinous chapel is roofed over by greenery. A spring [NG 717450] issuing from near the road, west of Applecross House, is said to be a holy well. A heritage centre is being set up at Clachan in Applecross.

Parking nearby.
Access at all reasonable times.
Tel: 01520 744478 (Applecross Heritage Centre)

K47 Ardclach Bell Tower (HS)

[Map: 3B, E10] Off A939, 8.5 miles SE of Nairn, Ardclach, Highland. (NGR: NH 953453 LR: 27)

The two-storey fortified bell tower was built in 1655 on the hill above the parish church. It was used to summon worshippers to the church, as well as to keep a lookout during times of conflict.

Access at all reasonable times – apply to key holder.
Tel: 01667 460232

K48 Auld Kirk of Kilbirnie

[Map: 6A, E6] Off B780, 7.5 miles E of Largs, Dalry Road, Kilbirnie, Ayrshire. (NGR: NS 314546 LR: 63)

The church dates from before the Reformation, and stands on the site of a 6th-century monastery of St Brendan of Clonfert. The nave dates from 1470, the tower from 1490, and an aisle from 1597. There is fine Italian Renaissance-style carving from 1642 in the Crawfurd aisle.

Sales area. WC. Disabled access. Parking nearby.
Open Jul-Aug, Tue-Fri 14.00-16.00; other times by appt.
Tel: 01505 683459

K49 Balnakeil Church

[Map: 3B, A8] Off A838, 0.5 miles NW of Durness, Balnakeil, Sutherland, Highland. (NGR: NC 391687 LR: 9)

There was a church here from early times, dedicated to St Maelrubha, but the ruins of the present building date from the 17th century. There are some interesting markers in the burial ground, including to Robert Calder Mackay (Rob Doun) the 'Burns of the North', who died in 1812.

Parking.
Access at all reasonable times.

K50 Balquhidder Kirkyard

[Map: 5B, C7] Off A84, 14 miles NW of Callendar, Balquhidder Kirkyard, Balquhidder, Stirlingshire. (NGR: NN 535209 LR: 57)

At the west end of the burial ground are three burial slabs, enclosed by railings, for Rob Roy MacGregor (who died on 28 December 1734), his wife, and two of his sons. His stone has a sword roughly carved on it. The old parish church is ruined, while on the north wall of the modern church is St Angus's Stone, which dates from the 8th century. The newer church has a 17th-century bell from the old church, and old Gaelic bibles. St Angus's Stone (Clach Aenais) was 'removed [from the old church] to destroy a superstitious desire that existed among the parishioners to stand or kneel on it during a marriage or baptism'. The stone is named after Angus, one of Columba's followers.

Parking nearby.
Access at all reasonable times.

K51 Birnie Kirk

[Map: 4, E3] Off B9010, 2.5 miles S of Elgin, Moray. (NGR: NJ 206587 LR: 28)

Standing on a kirkyard mound, Birnie Kirk dates from the 12th century, and the chancel arch, the north and south doorways and the font date from this time. The church is dedicated to St Brendan, and was altered in 1734 and 1891. Birnie was one of the places where the Bishops of Moray had their cathedral before moving to Elgin. A Pictish carved stone stands in the burial ground, carved with an eagle and notched rectangle and z-rod. Within the church are the fragments of a cross-slab.

Parking.
Stone: access at all reasonable times.
Tel: 01343 542621

T3 Bolton Parish Church

See main entry T3

K52 Borthwick Parish Church

[Map: 6B, E10] Off A7, 2 miles SE of Gorebridge, Borthwick, Midlothian. (NGR: NT 369597 LR: 66)

Borthwick Parish Church mostly dates from Victorian times, although an aisle and vault are 15th century, while the apse is 12th century. There are two fine 15th-century stone effigies, believed to be of William Borthwick and his wife. Borthwick was responsible for building the nearby and hugely impressive **Borthwick Castle [N7]** (which is now a hotel).

WC. Disabled access. Induction loop for church services. Car and coach parking.
Open all year, daily.

K53 Bowden Kirk

[Map: 6B, F10] Off A699, 5 miles E of Selkirk, Bowden, Borders. (NGR: NT 554303 LR: 73)

Founded in 1128, part of the present church probably dates from the 15th century or earlier, while most is 17th century. The church was remodelled in 1794 and again in 1909. There are interesting monuments, including burial vaults of the Dukes of Roxburghe, and a memorial to Lady Grizel Baillie, as well as notable tombstones in the graveyard. The church stands by the pilgrim route, St Cuthbert's Way, from **Melrose [J26]** to Lindisfarne.

WC. Disabled access. Parking nearby.
Open all year during daylight hours.

K54 Brough of Birsay (HS)

[Map: 2, B2] Off A966, 13 miles N of Stromness, Birsay, Orkney. (NGR: HY 239285 LR: 6)

On a tidal island is the Brough of Birsay, an early Christian settlement, which was later used by Norsemen, and became an important centre. Earl Thorfinn of Orkney had a house here, and there was a substantial 12th-century church. A fine Pictish sculptured stone decorated with figures was found here, now in the **Museum of Scotland [Y6]**, while there is a replica on the islet; there is also a Pictish well.

Parking nearby. £. Combined ticket available for all Orkney monuments.
Open mid Jun-Sep, daily 9.00-18.30, last ticket 18.00.
Tel: 01856 721205

K55 Burntisland Parish Church

[Map: 6B, D9] Off A921, 4 miles SW of Kirkcaldy, East Leven Street, Burntisland, Fife. (NGR: NT 234857 LR: 66)

One of the first post-Reformation churches, built between 1592-4, to an unusual square design, and is still in use. The General Assembly met here in 1601, in the presence of James VI, when a new translation of the Bible was approved.

Sales area. WC. Parking nearby. Church tours arranged by curator: also for visits to Burntisland Heritage Centre.
Open Jun-Aug, daily 10.00-12.00 and 14.00-16.00; other times key available from church officer or curator.
Tel: 01592 873275 curator/01592 872011 church officer

K56 Canisbay Parish Church

[Map: 3B, A11] On A836, 15 miles N of Wick, Kirkstyle, Caithness, Highland. (NGR: ND 343729 LR: 12)

The church, which dates from the 15th century and later, is mentioned in the 13th century and was dedicated to St Drostan. It is built on a mound covering the remains of a broch. There are some interesting burial markers, including for the de Groot or Groat family, best known from nearby John o' Groats.

Access at all reasonable times.

K57 Canongate Kirk, Edinburgh

[Map: 6B, E9] Canongate (Royal Mile), opposite Huntly House, Edinburgh. (NGR: NT 262738 LR: 66)

The Canongate Kirk is the parish church of **Holyroodhouse [N31]** and **Edinburgh Castle [N25]**, and is some 300 years old. It was recently restored and renovated. There is an interesting burial ground with fine memorials: David Rizzio is buried here, as well as Adam Smith, the poet Robert Ferguson, who was much admired by Robert Burns, and Agnes McLehose, Burns's 'Clarinda'.

Guided tours by arrangement. Information available in many languages. Refreshments. Disabled access. Parking nearby.

Church: open Jun-Sep, Mon-Sat 10.30-16.30; burial ground open all year.

Tel: 0131 556 3515   Fax: 0131 557 5847

K58 Carfin Grotto and Pilgrimage Centre

[Map: 6B, E8] Off A723, 2 miles E of Motherwell, 100 Newarthill Road, Carfin, Lanarkshire. (NGR: NS 775588 LR: 64)

The Pilgrimage Centre, situated adjacent to Carfin Grotto, features a unique audio-visual and gallery exhibition tracing the history and tradition of pilgrimage worldwide.

Guided tours on request. Explanatory displays. Gift shop. Cafe. Gardens and walkways. WC. Disabled access. Car and coach parking. Group concessions. £.

Open all year, daily 10.00-17.00.

Tel: 01698 268941   Fax: 01698 268941

K59 Castle Semple Collegiate Church (HS)

[Map: 6A, E6] Off B7776, 7 miles SW of Paisley, 2 miles E of Lochwinnoch, Castle Semple. (NGR: NS 377601 LR: 63)

A late Gothic church with a three-sided east end with windows of an unusual style. Roofless but standing to the wallhead, the church contains the elaborate tomb of its founder, John, 1st Lord Semple.

Parking nearby.

Access at all reasonable times.

K60 Chapel Finian (HS)

[Map: 6A, I6] On A747, 11 miles SE of Glenluce, Mochrum, Dumfries and Galloway. (NGR: NX 278489 LR: 82)

The foundations of a small rectangular chapel survive, dating from the 10th or 11th century, standing in a 50-foot-wide enclosure. It was dedicated to St Finian of Moville, who was educated at Findhorn and died around 579, and was used by pilgrims on their way to Whithorn.

Parking nearby.

Access at all reasonable times.

K61 Cille Bharra

[Map: 3A, G2] Off A888, 6 miles N of Castlebay, Eoligarry, N end of Barra. (NGR: NF 704077 LR: 31)

The ruinous medieval church was built about the 12th century and dedicated to St Barr. Two chapels also survive, one of which has been reroofed to shelter carved burial slabs, some used to mark the burials of the MacNeils of Barr. Other interesting slabs lie in the yard, while a fine 10th-century carved stone – with a cross and runic inscription – is kept in the **Museum of Scotland [Y6]**: a cast is displayed at Cille Bharra.

Parking nearby.

Access at all reasonable times.

R2 Crathie Parish Church

See main entry R2

N80 Cubbie Roo's Castle (HS)

The nearby ruined Romanesque chapel of St Mary [HY 442264] dates from the 12th century.

See main entry N80

K62 Dalmally Church

[Map: 5A, B5] Off A85, on B8077 Stronmilchan Road, Dalmally, Argyll. (NGR: NN 168275 LR: 50)

The present church was built in 1811 replaced a medieval building. There are several medieval grave slabs, attributed to the Loch Awe school of carving.

Access at all reasonable times.

K63 Dalmeny Parish Church

[Map: 6B, D9] Off B924, 8 miles NW of Edinburgh, Dalmeny, Lothian. (NGR: NT 144775 LR: 65)

A fine and largely unaltered medieval Romanesque church, founded in the 12th century, and dedicated to St Cuthbert. The south doorway is particularly interesting, and the arch stones are carved with animals, figures and grotesque heads. There is also a historic burial ground.

WC. Disabled access. Parking nearby. Donations welcome.

Open Apr-Sep, Sun 14.00-16.30 – key available from manse or post office, 5 main street at times outwith above. Coach parties should tel in advance.

Tel: 0131 331 1479

K64 Deskford Church (HS)

[Map: 4, E4] Off B9018, 4 miles S of Cullen, Deskford, Aberdeenshire. (NGR: NJ 509616 LR: 29)

The ruins of a small church, dating from medieval times, with a fine sacrament house of 1551. The sacrament house was provided by Alexander Ogilvie of Deskford, and is characteristic of north-east Scotland.

Access at all reasonable times.
Tel: 01466 793191

K65 Duddingston Kirk

[Map: 6B, E9] Off A199, Old Church Lane, Duddingston, Edinburgh. (NGR: NT 284726 LR: 66)

The fine old church dates from the 12th century, and stands in the pretty village of Duddingston on the edge of **Holyrood Park [A8]**.

Sales area. Refreshments. WC. Disabled access. Parking nearby.
Open Jun-Sep, Sat 11.00-17.00, Sun 14.00-17.00.

N93 Dunstaffnage Castle (HS)

There is a fine ruined chapel near the castle.

See main entry N93

K66 Durisdeer Church

[Map: 6B, G8] Off A702, 6 miles NE of Thornhill, Durisdeer, Dumfries and Galloway. (NGR: NS 897037 LR: 78)

The cruciform church, built in 1699, houses the 'Queensberry Marbles', the stone recumbent effigies in black and white marble of the 2nd Duke and Duchess of Queensberry. The tomb dates from 1711, and is in a burial aisle occupying one 'arm' of the church. In the vault below are 29 lead coffins containing the remains of the Douglas family. At one end of the church is a two-storey block once used as a school. The Well Path runs through the village, a Roman road which was used as a pilgrimage route to **Whithorn [J33]** in medieval times. About 1 mile to the northeast [NS 903049] are the well-preserved earthworks of a Roman fortlet. **Drumlanrig [N20]** is nearby.

Parking.
Open all year.

N25 Edinburgh Castle (HS)

The oldest building in the castle is a small Norman chapel of the 12th century, dedicated to St Margaret.

See main entry N25

K67 Edrom Church (HS)

[Map: 6B, E12] Off A6105, 3.5 miles NE of Duns, Edrom, Berwickshire, Borders. (NGR: NT 827558 LR: 67)

The fine Norman doorway survives from the old parish church, as does a chancel arch from a building erected by Thor Longus about 1105.

Car parking.
Access at all reasonable times.

N98 Edzell Castle (HS)

The Lindsay burial aisle, in Edzell kirkyard [NO 582688], dates from the 16th century and is open to the public.

See main entry N98

G5 Eilean Mor

See main entry G5

K68 Eynhallow Church (HS)

[Map: 2, B2] S side of island of Eynhallow, W of Rousay, Orkney. (NGR: HY 359288 LR: 6)

The existing building, dating from the 12th century, was probably once part of a monastic establishment. The church consisted of a rectangular nave with a porch at one end and a square-ended chancel. The building was remodelled in the 16th century to make it a dwelling, and the older origins were not revealed until 1854.

Access at all reasonable times – access is by private boat hire.
Tel: 01856 841815

K69 Forteviot

[Map: 5B, C9] On B935, 4.5 miles SW of Perth, Forteviot, Perthshire. (NGR: NO 055176 LR: 58)

Forteviot was the site of a palace of the Pictish kings, traditionally at Halyhill to the west of the village. Kenneth MacAlpin slaughtered his rivals here at a drunken feast to secure his position as ruler of Dalriada and Pictland. A bronze bell, dated 900, is preserved at Forteviot Parish Church, and there are medieval carved stones, including the remains of the Dronachy Cross, which formerly stood at Invermay.

Church open by arrangement: tel 01738 625854.

G6 Fortingall Church and Yew Tree

See main entry G6

K70 Fowlis Easter Church

[Map: 4, J3] Off A923 or A90, 5 miles W of Dundee, Fowlis, Angus. (NGR: NO 323335 LR: 53)

A fine small simple-rectangular church, probably dating from the 15th century but on a much older site. It was dedicated to St Marnan or Marnock, and was made into a collegiate establishment in 1454 by Lord Gray. It survived the Reformation more or less intact, and still has part of the original rood screen, large medieval board paintings (the Crucifixion, the Saints and St Catherine), alms dish, sacrament house and font.

Parking nearby. Donations welcome.
Open: on request or by key available from neighbouring houses.
Email: william.horspool@tesco.net

F17 Glamis Church, Pictish Stone and Well
See main entry F17

K71 Govan Old Parish Church
[Map: 6B, E7] Off A739, 866 Govan Road, Govan, Glasgow. (NGR: NS 553658 LR: 64)

The present church, dedicated to St Constantine and dating from 1888, was built on the site of a much older establishment, and is surrounded by an interesting graveyard. The church houses a fine collection of early Christian stones, including a decorated sarcophagus, five hogback tombstones, two cross shafts and upright crosses, and a number of recumbent slabs.

Sales area. WC. Parking nearby.

Open by arrangement only.

Tel: 0141 445 1941 Fax: 0141 401 7189 Web: www.govanold.org.uk

K72 Greyfriars Kirk
[Map: 6B, E9] Greyfriars Place, near Museum of Scotland, Edinburgh. (NGR: NT 258734 LR: 66)

Built by the site of the Franciscan friary – hence the name 'Greyfriars' – this was the first post-Reformation church built in Edinburgh, and completed in 1620. It was altered in the following centuries. The National Covenant was signed here in 1638, and a copy is on display. The historic kirkyard has old burial monuments, and was used as a Covenanters' prison after the Battle of Bothwell Brig in 1679. The memorial to **Greyfriars Bobby [Z7]** is nearby – there is information and memorabilia about the 'wee dug'.

Guided tours by arrangement. Visitor centre with explanatory displays and videos. Gift shop. WC. Disabled access and car parking. Parking nearby.

Open Apr-Oct, Mon-Fri 10.30-16.30, Sat 10.30-14.30; Nov-Mar, Thu 13.30-15.30; kirkyard open all year, 9.00-18.00.

Tel: 0131 225 1900/226 5429 Fax: 0131 225 1900 Email: greyfriarskirk@compuserve.com

K73 Greyfriars, Kirkcudbright
[Map: 6B, I7] Off A711, near MacLellan's Castle, Kirkcudbright, Dumfries and Galloway. (NGR: NX 683511 LR: 83)

A Franciscan friary was founded here in 1455 by James II, although the remains of the present church may date from the 13th century. Part of the building was remodelled in 1730, then fell into disuse, then became part of a school. The church was restored in 1922.

Parking nearby.

Access at all reasonable times.

K74 Howmore
[Map: 3A, F2] Off A865, 11.5 miles N of Lochboisdale, Howmore, South Uist. (NGR: NF 758365 LR: 22)

The complex at Howmore, once surrounded by marshes, consists of the ruinous remains of two churches, two chapels – while a third was demolished in 1866 – and associated burial ground. The area is enclosed by a stone bank, and there was probably an early Christian community here.

Parking nearby.

Access at all reasonable times.

K75 Inchkenneth Chapel (HS)
[Map: 5A, B3] E side of island of Inch Kenneth, 1 mile W of Inchkenneth, E side of Mull, Argyll. (NGR: NM 437354 LR: 47)

The fine ruinous rectangular church, which dates from the 13th century, was dedicated to St Cainnech of Aghaboe, a contemporary of St Columba. In the burial ground and protected within the chapel are several fine carved medieval grave slabs. There are also a number of later table gravestones, and a 16th-century ring-headed cross of slate.

Access at all reasonable times.

K76 Innerpeffray Library and Chapel
[Map: 5B, C8] On B8062, 4.5 miles SE of Crieff, Innerpeffray, Perthshire. (NGR: NN 902183 LR: 58)

The library, Scotland's oldest free lending library, was founded in 1680 by David, Lord Madderty, and housed in a late 18th-century building. There is a notable collection of bibles and rare books. Adjacent is St Mary's Chapel, original home of the library and Drummond family burial place. The chapel was founded by Lord Drummond about 1508, although there was a church here from 1342 or earlier. The chapel is in the care of Historic Scotland.

Sales area. Refreshments. Parking. £.

Library open all year: Mon-Wed & Fri-Sat 10.00-12.45 & 14.00-16.45, Sun 14.00-16.00; closed Thu; Oct-Mar, closes 16.00; Dec-Jan, by appt only; Chapel open all year except Thu & Sun.

Tel: 01764 652819/0131 668 8800 (chapel)

F19 Inverallan
See main entry F19

F20 Inveravon Church
See main entry F20

Y108 Jura Parish Church
See main entry Y108

L8 Keills Chapel (HS)
See main entry L8

K77 Kilarrow (Bowmore) Parish Church
[Map: 5A, E2] On A846, Main Street, Bowmore, Islay. (NGR: NR 312596 LR: 60)

The church was built by the Campbells of Shawfield in 1767, and is unusual in being round: no corners

for the devil to hide in. The church can hold 500 souls.
Parking nearby.
Open all year, daily.

L11 Kildalton Cross and Chapel (HS)
See main entry L11

K78 Killean Old Parish Church
[Map: 5A, F4] Off A83, 1 mile S of Tayinloan, Killean, Kintyre. (NGR: NR 695445 LR: 62)
Dedicated to St John, the ruined church has a 12th-century nave, 13th-century chancel, and a 15th-century north aisle – and is now the burial place of the MacDonalds of Largie. The church was abandoned in 1770. An early Christian cross from the site is now in the **Campbeltown Museum [Y54]**, but there are several fine carved slabs in the church and burial ground.
Limited disabled access. Parking nearby.
Access at all reasonable times.

L12 Kilmartin Sculpted Stones and Parish Church (HS)
See main entry L12

L14 Kilmory Knap Chapel (HS)
See main entry L14

K79 Kilmun Church
[Map: 5A, D5] On A880, 6 miles N of Dunoon, NE shore of Holy Loch, Kilmun, Argyll. (NGR: NS 166821 LR: 56)
The parish church stands on the site of a Celtic monastery, dates from 1841 and features excellent stained glass. The tower of a collegiate church, built by Sir Duncan Campbell in 1442, also survives. The site is dedicated to St Munn, who was a friend of St Columba. The mausoleum of the Dukes of Argyll, 18th-century markers and the resting place of the first lady doctor are found in the kirkyard.
Guided tours. Gift shop. Tearoom. WC. Car and coach parking. Donations welcome.
Open Apr-Sep, Tue-Thu 13.30-16.30; all other times by arrangement.
Tel: 01369 840342

K80 Kincardine O'Neil Old Parish Church
[Map: 4, G4] About 7 miles W of Banchory, just S of A93, Kincardine O'Neil, Aberdeenshire. (NGR: NO 593995 LR: 44)
The ruinous remains of a church, which formerly had a two-storey hospice at one end. There is a 14th-century moulded doorway and interesting old burial markers. The site is associated with St Erchan, an early saint. His well stands across the road from the church,

and is now enclosed in a small building of 1858, although there is apparently now no water.
Access at all reasonable times.

K81 King's College Chapel
[Map: 4, G5] Off A92, College Bounds, Old Aberdeen, N of Aberdeen. (NGR: NJ 940081 LR: 38)
The collegiate chapel is a fine old building with a striking crown steeple and choir stalls dating from the 15th century. It was dedicated to St Mary, and was founded by William Elphinstone, Bishop of Aberdeen, in 1495. There is also a visitor centre at King's College (01224 273702) on the history of the university.
Opening by arrangement.
Tel: 01224 273325/272137

K82 Kinkell Church (HS)
[Map: 4, G5] Off A96 and B993, 2 miles S of Inverurie, Kinkell, Aberdeenshire. (NGR: NJ 785190 LR: 38)
The ruinous remains of a 16th-century church, dedicated to St Michael, which may have been a property of the Knights of Jerusalem. There is a fine sacrament house of 1524, as well as the richly carved grave slab of Gilbert de Greenlaw, who was killed at the bloody Battle of Harlaw in 1411. A monument to the battle is located at **Harlaw [Q13]**.
Limited disabled access. Parking nearby.
Access at all reasonable times.
Tel: 01466 793191

K83 Kinneff Old Parish Church
[Map: 4, H5] Off A92, 9 miles NE of Laurencekirk, Kincardine and Deeside. (NGR: NO 855749 LR: 45)
The present church was rebuilt in 1783, but incorporates much older work. It was dedicated to St Arnold (possibly St Adamnan), and a Pictish cross-slab was found here, although this is now in the **Museum of Scotland [Y6]**. The Scottish crown jewels were hidden in the church between 1651-60 after being smuggled out of **Dunnottar Castle [N90]**.

K84 Kirk of Calder
[Map: 6B, E9] On B7015, 12 miles W of Edinburgh, 1 mile SE of Livingston, Main Street, Mid Calder, West Lothian. (NGR: NT 075675 LR: 65)
The parish church, which dates from the 16th century, has fine stained-glass windows and information on four centuries of Scottish history. Famous visitors include John Knox, David Livingstone and James 'Paraffin' Young.
Guided tours. Explanatory displays. Gift shop. Tearoom. WC. Disabled access. Car and coach parking.
Open May-Sep, Sun 14.00-16.00.
Tel: 01506 880207   Web: www.kirkofcalder.com   Email: kirkofcalder@netscape.net

K85 Largs Old Kirk (HS)

[Map: 6A, E5] Off A78, Bellman's Close, off High Street, Largs, Ayrshire. (NGR: NS 200594 LR: 63)
Little remains of the old kirk except the Skelmorlie Aisle, a burial vault and loft built by the Montgomerys of Skelmorlie in 1636. There are a number of burial monuments, as well as a superb 17th-century painted ceiling. The key holder is **Largs Museum [Y116]**, which is nearby.
Parking nearby.
Open Apr-Sep, daily 14.00-17.00.
Tel: 0131 668 8800 (HS)/01475 687081 (Largs Museum)

K86 Logie Old Kirk

[Map: 5B, D8] Off A91, 2.5 miles N of Stirling, Logie, Airthrey Castle, Bridge of Allan, Stirlingshire. (NGR: NS 815970 LR: 57)
Standing by the Logie Burn, the picturesque ruined church mostly dates from 1784, although there was a church from 1178 or earlier. It stands in an oval kirk-yard, and there are two hogback grave stones dating from the 11th century. The church may have been dedicated to St Serf, who is associated with the area.
Access at all reasonable times.

K87 Magdalen Chapel

[Map: 6B, E9] 41 Cowgate, Edinburgh. (NGR: NT 258735 LR: 66)
The chapel was built in 1541 and dedicated to St Mary Magdalene, and is one of the oldest buildings in the city. It has been used by various denominations, and also as a guildhall by the Incorporation of Hammer-men until 1862, when it was taken over by the Protestant Institute of Scotland, and then from 1965 by the Scottish Reformation Society. There is rare medieval stained glass in the original setting, as well as a bell and clock dating from the early 17th century.
Guided tours. Explanatory displays. Gift shop. WC. Disabled access. Parking nearby.
Open all year: Mon-Fri, 9.30-16.00; at other times by appt.
Tel: 0131 220 1450 Fax: 0131 220 1450

K88 Maybole Collegiate Church (HS)

[Map: 6A, G6] Off A77, Maybole, Ayrshire. (NGR: NS 301098 LR: 76)
The ruinous chapel housed a college of priests, and was dedicated to St Mary. It was founded in 1384 by John Kennedy of Dunure, although the present build-ing is believed to be 15th century. The chapel was abandoned in 1563, and the Kennedy family took over the sacristy as their burial vault.
Parking nearby.
Access at all reasonable times.

K89 Mortlach Parish Church

[Map: 4, F3] Off A941, Dufftown, Moray. (NGR: NJ 323392 LR: 28)
The present church, dedicated to St Moluag, dates from the 11th or 12th century, but stands on the site of an early Christian site, said to date from 566. In 1016 the church was lengthened by three spears' length on the command of Malcolm II after his vic-tory over the Norsemen. The Battle Stone, a Pictish symbol stone, survives in the interesting graveyard, along with another stone built into the church.
Explanatory displays. Induction loop. Car and coach parking. Donations welcome.
Open Easter-Oct, daily 10.00-16.00.
Tel: 01340 820268

K90 Muthill Old Church and Tower (HS)

[Map: 5B, C8] On A822, 3 miles S of Crieff, Muthill, Perthshire. (NGR: NN 869170 LR: 58)
The ruinous remains of a mostly 15th-century church, consisting of an aisled nave and a tall tower, itself built in the 12th or 13th centuries. The church was altered after the Reformation, when the chancel was aban-doned and then completely demolished. Also see **Muthill Village and Parish Museum [Y141]**.
Parking nearby.
Access at all reasonable times.

L20 Netherton Cross
See main entry L20

K91 Old Steeple, Dundee

[Map: 4, J3] Off A90, Nethergate, Dundee. (NGR: NO 401301 LR: 54)
The old steeple, dating from the 15th century, is all that remains of the medieval church of St Mary's, which was founded in 1198. The tower is some 156 feet high, and has walls eight feet thick in places. There are fine views from the tower. Dundee's Mercat Cross, dating from 1586 but crowned by a modern unicorn, is nearby.
Parking nearby. £.
Open all year: Apr-Sep, Mon-Sat 10.00-17.00, Sun 12.00-16.00; Oct-Mar, Mon-Sat 11.00-16.00, Sun 12.00-16.00.
Tel: 01382 206790 Fax: 01382 206790 Email: admin@dundeeheritage@sol.co.uk

K92 Orphir Church and Earl's Bu (HS)

[Map: 2, C2] Off A964, 8 miles SW of Kirkwall, Orphir, Orkney. (NGR: HY 334044 LR: 6)
The ruined remains of the only surviving medieval round church in Scotland, dating from the 12th cen-tury. The apse survives but the rest was demolished for the building of a later church, itself now gone. The church was dedicated to St Nicholas, and was

probably started by Earl Haakon Paulsson before 1122, whose hall – 'bu' – was nearby. The **Orkneyinga Saga Centre [G8]** is nearby.

Car and coach parking nearby.
Access at all reasonable times.
Tel: 01856 841815

K93 Pennygown Chapel

[Map: 5A, B3] Off A849, 2 miles E of Salen, Pennygown, Mull. (NGR: NM 604432 LR: 49)
The shell of a rectangular 13th-century chapel stands within the old burial ground. Within the chapel is the base of a 16th-century cross-shaft, carved with a crucifix, a griffin and a galley in sail on one side, and the Virgin and Child on the other. In the interesting burial ground are two 17th-century slabs with effigies of a man and a woman, as well as 18th-century memorials.

Parking.
Access at all reasonable times.

K94 Pierowall Church (HS)

[Map: 2, A2] ON B9066, Pierowall, E side of Westray, Orkney. (NGR: HY 438487 LR: 5)
The ruins of a medieval church, with some interesting grave markers.
Access at all reasonable times.
Tel: 01856 841815

F28 Raven Stone, Tyrie Church
See main entry F28

G9 Rona
See main entry G9

K95 Sanquhar Church

[Map: 6B, G7] Off A76, Sanquhar, Dumfries and Galloway. (NGR: NS 795095 LR: 78)
The church, which dates from the 19th century, houses a medieval stone effigy of a monk, a cross-slab and an effigy of St Nicholas, which was found on a site to the south of the town.
Key available from session clerk: tel 01659 50596.
Tel: 01659 50596

N143 Skipness Castle (HS)

The ruins of a 13th-century chapel, Kilbrannan, dedicated to St Brendan, lie to the south-east of the castle [NR 910575]. There are fine grave slabs, an interesting burial ground, and grand views across to Arran.
See main entry N143

K96 Soutra Aisle

[Map: 6B, E10] On B6368, 8 miles SE of Gorebridge, Soutra, Fala, Lothian. (NGR: NT 453583 LR: 66)
Nothing remains of a church and hospital except one

aisle, later used as a burial vault. The hospital was founded by Malcolm IV around 1164, and dedicated to the Holy Trinity. It was for use by travellers, pilgrims and poor people, and had an infirmary. Nearby was the Trinity Well [NT 452588] which was famous for the healing power of the waters. It existed in 1853 but had gone by the 1930s. A stretch of **Dere Street [E10]**, a Roman road, runs nearby.
Open all year: tel to arrange tours or lectures.
Tel: 01875 833248 between 10.00-12.00

K97 St Athernase Church

[Map: 6B, C10] Off A919, Leuchars, Fife. (NGR: NO 455215 LR: 59)
One of the finest Romanesque churches in Scotland, the chancel and apse, with blind arcades, survive from a 12th-century church. The belfry was added about 1700, and the nave restored in 1858.
Sales area. WC. Parking nearby.
Open Mar-Oct, daily 9.30-18.00.
Tel: 01334 839226

K98 St Bean's Church, Fowlis Wester

[Map: 5B, C8] Off A85, 5 miles E of Crieff, Fowlis Wester, Perthshire. (NGR: NN 928241 LR: 52)
The church, which dates from the 13th century, was dedicated to St Bean. It has been rebuilt several times down the centuries, and now house houses **Fowlis Carved Wester Stone [F16]**, as well as a Class 2 Pictish carved stone.
Parking nearby.
Open by appt.
Tel: 01764 683205

K99 St Blane's Church (HS)

[Map: 5A, E5] Off A844, 2 miles S of Kingarth, Bute. (NGR: NS 094535 LR: 63)
In a peaceful and pleasant location is the site of a 6th-century Christian community, founded by St Blane, who was born on Bute. The site is surrounded by an enclosure wall, and there are several ruinous buildings, including a 12th-century chapel, with a finely decorated chancel arch. An upper and lower burial yard have some fine gravestones: the upper used for burying men, the lower for women. There is a reputed holy and wishing well nearby.
Parking.
Access at all reasonable times.

K100 St Boniface Church

[Map: 2, A3] W side of Papa Westray, Orkney. (NGR: HY 488527 LR: 5)
The church dates from the 12th century, and early Christian cross-slabs have been found here. There is a Norse hogbacked burial marker.

K101 St Bride's Church (HS)

[Map: 6B, F8] Off A70, 9 miles S of Lanark, Main Street, Douglas, Lanarkshire. (NGR: NS 835309 LR: 72)

Although there was probably a church here from earlier times, the present fragmentary ruin dates from 1330 and later. The remains consist of the chancel, and the south transept. The church houses the stone effigy of the Good Sir James Douglas, who died in 1331 at Granada in Spain. Other memorials include that of Archibald Douglas, 5th Earl of Douglas, who died in 1438; James 7th Earl who died in 1443; and his wife Beatrice Sinclair.

Parking nearby.

Access at all reasonable times – instruction for obtaining key on notice on gate.

Tel: 01555 851657/0131 668 8800

K102 St Bridget's Kirk (HS)

[Map: 6B, D9] Off A921, 5 miles SE of Dunfermline, Dalgety, Fife. (NGR: NT 169838 LR: 66)

The ruins of a church, dating from the 12th century but altered in the 17th century for Protestant worship. It was dedicated to St Bridget, an ancient Christian saint. There is a burial vault at one end with a laird's loft above, and Alexander Seton, Earl of Dunfermline and Chancellor of Scotland, who died in 1622, is buried here.

Parking nearby.

Church: access at all reasonable times.

G11 St Columba's Cave

See main entry G11

K103 St Columba's Church (Ui), Aignish

[Map: 3A, B5] Off A866, 3.5 miles E of Stornoway, Aignish, Lewis. (NGR: NB 484322 LR: 8)

Said to be built on the site of a 6th- or 7th- century cell of St Catan, a contemporary of St Columba, the existing ruinous rectangular church dates from medieval times. The burial place of the MacLeods of Lewis, there are two carved stones within the church: one of the effigy of a warrior and is believed to be Roderick, 7th chief; while the other is for Margaret, daughter of Roderick MacLeod, who died in 1503.

Car parking.

Access at all reasonable times.

G12 St Columba's Footprint

See main entry G12

K104 St Conan's Kirk

[Map: 5A, B5] On A85, 4 miles E of Dalmally, 0.5 miles W of Lochawe, Argyll. (NGR: NN 116268 LR: 50)

Fine and interesting modern church, built in various styles, with a cloister garth and semi-circular apse and ambulatory. Other features of interest include the Bruce Chapel, which has a fragment of bone reputed to be from Robert the Bruce, and effigy of the Campbell builder. St Conan is said to have lived in Glenorchy, and is the patron saint of Lorn.

Open at all reasonable times.

K105 St Congan's Church

[Map: 4, E5] Off B9025, Turriff, Aberdeenshire. (NGR: NJ 722498 LR: 29)

The long and ruinous church dates from the 13th century, and is dedicated to St Congan or Cowan, an 8th-century saint from Ireland, who had a Christian community here. There are also several carved burial markers, dating from the 16th and 17th centuries, and fragments of other carved stones.

Access at all reasonable times.

K106 St Duthac's Chapel, Tain

[Map: 3B, D10] On B9174, Tain, near the sea, Ross-shire. (NGR: NH 786823 LR: 21)

The ruins of a church, dating from the 13th century and dedicated to St Duthac. It was from near here that Elizabeth, wife of Robert the Bruce, and other womenfolk, were captured by the Earl of Ross in 1306. Despite being an area of sanctuary, they were delivered to Edward I of England. The church was torched in 1429 when MacNeil of Creich burned Mowat of Freswick and his men here. Also **St Duthac's Church [K29]** and **Tain through Time [Y189]**.

Parking nearby.

Access at all reasonable times.

G13 St Fillan's Cave

See main entry G13

K107 St Fillan's Church

[Map: 6B, D9] Off A921, 6.5 miles SW of Kirkcaldy, Aberdour, Fife. (NGR: NT 194856 LR: 66)

Standing in the picturesque village of Aberdour, the church, which is dedicated to St Fillan, is a fine example of Norman church architecture, and dates from the 12th century. It was enlarged in the 15th century, then again in the 17th. It fell into disrepair, but was restored in 1925. There is an interesting burial ground. Near to **Aberdour Castle [N49]**.

Open all year.

K108 St John the Baptist's Church, Ayr

[Map: 6A, F6] Off A719, Ayr, Ayrshire. (NGR: NS 334220 LR: 70)

Only the strong tower remains of the former parish church of Ayr, which was cruciform in plan and some 140 feet long. A church is mentioned in 1233, and Robert the Bruce held a parliament here in 1315. In the 1650s the church and burial ground were enclosed by a fort built by Cromwell, and most of the church was demolished in the 18th century.

Open to the public by arrangement; other times view from exterior.

Tel: 01292 286385

K109 St John's Church, Edinburgh

[Map: 6B, E9] W end of Princes Street, Edinburgh. (NGR: NT 248736 LR: 66)

The church was designed by William Burn and dates from the early 19th century, and has a fine collection of stained glass, as well as modern paintings and sculpture. Many famous Scots are buried in the kirkyard, including Sir Henry Raeburn, the famous portrait painter, and James Donaldson, founder of Donaldson's School for the Deaf.

Guided tours by arrangement. Gift shop. Cafe. WC. Disabled access. Parking nearby.

Open all year, daily from 7.30.

Tel: 0131 229 7565   Fax: 0131 229 2561   Email: saintjohnsoffice@btconnect.com

K110 St John's Church, Gamrie

[Map: 4, E5] Off B9031, 6 miles E of Banff, W of Gardenstown, Gamrie, Banff and Buchan. (NGR: NJ 791644 LR: 30)

The ruinous remains of a church, probably dating from the 16th century, but founded in 1004. It was dedicated to St John, and was formerly known as the Kirk of Skulls, as three skulls were kept within the church, probably the remains of Norsemen. There are fine views.

Access at all reasonable times.

K111 St Magnus Church, Egilsay (HS)

[Map: 2, B3] W side of Egilsay, E of Rousay, Orkney. (NGR: HY 467303 LR: 6)

Standing on the peaceful island, the ruinous church, dating from the 12th century, consists of a nave, square-ended chancel, and round tower of the Irish type. Some have suggested that this was the church where Earl Magnus prayed before his murder by beheading in 1117.

Access at all reasonable times.

Tel: 01856 841815

K112 St Magnus Church, Birsay

[Map: 2, B2] On A966, 12 miles N of Stromness, Birsay, Orkney. (NGR: HY 248276 LR: 6)

The church, which was first built in 1064 then rebuilt in 1664 and 1760, and restored in 1986, is said to be where the body of St Magnus was brought after he was slain in 1115. His remains were later placed in **St**

Magnus Cathedral [K33]. The **Earl's Palace, Birsay [N96]**, is across the road.

WC nearby. Parking nearby.

Open Apr-Sep, daily: key available all year from the village shop.

K113 St Margaret's Cave

[Map: 6B, D9] Off A994, Bruce Street car park, Dunfermline. (NGR: NT 087873 LR: 65)

The cave is associated with St Margaret, wife of Malcolm Canmore in the 11th century, and was a place of pilgrimage. The church and remains of **Dunfermline Abbey and Palace [J14]** are nearby, as is **Abbot House [Y18]**.

Explanatory displays. Gift shop. Car and coach parking.

Open Easter-Sep, daily 11.00-16.00.

Tel: 01383 314228/313838

K114 St Martin's Kirk, Haddington (HS)

[Map: 6B, E10] Off A1, E side of Haddington, East Lothian. (NGR: NT 521739 LR: 66)

The ruinous remains of a formerly splendid church, associated with the Cistercian nunnery of St Mary's, which was founded in Haddington in the 12th century.

Parking nearby.

Access at all reasonable times.

K115 St Mary's Chapel, Crosskirk (HS)

[Map: 3B, A10] Off A836, 6 miles NW of Thurso, Crosskirk, Caithness. (NGR: ND 024700 LR: 12)

The simple dry-stone chapel, possibly built in the 12th century, is roofless but the walls are complete. The building probably had a thatched roof. Part of the church was used as a burial place for the Gunn family from the late 19th century, and to the south is a healing well, also dedicated to St Mary.

Parking nearby.

Access at all reasonable times – may be muddy.

Tel: 01667 460232

K116 St Mary's Chapel, Dunvegan

[Map: 3A, E4] On A850, E of Dunvegan, Skye. (NGR: NG 256478 LR: 23)

The ruins of St Mary's Chapel stand within a burial ground, which has a memorial to the MacCrimmons, pipers to the MacLeods of **Dunvegan [N24]**, and to the MacLeods themselves in the church, where they have a burial enclosure: a lintel is inscribed 'I ML 1694'. There are three carved grave slabs, decorated with a claymore and foliage, as well as other old burial markers.

K117 St Mary's Church, Grandtully (HS)

[Map: 5B, B8] Off A827, 3 miles NE of Aberfeldy, Grandtully, Perthshire. (NGR: NN 886505 LR: 52)

Dating from the 16th century, St Mary's Church was remodelled in 1633, when a finely painted ceiling, illustrating heraldic and symbolic subjects, was added.

Parking.

Access at all reasonable times.

K118 St Mary's Church, Monymusk

[Map: 4, G5] Off B993, 6.5 miles SW of Inverurie, Monymusk, Aberdeenshire. (NGR: NJ 684152 LR: 38)

Part of the fine church may date from 12th century, and a priory of Augustinian canons was founded here. Housed in the church is the Monymusk Stone, a Pictish symbol stone, as well as other stones dating from the 7th-9th centuries. The Monymusk Reliquary, which once held the relics of St Columba, was also sometimes displayed here. It was carried before Bruce's army at Bannockburn, and is now kept in the **Museum of Scotland [Y6]** in Edinburgh. There are fine modern stained-glass windows.

Parking nearby. Disabled access on request.

Open Apr-Oct, daylight hours; Sun all year for worship; other times by arrangement.
Tel: 01467 651470   Email: euanglen@aol.com

K119 St Mary's Church, Rothesay (HS)

[Map: 5A, E5] On A845, 0.5 miles S of Rothesay Castle, Bute. (NGR: NS 086637 LR: 63)

The chapel, dedicated to St Mary and also known as Ladykirk, stands next to the modern parish church, and may date from as early as the 13th century. It is all that remains of a larger building, which was also dedicated to St Brioc, a 6th-century saint, and used as the Cathedral of the Isles. It houses two well-preserved stone effigies: one of a warrior from the 14th century, probably a Stewart of Menteith. A sculpted stone, dating from around the 8th century, was found here and is now in the **Bute Museum [Y50]**. A spring, housed in a small building, is known as 'St Mary's Well'. Interesting burial ground with outstanding Victorian markers.

Parking nearby.

Open Apr-Sep, daily 8.00-17.00; Oct-Mar, Sat-Thu 8.00-17.00.

K120 St Mary's Kirk, Auchindour (HS)

[Map: 4, G4] Off A97, 8 miles NW of Alford, near Lumsden, Aberdeenshire. (NGR: NJ 477244 LR: 37)

The fine ruinous shell of a medieval parish church with a Romanesque doorway and 14th-century sacrament house. About 100 yards to the west is St Mary's Well, which was used for healing and to alleviate toothache.

Parking nearby.

Access to church at all reasonable times: keys available locally.
Tel: 01667 460232

K121 St Moluag's Church

[Map: 3A, A5] Off B8014 or B8013, 26 miles N of Stornoway, Eorrapaidh, Lewis. (NGR: NB 519652 LR: 8)

Although there was probably a Christian settlement here from the 6th century, the present church dates from the 12th century, and was dedicated to St Moluag or St Olaf. The church has round arched windows and door. An adjoining chapel, possibly used by lepers, only has a squint – or viewing hole – into the main church. The church was associated with 'hallow-tide sacrifices', probably a fertility rite, to the seagod Shony as late as the 17th century.

Parking nearby.

Open Easter-Sep during daylight hours: short walk – path may be muddy.

G14 St Ninian's Cave (HS)

See main entry G14

K122 St Ninian's Chapel, Isle of Whithorn (HS)

[Map: 6A, J6] Off A750, 2 miles DE of Whithorn, S end Isle of Whithorn, Dumfries and Galloway. (NGR: NX 479362 LR: 83)

Occupying a site associated with St Ninian, the present ruined and roofless chapel dates from the 13th century, and occupies the site of an earlier building. It was used by pilgrims on their way from Ireland and the Isle of Man to St Ninian's shrine at **Whithorn [J33]**.

Car and coach parking nearby.

Access at all reasonable times – involves walk.

K123 St Peter's Church, Duffus (HS)

[Map: 4, E3] Off B9012, Duffus, Moray. (NGR: NJ 175688 LR: 28)

The roofless ruins consist of the base of a 14th-century tower, now the Sutherland burial vault, and a fine 16th-century porch with a groined vault – while the body of the church is 18th century. St Peter's Cross, a typical medieval market cross dating from the 14th century (markets were regularly held in kirkyards) and table tombs survive in the burial ground.

Parking nearby.

Access at all reasonable times.

K124 St Peter's Church, Thurso

[Map: 3B, A11] Off A882, Wilson Lane, Thurso, Caithness, Highland. (NGR: ND 120686 LR: 12)

The ruins of a cruciform church, dedicated to St Peter, which probably dates mostly from the 16th century, but may incorporate work from the 12th century. It has a small vaulted cell, stair tower and passageway, and there is a runic inscription on one wall.

Access at all reasonable times: open summer; other times key available from the Town Hall.

K125 St Serf's Church, Dunning (HS)

[Map: 5B, C9] On B8062 or B934, 5 miles E of Auchterarder, Dunning, Perthshire. (NGR: NO 019145 LR: 58)

The parish church, which was rebuilt in 1810, still has a square 75-foot-high Romanesque tower and tower arch, dating to about 1200-10. A church was founded here in the 6th century by St Serf, and the present building was dedicated to him. The fine **Dupplin Cross [L4]** is to be housed in the tower in 2002 to protect it from the elements.

Parking nearby.
Keys available locally.

K126 St Serf's Church, Tullibody

[Map: 5B, D8] On B9140, 5 miles NE of Stirling, Menstrie Road, N of Tullibody, Clackmannanshire. (NGR: NS 860953 LR: 58)

The ruins of a 16th-century church, rebuilt after being destroyed by forces of Mary of Guise in 1559 to replace a demolished bridge. The church was dedicated to St Serf, but was stripped and unroofed in 1916. It served as the mausoleum of the Abercrombies of Tullibody.

Access at all reasonable times.

K127 St Ternan's Church, Arbuthnott

[Map: 4, H5] Off B967, 5.5 miles NE of Laurencekirk, SE of Arbuthnott, Kincardine and Deeside. (NGR: NO 801746 LR: 45)

The chancel of the present building dates from 1242, although an earlier church probably stood on the site. It was dedicated to St Ternan, a 5th-century saint, who is said to have been born at Arbuthnott. The bell tower and west end were built about 1500, and the church houses a carved monument to Hugh Arbuthnott. Above this aisle is the Priest's Room. Lewis Grassic Gibbon is buried in the graveyard – the **Grassic Gibbon Centre [T14]** is nearby.

Disabled limited access. Parking nearby.
Open all year.

K128 St Triduana's Chapel (HS)

[Map: 6B, E9] On Restalrig Road South, to E of Edinburgh. (NGR: NT 282745 LR: 66)

The church, which is dedicated to St Mary and The Trinity, was founded as a collegiate establishment by James III in the 1460s, although it is a much older site. There is an extremely unusual hexagonal vaulted chamber, known as St Triduana's Chapel or Well, probably the lower part of a two-storey building. Water still flows from a spring here. Visiting Triduana's shrines were supposed to help blindness and other conditions of the eye. There is an interesting kirkyard.

Parking nearby.
Access can be arranged by contacting St Margaret's Parish Church, Restalrig.
Tel: 0131 554 7400/0131 668 8800

K129 St Vigeans Church

[Map: 4, I4] Off A933, 0.5 miles N of Arbroath, St Vigeans, Angus. (NGR: NO 639429 LR: 54)

Perched upon a steep mound in the peaceful hamlet, the interesting church dates from the 12th century and is dedicated to St Vigean (St Fechin), an Irish saint, who died in 664. This was the parish church for Arbroath. **St Vigeans Museum [F30]** is across the road.

Music in St Vigeans – every Sun in Jun, 14.30. Parking nearby at Church Hall.
Key available from no 7, over the road from the church.
Tel: 01241 873206 Email: gaz71@dial.pipex.com

K130 Stenton

[Map: 6B, D11] On B6370, 5 miles SW of Dunbar, Stenton, East Lothian. (NGR: NT 633743 LR: 66)

In the picturesque and peaceful village of Stenton is the Wool Stone, formerly used for weighing wool at Stenton Fair. Nearby is the Cardinal's Hat, a rood well dating from the 14th century, which is housed in small chamber resembling a cardinal's hat, hence the name. There is also an old doocot, and the tower and ruins of a 16th-century church, with added pigeons. There are several interesting memorials in the burial ground.

Car parking.
Access at all reasonable times.

K131 Stobo Kirk

[Map: 6B, F9] Off B712, 4.5 miles SW of Peebles, Stobo, Borders. (NGR: NT 182376 LR: 72)

Dating from the 12th century, the nave and chancel of the church are Norman, and a fine doorway survives within a 16th-century porch. The church was dedicated to St Mungo or Kentigern, who probably founded a church here in the 6th century. The tower was altered in the 16th century, although the base is also probably Norman. The church houses fine re-

cumbent tombstones, and there are interesting 17th- and 18th-century gravestones in the burial ground.
Disabled limited access. Parking nearby.
Open all year.
Tel: 01899 830331   Email: revracheldobie@cs.com

K132 Symington Parish Church

[Map: 6B, F8] Off A72, 3 miles SW of Biggar, Symington, Lanarkshire. (NGR: NS 999352 LR: 72)
The fine small church dates from the 12th century, and retains many features including Norman arched windows, piscina and an old oak-beam ceiling. The village (Simon's town) is named after Simon Loccard (or Lockhart), whose descendants were the Lockharts of the Lee. He also founded the church in about 1160.
Wheelchair access available. Parking nearby.
Open Jul-Aug, Sun 14.00-16.00; other times by appt.
Tel: 01563 830205   Web: www.symingtonchurch.com   Email: alel@sanderson29.fsnet.co.uk

K133 Tarves Medieval Tomb (HS)

[Map: 4, F5] On B999, 15 miles NW of Aberdeen, 3 miles N of Pitmedden, Tarves, Aberdeenshire. (NGR: NJ 869303 LR: 30)
The finely carved tomb of William Forbes, who was responsible for rebuilding **Tolquhon Castle [N151]**.
Parking nearby.
Access at all reasonable times.
Tel: 01466 793191

K134 Teampull na Trionaid

[Map: 3A, E2] Off A865, 4 miles NE of Balivanich, Carinish, North Uist. (NGR: NF 816602 LR: 22)
The Church of The Trinity dates from the 13th or 14th century, and was one of the largest pre-Reformation churches in the Western Isles. It is believed to have been built by Beatrice, daughter of Somerled, about 1203, or by Amy MacRuari, first wife of John, Lord of the Isles. The buildings are now ruinous, but this was an important centre of learning in medieval times. There was a holy well nearby [NF 814601], known as Tobar na Trionaid
Parking nearby.
Access at all reasonable times.

K135 Temple Preceptory

[Map: 6B, E10] Off B6372, 3 miles SW of Gorebridge, Temple, Midlothian. (NGR: NT 315588 LR: 66)
Temple Preceptory was the main seat of the Knights Templar in Scotland. They were founded to protect pilgrims in the Holy Land, but their order was suppressed in 1312. The property was given to the Order of St John. Little or nothing of the Preceptory remains, except possibly in the ruined parish church, dating from the mid 14th century. The church was

repaired in the 1980s, and stands in an interesting burial ground.
Access at all reasonable times.

K136 Torphichen Preceptory (HS)

[Map: 6B, E8] Off B792, 4 miles SW of Linlithgow, Torphichen, West Lothian. (NGR: NS 972727 LR: 65)
A rather unusual and eerie place, the preceptory has been reduced to the crossing and transepts of the church, and traces of other buildings. It dates from the 12th century, and the parish church was built on the nave. This was the main seat of the Knights Hospitallers from the 12th century. William Wallace held a convention of barons here in 1298.
Exhibition. Sales area. WC. Car and coach parking. £.
Preceptory and parish church open Apr-Sep, Sat 11.00-17.00, Sun and Bank Hols 14.00-17.00.
Tel: 01506 653475/0131 668 8800

K137 Trumpan Church

[Map: 3A, E4] Off B886, 8 miles NE of Dunvegan, Trumpan, Skye. (NGR: NG 225613 LR: 23)
The ruins of a medieval church, formerly with a thatched roof. It was dedicated to St Conan, and stands in an old burial ground. The church is the scene of a cruel massacre when the congregation of MacLeods were burned to death in the church by raiding MacDonalds. In the graveyard is the Trial Stone, which has a small hole near the top. The trial was carried out by blindfolding the accused, who would be proved to be telling the truth if they succeeded in putting their finger in the hole at the first attempt. Lady Grange, who was imprisoned in the outer isles after discovering her husband's Jacobite plottings, is believed to be buried in the graveyard, and there are also two medieval carved slabs.
Parking Nearby.
Access at all reasonable times.

K138 Tullibardine Chapel (HS)

[Map: 5B, C8] Off A823, 6 miles SE of Crieff, Tullibardine, Perthshire. (NGR: NN 909134 LR: 58)
An unaltered medieval church, founded by Sir David Murray of Tullibardine in 1446: it has been used as a burial place by the Murrays since the Reformation. It was rebuilt about 1500, and is one of the most complete examples of a small collegiate church in Scotland.
Exhibition. Parking nearby.
Open Apr-Sep.

K139 Tullich Kirk

[Map: 4, G3] By A93, 2 miles NE of Ballater, Tullich, Aberdeenshire.
(NGR: NO 390975 LR: 44)

The ruins of a medieval church, dating from about 1400, stand within an oval burial ground with old markers. There is a Class I Pictish symbol stone with double-disc and z-rod, mirror and Pictish beast, as well as other carved stones, although they are much weathered. The site is associated with St Nathalan, who died in 678. He is said to have spent his childhood at Tullich and later established a church here.

Access at all reasonable times.

K140 Westside Church (Crosskirk), Westray (HS)

[Map: 2, B2] Off B9067, 3.5 miles S of Pierowall, Tuquoy, SE side of Westray, Orkney. (NGR: HY 455432 LR: 5)

The ruins of a church, dating from the 12th century but with later modifications, which is said to have been built by the Norseman Hafliki Thorkelsson. There was a Norse settlement here, some remains of which survive.

Parking nearby.

Access at all reasonable times: walk to site.
Tel: 01856 841815

Top *Teampull na Trionaid*
Right *St John's Church,*
Edinburgh
Bottom *St Conan's Church,*
Lochawe

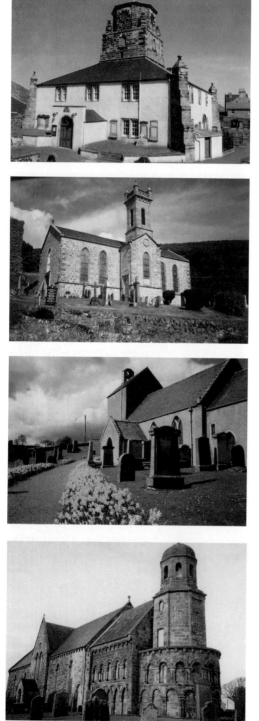

Top left *Burntisland Parish Church*
Above *Symington Parish Church*
Above left *Kilmun Church*
Below left *Stobo Kirk*
Bottom left *St Athernase Church, Leuchars*
Below *Round Tower, Abernethy*

L: Carved Crosses and Memorials

Also see the section on the Picts, and sections on Cathedrals and Churches.

K41 Abercorn Church and Museum
See main entry K41

K42 Aberlady Parish Church
See main entry K42

L1 Barochan Cross (HS)
[Map: 6A, E6] Off A737, Paisley Abbey, Paisley, Renfrewshire. (NGR: NS 486640 LR: 64)
A fine free-standing Celtic cross, sculpted with warriors and human figures, dates from as early as the 8th century. It formerly stood at Barochan, in Houston parish west of Paisley. Also see **Paisley Abbey [J28]**.
Guided tours by arrangement. Explanatory displays. Gift shop. Tearoom. WC. Parking nearby.
Paisley Abbey: open all year, Mon-Sat 10.00-15.30, Sun for services only.
Tel: 0141 889 7654

L2 Campbeltown Cross
[Map: 5A, F4] Off A83, NE of Main Street, Campbeltown, Kintyre, Argyll. (NGR: NR 720204 LR: 68)
A fine 15th-century carved cross, decorated on both sides with figures of saints, including St Michael slaying the dragon, and decorative motifs. The cross was brought here from Kilkivan in the 17th century, and is similar in style to the cross at **Kilchoman [L10]**.
Parking nearby.
Access at all reasonable times.

S75 Colonsay House Gardens
See main entry S75

L3 Crosshall Cross
[Map: 6B, E11] On B6461, 5 miles NE of Kelso, 0.5 miles N of Eccles, Crosshall, Borders. (NGR: NT 760422 LR: 74)
The cross, which is about ten feet high, is carved on all four sides, and dates from medieval times. It has a round head, and decorative features include crosses, a rough figure and a hound.
Disabled access. Parking nearby.
Access at all reasonable times.

K62 Dalmally Church
See main entry K62

Y70 Dumfries Museum
See main entry Y70

L4 Dupplin Cross (HS)
[Map: 5B, C9] On B8062 or B934, 5 miles E of Auchterarder, St Serf's Church, Dunning, Perthshire. (NGR: NO 019146 LR: 15)
A beautifully carved free-standing cross, some six feet high. It dates from the 9th or 10th century and has fine interlace knotwork and scrolled designs, along with a Latin inscription, recently identified as CU [...]NTIN FILIUS FIRCUS – Constantine Mac Fergus, a Pictish king, who ruled over both Picts and Scots. The cross has been moved from Cross Park Field near Forteviot to the **Museum of Scotland [Y6]**, but is due to be installed at **St Serf's Parish Church, Dunning [K125]** in 2002.
Access at all reasonable times.

L5 Edderton Cross-Slab
[Map: 3B, D9] Off A836, 5 miles NW of Tain, 0.5 miles E of crossroads at Edderton, Ross and Cromarty, Highland. (NGR: NH 719842 LR: 21)
Standing in the graveyard of the 18th-century church is a carved cross-slab, which now leans. On one side is a cross, below which is a rider within a curved frame, while on the other side is a large ringed cross on a tall stem. There are the ruins of an earlier church to the east of the modern building. The first letters of names of trees and shrubs in the burial ground spell 'Eader Dun', the old name for the Edderton. Other Pictish fragments from here are held at **Tain Through Time [Y189]**. The church can be visited, contact Edderton Old Church Trust.
Disabled access. Parking nearby.
Access at all reasonable times.
Tel: 01862 812245 (Edderton Old Church Trust)

N103 Finlaggan
See main entry N103

K71 Govan Old Parish Church
The church houses a fine collection of early Christian stones, including a decorated sarcophagus, five hogback tombstones, two cross shafts and upright crosses, and a number of recumbent slabs.
See main entry K71

L6 Hilton of Cadboll Carved Stone and Chapel (HS)
[Map: 3B, D10] Off B9165 or B9166, 7 miles SE of Tain, Hilton of Cadboll, Ross and Cromarty, Highland. (NGR: NH 873768 LR: 21)
The remains of a small rectangular chapel, dedicated to the Virgin Mary. It was nearby that the fine Pictish carved stone, decorated with Pictish symbols and panels of figures, was found, dating from the 8th or 9th century. It had been reused as a 17th-century grave

marker erasing one side, but in 1922 was moved to what is now the **Museum of Scotland [Y6]**. A copy was recently put back here, and excavations have revealed the base of the original stone as well as other fragments.

Parking nearby.
Access at all reasonable times: short walk.
Tel: 01667 460232

L7 Inchinnan Early Christian Stones

[Map: 6A, E6] Off A8, 3 miles N of Paisley, Inchinnan, Renfrewshire. (NGR: NS 479689 LR: 64)

Three sculpted stones lie in a covered area between the church and bell-tower, and consist of a carved sarcophagus, grave-slab and cross-slab. Inchinnan was an early Christian site, dedicated to St Conval, a saint from Ireland, and became a place of pilgrimage. The present church was built when the medieval church was demolished to make way for Glasgow airport.

Disabled access. Parking.
Access at all reasonable times; church open Thu during term time 12.00-13.30.

K75 Inchkenneth Chapel (HS)

See main entry K75

J20 Iona Abbey (HS)

The magnificent St Martin's Cross and St John's Cross – the latter a replica: the original is reconstructed and displayed in the Infirmary Museum – stand just outside the church, and the Infirmary Museum houses a splendid collection of sculpted stones and crosses, one of the largest collections of early Christian carved stones in Europe.

See main entry J20

L8 Keills Cross (HS)

[Map: 5A, D4] Off B8025, 6 miles SW of Tayvallich, Keills, Argyll. (NGR: NR 690806 LR: 55)

In the old chapel, which has been reroofed, is the Keills Cross, which is believed to date from the second half of the 8th century. The cross is carved with a central boss, panels of interlace, as well as figures. It formerly stood just behind the chapel. Keills was an important ecclesiastical centre, and there is also a fine collection of carved grave slabs.

Explanatory panels. Parking nearby.
Access at all reasonable times – short walk to chapel: may be muddy.

L9 Kilberry Sculpted Stones (HS)

[Map: 5A, E4] Off B8024, 17 miles SW of Lochgilphead, Kilberry Castle, Argyll. (NGR: NR 709642 LR: 62)

An important collection of early stone crosses and sculpted stones, which date from medieval times, is located here. The stones were collected from the estate around Kilberry.

Sculpted stones: access at all reasonable times.

L10 Kilchoman Cross

[Map: 5A, E2] Off B8018, 3 miles NW of Bruichladdich, Kilchoman, Islay. (NGR: NR 214631 LR: 60)

A fine eight-foot-high disc-headed cross, which was carved about 1500, and is similar to the **Campbeltown Cross [L2]**, is located in the burial ground. One face has the depiction of the Crucifixion, with other figures including a horseman and knotwork decoration. In the base are cups and a stone. Wishes are said to be granted if the stone is turned in the holes in the correct order – towards the sun. There are several carved grave slabs, and a stone known as the Sanctuary Cross.

Parking nearby.
Access at all reasonable times.

L11 Kildalton Cross and Chapel (HS)

[Map: 5A, E3] Off A846, 7 miles NE of Port Ellen, Kildalton, Islay. (NGR: NR 458508 LR: 60)

The finest surviving intact cross in Scotland, dating from the 8th century, and carved from a single slab. The ringed cross has a representation of the Virgin and Child flanked by angels on one side, while the other has serpent and boss patterns with four lions around the central boss. Other representations illustrate biblical scenes. The remains of a Norse ritual killing are said to have been found beneath the cross when it was excavated in 1890; and there may have been an early Christian community here. The small ruined chapel, dedicated to St John the Beloved, dates from the 12th or 13th century, and is a simple rectangular building. It houses several carved grave slabs, some with effigies of warriors, and there are more in the churchyard, dating from the 15th-17th centuries. The 15th-century Thief's Cross is nearby.

Parking nearby.
Access at all reasonable times.

K78 Killean Old Parish Church

See main entry K78

L12 Kilmartin Sculpted Stones and Parish Church (HS)

[Map: 5A, D4] On A816, Kilmartin, Argyll. (NGR: NR 834988 LR: 55)

Located in the burial ground of the church is a fine collection of West Highland grave slabs, and in the church, which dates from 1835, are two crosses, one very weathered, which has a Christ figure and now looks quite scary. **Kilmartin House Museum [A9]** is nearby, as are many burial cairns and other prehistoric sites in Kilmartin glen.

Parking.
Access to churchyard at all reasonable time; church open Apr-Oct, daily 9.30-18.00.

L13 Kilmodan Sculpted Stones (HS)

[Map: 5A, D5] On A886, 8 miles N of Colintrave, Kilmodan, Clachan of Glendaruel, Argyll. (NGR: NR 995862 LR: 55)

A group of West Highland carved burial slabs are situated in the burial ground.

Parking nearby.
Access at all reasonable times.

L14 Kilmory Knap Chapel (HS)

[Map: 5A, D4] Off B8025, Kilmory Knap, 14 miles SE of Lochgilphead, Loch Sween, Knapdale, Argyll. (NGR: NR 703752 LR: 62)

The chapel, which has been reroofed, houses MacMillan's Cross, a fine medieval carved stone cross, and a collection of West Highland burial slabs, moved here for protection from the burial ground.

Explanatory panel. Parking nearby.
Access at all reasonable times.

L15 Kinord Cross-Slab

[Map: 4, G4] Off B9119, 4.5 miles E of Ballater, Muir of Dinnet National Nature Reserve, Aberdeenshire. (NGR: NO 440997 LR: 37)

This is a fine cross-slab, dating from the 9th century. The cross is filled with interlace knotwork. **New and Old Kinord [A13]** are nearby.

Disabled limited access. Parking nearby.
Access at all reasonable times.

L16 Kirkmadrine Early Christian Stones (HS)

[Map: 6A, I5] Off A716, 7 miles S of Stranraer, Kirkmadrine, Dumfries and Galloway. (NGR: NX 080483 LR: 82)

Displayed in the porch of the former 19th-century chapel are some of the oldest Christian monuments in Britain. A pillar stone, dating from the 5th century, is carved with a circled cross and Latin inscription 'Here lie the holy and chief priests, Ides, Viventius and Mavorius'. Two other 5th- or early 6th-century stones are also inscribed.

Disabled access. Parking nearby.
Access at all reasonable times.

L17 McLean's Cross (HS)

[Map: 5A, C2] Off unlisted road, Iona, Argyll. (NGR: NM 285242 LR: 48)

Located on the road between the abbey and the nunnery is MacLean's Cross, a fine 15th-century carved stone cross.

Walk to cross – on route to abbey from passenger ferry to island.
Access at all reasonable times.

L18 Merkland Cross (HS)

[Map: 6B, H9] Off M74, 6 miles SE of Lockerbie, Merkland Smithy, near Ecclefechan. (NGR: NY 250721 LR: 85)

A fine carved and decorated cross, dating from the 15th century.

Parking nearby.
Access at all reasonable times.

L19 Milnholm Cross

[Map: 6B, H10] On B6357, 1 mile S of Newcastleton, Mangerton, Borders. (NGR: NY 475862 LR: 79)

The cross, which was erected around 1320, is to commemorate Alexander Armstrong, who was murdered in **Hermitage Castle [N110]**, about 4 miles to the north. The cross is near the remains of Mangerton Castle, the stronghold of the Armstrongs for 300 years.

Car parking.
Access at all reasonable times.

Y139 Museum of Islay Life

Displays include an important collection of carved stones, dating from the 6th to 16th centuries.

See main entry Y139

Y6 Museum of Scotland

See main entry Y6

L20 Netherton Cross

[Map: 6B, E7] Off A724, Strathmore Road, Hamilton Old Parish Church, Hamilton, Lanarkshire. (NGR: NS 723555 LR: 64)

Standing in the burial ground of Hamilton Old Parish Church is the Netherton Cross, a 10th-century sculpted cross, decorated with figures, animals and cross-weave. There are also Covenanting memorials. The present church was designed and built by William Adam in 1732-4: the only church designed by him. There are fine stained-glass windows.

Church: WC. Disabled access. Car and coach parking.
Church: open all year, Mon-Fri, 10.30-15.30, Sat 10.30-12.00, Sun after 10.45 service; evenings by appt.
Tel: 01698 281905 Web: www.hopc.fsnet.co.uk
Email: office@hopc.fsnet.co.uk

L21 Nith Bridge Cross

[Map: 6B, G8] Off A702, Thornhill, Dumfries and Galloway. (NGR: NX 868954 LR: 78)

The most complete Anglian Cross apart from the **Ruthwell Cross [L24]**, the Nith Bridge Cross stands to about a height of nine feet, and carvings include animals and winged beasts.

Parking nearby.
Access at all reasonable times.

K91 Old Steeple, Dundee

Dundee's Mercat Cross, dating from 1586 but crowned by a modern unicorn, is nearby.

See main entry K91

L22 Ormiston Market Cross (HS)

[Map: 6B, E10] On B6371, 7 miles E of Haddington, Ormiston, East Lothian. (NGR: NT 413694 LR: 66)

The free-standing cross, which dates from the 15th century, was to show that the inhabitants of Ormiston had the right to hold a market.

Parking nearby.

Access at all reasonable times.

J27 Oronsay Priory

The Oronsay Cross is a fine late-medieval carved cross. On one side is the figure of Christ being crucified, a pattern of foliage on both sides, as well as: 'this is the cross of Colinus, son of Cristinus MacDuffie'. More than 30 fine carved grave slabs are in the Prior's House.

See main entry J27

J28 Paisley Abbey

The striking Barochan Cross **[L1]** is housed here.

See main entry J28

K93 Pennygown Chapel

See main entry K93

L23 Pilgrims Way to Iona

[Map: 5A C3] Barvas and Rinns of Mull, Mull.

A series of standing stones is said to mark the old pilgrim route from Grass Point [NM 748310] to Fionnphort as markers for pilgrims on their way to **Iona [J20]**. Stones which survive include:

• Six foot standing stone at Uluvalt, W of A849 [NM 547300] • Seven foot standing stone at Rossal, S of A849 [NM 543282] • Seven foot standing stone at Taoslin, just S of A849 [NM 397224] • 6.5 foot standing stone at Suie, N of A849 near cairn [NM 371218] • 8.5 foot standing stone at Tirghoil, just N of A849 [NM 353224] • Eight foot standing stone at Achaban, just N of A849 [NM 313233].

There was a final standing stone at Catchean, near Fionnphort, but this was destroyed by accident in 1863.

L24 Ruthwell Cross (HS)

[Map: 6B, H9] Off B724, 9 miles SE of Dumfries, Ruthwell, Dumfries and Galloway. (NGR: NY 100682 LR: 85)

A magnificent Anglian sculpted cross, dating from the 7th century, standing about 17 feet high.

It was destroyed by the order of the General Assembly in 1640, but has since been reassembled from the smashed pieces – there is information about the reconstruction at the Savings Banks Museum **[Y170]**.

All four sides are decorated, the two wider sides with biblical scenes, while the other sides are carved with foliage and beasts.

Parking.

Access can be arranged by contacting the keyholder.
Tel: 01387 870429.

K95 Sanquhar Church

See main entry K95

L25 Shandwick Cross-Slab

[Map: 3B, D10] Off B9166, 4 miles SE of Tain, S of Balintore, Shandwick, Ross and Cromarty. (NGR: NH 855747 LR: 21)

Also known as Clach a' Charridh, 'stone of the monument', the Shandwick Stone is an impressive nine-foot-high cross-slab encased in a glass box. One side is decorated with a cross made of protruding bosses, as well as angels, beasts and interlaced snakes. The other side is divided into five carved panels. The stone was blown down in a gale of 1846 and broken. It was joined back together and then re-erected, although it may have been moved from its original position.

Parking nearby.

Access at all reasonable times: over stile.
Tel: 01862 832525 (Shandwick Stone Trust)

Y173 Shetland Museum

See main entry Y173

K26 St Andrews Cathedral (HS)

The museum houses a large and magnificent collection of Christian and early medieval sculpture, including the magnificent St Andrews Sarcophagus.

See main entry K26

K98 St Bean's Church, Fowlis Wester

See main entry K98

K28 St Clement's Church (HS)

See main entry K28

L26 St Demhan's Cross, Creich

[Map: 3B, D9] Off A9, 11 miles W of Dornoch, Creich, in field E of burial ground, Sutherland. (NGR: NH 636892 LR: 21)

A tall carved stone, dating from the 9th or 10th century, with the outline of a large cross. The cross is named after St Devenick, an early saint, and nearby are the ruins of an 18th-century parish church, built on the site of the medieval church of St Demhan or Devenick. Fairs were held here.

Parking nearby but take care.

Access at all reasonable times.

K119 St Mary's Church, Rothesay (HS)

See main entry K119

K123 St Peter's Church, Duffus (HS)

St Peter's Cross, a typical medieval market cross, dates from the 14th century (markets were regularly held in kirkyards).
See main entry K123

K125 St Serf's Church, Dunning (HS)

See main entry K125

F30 St Vigeans Museum (HS)

See main entry F30

L27 Stones, Stocks and Stories

[Map: 5B, C8] On A85, Town Hall, High Street, Crieff, Perthshire. (NGR: NN 865215 LR: 58)
The exhibition features Crieff Town Stocks, which are unique in design and one of the few sets remaining; the Drummond or Market Cross; and the 1000-year-old Burgh Cross, a Pictish cross-slab.
Open as Crieff TIC.
Tel: 01764 652578 Fax: 01764 655422

Y185 Strathnaver Museum

An 8th-century carved slab, incised with a cross and known as the Farr Stone, is located in the burial ground.
See main entry Y185

L28 Sueno's Stone (HS)

[Map: 4, E2] Off A96, on E edge of Forres, Moray. (NGR: NJ 809653 LR: 27)
Standing over 22-foot tall is the magnificent sculpted stone, which dates from around the 9th century. One face is carved with a large ring-headed cross filled with interlaced knotwork. The other side is divided into four panels relating the events of a battle. It has been suggested that this stone marks the end of the Pictish period, the final triumph of the Scots. This seems unlikely, and it probably commemorates a battle against the Norsemen.
Parking nearby.
Access at all reasonable times – stone is encased in a glass case for protection – viewing may be difficult in wet weather.
Tel: 01667 460232

J33 Whithorn Priory (HS)

A fine collection of early Christian sculpture is housed in the nearby museum, including the 'Latinus Stone', the earliest Christian memorial in Scotland; the 'St Peter's Stone'; and the 10th-century Monreith Cross.
See **Whithorn: Cradle of Christianity in Scotland [J34]**.
See main entry J33

Above *Kilmartin*

Above left *Campbeltown Cross*
Above right *Kilchoman Cross*
Left *MacMillan's Cross, Kilmory Knap*
Below *Infirmary Museum, Iona Abbey*

M: *Spiritual Places*

This is a small selection of sites which have or have had spiritual or religious significance, such as standing stones and healing wells.

D6 Burghead

The Well, rediscovered in 1809, consists of a rock-hewn chamber, reached down stone steps. It has been identified by some as being associated with St Ethan, a disciple of St Columba, and has a deep tank of water surrounded by a platform, with a basin and pedestal. Burghead is well known for the 'Burning of the Clavie', an old fire festival when a burning barrel of tar is taken around the streets on 12 January.
See main entry D6

S75 Colonsay House Gardens

In the garden is Tobar Oran, a round covered well with steps leading down to the water. Beside the well is St Oran's Cross, which is carved with the face of a man and dates from early Christian times.
See main entry S75

M1 Dagon Stone, Darvel

[Map: 6B, F7] Off A71, 9 miles E of Kilmarnock, Hastings Square, Darvel, Ayrshire. (NGR: NS 563374 LR: 71)
A standing stone known as the 'Dagon Stone', now with a round stone on top of it, was moved to Hastings Square in the 1960s. Newlyweds would walk around the stone for good luck.

M2 Fairy Bridge

[Map: 3A, E4] On A850, 3 miles NE of Dunvegan, Skye. (NGR: NG 278512 LR: 23)
The small bridge stands at the meeting of three roads, and is called the Fairy Bridge. It is said to be where the chief of MacLeods parted from his fairy wife, by whom he had had a child. The Fairy Flag, which is preserved at **Dunvegan Castle [N24]**, is said to have come from her.
Parking nearby.
Access at all reasonable times.

F17 Glamis Church, Pictish Stone and Well

In the adjacent garden of Glamis Manse (across the road from the church) is a fine carved Pictish stone. A healing well, St Fergus's Well, lies below the church, and is reached by a landscaped trail.
See main entry F17

A8 Holyrood Park (HS)

Within the park are the remains of St Anthony's Chapel and St Anthony's Well [NT 275736], a holy well.
See main entry A8

C33 Kempock Stone, Gourock

The stone, which is about six feet high, is known as Granny Kempock's Stone, and was used by fishermen in rituals to try to ensure good weather and fair winds, as well as a good catch of fish. Fisherman and others would walk around the stone seven times, carrying a basket of sand. The same ritual was used by betrothed and newly married couples to get Granny's blessing.
See main entry C33

L10 Kilchoman Cross

A fine eight-foot-high disc-headed cross, which was carved about 1500, is located in the burial ground. One face has the depiction of the Crucifixion, with other figures including a horseman and knotwork decoration. In the base are cups and a stone. Wishes are said to be granted if the stone is turned in the holes in the correct order – towards the sun.
See main entry L10

K80 Kincardine O'Neil Old Parish Church

The site is associated with St Erchan, an early saint. His well stands across the road from the church, and is now enclosed in a small building of 1858, although there is apparently no water.
See main entry K80

M3 Maggie Walls Monument

[Map: 5B, C9] On B8062, 4 miles E of Auchterarder, 1 mile W of Dunning, Perthshire. (NGR: NO 006141 LR: 58)
The monument, which consists of a rough plinth and a cross, is believed to commemorate the burning of Maggie Walls, a reputed witch, in 1657. The writing is regularly renewed and flowers are often left here.
Car and coach parking.
Access at all reasonable times.

M4 Rhymer's Stone Viewpoint

[Map: 6B F10] On Old Bogle Burn Road, the old road between Melrose and Newtown St Boswells, Borders.
This stone is said to mark the spot of the Eildon Tree, where in the 13th century Thomas the Rhymer or True Thomas, Thomas Learmoth of Ercildoune, met the Queen of the Fairies. Thomas spent seven years in the land of the fairies, and when he returned he had the power of prophecy – many of his prophecies are

said to have come true. He is said to later have disappeared, presumably returning to fairyland.
Access at all reasonable times.

K99 St Blane's Church (HS)

In a peaceful and pleasant location is the site of a 6th-century Christian community, founded by St Blane, who was born on Bute. There is a reputed holy and wishing well nearby.
See main entry K99

M5 St Curitan's Well, Munlochy

[Map: 3B, E9] Just S of A832, 5 miles N of Inverness, 0.5 miles NW of Munlochy, Hill o' Hirdie, Black Isle, Highland. (NGR: NH 641537 LR: 26)

St Curitan's Well, a clootie well, is still in use, and the trees and fence around the well are adorned with rags. The well was dedicated to St Curitan or Boniface, an 8th-century saint who was active among the Picts. To have a wish granted, a small amount of well water must be spilt on the ground three times, a rag tied on a nearby tree, the sign of the cross made, then a drink of water taken from the well. Anyone removing a rag from the well (or any well or healing site) will be afflicted by the misfortunes of the person who put it there.
Access at all reasonable times.

K115 St Mary's Chapel, Crosskirk (HS)

The simple dry-stone chapel, possibly built in the 12th century, is roofless but the walls are complete. The building probably had a thatched roof. Part of the church was used as a burial place for the Gunn family from the late 19th century, and to the south is a healing well, also dedicated to St Mary.
See main entry K115

K120 St Mary's Kirk, Auchindour (HS)

The fine ruinous shell of a medieval parish church with a Romanesque doorway and 14th-century sacrament house. About 100 yards to the west is St Mary's Well, which was used for healing and to alleviate toothache.
See main entry K120

K37 St Mary's Parish Church, Whitekirk

Whitekirk was a place of pilgrimage from around 1295 after Agnes, Countess of Dunbar, was healed at a nearby well [NT 598817?]. The number of miracles which occurred at the well was so great that a shrine was built in 1309 and dedicated to St Mary. It was visited by Aeneas Sylvius Piccolomini (later Pope Pious II) in 1435 who, after being saved from a storm, walked barefoot to Whitekirk from Dunbar. A fresco in the chapter house of Siena Cathedral records his visit. This well apparently dried up around 1830, and its location is not certain.
See main entry K37

M6 St Mary's Well, Culloden

[Map: 3B, F9] Off B9006, 3.5 miles E of Inverness, Culloden, Highland. (NGR: NH 723452 LR: 27)

Located in a forestry plantation and accessible by a forest trail, the spring here, which flows into a stone basin enclosed by a wall, is also known as Tobar na h'Oige ('well of youth'). It is a healing and clootie well, and rags were and are left on surrounding trees.
Access at all reasonable times.

M7 St Queran's Well, Islesteps

[Map: 6B, H8] Off A710, 2.5 miles SE of Dumfries, Islesteps, Troqueer, Dumfries and Galloway. (NGR: NX 956722 LR: 84)

The clootie well is dedicated to St Queran, a 9th-century Scottish saint. The water was used for healing, and especially employed for women and children. Hundreds of coins were found in the spring when it was cleared out in 1870. Other items included pins, and cloth or rags are still tied to nearby bushes.
Parking nearby.
Access at all reasonable times: walk to well.

Y181 St Ronan's Wells Interpretive Centre, Innerleithen

The centre features memorabilia of Sir Walter Scott with information and photographs about the local Cleikum ceremony and the St Ronan's Border Games. The site was visited by Scott and used in one of his novels. The well water can be tasted, and is said to have medicinal properties. In the 19th century it was recorded as being effective for 'ophthalmic, scorbutic, bilious and dyspeptic complaints'. The well, which was also known as the 'Dow-well', was dedicated to St Ronan and was an old healing well.
See main entry Y181

K128 St Triduana's Chapel (HS)

The church, which is dedicated to St Mary and The Trinity, was founded as a collegiate establishment by James III in the 1460s, although it is a much older site. There is an extremely unusual hexagonal vaulted chamber, known as St Triduana's Chapel or Well, only the lower parts of a two-storey building. Water still flows from a spring here. Visiting Triduana's shrines were supposed to help blindness and other conditions of the eye. Interesting kirkyard.

See main entry K128

K130 Stenton

The Cardinal's Hat, a rood well dating from the 14th century, which is housed in small chamber resembling a cardinal's hat, hence the name.

See main entry K130

K137 Trumpan Church

The Trial Stone, which has a small hole near the top, stands in the grave yard. The trial was carried out by blindfolding the accused, who would be proved to be telling the truth if they succeeded in putting their finger in the hole at the first attempt.

See main entry K137

M8 Wigtown Martyrs' Monument

[Map: 6A, I6] Off A714, Wigtown, Dumfries and Galloway. (NGR: NX 436555 LR: 83)

The marble monument in the burial ground commemorates the execution by drowning in 1685 of two women who had refused to repudiate the Covenant.

Graham of Claverhouse, 'Bloody Clavers' or 'Bonnie Dundee' presided at the executions, and had the women tied to a stake to be drowned by the incoming tide. A stone shaft on the shore is said to mark the spot, although it has been suggested that the women escaped death.

Access at all reasonable times.

M9 Witch's Stone, Dornoch

[Map: 3B, D10] Off A949, Littledown, Dornoch, Sutherland. (NGR: NH 797896 LR: 21)

The stone, an upright slab, is said to mark the place in 1722 where the last witch was burned in Scotland. Janet Horne was accused of, among other things, turning her daughter into a pony, getting her shod, and riding her to meetings with the devil. This accusation appears to have been in 1727, rather than 1722.

Access at all reasonable times.

Above *Rood Well, Stenton*
Above right *St Fergus Well, Glamis*
Right: St Anthony's Well, Holyrood Park

N1: Castles, Towers and Palaces – 1

There were as many as 3000 castles in Scotland. Although most of these were modest towers and fortalices, some were, and are, grand fortresses. The following castles are either still occupied or are furnished or are particularly impressive or grand.

Also see the sections on *N2: Castles, Towers and Palaces – 2*; *S1: Houses and Mansions*; and *Q: Clan Castles and Museums*.

N1 Aikwood Tower

[Map: 6B, F10] Off B7009, 4 miles W of Selkirk, Borders. (NGR: NT 420260 LR: 73)

Aikwood Tower, a 16th-century tower house, was a property of the Scotts. The tower is now home to Sir David Steel, Presiding Officer of the Scottish Parliament. There is an exhibition about James Hogg, the 'Ettrick Shepherd', the well-known Scottish writer and poet, and temporary exhibitions of art and sculpture.

Permanent exhibition: James Hogg, the Ettrick Shepherd; medieval-style garden. Temporary art exhibitions. Car parking. £.
Open May-Sep, Tue, Thu and Sun 14.00-17.00 until end 2002.
Tel: 01750 52253 Web: www.aikwoodscottishborders.com
Fax: 01750 52253 Email: steel@aikwoodscottishborders.com

N2 Alloa Tower (NTS)

[Map: 5B, D8] Off A907, 7 miles E of Stirling, Alloa, Clackmannan. (NGR: NS 889925 LR: 58)

Alloa Tower is a tall imposing building, altered down the years, and has a rare medieval timber roof. Alloa was held by the Erskines, and Mary, Queen of Scots, was reconciled with Darnley here in 1565, and gave the Earldom of Mar to the family. The 6th Earl 'Bobbing John' led the Jacobites in the 1715 Rising. The tower has been renovated.

Explanatory displays. Collection of portraits of the Erskine family. WC. Disabled WC & access to ground floor only. Parking nearby. Group concessions. £.
Open (2002) 25 Mar-27 Oct, daily 13.00-17.00; morning visits available for pre-booked groups.
Tel: 01259 211701

N3 Balgonie Castle

[Map: 6B, D9] Off A911, 6.5 miles NE of Kirkcaldy, Balgonie, Fife. (NGR: NO 313007 LR: 59)

A fine 14th-century keep within a courtyard enclosing ranges of buildings, many of which have been re-

stored. The property was held by the Sibbalds, Lundies, and the Leslies.

Guided tours. Picnic area. Disabled access to ground floor. Car and coach parking. Weddings. £.
Open all year, daily 10.00-17.00, unless hired for a private function, including Christmas & New Year.
Tel: 01592 750119 Fax: 01592 753103

N4 Ballindalloch Castle

[Map: 4, F3] On A95, 7.5 miles SW of Aberlour, Ballindalloch, Moray. (NGR: NJ 178365 LR: 28)

An impressive 16th-century Z-plan tower house, altered and extended in later centuries. One of the few castles that is still occupied by the same family who built it: the Macpherson-Grants.

Many rooms. Large collection of 17th-century Spanish paintings. Audio-visual presentation. Shop. Tea room. WC. Gardens and grounds. Rock garden. Rose garden. River walks. Famous breed of Aberdeen Angus cattle. Disabled access to ground floor and grounds. ££.
Open Good Fri-Sep, Sun-Fri 10.30-17.00, closed Sat; other times by appt throughout the year.
Tel: 01807 500206 Web: www.ballindallochcastle.co.uk
Fax: 01807 500210 Email: enquiries@ballindallochcastle.co.uk

N5 Barcaldine Castle

[Map: 5A, B4] Off A828, 8 miles N of Oban, 4 miles N of Connel, Barcaldine, Argyll. (NGR: NM 907405 LR: 49)

A fine restored 16th-century L-plan tower house with turrets and harled walls, completed by Sir Duncan Campbell of Glenorchy in 1609, and still held by the Campbells. There are secret stairs and a bottle dungeon. The ghost of Harriet Campbell, a 'Blue Lady', has reputedly been seen here, and it is said that a piano can be heard playing on windy nights.

Explanatory displays. Secret stairs. Bottle dungeon. Gifts. Garden. Car parking. £. B&B accommodation: 1 double ensuite room and 1 family bedroom with shower room.
Open: tel to confirm or check website for opening dates and times. Accommodation available Jul-Aug. Restricted access to bedrooms during public opening.
Tel: 01631 720598 Fax: 01631 720598
Web: www.oban.org.uk/attractions/barcaldine.html
Email: barcaldine.castle@tesco.net

N6 Blair Castle

[Map: 5B, A8] Off B8079, 7 miles N of Pitlochry, 1 mile NW of Blair Atholl, Perthshire. (NGR: NN 867662 LR: 43)

Set in acres of park land and white-washed and castellated, Blair Castle is a rambling mansion of the Dukes of Atholl. The Murray Earls of Atholl were made Marquises, then Dukes of Atholl in 1703. The Duke of Atholl has the unique distinction of having the only remaining private army in Europe, while Blair Castle is the last stronghold in Britain to be besieged, albeit unsuccessfully, having been attacked by the Jacobites in 1746.

Some 30 interesting rooms. Collections of paintings, tapestries, arms, armour, china, costumes and Jacobite mementoes. Fine Georgian plasterwork. Guided tours for groups. Gift shop. Licensed restaurant. Sun terrace. Walled garden. Picnic area. Deer park. Pony trekking. Play area. Disabled access & facilities. Car and coach parking. Group concessions. £££.

Open Apr-Oct, daily 10.00-18.00; last admission 17.00; winter tours by arrangement.
Tel: 01796 481207   Fax: 01796 481487
Web: www.blair-castle.co.uk   Email: office@blair-castle.co.uk

N7 Borthwick Castle

[Map: 6B, E10] Off A7, 2 miles SE of Gorebridge, Borthwick, Midlothian. (NGR: NT 370597 LR: 66)

One of the most impressive castles in Scotland, Borthwick is a magnificent looming tower house, rising to 110 feet high with walls up to 14 feet thick. The castle was built by Sir William Borthwick in 1430, whose stone effigy is in nearby **Borthwick Parish Church [K52]**. James Hepburn, Earl of Bothwell, and Mary, Queen of Scots, visited the castle in 1567 after their marriage and were besieged here: Mary only escaped disguised as a man.

10 rooms with ensuite facilities. Castle may be booked for exclusive use. Conferences, weddings, banquets and meetings. Not suitable for disabled. Garden.
Hotel: open mid-Mar to 2 Jan and to non-residents. Borthwick Church open all year, daily.
Tel: 01875 820514   Fax: 01875 821702

N8 Braemar Castle

[Map: 4, G3] On A93, 0.5 miles NE of Braemar, Kincardine & Deeside. (NGR: NO 156924 LR: 43)

Braemar Castle is an altered 17th-century tower house, with later star-shaped artillery defences. There is a pit-prison. The castle was built by the Erskines but passed to the Farquharsons. It was used by the government in the aftermath of the Jacobite Risings. *Many interesting rooms. Guided tours. Explanatory sheets. Gift shop. WC. Picnic area. Car and coach parking. Group concessions. £.*
Open Apr-Oct, daily 10.00-18.00, last entry 17.30, closed Fri; open Fri in Jul and Aug.
Tel: 01339 741219   Fax: 01339 741219
Web: www.braemarcastle.co.uk   Email: invercauld@freenet.com

N9 Brodick Castle (NTS)

[Map: 6A, F5] Off A841, 1.5 miles N of Brodick, Cladach, Arran. (NGR: NS 016378 LR: 69)

Occupying a magnificent site overlooking Brodick Bay, the large castle incorporates an ancient keep, while extensive castellated additions were made in 1844 by the architect James Gillespie Graham. Brodick was long a property of the Hamiltons, and saw much action down the centuries.
Collections of furniture, porcelain, pictures and silver. Gift shop. Licensed restaurant. WC. Gardens and country park, ice house, summer house and adventure playground. Nature trail and access to Goatfell. Disabled WC and access. Car and coach parking. £££.
Castle and walled garden open (2002) 25 Mar-27 Oct, daily 10.00-17.00; reception centre, restaurant and shop also open

1 Nov-22 Dec, Fri-Sun 10.00-17.00; country park open all year, daily 9.30-sunset.
Tel: 01770 302202   Fax: 01770 302312

N10 Brodie Castle (NTS)

[Map: 4, E2] Off A96, 4.5 miles W of Forres, Brodie, Moray. (NGR: NH 980578 LR: 27)

A large and impressive building, Brodie is a 16th-century tower house, with extensive additions, which was further enlarged in the 19th century by the architect William Burn. The property was owned by the Brodies from 1160, but was renovated in 1980 after passing to The National Trust for Scotland. A fine Pictish cross-slab stands in the avenue up to the castle.
Collection of paintings and furniture. Guided tours available. Explanatory displays. Gift shop. Tearoom. WC. Picnic area. Garden and adventure playground. Disabled facilities including Braille guides. Car and coach parking. Group concessions. £££.
Open (2002) 25 Mar-29 Sep, Thu-Mon 11.00-18.00; grounds open all year, daily 9.30-sunset.
Tel: 01309 641371   Fax: 01309 641600

N11 Castle Fraser (NTS)

[Map: 4, G5] Off B993 or B977, 6.5 miles SW of Inverurie, Aberdeenshire. (NGR: NJ 724126 LR: 38)

Magnificent and well preserved, Castle Fraser is a tall and massive Z-plan tower house, mostly dating from between 1575 and 1636. Two projecting wings form a courtyard, the final side being completed by other buildings, one with an arched gateway. The property was acquired by the Frasers in 1454, who held it until 1921.
Explanatory sheets. Many interesting rooms. Gift shop. Tea room. Picnic area. Garden and grounds. Adventure playground. Car and coach parking. Group concessions. £££.
Open (2002) 25 Mar-28 Jun and 2 Sep-27 Oct, Fri-Tue 12.00-17.00; 29 Jun-1 Sep, daily 10.00-17.00; shop also open 28 Oct-22 Dec, Sat-Sun 12.00-16.00.
Tel: 01330 833463

N12 Castle Menzies

[Map: 5B, B8] Off B846, 1.5 miles NW of Aberfeldy, Castle Menzies, Perthshire. (NGR: NN 837496 LR: 52)

Castle Menzies is a fine altered and extended castle, and was a property of the Menzies family until 1918. Bonnie Prince Charlie stayed here for two nights in 1746, but four days later the castle was seized by Hanoverian forces, led by the Duke of Cumberland, the 'Butcher of Culloden'. It was bought back by the Menzies Clan Society in 1957. A small museum about the Menzies clan has exhibits including Bonnie Prince Charlie's death mask.
Access to all old parts. Explanatory displays. Museum about Menzies Clan. Gift shop. Tea room. Disabled access to part of ground floor, tea room and gift shop. WC. Car and limited coach parking. Group concessions. £.
Open Apr or Easter-mid Oct, Mon-Sat 10.30-17.00, Sun 14.00-17.00; last entry 16.30.
Tel: 01887 820982

N13 Castle Stalker

[Map: 5A, B4] Off A828, 20 miles N of Oban, Portnacroish, Argyll. (NGR: NM 921473 LR: 49)

Standing dramatically on a small island in a magnificent location, Castle Stalker is a tall, massive and simple keep. It was built by Duncan Stewart of Appin, who was made Chamberlain of the Isles, and is believed to have been used by James IV as a hunting lodge. The castle was abandoned about 1780, but restored from ruin in the 1960s.

Parking nearby. Not suitable for coach parties. £££.

Open by appt from Apr-Sep – tel for details (£6.00 admission charge). Times variable depending on tides and weather as reached by boat.

Tel: 01883 622768   Fax: 01883 626238

N14 Cawdor Castle

[Map: 3B, E10] On B9090, off A96, 5 miles SW of Nairn, Cawdor, Highlands. (NGR: NH 847499 LR: 27)

One of the most magnificent strongholds in Scotland, Cawdor Castle consists of a tall keep within a courtyard and ditch. The 5th Thane of Cawdor built much of the present castle, but the Campbells obtained Cawdor in 1511 by kidnapping the girl heiress, Muriel Calder. The Campbells of Cawdor, her descendants, remained at the castle, and were made Earls of Cawdor in 1827.

Fine collections of portraits, furnishings and tapestries. Explanatory displays. Three shops: gift shop, wool and book shop. Licensed restaurant and snack bar. Gardens, grounds and nature trails. Golf course and putting. Disabled access to grounds; some of castle. Car and coach parking. Group concessions. Conferences. £££.

Open May-mid-Oct, daily 10.00-17.30; last admission 17.00.

Tel: 01667 404615   Fax: 01667 404674

Web: www.cawdorcastle.com   Email: info@cawdorcastle.com

N15 Craigievar Castle (NTS)

[Map: 4, G4] Off A980, 4.5 miles S of Alford, Aberdeenshire. (NGR: NJ 566095 LR: 37)

A well-preserved and picturesque castle, Craigievar Castle is a massive L-plan tower house of seven storeys, which was completed in 1626. Turrets, gables, chimney-stacks and corbelling crown the upper storeys, while lower storeys are very plain. The interior has contemporary plasterwork and panelling. The property belonged to the Mortimers, but passed to the Forbeses of Menie.

Guided tours only. No coaches. No groups. £££.

Open (2002) 25 Mar-27 Oct, Thu-Mon 12.00-17.00; grounds all year, daily 9.30-sunset.

Tel: 01339 883635

N16 Crathes Castle (NTS)

[Map: 4, G5] Off A93, 3 miles E of Banchory, Kincardine & Deeside. (NGR: NO 734968 LR: 45)

One of the finest surviving castles in Scotland, Crathes Castle is a massive 16th-century tower house. The upper storeys are adorned with much corbelling, turrets, and decoration, while the lower storeys are very plain. The interior is also particularly fine, and there are original painted ceilings. The property was owned by the Burnetts of Leys from the 14th century until 1951. The jewelled ivory 'Horn of Leys' is kept at Crathes, and was given to the Burnetts by Robert the Bruce.

Collections of portraits and furniture. Gift shop. Restaurant. Gardens, grounds and adventure playground. Plant sales. Disabled facilities, including access to ground floor and WC. Car and coach parking. £££.

Castle and visitor centre open (2002) 25 Mar-30 Sep, daily 10.00-17.30; Oct, daily 10.00-16.30; plant sales, same dates but wknds only in Oct; restaurant and shop, 20 Jan-24 Mar and 1 Nov-22 Dec, Wed-Sun 10.00-16.00; 25 Mar-30 Sep, daily 10.00-17.30, Oct, daily 10.00-16.30; to help enjoy visits and for safety reasons, admission to the castle is by timed ticked (limited numbers: entry may be delayed); garden and grounds all year, daily 9.00-sunset.

Tel: 01330 844525   Fax: 01330 844797

N17 Culcreuch Castle

[Map: 5B, D7] Off B822, 11 miles E of Stirling, 0.5 miles N of Fintry, Culcreuch, Stirlingshire. (NGR: NS 620876 LR: 57)

Set in 1600 acres of parkland, Culcreuch Castle is a fine old castle, and passed from the Galbraiths of Culcreuch to the Napiers. In 1796, it was acquired by Alexander Speirs, who built a large and profitable cotton mill on his estate. It is now a hotel. The country park features woodland, river and moorland walks and a fine Pinetum.

Restaurant and 2 bars. Gift shop. Accommodation and self-catering lodges. Country park. Parking.

Hotel – open all year and to non-residents; country park – open all year.

Tel: 01360 860228/555   Fax: 01360 860556

Web: www.culcreuch.com   Email: david@culcreuch.com

N18 Delgatie Castle

[Map: 4, E5] Off A947, 2 miles E of Turriff, Banff and Buchan, Aberdeenshire. (NGR: NJ 755506 LR: 29)

An imposing and interesting building, Delgatie Castle consists of a 15th-century keep, an adjoining 16th-century gabled house, and lower later buildings, although it is said to incorporate work from the 11th century. It was a property of the Hays from the 14th century, but passed from the family. It was then left uninhabited until bought back by the Hays, and Delgatie was made the Clan Hay centre in 1948.

Many rooms, two with original painted ceilings of 1592 and 1597. Guided tours available by arrangement. Explanatory boards. Collection of portraits. Gift shop. Tearoom. WC. Picnic area. Disabled access to tearoom and front hall only. Accommodation available including in castle. Short breaks available. £

Open Apr-Oct, daily 10.00-17.00.

Tel: 01888 563479   Web: www.delgatiecastle.com
Fax: 01888 563479   Email: jjohnson@delgatie-castle.freeserve.co.uk

N19 Drum Castle (NTS)

[Map: 4, G5] Off A93, 9.5 miles W of Aberdeen, 3 miles W of Peterculter, Kincardine and Deeside. (NGR: NJ 796005 LR: 38)

One of the oldest occupied houses in Scotland, Drum Castle consists of a plain 13th-century keep of four storeys to which have been added later extensions. Drum was a property of the Irvines from 1323 until 1975. Sir Alexander Irvine was killed at the Battle of **Harlaw [Q13]** in 1411, slain by and slaying MacLean of Duart, 'Hector of the Battles'.

Collections of furniture and pictures. Garden of historic roses. Woodland walks. Gift shop. Tearoom. WC. Disabled facilities. Parking. £££.

Castle and garden open 25 Mar-28 Jun and 2 Sep-27 Oct, daily 12.00-17.00; 29 Jun-1 Sep, daily 10.00-18.00; grounds all year, daily 9.30-sunset.

Tel: 01330 811204 Fax: 01330 911962

N20 Drumlanrig Castle

[Map: 6B, G8] Off A76, 3 miles NW of Thornhill, Drumlanrig, Dumfries and Galloway. (NGR: NX 851992 LR: 78)

Drumlanrig is an impressive 17th-century courtyard mansion, consisting of four ranges around a courtyard, with higher rectangular towers at the corners. The property was held by the Douglases, but later passed to the Scott Dukes of Buccleuch.

Fine collection of pictures, including paintings by Rembrandt, Holbein and Leonardo, as well as many other works of art. Guided tours. Gift shop. Tea room. Visitor centre. Park land, woodland walks and gardens. Visitor centre. WC. Picnic area. Adventure woodland play area. Working craft centre. Demonstrations of birds of prey (except Thu). Disabled access. Car and coach parking. Group concessions. ££ (local residents free).

Open late Mar-Oct, Mon-Sat 10.00-17.00, Sun 12.00-17.00; Jun and Sep, daily 10.00-17.30; Jul-Aug, daily 10.00-18.00.

Tel: 01848 330248 Fax: 01848 600244
Email: bre@drumlanrigcastle.org.uk

Y69 Drumlanrig's Tower

See main entry Y69

N21 Drummond Castle Gardens

[Map: 5B, C8] Off A822, 2.5 miles SW of Crieff, Drummond, Perthshire. (NGR: NN 844181 LR: 58)

Built on a rocky outcrop, Drummond Castle is a fine castle, dating from the 15th century, with splendid gardens. The terraces overlook a magnificent parterre, celebrating the saltire and family heraldry, surrounding a famous sundial by John Milne, Master Mason to Charles I. Drummond was a property of the Drummonds, who were made Earls of Perth, but they later lost the castle after being forfeited following the Jacobite Risings.

Gift shop. Disabled partial access. WC. Car and coach parking.

Castle not open. Gardens open Easter & May-Oct 14.00-18.00; last admission 17.00.

Tel: 01764 681257/433 Fax: 01764 681550
Email: thegardens@drummondcastle.sol.co.uk

N22 Duart Castle

[Map: 5A, B4] Off A849, 2E miles S of Craignure, Duart, Mull. (NGR: NM 749354 LR: 49)

An extremely impressive and daunting fortress, Duart Castle consists of a large keep and curtain wall, enclosing a courtyard on a rocky knoll. It was held by the MacLeans of Duart, but passed from the family and became ruinous. It was acquired in 1911 by Fitzroy MacLean, 26th Chief, who restored the castle.

13th-century keep, exhibitions, dungeons and state rooms. Tea room and gift shop. WC. Picnic areas. Disabled access to tea room and gift shop. Car and coach parking. Group concessions. ££ (castle).

Open May-mid Oct, daily 10.30-18.00.

Tel: 01680 812309/01577 830311 Web: www.duartcastle.com
Fax: 01577 830311 Email: duart@isle-of-mull.demon.co.uk

N23 Dunrobin Castle

[Map: 3B, C10] Off A9, 1.5 miles NE of Golspie, Dunrobin, Sutherland, Highland. (NGR: NC 852008 LR: 17)

Dunrobin, an elegant mansion designed like a fairytale castle, consists of an altered keep, which may date from the 1300s, and later mansion. It was held by the Sutherland family, who were created Earls of Sutherland in 1235, then later Dukes, and had a castle here from the 13th century: Dunrobin may be called after Robert or Robin, the 6th Earl. The museum, in the grounds, has a fine collection of 20 carved Pictish stones from Sutherland, including a cross-slab from St Andrews kirkyard with Pictish devices and an Ogham inscription.

Collections of furniture, paintings and memorabilia. Museum, which features a collection of Pictish stones. Formal gardens. Guided tours. Explanatory displays. Gift shop. Tea room. WC. Disabled access: phone to arrange. Car and coach parking. Group concessions. £££.

Open Apr-mid Oct: Apr, May and Oct, Mon-Sat 10.30-16.30, Sun 12.00-16.30; Jun and Sep, Mon-Sat 10.30-17.30, Sun 12.00-17.30; Jul and Aug, daily 10.30-17.30; last entry 30 mins before close.

Tel: 01408 633177 Web: www.great-houses-scotland.co.uk
Fax: 01408 634081 Email: dunrobin.est@btinternet.com

N24 Dunvegan Castle

[Map: 3A, E4] Off A850, 1 mile N of Dunvegan, Skye. (NGR: NG 247491 LR: 23)

Dunvegan Castle has been continuously occupied by the chiefs of MacLeod since 1270, who trace their ancestry back to Leod, a son of Olaf the Black, Viking King of the Isle of Man. His stronghold was developed down the centuries into a large mansion and castle, and it is still owned by the 29th Chief of MacLeod. It is home to the famous Fairy Flag.

Info cards in various languages in each of the public rooms. Guides on-hand. Audio-visual theatre. Gift shops. Restaurant. WC. Gardens. Boat trips (££) to seal colony. Dunvegan seal colony. Pedigree Highland cattle fold. Car and coach parking. Group/student/OAP

concessions. Holiday cottages available, also wedding venue. £££
**Open all year: Mar-Oct, daily 10.00-17.30; Nov-Mar, daily
11.00-16.00; closed 25/26 and 1/2 Jan; last entry 30 mins
before closing.**
Tel: 01470 521206   Web: www.dunvegancastle.com
Fax: 01470 521205   Email: info@dunvegancastle.com

N25 Edinburgh Castle (HS)

*[Map: 6B, E9] Off A1, in the centre of Edinburgh. (NGR: NT 252735
LR: 66)*

Standing on a high rock, Edinburgh Castle was one
of the strongest and most important fortresses in Scotland. The oldest building is a small Norman chapel of
the early 12th century, dedicated to St Margaret, wife
of Malcolm Canmore. The castle has a long and eventful history, and only a little of it can be recorded here.
It had an English garrison from 1296 until 1313 during the Wars of Independence, when the Scots, led
by Thomas Randolph, climbed the rock, surprised the
garrison, and retook it. The castle was slighted, but
there was an English garrison here again until 1341,
when it was retaken by a Scot's force disguised as
merchants. In 1566 Mary, Queen of Scots, gave birth
to the future James VI in the castle. The Jacobites
besieged the castle in both the 1715 and 1745 Risings
but were unsuccessful. The castle is the home of the
Scottish crown jewels, the huge 15th-century cannon
Mons Meg, the National War Museum of Scotland, and
the Stone of Destiny – on which the Kings of Scots
were inaugurated – and is an interesting complex of
buildings with spectacular views over the capital. Scottish War Memorial and Regimental Museum of the
Royal Scots.

*Explanatory displays. Audio-guide tour. Guided tours. Gift shop.
Restaurant. WC. Disabled access. Visitors with a disability can be
taken to the top of the castle by a courtesy vehicle; ramps and lift
access to Crown Jewels and Stone of Destiny. Car and coach parking
(except during Tattoo). £££*
**Open all year: Apr-Sep, daily 9.30-17.15 (last ticket sold);
Oct-Mar, daily 9.30-16.15 (last ticket sold), castle closes 45
mins after last ticket is sold; times may be altered during
Tattoo and state occasions; closed 25/26 Dec and 1/2 Jan.**
Tel: 0131 225 9846

N26 Eilean Donan Castle

*[Map: 3A, F6] On A87, 8 miles E of Kyle of Lochalsh, Dornie,
Highland. (NGR: NG 881259 LR: 33)*

One of the most beautifully situated of all Scottish
castles, Eilean Donan Castle consists of a 13th-cen-
tury wall, surrounding a courtyard, with a strong 14th-
century keep and other buildings. Although very ruinous, it was completely rebuilt in the 20th century.
It was a property of the Mackenzies, and there are
mementoes of Bonnie Prince Charlie and James VIII
and III. The castle has been used in many films, in-

cluding the James Bond film 'The World is Not
Enough' and 'Highlander'.

*Guided tours available. Visitor centre. New exhibitions. Gift shop.
Tearoom. WC and disabled WC. Car and coach parking. Group
concessions. ££.*
Open Apr-Oct, daily 10.00-17.30.
Tel: 01599 555202   Fax: 01599 555262
Web: www.eileandonan.com   Email: info@eileandonan.com

N27 Falkland Palace (NTS)

*[Map: 6B, C10] Off A912, 10 miles N of Kirkcaldy, Falkland, Fife.
(NGR: NO 254075 LR: 59)*

A splendid fortified residence, remodelled in Renaissance style, with ranges of buildings around an open
courtyard. The late 15th-century gatehouse range
survives complete, while an adjoining range is ruined,
and only traces remain of a range opposite the gatehouse. The restored cross house contains a refurbished room, reputedly the King's Room, where
James V died in 1542. Falkland was a favourite residence of the Stewart monarchs. There are extensive
gardens and a real tennis court, dating from 1539.
There are two Pictish Class 1 carved stones here on
display in the museum. In the nearby Town Hall an
exhibition tells the history of the palace and royal
burgh.

*Explanatory displays. Gift shop. Visitor centre. Picnic area. Extensive
gardens. Real tennis court. WC. Disabled access. Tape tour for
visually impaired. Car parking nearby. ££.*
**Palace, garden and Town Hall open 1 Mar-27 Oct, Mon-Sat
10.00-18.00, Sun 13.00-17.00.**
Tel: 01337 857397   Fax: 01337 857980

N28 Ferniehirst Castle

*[Map: 6B, F11] Off A68, 1.5 miles S of Jedburgh, Borders. (NGR: NT
653179 LR: 80)*

Ferniehirst Castle consists of an extended and altered
tower house, which incorporates the cellars from the
16th-century castle, with later wings and extensions.
It was and is a property of the Kerrs. Sir Thomas Kerr,
protector of Mary, Queen of Scots, invaded England
in 1570, hoping to have her released, but all that resulted was a raid on Scotland, during which Ferniehirst was damaged.

*Collection of portraits. Turret library. Guided tours. Explanatory
displays. Gift shop. WC. Riverside walk. Sheep of a breed of Viking
origin. Car and coach parking. £.*
Open Jul, Tue-Sun 11.00-16.00.
Tel: 01835 862201   Fax: 01835 863992

N29 Fyvie Castle (NTS)

*[Map: 4, F5] Off A947, 8 miles S of Turriff and 1 mile N of Fyvie
village, Fyvie, Banff & Buchan. (NGR: NJ 764393 LR: 29)*

Set in the rolling countryside of Aberdeenshire, Fyvie
Castle is one of the most magnificent castles in Scotland. The building consists of a massive tower house

with very long wings, and is adorned with turrets, dormer windows and carved finials, and corbiestepped gables. There are also many original interiors. Fyvie was destined to have a succession of owners: Lindsays, Prestons, Meldrums, Setons, Gordons and finally the Leiths.

Collections of portraits, arms and armour and tapestries. Gift shop. Tearoom. WC. Picnic area. Garden and grounds. Plant sales. Disabled access to tearoom and WC. Car parking. £££.
Open 25 Mar-28 Jun and 2 Sep-27 Oct, Sat-Wed 12.00-17.00; 29 Jun-1 Sep, daily 10.00-17.00; ground open all year, daily 9.30-sunset.
Tel: 01651 891266   Fax: 01651 891107

N30 Glamis Castle

[Map: 4, 13] Off A94, 5.5 miles SW of Forfar, 1 mile N of Glamis village, Angus. (NGR: NO 387481 LR: 54)
Glamis Castle is a hugely impressive and striking fortress, and consists of a greatly extended 14th-century keep with later ranges, set in an extensive park. It is a property of the Lyon Earls of Strathmore and Kinghorne, and the late Queen Mother came from this family.

In 1540 the young and beautiful wife of the 6th Lord, Janet Douglas, was burned to death on a suspect charge of witchcraft by James V, who hated the Douglases. The castle is reputed to be one the most haunted in Britain, not the least by the ghost of the Lindsay 4th Earl of Crawford, 'Earl Beardie', who is said to haunt a walled-up room where he played cards with the devil. A huge bearded ghost has apparently been seen on many occasions. The castle is also said to be haunted by the 'Grey Lady of Glamis', the ghost of Janet Douglas, the Lady Glamis who was burnt by James V.

Collections of historic pictures, porcelain and furniture. Guided tours. Three additional exhibition rooms. Four shops. Licensed restaurant. WC. Picnic area. Playpark. Extensive park, pinetum, nature trail and garden. Disabled access to gardens and ground floor; WC. Car and coach parking. Group concessions. £££.
Open Apr-Oct, daily 10.30-17.30; Jul-Aug, from 10.00; last admission 16.45; at other time groups by appt.
Tel: 01307 840393   Fax: 01307 840733
Web: www.glamis-castle.co.uk   Email: admin@glamis-castle.co.uk

N31 Holyroodhouse

[Map: 6B, E9] Off A1, at foot of Royal Mile, in Edinburgh. (NGR: NT 269739 LR: 66)
The official residence of the monarch in Scotland, Holyroodhouse is a fine historic palace. One range dates from the 16th century, and the building was remodelled and extended by Sir William Bruce for Charles II in 1671-8. Original 16th-century interiors survive in the old block. David Rizzio, favourite of Mary, Queen of Scots, was murdered here in 1566 in front of the pregnant queen. Ruins of **Holyrood Abbey [J17]** church adjoin.

Guided tours Nov-Mar. Gift shop. WC. Garden. Disabled access. Car and coach parking. Group concessions (10% groups of 15 or more). £££.
Open all year (except when monarch is in residence, Good Friday and 25/26 Dec): Apr-Oct daily 9.30-17.15; Nov-Mar daily 9.30-15.45.
Tel: 0131 556 1096/7371   Web: www.royal-collection.gov.uk
Fax: 0131 557 5256   Email: holyrood@royalcollection.org.uk

N32 Kelburn Castle

[Map: 6A, E5] Off A78, 2 miles S of Largs, Kelburn, Ayrshire. (NGR: NS 217567 LR: 63)
With fine views over the Clyde and set in parkland, Kelburn Castle is a tall 16th-century tower house, to which has been added a large symmetrical mansion, although part may date from the 13th century. The Boyles have held the property since the 13th century. The grounds are open to the public as a Country Centre, and there are walled gardens with rare shrubs and trees, and a Water Garden.

Guided tours of house. Explanatory displays. Gift shop. Licensed tea room. Cafe. WC. Picnic area. Riding centre open all year. Assault and adventure courses. Secret Forest. Disabled limited access and WC. Car and coach parking. Group concessions. ££ (+£ entrance to castle).
Castle open: Jul-1st week in Sep; daily tours 13.45, 15.00 and 16.15; other times by appt only. Country centre and gardens open: Easter-Oct, daily 10.00-18.00. Also grounds only open: Nov-Easter, daily 11.00-17.00.
Tel: 01475 586685/204 (castle)   Fax: 01475 568121/328 (castle)
Web: www.kelburncastle.com   Email: info@kelburncastle.com

N33 Kellie Castle (NTS)

[Map: 6B, C10] Off B9171, 4 miles N of Elie, Kellie, Fife. (NGR: NO 520052 LR: 59)
One of the finest castles in Scotland, Kellie Castle is a tall 16th-century tower house. The Vine Room, on one of the upper floors, has a ceiling painted by De Witt, and there are good plaster ceilings and painted panelling. The castle was built by the Oliphants, but passed to the Erskines, made Earls of Kellie in 1619. Robert Lorimer, the famous architect, spent most of his childhood here. The gardens feature a fine collection of old roses and herbaceous plants.

Victorian nursery, old kitchen, and audio-visual show. Explanatory displays. Gift shop. Tearoom. Magnificent walled garden. WC. Disabled access to ground floor and grounds. Car park. ££.
Castle open (2002) 25 Mar-29 Sep, Thu-Mon 12.00-17.00; garden and grounds open all year, daily 9.30-sunset.
Tel: 01333 720271   Fax: 01333 720326

N34 Kilravock Castle

[Map: 3B, E10] Off B9091, 6 miles SW of Nairn, Kilravock, Highland. (NGR: NH 814493 LR: 27)
Pronounced 'Kilrock', Kilravock Castle is an impressive stronghold, and was long held by the Roses of

Kilravock. Mary, Queen of Scots, visited the castle, as did Bonnie Prince Charlie and the Duke of Cumberland (although not at the same time), and Robert Burns.

Tearoom open Mon-Sat 10.00-16.00. WC. Car and coach parking. £.

Accsss to gardens (£). Dinner, bed and breakfast available Apr-Sep; open for conferences all year.
Tel: 01667 493258   Fax: 01667 493213
Web: www.kilravockcastle.com   Email: info@kilravockcastle.com

N35 Lauriston Castle, Edinburgh

[Map: 6B, E9] Off B9085, 3 miles W of Edinburgh Castle, Cramond Road South, Davidson's Mains, Edinburgh. (NGR: NT 204762 LR: 66)

Lauriston Castle is a much-altered 16th-century tower house, to which was added a two-storey Jacobean extension, designed by William Burn, in 1824-7. The castle was built by the Napiers of Merchiston, and one of the family, John Napier, was the inventor of logarithms. It passed through many hands until coming to the Reids in 1902, who gave it to the city of Edinburgh.

Good collections of Italian furniture, Blue John, Grossley wool mosaics, Sheffield plate, mezzotint prints, Caucasian carpets, and items of decorative art. Guided tours of house only. WC. Disabled access to grounds & WC. Japanese garden currently under construction – due to be completed spring 2002. Car and coach parking. Group concessions. ££ (castle).
Visit by guided tour only: Apr-Oct, Sat-Thu 11.20, 12.20, 2.20, 3.20 and 4.20, closed Fri; Nov-Mar, Sat-Sun only 2.20 and 3.20, closed Mon-Fri.
Tel: 0131 336 2060   Fax: 0131 312 7165   Web: www.cac.org.uk

N36 Leith Hall (NTS)

[Map: 4, F4] Off B9002, 8 miles S of Huntly, 3.5 miles NE of Rhynie, Leith Hall, Aberdeenshire. (NGR: NJ 541298 LR: 37)

Leith Hall is ranged around a courtyard and incorporates 17th-century work. The Leith family held the property from 1650 or earlier until 1945, when it was given to The National Trust for Scotland.

Jacobite mementoes. Exhibition on family's military history. Exhibition. Tearoom. WC. Picnic area. Garden and 286 acres of extensive grounds with trails, ponds and a bird hide. Disabled facilities and WC. Car and coach parking. Group concessions. £££.
House and tearoom open (2002) 25 Mar-27 Oct, Wed-Sun 12.00-17.00; garden and grounds open all year, daily 9.30-sunset.
Tel: 01464 831216   Fax: 01464 831594

N37 Lennoxlove

[Map: 6B, E10] Off A1, between B6369 and B6368, 1 mile S of Haddington, Lennoxlove, East Lothian. (NGR: NT 515721 LR: 66)

Originally known as Lethington, Lennoxlove incorporates an altered L-plan tower house, which includes work from the 14th century, with later additions and extensions. It was a property of the Maitlands, one of whom was secretary to Mary, Queen of Scots. In 1947

it passed to the Duke of Hamilton, since when it has been the family seat. Among the treasures it contains are the death mask of Mary, Queen of Scots, a sapphire ring given to her by Lord John Hamilton, and the casket which may have contained the 'Casket Letters'.

Hamilton Palace collection of pictures, furniture and porcelain. Fully guided tours. Explanatory displays. Garden cafe. WC. Disabled access to house and gardens. Parking. ££.
Open Easter-Oct, Wed, Thu, Sat and Sun, 14.00-16.30; check if house is open on Sat before setting out.
Tel: 01620 823720   Fax: 01620 825112
Web: www.lennoxlove.org   Email: fayangus@dial.pipex.com

N38 Loudoun Hall, Ayr

[Map: 6A, F6] Off A77, Boat Vennel, New Bridge Street, Ayr. (NGR: NS 337221 LR: 70)

Loudoun Hall dates from the beginning of the 16th century, and has a vaulted basement. It was built by James Tait, a burgess of Ayr, but sold to the Campbells of Loudoun around 1530.

Open: tel to confirm.
Tel: 01292 530353

I2 Mary Queen of Scots Visitor Centre, Jedburgh
See main entry I2

N39 Megginch Castle Gardens

[Map: 5B, C10] About 8 miles E of Perth, E of A85, Megginch, Perthshire. (NGR: NO 242246 LR: 59)

Surrounded by woodlands, Megginch Castle is an altered L-plan tower house, from 1460. It was bought by the Drummonds of Lennoch in 1646: the Drummond family still live at the castle. There are extensive gardens with 1000-year-old yews, 16th-century rose garden, astrological garden, kitchen garden, topiary and 16th-century physick garden. The courtyard of the castle was used for part of the film version of 'Rob Roy' with Liam Neeson in 1994.

Guided tours by arrangement and extra charge. Disabled partial access. Car and coach parking. £.
Castle not open; gardens open Jun- Sep, daily 14.30-17.00; other times by prior arrangement.
Tel: 01821 642222   Fax: 01821 642708

N40 Moniack Castle

[Map: 3B, F9] On A862, 7 miles SW of Inverness, Moniack, Kirkhill. (NGR: NH 552436 LR: 26)

Moniack Castle incorporates a 17th-century tower house and was a property of the Frasers of Lovat. It now gives its name to a range of wines and foods, including elderflower and silver birch wine, mead and sloe gin, and meat and game preserves. A carved Pictish stone, bearing a bird-headed man carrying a club as well as prehistoric cup and ring marks, is in the grounds of the castle.

Guided tours. Gift shop. Wine bar and bistro. Tearoom. Picnic area. WC. Car and coach parking.

Open Mar-Oct, daily 10.00-17.00, closed Sun; Nov-Feb, 11.00-16.00.

Tel: 01463 831283 Fax: 01463 831419

Email: jq@moniackcastle.freeserve.co.uk

N41 Old Buittle Tower

[Map: 6B, H8] Off A745, 1.5 miles W of Dalbeattie, Buittle, Dumfries and Galloway. (NGR: NX 817616 LR: 84)

A late 16th-century L-plan tower house, probably built from masonry from the nearby 13th-century stronghold. The lands of Buittle were held by the Balliol family, based at the earlier castle. The property passed to the Douglas family, then the Maxwells. There are displays of arms and armour, as well as mounted displays of Border reivers.

Refreshments. WC. Parking. £.

Check by tel.

Tel: 01556 612607

N42 Provand's Lordship

[Map: 6B, E7] Off M8, 3 Castle Street, opposite the Cathedral, Glasgow. (NGR: NS 605655 LR: 64)

Provand's Lordship, the oldest house in Glasgow, dates from 1471 and was built as part of St Nicholas's Hospital. There are period displays and furniture, as well as a recreated medieval herb garden.

Explanatory displays. Disabled access. Car and coach parking.

Open all year, Mon-Sat 10.00-17.00, Fri and Sun 11.00-17.00.

Tel: 0141 553 2557 Fax: 0141 552 4744

Web: www.glasgow.gov.uk/cls

N43 Provost Ross's House

[Map: 4, G5] Shiprow, Aberdeen. (NGR: NJ 935060 LR: 38)

Built in 1593, Provost Ross's House is the third oldest in Aberdeen, and now houses part of the Aberdeen Maritime Museum, which gives an insight into the maritime history of the city, including the oil industry. Unique collection of ship models, paintings, artefacts, computer interaction and set-piece exhibitions. Five star museum.

Explanatory displays. Gift shop. Restaurant. WC. Disabled access and induction loop. Public car parking nearby.

Open all year, Mon-Sat 10.00-17.00, Sun 11.00-17.00; closed 25-26 Dec and 1-2 Jan.

Tel: 01224 337700 Fax: 01224 213066 Web: www.aberdeencity.gov.uk

N44 Provost Skene's House

[Map: 4, G5] Off A92, 45 Guest Row, off Broad Street, Aberdeen. (NGR: NJ 943064 LR: 38)

Provost Skene's House is a fine 16th-century town house. Magnificent 17th-century plaster ceiling and wood panelling survive, and the Painted Gallery has a tempera painted ceiling with themes from the life of Christ. It was a property of George Skene of Rubis-

law. Other rooms include a suite of Georgian chambers, and an Edwardian nursery, and changing displays of local interest, archaeology and coins.

Period room settings. 17th-century ceiling and wall paintings, costume gallery, and local history exhibitions. Sales area. Coffee shop. WC. Public parking nearby.

Open all year, Mon-Sat 10.00-17.00, Sun 13.00-16.00; closed 25/26/31 Dec and 1/2 Jan.

Tel: 01224 641086 Fax: 01224 632133 Web: www.aagm.co.uk

N45 Sorn Castle

[Map: 6B, F7] Off B743, 3 miles E of Mauchline, Ayrshire. (NGR: NS 548269 LR: 70)

Sorn Castle is a 14th-century castle on a cliff above the River Ayr, with later additions of the 15th and 16th centuries. In 1865 the architect David Bryce restored it, with additions including the balcony, porch, and billiard room by Clifford in 1908. It is owned by the McIntyre family.

Guided tours: 2nd 2 weeks of Jul and 1st 2 weeks of Aug.

Tel: 01290 551555 Fax: 0290 551712

N46 Stirling Castle (HS)

[Map: 5B, D8] Off A872, Upper Castle Hill, in Stirling. (NGR: NS 790940 LR: 57)

One of the most important and powerful castles in Scotland, the castle stands on a high rock with fine views, and consists of a very impressive complex of buildings, including the restored Great Hall and the Chapel Royal. Other features of interest are the kitchens, the wall walk and the nearby 'King's Knot'.

The castle has a long and eventful history, only some of which can be recounted.

Alexander I died here in 1124, as did William the Lyon in 1214. Edward I of England captured the castle in 1304 when he used – although after the garrison had surrendered – a siege engine called the 'War Wolf'. William Wallace took the castle for the Scots, but it was retaken by the English until the Battle of Bannockburn in 1314.

James II was born here in 1430, as was James III in 1451. James II lured the 8th Earl of Douglas to it in 1452, murdered him, and had his body tossed out of one of the windows, despite promising safe conduct. Mary, Queen of Scots, was crowned in the old chapel in 1543, and the future James VI was baptised here in 1566. The garrison harried the Jacobites during both the 1715 and 1745 Risings.

The Argyll and Sutherland Highlanders Regimental Museum is housed in the castle, telling the story of the regiment from 1794 to the present day, and featuring uniforms, silver, paintings, colours, pipe banners and commentaries.

Some of the fine 16th-century town wall of Stirling also survives.

Guided tours are available and can be booked in advance. Exhibition of life in the royal palace, introductory display, medieval kitchen display. Museum of the Argyll and Sutherland Highlanders. Gift shop. Restaurant. WC. Disabled access and WC. Car and coach parking. Group concessions. £££.

Open all year: Apr-Sep daily 9.30-17.15 (last ticket sold); Oct-Mar daily 9.30-16.15 (last ticket sold); castle closes 45 mins after last ticket sold – joint ticket with Argyll's Lodging; closed 25/26 Dec and 1/2 Jan.

Tel: 01786 450000   Fax: 01786 464678

N47 Thirlestane Castle

[Map: 6B, E10] Off A68, E of Lauder, Borders. (NGR: NT 540473 LR: 73)

Thirlestane is an impressive and stately castle, much altered and extended in the 17th and 19th centuries. It was home of the Maitlands of Lauderdale, one of whom was John Maitland, Duke of Lauderdale, a very powerful man in Scotland in the 17th century. Bonnie Prince Charlie stayed here in 1745. The castle is still occupied by the same family.

Many rooms. Fine 17th-century plasterwork ceilings. Collection of portraits, furniture and china. Exhibition of historical toys and Border country life. Audio-visual presentation. Gift shop. Tea room. WC. Picnic tables. Adventure playground. Woodland walks. Car parking. Coaches by arrangement. Group concessions. £££.

Open Apr- Oct, Sun-Fri 10.30-17.00, closed Sat; last admission 16.15.

Tel: 01578 722430   Web: www.thirlestanecastle.co.uk
Fax: 01578 722761   Email: admin@thirlestanecastle.co.uk

N48 Traquair House

[Map: 6B, F10] Off B709, 1 mile S of Innerleithen, Borders. (NGR: NT 330354 LR: 73)

Reputedly the oldest continuously occupied house in Scotland, Traquair House dates from as early as the 12th century. It houses a collection of mementoes associated with Mary, Queen of Scots, who stayed here with Lord Darnley, and the Jacobites. The house passed through several families, including the Douglases and Stewarts, and now belongs to the Maxwell Stuarts.

Working 18th-century brewery. Guided tours by arrangement. Explanatory displays. 1745 Cottage Restaurant. WC. Gardens, woodland walks and maze. Craft workshops. Gift, antique and the Brewery shop. Brewery. Car and coach parking (coaches please book). Group concessions. £££. Accommodation available: contact house.

Open Easter-Oct, daily 12.30-17.30, Jun-Aug, daily 10.30-17.30; grounds open Easter-Oct, daily 10.30-17.30.

Tel: 01896 830323   Fax: 01896 830639
Web: www.traquair.co.uk   Email: enquiries@traquair.co.uk

Top left
Castle Fraser
Top right
Stirling Castle
Left
Traquair House

Above *Cawdor Castle*
Above Right *Craigievar Castle*
Right *Thirlestane Castle*
Below right *Braemar Castle*
Bottom right *Edinburgh Castle*
Below left *Blair Castle*
Bottom left *Lauriston Castle*

N2: Castles, Towers and Palaces – 2

The following castles are either ruins, are not occupied, or are used as museums. Many are spectacular ruins in picturesque locations.

Also see the following sections on *N1: Castles, Towers and Palaces – 1*; *S1: Houses and Mansions*; and *Q: Clan Castles and Museums*.

N49 Aberdour Castle (HS)

[Map: 6B, D9] On A921, 6.5 miles SW of Kirkcaldy, Aberdour, Fife. (NGR: NT 193854 LR: 66)

Standing in the picturesque village, Aberdour is a fine large and partly ruinous castle. A terraced garden has been restored, and there is also a walled garden and round doocot. It was a property of the Mortimers, but by 1342 had passed to the Douglases. James Douglas, Earl of Morton and Regent to James VI, held the castle. **St Fillans Church [K107]** is nearby.

Explanatory displays. Gift shop. Tearoom. WC. Disabled access and WC. Garden. Parking. £.
Open all year: Apr-Sep, daily 9.30-18.30; Oct-Mar, Mon-Wed and Sat, 9.30-16.30, Thu 9.30-12.00, Sun 14.00-16.30, closed Fri; closed 25/26 Dec and 1/2 Jan.
Tel: 01383 860519

N50 Ardvreck Castle

[Map: 3B, C7] Off A837, 1.5 miles NW of Inchnadamph, Ardvreck, Highland. (NGR: NC 240236 LR: 15)

In a lonely and picturesque situation, Ardvreck Castle is a stark ruin, and was a property of the MacLeods of Assynt. The castle was sacked in 1672, and replaced by nearby Calda House, itself burnt out in 1760.
Parking Nearby.
Access at all reasonable times – view from exterior only.

N51 Auchindoun Castle

[Map: 4, F3] Off A941, S of Dufftown, Moray. (NGR: NJ 348374 LR: 28)

An impressive ruinous castle, built within the ramparts of an Iron Age fort, and with fine views.

It was probably built by Robert Cochrane, a master mason, one of James III's favourites. In 1482 he was hanged from Lauder Bridge, and it later passed to the Gordons.

Auchindoun was sacked in 1591 in revenge for the murder of the Bonnie Earl o' Moray at Donibristle by the Marquis of Huntly and Sir Patrick Gordon of Auchindoun. Gordon was later killed in 1594 at the Battle of Glenlivet.
Parking nearby.
Access at all reasonable times: footpath is steep and may be muddy – view from exterior only.
Tel: 01466 793191

Y31 Balloch Castle
See main entry Y31

N52 Balvaird Castle (HS)

[Map: 5B, C9] Off A912, 7 miles SE of Perth, 4 miles S of Bridge of Earn, Balvaird, Perthshire. (NGR: NO 169118 LR: 58)

In a striking location, Balvaird Castle is a fine ruinous castle, dating from the 15th century. It was a Barclay property, but passed by marriage to the Murrays of Tullibardine in 1500, who built the castle. The family moved to **Scone Palace [S41]**.
Car and coach parking (when open). £.
Tel to check.
Tel: 0131 668 8800

N53 Balvenie Castle (HS)

[Map: 4, F3] Off A941, N of Dufftown, Moray. (NGR: NJ 326409 LR: 28)

In a pleasant location is a large ruined castle, with a strong curtain wall and ditch enclosing ranges of buildings. The castle was held by the Comyns, when it was called Mortlach, and sacked by Robert the Bruce in 1308. It passed to the Douglases, then to the Stewart Earl of Atholl, the Innes family, and the Duffs. Near to **Glenfiddich Distillery [W21]**.
Explanatory boards. Gift shop. Picnic area. WC. Disabled WC. Car parking. Group concession. £.
Open Apr-Sep, daily 9.30-18.30, last ticket sold 18.00.
Tel: 01340 820121

N54 Bishop's Palace, Kirkwall (HS)

[Map: 2, C3] On A960, W of Kirkwall, Orkney. (NGR: HY 449108 LR: 6)

The Bishop's Palace, incorporating work from the 12th century, consists of a rectangular block with a taller round tower at one end. The palace was the residence of the Bishops of Orkney from the 12th century, when held by the Norsemen. King Hakon Hakonson of Norway died here in 1263. The fine and complete medieval cathedral, **St Magnus Cathedral [K33]**, is nearby. Also see **Earl's Palace, Kirkwall [N97]**.
Explanatory displays. Parking nearby. £. Joint entry ticket for all Orkney monuments available.
Open Apr-Sep, daily 9.30-18.30; last ticket 30 mins before closing.
Tel: 01856 875461 Fax: 0131 668 8800

N55 Blackness Castle (HS)

[Map: 5B, D9] Off B903 or B9109, 4 miles NE of Linlithgow, 4 miles E of Bo'ness, Falkirk. (NGR: NT 056803 LR: 65)

A grim and impressive courtyard castle, built on a promontory in the Firth of Forth, which was used as a state prison. The oldest part is the tall central 15th-century keep, although the stronghold was strengthened for artillery in later centuries. Part of 'Hamlet', starring Mel Gibson, was filmed here.

Gift shop. Refreshments. WC. Picnic area. Parking. £.

Open all year: Apr-Sep, daily 9.30-18.30; Oct-Mar, Mon-Wed and Sat 9.30-16.30, Thu 9.00-12.00, Sun 14.00-16.30, closed Fri; closed 25/26 Dec and 1/2 Jan.

Tel: 01506 834807

N56 Bothwell Castle (HS)

[Map: 6B, E7] Off B7071 at Uddingston, 3 miles NW of Hamilton, Lanarkshire. (NGR: NS 688594 LR: 64)

In a fine setting overlooking the Clyde is one of the largest and most impressive early stone castles in Scotland. A once magnificent, but now ruinous, round keep stands by a walled courtyard, which rise to 60 feet. It was fought over during the Wars of Independence, and was long a property of the Douglases.

Exhibition. Explanatory boards. Gift shop. Refreshments. WC. Car and coach parking. £.

Open all year: Apr-Sep, daily 9.30-18.30; Oct-Mar, Mon-Wed and Sat 9.30-16.30, Thu 9.30-12.00, Sun 14.00-16.30, closed Fri; closed 25/26 Dec and 1/2 Jan.

Tel: 01698 816894

N57 Broughty Castle

[Map: 4, J4] Off A930, 4 miles E of Dundee, S of Broughty Ferry, Angus. (NGR: NO 465304 LR: 54)

Standing by the sea, Broughty Castle is a tall 15th-century keep with a later wing and artillery emplacements. It was held by the Grays, but was bought by the government in 1851, and restored and given gun emplacements. The castle now houses a museum of whaling and fishery, arms and armour, and local history. There are fine views of the Tay.

Explanatory displays. Sales area. Parking.

Open Apr-Sep, Mon-Sat 10.00-16.00, Sun 12.30-16.00; Oct-Mar, Tue-Sat 10.00-16.00, Sun 12.30-16.00, closed Mon.

Tel: 01382 436916 Fax: 01382 436951

Web: www.dundeecity.gov.uk Email: broughty@dundeecity.gov.uk

N58 Burleigh Castle (HS)

[Map: 5B, C9] On A911, 1.5 miles N of Kinross, Burleigh, Perthshire. (NGR: NO 130046 LR: 58)

Although once a large and imposing castle, Burleigh Castle now consists of a ruined 15th-century keep, a section of courtyard wall with a gate, and a corner tower. It was a property of the Balfours of Burleigh.

Parking nearby.

Access at all reasonable times: keys available locally.

N59 Cadzow Castle (HS)

[Map: 6B, E8] Off A72, 1.5 miles SE of Hamilton, Chatelherault, Lanarkshire. (NGR: NS 734538 LR: 64)

Standing in **Chatelherault [S13]** park, the present ruin dates from the first half of the 16th century. The castle was used by the kings of Scots, including David I, but passed to the Comyns, then to the Hamiltons. The Hamiltons were made Dukes of Chatelherault in France, and Mary, Queen of Scots, visited the castle in 1568 after escaping from **Lochleven Castle [N121]**. In 1579 the castle was captured, then dismantled to be left as a ruin.

Park open to the public except Christmas and New Year – castle: view from exterior.

Tel: 01698 426213 Fax: 01698 421537

N60 Caerlaverock Castle (HS)

[Map: 6B, H9] Off B725, 7 miles SE of Dumfries, Caerlaverock, Dumfries and Galloway. (NGR: NY 026656 LR: 84)

Once a formidable fortress and still a magnificent ruin, Caerlaverock Castle consists of a triangular courtyard with a gatehouse at one side, round towers at two corners, and ranges of buildings between, all still surrounded by a wet moat. The castle was built in the 13th century by the Maxwells, but was captured by Edward I of England in 1300 after a difficult siege. It was eventually retaken by the Scots, and was fought over down the centuries.

Visitor centre, children's park and nature trail to old castle. Shop. Tea room. Picnic area. Explanatory panels. Replica siege engine. Reasonable disabled access and WC. Car and coach parking. Group concessions. £.

Open all year: Apr-Sep, daily 9.30-18.30; Oct-Mar, Mon-Sat 9.30-16.30, Sun 14.00-16.30; last ticket 30 mins before closing; closed 25/26 Dec and 1/2 Jan.

Tel: 01387 770244 Fax: 0131 668 8800

N61 Caisteal Bharraich

[Map: 3B, A9] Off A838, 1 mile W of Tongue, Sutherland, Highland. (NGR: NC 581567 LR: 10)

Caisteal Bharraich, built on a promontory with fine views along the Kyle of Tongue, is a small two-storey ruined tower house of the Bishops of Caithness, then the Mackays. The castle can be reached by a steep path from the gate beside the Royal Bank of Scotland.

Parking nearby.

Access at all reasonable times: long walk and care should be taken.

N62 Cardoness Castle (HS)

[Map: 6B, I7] Off A75, 1 mile SW of Gatehouse of Fleet, Dumfries and Galloway. (NGR: NX 591552 LR: 83)

Standing on a rocky mound above the Water of Fleet is a ruinous but imposing late 15th-century rectangular keep and a courtyard which enclosed outbuildings. Cardoness passed to the MacCullochs by marriage around 1450 – they were a pretty unruly lot – then later to the Gordons in 1629, then to the Maxwells. There are fine views.

Visitor centre. Exhibition and scale model of the castle. Shop. Picnic area. WC. Car and coach parking. Group concessions. £.

Open Apr-Sep, Mon-Sun 9.30-18.30; open Oct-Mar wknds only, Sat 9.30-16.30, Sun 14.00-16.30; last ticket 30 mins before closing; closed 25/26 Dec and 1/2 Jan.

Tel: 01557 814427

N63 Carnasserie Castle (HS)

[Map: 5A, D4] Off A816, 8.5 miles N of Lochgilphead, 1 mile N of Kilmartin, Argyll. (NGR: NM 837009 LR: 55)

A ruined 16th-century tower house and lower hall-block which was built by John Carswell, who published the first ever book in Gaelic in 1567. He was Chancellor of the Chapel-Royal at Stirling, then Bishop of Argyll and the Isles. On his death in 1572, Carnasserie passed to the Campbells of Auchinbreck.

Picnic area. Car and coach parking.

Access at all reasonable times.

N64 Carsluith Castle (HS)

[Map: 6B, I7] On A75, 6/5 miles SW of Gatehouse of Fleet, Carsluith, Dumfries and Galloway. (NGR: NX 495542 LR: 83)

A 16th-century tower house, held by the Cairns family, the Lindsays, then to the Browns. Gilbert Brown of Carsluith was the last abbot of Sweetheart Abbey, and in 1605 was imprisoned in **Blackness Castle [N55]**. The Brown family emigrated to India in 1748, and abandoned the castle.

Parking nearby.

Open Apr-Sep, daily 9.30-18.30 – tel to confirm.

N65 Castle Campbell (HS)

[Map: 5B, D8] Off A91, 12 miles E of Stirling, 0.5 miles N of Dollar, Clackmannan. (NGR: NS 962994 LR: 58)

An impressive and picturesque ruin in a wonderful location, Castle Campbell was built where the Burns of Care and Sorrow join, overlooked by Gloom Hill, and was originally known as Castle Gloom. A large strong 15th-century keep, altered in later centuries, stands at one corner of a substantial ruinous courtyard, enclosed by a curtain wall. The castle was long held by the Campbells. There is a fine walk up to the castle through Dollar Glen.

Gift shop. Tearoom. WC. Car parking. Group concessions. £. Owned by NTS but administered by Historic Scotland.

Open all year: Apr-Sep, daily 9.30-18.30; Oct-Mar, Mon-Wed and Sat 9.30-16.30, Thu 9.30-12.00, Sun 14.00-16.30, closed Fri; last ticket 30 mins before closing; closed 25/26 Dec and 1/2 Jan.

Tel: 01259 742408

N66 Castle Kennedy

[Map: 6A, 15] Off A75, 3 miles E of Stranraer, Dumfries and Galloway. (NGR: NX 111609 LR: 82)

Set among gardens and originally on an island in a loch, Castle Kennedy is a large ruinous 17th-century E-plan tower house. It was built by the Kennedys, but passed to the Dalrymples of Stair around 1677. A fire gutted the castle in 1716, and it was never restored. The 75 acres of gardens are laid out between two lochs, originally in 1730, with impressive terraces and avenues around a large lily pond. There is a walled garden.

Gift shop. Tea room. Disabled access: admission free to disabled visitors. Disabled access. Car and coach parking. £.

Lochinch Castle not open to the public. Gardens open daily Apr-Sep daily 10.00-17.00.

Tel: 01776 702024 Fax: 01776 706248 Email: ckg@stair-estates.sol.co.uk

N67 Castle Roy

[Map: 3B, F10] On B970, 3 miles SW of Grantown on Spey, Highland. (NGR: NJ 007219 LR: 36)

Castle Roy (from Caisteal Ruadh 'Red Castle') consists of a ruined rectangular castle of enclosure, with a square tower at one corner. It was built by the Comyns in the 13th century.

Explanatory board. Parking.

Access at all reasonable times.

N68 Castle Sween (HS)

[Map: 5A, D4] Off B8025, 11 miles SE of Lochgilphead, E shore of Loch Sween, Argyll. (NGR: NR 712789 LR: 62)

Standing on a rocky ridge by the shore of a sea loch is an impressive early castle of enclosure, consisting of a curtain wall, enclosing a rectangular courtyard, and a strong 15th-century keep. It was built at a time when this part of Scotland was still under Norse rule, and was held by the MacSweens, although it later passed to the Campbells.

Parking nearby.

Access at all reasonable times.

N69 Castle of Old Wick (HS)

[Map: 3B, B12] Off A9, 1 mile S of Wick, Castle of Old Wick, Caithness. (NGR: ND 369488 LR: 12)

One of the oldest castles in Scotland, Castle of Old Wick consists of a simple square keep standing on a promontory on cliffs above the sea. It was built in the 12th century when this part of Scotland was ruled by Norsemen. It was held by the Cheynes, Oliphants, Dunbars of Hempriggs, the Sutherland Lord Duffus, then the Sinclairs. In 1569, during a feud, the castle was besieged and starved into submission.

Parking nearby.

Access at all reasonable times – great care must be taken.

Tel: 01667 460232

N70 Castle of St John

[Map: 6A, I5] Off A77, in centre of Stranraer, Dumfries and Galloway. (NGR: NX 061608 LR: 82)

A much-altered 16th-century L-plan tower house, held by the Adairs, Kennedys and Dalrymples. John Graham of Claverhouse, 'Bonnie Dundee' or 'Bloody Clavers', stayed here while suppressing Covenanters from 1682-5. The castle now houses displays telling the building's history from first construction to use as a town jail in the 19th century.

Explanatory displays and videos. Gift shop. Family activities. Parking nearby. £.

Open Easter-mid Sep, Mon-Sat 10.00-13.00 and 14.00-17.00; closed Sun.

Tel: 01776 705088/705544 Fax: 01776 705835
Web: www.dumgal.gov.uk/sevices/depts/comres/museums/facilities.asp Email: JohnPic@dumgal.gov.uk

N71 Castle of Troup

[Map: 4, E5] Off B9031, 9 miles W of Fraserburgh, 2.5 miles E of Gardenstown, Troup, Aberdeenshire. (NGR: NJ 838663 LR: 30)

Standing on a promontory above the sea is the site of a 13th-century castle, within the earthworks of an Iron Age fort. This may have been one of the Comyn strongholds destroyed by Robert the Bruce in 1307-8. Hell's Lum, which is nearby, is a fissure in the cliffs through which spray is forced by waves.

Parking.

Access at all reasonable times: walk to castle.

N72 Clackmannan Tower (HS)

[Map: 5B, D8] Off B910, 7 miles E of Stirling, W outskirts of Clackmannan. (NGR: NS 905920 LR: 58)

Standing on the summit of a hill with fine views, Clackmannan Tower is a large and impressive castle, and was a property of the Bruces from 1359 until 1796. In the adjoining but now demolished mansion, Henry Bruce's widow 'knighted' Robert Burns with the sword of Robert the Bruce.

Access at all reasonable times: view from exterior only.

N73 Claypotts Castle (HS)

[Map: 4, J4] Off A92, 3.5 miles E of Dundee, Angus. (NGR: NO 452319 LR: 54)

An unusual and impressive building, Claypotts Castle is a fine Z-plan tower house. It was held by the Strachans, before passing to the Grahams in 1620. One of the family was John Graham of Claverhouse, Viscount Dundee of Jacobite fame. The property passed to the Douglas Earl of Angus, then later to the Homes.

Parking nearby. £.

Tel to check.

Tel: 01786 450000

N74 Corgarff Castle (HS)

[Map: 4, G3] Off A939, 10 miles NW of Ballater, Corgarff, Aberdeenshire. (NGR: NJ 255086 LR: 37)

A 16th-century tower house, white-washed and re-stored, with later pavilions and star-shaped outworks. The castle was built about 1530 by the Elphinstones, and leased to the Forbes family. The castle was torched in 1571, killing Margaret Campbell, wife of Forbes of Towie, and 26 others of her household. Corgarff saw action in the Jacobite Risings, and was later used to help stop illicit whisky distilling.

Short but steep walk to castle. Exhibition: one of the floors houses a restored barrack room. Explanatory displays. Gift shop. Car and coach parking. Group concessions. £.

Open Apr-Sep, daily 9.30-18.30; last ticket 18.00; open Oct-Mar wknds only, Sat 9.30-16.30, Sun 14.00-16.30; last ticket 16.00.

Tel: 01975 651460

N75 Coulter Motte (HS)

[Map: 6B, F8] On A73, 1.5 miles SW of Biggar, Coulter, Lanarkshire. (NGR: NT 018362 LR: 72)

The remains of a motte and bailey castle consist of a fine example of a large castle mound.

Parking nearby.

Access at all reasonable times.

N76 Craigmillar Castle (HS)

[Map: 6B, E10] Off A68, 3 miles SE of Edinburgh Castle, Craigmillar, Edinburgh. (NGR: NT 288709 LR: 66)

A strong, imposing and well-preserved ruin, Craigmillar Castle consists of a large keep, surrounded by a curtain wall with round corner towers and an outer courtyard. The Prestons held the property from 1374. Mary, Queen of Scots, used Craigmillar often, and fled here after the murder of Rizzio. It was also here that the Earl of Moray, Bothwell and William Maitland of Lethington plotted Darnley's murder.

Exhibition and visitor centre. Gift shop. Refreshments. WC. Disabled WC. Car and coach parking. Group concessions. £.

Open all year: Apr-Sep, daily 9.30-18.30; Oct-Mar, Mon-Wed and Sat 9.30-16.30, Thu 9.30-12.00, Sun 14.00-16.30, closed Fri; last ticket 30 mins before closing; closed 25/26 Dec and 1/2 Jan.

Tel: 0131 661 4445

N77 Craignethan Castle (HS)

[Map: 6B, F8] Off A72, 4.5 miles W of Lanark, Craignethan, Lanarkshire. (NGR: NS 816464 LR: 72)

Standing on a promontory above a deep ravine, Craignethan is a ruinous castle, consisting of a strong tower surrounded by a curtain wall on three sides, with a thick rampart on the landward side. It was built by the Hamiltons as an early castle to withstand artillery, but, although attacked and eventually slighted, never withstood a determined siege.

Exhibition and explanatory boards. Gift shop. Tearoom. Car parking. Group concessions. £.

Open Apr-Sep, daily 9.30-18.30; last ticket 30 mins before closing.

Tel: 01555 860364   Fax: 0131 668 8800

N78 Crichton Castle (HS)

[Map: 6B, E10] Off B6367, 2 miles E of Gorebridge, Crichton, Midlothian. (NGR: NT 380612 LR: 66)

A complex, large and striking building, Crichton Castle consists of ruinous ranges of buildings enclosing a small courtyard. One particularly fine feature is the arcaded, diamond-faced facade in the courtyard. The castle was a property of the Crichtons, but later passed to the Hepburn Earl of Bothwell. Mary, Queen of Scots, attended a wedding here in 1562.

Walk to property. Sales area. Car and coach parking. Group concessions. £.

Open Apr-Sep, daily 9.30-18.30; last ticket 18.00.

Tel: 01875 320017

N79 Crookston Castle (HS)

[Map: 6A, F6] Off A736, 3 miles E of Paisley, off Brockburn Road, Crookston, Glasgow. (NGR: NS 524628 LR: 64)

Surrounded by a large ditch is an unusual ruined keep, dating from the 13th century. The lands were held by the Stewart Earls of Lennox, one of whom was Henry Stewart, Lord Darnley. James IV had bombarded the castle with the large cannon 'Mons Meg' in the 15th century, although the castle was subsequently repaired.

Parking nearby.

Access at all reasonable times – collect key from keeper (Mrs McCourt) at bottom of path. Owned by NTS; administered by Historic Scotland.

Tel: 0141 883 9606/0131 668 8800

N80 Cubbie Roo's Castle (HS)

[Map: 2, B2] North side of island of Wyre, Orkney. (NGR: HY 442264 LR: 6)

Standing on a small ridge, Cubbie Roo's Castle consists of a small keep surrounded by several rock-cut ditches. The name Cubbie Roo is a corruption of the Norseman Kolbein Hruga, who built the tower about 1150, as mentioned in the *Orkneyinga Saga*. The assassins of Earl John Haraldsson sought refuge here in 1231. The nearby ruined Romanesque chapel of St Mary [HY 442264] dates from the 12th century.

Access at all reasonable times.

Tel: 01856 875461

N81 Dean Castle

[Map: 6A, F6] Off B7038, 1 mile NE of Kilmarnock, Ayrshire. (NGR: NS 437394 LR: 70)

Interesting and well preserved, Dean Castle consists of a 14th-century keep and a 15th-century palace block within a courtyard. It was a property of the Boyds, later Earls of Kilmarnock, one of whom was executed by beheading for treason after the 1745-6 Jacobite Rising. The castle now houses a museum of armour and musical instruments, and is surrounded by 200 acres of woodland.

Guided tours. Explanatory displays. Museum of armour and musical instruments. Gift shop. Restaurant. WC. Picnic area. Park. Disabled access – but not into castle. Car and coach parking. Country park and castle free.

Open daily Apr-Oct 12.00-17.00; open Nov to end Mar wknds only; closed Christmas and New Year; park open daily dawn-dusk.

Tel: 01563 522702   Fax: 01563 572552

Web: www.deancastle.com   Email: rangers@east-ayrshire.gov.uk

N82 Dirleton Castle (HS)

[Map: 6B, D10] Off A198, 2 miles W of North Berwick, Dirleton, East Lothian. (NGR: NT 518840 LR: 66)

Standing on a rock, Dirleton Castle is a spectacular ruined castle with several towers and ranges of buildings around a courtyard. The castle was held by the De Vaux family, but was captured by the English after a hard siege in 1298. It passed to the Halyburton family, the Ruthvens, then the Erskines of Gogar, and was captured in 1650 by Cromwell's forces. There are fine gardens with ancient yews and hedges around the bowling green, as well as an early 20th-century Arts and Crafts garden and recreated Victorian garden.

Explanatory displays. Gift shop. WC. Limited disabled access. Disabled WC. Car and coach parking. Group concessions. £.

Open all year: Apr-Sep, daily 9.30-18.30; Oct-Mar, Mon-Sat 9.30-16.30, Sun 14.00-16.30; last ticket sold 30 mins before closing; closed 25/26 Dec and 1/2 Jan. Owned by NTS; administered by Historic Scotland.

Tel: 01620 850330

N83 Doune Castle (HS)

[Map: 5B, D8] Off A820, 7 miles NW of Stirling, SE of Doune, Stirlingshire. (NGR: NN 728011 LR: 57)

Standing on a strong site in a lovely location, Doune Castle is a powerful courtyard castle with two towers linked by a lower range. The fine Lord's Hall has a carved oak screen, musician's gallery and a double fireplace. The castle was built by Robert Stewart, Duke of Albany, but passed to the Crown and was used as a dower house. Doune was extensively used as a location in 'Monty Python and the Holy Grail'.

Explanatory displays. Gift shop. Picnic area. Car parking. Group concessions. £.

Open all year: Apr-Sep, daily 9.30-18.30; Oct-Mar, Mon-Wed and Sat-Sun 9.30-16.30, Thu 9.30-12.00, closed Fri; last admission 30 mins before closing; closed 25/26 Dec and 1/2 Jan.

Tel: 01786 841742

N84 Druchtag Motte (HS)

[Map: 6A, I6] Off A747, 11 miles SW of Whithorn, Mochrum, Dumfries and Galloway. (NGR: NX 349467 LR: 82)
The well-preserved motte of an early castle.
Access at all reasonable times – steep climb to top.

N85 Drumcoltran Tower (HS)

[Map: 6B, H8] Off A711, 6 miles NE of Dalbeattie, Drumcoltran, Dumfries and Galloway. (NGR: NX 869683 LR: 84)
Located in the middle of a farm, Drumcoltran Tower is a 16th-century L-plan tower house, which was held by the Maxwells, Irvings, Hynds and Herons. The tower was occupied until the 1890s.
Parking.
Access at all reasonable times – apply to key holder.

N86 Dryhope Tower

[Map: 6B, F10] Off A708, 9 miles S of Peebles, 2 miles E of Cappercleuch, Dryhope, Borders. (NGR: NT 267247 LR: 73)
Dryhope Tower is a ruined 16th-century tower house in a fine location. It was a property of the Scotts, and home of Mary (or Marion) Scott, the Flower of Yarrow. An old ballad records, in several versions, the bloody events surrounding her. In 1576 she married Walter Scott of Harden, 'Auld Wat', a famous Border reiver.
Access at all reasonable times.

N87 Duffus Castle (HS)

[Map: 4, E3] Off B9012 or B9135, 3 miles NW of Elgin, Moray. (NGR: NJ 189672 LR: 28)
One of the best examples of a 12th-century motte and bailey castle in Scotland, Duffus Castle consists of an extensive outer bailey with a small wet moat, a walled and ditched inner bailey, and a large motte with the ruins of a keep. It was held by the Cheynes, but passed to the Sutherland Lord Duffus. The castle was besieged and sacked several times, and part of the keep collapsed down the motte.
Car parking.
Access at all reasonable times – short walk.
Tel: 01667 460232

N88 Dumbarton Castle (HS)

[Map: 5A, D6] Off A814, in Dumbarton. (NGR: NS 400745 LR: 64)
Standing on a commanding rock on the north shore of the Clyde, little remains of the medieval Dumbarton Castle, except the 14th-century entrance. Most of the remains are 18th and 19th century fortifications.
  Meaning 'fortress of the Britons', Dumbarton is mentioned around 450 as the stronghold of the kings of Strathclyde. In 756 it was captured by Picts and Northumbrians, and in 870 was besieged by Irish raiders. Owen the Bald, the last King of Strathclyde, died at

the Battle of Carham in 1018, and Strathclyde was absorbed into the kingdom of Scots. Dumbarton became a royal castle, and was a formidable fortress, used as a place of refuge and a prison. The infant Mary, Queen of Scots, was kept at Dumbarton before being taken to France. Regent Morton and Patrick Stewart, 3rd Earl of Orkney, were imprisoned here before execution in 1581 and 1614 respectively.
Exhibition in Governor's House. Gift shop. Refreshments. WC. Car parking. Group concessions. £.
Open all year: Apr-Sep, daily 9.30-18.30; Oct-Mar, Mon-Wed and Sat 9.30-16.30, Thu 9.30-12.00, Sun 14.00-16.30, closed Fri; last ticket 30 mins before closing; closed 25/26 Dec and 1/2 Jan.
Tel: 01389 732167

N89 Dundonald Castle

[Map: 6A, F6] Off B730, 3.5 miles SE of Irvine, Dundonald, Ayrshire. (NGR: NS 364345 LR: 70)
Dundonald Castle consists of an ancient keep and adjoining courtyard, and is a fine building. It was extended and remodelled around 1350 by Robert II, King of Scots, who died at Dundonald in 1390. Robert III also used the castle, and he may have died here in 1406. The visitor centre features an interpretive display charting the history of the castle.
Visitor centre. Gift shop. Coffee shop. WC. Disabled access only to visitor centre. Car and coach parking. £.
Open Apr-Oct, daily 10.00-17.00. Managed by the Friends of Dundonald Castle.
Tel: 01563 850201 Web: www.royaldundonaldcastle.co.uk Email: royaldundonaldcastle@linel.net

J14 Dunfermline Palace (HS)
See main entry J14

N90 Dunnottar Castle

[Map: 4, H5] Off A92, 2 miles S of Stonehaven, Kincardine & Deeside. (NGR: NO 882839 LR: 45)
Built on a promontory on cliffs high above the sea, Dunnottar Castle is a spectacular ruined courtyard castle, parts of which date from the 12th century, and covers a large site. The entrance and tunnel up to the castle are especially impressive.
  There was a stronghold here from early times, and it was besieged by the Picts, and then in 900 by Vikings when Donald II, King of Scots was slain. Dunnottar was captured by William Wallace from the English in 1296, one story relating that he burnt 4000 Englishmen.
  It was held by the Keith Earls Marischal from 1382. In 1651 the Scottish crown jewels were brought here for safety, and Cromwell had the castle besieged in 1652. Before the garrison surrendered, the regalia and state papers were smuggled out to be hidden in

nearby **Kinneff Old Parish Church [K83]** until re-covered at the Restoration.

Getting to the castle involves a walk, steep climb, and a steeper one back. Exhibition. Sales area. WC. Car and coach parking. Group concessions. £.

Open Easter-Oct, Mon-Sat 9.00-18.00, Sun 14.00-17.00; winter Mon-Fri only, 9.00 to sunset; last admission 30 mins before closing.

Tel: 01569 762173 Fax: 01330 860325

Web: www.dunectestates.com Email: info@dunectestates.com

N91 Dunollie Castle

[Map: 5A, B4] Off A85, 1 mile N of Oban, Dunollie, Argyll. (NGR: NM 852314 LR: 49)

Standing on a rocky ridge overlooking the sea, Du-nollie Castle consists of an impressive ruined castle. It was built by the MacDougalls, who were bitter en-emies of Robert the Bruce. A MacDougall force de-feated Bruce at Dalry, nearly killing him and wrench-ing a brooch from his cloak. This was known as the Brooch of Lorne and kept at the castle, then at **Gylen [N108]**. Bruce returned and ravaged MacDougall lands after defeating them at **Loch Aweside [H9]**.

Can be reached from a lay-by on the Ganavan road, but not from the drive to Dunollie House, which is NOT open to the public. Care should be taken.

N92 Dunskey Castle

[Map: 6A, I5] Off A77, 5.5 miles SW of Stranraer, Dunskey, Portpatrick, Dumfries and Galloway. (NGR: NX 994534 LR: 82)

Set on a windswept and oppressive headland above the sea, Dunskey Castle is a ruinous tower house, mostly dating from the 16th century. It was held by the Adairs, and it was here that the abbot of Soulseat Abbey was imprisoned and tortured to force him to sign away the abbey lands.

Parking nearby.

View from exterior – climb and walk to castle from Portpatrick: care should be taken.

N93 Dunstaffnage Castle (HS)

[Map: 5A, B4] Off A85, 3.5 miles NE of Oban, Dunstaffnage, Argyll. (NGR: NM 882344 LR: 49)

On a rock on a promontory in the Firth of Lorne, the castle consists of a massive strong wall and a later gatehouse, which was built by the MacDougalls. The castle was besieged and captured by Robert the Bruce. Flora MacDonald was imprisoned here, albeit briefly. There is a fine ruined chapel nearby.

Explanatory panels. Gift shop. WC. Car and coach parking. Group concessions. £. Joint entry ticket available with Bonawe Iron Furnace.

Open Apr-Sep, daily 9.30-18.30; Oct-Mar, Sat-Wed 9.30-16.30, Thu 9.30-1200, closed Fri; last ticket 30 mins before closing; closed 25/26 Dec and 1/2 Jan.

Tel: 01631 562465

N94 Duntulm Castle

[Map: 3A, E4] Off A855, 6.5 miles N of Uig, Duntulm, Skye. (NGR: NG 410743 LR: 23)

On a strong and scenic site is a very ruinous castle, once a strong and comfortable fortress and residence. The Norsemen had a stronghold here, known as Dun-david or Dun Dhaibhidh, and it was later held by the MacLeods, then the MacDonalds. James V had visited the castle in 1540. The castle was abandoned around 1730 when the MacDonalds moved to Monkstadt House, then **Armadale Castle [Q1]** in Sleat.

Parking nearby.

View from exterior as dangerously ruined.

N95 Dunyvaig Castle

[Map: 5A, F3] Off A846, 2 miles E of Port Ellen, Lagavulin, Islay. (NGR: NR 406455 LR: 60)

Little remains of Dunyvaig Castle, except the remains of a small keep on top of a rock as well as a courtyard. The castle was long held by the MacDonalds, and was besieged several times in the 17th century. The prop-erty passed to the Campbells.

Parking nearby.

Access at all reasonable times – care should be taken.

N96 Earl's Palace, Birsay (HS)

[Map: 2, B2] Off A966, 12 miles N of Stromness, Birsay, Orkney. (NGR: HY 248279 LR: 6)

Once a fine and stately building, the Earl's Palace at Birsay is a ruined 16th-century courtyard castle, started by Robert Stewart, Earl of Orkney about 1574 and completed by his son, Patrick Stewart, before 1614. Both of them were executed in 1615. Nearby is the **Brough of Birsay [K54]**.

Parking nearby

Access at all reasonable times.

Tel: 01856 721205/841815

N97 Earl's Palace, Kirkwall (HS)

[Map: 2, C3] On A960, W of Kirkwall, Orkney. (NGR: HY 449107 LR: 6)

The Earl's Palace is a fine ruinous palace, dating from the beginning of the 17th century, dominated by large oriel windows. The palace was built by Patrick Stew-art, Earl of Orkney, illegitimate half-brother of Mary, Queen of Scots. He oppressed the Orcadians, and was imprisoned then executed in 1615. The Bishops of Orkney occupied the palace until 1688. (Also see **Bishop's Palace [N54]**). The fine medieval cathe-dral, **St Magnus Cathedral [K33]**, stands nearby.

Explanatory displays. Parking nearby. £. Joint entry ticket for all Orkney monuments available.

Open Apr-Sep, daily 9.30-18.30, last ticket 18.00.

Tel: 01856 875461

N98 Edzell Castle (HS)

[Map: 4, H4] Off B966, 6 miles N of Brechin, Edzell, Angus. (NGR: NO 585693 LR: 44)

A fine tower house, later enlarged and extended with ranges of buildings around a courtyard, all now ruinous. A large pleasance, or garden, was created in 1604, and is surrounded by an ornamental wall, to which a summerhouse and a bath-house were added. The fine carved decoration of the garden walls is unique. The castle was built by the Lindsay Earls of Crawford, but passed to the Maule Earl of Panmure in 1715. The Lindsay burial aisle, in Edzell kirkyard [NO 582688], dates from the 16th century and is also open to the public.

Visitor centre. Exhibition and explanatory panels. WC. Garden. Picnic area. Reasonable disabled access and WC. Car and coach parking. Group concessions. £.

Open all year: Apr-Sep, daily 9.30-18.30; Oct-Mar, Mon-Wed and Sat 9.30-16.30, Thu 9.30-12.00, Sun 14.00-16.30, closed Fri; last ticket 30 mins before closing; closed 25/26 Dec and 1/2 Jan.

Tel: 01356 648631

N99 Eglinton Castle

[Map: 6A, F6] Off B7080, 1.5 miles N of Irvine, near Eglinton Park visitor centre, Ayrshire. (NGR: NS 323423 LR: 70)

A huge, but very ruinous, 18th-century castellated mansion, built on the site of a 16th-century stronghold of the Montgomery Earls of Eglinton. It was here that the Eglinton Tournament was held in 1839, a medieval-style extravaganza, which attracted thousands of visitors. The ruins stand in a public park, and the visitor centre has displays about the tournament and natural history.

Explanatory displays. Visitor centre. Gardens. Children's play areas. Ranger service.

Access at all reasonable times.

Tel: 01294 551776   Fax: 01294 556467

N100 Elcho Castle (HS)

[Map: 5B, C9] Off A912, 4 miles E of Perth, Elcho, Perthshire. (NGR: NO 165211 LR: 58)

Both stronghold and comfortable residence, Elcho Castle is a 16th-century castle, with a long rectangular main block and several towers. There is a fine quarry garden. The Wemyss family held the property from 1468, and were made Lords Elcho in 1633, as well as Earls of Wemyss.

Kiosk. Picnic area. WC. Parking. £.

Open Apr-Sep, daily 9.30-18.30; last ticket sold 30 mins before closing.

Tel: 01738 639998

N101 Fast Castle

[Map: 6B, E12] Off A1107, 6 miles NW of Eyemouth, Borders. (NGR: NT 862710 LR: 67)

Standing on a cliff-top promontory, little remains of Fast Castle, an ancient castle, which was once approached by a drawbridge over the steep chasm. It was held by the Homes, Douglases, Arnots, Logans and Halls, and has a long eventful history. It was reputedly used by smugglers, having a 'secret' cave below the castle. There are tales of treasure buried here, possibly hidden by Sir Robert Logan of Restalrig, who died in 1606.

Car parking nearby.

Access at all times – visit involves walk and care must be taken (joined to the 'mainland' by a gangway).

N102 Findlater Castle

[Map: 4, E4] Off A98, 2 miles E of Cullen, Findlater, Sandend, Banff and Buchan. (NGR: NJ 542673 LR: 29)

Built on a dizzying cliff-top promontory, not much remains of a 14th-century keep and castle, the large fortress of the Ogilvies of Findlater, later Earls of Findlater, who held it from 1445 or earlier.

Access at all reasonable times – care should be taken.

N103 Finlaggan

[Map: 5A, E2] Off A846, 3 miles W of Port Askaig, Loch Finlaggan, Islay. (NGR: NR 388681 LR: 60)

Finlaggan was a very important centre of the MacDonald Lords of the Isles in medieval times, but not much remains except foundations on two islands. Traces have recently been found of a 15th-century keep on the smaller, or council, island. The ruins of a chapel, dedicated to St Finlaggan a contemporary of St Columba, and many other buildings stand on the larger island, Eilean Mor. There are several carved gravestones, thought to be for relatives of the Lords of the Isles, who were themselves buried on **Iona [J20]**.

Visitor centre. Parking nearby.

Open Apr-Oct: tel to confirm.

Tel: 01496 810629   Fax: 01496 810856

Web: www.islay.com   Email: lynmags@aol.com

N104 Gilnockie Tower

[Map: 6B, H10] Off A7, 9 miles N of Gretna, 2 miles N of Canonbie, Hollows Village, Dumfries. (NGR: NY 383787 LR: 85)

Gilnockie Tower is a 16th-century tower house, and was a stronghold of the unruly Armstrongs. Johnnie Armstrong of Gilnockie was hanged without trial by James V in 1530, with 36 of his followers. The tower has been restored, and occupied since 1992 by the Clan Armstrong Centre.

Guided tour. Explanatory displays. Gift shop. WC. Car parking. Group concessions – groups must book in advance. £.

Open summer months, guided tour at 14.30: check with Gilnockie Tower.

Tel: 01387 371876   Fax: 01387 371876

Web: www.armstrong-clan.co.uk   Email: tedarmclan@aol.com

N105 Girnigoe Castle

[Map: 3B, B12] Off A9, 3 miles N of Wick, Caithness, Highland (NGR: ND 379549 LR: 12)

Standing on a rocky promontory in the sea, Girnigoe Castle and Castle Sinclair were two ruinous fortresses. It was the seat of the Sinclair Earls of Caithness. In 1571 the 4th Earl had John, Master of Caithness, his son and heir, imprisoned in the dungeons for seven years. The Master was fed on salted beef, and denied water so that he died mad with thirst. There is more information at the **Wick Heritage Centre [Y208]**.

Car parking.

Access at all reasonable times: medium walk to site – view from exterior and great care should be taken.

N106 Glenbuchat Castle (HS)

[Map: 4, G3] Off A97, 10 miles W of Alford, 4.5 miles W of Kildrummy, Aberdeenshire. (NGR: NJ 397149 LR: 37)

A roofless but mostly complete 16th-century Z-plan tower house with round and square turrets. The castle was built by the Gordons. Brigadier-General John Gordon of Glenbuchat fought for the Jacobites, and led the Gordons and Farquharsons at the Battle of Culloden in 1746 – when already 70. He was hunted after the battle, but managed to escape to Norway disguised as a beggar, and died in France.

Parking nearby.

Access at all reasonable times.

Tel: 01466 793191

N107 Greenknowe Tower (HS)

[Map: 6B, E11] On A6105, 7 miles NW of Kelso, 0.5 miles W of Gordon, Borders. (NGR: NT 639428 LR: 74)

Built for comfort as well as defence is a 16th-century L-plan tower house, with turrets crowning the corners of the building. Greenknowe passed by marriage from the Gordons to the Setons of Touch, later coming to the Pringles of Stichel.

Parking nearby.

Access at all reasonable times.

N108 Gylen Castle

[Map: 5A, C4] Off unlisted track, 2 miles SW of Balliemore, Gylen, S side of Kerrera. (NGR: NM 805265 LR: 49)

On a rocky promontory jutting into the sea, Gylen – 'castle of fountains' – is a ruinous 16th-century L-plan tower house. Gylen was a property of the MacDougalls, and this may have been where Alexander II died. The castle was captured and burnt by a Covenanter army in 1647.

Access at all reasonable times – care should be taken (take the Kerrera ferry then 3 mile walk).

N109 Hailes Castle (HS)

[Map: 6B, D11] Off A1, 4 miles E of Haddington, 1.5 miles W of East Linton, East Lothian. (NGR: NT 575758 LR: 67)

In a lovely location above the River Tyne, Hailes Cas-

tle is a picturesque ruinous castle, which dates from the 13th century, and has two pit-prisons. Hailes was long a Hepburn property, and saw much action down the centuries. The Earl of Bothwell brought Mary, Queen of Scots, here after abducting her in 1567, and they married soon afterwards. The castle was abandoned for the mansion of **Newhailes [S36]**, near Musselburgh.

Picnic area. Parking.

Access at all reasonable times.

N110 Hermitage Castle (HS)

[Map: 6B, G10] Off B6399, 5 miles N of Newcastleton, Borders. (NGR: NY 494960 LR: 79)

One of the most impressive and oppressive of Scottish fortresses, Hermitage Castle is a large brooding fortress in a bleak location. It had many owners, including the Hepburn Earls of Bothwell. In 1566 James Hepburn, 4th Earl, was badly wounded in a skirmish with the Border reiver 'Little Jock' Elliot of Park, and was paid a visit by Mary, Queen of Scots.

Sales area. Picnic area. Car and coach parking. Group concessions. £.

Open Apr-Sep, daily 9.30-18.30, last ticket sold 18.00.

Tel: 01387 376222

N111 Hume Castle

[Map: 6B, F11] On B6364, 6 miles N of Kelso, Hume, Borders. (NGR: NT 704414 LR: 74)

Standing on a commanding position with fine views over the Tweed valley, Hume Castle was an important stronghold of the Home family. It was considered impregnable before the advent of gunpowder. In 1651 the castle was surrendered to Cromwell's forces, and demolished, and the family moved to **The Hirsel [Y193]**. The castle was rebuilt as a folly in 1794, incorporating the foundations of the old castle.

Explanatory displays. Car and coach parking.

Open all year, daily 9.00-21.00; in winter months, key available from the large house opposite castle.

N112 Huntingtower Castle (HS)

[Map: 5B, C9] Off A85, 2 miles NW of Perth, Huntingtower, Perthshire. (NGR: NO 083252 LR: 58)

A well-preserved and interesting castle, Huntingtower consists of two towers and a later small connecting range. Some rooms have fine painted ceilings, mural paintings and plasterwork, as well as decorative beams in the hall. The property was held by the Ruthvens, but they were forfeited, their lands seized, and their name proscribed.

Gift shop. Picnic area. Car parking. Group concessions. £.

Open all year: Apr-Sep, daily 9.30-18.30; Oct-Mar, Mon-Wed and 18.30-16.30, Thu 9.30-12.00, Sun 14.00-16.30, closed Fri; last ticket sold 30 mins before closing; closed 25/26 Dec and 1/2 Jan.

Tel: 01738 627231 Fax: 0131 668 8800

N113 Huntly Castle (HS)

[Map: 4, F4] Off A920, N of Huntly, Aberdeenshire. (NGR: NJ 532407 LR: 29)

A fine building with a long and violent history, Huntly Castle consists of a strong and sophisticated main block, rectangular in plan, with an adjoining large courtyard. It was long held by the Gordon Earls of Huntly, and was besieged and torched on several occasions. The 4th Earl was defeated (and died, reportedly from apoplexy) at the Battle of Corrichie in 1562 by the forces of Mary, Queen of Scots, and his son was executed and buried in **Kirk of St Nicholas [K20]**.

Exhibition. Gift shop. WC. Disabled WC. Parking. £

Open all year: Apr-Sep, daily 9.30-18.30; Oct-Mar, Mon-Wed and Sat 9.30-16.00, Thu 9.30-12.00, Sun 14.00-16.30, closed Fri; last ticket sold 30 mins before closing; closed 25/26 Dec and 1/2 Jan.

Tel: 01466 793191

N114 Inverlochy Castle (HS)

[Map: 3B, H7] Off A82, 1.5 miles NE of Fort William, Inverlochy, Highland. (NGR: NN 120754 LR: 41)

A ruined 13th-century castle of enclosure, with corner towers, of the Comyns of Badenoch. There were two entrances, opposite each other, with portcullises. The Comyns were destroyed by Robert the Bruce around 1308, and the castle was later held by the Gordons of Huntly. Major consolidation work is underway.

Parking nearby.

Access at all reasonable times.

Tel: 01667 460232

N115 Kilchurn Castle (HS)

[Map: 5A, B5] Off A85, 2 miles W of Dalmally, Kilchurn, Argyll. (NGR: NN 133276 LR: 50)

A picturesque and much photographed ruin, Kilchurn Castle is a large ruinous courtyard castle, dating from the 15th century. The lands originally belonged to the MacGregors, but were acquired by the Campbells of Glenorchy, who built or rebuilt the castle. There are apparently regular sailings from Loch Awe pier to Kilchurn by steamer, although it was closed at time of visiting – phone ferry company 01838 200400/200449. The castle can also be reached across land off A85.

Parking nearby: through gate off A85.

Open Apr-Sep, daily 9.30-18.30 – tel to check if ferry operating.

Tel: 01838 200440/200449 (ferry co.)

N116 Kildrummy Castle (HS)

[Map: 4, G4] Off A97, 10 miles SW of Alford, Kildrummy, Aberdeenshire. (NGR: NJ 454164 LR: 37)

Although now ruinous, this was one of the largest early castles in Scotland. The high curtain wall enclosed a courtyard with six round towers. It was captured by the English in 1306 from a garrison led by Nigel Bruce, younger brother of Robert the Bruce. The castle was badly damaged in 1690, but was complete enough for the Earl of Mar to use it as his base when he led the Jacobite Rising in 1715.

Gift shop. WC. Disabled WC. Parking. £

Open Apr-Sep, daily 9.30-18.30; last admission 18.00.

Tel: 01975 571331

N117 Kindrochit Castle

[Map: 4, G3] Off A93, by car par, S of Braemar, Kincardine and Deeside. (NGR: NO 152913 LR: 43)

Little remains of a once strong castle, held for many years by the Drummonds. It was reputedly destroyed by cannon in the 17th century after plague had struck.

Parking.

Access at all reasonable times.

X26 Kinnaird Head Castle (HS)

A large altered 15th-century keep, rectangular in plan, the walls of which are harled and whitewashed. It was a property of the Frasers of Philorth. A lighthouse was built into the top of the castle in 1787, and the outbuildings were built around it in 1820 by Robert Stevenson, grandfather of Robert Louis Stevenson. It now forms part of a Scotland's National Lighthouse Museum. The Wine Tower, a lower tower, stands nearby. Managed by the Kinnaird Head Trust.

See main entry X26

N118 Kisimul Castle (HS)

[Map: 3A, G2] Off A888, on island S of Castlebay, Barra. (NGR: NL 665979 LR: 31)

Kisimul Castle consists of curtain wall shaped to fit the island on which it stands, enclosing a three-storey keep, hall and other ranges of buildings including a chapel. It was held by the MacNeils, and Neil of the Castle may have built a stronghold here in 1030. The family was forced to sell Barra in 1840 to the Gordons of Cluny, but the castle was bought back in 1937, and restored in the 1950s and 60s. It is managed by Historic Scotland.

Parking nearby. £. Boat trip.

Open Apr-Sep, daily 9.30-18.30; Oct, Mon-Wed and Sat, 9.30-16.30, Thu 9.30-12.00, Sun , 14.00-16.30, closed Fri; last ticket 30 mins before closing.

Tel: 01871 810313

N119 Linlithgow Palace (HS)

[Map: 6B, D8] Off A803, in Linlithgow, West Lothian. (NGR: NT 003774 LR: 65)

Once a splendid palace and still a spectacular ruin, Linlithgow Palace consists of ranges of buildings set around a rectangular courtyard with a fountain, and may include 12th-century work. There was a 12th-century castle here, which was captured and strengthened by Edward I of England in 1301 during the Wars of Independence, then known as the Peel of Linlithgow. It was slighted, after being retaken by the Scots by driving a cart under the portcullis, and remained a ruin until about 1350. It was repaired by David II, then mostly rebuilt by James I at the beginning of the 15th century. It became a favourite residence of the monarchs of Scots, and the work continued under James III and James IV. James V was born here in 1512, as was Mary, Queen of Scots, in 1542. It was burnt out in 1746.

Explanatory panels and exhibition. Gift shop. WC. Picnic area. Disabled access. Car parking. Group concessions. £.

Open all year: Apr-Sep, daily 9.30-18.30; Oct-Mar, Mon-Sat 9.30-16.40, Sun 14.00-16.30; last ticket sold 30 mins before closing; closed 25/26 Dec and 1/2 Jan.

Tel: 01506 842896

N120 Loch Doon Castle (HS)

[Map: 6A, H6] Off A713, 7 miles S of Dalmellington, Ayrshire. (NGR: NX 483509 LR: 77)

A ruined 13th-century courtyard castle, polygonal in plan. It originally stood on an inland in the loch, but when the water level was raised by a hydroelectric scheme, the castle was moved to its present site. It was built by the Bruce Earls of Carrick, and in 1333 was one of the six strongholds which held out for David II against Edward Balliol.

Parking.

Access at all reasonable times.

N121 Lochleven Castle (HS)

[Map: 5B, C9] Off B996, 1 mile E of Kinross, Loch Leven, Perthshire. (NGR: NO 138018 LR: 58)

Standing on an island in a picturesque loch is a small ruinous rectangular keep, standing at one corner of a courtyard. It was a royal castle from 1257, and stormed by William Wallace, but passed to the Douglases. Mary, Queen of Scots, was held here from 1567 until she escaped in 1568, during which time she signed her abdication. The island was landscaped for nearby **Kinross House [S94]**.

Gift shop. WC. Picnic area. Car parking at Kinross. £.

Open Apr-Oct, daily 9.30-18.30; last ticket 18.00 – includes boat trip from Kinross.

Tel: 01786 450000

N122 Lochmaben Castle (HS)

[Map: 6B, H9] Off B7020, 3 miles W of Lockerbie, Lochmaben, Dumfriesshire. (NGR: NY 088812 LR: 78)

Once an important and powerful castle, Lochmaben Castle consists of a complex of very ruined buildings, dating from the 13th century, but remodelled by James IV. It saw much action in the Wars of Independ-

ence. It was here in 1542 that the Scottish army was mustered before going to defeat at Solway Moss. Mary, Queen of Scots, and Darnley attended a banquet here in 1565.

Car parking

Access at all reasonable times – view from exterior.

N123 Lochranza Castle (HS)

[Map: 6A, E4] Off A841, 10 miles N of Brodick, Lochranza, Arran. (NGR: NR 933507 LR: 69)

In a beautiful location, Lochranza Castle is a ruined L-plan building, much of which dates from the 13th or 14th century. Lochranza was used as a hunting lodge by the kings of Scots, and is said to have been visited by Robert the Bruce.

Car parking.

Key available locally.

N124 Loudoun Castle

[Map: 6A, F6] Off A77, 4 miles E of Kilmarnock, 1 mile N of Galston, Loudoun, Ayrshire. (NGR: NS 506378 LR: 70)

Loudoun Castle, a large ruined castellated mansion, incorporates an old stronghold. It was a property of the Crawfords in the 14th century, but passed by marriage to the Campbells. John Campbell, Chancellor of Scotland, was made Earl of Loudoun in 1641. In 1941 was accidentally torched and gutted. It remains a large impressive ruin, and is now the centre piece of a theme park.

Guided tours for school parties. Woodland and country walks. Theme park with rollercoasters, go karts, log flume, carousel and much else (!). Gift shop. Restaurant. Tearoom. WC. Picnic area. Disabled limited access and WC. Car and coach parking. Group concessions. £££.

Loudoun Castle Park open Easter-Oct from 10.00.

Tel: 01563 822296   Web: www.loudouncastle.co.uk
Fax: 01563 822408   Email: loudouncastle@btinternet.com

N125 MacLellan's Castle (HS)

[Map: 6B, I7] On A711, in Kirkcudbright, Galloway. (NGR: NX 683511 LR: 83)

A fine but ruinous 16th-century tower house, built by Sir Thomas MacLellan of Bombie, Provost of Kirkcudbright, in 1582. The MacLellans abandoned the castle around 1752, because of financial troubles.

Sales area. Exhibition. WC. Parking. £.

Open Apr-Sep, daily 9.30-18.30; last ticket 18.00.

Tel: 01557 331856

N126 Mar's Wark (HS)

[Map: 5B, D8] Off A9, Castle Wynd, Stirling. (NGR: NS 794937 LR: 57)

A ruinous Renaissance-style mansion, which was built in 1570 by the 1st Earl of Mar, Regent of Scotland and hereditary keeper of Stirling Castle. The main surviving part is the fine facade with the gatehouse decorated by sculptures. The building was converted into a barracks, but damaged by cannon during the 1745-6 Jacobite Rising.

Parking nearby.

Access at all reasonable times.

N127 Menstrie Castle

[Map: 5B, D8] Off A91, 5 miles NE of Stirling, 3 miles NW of Alloa, Castle Street, Menstrie, Clackmannan. (NGR: NS 852968 LR: 58)

A small 16th-century tower house, the wing of which was later greatly extended into a long block. It was a property of the Alexander family from around 1481. Sir William Alexander of Menstrie, 1st Earl of Stirling, was the founder of Nova Scotia, although he was later ruined and died bankrupt. The house was saved from demolition in the 1950s, and the museum tells the story of Sir William and the Nova Scotia Baronetcies.

Parking nearby.

Open Easter wknd, then May-Sep, Wed and Sun 14.00-16.00; administered by NTS and staffed by Clackmannanshire Council.

Tel: 01259 213131

N128 Morton Castle (HS)

[Map: 6B, G8] Off A76, 2.5 miles NE of Thornhill, Morton, Dumfries and Galloway. (NGR: NX 891992 LR: 78)

Built on a strong site, Morton Castle consists of a ruined 13th-century castle, although little remains of two sides. It was long a property of the Douglases, later Earls of Morton. The castle was occupied until about 1715.

Parking nearby

Access at all reasonable times – view from exterior.

N129 Motte of Urr

[Map: 6B, H8] Off B794, 2.5 miles NW of Dalbeattie, Urr, Dumfries and Galloway. (NGR: NX 815647 LR: 84)

Probably the best example of a motte and bailey earthwork castle in Scotland, dating from the 12th century, covering some five acres and incorporating a hill fort. It was a stronghold of the Lords of Galloway before they moved to Buittle in the 1240s. Devorgilla of Galloway, heiress of Allan, Lord of Galloway, married John Balliol, and their son became John I of Scots. They founded Balliol College, Oxford, and she built **Sweetheart Abbey [J32]**, where they are buried.

Parking nearby.

Access at all reasonable times.

N130 Mugdock Castle

[Map: 5B, D7] Off A81, 8 miles N of Glasgow, Craigallian Road, 1.5 miles N of Milngavie, East Dunbartonshire. (NGR: NS 549772 LR: 64)

Formerly a large fortress of great strength, Mugdock Castle is a ruinous courtyard castle, dating from the 14th century. It was a property of the Grahams, and one of the family was James Graham, the famous Marquis of Montrose. The ruins of the castle were presented to the local council, have been consolidated, and are in a 740-acre public park. The park includes lakes, woodland and heather.

Explanatory displays. Gift shop. Restaurant. Tearoom. Picnic and barbecue areas. WC. Play areas and walks. Craigend stables and bridle routes. Disabled access and WC. Tactile map. Car and coach parking.

Park open all year: summer 9.00-21.00; winter 9.00-17.30.

Tel: 0141 956 6100 Web: www.mugdock-country-park.org.uk
Fax: 0141 956 5624 Email: iain@mcp.ndo.co.uk

N131 Muness Castle (HS)

[Map: 1, B4] Off A968, SE end of island of Unst, Muness, Shetland. (NGR: HP 629012 LR: 1)

The most northerly castle in the British Isles, Muness Castle is a ruined 16th-century Z-plan tower house. The castle was built by Laurence Bruce of Cultmalindie, a Scottish incomer to Shetland. In 1573 he was appointed Chamberlain of the Lordship of Shetland, but his was a corrupt and repressive regime.

Access at all reasonable times.

Tel: 01466 793191

N132 Neidpath Castle

[Map: 6B, F9] Off A72, 1 mile W of Peebles, Borders. (NGR: NT 236405 LR: 73)

Standing on a steep bank of the Tweed in a wooded gorge, Neidpath is a splendid 14th-century castle with a small courtyard. It was held by the Frasers, Hays, and Douglases, then the Earls of Wemyss and March. It was besieged by Cromwell in 1650, and held out longer than any other stronghold south of the Forth.

Gift shop. Museum. Unique batiks depicting Mary Queen of Scots. Tartan collection. WC. Disabled access only to museum and ground floor of castle (up 5 steps). Picnic area. Group concessions. Car and coach parking. £.

Open (2002) Easter 13-22 Apr, 14.00-19.00, then 25-28 May, 29 Jun-Sep, daily 11.00-18.00

Tel: 01721 720333 Fax: 01721 720333

N133 Newark Castle (HS)

[Map: 6A, D6] On A8, 3 miles E of Greenock, Newark, Port Glasgow, Renfrewshire. (NGR: NS 331745 LR: 63)

Standing on a spit of land into the sea, Newark Castle is a large and imposing building, which was built by the Maxwells. James IV was a frequent visitor. One of the family, Patrick Maxwell, was involved in the murders of Patrick Maxwell of Stanely and the Montgomery Earl of Eglinton, in 1584 and 1596 respectively, during a series of feuds.

Exhibition. Sales area. WC. Car and coach parking. Group concessions. £.

Open Apr-Sep, daily 9.30-18.30; last ticket 18.00.

Tel: 01475 741858

N134 Noltland Castle (HS)

[Map: 2, B2] Off B9066, NE side of island of Westray, Orkney. (NGR: HY 430487 LR: 5)

A strong and grim stronghold, Noltland Castle is a large ruined 16th-century Z-plan tower house. The present castle was built by Gilbert Balfour, who was Master of the Household to Mary, Queen of Scots. He was involved in the murders of Cardinal Beaton in 1546, for which he was imprisoned, and Lord Darnley in 1567.

Open Jul-Sep, daily 9.30-18.30; last ticket 18.00.
Tel: 01856 841815

N135 Orchardton Tower (HS)

[Map: 6B, I8] Off A711, 4 miles S of Dalbeattie, Orchardton, Dumfries and Galloway. (NGR: NX 817551 LR: 84)

A ruinous round tower house of four storeys, unique in Scotland. It was held by the Cairns family, then the Maxwells. Sir Robert Maxwell, was captured at Culloden in 1746 and taken to Carlisle for probable execution. After his commission as an officer in the French army was found, he was treated as a prisoner of war and sent to France instead of being executed. *Car parking.*

Access at all reasonable times.

N136 Peel Ring of Lumphanan (HS)

[Map: 4, G4] Off A93, 5 miles NE of Aboyne, Lumphanan, Kincardine & Deeside. (NGR: NJ 576037 LR: 37)

Site of 12th-century castle of enclosure, now consisting of a large but low motte with a ditch. It was held by the Durwards in the 13th century, and visited by Edward I of England in 1296. It was at Lumphanan that Macbeth was slain in battle with the forces of Malcolm Canmore in 1057. There is a large boulder – Macbeth's Stone – at which he is said to have died [NJ 575034] and spring – Macbeth's Well – where he drank before the battle [NJ 580039]. Macbeth's Cairn [NJ 578053] is where he is believed to have been buried before his body was taken to Iona – although the robbed and disturbed mound is probably a prehistoric burial cairn. *Parking.*

Access at all reasonable times.
Tel: 01466 793191

N137 Ravenscraig Castle (HS)

[Map: 6B, D10] Off A955, 1 mile NE of Kirkcaldy, Ravenscraig, Fife. (NGR: NT 291925 LR: 59)

A ruinous altered 15th-century castle and courtyard, built to withstand and return artillery. James II, who died when a cannon exploded during the siege of Roxburgh Castle, started to build Ravenscraig for Mary

of Gueldres before 1460. She died at the castle in 1463. It was later held by the Sinclairs. *Parking.*

Access at all reasonable times – some of the building cannot be entered.
Tel: 01592 412690

N138 Red Castle

[Map: 4, I4] Off A92, 5 miles S of Montrose, Lunan, Angus. (NGR: NO 687510 LR: 54)

A ruinous castle, dating from the 12th century, with an impressive section of curtain wall and one half of the keep. The original castle was built by the Berkleys, but passed to Hugh, 6th Earl of Ross, then to the Stewart Lord Innermeath. It was attacked by Protestants when occupied by an Episcopal minister, James Rait, and later passed to the Guthries. *Parking nearby.*

Access at all reasonable times – the castle may be in a dangerous condition.

N139 Rothesay Castle (HS)

[Map: 5A, E5] Off A845, Rothesay, Bute. (NGR: NS 086646 LR: 63)

Surrounded by a wet moat, Rothesay Castle is a ruinous 12th-century castle, with four later round towers and a gatehouse. The castle was seized by Norsemen in the 1230s, and captured in 1263 by King Hakon of Norway. It was a favourite residence of Robert II and Robert III, who may have died here, rather than at **Dundonald [N89]**, in 1406. In 1401 Robert III made his son Duke of Rothesay, a title since taken by the eldest son of the kings of Scots and currently held by Prince Charles. Finds from here are in the **Bute Museum [Y50]**.

Explanatory displays and panels. Audio-visual display. Kiosk. WC. Car parking nearby. Group concessions. £.
Open all year: Apr-Sep, daily 9.30-18.30; Oct-Mar, Mon-Wed and Sat 9.30-16.30, Thu 9.30-12.00, Sun 14.00-16.30, closed Fri; last ticket sold 30 mins before closing; closed 25/26 Dec and 1/2 Jan.
Tel: 01700 502691

N140 Roxburgh Castle

[Map: 6B, F11] Off A699, 1 mile W of Kelso, Borders. (NGR: NT 713337 LR: 74)

This was once one of the most important strongholds in Scotland, although not much now remains. Mary, sister of Robert the Bruce, was hung by the English from a cage suspended from the walls. In 1460 James II was killed when one of the cannons, with which he was bombarding the castle, blew up beside him. A holly tree between Floors and the River Tweed is said to mark the spot where James was killed.
Parking nearby.

Access at all reasonable times.

N141 Scalloway Castle (HS)

[Map: 1, D3] Off A970, Scalloway, Shetland. (NGR: HU 404392 LR: 4)

A ruinous 17th-century tower house, consisting of a main block and a smaller square offset wing. The castle was built by Patrick Stewart, Earl of Orkney, in 1600. He was unpopular with both the Orcadians and the folk of Shetland, and executed in 1615.

Explanatory displays. Car parking.

Open Mon-Sat 9.30-17.00 (or as Shetland Woollen Company shop). Sun key available from the Royal Hotel.

Tel: 01466 793191

N142 Scotstarvit Tower (HS)

[Map: 6B, C10] Off A916, 2 miles S of Cupar, Hill of Tarvit, Fife. (NGR: NO 370113 LR: 59)

A fine and well-preserved tower, Scotstarvit is a 15th- and 16th-century tower house. It was held by the Inglis family, the Scotts, Gourlays, Wemyss family and the Sharps. Sir John Scott of Scotstarvit was an eminent historian. It was given to The National Trust for Scotland in 1949 – see **Hill of Tarvit [S26]**.

Owned by NTS; administered by Historic Scotland. Key available at Hill of Tarvit, which is open Easter, May to September, wknds in October.

Tel: 01334 653127

N143 Skipness Castle (HS)

[Map: 5A, E4] Off B8001, 7 miles S of Tarbert, Skipness, Argyll. (NGR: NR 907577 LR: 62)

A large ruinous 13th-century castle of enclosure. The main entrance was from the sea, which was defended by a gatetower. The first castle was probably built by the MacSweens around 1247, and it was later held by the MacDonalds, Forresters and Campbells. The ruins of a 13th-century chapel, Kilbrannan, dedicated to St Brendan, lie to the south-east of the castle [NR 910575]. There are fine grave slabs, an interesting burial ground, and grand views across to Arran.

Explanatory boards. Car parking.

Access at all reasonable times: short walk to castle, then walk to chapel which may be muddy.

N144 Smailholm Tower (HS)

[Map: 6B, F11] Off B6397, 6 miles W of Kelso, Smailholm, Borders. (NGR: NT 637346 LR: 74)

Standing on a rocky outcrop is a plain tower house, a property of the Pringle family from 1408. David Pringle of Smailholm was killed, together with his four sons, at the Battle of Flodden in 1513. The property was sold to the Scotts of Harden. The tower houses an exhibition of dolls illustrating some of the Border ballads from Walter Scott's 'Minstrelsy of the Scottish Borders'.

Explanatory displays. Sales area. Car and coach parking. £.

Open Apr-Sep, daily 9.30-18.30; open Oct-Mar wknds only,

Sat 9.30-16.30, Sun 14.00-16.30; last ticket 30 mins before closing; closed 25/26 Dec and 1/2 Jan.

Tel: 01573 460365

N145 Spynie Palace (HS)

[Map: 4, E3] Off A941, 2.5 miles N of Elgin, Spynie, Moray. (NGR: NJ 231658 LR: 28)

One of the finest castles in Scotland, the palace consists of a massive keep, Davy's Tower, at one corner of a large courtyard, enclosing ranges of buildings. All are now ruinous. The palace was probably built by Bishop Innes, after **Elgin Cathedral [K17]** had been burnt by the 'Wolf of Badenoch'. Mary, Queen of Scots visited in 1562, as did the Earl of Bothwell. There are fine views from the tower.

Explanatory panels. Gift shop. WC. Picnic area. Car and coach parking. £. Joint ticket with Elgin Cathedral available (£).

Open Apr-Sep, daily 9.30-18.30; Oct-Mar wknds only, Sat 9.30-16.30, Sun 14.00-16.30; last ticket sold 30 mins before closing; closed 25/25 Dec and 1/2 Jan.

Tel: 01343 546358

N146 St Andrews Castle (HS)

[Map: 6B, C10] Off A91, St Andrews, Fife. (NGR: NO 513169 LR: 59)

A ruined courtyard castle, enclosed by a wall with a gatehouse and towers, one of which contains a bottle dungeon cut into the rock. The first castle here was built by Bishop Roger, and it was held by the bishops and archbishops. In 1546 a band of Protestants murdered Cardinal David Beaton, and hung his naked body from one of the towers. There are tunnels from the resultant siege, which can be entered and are some of the finest siege works in Europe.

Visitor centre with fine exhibition. Explanatory panels. Gift shop. WC. Disabled access and WC. Car parking nearby. Group concessions. £. Combined ticket for cathedral & castle is available (££).

Open all year: Apr-Sep, daily 9.30-18.30; Oct-Mar, daily 9.30-16.30; last ticket sold 30 mins before closing; closed 25/26 Dec and 1/2 Jan.

Tel: 01334 477196

N147 Strome Castle (NTS)

[Map: 3A, F6] Off A896, 8 miles NE of Kyle of Lochalsh, Strome, Wester Ross, Highland. (NGR: NG 862354 LR: 24)

On a rock by the sea is a very ruinous castle, dating from the 15th century. Part of the courtyard or hall wall stands to some height, but little remains of the keep except a mound. It may have been held by the Camerons of Lochiel, then the MacDonalds of Glengarry. It was besieged, sacked after a long siege and blown-up by Kenneth Mackenzie of Kintail in 1602. There is no ferry at Strome Ferry.

Parking nearby.

Access at all reasonable times.

N148 Tantallon Castle (HS)

[Map: 6B, D11] Off A198, 3 miles E of North Berwick, Tantallon, East Lothian. (NGR: NT 596851 LR: 67)

One of the most impressive castles in southern Scotland, Tantallon is a large and strong 14th-century courtyard castle, which is now ruinous. It has a thick 80-foot-high curtain wall, blocking off a high promontory, with towers at each end and a central gatehouse. The castle was built by the Douglases, later the Earls of Angus, and has a long and violent history. In 1651 it fell to Cromwell after being bombarded for 12 days.

Short walk to castle. Explanatory boards and exhibitions. Gift shop. WC. Limited disabled access. Car and coach parking. £.
Open Apr-Sep, daily 9.30-18.30; Oct-Mar, Mon-Wed and Fri 9.30-16.30, Thu 9.30-12.00, Sun 14.00-16.30, closed Fri; last ticket 30 mins before closing; closed 25/26 Dec and 1/2 Jan.
Tel: 01620 892727

N149 Tarbert Castle

[Map: 5A, E4] Off A8015, E of Tarbert, Argyll. (NGR: NR 867687 LR: 62)

A ruined royal castle of enclosure with a tower house. Around 1098 Magnus Barelegs, King of Norway, had his longship taken across the isthmus here to symbolise his possession. Robert the Bruce strengthened the castle, as did James IV during his campaign against the MacDonald Lord of the Isles.

Parking in Tarbert.
Access by footpath beside old police station, opposite Fish Quay.

N150 Threave Castle (HS)

[Map: 6B, H8] Off A75, 6 miles W of Dalbeattie, Threave, Dumfries and Galloway. (NGR: NX 739623 LR: 84)

Standing on an island is a massive 14th-century keep, rectangular in plan, which stood within a courtyard, enclosed by a wall and ditch with drum towers at each corner, only one of which survives. The present castle was started by Archibald the Grim – so named because his face was terrible to look upon in battle – 3rd Earl of Douglas, and Lord of Galloway from 1369. He died at Threave in 1400. The castle was besieged and captured by James II in 1455.

Sales area. Picnic area. WC. Car and coach parking. £.
Open Apr-Sep, daily 9.30-18.30; last ticket 18.00. Owned by NTS; administered by Historic Scotland – includes walk and short ferry trip.
Tel: 01831 168512

N151 Tolquhon Castle (HS)

[Map: 4, F5] Off A999, 8 miles NE of Inverurie, Tolquhon, Aberdeenshire. (NGR: NJ 873286 LR: 38)

Once a strong but comfortable fortress, the castle consists of a ruined 15th-century keep in one corner of a courtyard enclosed by ranges of buildings, including a drum-towered gatehouse. It was held by the Prestons of Craigmillar, but passed to the Forbes family in 1420, who built most of the present castle. It was later held by the Farquhars. Also see **Tarves Medieval Tomb [K133]**.

Sales area. Picnic area. WC. Disabled limited access and WC. Car and coach parking. £.
Open Apr-Sep, daily 9.30-18.30; open Oct-Mar wknds only, Sat 9.30-16.30, Sun 14.00-16.30; last ticket sold 30 mins before closing; closed 25/26 Dec and 1/2 Jan.
Tel: 01651 851286

H12 Turnberry Castle

See main entry H12

D63 Tynron Doon

See main entry D63

N152 Urquhart Castle (HS)

[Map: 3B, F9] Off A82, 1.5 miles E of Drumnadrochit, Urquhart, Highland. (NGR: NH 531286 LR: 26)

Standing in a picturesque location on the shore of Loch Ness is the large ruinous courtyard castle. The Picts had a fort here in the 6th century, near where St Columba is said to have confronted a kelpie or beastie in Loch Ness. The castle saw action in the Wars of Independence, and in 1308 was besieged by Robert the Bruce. It was fought over many times, but dismantled in 1691. There have been many sightings of the Loch Ness Monster nearby – there are two exhibition centres in nearby Drumnadrochit **[Y120/Y154]**.

New visitor centre and car park. Audio-visual show. Walk to castle. Gift shop. Cafe. WC. Car and coach parking. Group concessions. ££.
Open all year: Apr-Sep, daily 9.30-18.30; Oct-Mar, daily 9.30-16.30; last ticket 45 mins before closing; closed 25/26 Dec and 1/2 Jan.
Tel: 01456 450551 Fax: 0131 668 8800

N153 West Port, St Andrews (HS)

[Map: 6B, C10] Off A91, South Street, St Andrews, Fife. (NGR: NO 506165 LR: 59)

The city gate, built in 1589, was restored in 1843.
Parking nearby.
Access at all reasonable times – view from exterior.

Top left *Skipness Castle*
Above left *Scalloway Castle*
Top right *Blackness Castle*
Right *Huntly Castle*
Bottom Right
Castle Campbell

O: The Jacobites

Some sites which are associated with the times of the Jacobites, including Rob Roy and Bonnie Prince Charlie.

N2 Alloa Tower (NTS)

The tower was held by John Erskine, the 6th Earl of Mar, 'Bobbing John', who led the Jacobites in the 1715 Rising.

See main entry N2

K50 Balquhidder Kirkyard

Rob Roy MacGregor (who died on 28 December 1734), his wife, and two of his sons are buried here, there graves marked by three slabs, enclosed by railings, at the west end of the burial ground. His stone has a sword roughly carved on it.

See main entry K50

O1 Bernera Barracks

[Map: 3A, G6] Off A87 at Shiel Bridge, 6 miles SE of Kyle of Lochalsh, 0.3 miles N of Glenelg, Highlands. (NGR: NG 815197 LR: 33)

Built to control the crossing to Skye, Bernera Barracks, dating from the 1720s, consists of ruined ranges of buildings around a courtyard, and had accommodation for over 200 men. The garrison was reduced after the failure of the Jacobite rising in 1746, and abandoned about 1800. The road to Glenelg mostly follows the course of an old military way.

N6 Blair Castle

Blair Castle is the last stronghold in Britain to be besieged, albeit unsuccessfully, having been attacked by the Jacobites in 1746.

See main entry N6

N12 Castle Menzies

Bonnie Prince Charlie stayed here for two nights in 1746, but four days later the castle was seized by Hanoverian forces, led by the Duke of Cumberland, the 'Butcher' of Culloden. It was bought back by the Menzies Clan Society in 1957. A small museum about the Menzies clan has exhibits including Bonnie Prince Charlie's death mask.

See main entry N12

Q6 Clan Cameron Museum

Site of house of the Camerons of Lochiel, the ruins of which remain, destroyed by Hanoverian troops after the Jacobite Rising of 1745. The museum, in a converted cottage, charts the history of the Camerons.

See main entry Q6

Q8 Clan Macpherson House and Museum

The house and museum feature mementoes and information on the Macphersons and Bonnie Prince Charlie. There are letters from the Prince to the clan chief in 1745 and one to the Prince from his father, James VIII and III.

See main entry Q8

N74 Corgarff Castle (HS)

A 16th-century tower house, white-washed and restored, with later pavilions and star-shaped outworks. Corgarff saw action in the Jacobite Risings, and there is a reconstructed barrack room.

See main entry N74

O2 Culloden Moor (NTS)

[Map: 3B, F9] On B9006, 5 miles E of Inverness, Culloden, Highland. (NGR: NH 745450 LR: 27)

It was here at the bleak moor of Drumossie that on 16 April 1746 the Jacobite army of Bonnie Prince Charlie was crushed and slaughtered by Hanoverian forces led by the Duke of Cumberland – the last major battle to be fought on British soil. Sites of interest include Old Leanach Cottage, Graves of the Clans, Wells of the Dead, Memorial Cairn, Cumberland Stone, and Field of the English.

Guided tours available in summer. Visitor centre with audiovisual programme. Bookshop. Restaurant. WC. Disabled access to visitor centre, WC and facilities. Car and coach parking. Group concessions. £.

Site open all year, daily; visitor centre, restaurant and shop, 20 Jan-24 Mar and 28 Oct-24 Dec, daily 10.00-16.00; 25 Mar-27 Oct, daily 9.00-18.00.
Tel: 01463 790607 Fax: 01463 794294

N26 Eilean Donan Castle

The castle was used by the Jacobites, including Spaniards, in the 1719 Rising, when it was blown up with gunpowder. There are mementoes of Bonnie Prince Charlie and James VIII and III.

See main entry N26

Y80 Fort Augustus

Fort Augustus was built in 1716, and subsequently strengthened by General Wade. The fort was captured by the Jacobites in 1746. Part of the complex houses a heritage centre with displays on Loch Ness and the Great Glen, the Jacobite Risings, the capturing of the fort, and the history of the Scottish Highlander. The Clansmen Centre features a turf house, weapon demonstrations, and life in the 17th century.

See main entry Y80

P6 Fort George (HS)

Fort George is a magnificent example of a massive Georgian artillery fort. It was built after the Jacobite rising of 1745-6 to designs by William Skinner, but was not completed until 1769, by which time it was redundant. Many of the buildings were designed by William and John Adam. It extends over 16 acres and could accommodate nearly 2000 men; and is still used as a barracks. There is a reconstruction of barrack rooms in different periods, and a display of muskets and pikes. The Regimental Museum of the Queen's Own Highlanders features uniforms, medals and pictures.

See main entry P6

O3 Garva Bridge

[Map: 3B, G9] Off A86, 11.5 miles SE of Newtonmore, 6 miles W of Laggan Bridge, Garvamore, Highland. (NGR: NN 522948 LR: 35)
The two-arched bridge was built by General Wade in 1735, between the 1715 and 1745-6 Jacobite Risings. It is located at the south side of the important Corrieyairack Pass, and was built to facilitate the moving of Hanoverian forces.

Access at all times.

C30 Gathering Stone, Sheriffmuir

The stone, which is about seven feet long and split into three parts, is believed to be where the Jacobite forces gathered before the Battle of **Sheriffmuir [O12]** in 1715. The stone, also known as the Battle Stone, had previously been called the Beltane Stone.

See main entry C30

O4 Glencoe (NTS)

[Map: 3B, I7] On A82, 17 miles S of Fort William, Glencoe, Highlands. (NGR: NN 127564 LR: 41)
Glencoe, one of the most picturesque and accessible parts of Scotland, was the site of the infamous massacre in 1692, executed by government forces under Campbell of Glenlyon. Thirty eight members of the MacDonalds of Glencoe, including their chief MacIain, were slaughtered by men from the garrison of Fort William, who had been billeted on the MacDonalds. One of the sites of the massacre at Inverglen can be visited; as can the Signal Rock, reputedly from where the signal was given to begin the massacre. A new eco-friendly visitor centre has fascinating exhibitions about the area.

Video programme on the massacre. Exhibition on the history of mountaineering. Guided walks in glen. Gift shop. Snack bar. WC. Picnic area. Disabled access to visitor centre. Walks. Climbing. Car and coach parking. Group concessions. £ (visitor centre).
Site open all year; visitor centre, shop and cafe open 1 May-27 Oct, daily 10.00-18.00.
Tel: 01855 811307 Fax: 01855 811772

V36 Glencoe and North Lorn Folk Museum

The museum, which is housed in two thatched cottages, features displays on the MacDonalds and the Jacobite Risings.

See main entry V36

O5 Glenfinnan Monument (NTS)

[Map: 3A, H6] On A830, 15 miles NW of Fort William, Glenfinnan, Highland. (NGR: NM 906805 LR: 41)
In the grand and scenic area at the head of Loch Shiel, it was here on 19 August 1745 that the standard was raised by the Jacobites led by Bonnie Prince Charlie for James VIII and III, so beginning the 1745 Rising. The Glenfinnan Monument was built in 1815 to commemorate the many who fought and died for Bonnie Prince Charlie.

Visitor centre. Gift shop. Snack bar. WC. Disabled facilities. Parking. £.
Site open all year; visitor centre, shop and snack bar open 25 Mar-27 Oct, daily 10.00-18.00.
Tel: 01397 722250

O6 Glenshiel (NTS)

[Map: 3A, F6] Off A87, 16 miles E of Kyle of Lochalsh, Morvich, Kintail, Highland. (NGR: NH 962211 LR: 33)
The site of the Battle of Glenshiel, where a Jacobite force mainly made up of Spaniards was defeated by government forces in 1719, some five miles east of the village near the main road – there is an information board. The picturesque estate of Kintail and Morvich covers 17,422 acres and the Five Sisters of Kintail, four of which are Munros (over 3000 feet), as well as the Falls of Glomach. Access to the mountains is best gained from the countryside centre at Morvich.

Explanatory board. Sales area. WC. Parking. Outdoor centre: accommodation. Caravan site. £.
Access at all reasonable times. Countryside centre at Morvich open (2002) May-Sep, daily 9.00-22.00.
Tel: 01599 511231 Fax: 01599 511417

O7 Inversnaid

[Map: 5A, D6] Off B829, 16 miles NW of Aberfoyle, west end of Glen Arklet, at Garrison, Stirlingshire. (NGR: NN 348097 LR: 56)
Not much remains of a barracks, dating from 1719. The barracks was built after the Jacobite Rising of 1715 to protect against the MacGregors, and Rob Roy's men attacked the workmen during construction.

N116 Kildrummy Castle (HS)

The castle was used by the Earl of Mar when he led the Jacobite Rising of 1715.

See main entry N116

O8 Killiecrankie (NTS)

[Map: 5B, A9] On B8079, 3 miles N of Pitlochry, Perthshire. (NGR: NN 917627 LR: 43)

Set in a fine and picturesque wooded gorge, it was here that the Jacobites, led by John Graham of Claverhouse, Viscount Dundee, defeated a government army in 1689. Claverhouse was mortally wounded at the battle. The 'Soldier's Leap' is where one government soldier escaped from Jacobites by jumping across the River Garry. The exhibition in the visitor centre features the battle, with models and maps, and there are also displays on natural history.

Exhibition. Gift shop. Snack bar. WC. Disabled WC. Car park. £.

Site open all year; visitor centre, shop and snack bar open (2002) 25 Mar-23 Dec, daily 10.00-18.00.

Tel: 01796 473233   Fax: 01796 473233

O9 Loch nam Uamh Cairn

[Map: 3A, H5] Off A830, 8 miles S of Mallaig, Cuildarrach, Loch nan Uamh, Highland. (NGR: NM 720844 LR: 40)

The cairn commemorates the association of the Loch with Bonnie Prince Charlie, and it is from near here that the Prince sailed for France, never to return, on 20 September 1746, after having been hunted by the forces of 'Butcher Cumberland'.

Car parking.

Access at all reasonable times.

O10 Milton

[Map: 3A, F2] Off A865, 6 miles NW of Lochboisdale, Milton, South Uist. (NGR: NF 741269 LR: 22)

This ruined cottage is where Flora MacDonald may have been born in 1722. Flora helped Bonnie Prince Charlie escape from Benbecula to Trotternish on Skye. There is a memorial cairn.

Access at all reasonable times.

O11 Prestonpans Battle Cairn

[Map: 6B, D10] Off A198, 6.5 miles W of Haddington, E of Prestonpans, East Lothian. (NGR: NT 403744 LR: 66)

The site of the Jacobite victory in 1745, led by Bonnie Prince Charlie, over a government army under Sir John Cope. A memorial cairn marks the site.

Access to site at all reasonable times.

Y165 Rob Roy and Trossachs Visitor Centre, Callander

The centre tells the story of Scotland's most famous outlaw, Rob Roy MacGregor, in a multimedia theatre and the 'Life and Times' interactive exhibition. There is a Highland cottage, detailed visitor information on the Trossachs, and a Scottish bookshop.

See main entry Y165

P13 Ruthven Barracks (HS)

In 1718 a castle here was demolished and replaced by a barracks for Hanoverian troops. It was held by government forces in 1746, but was eventually taken and burnt by Jacobite forces. It was not restored, and the buildings are ruinous.

See main entry P13

O12 Sheriffmuir

[Map: 5B, D8] Off A9, 6 miles N of Stirling, 3 miles E of Dunblane, Sheriffmuir, Stirlingshire. (NGR: NN 830028 LR: 57)

The site of the battle fought on 13 November 1715 between Jacobites, under the Earl of Mar, and a Hanoverian army led by the Duke of Argyll. The Jacobites were left holding the field, but by early 1716 the rising was over. A memorial cairn marks the spot. The **Gathering Stone [C30]** is traditionally where the Jacobite army was marshalled, and the White Stone [NN 806042], also known as MacGregor's Stone, is also associated with the battle.

V73 Skye Museum of Island Life, Kilmuir

Flora MacDonald is buried in the nearby churchyard at Kilmuir, her grave marked by a Celtic cross.

See main entry V73

N48 Traquair House

The house has a collection of mementoes associated with the Jacobites, and Bonnie Prince Charlie stayed here in 1745 on his way to England.

See main entry N48

O13 Wade's Bridge, Aberfeldy

[Map: 5B, B8] On B846, N of Aberfeldy, Perthshire. (NGR: NN 851493 LR: 52)

The fine bridge, which crosses the River Tay, was built by General Wade from 1733 and designed by William Adam – it was built to hasten the passage of Hanoverian troops against the Jacobite threat. There is a memorial to the **Black Watch [P3]** nearby.

Car parking.

Access at all reasonable times.

V89 West Highland Museum, Fort William

The museum features displays on traditional Highland life and culture. There are many Jacobite mementoes.

See main entry V89

P: Military

P1 Argyll and Sutherland Highlanders Regimental Museum

[Map: 5B, D8] Off A9, Stirling Castle, Stirling. (NGR: NS 790940 LR: 57)

The museum charts the history of the Regiment from 1794 until the present day. It has a fine collection of weapons, silver, colours, uniforms, medals, pictures, and music. There is a First World War trench. Also see **Stirling Castle [N46]**.

Explanatory displays. Gift shop. Refreshments. WC. Car and coach parking. Free but ££ for Stirling Castle.

Open Easter-Sep, Mon-Sat 10.00-17.45, Sun 11.00-16.45; Oct-Easter daily 10.00-16.15.

Tel: 01786 475165

P2 Balhousie Castle

[Map: 5B, C9] Hay Street, Perth. (NGR: NO 115244 LR: 58)

Balhousie Castle was taken over by the army after World War II, and in 1962 became the regimental headquarters and museum of the Black Watch. The museum features pictures, medals, uniforms and other military mementoes, telling the story of the Black Watch from its founding in 1739 to the present day.

Explanatory displays. Audiotours. Gift shop. WC. Car parking.

Open May-Sep Mon-Sat 10.00-16.30; Oct-Apr, Mon-Fri 10.00-15.30; closed 23 Dec-4 Jan; closed last Sat of Jun; other times by appt.

Tel: 0131 310 8530   Email: bw.rhq@btclick.com

O1 Bernera Barracks

See main entry O1

P3 Black Watch Memorial

[Map: 5B, B8] On B846, Wade's Bridge, E of Aberfeldy, Perthshire. (NGR: NN 852492 LR: 52)

The monument commemorates the raising of this world-renowned regiment.

Access at all reasonable times.

Q6 Clan Cameron Museum

There are displays on the Queen's Own Cameron Highlanders, and Commandos who trained here in World War II.

See main entry Q6

Y60 Coldstream Museum

The museum has local history displays and information on the Coldstream Guards.

See main entry Y60

P4 Commando Memorial

[Map: 3B, H8] Off A82, 11 miles NE of Fort William, 1 mile W of Spean Bridge, Highlands. (NGR: NN 208824 LR: 41)

The monument, which was built in 1952 and executed by Scott Sutherland, commemorates the commandos of World War II who trained at Achnacarry and in the area. Fine views over Lochaber and of Ben Nevis.

Car parking.

Access at all reasonable times.

N25 Edinburgh Castle (HS)

At the castle is the Scottish War Memorial, the National War Museum of Scotland, and the Regimental Museum of the Royal Scots.

See main entry N25

P5 Fort Charlotte (HS)

[Map: 1, D3] Off A970, overlooking harbour, Lerwick, Shetland. (NGR: HU 475415 LR: 4)

Fort Charlotte is a 17th-century pentagonal artillery fort, which had accommodation for 100 men. It was first built in 1665 to defend the harbour from the Dutch, who – nevertheless – burnt the barrack block and much of the town of Lerwick in 1673. The fort was rebuilt in 1781, and called Fort Charlotte after the wife of George III. The fort never saw action, but it is well preserved, although modern buildings encroach on all sides.

Parking nearby.

Keys available locally.

Tel: 01466 793191

P6 Fort George (HS)

[Map: 3B, E9] Off B9006, 10 miles NE of Inverness, Fort George, Ardersier, Highland. (NGR: NH 763566 LR: 27)

Fort George is a magnificent example of a massive Georgian artillery fort. It was built after the Jacobite rising of 1745-6 to designs by William Skinner, but was not completed until 1769, by which time it was redundant. Many of the buildings were designed by William and John Adam. It extends over 16 acres and could accommodate nearly 2000 men; and is still used as a barracks. There is a reconstruction of barrack rooms in different periods, and a display of muskets and pikes. The Regimental Museum of the Queen's Own Highlanders features uniforms, medals and pictures.

Reconstruction of barrack rooms in different periods, and display of muskets and pikes. Visitor centre with explanatory panels. Gift shop. Tea room. WC. Picnic area. Disabled access and WC. Car and coach parking. Group concessions. ££.

Open all year: Apr-Sep, daily 9.30-18.30; Oct-Mar, Mon-Sat 9.30-16.30, Sun 14.00-16.30; last ticket 45 mins before closing; closed 25/26 Dec and 1/2 Jan.

Tel: 01667 462777   Fax: 01667 462698

P7 Gordon Highlanders Museum, Aberdeen

[Map: 4, G5] Off A944, St Luke's, Viewfield Road, Aberdeen. (NGR: NJ 940060 LR: 38)

The museum has fine displays from the regiment's collection, covering some 200 years. The museum is housed in the home and studio of Sir George Reid PRSA, the well-known Victorian artist.

Audio-visual and interactive displays. Temporary exhibitions. Gift shop. Tearoom. Gardens. WC. Disabled access. Car parking. £.

Open Apr-Oct, Tue-Sat 10.30-16.30, Sun 13.30-16.30; closed Mon; other times by appt.

Tel: 01224 311200   Web: www.gordonhighlanders.com
Fax: 01224 319323   Email: museum@gordonhiglanders.com

P8 H. M. Frigate *Unicorn*

[Map: 4, J3] Off A92, Victoria Dock, Dundee, Angus. (NGR: NO 415305 LR: 54)

The *Unicorn* is the oldest British warship still afloat, having been launched in 1824, and is Scotland's only example of a wooden warship. She was used as a navy drill ship until 1968, and now has a museum of life in the Royal Navy during the days of sail, with guns, models and displays.

Explanatory displays. Gift shop. Tearoom. Picnic area. WC. Car and coach parking. Group concessions. £.

Open Apr-Oct, daily 10.00-17.00; Nov-Mar, Wed-Sun 10.00-16.00.

Tel: 01382 200900   Web: www.frigateunicorn.org
Fax: 01362 200923   Email: frigateunicorn@hotmail.com

P9 Hackness Martello Tower and Battery (HS)

[Map: 2, D2] Off B9047, SE of Hoy, Hackness, Orkney. (NGR: ND 338912 LR: 7)

The tower here is one of a pair which was built between 1813-15 to protect Longhope and Scapa Flow, and the British ships which were moored there, against French and American pirates. The squat round tower housed a 25 pounder gun and its crew, and was refortified in 1866. The nearby Battery is being conserved. There is also a Martello Tower at Crockness, on the north side of Longhope [ND 324934].

For access contact key holder – a visit involves a walk.

Tel: 01856 841815

O7 Inversnaid

See main entry O7

P10 Italian Chapel, Orkney

[Map: 2, D3] Off A961, 7 miles S of Kirkwall, Lamb Holm, St Mary's, Holm, Orkney. (NGR: HY 489007 LR: 6)

The Italian Chapel is located in two Nissen huts which were once within an Italian prisoner of war camp – the prisoners were building the Churchill Barriers.

The huts have been lavishly decorated, and have a surprising and remarkable interior.

Booklets. Disabled access. Car and coach parking.

Open all year, daily during daylight hours.

Tel: 01856 781268   Fax: 01856 781268   Email: jamuir@lineone.net

Y122 Low Parks Museum

The museum, housed in a restored 17th-century house, features displays including the Cameronians Regimental Museum.

See main entry Y122

P11 Orkney Wireless Museum

[Map: 2, C2] Off A964, Kiln Corner, near harbour, Junction Road, Kirkwall, Orkney. (NGR: HY 455110 LR: 6)

The museum charts Orkney's military history during the wars, which involved a complex network of communications to protect the ships anchored in Scapa Flow. Features include details of a secret radar station, and displays of receivers, valves, gramophones, transistors and special equipment. There is also a exhibition of Italian POW crafts.

Explanatory displays. Gift shop. WC. Disabled access. Parking nearby. £.

Open Apr-Sep, Mon-Sat 10.00-16.30, Sun 14.00-16.30.

Tel: 01856 871400/874272

P12 Royal Highland Fusiliers Regimental Museum, Glasgow

[Map: 6B, E7] Off M8, 518 Sauchiehall Street, Charing Cross, Glasgow. (NGR: NS 575657 LR: 64)

The museum charts the history of the Royal Scots Fusiliers, the Highland Light Infantry and the Royal Highland Fusiliers, Princess Margaret's Own Glasgow and Ayrshire Regiment with displays of medals, badges, uniforms and records.

Guided tours. Explanatory displays. Gift shop. WC. Disabled access. Car parking.

Open all year, Mon-Thu 9.00-16.30, Fri 9.00-16.00.

Tel: 0141 332 0961

P13 Ruthven Barracks (HS)

[Map: 3B, G9] Off A9, 1 mile S of Kingussie, Ruthven Barracks, Highland. (NGR: NN 764997 LR: 35)

Nothing remains, except the substantial earthworks, of a 13th-century castle of the Comyns, later held by the 'Wolf of Badenoch'. In 1718 the castle was demolished and replaced by a barracks for Hanoverian troops. It was held by government forces in 1746, but was eventually taken and burnt by Jacobite forces. It was not restored, and the buildings are ruinous.

Car parking.

Access at all reasonable times.

Tel: 01667 460232

Y171 Scalloway Museum

The museum features local and war-time history, with exhibitions of local artefacts and a display on the secret exploits of the Norwegian resistance movement.
See main entry Y171

P14 Scapa Flow Visitor Centre

[Map: 2, D2] On B9047, Lyness, E side of Hoy, Orkney. (NGR: ND 305945 LR: 7)
Scapa Flow was a major naval anchorage in both wars and the scene of the surrender and scuttling of the German High Seas Fleet in 1919. It is also where the *Royal Oak* was sunk by a German U-boat in 1939 with the loss of many lives. There was a British Royal Navy base at Lyness, although it was closed in 1957. The pump house of the base now tells the war-time story of Scapa Flow.
Explanatory displays. Audio-visual show. Gift shop. Cafe. WC. Parking.
Open all year, Mon-Fri 9.30-16.30; mid May-Oct, also Sat-Sun 10.30-13.30.
Tel: 01856 791300   Web: www.orkneyheritage.com
Fax: 01856 871560   Email: steve.callaghan@orkney.gov.uk

P15 Scotland's Secret Bunker

[Map: 6B, C10] Off B940, 6 miles SE of St Andrews, 4 miles N of Anstruther, Troywood, Fife. (NGR: NO 562090 LR: 59)
The bunker, which is some 100 feet underground, housed the centre of government operations in the event of a nuclear war, including an operations room, cinemas and restaurants.
Guided tours. Explanatory displays. Gift shop. Cafe. WC. Car and coach parking. £££.
Open Apr-Oct, daily 10.00-17.00.
Tel: 01333 310301   Fax: 01333 312040
Web: www.secretbunker.co.uk   Email: mod@secretbunker.co.uk

N46 Stirling Castle (HS)

The Museum of the **Argyll and Sutherland Highlanders [P1]** is housed in the castle, telling the story of the regiment from 1794 to the present day, and featuring uniforms, silver, paintings, colours, pipe banners and commentaries.
See main entry N46

Y187 Stromness Museum

The museum houses many interesting displays, including on the German fleet in Scapa Flow.
See main entry Y187

Q: Clan Castles and Museums

The following castles and museums are strongly associated with and have information about many clans and families. Also see the following sections on *N1: Castles, Towers and Palaces – 1*; *N2: Castles, Towers and Palaces – 2*; and *S1: Houses and Mansions.*

Q1 Armadale Castle and Museum of the Isles

[Map: 3A, G5] Off A881, Armadale, SE of Sleat, Skye. (NGR: NG 640047 LR: 32)

The main part of Armadale Castle is burnt out and ruined. Housed in outbuildings is the Clan Donald centre and 'The Museum of the Isles', an exhibition and slide show covering 1300 years of the MacDonald clan and Lord of the Isles. A library and study centre offer genealogical research, and there is a countryside information service. Around the castle are 40 acres of woodland gardens and nature trails, as well as a walled kitchen garden.

Guided tours. Explanatory displays. Gift shops. Licensed restaurant. Tea room. Picnic area. WC. Disabled access. Car and coach parking. Self-catering accommodation available all year. Group concessions. ££.

Open Apr-Oct, daily 9.30-17.30, last entry 17.00; gardens open all year.

Tel: 01471 844305/227   Fax: 01471 844275

Web: www.cland.demon.co.uk   Email: office@cland.demon.co.uk

Q2 Armstrong Clan Museum

[Map: 6B, H10] Lodge Walk, Castleholm, Langholm, Dumfries and Galloway. (NGR: NY 363845 LR: 79)

The museum charts the history of the Armstrong family, who were once very powerful in the Borders. Arms, armour and heraldry, as well as a library and archives.

Disabled access with assistance. Parking. £.

Open mid-Apr-Oct, Tue-Sun 14.00-17.00; also Mon Bank Hols; winter by appt only.

Tel: 01387 380610

Q3 Beheading Stone, Stirling

[Map: 5B, D8] Off A9 or M9, Gowan Hill, access from Upper Castlehill, Stirling. (NGR: NS 793942 LR: 57)

The stone is believed to have been used for executions, and Murdoch Stewart, Duke of Albany and former Regent of Scotland, was beheaded here in 1425.

Y41 Braemar Highland Heritage Centre

The heritage centre features include a clan heritage service, with a range of Scottish and clan gifts available. The centre also stocks a wide range of tartan, tweed, knitwear and Highland dress.

See main entry Y41

Y44 Breadalbane Folklore Centre

The folklore centre features the history of local clans, such as the MacLarens, MacNabs, Campbells and MacGregors.

See main entry Y44

Q4 Carmichael Heritage Centre

[Map: 6B, F8] On A73, 6 miles W of Biggar, Carmichael Estate, Warrenhill Farm, Thankerton, Lanarkshire. (NGR: NS 948388 LR: 72)

The heritage centre has Scotland's only wax model collection, and charts the history of Scotland and Carmichael using Madame-Tussaud-quality models. The Clan Centre for southern Scotland concentrates on the Carmichaels, who lived here for hundreds of years, as well as many other southern Scottish families.

Guided tours by arrangement. Explanatory displays. Gift shop. Nightingales Ladies Fashion Outlet Shop. Restaurant. Picnic area. WC. Deer park. Venison farm shop. Adventure playground. Animal farm. Horse and pony trekking. Clydesdale horse and cart rides. Heritage walks. Disabled access. Car and coach parking. Group concessions. ££.

Open all year: daily 10.00-17.00; closed Jan & Feb; farm and gift shop open daily all year 10.00-17.00, except closed Christmas and New Year; Oct-Mar, winter opening call 01899 308336 to check.

Tel: 01899 308169/308336   Web: www.carmichael.co.uk/visitorcentre

Fax: 01899 308481   Email: visitors@carmichael.co.uk

N12 Castle Menzies

The castle houses a small museum about the Menzies clan.

See main entry N12

Q5 Chisholms Highland Dress

[Map: 3B, F9] Off A82, 47-51 Castle Street, Inverness, Highland. (NGR: NH 667450 LR: 26)

Chisholms Highland Dress features a display of kiltmaking and of Scottish Highland dress, with models and uniforms from the period of 1745 to the present. Tartans, swords and other weapons are on show.

Guided tours on request. Explanatory displays. Gift shop. Disabled access. Parking nearby.

Open all year: Mon-Sat 9.00-17.30; summer, 19.00-21.00.

Tel: 01463 234599   Fax: 01463 223009

Web: www.kilts.co.uk   Email: info@kilts.co.uk

Q6 Clan Cameron Museum

[Map: 3B, H8] Off B8005, 9 miles NE of Fort William, Achnacarry, Spean Bridge, Highland. (NGR: NN 175878 LR: 41)

Site of house of the Camerons of Lochiel, the ruins of which remain, destroyed by Hanoverian troops after the Jacobite Rising of 1745. Achnacarry House is still occupied by the Camerons, but is not open to the public. The museum, housed in a converted cottage, charts the history of the Camerons, and there are displays on the Queen's Own Cameron Highlanders, and Commandos who trained here in World War II.

Guided tours on request. Explanatory displays. Gift shop. Garden. WC. Disabled access. Car and coach parking. Group concessions. £.

House not open. Museum open Apr-mid Oct, daily 13.30-17.00; Jul & Aug, daily 11.00-17.00.

Tel: 01397 712090 Web: www.clan-cameron.org
Email: museum@achnacarry.fsnet.co.uk

Q7 Clan Gunn Heritage Centre and Museum, Latheron

[Map: 3B, B11] On A99, 4 miles NE of Dunbeath, Latheron, Caithness. (NGR: ND 203335 LR: 11)

The centre features the story of the Gunns, one of Scotland's oldest families, from Norse times until the present day. There is an audio-visual presentation and clan archive.

Explanatory displays. Shop. Parking nearby. £.

Open Jun-Sep, Mon-Sat 11.00-13.00 and 14.00-16.00; Jul-Aug also Sun 14.00-16.00.

Tel: 01593 741700 (during season)/721325

Q8 Clan Macpherson House and Museum

[Map: 3B, G9] On A86, Clan House, Main Street, Newtonmore, Highlands. (NGR: NN 712991 LR: 35)

The house and museum feature mementoes and information on the Macphersons and Bonnie Prince Charlie. There are letters from the Prince to the clan chief in 1745 and one to the Prince from his father, James VIII and III. Other features include royal warrants, the green banner of the clan, and James Macpherson's fiddle, sword, pictures, decorations and medals.

Guided tours. Explanatory displays. Gift shop. WC. Disabled access. Car and coach parking. Group concessions. £.

Open Apr-Oct, Mon-Sat 10.00-17.00.

Tel: 01540 673332 Fax: 01540 673332
Web: www.clan-macpherson.org

Q9 Clan Tartan Centre, Edinburgh

[Map: 6B, E9] Off A902, 2 miles N of Edinburgh Castle, 70-74 Bangor Road, Leith, Edinburgh. (NGR: NT 265766 LR: 66)

The Clan Tartan Centre, located in James Pringle

Weavers Leith Mills, has a computer archive which can provide information about any clan connection, clan chief, origins, heraldic emblems and other historical information. There is also a large shop which sells woollens, tartans, clothing and gifts.

Gift shop. Restaurant. WC. Disabled access. Car and coach parking.

Open all year: Mon-Sat 9.30-17.30, Sun 10.00-17.00; closed Christmas and New Year.

Tel: 0131 553 5161 Fax: 0131 553 4415
Web: www.clantartan.com Email: simplythebest@ewm.co.uk

V20 Clansman Centre

The centre features clan life in the Highlands with a live presentation inside a reconstructed Highland turf house. There is information on how a family of the 17th century lived, ate and survived, including clothing and weapon demonstrations.

See main entry V20

N18 Delgatie Castle

Delgatie was made the Clan Hay centre in 1948.

See main entry N18

N22 Duart Castle

Duart Castle is home of the MacLeans, and there is information about the clan.

See main entry N22

N24 Dunvegan Castle

Dunvegan Castle has been continuously occupied by the chiefs of MacLeod since 1270, and there is information and displays about the clan.

See main entry N24

Q10 Falls of Dochart, Killin

[Map: 5B, C7] On A827, Killin, Stirlingshire. (NGR: NN 570324 LR: 51)

The picturesque, dramatic waterfalls are located in the scenic village of Killin. On Inchbuie, an island in the river, is the burial ground of the MacNabs – information and key from the Tourist Information Centre.

Parking nearby.

Access at all reasonable times.

N103 Finlaggan

Finlaggan was a very important centre of the MacDonald Lords of the Isles in medieval times.

See main entry N103

Q11 Finlaystone House

[Map: 6A, D6] On A8, 5.5 miles E of Greenock, Finlaystone, Renfrewshire. (NGR: NS 365737 LR: 63)

Overlooking the Clyde and set in fine gardens and woodland, Finlaystone House is a grand symmetrical mansion mostly dating from 1760. It was a property of the Cunningham Earls of Glencairn, but is now held by the MacMillans. There is a visitor centre with MacMillan clan exhibits

Visitor centre with Clan MacMillan exhibits, doll museum, and Celtic art display. Gift shop. Tearoom. WC. Gardens. Disabled access to grounds & WC. Parking. £.

House not open; gardens and grounds open all year, daily 10.30-17.00; visitor centre and refreshments open May-Sep, daily 11.00-16.30.

Tel: 01475 540505 Fax: 01475 540285 Web: www.finlaystone.co.uk

V33 Fraserburgh Heritage Centre

The heritage centre's features include information on the Frasers.

See main entry V33

N104 Gilnockie Tower

The tower is home to the Clan Armstrong Centre.

See main entry N104

Q12 Glen Fruin

[Map: 5A, D6] Off A814, 10.5 miles NE of Dumbarton, Auchengaich, Glen Fruin, Dunbartonshire. (NGR: NS 276894 LR: 56)

The site of a clan battle near Auchengaich, fought between the MacGregors and the Colquhouns of Luss on 7 February 1603. Some 140 or more of the Colquhouns were slain in the following rout. The battle resulted in dire retribution for the MacGregors. The clan, and even their name, were proscribed by James VI in April, and by March the following year 35 of the clan had been executed, including Alasdair, the chief. A cairn commemorates the battle.

S24 Glenbarr Abbey

Glenbarr Abbey is a striking Gothic revival house, built in the 18th century. It has been the home of the lairds of Glenbarr since 1796. There are tours, which are conducted by the 5th laird, Angus MacAlister, who also owns the property.

See main entry S24

O4 Glencoe (NTS)

See main entry O4

V36 Glencoe and North Lorn Folk Museum

The museum, which is housed in two thatched cottages, features displays on the MacDonalds and the Jacobite Risings.

See main entry V36

Q13 Harlaw Monument

[Map: 4, G5] Off B9001 or A96, 2 miles N of Inverurie, Harlaw, Aberdeenshire. (NGR: NJ 751241 LR: 38)

The monument commemorates the bloody battle of Harlaw on 24 July 1411. An army of Highlanders and Islanders, led by Donald MacDonald, Lord of the Isles, was defeated by Alexander Stewart, Earl of Mar and son of the 'Wolf of Badenoch'. Such was the loss of life that the battle is known as the Red Harlaw in ballad.

Access at all reasonable times.

S30 Inveraray Castle

Inveraray Castle is the seat of the Campbell Dukes of Argyll, and there is a clan room.

See main entry S30

Q14 Johnnie Armstrong of Gilnockie Memorial

[Map: 6B, G10] Off A7, 10 miles SW of Hawick, Caerlanrig, memorial next to churchyard, Dumfries and Galloway. (NGR: NT 403048 LR: 79)

A stone memorial marks the mass grave of the Border reiver Johnnie Armstrong of Gilnockie and about 50 of his men – who were hanged from nearby trees without trial by James V in 1530. An old ballad tells the story.

Information plaque. Wheel chair access via nearby field gate. Car parking.

Access at all reasonable times.

L19 Milnholm Cross

The cross, which was erected around 1320, is to commemorate Alexander Armstrong, who was murdered in **Hermitage Castle [N110]**, about 4 miles to the north. The cross is near the remains of Mangerton Castle, the stronghold of the Armstrongs for some 300 years.

Car parking

See main entry L19.

Q15 Museum of Piping

[Map: 6B, E7] Off M8, 30-34 McPhater Street, Cowcaddens, Glasgow. (NGR: NS 580664 LR: 64)

Housed in a fine building, this is a centre for the bagpipes. There is a museum and interpretation centre, a school with rehearsal rooms, a performance hall, and a reference library.

Guided tours. Explanatory displays. Gift shop. Brasserie/bar. WC. Conference facilities. Parking nearby. Group concessions. £.

Open all year: museum, daily 10.00-16.00; brasserie/bar 10.30-23.00.

Tel: 0141 353 0220   Web: www.thepipingcentre.co.uk
Fax: 0141 353 1570   Email: eminty@thepipingcentre.co.uk

Q16 Scottish Kiltmaker Visitor Centre, Inverness

[Map: 3B, F9] Off A82, Hector Russell House, 4-9 Huntly Street, Inverness, Highlands. (NGR: NH 663447 LR: 26)

The visitor centre features the history and development of the kilt, including tradition and culture, and how it should be worn. The manufacture of kilts can be viewed, and there is an audio-visual presentation, as well as costume and tartan displays.

Explanatory displays. Gift shop. Parking nearby. Group concessions. £.

Open May-Sep, Mon-Sat 9.00-19.00, Sun 10.00-17.00; Oct-May, Mon-Sat 9.00-17.00.

Tel: 01463 222781   Fax: 01463 713414

Web: www.hector-russell.com   Email: kilts@hector-russell.com

Q17 Scottish Tartans Museum, Edinburgh

[Map: 6B, E9] On A1, Princes Street, Edinburgh. (NGR: NT 255738 LR: 66)

The museum covers every aspect of tartan, from its development in Highland dress to the plants used for dying the different colours. There are some 600 examples of tartan, and there are displays on the development of the kilt. Family tartans can be traced.

Explanatory displays. Gift shop. WC. Disabled access.

Open all year, except closed Sun.

Tel: 0131 556 1252

Q18 Scottish Tartans Museum, Keith

[Map: 4, E4] Off A95, The Institute Hall, Mid Street, Keith, Moray. (NGR: NJ 428507 LR: 28)

The museum has information on the history and development of tartan and kilts, and there are 700 tartans on display. Family tartans can be traced.

Gift shop.

Tel: 01542 888419

Q19 Storehouse of Foulis

[Map: 3B, E9] On A9, 15 miles N of Inverness, 1 mile N of Cromarty Bridge, Foulis Ferry, Evanton, Highland. (NGR: NH 599635 LR: 21)

Situated on the shore of the Cromarty Firth, the centre is housed in an 18th-century building and features educational exhibitions, interactive displays and an audio-visual show with displays on history, boats, the Munro clan and wildlife. There is a hide for seal watching, and a children's fish maze.

Explanatory displays. Audio-visual presentation. Gift shop. Restaurant/coffee shop, member of 'Taste of Scotland 2002'. Picnic area. WC. Baby changing facility. Disabled access. Car and coach parking. Group concessions. ££.

Open all year: daily 10.00-17.00; closed Xmas and New Year.

Tel: 01349 830000   Web: www.storehouseoffoulis.co.uk

Fax: 01349 830033   Email: info@storehouseoffoulis.co.uk

Y185 Strathnaver Museum

The museum features include a Clan Mackay room.

See main entry Y185

Y189 Tain Through Time

There is information about the Ross clan.

See main entry Y189

Q20 Tartan Weaving Mill and Exhibition, Edinburgh

[Map: 6B, E9] 555 Castlehill (Royal Mile), near Castle, Edinburgh. (NGR: NT 255736 LR: 66)

The working mill and exhibition features a hands-on experience of the production of tartan from the sheep to the shop. Tartan can be made by the visitor on a pedal-operated loom.

Explanatory displays. Guided tour: weaving for the visitor. Highland Dress through the ages. Photo in Scottish costume. Clan and tartan information centre. Gift shop. Cafe and restaurant. WC. Disabled access. Car and coach parking nearby. Group concessions. ££.

Open all year Mon-Sat, 9.00-17.30, Sun 10.00-17.00, slightly later in summer months; closed Christmas and New Year.

Tel: 0131 226 1555   Fax: 0131 225 4846

Web: www.scotweb.co.uk/edinburgh/weaving

Email: castlehill@geoffreykilts.co.uk

Q21 Well of Seven Heads

[Map: 3B, G8] On A82, 6 miles SW of Fort Augustus, W shore of Loch Oich, Highlands. (NGR: NN 304990 LR: 34)

The monument, 'Tobar nan Ceann' in Gaelic, commemorates the execution by beheading of seven brothers for the murder of two sons of a 17th-century MacDonald chief of Keppoch. It stands near a spring, and is inscribed in Gaelic, English, French and Latin – and is decorated by the carved heads of seven men.

Picnic area. Car parking.

Access at all reasonable times.

Top left *Dunvegan*
Top right *Storehouse of Foulis*
Above *Corgarff*
Left *Delgatie*
Below *Duart*

R: Royalty

R1 Balmoral Castle

[Map: 4, G3] Off A93, 7 miles W of Ballater, Kincardine and Deeside. (NGR: NO 255952 LR: 44)

Balmoral Castle is a large castellated mansion, dominated by a tall turreted and battlemented tower. In 1852 Prince Albert bought the estate, and in 1855 had the present mansion built, demolishing the remains of an old castle. Balmoral became their holiday home, and it is still often used by the royal family.

Display of carriages. Exhibition of paintings, works of art and Royal Tartans in the Castle Ballroom. Pony trekking and pony cart rides. Gift shop. Cafe. WC. Disabled access to exhibition, shops, cafe, gardens and WC. Car and coach parking. ££.

Gardens, grounds and exhibitions open mid Apr-Jul 10.00-17.00 (check opening); last recommended admission 16.00.

Tel: 01339 742334 Fax: 01339 742034
Web: www.balmoralcastle.com Email: info@balmoralcastle.com

R2 Crathie Parish Church

[Map: 4, G3] On A93, 6 miles W of Ballater, Crathie, Kincardine and Deeside. (NGR: NO 265949 LR: 44)

Overlooking the ruins of an earlier building, the church was begun in 1893, and Queen Victoria laid the foundation stone. The church is cruciform in plan, and there are memorial stones, plaques and stained glass which commemorate royalty and ministers.

Parking.

Open Apr-Oct, Mon-Sat 9.30-17.00, Sun 12.45-17.00.

N30 Glamis Castle

The Queen Mother, who died recently, came from the Bowes-Lyon family of Glamis.

See main entry N30

N31 Holyroodhouse

The official residence of the monarch in Scotland.

See main entry N31

R3 Old Royal Station, Ballater

[Map: 4, G3] Off A93, Station Square, Ballater, Aberdeenshire. (NGR: NO 370958 LR: 44)

The fine Victorian railway station has been restored, and has displays charting the 100 years history of the railway (which has been dismantled) being used by royalty. There is the waiting room specially built for Queen Victoria, as well as the Deeside Orientation Centre.

Explanatory displays. Gift shop. Restaurant. WC. Disabled access. Tourist Information Centre. Parking.

Open all year: tel 01339 755306 to confirm.

Tel: 01339 755306 Web: www.castlesandwhisky.com
Fax: 01339 754088 Email: info@castlesandwhisky.com

R4 Royal Yacht *Britannia*

[Map: 6B, E9] Off A901, 2 miles N of Edinburgh Castle, Ocean Terminal, Leith, Edinburgh. (NGR: NT 260773 LR: 66)

Permanently moored in the historic port of Leith, Royal Yacht *Britannia* is the famous ship used by the Royal Family around the world. There is a visitor centre, and since Britannia's reberth at Ocean Terminal, Leith, in October 2001 there are newly opened areas: the Laundry, Sick Bay, and Royal Marines' Barracks.

Explanatory displays. Visitor centre. Gift shop. Audio tour. Dedicated bus service from Waverley Bridge. Groups should book: tel 0131 555 8800. Parking. £££.

Open all year (2002): Jan-Mar, daily 10.00-15.30 (closes 17.00); Apr-Sep, daily 9.30-16.30 (closes 18.00); Oct-Dec, daily 10.00-15.30 (closes 17.00).

Tel: 0131 555 5566 Web: www.royalyachtbritannia.co.uk
Fax: 0131 555 8835 Email: enquiries@tryb.co.uk

Above *Royal Yacht* Britannia

S1: Houses and Mansions

Also see the sections on *N1: Castles, Towers and Palaces – 1*; *N2: Castles, Towers and Palaces – 2*; *Q: Clan Castles and Museums*; and *S1: Gardens.*

S1 Abbotsford

[Map: 6B, F10] On B6360, 2 miles W of Melrose, Borders. (NGR: NT 508343 LR: 73)

Sir Walter Scott, the famous Scottish writer and historian, bought Cartley Hole farmhouse, by the Tweed, in 1812, which he renamed Abbotsford. He had the old house demolished in 1822, and it was replaced by the main block of Abbotsford as it is today. Scott collected many historic artefacts, and there is an impressive collection of armour and weapons at the house, including Rob Roy MacGregor's gun and the Marquis of Montrose's sword.

Guided tours. Gift shop. Tearoom. Extensive gardens and grounds. WCs. Disabled access by private entrance. Car and coach parking. Group concessions. ££.
Open daily: 3rd Monday in Mar-Oct, Mon-Sat 9.30-17.00, Sun 14.00-17.00; Jun-Sep, daily including Sun 9.30-17.00; other dates by appt.
Tel: 01896 752043 Fax: 01896 752916 Email: abbotsford@melrose.bordernet.co.uk

S2 Arbuthnott House

[Map: 4, H5] Off B967, 5.5 miles NE of Laurencekirk, Arbuthnott, Kincardine and Deeside. (NGR: NO 795750 LR: 45)

Arbuthnott House incorporates some very old work and has some fine ceilings from about 1685. The house was remodelled to create a symmetrical mansion. It has been a property of the Arbuthnotts from the 12th century. The gardens are open all year, as is the house on specified occasions.

Guided tours only. WC. Disabled access to ground floor. Parking. £.
Gardens open all year, daily 9.00-17.00. House open certain days and by arrangement: tel to check.
Tel: 01561 320417/361226 Fax: 01561 320476
Web: www.arbuthnott.co.uk Email: keith@arbuthnott.co.uk

S3 Argyll's Lodging (HS)

[Map: 5B, D8] Off A9, Castle Wynd, Stirling. (NGR: NS 793938 LR: 57)

A fine, well-preserved 17th-century town house surrounding a courtyard with one side enclosed by a wall. Many of the rooms within the lodging have recently been restored and furnished in 17th-century style. The Lodging was built by Sir William Alexander of Menstrie, 1st Earl of Stirling and Viscount Canada, but passed to the Campbell Earls of Argyll.

Visitor centre with explanatory displays. Gift shop. WC. Disabled access. Car and coach parking. £ (Joint ticket available with Stirling Castle).
Open all year: Apr-Sep, daily 9.00-17.15 (last ticket sold); Oct-Mar, daily 9.30-16.15 (last ticket sold); closed Christmas and New Year.
Tel: 01786 461146/450000 Fax: 01786 448194

S4 Arniston House

[Map: 6B, E10] Off B6372, 2 miles SW of Gorebridge, Arniston, Midlothian. (NGR: NT 326595 LR: 66)

Arniston is a symmetrical classical mansion, built for Robert Dundas of Arniston by the architect William Adam in 1726. The house was altered in 1754 and 1877. A section was gutted because of dry rot, and is undergoing restoration. The house retains grand plasterwork and period furniture, and the garden is in a fine country setting.

Guided tours. WC. Disabled WC. Car and coach parking. ££ (house).
Open Apr-Jun: guided tours on Tue and Wed starting at 14.00 and 15.30; Jul-mid Sep, Mon-Fri and Sun at 14.00 and 15.30; private groups of 10-50 accepted all year by prior arrangement.
Tel: 01875 830230/515 Web: www.arniston-house.co.uk
Fax: 01875 830515 Email: henrietta.d.bekker2@btinternet.com

S5 Ayton Castle

[Map: 6B, E12] Off B9635, 2.5 miles SW of Eyemouth, Borders. (NGR: NT 929614 LR: 67)

A rambling castellated mansion with a profusion of turrets, battlements and towers. The property was held by the Aytons, the Homes, then the Fordyce family in 1765. In 1834 the old castle was burnt to the ground, and a new mansion, designed by James Gillespie Graham, was built and then extended by the architect David Bryce. It passed to the Liddell-Grainger family, whose descendants still occupy it.

Guided tours. Woodlands. Disabled access. Car and coach parking. £.
Open May-Sep, Sat-Sun 14.00-17.00 or by appt at any time.
Tel: 01890 781212/781550 Fax: 01890 781550

S6 Balfour Castle

[Map: 2, C3] Off B9059, Balfour, SW side of Shapinsay, Orkney. (NGR: HY 475165 LR: 6)

Balfour Castle, a castellated mansion, was begun in 1847 for David Balfour, and designed by the architect David Bryce. The Balfours sold the property in 1961, and the castle is now run as a small private hotel. There is a large walled garden.

Guided tours of castle and gardens. £££ including boat fare (£16 2002).
Hotel – private guests only. Castle and garden open May-Sep, Sun afternoons: bookings from Balfour Castle.
Tel: 01856 711282 Web: www.balfourcastle.co.uk
Fax: 01856 711283 Email: balfourcastle@btinternet.com

R1 Balmoral Castle

See main entry R1

S7 Bardrochat

[Map: 6A, H5] Off A77, 6 miles S of Girvan, Colmonell, Bardrochat, Ayrshire. (NGR: NX 153853 LR: 76)

Bardrochat was built in 1893 by the architect George M. Watson for Robert McEwen, then extended in 1906-8 by the architect Sir Robert Lorimer. Robert McEwen was a noted philanthropist, and the same family still live at the house.

Partial disabled access. Accommodation available. Parking. £.
Open Apr-Sep, Mon-Fri 9.00-17.00.
Tel: 01465 881242 Fax: 01465 881330

S8 Blairquhan

[Map: 6A, G6] Off B7045, 7 miles SE of Maybole, Ayrshire – signposted from A77. (NGR: NS 367055 LR: 70)

Blairquhan, a large castellated mansion designed by William Burn in 1821-4, replaced a castle dating from 1346. There is a walled garden. It has been owned by the Hunter Blair family since 1798. There is a good collection of furniture and pictures, including Scottish Colourists.

Self-guided tours – guided tours by arrangement. Gift shop. Tea room. WC. Walled garden. Picnic area. Partial disabled access and WC. Car and coach parking. £££.
Open mid Jul-mid Aug, daily 13.30-17.00, closed Mon; last admission 16.15; check exact dates with castle; grounds open until 18.00; open at all other times by appt.
Tel: 01655 770239 Fax: 01655 770278
Web: www.blairquhan.co.uk Email: enquiries@blairquhan.co.uk

S9 Bowhill

[Map: 6B, F10] Off A708, 3 miles W of Selkirk, Borders (NGR: NT 426278 LR: 73)

Bowhill is an extensive rambling mansion, dating mainly from 1812, although part may date from 1708. The house was remodelled in 1831-2 by the architect William Burn. It is the home of the Duke and Duchess of Buccleuch. The interesting ruins of Newark Castle are in the grounds.

Fine collections of paintings and artefacts, including the Duke of Monmouth's saddle and execution shirt. Audio-visual presentation. Restored Victorian kitchen and fire engine display. Sales area (gift shop Jul). Restaurant. WC. Garden and country park. Disabled facilities; wheelchair visitors free. Ruins of Newark Castle in grounds. Car and coach parking. ££.
Park open Easter-end Aug, daily 12.00-17.00, except closed Fri, also open Fri in Jul, 12.00-17.00; house open Jul, daily 13.00-16.30; other times by appt for educational groups.
Tel: 01750 22204 Fax: 01750 22204
Web: www.heritageontheweb.co.uk Email: bht@buccleuch.com

S10 Broughton House (NTS)

[Map: 6B, I7] Off A711 or A755, 12 High Street, Kirkcudbright, Dumfries and Galloway. (NGR: NX 684509 LR: 83)

Situated in the picturesque town of Kirkcudbright, Broughton House, which dates from the 18th century, was a property of Murrays of Broughton and Cally. It was the home and studio of the artist E. A. Hornel, one of the 'Glasgow Boys', from 1901-33 . It contains many of his works, along with other paintings by contemporary artists, as well as rare copies of the poems of Robert Burns and material on local history. There is a Japanese-style garden.

Explanatory displays. Garden. WC. Car parking. Group concessions. £.
Open (2002) 25 Mar-28 Jun and 2 Sep-27 Oct, Mon-Sat 12.00-17.00, Sun 13.00-17.00; 29 Jun-1 Sep, Mon-Sat 10.00-18.00, Sun 13.00-17.00; garden also open, 1 Feb-22 Mar, Mon-Fri 11.00-16.00; wknd 23/24 Feb, 11.00-16.00.
Tel: 01577 330437

S11 Callendar House

[Map: 5B, D8] Off A803, Callendar Park, in Falkirk. (NGR: NS 898794 LR: 65)

Callendar House, a large ornate mansion of the 1870s with towers and turrets, incorporates a 14th- or 15th-century castle. It was held by the Livingstone family, who were made Earls of Callendar in 1641, then the Boyd Earls of Kilmarnock, and later William Forbes, a copper merchant. It is now in the care of the local council, and is set in a public park. There is a new exhibition on 'William Forbes' Falkirk', as well as Roman finds from the area.

Permanent displays. Temporary exhibitions. Restored 1820s kitchen with costumed interpretation. History research centre. Contemporary art gallery. Gift shop. Tea room. Garden. Park with boating, pitch and putt. Woodland walks. Children's play area. WC. Disabled access. Car and coach parking. Group concessions. £.
Open all year: Mon-Sat 10.00-17.00; also Apr-Sep, Sun 14.00-17.00; open most public hols; park open all year.
Tel: 01324 503770 Fax: 01324 503771
Web: www.falkirkmuseums.demon.co.uk
Email: callendarhouse@falkirkmuseums.demon.co.uk

S12 Carrick House, Eday

[Map: 2, B3] Off B9063, Carrick, N of Eday, Orkney. (NGR: HY 567384 LR: 5)

Carrick House, a 17th-century harled and corbiestepped house, has an arched entrance to the courtyard dated 1633. It was built by John Stewart, Earl of Carrick, younger brother of the notorious Patrick Stewart, Earl of Orkney, but passed on his death to the Buchanans, then to James Fea of Clestrain, who captured the pirate John Gow in 1725. It is still occupied. Guided tours take in the house, garden and other parts of the island. There are spectacular views.

Guided tours. Picnic area. WC. Limited disabled access. Car parking. £.
Open Jun-Sep, Sun 14.00 onwards – tel to check; other times by arrangement.
Tel: 01857 622260 Fax: 01857 622260

S13 Chatelherault

[Map: 6B, E8] Off A72, 2 miles SE of Hamilton, Carlisle Road, Chatelherault, Lanarkshire. (NGR: NS 737540 LR: 64)

Chatelherault is a magnificent hunting lodge and kennels, built in 1732-44 by the architect William Adam for James Hamilton, 5th Duke of Hamilton. The building has been restored, and houses an exhibition about the Clyde valley, geology and natural history of the park. The country park, which covers some 500 acres, has 18th-century gardens, terraces and parterre, as well as extensive country walks. There are also the ruins of **Cadzow Castle [N59]**.

Guided tours. Explanatory displays. Tearoom. Picnic area. Garden. WC. Disabled access. Car and coach parking.

Open all year, Mon-Sat 10.00-17.00, Sun 12.00-17.00; Easter Sun-Sep open until 17.30; house closed Fri all year; closed Christmas and New Year.

Tel: 01698 426213 Web: www.southlanarkshire.gov.uk
Fax: 01698 421532 Email: liz.macgill@southlanarkshire.gov.uk

S14 Cowane's Hospital and Guildhall, Stirling

[Map: 5B D8] St John Street, Old Town, Stirling.

The hospital was built in 1639-49 by the wealthy Stirling merchant John Cowane for merchants of the burgh who had fallen on hard times. The building was later used as a school and epidemic hospital, and now hosts ceilidhs, banquets and concerts, as well as housing the Family History Project and displays on the building's history.

Venue for ceilidhs, medieval banquets and concerts.

Tel: 01786 473544 Fax: 01786 462264

Web: www.cowanes.org.uk Email: gerry@cowanes.org.uk

T11 Craigieburn

See main entry T11

S15 Culross Palace (NTS)

[Map: 6B, D8] Off B9037, 6.5 miles W of Dunfermline, Culross, Fife. (NGR: NS 986862 LR: 65)

Set in the picturesque village of Culross on the banks of the Forth, the Palace, built between 1597 and 1611, consists of yellow-washed ranges of gabled buildings, with decorative paint work and original interiors. There is an unusual steeply terraced garden. It was built for Sir George Bruce of Carnock, who made a fortune in coal mining, but about 1700 it passed to the Erskines. The building has been carefully restored by The National Trust for Scotland. The Trust has a visitor centre and exhibition in the Town House of 1626. The house of 1610 called The Study is also open to visitors to view the Norwegian painted ceiling in the drawing room. Many other 16th- and 17th-century houses survive in the narrow streets of this an-

cient royal burgh, and can be viewed from outside.

Audio-visual show. Explanatory displays. Tea room. Town trail. Induction loop & Braille guide. ££. Combined ticket for Palace, Study and Town House available (£££).

Palace, Study, Town House, shop and tearoom open 25 Mar-28 Jun and 2 Sep-27 Oct, daily 12.00-17.00; 29 Jun-1 Sep, daily 10.00-18.00.

Tel: 01383 880359 Fax: 01383 882675

S16 Culzean Castle (NTS)

[Map: 6A, G5] Off A77, 4.5 miles W of Maybole, Culzean, Ayrshire. (NGR: NS 233103 LR: 70)

Pronounced 'Cul-lane', Culzean Castle, a magnificent sprawling castellated mansion built between 1777-92, incorporates part of the original castle, which itself was built on the site of an older stronghold. Culzean was a property of the Kennedys from the 12th century. The castle was completely rebuilt for the 9th and 10th Earls of Cassillis by the architect Robert Adam. In 1945 it passed to The National Trust for Scotland. A flat within the building was reserved for use by President Dwight Eisenhower for his services to Britain during World War II. The elegant interior includes the spectacular Oval Staircase and the Circular Saloon.

Fine interiors. Collections of paintings and furniture. Gift shops. Two restaurants. WC. Picnic areas. Gardens and adventure playground. Country park and visitor centre – one of the foremost attractions in Scotland. Car and coach parking. Group concessions. £££

Castle, visitor centre, restaurants and shops open 25 Mar-27 Oct, daily 10.00-17.00; 2 Nov-22 Dec, Sat-Sun 10.00-16.00; visitor facilities (not castle) also open 20 Jan-24 Mar, Sat-Sun 10.00-16.00; country park open all year, daily 9.30-sunset.

Tel: 01655 884455 Fax: 01655 884503

S17 Dalmeny House

[Map: 6B, D9] Off A90, 6 miles NW of Edinburgh, South Queensferry, Edinburgh. (NGR: NT 167779 LR: 65)

Dalmeny House is home to the Earl and Countess of Rosebery, whose family have lived here for over 300 years. The house dates from 1815 and was built in Tudor Gothic style. There are vaulted corridors and a splendid hammerbeam hall, but the main rooms are classical in style. The house has French furniture, tapestries and porcelain, as well as 18th-century portraits by Gainsborough, Raeburn, Reynolds and Lawrence, racing mementos, and items associated with Napoleon. There are fine walks in the wooded grounds and along the shore.

Guided tours. Tea room. Disabled access and WC. Car and coach parking. Group concessions. ££

Open Jul-Aug, Sun-Tue 14.00-17.30; last admission 16.30; open other times by appt only.

Tel: 0131 331 1888 Fax: 0131 331 1788

Web: www.dalmeny.co.uk Email: events@dalmeny.co.uk

S18 Duff House, Banff (HS)

[Map: 4, E4] Off A97, in Banff, Aberdeenshire (NGR: NJ 692633 LR: 29)

Duff House is a fine classical mansion with colonnades and corner towers, dating from 1735, and designed by William Adam for William Duff of Braco, later Earl of Fife. Adam and Duff fell out over the cost of building the house, and work stopped in 1741. The house is now used to display works of art from the **National Galleries of Scotland [U13]**, and there is a programme of changing exhibitions, as well as musical and other events.

Exhibitions. Sales area. Refreshments. WC. Picnic area. Disabled facilities including lift and toilets. Parking. £ (free admission to shop, tearoom, grounds and woodland walks).

Open all year: Apr-Oct, daily 11.00-17.00; Oct-Mar, Thu-Sun 11.00-16.00.

Tel: 01261 818181   Fax: 01261 818900

S19 Dunninald

[Map: 4, I5] Off A92, 2.5 miles S of Montrose, Dunninald, Angus (NGR: NO 704543 LR: 54)

Dunninald was built to replace Black Jack Castle [NO 708535] in the 16th century, itself replaced by a mansion dating from 1824 and designed by James Gillespie Graham. The 16th-century Dunninald survives as a ruin in the grounds of the newer building. There is a fine walled garden and a planned landscape of 1740. *££*

Open Jul, Tue-Sun 13.00-17.00: 29 Jun-28 Jul for 2002.

Tel: 01674 674842

S20 Fasque

[Map: 4, H5] Off B974, 5 miles NW of Laurencekirk, Kincardine and Deeside. (NGR: NO 648755 LR: 45)

Fasque, a fine castellated mansion started in 1809, passed to the Gladstones in 1829, one of whom, William Ewart Gladstone, was Prime Minister four times between 1830 and 1851.

William Gladstone library, state rooms, kitchen, extensive domestic quarters and family church. Explanatory displays. Sales area. WC. Picnic area. Collections of farm machinery. Deer park with Soay sheep and walks. Car and coach parking. ££

Open May-Sep, daily 11.00-17.30; last admission 17.00.

Tel: 01561 340569   Fax: 01561 340569

S21 Floors Castle

[Map: 6B, F11] Off A6089, 1 mile NW of Kelso, Floors, Borders. (NGR: NT 711346 LR: 74)

The largest inhabited castle in Scotland, the present house consists of a large towered and turreted central block with other wings and ranges. The building dates from 1721, and was designed by William Adam for the 1st Duke of Roxburghe. In the 19th century the house was remodelled with a profusion of spires and domes, corbelling and battlements, by William Playfair. Floors is still the home of the Duke and Duchess of Roxburghe.

Collections of furniture, tapestries, works of art and porcelain. Gift shop. Licensed restaurant. WC. Playground. Walled garden and park. Disabled access to house; lift for wheelchairs; WC. Car and coach parking. Group concessions. £££

Open mid Apr-mid Oct, daily 10.00-16.30; last admission 16.00.

Tel: 01573 223333   Fax: 01573 226056
Web: www.floorscastle.com   Email: estates@floorscastle.com

S22 Georgian House (NTS)

[Map: 6B, E9] 7 Charlotte Square, Edinburgh. (NGR: NT 247740 LR: 66)

The Georgian House is part of the north side of Charlotte Square, in the New Town of Edinburgh, and was designed by Robert Adam. The lower floors of No 7 have been restored, and there is a fine display of china and silver, pictures and furniture, and other items.

Explanatory displays. Gift shop. Audio-visual presentation with induction loop. Disabled facilities. Parking nearby. ££

House and shop open 20 Jan-24 Mar and 28 Oct-24 Dec, daily 11.00-16.00; 25 Mar-27 Oct, daily 10.00-18.00.

Tel: 0131 226 3318   Fax: 0131 226 3318

S23 Gladstone's Land (NTS)

[Map: 6B, E9] 477b Lawnmarket, High Street, Edinburgh. (NGR: NT 255736 LR: 66)

Gladstone's Land, built in 1620 and retaining an arcaded front, is a typical six-storey tenement and was the home of prosperous Edinburgh merchant, Thomas Gledstanes. There are unusual tempera paintings, and the rooms and ground-floor shop are furnished and equipped as they would have been in the 17th century.

Explanatory displays. Gift shop. Tours for the blind by appt. Disabled access to ground floor. Parking nearby. £

Open 25 Mar-27 Oct, daily 10.00-17.00, Sun 13.00-17.00; Sun 13.00-14.00 guided tour only (max 10 people).

Tel: 0131 226 5856   Fax: 0131 226 4851

S24 Glenbarr Abbey

[Map: 5A, F3] On A83, 12 miles N of Campbeltown, Glenbarr, Kintyre, Argyll. (NGR: NR 669365 LR: 68)

Glenbarr Abbey is a striking Gothic revival house, built in the 18th century. It has been the home of the lairds of Glenbarr since 1796. There are tours, which are conducted by the 5th laird, Angus MacAlister, who also owns the property.

Guided tours. Museum. Explanatory displays. Gift shop. Tearoom. Grounds. Woodland and riverside walk. Picnic facilities. WC. Car and coach parking. Group concessions. £

Open Easter-Oct, daily 10.00-17.30; closed Tue.

Tel: 01583 421247   Fax: 01583 421255
Web: www.kintyre-scotland.org.uk/glenbarr

S25 Haddo House (NTS)

[Map: 4, F5] Off B9005, 10 miles NW of Ellon, Haddo, Aberdeenshire. (NGR: NJ 868347 LR: 30)

A fine classical mansion with two sweeping wings, built in 1731-6 and designed by William Adam for William Gordon, 2nd Earl of Aberdeen. The house was restored in the 1880s. Nothing survives of a castle of the Gordons, who had held the lands from 1429. In 1644 Sir John Gordon of Haddo, who supported the Marquis of Montrose, was captured and executed after being besieged in the old castle.

Generally guided tours, Mon-Sat. Exhibition of paintings. Explanatory displays. Gift shop. Restaurant. WC. Adjoining country park (01651 851489). Disabled access. Car and coach parking. Group concessions. £££.

House and garden open (2002) 29 Jun-1 Sep, daily 10.00-17.00; shop and tearoom 29 Mar-27 Sep, daily 10.00-17.00; Oct, wknds only, 10.00-17.00; country park (Aberdeenshire Council) open all year, daily 9.30-sunset.
Tel: 01651 851440   Fax: 01651 851888

S26 Hill of Tarvit Mansion House (NTS)

[Map: 6B, C10] Off A916, 2.5 miles S of Cupar, Hill of Tarvit, Fife. (NGR: NO 380119 LR: 59)

The original house dating from 1696, with 19th-century wings, was virtually rebuilt in 1906 by Sir Robert Lorimer for Mr F. B. Sharp, a Dundee industrialist. Sharp wanted to house his fine collections of paintings and pictures including by Raeburn and Ramsay, furniture by Chippendale, Flemish tapestries and Chinese porcelain and bronzes. There are also formal gardens, designed by Lorimer.

Explanatory displays. Gift shop. Tearoom. Picnic area. Restored Edwardian laundry. Woodland walk. Scotstarvit Tower is nearby. Disabled access to ground floor and grounds suitable and WC. ££.

Open (2002) 25 Mar-27 Oct, daily 12.00-17.00; tearoom, same dates but wknds only in Oct; garden and grounds open all year, daily 9.30-sunset.
Tel: 01334 653127   Fax: 01334 653127

S27 Holmwood House (NTS)

[Map: 6B, E7] Off A77 or B767, Netherlee Road (off Clarkston Road), Cathcart, Glasgow. (NGR: NS 580593 LR: 64)

The classical Greek-style house was designed by Alexander 'Greek' Thomson in the middle of the 19th century for James Couper, a paper mill owner. Many rooms are richly ornamented in wood, plaster and marble. The conservation work is ongoing.

Limited parking. Groups MUST pre-book. £.

Open (2002) 25 Mar-27 Oct, daily 12.00-17.00; morning visits available for pre-booked groups.
Tel: 0141 637 2129   Fax: 0141 637 2129

S28 Hopetoun House

[Map: 6B, D9] Off A904, 6 miles E of Linlithgow, Hopetoun, West Lothian. (NGR: NT 089790 LR: 65)

Situated on the shores of the Firth of Forth, Hopetoun House is a large and stately palatial mansion, built between 1699 and 1707 for the Hope family. The house was remodelled by William Adam from 1721, the work being continued by John and Robert Adam. The house was transferred to a charitable trust in 1974.

Fine interiors. Collections of furniture, tapestries and pictures. Gift shop. Restaurant. WC. Picnic area. Exhibitions. 100 acres of park land. Woodland walks. Red deer park. Croquet. Car and coach parking. Group concessions. ££.

Open daily 2 Apr-26 Sep 10.00-17.30; wknds only in Oct; last admission 16.30; other times closed except for group visits by prior appt.
Tel: 0131 331 2451   Web: www.hopetounhouse.com
Fax: 0131 319 1885   Email: dayvisits@hopetounhouse.com

S29 House of Dun (NTS)

[Map: 4, I4] Off A935, 3 miles NW of Montrose, Angus. (NGR: NO 667599 LR: 54)

The present House of Dun, a fine classical mansion, was built in 1730 by William Adam for David Erskine Lord Dun. The mansion has fine plasterwork. The Erskine family held the lands from 1375, and had a castle nearby, one archway of which survives. The Erskines got embroiled in a dispute about ownership, and several of the family were executed after poisoning the then heir.

Explanatory displays. Gift shop. Restaurant. Adventure playground. Fine plasterwork and a collection of portraits, furniture and porcelain. Walled garden and handloom weaving workshop. Woodland walk. Disabled access to ground floor and basement and WC. Info in Braille. £££.

House open (2002) 25 Mar-27 Oct, Fri-Tue 12.00-17.00; 29 Jun-1 Sep, Fri-Tue 11.00-18.00; restaurant same dates, daily 11.00-18.00; garden and grounds open all year, daily 9.30-sunset.
Tel: 01674 810264   Fax: 01674 810722

Y97 Hutchesons' Hall (NTS)

Said to be one of Glasgow's most elegant buildings, Hutchesons' Hall dates from 1802-5, and was designed by David Hamilton.

See main entry Y97

S30 Inveraray Castle

[Map: 5A, C5] Off A83, N of Inveraray, Argyll. (NGR: NN 096093 LR: 56)

Inveraray Castle, a large classical mansion with corner towers and turrets, was begun in 1744 for the Campbell Dukes of Argyll. It was remodelled by William and John Adam, and then again in 1877 after a fire. The castle is still the seat of the Dukes of Argyll. Nearby, but now demolished, was the 15th-century castle of the Campbells.

Guided tours. Collections of tapestries and paintings. Displays of weapons. Rob Roy MacGregor's sporran and dirk handle. Clan Room. Gift shop. Tea room. WC. Picnic area. Woodland walks. Disabled access to ground floor only. Car and coach parking. Group concessions. ££.

Open Apr-Oct, Mon- Thu and Sat 10.00-13.00 and 14.00-17.45,
Sun 13.00-17.45, closed Fri; Jul and Aug, Mon-Sat 10.00-17.45,
Sun 13.00-17.45; last admissions 12.30 and 17.00.
Tel: 01499 302203 Web: www.inveraray-castle.com
Fax: 01499 302421 Email: enquiries@inveraray-castle.com

S31 John Knox House

[Map: 6B, E9] The Netherbow, 43-45 High Street, Edinburgh. (NGR: NT 262738 LR: 66)

John Knox House, which may be the oldest house in Edinburgh, dates from the 15th century and John Knox is said to have died here. The house was home to James Mossman, keeper of the Royal Mint for Mary, Queen of Scots. The original floor in the Oak Room survives, and there is a magnificent painted ceiling. An exhibition covers the life and times of John Knox, and information about Mossman.

Explanatory displays. Gift shop. Cafe. WC. Parking nearby. £.
Open all year: Mon-Sat 10.00-17.00; closed Christmas; last admission 30 mins before closing.
Tel: 0131 556 9579

S32 Kinneil House (HS)

[Map: 5B, D9] Off A993, 5 miles E of Falkirk, 1 mile SW of Bo'ness, Kinneil, West Lothian. (NGR: NS 983806 LR: 65)

Set in a public park, Kinneil House, dating from the 16th century, is a fine old mansion with original tempera paintings in two rooms. The lands were long held by the Hamiltons. A museum occupies the renovated stable block. James Watt had a workshop here, where he carried out experiments on the development of the steam engine.

Car parking.
Access at all reasonable times – view from exterior.

S94 Kinross House Gardens

The house, which is one of the finest examples of 17th-century architecture in Scotland, was built by Sir William Bruce, who was Royal Architect to Charles II. There are formal walled gardens with yew hedges, roses and herbaceous borders, which are open to the public.

See main entry S94

S33 Manderston

[Map: 6B, E12] Off A6105, 1.5 miles E of Duns, Manderston, Borders. (NGR: NT 810545 LR: 74)

Featuring the only silver staircase in the world, Manderston is a fine Edwardian mansion, part of which dates from the original house of 1790, when it was a property of the Homes. The house was virtually rebuilt between 1903-5 by John Kinross for Sir James Miller, a millionaire racehorse owner, whose family had acquired the property in 1890.

Fine interiors, above and below stairs. Museum. Tea room. WC. Gardens. 56 acres of park land. Woodland and loch-side walks.

Car and coach parking. £££.
Open mid May-end Sep, Thu and Sun 14.00-17.00; Bank Holiday open Mon May and Aug, 14.00-17.00; other times group visits by appt.
Tel: 01361 883450/882636 Fax: 01361 882010
Web: www.manderston.co.uk Email: palmer@manderston.co.uk

S34 Mellerstain

[Map: 6B, F11] Off A6089, 5.5 miles NW of Kelso, Mellerstain, Borders. (NGR: NT 648392 LR: 74)

Mellerstain House is a magnificent castellated mansion, which was designed by William and Robert Adam. The wings date from 1725, while the central block was not completed until 1778, and replaced an earlier building. Mellerstain was built for George Baillie of Jerviswood, and is now owned by the Baillie-Hamiltons, Earls of Haddington.

Collections of paintings and furniture. Fine interiors. Gift shop. Tearoom. Gardens and grounds. Disabled access to ground floor and grounds. Car and coach parking. £££.
Open Easter weekend (Fri-Mon), then May-Sep, daily except Sat 12.30-17.00; groups at other times by appt; restaurant, 11.30-17.30.
Tel: 01573 410225 Fax: 01573 410636
Web: http://muses.calligrafix.co.uk/mellerstain
Email: mellerstain.house@virgin.net

S35 Mount Stuart House

[Map: 5A, E5] Off A844, 5 miles S of Rothesay, Mount Stuart, Bute. (NGR: NS 105595 LR: 63)

A fine Victorian Gothic stately home with splendid interior decoration, Mount Stuart was designed by the Scottish architect Robert Rowand Anderson for the 3rd Marquess of Bute. A Special Day Return Ticket is available, which includes travel from Glasgow and admission to house and gardens – tel. for details.

Fine collection of family portraits. Visitor reception area. Guided tours. Gift shop. Tearoom. Picnic areas. Audio-visual presentation. WC. 300 acres of landscaped grounds, gardens and woodland. Glass pavilion with tropical plants. Adventure play area. Disabled facilities: access to house and most of gardens. Car and coach parking. Group concessions available. £££.
House and garden open Easter, then May-mid Oct, daily except closed Thu and Thu: house 11.00-16.30, last tour 15.30, gardens 10.00-17.00.
Tel: 01700 503877 Web: www.mountstuart.com
Fax: 01700 505313 Email: contactus@mountstuart.com

S36 Newhailes (NTS)

[Map: 6B, D10] On A6095, 4.5 miles E of Edinburgh, Newhailes Road, Musselburgh, East Lothian. (NGR: NT 267725 LR: 66)

A plain symmetrical mansion, built in 1686 by the architect James Smith. It was then known as Whitehill, but the name was changed to Newhailes when the property was purchased by Sir David Dalrymple, calling it after his East Lothian estate of Hailes (see **Hailes Castle [N109]**). It was extended about 1750. Newhailes was visited by many leading figures of the

Scottish Enlightenment, and is currently undergoing a major programme of restoration.

One-hour guided tours of house from 13.00 – booking essential. Visitor centre. Plant centre. Parking. ££.

House and visitor centre open (2002) 1 Jun-27 Oct, Thu-Mon 12.00-17.00; estate open all year, daily 10.00-18.00.
Tel: 0131 665 1546

S37 No 28 Charlotte Square, Edinburgh (NTS)

[Map: 6B, E9] In Edinburgh city centre, N of W end of Princes Street, Charlotte Square, Edinburgh. (NGR: NT 247738 LR: 66)

The house in Charlotte Square, designed by Robert Adam, is in probably the finest Georgian square in Britain. The National Trust for Scotland purchased part of the square for a new head office, with exhibition, retail and catering areas. There is a fine collection of 20th-century Scottish paintings as well as Regency furniture.

Explanatory displays. Gift shop. Coffee House. Restaurant at No 27 (open 18.00-2300). WC. Disabled access. Parking nearby.

Open all year: Drawing Room Gallery, Mon-Sat 10.00-17.00, Sun 12.00-17.00; shop open, Mon-Sat 10.00-17.00, Sun 12.00-18.00; Coffee House and Restaurant open, Mon-Sat 10.00-18.00, Sun 12.00-17.00; Restaurant at No 27 open Tue-Sat from 18.00 (restaurant reservations 0131 243 9339).
Tel: 0131 243 9300   Fax: 0131 243 9301

S38 Paxton House

[Map: 6B, E12] Off B6461, 7 miles S of Eyemouth, Paxton, Borders. (NGR: NT 935530 LR: 74)

In a picturesque setting overlooking the Tweed, Paxton House, a fine classical mansion, was built in 1756 for Patrick Home of Billie. The house was probably designed by Robert, John and James Adam, with later additions. There is access to 12 period rooms, and a fine collection of furniture. Paxton is now an outstation of the **National Galleries of Scotland [U13]**, and houses 70 paintings.

Exhibitions of pictures and furniture. Gift shop. Licensed tearoom. Gardens, woodlands and 80 acres of park land. Picnic area. Plant centre. Adventure playground. Partial disabled access to house. Car and coach parking. ££. Function suite for hire.

Open Good Fri-Oct, daily 11.00-17.00; last admission 16.15; shop and tearoom, 10.00-17.30; grounds 10.00-sunset; open to groups/schools all year by appt.
Tel: 01289 386291   Fax: 01289 386660
Web: www.paxtonhouse.com   Email: info@paxtonhouse.com

Y161 Pittencrieff House

See main entry Y161

S39 Pollok House (NTS)

[Map: 6B, E7] Off B768, Pollok Country Park, Pollokshaws area of Glasgow. (NGR: NS 549619 LR: 64)

Pollok House, first built about 1750, was a property of the Maxwells from the mid 13th century. Pollok was gifted to the City of Glasgow in 1966, and the

Burrell Collection is situated within the grounds. The house contains the Stirling Maxwell collection of Spanish and European paintings, furniture, ceramics and silver. The house stands within a country park with fine woodland and shrubbery. Managed by The National Trust for Scotland on behalf of Glasgow City.

Guided tours. Gift shop. Licensed restaurant. WC. Partial disabled access. Parking. ££.

Open all year, daily 10.00-17.00; closed 25-26 Dec & 1-2 Jan.
Tel: 0141 616 6410   Fax: 0141 616 6521

S40 Rammerscales House

[Map: 6B, H9] On B9020, 3 miles SW of Lockerbie, Dumfries and Galloway. (NGR: NY 081777 LR: 85)

Standing high overlooking the Annan valley, Rammerscales is a fine 18th-century mansion, with magnificent grounds, surrounded by mature trees. In Adam style and mostly unaltered, the mansion was home to the Mounsey family in the 18th century, but is now a property of the Bell Macdonald family. It is now possible to stay at Rammerscales: contact house.

Guided tours for parties. Extensive and attractive grounds with walled gardens. Car and coach parking. £££.

Last week in Jul; 1st three weeks in Aug: Sun-Fri 14.00-17.00, closed Sat.
Tel: 01387 810229   Web: www.rammerscales.co.uk
Fax: 01387 810940   Email: estate@rammerscales.co.uk

U17 Rozelle House, Ayr

See main entry U17

S41 Scone Palace

[Map: 5B, C9] Off A93, 2 miles N of Perth, Scone, Perthshire. (NGR: NO 114267 LR: 58)

Scone Palace (pronounced 'Scoon'), a large castellated mansion dating from 1802, incorporates part of the palace built by the Ruthvens in the 1580s, and stands on the site of an abbey. The property passed to the Murrays, made Viscounts Stormont and Earls of Mansfield. The Kings of Scots were inaugurated at the Moot Hill, near the present palace, the last king to be so was Charles I in 1651. The Stone of Destiny, also called the Stone of Scone, was kept here, until taken to Westminster Abbey by Edward I in 1296 – it was returned to **Edinburgh Castle [N25]** in 1996.

Fine collections of furniture, clocks, needlework and porcelain. Gift shops. Restaurant. Tearoom. WC. Picnic area. 100 acres of wild gardens. Maze. Adventure playground. Meetings and conferences. Disabled access to state rooms & restaurant. Car and coach parking. Group concessions. £££.

Open 31 Mar-Oct (2002), daily 9.30-17.15; last admission 16.45; grounds close at 17.45; other times by appt.
Tel: 01738 552300   Fax: 01738 552588
Web: www.scone-palace.co.uk   Email: visits@scone-palace.co.uk

Y14 Shambellie House

See main entry Y14

S42 Skaill House

[Map: 2, C2] Off B9056, 6 miles N of Stromness, Skaill, Breckness, Orkney. (NGR: HY 234186 LR: 6)

Standing close by the hugely impressive Neolithic village of **Skara Brae [A21]**, Skaill House is the most complete 17th-century mansion house in Orkney. It was built for Bishop George Graham in the 1620s, and has fine gardens. On display is the dinner service from Captain Cook's ship, *The Discovery*.

Guided tours. Explanatory displays. Gift shop. WC. Disabled access. Garden. Car and coach parking. Group concessions. ££. Joint entry ticket for all Orkney monuments (£££).

Skaill House open Apr-Sep, daily 9.30-18.30; last ticket sold 18.00. (Skara Brae also Oct-Mar Mon-Sat 9.30-16.30, Sun 2.00-4.30; last ticket sold 16.00; closed 25/26 Dec &1-3 Jan).

Tel: 01856 841501 Web: www.skaillhouse.com
Fax: 01856 841668 Email: janette@skaillhouse.freeserve.co.uk

S43 The Binns (NTS)

[Map: 6B, D9] Off A904, 3 miles NE of Linlithgow, West Lothian. (NGR: NT 051785 LR: 65)

A fine castellated mansion, built between 1612 and 1630, with later additions and remodelling. It was held by the Livingstones, then the Dalziels. General Tom Dalyell of The Binns was taken prisoner in 1651 at Worcester, but escaped from the Tower of London. He served with the Tsar's cossacks, when reputedly he roasted prisoners. Dalyell returned to Scotland, defeated the Covenanters at Rullion Green in 1666, and raised the Royal Scots Greys in 1681.

Collections of portraits, furniture and china. Guided tours. Explanatory displays. WC. Park land. Disabled access to ground floor and grounds and WC. Car parking. ££.

House open (2002) 1 May- 29 Sep, Sat-Thu 13.00-17.00, closed Fri; parkland open 1 Jan-24 Mar and 28 Oct-31 Dec, daily 10.00-16.00; 25 Mar-27 Oct, daily 10.00-19.00.

Tel: 01506 834255

S44 Threave Garden and Estate (NTS)

[Map: 6B, H8] Off A75, 6 miles W of Dalbeattie, Threave, Dumfries and Galloway. (NGR: NX 752605 LR: 84)

Threave House, a castellated mansion, was built in 1873 by the Gordon family, who acquired the estate in 1870. The garden has peat and woodland plants, a rock garden, some 200 varieties of daffodil, and herbaceous borders. There is also a walled garden and glasshouses. The house is The National Trust for Scotland's School of Horticulture.

Guided tours of house. Visitor centre, countryside centre and exhibition. Gift shop. Restaurant. WC. Disabled access and WC. Parking. ££.

Estate and garden open (2002) all year, daily 9.30-sunset; walled garden and glasshouses open all year, daily 9.30-17.00; visitor centre, countryside centre and exhibition open 1-24 Mar and 28 Oct-23 Dec, daily 10.00-16.00; 25 Mar-27 Oct,

daily 9.30-17.30; house open 1 Mar-27 Oct, Wed-Fri and Sun 11.00-16.00: guided tours only, max 10 people, two per hour, admission by time ticket.

Tel: 01556 502575 Fax: 01556 502683

S45 Torosay Castle

[Map: 5A, B4] On A849, 1 mile S of Craignure, Torosay, Mull. (NGR: NM 729353 LR: 49)

Torosay Castle is a fine castellated mansion of 1858, designed by David Bryce for the Campbells of Possel. It was sold to the Guthrie family in 1865, and remains with their descendants. The principal rooms are open to the public. The 12 acres of gardens, laid out by Sir Robert Lorimer in 1899, include formal terraces, an Italian statue walk, Japanese garden, walled garden and woodland, and there are fine views.

Guided tours by arrangement. Gift shop. Tearoom. WC. Disabled access. Pedigree cattle. Isle of Mull Weavers. Miniature steam railway from Craignure. Car and coach parking. Group concessions. ££.

House open April-mid-Oct, daily 10.30-17.30; last admission 17.00; gardens open all year, daily 9.00-19.00 or daylight hours in winter.

Tel: 01680 812421 Fax: 01680 812470 Email: torosay@aol.com Web: www.holidaymull.org/members/torosay

S46 Trinity House (HS)

[Map: 6B E9] 99 Kirkgate, Leith, Edinburgh

The fine Georgian building houses a unique collection of maritime displays. Trinity House is home to the Incorporation of Shipowners and Shipmasters, who have been closely involved in the history of Leith from the 14th century. The building stands on the site of a medieval sailors' hospital.

Parking nearby.

Open all year: guided tour only– tel in advance to book.

Tel: 0131 554 3289 Fax: 0131 554 1273

S47 Winton House

[Map: 6B, E10] Off A1, 4.5 miles W of Haddington, Winton, East Lothian. (NGR: NT 439696 LR: 66)

Winton House, a Renaissance mansion dating from 1620 with later additions, has famous stone twisted chimneys and some fine 17th-century plaster ceilings, decorated in honour of Charles I. Winton was long held by the Setons, who were made Earls of Winton in 1600, but later passed to the Hamiltons, then the Ogilvys, who still own it.

Guided tours. Collections of pictures, furniture, and family exhibitions of costumes and photographs. Tearoom. WC. Picnic area. Terraced gardens and specimen trees. Woodland walks. WC. Limited disabled access. WC. Car and coach parking. Group concessions. ££. Corporate and private hospitality.

Tel to confirm.

Tel: 01620 824986 Web: www.wintonhouse.co.uk
Fax: 01620 823961 Email: enquiries@wintonhouse.co.uk

Top *Ayton Castle* Above *Bowhill*
Left *Scone* Below left *Mellerstain*
Bottom left *Duff House*
Below right *House of Dun*
Bottom right *Dunninald*

S2: Gardens

Also see the sections on *N1: Castles, Towers and Palaces – 1*; *N2: Castles, Towers and Palaces – 2*; and *Q: Clan Castles and Museums*.

S1 Abbotsford
See main entry S1

N49 Aberdour Castle (HS)
A terraced garden has been restored, and there is also a walled garden.
See main entry N49

S48 Abriachan Garden Nursery
[Map: 3B, F9] Off A82, 9 miles SW of Inverness, Abriachan, Highland. (NGR: NH 558353 LR: 26)
The garden, which stands in a grand woodland setting on the banks of Loch Ness, features many native and exotic plants. Hardy perennials are a speciality, and the adjacent nursery sells many unusual plants.
Guided tours. Explanatory displays. Plant sales. Picnic seats. Disabled access. Parking Nearby. £.
Open Feb-Nov daily 9.00-19.00 or dusk of earlier.
Tel: 01463 861232   Fax: 01463 861232

S49 Achamore Gardens
[Map: 5A, E3] Off unlisted road, 1 miles SW of Ardminish, Achamore, Gigha. (NGR: NR 644477 LR: 62)
The fine woodland gardens of rhododendrons and azaleas were created by Sir James Horlick, who purchased the estate in 1944. Many of the plants were brought in laundry baskets from his former home in Berkshire, and others were added over the following 29 years. Sub-tropical plants flourish in the virtually frost-free climate, and there is a walled garden for some of the finer specimens. There are good views over Islay and Jura, and two self-guided garden routes, one of 40 minutes, the other two hours. The house was built in 1884 by Captain William Scarlett, Lord Abinger, after he had bought the island, but is not open to the public.
WC. Disabled access. Parking. £.
Open daily all year, dawn to dusk.
Tel: 01583 505254   Fax: 01583 505244

S50 Achiltibuie Hydroponicum
[Map: 3A, C6] Off A835 (many miles), 13 miles NW of Ullapool, Achiltibuie, Highland. (NGR: NC 025085 LR: 15)
The hydroponicum, overlooking the Summer Isles, is an unusual indoor garden which does not use soil. There is a one hour guided tour around the four greenhouses, each of which has different climates, with flowers, exotic fruit, vegetables and herbs.
Hourly guided tours. Picnic lawns. Gift shop. Cafe. WC. Access to shore. Disabled access. Car parking. ££.
Open Apr-Sep, daily 10.00-18.00.
Tel: 01854 622202 Fax: 01854 622201
Email: info@thehydroponicum.com

S51 Achnacloich Gardens
[Map: 5A, B5] Off A85, 8 miles E of Oban, Achnacloich, Argyll. (NGR: NM 981289 LR: 49)
The woodland garden, which covers about 35 acres, was developed over a period of 130 years. There is a small walled garden, planted ponds, and a wide variety of shrubs, many from the Southern Hemisphere.
WC. Car parking. £.
Open Apr-Oct, daily 10.00-18.00.
Tel: 01631 710221

S52 An Cala Garden, Easdale
[Map: 5A, C4] On B844, 13.5 miles SW of Oban, Easdale, Seil. (NGR: NM 745175 LR: 55)
The fine garden, designed by Mawson in the 1930s, features meandering streams, winding paths, formal terraces and lawns. A 15-foot-high wall protects the plants from winter gales, and much of the original planting still survives.
Parking. Refreshments in village. Plants for sale (later in season). WC. £.
Open Apr-Oct, daily 10.00-18.00.
Tel: 01852 300237 Fax: 01852 300237

S2 Arbuthnott House
See main entry S2

S53 Ardanaiseig Gardens
[Map: 5A, C5] Off B845, 4 miles SW of Dalmally, 10 miles E of Taynuilt, Ardanaiseig, Kilchrenan, Argyll. (NGR: NN 089249 LR: 50)
The woodland garden, which covers some 100 acres of woodland, was laid out in 1834 when Ardanaiseig House was built. There are many exotic shrubs and trees, as well as rhododendrons, azaleas and magnolias.
Explanatory displays. Refreshments and WC in Ardanaiseig Hotel. Car parking. Donation. Hotel.
Open all year, daily 9.00-dusk; closed Jan & 1st wks of Feb.
Tel: 01866 833333 Fax: 01866 8332222

J3 Ardchattan Priory (HS)
There are fine gardens by the remains of the priory.
See main entry J3

S54 Ardencraig Garden
[Map: 5A, E5] Off A844, S of Rothesay, Ardencraig, Bute. (NGR: NS 106635 LR: 63)
Ardencraig Gardens feature a wide range of fine floral displays. The Cactus House has a huge variety of cacti, some large in size; and a Fuchsia House with an

impressive display of colour. There is a small aviary, stream and fish pond. Plants are available for sale.

Gift shop. Plant sales. Tearoom. WC. Disabled access. Car and coach parking.
Open May-Sep, Mon-Fri 9.00-16.30, Sat and Sun 13.00-16.30.
Tel: 01700 504225 ext 204 (council)/504644 (gardens) Fax: 01700 504225

S55 Ardkinglas Woodland Garden

[Map: 5A, C5] Off A83 Loch Lomond to Inveraray Road, 5 miles E of Inveraray, Cairndow, Argyll. (NGR: NN 175104 LR: 56)

In a picturesque location with fine views over Loch Fyne, the woodland garden is set on a hillside and has a fine collection of rhododendrons and conifers. The present Ardkinglas House, built in 1906, was designed by Sir Robert Lorimer for Sir Andrew Noble, and is still occupied by the Noble family.

Guided tours for groups by appt. Picnic area. Plant and craft sales and refreshments available from Tree Shop nearby. WC. £.
Ardkinglas Woodland Garden open, daily dawn to dusk; Ardkinglas House open strictly for groups by appt only.
Tel: 01499 600261/263 Fax: 01499 600241
Web: www.ardkinglas.com Email: ardkinglas@btinternet.com

S56 Ardmaddy Castle

[Map: 5A, C4] Off B844, 12 miles S of Oban, 5 miles SW of Kilninver, Ardmaddy, Argyll. (NGR: NM 788164 LR: 55)

Ardmaddy Castle, a mansion mostly dating from 1737, incorporates the basement of a 15th-century castle. It was a property of the MacDougalls, who built the castle, but passed to the Campbells. The fine walled garden features rhododendrons, azaleas and climbing plants, shrubs and herbaceous perennials. There are woodland walks, with fine views, as well as a water garden.

Plant sales. Walled garden, water features and woodland walks. Parking. £.
Gardens open all year, daily dawn to dusk; castle not open.
Tel: 01852 300353 Fax: 01852 300353 Email:
c.m.struthers@lineone.net

S57 Ardtornish Estate

[Map: 3A, I5] On A884, 40 miles SW of Fort William by Corran Ferry, 3 miles N of Lochaline, Ardtornish, Morvern, Highland. (NGR: NM 700475 LR: 49)

Set in the picturesque peninsula of Morvern, Ardtornish Estate is a 35 000 acres Highland estate with 24 acres of established gardens around the Grade A listed Ardtornish House. The house was completed in 1892, and designed by Alexander Ross. There is a market garden and self-catering properties.

Explanatory displays. Gift shop. Picnic areas. WC. Car and coach parking. £ (gardens). Accommodation available.
Open Mar-Oct, daily 9.00-18.00; market garden open all year, daily 9.00-16.00 except closed Thu.
Tel: 01967 421288 Fax: 01967 421211
Web: www.ardtornish.co.uk Email: tourism@ardtornish.co.uk

S58 Arduaine Garden (HS)

[Map: 5A, C4] Off A816, 20 miles S of Oban, 3 miles SW of Kilmelford, Arduaine, Argyll. (NGR: NM 798105 LR: 55)

Arduaine, a fine 18 acre garden, has a good collection of rhododendrons, azaleas, magnolias and rare trees and shrubs. There are also blue Tibetan poppies, perennial borders, lily ponds, and a woodland garden with a picturesque walk to a coastal viewpoint.

Explanatory displays. WC. Disabled access. Car and coach parking. £.
Open all year, daily 9.30-18.00.
Tel: 01852 200366 Fax: 01852 200366

S59 Ardwell House Gardens

[Map: 6A, I5] Off A716, 9.5 miles S of Stranraer, Ardwell, Dumfries and Galloway. (NGR: NX 103455 LR: 82)

Ardwell House, an 18th-century mansion, replaced a nearby castle of the MacCullochs. The country house gardens and grounds have flowering shrubs and woodland walks, as well as daffodils, azaleas, camellias, and rhododendrons. There is also a walled garden and herbaceous border, and fine views over Luce Bay.

Plant centre & gift shop. Picnic area. Partial disabled access and WC. Car and coach parking. £.
Garden and grounds open Apr-Oct, 10.00-17.00; walled garden and green house close 15.00.
Tel: 01776 860227 Fax: 01776 860288

Q1 Armadale Castle

Around the castle are 40 acres of woodland gardens and nature trails, as well as a walled kitchen garden.
See main entry Q1

S60 Ascog Hall Fernery and Garden

[Map: 5A, E5] On A886, 3 miles S of Rothesay, Ascog, Bute. (NGR: NS 106634 LR: 63)

Built around 1870, the Victorian fernery, with fine rock work and water pools, has been restored and refurnished with a collection of sub-tropical ferns. The only surviving fern from the original collection, the *Todea barbara*, is said to be around 1000 years old.

Guided tours. Partial disabled access. No dogs. Car parking; coaches by appt only. £.
Open Apr-Oct, Wed-Sun 10.00-17.00; last admission 16.30; closed Mon & Tue.
Tel: 01700 504555

S61 Attadale Garden

[Map: 3A, F6] On A890, 12 miles NE of Kyle of Lochalsh, Attadale, Strathcarron, Ross, Highland. (NGR: NG 927388 LR: 25)

Attadale House was built in 1755 by Donald Matheson. The gardens and woodlands were started in 1890 by Baron Schroder, and planted with rhododendrons, azaleas and specimen trees. Since the storms of the 1980s, more old paths have been revealed. There is also a restored sunken garden, vegetable and herb gardens.

Guided tours by arrangement. Explanatory displays. Visitors are advised to wear waterproof shoes. WC. Disabled access. Car and coach parking. Group concessions. £.

Open Apr-Oct, Mon-Sat 10.00-17.30.

Tel: 01520 722217 Fax: 01520 722546

Web: www.attadale.com Email: gardens@attadale.com

S62 Balmacara (Lochalsh Woodland Garden) (NTS)

[Map: 3A, F6] Off A87, 2 miles E Kyle of Lochalsh, Balmacara, Kyle, Lochalsh, Highland (NGR: NG 800277 LR: 33)

Balmacara estate, covering some 5600 acres, includes the picturesque village of Plockton where 'Hamish Macbeth' was filmed. Lochalsh Woodland Garden features sheltered loch-side walks, as well as pine trees, oaks, beeches, ferns, bamboos, fuchsias, hydrangeas and rhododendrons.

Information kiosk. Explanatory displays. Car parking. £.

Estate: open all year; garden: open all year, daily 10.00-18.00.

Tel: 01599 566325 Fax: 01599 566359

R1 Balmoral Castle

See main entry R1

S63 Bargany Castle Gardens

[Map: 6A, G5] Off B734, 4 miles E of Girvan, Ayrshire. (NGR: NS 244003 LR: 76)

The fine gardens consist of a lily pond, rock garden, and a collection of hard and soft-wood trees.

Disabled access. Parking. £ (contributions box).

Garden: open Mar-Oct, daily 10.00-19.00.

Tel: 01465 871249 Fax: 01465 871282

S64 Bell's Cherrybank Gardens, Perth

[Map: 5B, C9] Off A93, Cherrybank, W of Perth. (NGR: NO 095225 LR: 58)

The garden contains Bell's National Heather Collection, the largest collection in Britain with over 900 varieties from all over the world. Different heathers flower every month of the year. Other features include a doocot, aviary, play area and putting green, sundial, acoustic pool, hidden pool, pond, The Rocky Island, natural burn, sculpture collection, and a fountain.

Guided tours. Explanatory displays. Tearoom. WC. Disabled access. Car and coach parking. Group concessions. £.

Open Easter-Oct, Mon-Sat 9.00-17.00, Sun 12.00-14.00; Oct-Easter, Mon-Fri 10.00-16.00.

Tel: 01738 627330

S65 Benmore Botanic Garden

[Map: 5A, D5] On A815, 7 miles N of Dunoon, Benmore, Argyll. (NGR: NS 142857 LR: 56)

The woodland garden, which has magnificent views, features many conifers, magnolias and more than 250 species of rhododendron. There is a formal garden and way-marked trails, while the Redwood Avenue, planted in 1863, has some of the largest conifers in Britain. Benmore has been a specialist garden of the **Royal Botanic Garden [S102]**, since the 1930s.

Botanics shop. Cafe. WC. Disabled limited access and WC. Car and coach parking. Dogs permitted on short lead. £.

Open mid Mar-Oct, daily 9.30-18.00.

Tel: 01369 706261 Fax: 01369 700639

S66 Biblical Garden, Elgin

[Map: 4, E3] Off A96, King Street, Cooper Park by Cathedral, Elgin, Moray. (NGR: NJ 216633 LR: 28)

The garden, which covers some three acres, uses the Bible as a reference, and is planted with every species mentioned in the good book. A desert area depicts Mount Sinai and the cave of resurrection, and the central walkway is laid in the shape of a Celtic cross. Life-size statues depict various parables.

Explanatory display. Disabled access. Car and coach parking.

Open daily, May-Sep 10.00-19.30.

N6 Blair Castle

See main entry N6

S67 Bolfracks Garden

[Map: 5B, B8] On A827, 2 miles W of Aberfeldy, Bolfracks, Perthshire. (NGR: NN 822481 LR: 52)

Bolfracks Garden, which overlooks the Tay, features a wide range of plants, trees, shrubs, perennials and bulbs. Specialities are rhododendrons, mecanopsis, azaleas and primulas, as well as old, rambling roses within a walled garden. There is also a less formal wooded garden.

Guided tours by appt. Plant sales. Guide dogs not permitted. Parking nearby. £.

Open Apr-Oct, daily 10.00-18.00.

Tel: 01887 820207

S68 Botanic Gardens, Glasgow

[Map: 6B, E7] Off A82, 730 Great Western Road, Queen Margaret Drive, Glasgow. (NGR: NS 568674 LR: 64)

The botanic gardens were established in 1817 from an older university physic garden, and moved to this site in 1842. There is an outstanding plant collection. The Kibble Palace, a magnificent glasshouse which covers some 23,000 square feet, has huge tree ferns. There are also other glasshouses with orchids and other exotic plants. The fine grounds are laid out with lawns and beds, as well as a herb garden.

Guided tours by arrangement. Explanatory displays. Disabled access. Parking nearby.

Kibble Palace open 10.00-16.45, 16.15 in winter; main glasshouse open Mon-Sat 13.00-16.45, 16.15 in winter, Sun 12.00-16.45, 16.15 in winter; gardens open daily 7.00-dusk.

Tel: 0141 334 2422/3354 Web: www.glasgow.gov.uk

Fax: 0141 339 6964 Email: ewen.donaldson@ls.glagow.gov.uk

S9 Bowhill
See main entry S9

S69 Branklyn Garden (NTS)
[Map: 5B, C9] On A85, Dundee Road, Branklyn, Perth. (NGR: NO 125225 LR: 58)
Branklyn Garden, which was first laid out in 1922, covers just two acres but is well known for the collection of rhododendrons, shrubs, herbaceous borders, peat garden plants and alpines. There is also a rock garden.
Guided garden walks. Explanatory displays. Shop and plant centre. Limited disabled access. Painting courses. Car and coach parking nearby. Group concessions. £.
Open all year, daily 9.30-18.00; walk to garden.
Tel: 01738 625535   Fax: 01738 625535

N9 Brodick Castle (NTS)
See main entry N9

N10 Brodie Castle (NTS)
See main entry N10

S10 Broughton House (NTS)
There is a Japanese-style garden.
See main entry S10

S70 Broughton Place
[Map: 6B, F9] Off A701, 5 miles E of Biggar, Broughton Place, Lanarkshire. (NGR: NT 117372 LR: 72)
Although Broughton Place appears to be a tower house, it was built in 1938 and designed by Sir Basil Spence. The drawing room and hall are open to the public, and have paintings and crafts by living British artists for sale. The gardens are open and have fine views of the Tweeddale hills. There are also national collections of Thalictrum and Tropaeolum.
Gift shop. Garden. Garden centre. WC. Disabled access. Car and coach parking.
Gallery open Apr-mid Oct and mid Nov-Christmas.
Tel: 01899 830234

S71 Bughtrig Gardens
[Map: 6B, E12] On B6461, 4 miles NW of Coldstream, Leitholm, Borders. (NGR: NT 797447 LR: 74)
Bughtrig House is a classical family house of about 1785, much altered in later years. The formal garden features herbaceous plants, roses, shrubs, annuals, fruit, vegetables and tree nursery.
Accommodation. Small picnic area. Disabled limited access. Limited parking. £.
Garden open Jun-Sep, daily 11.00-17.00; house by appt only.
Tel: 01890 840678   Fax: 01890 840509

T10 Burns Monument and Gardens, Alloway
See main entry T10

S72 Cambo
[Map: 6B, C11] Off A917, 3 miles N of Crail, Kingsbarns, Cambo, Fife. (NGR: NO 604115 LR: 59)
Set about the Cambo Burn, the walled garden features snowdrops and bulbs in spring, magnificent herbaceous borders, an extensive rose collection of 200 varieties and ornamental potager. There is a September border and a colchicum meadow in autumn. Woodland walks follow the burn to a secluded sandy beach.
Guided tours can be arranged. Picnics allowed. Victorian walled garden. Woodland walks. Golf course. Disabled access. Car and coach parking. £. Self-catering and b&b accommodation available.
Garden: open all year, daily 10.00-dusk; house not open.
Tel: 01333 450313   Web: www.camboestate.com
Fax: 01333 450987   Email: cambohouse@compuserve.com

S73 Candacraig
[Map: 4, G3] On A944, 10 miles N of Ballater, Candacraig, Kincardine & Deeside. (NGR: NJ 339111 LR: 37)
The walled garden, dating from the 1820s, features specialist hardy plants, some from the Himalayas and the Far East, as well as cottage garden plants.
Explanatory displays. Gift shop. Plant centre. WC. Disabled access. Car parking. Coach parking by arrangement only. £ (donation). Accommodation available.
House not open. Garden open May-Sep, daily 10.00-18.00.
Tel: 01975 651226   Fax: 01975 651391

N66 Castle Kennedy
The 75 acres of gardens were laid out between two lochs, originally in 1730, and have impressive terraces and avenues around a large lily pond. There is a walled garden.
See main entry N66

N14 Cawdor Castle
See main entry N14

S13 Chatelherault
The country park, which covers some 500 acres, has 18th-century gardens, terraces and parterre, as well as extensive country walks.
See main entry S13

S74 Cluny House Garden
[Map: 5B, B8] Off A827, 2 miles NE of Aberfeldy, Cluny House, Perthshire. (NGR: NN 879513 LR: 52)
Cluny is a Himalayan woodland garden, which was created and planted from 1950 by the late Mr and Mrs Robert Masterton. Plants include primulas, mecanopsis, rhododendrons, lilies, trillums and spring bulbs.
Guided tours. Explanatory displays. Plant stall. Picnic area. £.
Open Mar-Oct, daily 10.00-18.00.
Tel: 01887 820795

S75 Colonsay House Gardens

[Map: 5A, D3] Off A871, 2 miles N of Scalasaig, Kiloran, Colonsay. (NGR: NR 395968 LR: 61)

The well-known rhododendron garden of 20 acres is adjacent to Colonsay House. The house dates from 1722, was extended in the 19th century. In the woods surrounding the house, rocks, streams and contours of land have been used to create a natural woodland garden. There are various, more formal, walled gardens surrounding the house, including a fine terraced area where refreshments are served. In the garden is Tobar Oran, a round covered well with steps leading down to the water. Beside the well is St Oran's Cross, which is carved with the face of a man and dates from early Christian times.

Lunches and afternoon teas. Shop selling local produce and crafts. Picnic area. Parking. Self-catering accommodation available in Colonsay House (and island cottages).

Open Apr-Sep: Wed, 12.00-17.00; Fri, 15.00-17.30,

Tel: 01951 200211   Fax: 01951 200369   Web: www.colonsay.org.uk

T11 Craigieburn

The garden specialises in rare and unusual plants from south-east Asia. There is a fine gorge, sheltered woodland, formal borders, roses, a bog garden and alpines.

See main entry T11

S76 Crarae Gardens

[Map: 5A, D5] On A83, 10 miles S of Inveraray, Crarae, Argyll. (NGR: NS 987975 LR: 55)

Set in a picturesque natural gorge with a series of waterfalls and extensive walks, there is a fine collection of rhododendrons, azaleas, conifers and eucalyptus, as well as Himalayan Blue Poppies and ferns from Tasmania. The Clan Garden features plants associated the families of Argyll and the Isles

Guided tours (prearranged only). Explanatory displays. Visitor centre. Gift shop. Refreshments. Picnic area. Four trails. WC. Disabled access. Car and coach parking. £. Free to visitors in wheelchairs.

Open all year: summer, Mar-Oct 9.00-18.00; Nov-Mar, daily daylight hours only.

Tel: 01546 886388 (visitor centre 01546 886614   Fax: 01546 886388
Web: www.crarae-gardens.org   Email: info@crarae-gardens.org

N16 Crathes Castle (NTS)

See main entry N16

S77 Cruickshank Botanic Garden, Aberdeen

[Map: 4, G5] St Machar Drive, University of Aberdeen, Old Aberdeen. (NGR: NJ 938084 LR: 38)

Cruickshank Botanic Garden, which was developed at the end of the 19th century, covers some 11 acres, including rock and water gardens, a rose garden, a fine herbaceous border, an arboretum and a patio garden. There are collections of spring bulbs, gentians and alpine plants, and fine trees and shrubs. Enter by gate in Chanonry, Old Aberdeen

Guided tours. Disabled access. Parking nearby.

Open all year, Mon-Fri 9.00-16.30; also May-Sep, Sat and Sun 14.00-17.00.

Tel: 01224 272704   Fax: 01224 272703

S16 Culzean Castle (NTS)

See main entry S16

S78 Dawyck Botanic Garden

[Map: 6B, F9] On B712, 8 miles SW of Peebles, Stobo, Borders. (NGR: NT 168352 LR: 72)

Dawyck is well known for the historic arboretum, a specialist garden of the **Royal Botanic Garden [S102]** in Edinburgh. Three of the oldest European larches survive from 1725, as do silver firs planted in 1686. Among the mature specimen trees – some over 130 feet tall – are a variety of flowering trees, shrubs and herbaceous plants.

Swiss Bridge. Explanatory displays. Gift shop. Plant centre. Tea room. WC. Partial access for disabled and WC. Car and coach parking. Group concessions. £.

Botanic garden: open Mar-Oct, daily 9.30-18.00; other times by arrangement.

Tel: 01721 760254   Fax: 01721 760214

N82 Dirleton Castle (HS)

There are fine gardens with ancient yews and hedges around the bowling green, as well as an early 20th-century Arts and Crafts garden and recreated Victorian garden.

See main entry N82

S79 Dochfour Gardens

[Map: 3B, F9] On A82, 5 miles SW of Inverness, Dochgarroch, Highlands. (NGR: NH 620610 LR: 26)

The fine Victorian terraced garden, covering some 15 acres, is located at the north end of the Great Glen with superb views over Loch Dochfour.

Guided tours by arrangement. Disabled access. Car parking. £.

Open Apr-Sep, Mon-Fri 10.00-17.00; Jul & Aug Sat-Sun 14.00-17.00.

Tel: 01463 861218   Fax: 01463 861336

N19 Drum Castle (NTS)

See main entry N19

N21 Drummond Castle Gardens

Built on a rocky outcrop, Drummond Castle is a fine castle, dating from the 15th century, with splendid gardens. The terraces overlook a magnificent parterre, celebrating the saltire and family heraldry, surrounding a famous sundial by John Milne, Master Mason to Charles I.

See main entry N21

N23 Dunrobin Castle
See main entry N23

S80 Duthie Park Winter Gardens, Aberdeen
[Map: 4, G5] Polmuir Road, 1 mile S of city centre, Duthie Park, Aberdeen. (NGR: NJ 970044 LR: 38)
The winter gardens have two acres of covered gardens, the largest in Europe. There are plants from around the world. Features include the cacti and succulent hall, Victorian corridor and outside gardens, floral hall, corridor of perfumes, and fern house.
Guided tours (£) by arrangement. Explanatory displays. Gift shop. Plant sales. Restaurant. WC. Disabled access. Car and limited coach parking.
Open all year: daily from 9.30.
Tel: 01224 585310 Fax: 01224 210532

N98 Edzell Castle (HS)
A large pleasance, or garden, was created in 1604, and is surrounded by an ornamental wall, to which a summerhouse and a bath-house were added. The fine carved decoration of the garden walls is unique.
See main entry N98

N100 Elcho Castle (HS)
See main entry N100

N27 Falkland Palace (NTS)
See main entry N27

Q11 Finlaystone House
See main entry Q11

S21 Floors Castle
See main entry S21

S81 Foreland Walled Garden
[Map: 5A, E2] Off B8018, 3 miles N of Bruichladdich, Foreland, Islay. (NGR: NR 267644 LR: 60)
Set in scenic countryside, the walled garden stands among woods and has views over Loch Gruinart and Colonsay. It features a herb garden, herbaceous border and wild flower garden.
Plants and garden gift items for sale. Parking.
Open all year, Tue-Sat 11.00-17.00, Sun 15.00-17.00; Oct-Feb, Thu 12.00-15.00, closed Fri-Wed.
Tel: 01496 850483 Fax: 01496 850483

S82 Galloway House Gardens
[Map: 6A, I6] On B7004, 15 miles S of Newton Stewart, 6 miles SE of Wigtown, Garlieston, Galloway. (NGR: NX 478453 LR: 83)
Commanding fine views over Wigtown Bay and the Solway Firth, Galloway House dates from 1740. The property was owned by the Stewart Earls of Galloway, descended from Stewart of Bonkyl. The family were made Lord Garlies in 1607 then Earls of Galloway in 1623. The gardens, created in 1740 by Lord Garlies, are currently under restoration but are open to the public.
Parking. £.
Gardens open Mar-Oct, daily 9.00-17.00; house not open.
Tel: 01988 600680

S83 Geilston Garden (NTS)
[Map: 5A, D6] On A814, 3 miles NW of Dumbarton, E of Cardross, Geilston, Dunbartonshire. (NGR: NS 339783 LR: 63)
Geilston is a two-storey L-plan house, which may incorporate work from the 15th century, although it appears to mostly date from the 17th century and later. The walls are harled, and the house has corbiestepped gables. There is a magnificent walled garden as well as a wooded glen.
Parking. £.
Garden open 25 Mar-27 Oct (2002), daily 9.30-17.00; house not open.
Tel: 01389 841867 Fax: 01389 841189

S84 Glenwhan Garden
[Map: 6A, I5] Off A75, 6 miles E of Stranraer, Dunragit, Dumfries and Galloway. (NGR: NX 150580 LR: 82)
Glenwhan, which has fine views of Glenluce Bay, covers some 12 acres, and was begun in 1979. Features include two ponds, alpines, scree plants, conifers, rhododendrons, azaleas and shrub roses. There is also woodland with bluebells, snowdrops and daffodils in spring, as well as rare ducks and the Primula Arena.
Visitor centre. Guided tours. Explanatory displays. Gift shop. Restaurant. Plant centre. Disabled access. WC. Parking. £.
Open Apr-Sep, daily 10.00-17.00; other times by appt.
Tel: 01581 400222 Fax: 01581 400295

S85 Greenbank Garden (NTS)
[Map: 6B, E7] Off A726, Flenders Road, Clarkston, S of Glasgow. (NGR: NS 563566 LR: 64)
Walled and woodland gardens laid out in the grounds of a Georgian house, featuring fountain garden, woodland walks, ornamental plants, annuals, perennials, shrubs and trees, although the garden is best seen between April and October. There is a garden and greenhouse designed for disabled visitors, with special gardening tools.
Guided garden walks. Explanatory displays. Gift shop and tearoom in summer. Plant sales. WC. Disabled access and WC. Parking. £.
Garden open all year, daily 10.00-sunset; shop and tearoom, 25 Mar-27 Oct, daily 11.00-17.00; 2 Nov-29 Dec, Sat-Sun 14.00-16.00.
Tel: 0141 639 3281

S86 Harmony Garden (NTS)
[Map: 6B, F10] Off B6361, St Mary's Road, opposite the Abbey, Melrose, Borders. (NGR: NT 549341 LR: 73)
A small, peaceful garden, which has herbaceous and mixed borders, and lawns as well as vegetable and

fruit areas. There are fine views of nearby **Melrose Abbey [J26]** and **Eildon Hill [D42]**, and the garden is laid out by a 19th-century house.

Parking nearby. £

Open end Mar-end Oct, Mon-Sat 10.00-18.00, Sun 13.00-17.00.

Tel: 01721 722502 Fax: 01721 724700

S26 Hill of Tarvit (NTS)

There are formal gardens, designed by Sir Robert Lorimer.

See main entry S26

S29 House of Dun (NTS)

See main entry S29

S87 Inveresk Lodge Garden (NTS)

[Map: 6B, E10] On A6124, 6.5 miles E of Edinburgh, S of Musselburgh, 24 Inveresk Village, East Lothian. (NGR: NT 348716 LR: 66)

Inveresk Lodge incorporates old work. The lands of Little Inveresk passed to the Maitlands of Thirlestane after the Reformation, until sold to the Scotts of Buccleuch in 1709. The terraced gardens of the house are open to the public, and feature a large range of plants including shrubs and roses.

Restored Edwardian conservatory. Explanatory displays. No dogs. Disabled access. Limited parking by garden wall. £

House not open; gardens open all year: 1 Nov-24 Mar, daily 10.00-16.30 or dusk; 25 Mar-31 Oct, daily 10.00-18.00.

Tel: 01721 722502

S88 Inverewe Garden (NTS)

[Map: 3A, D6] On A832, 6 miles NE of Gairloch, Loch Ewe, Poolewe, Wester Ross, Highland. (NGR: NG 860820 LR: 19)

Standing in a fine location on the shores of Loch Ewe, the garden features a range of exotic plants which grow here in the relatively warm climate. There is a visitor centre and woodland restaurant.

Guided walks (mid-Apr-mid Sep, daily 13.30). Visitor centre. Gift shop. Restaurant. WC. Disabled access although some paths difficult. Car and coach parking. £££

Garden open (2002) 25 Mar-31 Oct, daily 9.00-21.00; visitor centre, shop and restaurant 25 Mar-31 Oct 10.00-17.00.

Tel: 01445 781200 Fax: 01445 781497

S89 Jura House Walled Garden

[Map: 5A, E3] On A846, 4 miles SW of Craighouse, Ardfin, Jura. (NGR: NR 486636 LR: 61)

The walled organic garden has a wide variety of unusual plants and shrubs, suited to the protected west-coast climate, including a large Australasian collection. There are woodland and cliff walks featuring local historical interest and wildlife and flowers.

Explanatory boards. Tea tent in season. Picnic area. WC. Car and coach parking. £

House not open; garden open all year, daily 9.00-17.00.

Tel: 01496 820315

S90 Kailzie Gardens

[Map: 6B, F10] Off B7062, 2.5 miles E of Peebles, Kailzie, Borders. (NGR: NT 280385 LR: 73)

The traditional walled garden of 1812 has herbaceous, rose and shrub borders and a range of greenhouses. The 17 acres of gardens feature woodland and burnside walks, as well as a duck and fish pond.

Guided tours. Explanatory displays. Video presentation. Gift shop. Restaurant. Tearoom. Picnic area. WC. Children's play area. Fishing pond. Art gallery. Car and coach parking. Group concessions. £

Open all year: summer, daily 11.00-17.30; winter, daylight hours; shop open wknds in Dec.

Tel: 01721 720007

N32 Kelburn Castle

The grounds are open to the public as a Country Centre, and there are walled gardens with rare shrubs and trees, and a Water Garden.

See main entry N32

N33 Kellie Castle (NTS)

The gardens feature a fine collection of old roses and herbaceous plants.

See main entry N33

S91 Kildrummy Castle Gardens

[Map: 4, G4] On A97, 10 miles W of Alford, Kildrummy, Aberdeenshire. (NGR: NJ 456164 LR: 37)

The fine gardens, which are overlooked by the ruins of **Kildrummy Castle [N116]**, consist of an alpine garden, water garden and woodland. A small museum features a video on the garden throughout the year.

Guided tours. Explanatory displays. Video. Gift shop. Tearoom. Picnic area. WC. Children's play area. Sales area with unusual plants. Disabled access. Car and coach parking. £

Open Apr-Oct, daily 10.00-17.00.

Tel: 01975 571277/03

S92 Kilmory Castle Gardens

[Map: 5A, D4] On A83, 1 mile S of Lochgilphead, Kilmory, Argyll. (NGR: NR 870868 LR: 55)

The castle is said to date from the 14th century, but has been much enlarged and modified down the centuries. It was a property of the Campbells from 1828, but is now local council buildings. The garden, which was first planted in the 1770s, has over 100 species of rhododendron and has been fully restored. There are woodland walks, nature trails, herbaceous borders, as well as a sensory trail.

Disabled access. Car parking.

Garden: open all year, daylight hours; closed Christmas and New Year; castle not open.

Tel: 01546 604360 Fax: 01546 604208

S93 Kinlochlaich House Gardens

[Map: 5A, B5] On A828, 13.5 miles NE of Oban, 7 miles NE of Benderloch, Kinlochlaich House, Appin, Argyll. (NGR: NM 939466 LR: 49)

Located in a picturesque site, the house, which dates from the 18th century, was built by John Campbell who also laid out the gardens. The walled garden is surrounded by mature trees, and there is a garden plant centre with an extensive range of plants. No dogs.

Garden Plant Centre. WC. Car parking. Donations.
Open Apr-mid Oct, Mon-Sat 9.30-17.30, Sun 10.30-17.30; mid Oct-Mar, Mon-Sat 9.30-17.00.
Tel: 01631 730342   Fax: 01631 730482
Web: www.robbins-associate.co.uk/kinlochlaich
Email: 101602.3101@compuserve.com

S94 Kinross House Gardens

[Map: 5B, C9] Off B996, E of Kinross, W side of Loch Leven, Perthshire. (NGR: NO 126020 LR: 58)

The house, which is one of the finest examples of 17th-century architecture in Scotland, was built by Sir William Bruce, who was Royal Architect to Charles II. There are formal walled gardens with yew hedges, roses and herbaceous borders, which are open to the public. **Lochleven Castle [N121]** is an integral part of the landscape.

Gift shop. Disabled access. Car parking. £.
House not open; gardens open Apr-Sep, daily 10.00-19.00.
Tel: 01577 863497

N36 Leith Hall (NTS)

See main entry N36

N37 Lennoxlove

See main entry N37

B29 Lews Castle

The park is set in the pleasant wooded grounds and gardens of Lews Castle, built by the Mathesons in the 19th century, on the west side of Stornoway Harbour. The park has shore, woodland, river walks and moorland.

See main entry B29

S95 Linn Botanic Gardens

[Map: 5A, D5] On B833, 11 miles W of Dumbarton, The Linn, Cove, Dunbartonshire. (NGR: NS 220850 LR: 56)

The garden features a wide range of unusual and exotic plants. There are herbaceous borders, ponds and fountains, an extensive water garden, cliff garden and rockery, as well as a glen with a waterfall. The garden, which has been developed since 1971, is centred around a small mansion in the style of 'Greek' Thomson.

Plants for sale. Car and coach parking. Group concessions. £. Dogs on leads.
Garden open all year: dawn to dusk; plant sales, daily 10.00-17.30.
Tel: 01436 842242   Fax: 01436 842242

S96 Logan Botanic Garden

[Map: 6A, I5] Off B7065, 14 miles S of Stranraer, Logan, Dumfries and Galloway. (NGR: NX 097426 LR: 82)

Logan Botanic Garden features a wide range of unusual and exotic plants, able to survive in the relatively mild climate. There are tree ferns, cabbage palms, unusual shrubs, climbers and tender perennials, set in the walled, water, terrace and woodland gardens. It is a specialist garden of the **Royal Botanic Garden [S102]** in Edinburgh. There was a castle here, a property of the MacCullochs.

Botanic garden: Gift shop. Licensed salad bar. WC. Guided tours by arrangement. Plant centre. Discovery Centre. Soundalive self-guided tours. Disabled access. Parking. Group concessions. £.
Gardens open Mar-Oct, daily 10.00-18.00
Tel: 01776 860231   Fax: 01776 860333

S97 Malleny House Gardens (NTS)

[Map: 6B, E9] Off A70, E of Balerno, Edinburgh (NGR: NT 166667 LR: 65)

Malleny House is an extended 17th-century mansion with work from 1589 or earlier. The property belonged to the Hamiltons, but passed to the Kerrs, Murrays of Kilbaberton, the Scotts of Murdieston, then the Primrose Lord Rosebery. The garden features a good selection of shrub roses, a woodland garden, and a group of clipped yews first planted in 1603. The National Bonsai Collection for Scotland is also at Malleny.

Disabled access to garden. Car and coach parking. £.
House not open; garden open all year, daily 10.00-18.00 or dusk if earlier.
Tel: 0131 449 2283

S33 Manderston

See main entry S33

N39 Megginch Castle Gardens

There are extensive gardens with 1000-year-old yews, 16th-century rose garden, astrological garden, kitchen garden, topiary and 16th-century physic garden.
See main entry N39

S34 Mellerstain

See main entry S34

S98 Mertoun House Gardens

[Map: 6B, F11] Off B6404, 7 miles W of Kelso, Mertoun, Borders. (NGR: NT 618318 LR: 74)

Mertoun House, built in 1702 and later altered and extended, was designed by Sir William Bruce. Mertoun was held by the Halyburtons, then the Scotts.

The gardens consist of 26 acres of grounds with fine walks and river views. There are also impressive trees, herbaceous borders, and flowering shrubs, as well as a walled garden and well-preserved round doocot, dated 1576.

Guided tours. Disabled access. WC. Parking. £.
House not open; gardens open Apr-Sep wknds and Mon Bank Holidays 14.00-18.00; last admission 17.30.
Tel: 01835 823236   Fax: 01835 822474

S99 Monteviot House Gardens

[Map: 6B, F11] Off B6400, 3 miles N of Jedburgh, Borders. (NGR: NT 648247 LR: 74)
With fine views of the River Teviot, Monteviot House, dating from 1740, was later altered and extended. It was a property of the Kerr Marquis of Lothian, and it was here that Jean Elliot, author of 'The Flowers of the Forest', died in 1805. The fine gardens, which have views over the River Teviot, consist of an arboretum, rose garden, herbaceous shrub borders, and the water garden of islands linked by bridges.

Greenhouse and plant stall. WC. Disabled limited access and WC. Parking. Coach parties by prior arrangement only. £.
Garden open Apr-Oct, daily 12.00-17.00; last admission 16.45; house not open.
Tel: 01835 830380 (mornings only)   Fax: 01835 830288

S35 Mount Stuart House

See main entry S35

S38 Paxton House

See main entry S38

V62 Pitmedden Garden (NTS)

There is a 17th-century five-acre walled garden, which is open to the public, and features sundials, pavilions and fountains dotted among formal flower beds. There is also the Museum of Farming Life and visitor centre, as well as a wildlife garden and woodland walk.
See main entry V62

S100 Pitmuies Gardens and Grounds

[Map: 4, 14] Off A932, 7 miles E of Forfar, House of Pitmuies, Guthrie, Angus. (NGR: NO 567497 LR: 54)
The gardens feature mixed herbaceous perennials, delphiniums, old style roses, as well as paved areas with dianthus, violas and other rock plants. There are river and woodland walks, and a woodland and rhododendron garden. House of Pitmuies dates from the 18th century.

Guided tours. Explanatory displays. Picnic areas. WC. Limited disabled access. Car and coach parking. £.
Open Apr-Oct, daily 10.00-17.00.
Tel: 01241 818245

Y161 Pittencrieff House

See main entry Y161

S101 Priorwood Garden and Dried Flower Shop (NTS)

[Map: 6B, F10] Off B6361, in Melrose, by the Abbey, Borders. (NGR: NT 549341 LR: 73)
Overlooked by the ruins of the picturesque abbey, most of the plants in this unusual garden are grown for drying. There is a wide variety of dried flowers in the shop, and the orchard has many old varieties of apple tree.

Explanatory displays. Gift shop. Disabled access to grounds & WC. Parking nearby. £.
Open end Mar-24 Dec, Mon-Sat 10.00-17.00, Sun 13.00-17.00.
Tel: 01896 822493

S40 Rammerscales House

See main entry S40

S102 Royal Botanic Garden

[Map: 6B, E9] 20A Inverleith Row, 1 mile N of Edinburgh Castle, Edinburgh. (NGR: NT 249751 LR: 66)
The Botanic Garden, which covers some 70 acres, was founded as a physic garden in 1670 at Holyrood and moved to Inverleith in 1823. It has the largest rhododendron collection in Britain, and the different areas include an arboretum, a peat garden, as well as rock and heath gardens. There is also a fine herbaceous border, and the plant houses have orchids, cacti and other specialities from a variety of places and climates. The exhibition hall has informative displays, and Inverleith House Gallery features art exhibitions. Full-colour guidebook and map leaflet on sale.

Gift shop. Plant centre. Licensed restaurant and snack bar. WC. Disabled access and WC. Parking. Donations welcome.
Open all year: Feb, daily 9.30-17.00; Mar, daily 9.30-18.00; Apr-Aug, daily 9.30-19.00; Sep, daily 9.30-18.00; Oct, daily 9.30-18.00; Nov-Jan, daily 9.30-16.00; closed Christmas Day and New Year's Day.
Tel: 0131 552 7171   Fax: 0131 552 0382

U17 Rozelle House Galleries and Gardens, Ayr

See main entry U17

S103 Sir Douglas Bader Disabled Garden, Cupar

[Map: 6B, C10] On A913, Duffus Park, Carslogie Road, Cupar, Fife. (NGR: NO 368145 LR: 59)
The Sir Douglas Bader Disabled Garden was opened in 1982 and designed specifically for disabled visitors. There is a small public garden with raised flower borders, raised ponds, an aviary and picnic facilities.

Picnic area. Disabled access. Car parking.
Open all year, daily.
Tel: 01334 412820

S42 Skaill House

See main entry S42

S104 Speyside Heather Centre

[Map: 3B, F10] Off A95, 9 miles SE of Aviemore, Skye of Curr, Dulnain Bridge, Highland. (NGR: NH 980227 LR: 36)

The centre features an indoor exhibition 'Heather Story Exhibition', garden centre specialising in heathers and show garden, craft shop, as well as a gallery and antiques shop.

Guided tours. Explanatory displays. Gift shop. Tearoom/restaurant. Picnic area. WC. Play area and show garden. Disabled access. Car and coach parking. Group concessions. £.

Open Feb-Dec, daily 9.00-18.00, reduced hours in winter – tel to confirm.

Tel: 01479 851359 Fax: 01479 851396
Email: enquiries@heathercentre.com

S105 St Andrews Botanic Garden

[Map: 6B, C10] Off A91, Bassaguard, The Canongate, St Andrews, Fife. (NGR: NO 500162 LR: 59)

The garden, which was founded in 1887-8, was moved to its present site in 1960. It covers some 18 acres, and features a wide range of plants in peat, rock, heath and water gardens, as well as glasshouses.

Guided tours. Explanatory displays. Gift shop. Tea hut. WC. Disabled access. Car and coach parking. Group concessions. £.

Open May-Sep, Mon-Fri 10.00-19.00, Sat-Sun 10.00-16.00; Oct-Apr, Sat-Sun 10.00-16.00.

Tel: 01334 476452

S106 St Mary's Pleasance Gardens, Haddington

[Map: 6B, E10] Off A1, Haddington, East Lothian. (NGR: NT 520736 LR: 66)

The walled garden of a 17th-century house which has been developed as a period Scottish garden.

Parking nearby.

Garden open all year, daily dawn to dusk; house not open.

Tel: 01620 822838

S107 Stonefield Castle Gardens

[Map: 5A, E4] Off A83, 2 miles N of Tarbert, Stonefield, Argyll. (NGR: NR 864717 LR: 62)

Stonefield Castle is a modern mansion, built in 1837, and was held by the Campbells at the end of the 19th century. It is now used as a hotel, and the gardens are open to the public. The gardens feature rhododendrons, rare shrubs, fuchsia, and conifers.

Hotel. Gardens. Parking.

Hotel: accommodation available. Gardens open all year, dawn to dusk.

Tel: 01880 820836 Fax: 01880 820929

S108 Teviot Water Gardens

[Map: 6B, F11] On A698, 5 miles SW of Kelso and 5 miles NE of Jedburgh, Kirkbank House, Eckford, Borders. (NGR: NT 705268 LR: 74)

Located in picturesque Borders countryside, the water gardens are set on four levels and flow into the River Teviot.

Guided tours by appt. Explanatory displays. Gift shop. Smokery. Tearoom. WC. Disabled access. Car parking. Coached by arrangement.

Open Apr-Sep, daily 10.00-17.00, or by appt.

Tel: 01835 850253

Y193 The Hirsel Country Park

See main entry Y193

S44 Threave Garden and Estate (NTS)

The garden has peat and woodland plants, a rock garden, some 200 varieties of daffodil, and herbaceous borders. There is also a walled garden and glasshouses.

See main entry S44

S45 Torosay Castle

The 12 acres of gardens, laid out by Sir Robert Lorimer in 1899, include formal terraces, an Italian statue walk, Japanese garden, walled garden and woodland, and there are fine views.

See main entry S45

S109 University Botanic Garden, Dundee

[Map: 4, J3] Off A85, Riverside Drive, Dundee, Angus. (NGR: NO 394295 LR: 54)

The Botanic Garden, which was founded in 1971, has a fine collection of trees and shrubs in a natural landscape. There are two large tropical and temperate plant houses, as well as an award-winning visitor centre.

Guided tours. Explanatory displays. WC. Disabled access. Car and coach parking. Group concessions. £.

Open Mar-Oct, daily 10.00-16.30; Nov-Feb, daily 10.00-15.30; closed Christmas and New Year.

Tel: 01382 566939

S110 Wilton Lodge Walled Garden, Hawick

[Map: 6B, G10] Off A7, 0.5 miles W of Hawick, Wilton Park, Borders. (NGR: NT 495148 LR: 79)

The garden covers some 107 acres, and there is a wide range of mature trees and extensive shrubberies.

Tearoom. WC. Car and coach parking.

Open all year, daily 7.30-16.00.

Tel: 01450 378023

Top *Inveresk Lodge*
Top right *Arduaine*
Above *Edzell Castle*
Right *Crathes Castle*
Below *Pitmedden Garden*

T: Poets and Writers

The following museums and other sites are associated with Scotland's many poets and writers, including Robert Burns, Walter Scott and Robert Louis Stevenson.

S1 Abbotsford

Sir Walter Scott, the famous Scottish writer and historian, bought Cartley Hole farmhouse, by the Tweed, in 1812, which he renamed Abbotsford. He had the old house demolished in 1822, and it was replaced by the main block of Abbotsford as it is today.
See main entry S1

N1 Aikwood Tower

There is an exhibition about James Hogg, the 'Ettrick Shepherd', the well-known Scottish writer and poet.
See main entry N1

K44 Alloway Old Kirk

The ruin of this old church is where Tam – in Robert Burns's poem 'Tam o' Shanter' – saw the dancing witches. It was already a ruin in Burns's day, and William Burnes, Burns's father, is buried here.
See main entry K44

T1 Bachelors' Club (NTS)

[Map: 6A, F6] Off B744 or B730, 7.5 miles NE of Ayr, Sandgate Street, Tarbolton, Ayrshire. (NGR: NT 430270 LR: 70)
It was here, in an upstairs room, that Robert Burns was initiated into Freemasonry, attended dancing classes, and help found the Bachelors' Club debating society. It is furnished with period items, and contains mementoes of the poet.
Disabled access to ground floor. Car parking. Group concessions. £.
Open (2002) 25 Mar-27 Oct, daily 13.00-17.00; morning visits available for pre-booked groups.
Tel: 01292 541940

T2 Beatrix Potter Exhibition

[Map: 5B, B9] On A9, 15 miles N of Perth, Birnam, Dunkeld, Perthshire. (NGR: NO 035415 LR: 52)
Housed in the 19th-century Birnam Institution, the exhibition will be of interest to children and adults alike in the celebration of Beatrix Potter's literary characters, such as Peter Rabbit, Mr Jeremy Fisher and Mrs Tiggywinkle. The exhibition features the creation of these characters, born from her childhood holidays taken in this picturesque area of Perthshire, using interactive activities.
Explanatory displays. Gift shop. Cafe. Picnic area. WC. Disabled access. Library and IT facilities. Car and coach parking.
Open all year, daily 10.00-17.00; closed Christmas Day and New Year's Day.
Tel: 01350 727674   Fax: 01350 727748
Web: www.birnaminstitute.com Email: birnaminst@aol.com

T3 Bolton Parish Church

[Map: 6B, E10] On B6368, 3 miles S of Haddington, Bolton, East Lothian. (NGR: NT 507701 LR: 66)
Agnes Brown, mother of the poet Robert Burns, as well as his sister Annabella and brother Gilbert are buried in the graveyard of Bolton Parish Church. There has been a church here since 1244, although the present building dates from 1809: the church is open to the public. There is a mort-guard and other items from bodysnatching days in the porch.
Access at all reasonable times; church open daily.

T4 Brig o' Doon, Alloway

[Map: 6A, F6] Off B7024, 2 miles S of Ayr, Alloway, Ayrshire. (NGR: NS 333177 LR: 70)
This old bridge, which crosses the River Doon in a single span, is featured in Robert Burns's poem 'Tam o' Shanter', and is where Tam at last escaped from the witches.
Access at all reasonable times.

Y46 Bright Water Visitor Centre, Kyleakin

Set amid stunning scenery, the inspiring interpretive centre illustrates the cultural and natural history of the area. Exclusive boat trips operate to the island haven on Eilean Ban, featuring a Stevenson Lighthouse, wildlife hide, and Gavin Maxwell's Long Room.
See main entry Y46

T5 Burns Club and Museum, Irvine

[Map: 6A, F6] Off A737, Eglinton Street, Irvine, Ayrshire. (NGR: NS 325388 LR: 70)
The club was founded in 1826 by friends of Robert Burns. The museum contains manuscripts of the first edition of his poems and other mementoes of his life.
Parking. WC.
Open Easter-Sep, Mon, Wed, Fri and Sat 14.30-16.30.
Tel: 01294 274511

T6 Burns Cottage and Museum, Alloway

[Map: 6A, F6] Off B7024, 2 miles S of Ayr, Alloway, Ayrshire. (NGR: NS 335190 LR: 70)
Robert Burns was born in the thatched cottage in

1759. The cottage has been extensively refurbished and features an audio-visual presentation. The adjacent museum contains many mementoes and manuscripts belonging to Scotland's favourite poet, including the original manuscripts of 'Auld Lang Syne' and 'Tam o' Shanter'.

Explanatory displays. Audio-visual presentation. Gift shop. Restaurant. Tea room. WC. Picnic area. Gardens. Children's play area. Combined admission with 'Tam o' Shanter Experience'. Disabled access & WC. Car and coach parking. £.

Open all year: Apr-Oct, daily 9.00-18.00; Nov-Mar 10.00-16.00; Sun 12.00-16.00.

Tel: 01292 441215 Fax: 01292 441750
Web: www.robertburns.org

T7 Burns House Museum, Mauchline

[Map: 6A, F6] Off A716, Mauchline town centre, Ayrshire. (NGR: NS 495272 LR: 70)

Robert Burns once lived in this house. As well as mementos belonging to the poet, there is a large collection of Mauchline boxware, for which the town is famous, and an exhibition devoted to curling and curling stones. There are full audio-visual presentations. A number of Burns' contemporaries are buried in Mauchline Kirkyard, opposite the museum, including 'Holy Willie', Gavin Hamilton and 'Poosie Nansie' (whose tavern is nearby), as well as four of Burns' young daughters.

Guided tours by appt. Explanatory displays. Gift shop. Garden available for picnics. WC. Disabled access. Car and coach parking. £.

Open Easter wknd, then May-Sep, Tue-Sat 11.00-18.00, Sun 14.00-17.00. Telephone to confirm.

Tel: 01290 550045 Fax: 01563 554702

T8 Burns House, Dumfries

[Map: 6B, H8] Off A766, Burns Street, Dumfries, Dumfries and Galloway. (NGR: NX 974758 LR: 84)

Robert Burns and his family lived here from May 1793 until his death in 1796. Furnishings are contemporary with the poet, and there are many mementoes. One of the windows has his name scratched on the pane, which was his habit using his diamond ring. There is also the chair from which he wrote his last poems, and many original letters and manuscripts. The famous Kilmarnock and Edinburgh editions of his work are also on display.

Explanatory displays. Gift shop. WC nearby. Disabled access. Car parking.

Open Apr-Sep, Mon-Sat 10.00-17.00, Sun 14.00-17.00; Oct-Mar, Tue-Sat 10.00-13.00 & 14.00-17.00.

Tel: 01387 255297 Fax: 01387 265081
Web: www.dumgal.gov.uk/sevices/depts/comres/museums/facilities.asp

T9 Burns Mausoleum, Dumfries

[Map: 6B, H8] Off A756, corner of St Michael Street & Brooms Road, Dumfries, Dumfries and Galloway. (NGR: NY 975758 LR: 84)

The mausoleum is in the form of a Greek temple, and contains the tombs of Robert Burns, his wife Jean Armour and six of their children. St Michael's Church is also often open – Burns had a family pew here.

Open at all reasonable times. Get key from Burns House.

Tel: 01387 253374 Fax: 01387 265081

T10 Burns Monument and Gardens, Alloway

[Map: 6A, F6] Off B7024, 2 miles S of Ayr, Alloway, Ayrshire. (NGR: NS 334180 LR: 70)

The Grecian monument to Robert Burns was built in 1823. There are fine garden walks and statues of characters from his poems.

[Burns National Heritage Park] Gift shop. Restaurant. Tea room. WC. Picnic area. Gardens. Children's play area. 'Tam o' Shanter Experience'. Disabled access & WC. Car and coach parking.

Open all year: Apr-Sep 9.00-18.00; Nov-Mar 10.00-16.00; Sun 12.00-16.00.

Y57 Castle House Museum, Dunoon

Features include Highland Mary's Cottage, Mary Campbell, who was from near Dunoon and romantically entwined with Robert Burns.

See main entry Y57

T11 Craigieburn

[Map: 6B, G9] Off A708, 2.5 miles E of Moffat, Craigieburn, Dumfries and Galloway. (NGR: NT 117053 LR: 78)

Craigieburn House, a mansion, was the birthplace of Jean Lorimer, Robert Burns's 'Chloris', and Craigieburn Wood was frequented by Burns about 1789. The garden specialises in rare and unusual plants from south-east Asia. There is a fine gorge, sheltered woodland, formal borders, roses, a bog garden and alpines.

Plants for sale. Parking. £.

Open Easter-Oct, Tue-Sun 12.30-18.00.

Tel: 01683 221250 Fax: 01683 221250

Y72 Dunbeath Heritage Centre

There is an extensive archive of the work of the author Neil M. Gunn. Dunbeath was his birthplace, and he went to school here.

See main entry Y72

T12 Ellisland

[Map: 6B, H8] Off A76, 6 miles N of Dumfries, Ellisland, Dumfries and Galloway. (NGR: NX 930838 LR: 78)

The home of Robert Burns from 1788-91. It was here that Burns tried to farm using new methods. He was unsuccessful and had to become an exciseman, and then moved to Dumfries. Burns wrote 'Tam o' Shanter' here, as well as 'Auld Lang Syne'. The house has been restored. There are displays, an audiovisual presentation, and fine riverside walks.

Guided tours. Explanatory displays. Riverside walks. WC. Car and coach parking. £.
Open Easter-Sep, Mon-Sat 10.00-17.00, Sun 14.00-17.00; Oct-Easter, closed Sun and Mon.
Tel: 01387 740426   Fax: 01387 740426

T13 Globe Inn, Dumfries

[Map: 6B H8] Off A756, 56 High Street, Globe Inn, Dumfries, Dumfries and Galloway.

This has been a hostelry since 1610, and Robert Burns visited the pub often. There is some fine 18th-century panelling, and the bedroom he used has been preserved.

Refreshments and meals. WC. Baby changing facilities. Disabled access with assistance and WC. Car and coach parking
Public house: open Mon-Thu 10.00-23.00, Fri-Sat 10.00-00.00, Sun 12.00-23.00.
Tel: 01387 252335

T14 Grassic Gibbon Centre, Arbuthnott

[Map: 4, H5] On B967, 5.5 miles NE of Laurencekirk, Arbuthnott, Kincardine and Deeside. (NGR: NO 795755 LR: 45)

The centre is dedicated to the life and times of the writer Lewis Grassic Gibbon. His real name was James Leslie Mitchell, and he is the author of *The Scots Quair*, the first volume of which was *Sunset Song*. The centre features information on his life, as well as many mementoes and photographs. All of his titles currently in print are available from the shop, as well as limited editions published by the centre. There is a mail order facility. Grassic Gibbon is buried in the nearby **St Ternan's Church [K127]** at Arbuthnott.

Audiovisual display and exhibition. Gift shop. Tearoom. Picnic area. Children's play area. WC. Disabled access. Groups welcome by appt. Car and coach parking. Group concessions. £.
Open Apr-Oct, daily 10.00-16.30.
Tel: 01561 361668   Fax: 01561 361742
Web: www.grassicgibbon.com Email: lgginfo@grassicgibbon.com

T15 Highland Mary's Monument, Failford

[Map: 6A, F6] On B743, 3 miles W of Mauchline, Failford, Ayrshire. (NGR: NS 458262 LR: 70)

This is believed to be the place where Robert Burns parted from Mary Campbell, his 'Highland Mary', for the last time. They had apparently intended to marry, but the wedding never took place. A monument commemorates the event.

Parking nearby.
Access at all reasonable times.

T16 Highland Mary's Statue, Dunoon

[Map: 5A, D5] Off A815, near pier, Dunoon, Argyll. (NGR: NS 175763 LR: 63)

The statue of Mary Campbell, who is known as 'Highland Mary' from her association with Robert Burns. She was born near Dunoon, and is believed to have been betrothed to Burns. The marriage never took place, and she died the following year.

Car parking.
Access at all reasonable times.

T17 Hugh Miller's Cottage (NTS)

[Map: 3B, E9] Off A832, Church Street, Cromarty, Ross-shire, Highland. (NGR: NH 787675 LR: 21)

Hugh Miller's Cottage features an exhibition about Hugh Miller, a stonemason who became an eminent geologist and writer. Miller was born in this thatched cottage in 1802, although it was built by his great-grandfather about 1698. The cottage garden was re-developed in 1988.

Explanatory displays. Cottage garden. Car and coach parking. Group concessions. £.
Open (2002) 1 May-29 Sep, daily 12.00-17.00.
Tel: 01381 600245

T18 J. M. Barrie's Birthplace, Kirriemuir (NTS)

[Map: 4, I3] On A936, 9 Brechin Road, Kirriemuir, Angus. (NGR: NO 388542 LR: 54)

Sir James Matthew (J. M.) Barrie, creator of Peter Pan, was born in Kirriemuir in 1860. The upper floors of the house are furnished as they might have been when he lived here, while the adjacent house features an exhibition covering his works.

Explanatory displays. Shop. Tearoom. WC. Disabled access & stairlift. Car and coach parking. Group concessions. Parties welcome but must book. £.
Open (2002) 25 Mar-27 Oct, Sat-Wed 12.00-17.00.
Tel: 01575 572646

T19 James Hogg Monument

[Map: 6B, G9] Off B7009, 14 miles W of Hawick, Ettrick, Borders. (NGR: NT 265145 LR: 79)

The monument stands on the site of the birthplace in 1770 of the poet and writer, James Hogg, the 'Ettrick Shepherd', who was a contemporary of Sir Walter Scott. Hogg died in 1835, and is buried in the nearby churchyard.

Car parking.
Access at all reasonable times.

T20 Jane Welsh Carlyle Museum

[Map: 6B, E10] Off A1, Lodge Street, W end of High Street, Haddington, East Lothian. (NGR: NT 511739 LR: 66)

The museum, housed in the restored childhood

home of Jane Baillie Welsh, features Jane Welsh Carlyle. Jane was the only child of Dr John Welsh, a 19th-century Haddington medical practitioner. In 1821 she met Thomas Carlyle, the writer and philosopher, who she later married, see **Thomas Carlyle's Birthplace, Ecclefechan [T31]**.
Explanatory displays. Garden. WC. Parking nearby. Group concessions. £.
Open Apr-Sep, Wed-Sat 14.00-17.00.
Tel: 01620 823738 Fax: 01620 825147 Email: lamp_of_lothian@hotmail.com

T21 John Buchan Centre

[Map: 6B, F9] On A701, 5 miles E of Biggar, Broughton, Borders. (NGR: NT 113356 LR: 72)
The centre, housed in the Old Free Kirk, features John Buchan, 1st Lord Tweedsmuir, author of *The Thirty Nine Steps*. Buchan was also a lawyer, politician, soldier, historian, and the Governor-General of Canada. Broughton village was his mother's birthplace and he regularly holidayed here.
Explanatory displays. Bookshop. WC. Disabled access. Car and coach parking. £.
Open Easter wknd, then May-Sep , daily 14.00-17.00.
Tel: 01899 221050 Fax: 01899 221050

T22 Michael Bruce's Cottage

[Map: 5B, C9] Off A911, 4 miles E of Milnathort, The Coddles, Kinnesswood, Perthshire. (NGR: NO 175030 LR: 58)
The 18th-century pantiled crofter's cottage houses displays relating to the life of Michael Bruce, the poet who was born here in 1746, as well as on local history, including the manufacture of vellum and parchment.
Guided tours by appt. Garden. Guide dogs not permitted. Parking nearby.
Open Apr-Sep, daily 10.00-18.00.
Tel: 01592 840203

T23 National Burns Memorial Tower, Mauchline

[Map: 6A, F6] Off A76, Mauchline, Ayrshire. (NGR: NS 495274 LR: 70)
Opened in 1896 as a memorial to Robert Burns on the centenary of his death, there is an interpretation centre on the upper floors charting the life of Robert Burns in Mauchline.
Open on selected days and by arrangement.
Tel: 01290 551916

T24 Neil M. Gunn Memorial Viewpoint

[Map: 3B, E9] Off A834, Heights of Brae, Strathpeffer, Ross-shire. (NGR: NH 480580 LR: 26)
Neil M. Gunn, the well-known Scottish author, lived nearby, and there are fine views from the memorial.
Parking.
Access at all reasonable times.

T25 Robert Burns Centre, Dumfries

[Map: 6B, H8] Off A756, Mill Road, Dumfries, Dumfries and Galloway. (NGR: NX 969760 LR: 84)
Housed in the town's 18th-century water mill on the banks of the River Nith, the award-winning museum covers the years that Robert Burns spent in Dumfries in the 1790s. There is an audio-visual presentation, as well as many items connected with the poet.
Explanatory displays. Audio-visual presentation. Gift shop. Gallery. Cafe bistro. WC. Disabled access. Induction loop. Car and coach parking. £ (audio-visual only).
Open all year: Apr-Sep, Mon-Sat 10.00-20.00, Sun 14.00-17.00; Oct-Mar, Tue-Sat 10.00-13.00 & 14.00-17.00.
Tel: 01387 264808 Fax: 01387 265081
Web: www.dumgal.gov.uk/sevices/depts/comres/museums/facilities.asp

T26 Robinson Crusoe Statue

[Map: 6B, C10] Off A915, 3.5 miles NE of Methil, Lower Largo, Fife. (NGR: NO 415025 LR: 59)
The bronze statue of Alexander Selkirk, the real-life sailor on whom Daniel Defoe based his famous character in *Robinson Crusoe*. The statue stands on the site of Selkirk's house, although the real-life Selkirk seems to have been a lot less sympathetic than Robinson Crusoe.
Access at all reasonable times.

T27 Scott Monument

[Map: 6B, E9] On A1, Princes Street, East Princes Street Gardens, near Waverley Station, Edinburgh. (NGR: NT 258739 LR: 66)
The Scott Monument is a prominent Gothic memorial to Sir Walter Scott, one of Scotland's most influential writers, in the heart of Edinburgh, close to Waverley station – named after his novels. It is possible to climb the 287 steps (200 feet) to the top of the monument, from where there are fine views of the city. Not for the terminally unfit or claustrophobic: although there is a souvenir ticket/certificate for those willing to try.
Small gift area. £.
Open Mar-May, daily 10.00-18.00; Jun-Sep, Mon-Sat 9.00-20.00, Sun 10.00-18.00; Oct, daily 10.00-18.00; Nov-Feb daily 10.00-16.00; closed at dusk if earlier than above.
Tel: 0131 529 4068 Web: www.cac.org.uk

T28 Scott's View

[Map: 6B, F11] On B6536, 3 miles E of Melrose, Borders. (NGR: NT 394343 LR: 74)
This spot is associated with Sir Walter Scott, the famous writer, who is buried at **Dryburgh Abbey [J12]**. He is said to have come here for inspiration and loved the view, and when his mile-long funeral procession passed by here on the way to the abbey, his horse halted here of its own accord.
Access at all reasonable times.

Y175 Sir Walter Scott's Courtroom, Selkirk

In the courtroom are the bench and chair from which Sir Walter Scott, who was Sheriff of Selkirk, judged cases for some 30 years. Also on display are portraits of Scott himself, James Hogg, Mungo Park, as well as watercolours. There is an audio-visual presentation, and information on the history of the building and the civic history of the Royal Burgh of Selkirk.
See main entry Y175

T29 Souter Johnnie's Cottage, Kirkoswald (NTS)

[Map: 6A, G6] Off A77, 4 miles SW of Maybole, Kirkoswald, Ayrshire. (NGR: NS 240070 LR: 70)
The home of John Davidson the 'souter' – cobbler – in Robert Burns' poem 'Tam o' Shanter'. The thatched cottage features mementoes of Burns, as well as tools and exhibits of the cobbler's craft. The adjacent 'ale-house' has life-size stone statues of Burns' characters.
Explanatory displays. Cottage garden. WC. Disabled access. Limited parking. £
Open (2002) 25 Mar-27 Oct, daily 11.30-17.00.
Tel: 01655 760603

Y181 St Ronan's Wells Interpretive Centre

The centre features memorabilia of Sir Walter Scott with information and photographs about the local Cleikum ceremony and the St Ronan's Border Games. The site was visited by Scott and used in one of his novels.
See main entry Y181

K127 St Ternan's Church

Lewis Grassic Gibbon is buried in the graveyard – the **Grassic Gibbon Centre [T14]** is nearby.
See main entry K127

T30 Tam o' Shanter Experience

[Map: 6A, F6] Off A719, 2 miles S of Ayr, Murdoch's Loan, Alloway, Ayrshire. (NGR: NS 325185 LR: 70)
Tam o' Shanter Experience features audio-visual presentations using all the latest multimedia techniques. Brings to life 'Tam o' Shanter', one of Burns's best-loved poems. Other local places described in the poem are **Alloway Kirkyard [K44]**, where his father is buried, and the **Brig o' Doon [T4]**, where Tam finally escaped from the witches. Nearby is **Burns Cottage and Museum [T6]**, and **Burns Monument and Gardens [T10]**.
Audio-visual presentations. Gift shop. Restaurant. Gardens and

children's play area. WC. Disabled access. Car and coach parking. Group concessions. £
Open all year, daily 9.00-17.00; closed Christmas and New Year.
Tel: 01292 443700   Fax: 01292 441750   Web: www.robertburns.org

T31 Thomas Carlyle's Birthplace, Ecclefechan (NTS)

[Map: 6B, H9] Off M74, 6 miles SE of Lockerbie, The Arched House, Ecclefechan, Dumfries and Galloway. (NGR: NY 193745 LR: 85)
Thomas Carlyle was born here in the Arched House in 1795, the year before Burns died. Carlyle was a fine essayist, historian, and social reformer. There is the bedroom where Carlyle was born, and a small museum with a collection of photographs, manuscripts and other documents. There is also a museum to his wife, **Jane Welsh Carlyle Museum [T20]**, at Haddington.
Explanatory displays. WC. Car and coach parking. Group concessions. £
Open (2002) 25 Mar-29 Sep, Thu-Mon 13.00-17.00.
Tel: 01576 300666

T32 Vennel Gallery, Irvine

[Map: 6A, F6] Off A737, Irvine, Ayrshire. (NGR: NS 325388 LR: 70)
A contemporary gallery showing a wide range of art and craft exhibitions. It also includes the heckling shop where Robert Burns used to live and work.
Parking nearby. Sales area and craft shop. WC. Disabled facilities.
Open all year.
Tel: 01294 275059   Web: www.northayrshiremuseums.org.uk
Fax: 01294 275059   Email: vennel@globalnet.co.uk

T33 Writers' Museum

[Map: 6B, E9] Lady Stair's Close, Lawnmarket, Royal Mile, Edinburgh. (NGR: NT 255735 LR: 66)
The Writers' Museum, located in Lady Stair's Close of 1622, houses a museum displaying various mementoes and portraits Robert Burns, Sir Walter Scott and Robert Louis Stevenson. Items include Burns's writing desk, Scott's chessboard, dining table and the printing press on which the Waverley novels were produced, and a significant collection about Stevenson. A programme of temporary exhibitions feature other Scottish writers.
Sales area. Parking nearby.
Open all year, daily 10.00-17.00; during Festival only, also Sun 14.00-17.00.
Tel: 0131 529 4901   Web: www.cac.org.uk
Fax: 0131 220 5057   Email: enquiries@writersmuseum.demon.co.uk

U: *Artists*

The following museums, galleries and other sites are associated with (or have collections of work by) many of Scotland's artists.

U1 Aberdeen Art Gallery

[Map: 4, G5] Off Union Street, Schoolhill, Aberdeen (NGR: NJ 940065 LR: 38)
The gallery features 18th- to 20th-century Scottish art and a fine collection of modern paintings, including works by Spencer, Nash and Bacon. There are also watercolours, sculpture and decorative arts, and a print room and art library.
Guided tours. Special events and exhibitions. Gift shop. Tearoom. WC. Disabled access. Car parking nearby.
Open all year: Mon-Sat 10.00-17.00, Sun 14.00-17.00; closed 25/26 Dec and 1/2 Jan.
Tel: 01224 523700 Fax: 01224 632133
Web: www.aberdeencity.gov.uk Email: info@aagm.co.uk

S8 Blairquhan

There is a good collection of pictures, including Scottish Colourists.
See main entry S8

S10 Broughton House and Garden (NTS)

This was the home and studio of the artist E. A. Hornel, one of the 'Glasgow Boys', from 1901-33 . It contains many of his works, along with other paintings by contemporary artists.
See main entry S10

S70 Broughton Place

There are paintings and crafts by living British artists for sale.
See main entry S70

U2 City Art Centre

[Map: 6B, E9] 2 Market Street, near Waverley Station, Edinburgh. (NGR: NT 261739 LR: 66)
City Art Centre houses a permanent fine art collection, including works by McTaggart, Peploe, Fergusson, Davie, Blackadder, Paolozzi and Bellany. It also stages a changing programme of temporary international exhibitions. Educational programme of workshops, events and lectures.
Explanatory displays. Gift shop. Restaurant/cafe. Parking nearby. Disabled access. £ (special exhibitions only).
Open all year, Mon-Sat, 10.00-17.00, Sun during Festival and special exhibitions.
Tel: 0131 529 3993 Fax: 0131 529 3986 Web: www.cac.org.uk
Email: enquiries@city-art-centre.demon.co.uk

U3 Dean Gallery, Edinburgh

[Map: 6B, E9] Off A90 or A8, 73 Belford Road, Edinburgh. (NGR: NT 235739 LR: 66)
The modern art gallery is home to the Paolozzi Gift of sculpture and graphic art. It has an important collection of Dada and Surrealism, including works by Dali, Magritte, Picasso and Miro. There is a programme of temporary exhibitions.
Explanatory displays. Shop. Cafe. Parking.
Open daily.
Tel: 0131 624 6200 Web: www.natgalscot.ac.uk Email: deaninfo@natgalscot.ac.uk

S18 Duff House, Banff (HS)

The house is now used to display works of art from the **National Galleries of Scotland [U13]**, and there is a programme of changing exhibitions, as well as musical and other events.
See main entry S18

U4 Fergusson Gallery, Perth

[Map: 5B, C9] Off A912, Marshall Place on corner with Tay Street, Perth. (NGR: NO 115235 LR: 58)
The gallery is devoted to the work of John Duncan Fergusson (1874-1961), a Scottish colourist painter, and houses the largest collection of his work. There is also an extensive archive, which can be consulted by appointment.
Explanatory displays. Gift shop. WC. Car and coach parking.
Open all year, Mon-Sat 10.00-17.00; closed Christmas and New Year.
Tel: 01738 441944 Fax: 01738 621152
Web: www.pkc.gov.uk/fergussongallery.htm

U5 Gallery of Modern Art

[Map: 6B, E7] Off M8, Queen Street, Glasgow. (NGR: NS 590655 LR: 64)
Opened in 1996, the Gallery of Modern Art is set in a fine refurbished neoclassical building in the centre of the city. It houses a collection of post-war art and design, covering some four floors of display areas, themed to reflect the elements of fire, earth, water and air. Works are by Niki De Saint Phalle, Salgado and Bersudsky, as well as by Scottish artists such as Howson, Bellany, Davie, Wiszniewski and Watt.
Shop. Refreshments. WC. Disabled access. Parking nearby.
Open all year, Mon-Thu and Sat 9.30-18.00, Fri and Sun 11.00-17.00.
Tel: 0141 229 1996 Fax: 0141 204 5316 Web: www.glasgow.gov.uk

U6 Glasgow School of Art

[Map: 6B, E7] Off M8, 167 Renfrew Street, Glasgow. (NGR: NS 593659 LR: 64)
The Glasgow School of Art is Charles Rennie Mackintosh's architectural masterpiece. Still a working art school, the regular guided tours take the visitor along

the corridors of the school, through the Mackintosh Room, and finish in one of Mackintosh's most celebrated interiors, the Library.

Guided tours and brochure. Gift shop. Cafe. WC. Parking nearby. ££.
Open all year, Mon-Fri 10.00-17.00, Sat 10.00-13.00; Jul-Aug, Sat-Sun 10.00-15.00; guided tours Mon-Fri 11.00 and 14.00, Sat 10.30 and 11.30; Jul-Aug, Sat-Sun 10.30, 11.30 and 13.00; closed Christmas and New Year.
Tel: 0141 353 4526 Fax: 0141 353 4526
Web: www.gsa.ac.uk Email: shop@gsa.ac.uk

U7 Gracefield Art Centre

[Map: 6B, H8] Off A75, 28 Edinburgh Road, Dumfries, Dumfries and Galloway. (NGR: NY 975765 LR: 78)

The centre has a permanent collection of Scottish painting from the 1890s until the present day. There is a shop with local arts and crafts, and temporary exhibitions of local, national and international artists.
Explanatory displays. Cafe and bar. WC. Garden and play area. Disabled access to ground floor only. Car and coach parking.
Open all year, Tue-Sat 10.00-17.00; gallery building open Apr-Sep, 12.00-16.00 (galleries closed 12.00-14.00 Sat).
Tel: 01387 262084

U8 House for an Art Lover

[Map: 6B, E7] Off M8, 2 miles W of city centre, Bellahouston Park, Glasgow. (NGR: NS 547637 LR: 64)

Situated in a park with Victorian walled gardens, the house was completed in 1996 although it was designed by Charles Rennie Mackintosh in 1901. There is an exhibition on Mackintosh, and audio-visual presentation on the building of the house, as well as the Art Lovers Shop and Cafe.
Guided tours. Explanatory displays. Audiovisual presentation. Gift shop. Cafe. WC. Disabled access. Car and coach parking. Group concessions. ££
Open: Exhibition Apr-Sep, Sun-Thu 10.00-16.00; Fri closed; Sat 10.00-15.00; Oct-Mar, Sat-Sun 10.00-16.00, Mon-Fri tel to check; Art Lovers Cafe and Shop open all year, daily 10.00-17.00.
Tel: 0141 353 4770 Web: www.houseforanartlover.co.uk
Fax: 0141 353 4771 Email: info@houseforanartlover.co.uk

U9 Hunterian Art Gallery

[Map: 6B, E7] Off M8, 82 Hillhead Street, University of Glasgow, Glasgow. (NGR: NS 597655 LR: 64)

The gallery is named after Dr William Hunter, who bequeathed the core of the collection to the university. The collection has since grown, and there are important works by Whistler, Spanish paintings, British art and sculpture, and a recreation of Charles Rennie Mackintosh's home at 6 Florentine Terrace, as well as changing selections from the University's large collection of Mackintosh's work. The print collection has some 15,000 items, from Old Masters to modern day, and there is a programme of print exhibitions.
Explanatory displays. Gift shop. Sculpture courtyard. WC. Parking nearby.

Open all year: main gallery Mon-Sat 9.30-17.00; Mackintosh House 9.30-12.30 and 13.30-17.00; tel for Public Hols closures.
Tel: 0141 330 5431 Web: www.hunterian.gla.ac.uk
Fax: 0141 330 3618 Email: hunter@museum.gla.ac.uk

U10 James Paterson Museum

[Map: 6B, H7] On A702, 9 miles SW of Thornhill, Meadowcroft, North Street, Moniaive, Dumfries and Galloway. (NGR: NX 780909 LR: 78)

The museum charts the life and times of the artist James Paterson, one of the Glasgow Boys, who is well known for his painted landscapes, portraits and flowers. There is memorabilia, works and a reference library, as well as a 'Monet' garden and records of the location of James Paterson's works.
Explanatory displays. Free tea and coffee. WC. Garden. Disabled access and WC. Parking nearby.
Open Easter-Sep, Fri-Sun 10.00-18.00, holiday Mons 10.00-18.00, Tue-Thu by appt.
Tel: 01848 200583

U11 Kelvingrove Art Gallery and Museum

[Map: 6B, E7] Off M8, Argyll Street, Kelvingrove, 1 mile W of centre, Glasgow. (NGR: NS 570665 LR: 64)

The art gallery houses a good collection of pictures, from works by Giorgione and Rembrandt to French Impressionists, Post-Impressionists, and Scottish artists from the 17th century to the present day. There are also displays of sculpture, porcelain, silver and a magnificent collection of arms and armour. One area concentrates on the 'Glasgow Style', and features furniture by Charles Rennie Mackintosh. There are also displays on archaeology, ethnology and natural history, as well as an area devoted to Scottish wildlife.
Guided tours. Explanatory displays. Gift shop. Cafe. Picnic area. WC. Disabled access. Car and coach parking.
Open all year, Mon-Sat 10.00-17.00, Sun 11.00-17.00; closed Christmas and New Year.
Tel: 0141 287 2699 Fax: 0141 287 2690 Web: www.glasgow.gov.uk/cls

Y112 Kirkcaldy Museum and Art Gallery

Set in lovely grounds, the museum features a fine collection of 18th- and 21st-century Scottish paintings, including works by McTaggart and Peploe. There are also colourful displays of Kirkcaldy's famous Wemyss ware pottery in the museum cafe.
See main entry Y112

U12 Lillie Art Gallery

[Map: 6A, D6] Off A867, Station Road, Milngavie, Glasgow. (NGR: NS 545745 LR: 64)

The gallery has a collection of mainly 20th-century Scottish painting, prints, sculpture and ceramics. Tem-

porary exhibition programme of fine and applied art, as well as exhibitions from the permanent collection. *Shop. Disabled access. Parking.*
Open all year: Tue-Fri 10.00-13.00 and 14.00-17.00, Sat 14.00-17.00.
Tel: 0141 578 8847   Web: www.eastdunbarton.gov.uk
Fax: 0141 570 0244   Email: hildegarde.berwick@eastdunbarton.gov.uk

Y133 Montrose Museum and Art Gallery

The museum has displays of paintings by local artists and sculpture by William Lamb.
See main entry Y133

U13 National Gallery of Scotland, Edinburgh

[Map: 6B, E9] The Mound, Princes Street, Edinburgh. (NGR: NT 255738 LR: 66)
Recognised as one of Europe's best smaller galleries, the National Gallery of Scotland is housed in a fine classical building, designed by William Playfair and opened in 1859. It features works by Raphael, Monet, El Greco, Vermeer, Rembrandt, Constable, Titian, Velaquez, Van Gough, Turner and Gauguin. It also houses a major Scottish collection, including Wilkie, Ramsay, Raeburn and McTaggart.
Guided tours by arrangement. Gift shop. WC. Acoustic guide for visually impaired. Disabled access. Parking nearby. Charge for major exhibitions.
Open all year: Mon-Sat 10.00-17.00, Sun 14.00-17.00; closed Christmas and New Year.
Tel: 0131 624 6200   Web: www.natgalscot.ac.uk
Fax: 0131 332 4939   Email: nginfo@natgalscot.ac.uk

S37 No 28 Charlotte Square, Edinburgh (NTS)

There is a fine collection of 20th-century Scottish paintings.
See main entry S37

Y157 Paisley Museum and Art Galleries

The gallery has many 19th-century Scottish paintings, and there is a fine ceramic collection.
See main entry Y157

S38 Paxton House

Paxton is now an outstation of the **National Galleries of Scotland**, and houses 70 paintings.
See main entry S38

U14 Peter Anson Gallery

[Map: 4, E3] Off A942, Town House West, Cluny Place, Buckie, Moray. (NGR: NJ 425655 LR: 28)
The gallery, housed in the public library, features watercolours of coastal fishing communities by Peter Anson. The works cover fishing and fishing life throughout Scotland, as well as in other countries.
Explanatory displays. Museum shop. Parking nearby.
Open all year: Mon-Fri 10.00-20.00, Sat 10.00-12.00.
Tel: 01309 673701   Web: www.moray.org/museums/
Fax: 01309 675863   Email: museums@moray.gov.uk

U15 Queen's Cross Church

[Map: 6B, E7] Off M8, 0.5 miles W of centre, 870 Garscube Road, Glasgow. (NGR: NS 575655 LR: 64)
The church, now the headquarters for the Charles Rennie Mackintosh Society, is the only church which was designed by Mackintosh, and has Gothic and Japanese influences. It was built in 1898, and has been extensively restored, and has fine stained glass and relief carving on wood and stonework. There is a small exhibition area, reference library and specialist shop.
Guided tours by appt. Explanatory displays. Gift shop. Refreshments. WC. Car and some coach parking. Donations.
Open all year, Mon-Sat 10.00-17.00, Sun 14.00-17.00; closed some pub hols.
Tel: 0141 946 6600   Fax: 0141 945 2321
Web: www.crmsociety.com   Email: info@crmsociety.com

U16 Robert Clapperton's Daylight Photographic Studio

[Map: 6B, F10] Off A7, The Studio, 28 Scotts Place, Selkirk, Borders. (NGR: NT 475285 LR: 73)
One of the oldest surviving daylight photographic studios in Britain, which is located in the building used by Robert Clapperton in 1867. The studio is set up as a working museum, and demonstrations of black and white print processing in the original dark room can be arranged. Archive photographs and postcards are for sale.
Guided tours. Explanatory displays. Disabled access. Parking nearby. Group concessions. £.
Open May-Aug, Fri-Sun 14.00-16.00; tel for other times.
Tel: 01750 20523

U17 Rozelle House Galleries and Gardens, Ayr

[Map: 6A, F6] Off B7024, to S of Ayr, Monument Road, Rozelle Park, Ayrshire. (NGR: NS 338190 LR: 70)
The gallery, housed in an 18th-century building remodelled by David Bryce in 1830, holds art and museum exhibitions. There is a temporary exhibition programme throughout the year featuring British and international artists. Henry Moore bronze sculptures are in the sculpture park, and there are also high quality craft exhibitions. There are also fine gardens, and items of historical interest. Near **Burns Cottage [T6]**.
Craft shop. Coffee shop. Picnic area. WC. Disabled access. Car parking.
Open Apr-Oct, Mon-Sat 10.00-17.00, Sun 14.00-17.00; Nov-Mar, Mon-Sat 10.00-17.00; closed Xmas and New Year's day.
Tel: 01292 445447   Fax: 01292 442065

Y10 Scotland Street School Museum, Glasgow

The Scotland Street School was designed by Charles Rennie Mackintosh in 1904, and has fine leaded glass towers and tiled entrance hall.

See main entry Y10

U18 Scottish National Gallery of Modern Art, Edinburgh

[Map: 6B, E9] 75 Belford Road, Edinburgh. (NGR: NT 235737 LR: 66)
This gallery houses Scotland's finest collection of 20th-century paintings and graphic art, and includes works by Picasso, Matisse, Giacometti, Sickert and Hockney. It also an unrivalled collection of 20th-century Scottish art, from the Colourists to the contemporary scene, German expressionism and French art. One of the most important Dada and Surrealist collections in the world.

Sales area. Refreshments. WC. Disabled access & WC. Parking.
Open all year: Mon-Sat 10.00-17.00 & Sun 14.00-17.00; extended opening during Festival; closed 25/26 Dec & 1 Jan.
Tel: 0131 624 6200 Web: www.natgalscot.ac.uk Email: gmaininfo@natgalscot.ac.uk

Y12 Scottish National Portrait Gallery, Edinburgh

The gallery building, designed by the architect Sir Robert Rowland Anderson in the 1880s, resembles a Florentine palace. The gallery provides a visual history of Scotland from the 16th century until the present day, with portraits of the people who shaped it: royals and rebels, poets and philosophers, heroes and villains. Among the most famous are Mary Queen of Scots, Ramsay's portrait of David Hume and Raeburn's Sir Walter Scott. Other artists include Van Dyck, Gainsborough, Copley, Rodin, Kokoschka and Torvaldsen. The building also houses the Scottish National Collection of Photography.

Guided tours if booked in advance (0131 624 6506). Gift shop. Restaurant. WC. Disabled access and WC. Parking nearby.
Open all year, Mon-Sat 10.00-17.00, Sun 12.00-17.00; extended hours during Festival; closed 25 Dec-1 Jan.
Tel: 0131 556 8921 Fax: 0131 332 4939
Web: www.natgalscot.ac.uk Email: enquiries@natgalscot.ac.uk

Y182 Stewartry Museum

The museum's features include illustrations, pottery and jewellery by Jesse M. King, and the work of E. A. Taylor, her husband. There are also displays on Phyllis Bone and other Kirkcudbright artists.

See main entry Y182

U19 The Hill House (NTS)

[Map: 5A, D6 On B832, 7.5 miles NE of Dumbarton, Upper Colquhoun Street, N of Helensburgh. (NGR: NS 300838 LR: 56)
The Hill House was designed by Charles Rennie Mackintosh after being commissioned by Walter Blackie, the Glasgow publisher, in 1902. It is the finest of his domestic creations, as the commission included the house, garden, fittings, decoration and furniture, creating an elegant and stylish home.

Explanatory displays. Gift shop in the original laundry. Tearoom in the original kitchen. WC. Parking. Groups must pre-booked. £££.
Open (2002) 25 Mar-27 Oct, daily 13.30-17.30.
Tel: 01463 673900 Fax: 01463 674685

Y17 The Lighthouse

The centre, housed in a building designed by Charles Rennie Mackintosh, features a Mackintosh Interpretation Centre, interactive exhibits, Young Designers' Gallery, IT hotspot, and temporary exhibitions.

See main entry Y17

U20 Tolbooth Art Centre

[Map: 6B, I7] Off A711, High Street, Kirkcudbright, Dumfries and Galloway. (NGR: NX 684509 LR: 83)
The centre, which is housed in the 17th-century tolbooth, features displays on the town's history as an artists' colony from the 1880s, with paintings by Kirkcudbright artists.

Guided tours by appt. Audiovisual presentation. Explanatory displays. Gift shop. Tearoom. WC. Disabled access. Parking nearby. Group concessions. £.
Open all year, Mon-Sat 11.00-16.00.
Tel: 01557 331556 Fax: 01557 331643
Web: www.dumgal.gov.uk/sevices/depts/comres/museums/facilities.asp Email: davidd@dumgal.gov.uk

U21 William Lamb Memorial Studio, Montrose

[Map: 4 I5] In Montrose, Market Street, off the High Street, Montrose, Angus.
The studio of the sculptor William Lamb, born in 1893, has been preserved, and on show are examples of his sculptures, etchings, paintings and drawings. His studio features many of his modelling and etching tools.

Guided tours on request. Explanatory displays. Sales area. WC. Limited disabled access. Parking nearby.
Open Jul-mid Sep, daily 14.00-17.00; other times by appt.
Tel: 01674 673232 Web: www.angus.gov.uk Email: montrose.museum@angus.gov.uk

U22 Willow Tearooms

[Map: 6B, E7] Off M8, 217 Sauchiehall Street, Glasgow. (NGR: NS 585655 LR: 64)
Located in a building designed by Charles Rennie Mackintosh, and dating 1904-28, the Willow Tearoom features original glass and mirror work, and doors. The tearoom serves light meals, teas and coffee.

Restaurant. WC. Parking nearby.
Open all year, Mon-Sat 9.00-17.00, Sun 12.00-17.00, closed Christmas Day.
Tel: 0141 332 0521 Web: www.willowtearooms.co.uk
Fax: 0141 204 5242 Email: tea@willowtearooms.co.uk

Above *Burns Mausoleum*
Left *Fergusson Gallery*
Below left *Scott Monument*
Below *Canongate Cemetery*
Bottom *Ellisland*

V1: Folk, Fishing and Agriculture

The following museums all have significant collections of material on folk, fishing or agriculture.

V1 Aberdeenshire Farming Museum, Mintlaw

[Map: 4, E5] On A950, 8 miles W of Peterhead, 1 mile W of Mintlaw, Aden Country Park, Aberdeenshire. (NGR: NJ 994480 LR: 30)

The award-winning heritage centre, housed in 19th-century farm buildings, features fine displays charting 200 years of farming history and innovation. The newly reconstructed farm of Hareshowe illustrates a 1950s' family farm.

Tearoom. WC. Disabled access. Car and coach parking.
Open May-Sep daily 11.00-16.30; Apr & Oct wknds only 12.00-16.30; last admission 30 mins before closing; park open all year daily 7.00-22.00.
Tel: 01771 622906/813390 Web: www.aberdeenshire.gov.uk/heritage
Fax: 01771 622884 Email: heritage@aberdeenshire.gov.uk

V2 Aberfeldy Water Mill

[Map: 5B, B8] Off A827, Mill Street, Aberfeldy, Perthshire. (NGR: NN 855490 LR: 52)

The mill was built in 1825 and restored in 1983. It stands on a site where there has been a mill for some 400 years. The process of grinding oatmeal can be viewed, and stone-ground oatmeal and other products purchased. There is an audio-visual presentation on the importance of the miller in Scottish society.

Guided tours available. Explanatory displays. Gift shop. Tearoom. WC. Car and coach parking. Group concessions. £.
Open Easter-Oct, Mon-Sat 10.00-16.30, Sun 12.00-16.30.
Tel: 01887 820803 Web: www.aberfeldy-watermill.co.uk
Fax: 01334 652912 Email: reception@aberfeldy-watermill.fsnet.co.uk

V3 Aldie Water Mill and the Tain Pottery

[Map: 3B, D10] Off A9, 1 mile S of Tain, Aldie, Ross-shire, Highland. (NGR: NH 795804 LR: 21)

The water mill, which dates from 1860, although there has been a mill here since the 16th century, has been restored to working order. Crafts are for sale, including items from the Tain Pottery, baskets, carving and weaving.

Explanatory displays. Gift shop. WC. Limited disabled access. Car and coach parking. Group concessions. £.
Open Apr-Sep, daily 9.30-17.30; Oct-Mar, Mon-Sat 11.00-16.00.
Tel: 01862 893786 Fax: 01862 893787

V4 Angus Folk Museum (NTS)

[Map: 4, 13] Off A94, 4.5 miles W of Forfar, Kirkwynd Cottages, Glamis, Angus. (NGR: NO 385467 LR: 54)

Housed in row of picturesque stone-roofed 19th-century cottages, the museum features the fine Angus Folk Collection of domestic equipment and cottage furniture. A stone steading, across the Wynd, has 'The Life on the Land Exhibition', illustrating rural life in Angus over the past 200 years. Also in Glamis is a fine carved Pictish stone, and the church and healing well of St Fergus (see **Glamis Church [F17]**). **Glamis Castle [N30]** is also nearby.

Parking nearby. Explanatory displays. Gift shop. Disabled access. WC.
Open (2002) 25 Mar-27 Oct, Sat-Wed 12.00-17.00.
Tel: 01307 840288 Fax: 01307 840233

V5 Arbuthnott Museum and Art Gallery, Peterhead

[Map: 4, E6] Off A952, St Peter Street, Peterhead, Aberdeenshire. (NGR: NK 132464 LR: 30)

The museum features displays of local exhibits on fishing, whaling and maritime history, and there is also a large collection of British coins and Inuit art. There is a programme of changing exhibitions.

Guided tours. Gift shop. Parking nearby.
Open all year: Mon-Tue and Thu-Sat 10.30-13.30 and 14.30-17.00; Wed 10.30-13.00; closed Sun and pub hols.
Tel: 01779 477778 Web: www.aberdeenshire.gov.uk/ahc.htm
Email: general@abheritage.demon.co.uk.

V6 Arnol Blackhouse Museum (HS)

[Map: 3A, B4] Off A858, 12 miles NW of Stornoway, Arnol, Lewis. (NGR: NB 312495 LR: 8)

A traditional Lewis dwelling, a 'blackhouse', built without mortar and roofed with thatch on a timber framework. The people lived at one end of the house, while the beasts were housed at the other. It has a central peat fire in the kitchen, although no chimney, and retains many of its original furnishings. Blackhouses are said to have been used for hundreds of years, but were still being built as late as 1885 and their use only declined after World War I.

Kiosk. Parking nearby. £.
Open Apr-Sep, Mon-Sat 9.30-18.30; Oct-Mar, Mon-Sat 9.30-4.30; closed Sun all year.
Tel: 01851 710395

V7 Arran Heritage Museum

[Map: 6A, F5] On A841, 1.5 miles N of Brodick, Rosaburn, Arran. (NGR: NS 013377 LR: 69)

The museum features an original 18th-century croft farm with smiddy, cottage, dairy, coach house and stables. There is a large garden and special display area, which is changed annually, as well as exhibits on shipping, geology, archaeology, the Vikings and local history.

Guided tours. Explanatory displays. Gift shop. Tearoom. Picnic area. Garden. WC. Disabled access. Car and coach parking. Group concessions. £.

Open Easter-Oct, daily 10.30-1630.

Tel: 01770 302636 Email: tom.k.macleod@btinternet.com

V8 Atholl Country Life Museum, Blair Atholl

[Map: 5B, A8] On B8079, 7 miles NW of Pitlochry, Old School, Blair Atholl, Perthshire. (NGR: NN 875653 LR: 43)

The collection consists of artefacts and photographs illustrating local life from 1850. Displays include a crofter's kitchen, smiddy, byre, and gamekeeper's corner, as well as road, rail and postal communications, and the church and school.

Explanatory displays. Gift shop. Picnic area. WC. Disabled access. Car and coach parking. Group concessions. £.

Open Easter, then Jun-Oct, 13.30-17.00; Jul-Sep, Mon-Fri 9.30-17.00.

Tel: 01796 481232

V9 Auchindrain Township Open Air Museum

[Map: 5A, C5] Off A83, 6 miles SW of Inveraray, Auchindrain, Argyll. (NGR: NN 032031 LR: 55)

Auchindrain is a fine open air museum. The township buildings have been furnished and equipped in the styles of various periods to illustrate what life was like for the Highlander.

Explanatory displays. Gift shop. Picnic area. WC. Car and coach parking. Group concessions. ££.

Open Apr-Sep, daily 10.00-17.00.

Tel: 01499 500235

V10 Auldearn and Boath Doocot (NTS)

[Map: 3B, E10] Off A96, 2.5 miles E of Nairn, NW of village of Auldearn, Highlands. (NGR: NH 917557 LR: 27)

Just to the south of the village of Auldearn is the site of the battle in 1645 when the Marquis of Montrose defeated an army of Covenanters, led by General Hurry (or Urie) – a battle plan is on display. A round 17th-century doocot in the earthworks was presented to The National Trust for Scotland in 1947.

Explanatory board. Parking nearby. £.

Access at all reasonable times.

V11 Barony Mills, Birsay

[Map: 2, B2] On A967, 12 miles N of Stromness, Boardhouse, Birsay, Orkney. (NGR: HY 255275 LR: 6)

There are three mills on the site, two meal mills and threshing mill. Two are ruinous, while the third is the last working water-powered meal mill on Orkney.

There have been mills on the site dating back to Viking times.

Guided tours. Parking.

Open Apr-Sep, 10.00-13.00 and 14.00-17.00.

Tel: 01856 771276 Email: johnnyjohnston@talk21.com

Y34 Barra Heritage and Cultural Centre

Among its other attractions, the centre houses an extensive collection of old photographs including herring fishing, people, thatched houses and boats.

The centre also runs Dubharaidh, a restored traditional white house type thatched cottage in a magnificent, secluded location, 15 minutes walk from Craigston village, (which is 3 miles north-west of Castlebay). No cars at museum. Open May-Sep, Mon-Fri 11.00-17.00 – but check with centre (£).

See main entry Y34

V12 Barry Mill (NTS)

[Map: 4, J4] Off A930, 2 miles W of Carnoustie, Barry, Angus. (NGR: NO 533349 LR: 54)

The restored 18th-century mill, which milled and supplied oats for local farms, works on a demonstration basis on weekend afternoons and by arrangement. There has been a mill here from the 16th century, and there are displays and information on the mill.

Explanatory displays. Picnic area. Waymarked walk and picnic area. WC. Car and coach parking. Group concessions. £.

Open (2002) 25 Mar-27 Oct, Sat-Wed 12.00-17.00.

Tel: 01241 856761

V13 Bayanne House, Yell

[Map: 1, B3] Off A968, Bayanne House, Sellafirth, NE side of Yell, Shetland. (NGR: HU 520980 LR: 1)

Bayanne House features a working croft, craft workshop and archaeological site, as well as facilities for ancestral research and Shetland family history.

Open: tel to confirm.

Tel: 01597 744219 Fax: 01597 744219

V14 Blair Atholl Water Mill

[Map: 5B, A8] On B8079, 7 miles NW of Pitlochry, Ford Road, Blair Atholl, Perthshire. (NGR: NN 875655 LR: 43)

The working water mill, which dates from 1613, produces oatmeal and flour, which are on sale. Milling of the flour can be viewed, and home baking in the tearoom is made from the mill's own stone-ground flour. Honey from the mill's beehives is also available.

Guided tours by arrangement. Explanatory displays. Gift shop. Tearoom. WC. Disabled access. Car and coach parking. Group concessions. £.

Open Apr-Oct, Mon-Sat 10.30-17.30, Sun 12.00-17.30.

Tel: 01738 710610

V15 Bod of Gremista, Lerwick

[Map: 1, D3] Off A970, 1.5 miles N of Lerwick, Gremista, Shetland. (NGR: HU 465433 LR: 4)

Bod of Gremista is a restored 18th-century fishing booth, and was the birthplace of local shipowner and politician Arthur Anderson, co-founder of P&O Ferries. There is information on his life and of fisheries some 200 years ago, and recreated room interiors.

Guided tours. Explanatory displays. WC. Limited disabled access. Car and coach parking.

Open Jun-Sep, Wed-Sun 10.00-13.00 and 14.00-17.00.

Tel: 01595 694386 Fax: 01595 696729

Web: www.shetland-museum.org.uk

V16 Buckie Drifter

[Map: 4, E3] Off A942 or A990, Freuchny Road, Buckie, Moray. (NGR: NJ 425656 LR: 28)

Buckie Drifter charts the history of the herring industry and the lives of the fishing communities. Features include a recreated quayside of the 1920s, information about the herring, rare archive film footage of steam drifters, and an Oakley Class RNLI lifeboat.

Explanatory displays. Shop. Restaurant. WC. Baby changing facilities. Disabled access. Car and coach parking. Group concessions. £.

Open Apr-Oct, Mon-Sat 10.00-17.00, Sun 12.00-17.00.

Tel: 01542 834646 Fax: 01542 835995

Web: www.moray.org/area/bdrifter/mbdrifter.html

Email: buckie.drifter@moray.gov.uk

V17 Buckie Fishing Heritage Museum

[Map: 4, E3] Off A942 or A990, Buckie, Moray. (NGR: NJ 425656 LR: 28)

Fishing heritage museum.

Open: tel to confirm.

Tel: 01542 840944/835836

V18 Carradale Heritage Centre

[Map: 5A, F4] Off B879, 12.5 miles N of Campbeltown, Carradale, Kintyre, Argyll. (NGR: NR 816386 LR: 68)

The heritage centre features displays on the history of fishing, farming and forestry, and there are hands-on activities for children.

Explanatory displays. Craft shop. Tearoom. WC. Parking.

Open Easter-mid Oct: high season, Mon-Sat 10.30-17.00, Sun 12.30-16.00; low season, Tue-Wed, Fri-Sat 10.30-17.00, Sun 12.30-16.00.

Tel: 01586 431296 Fax: 01586 431296 Email: stuartirvine@talk21.com

V19 Choraidh Croft Farm Park

[Map: 3B, A8] On A838, 6 miles SE of Durness, 94 Laid, Loch Eribollside, Sutherland, Highland. (NGR: NC 415592 LR: 9)

The farm park, which is the most northerly in mainland Britain, has over 40 different breeds of animals, a pets corner, and a museum illustrating crofting life over the last 150 years.

Explanatory displays. Restaurant. Tearoom. Picnic area. WC. B&B accommodation available. Disabled access. Car and coach

parking. Group concessions. £.

Open mid May-end Sep, daily 10.30-18.30.

Tel: 01971 511235 Email: lesley@94croft.freeserve.co.uk

V20 Clansman Centre

[Map: 3B, G8] On A82, Fort Augustus, Highlands. (NGR: NH 380094 LR: 34)

The centre features clan life in the Highlands with a live presentation inside a reconstructed Highland turf house. There is information on how a family in the 17th century lived, ate and survived, including clothing and weapon demonstrations.

Guided tours. Explanatory displays. Gift shop with local crafts and Celtic jewellery. Scottish Armoury: range of swords, sgians, targes, axes and clothing: made to order. Picnic area. Disabled access. Car and coach parking. Group concessions. £.

Open Mar-Oct, daily 10.00-20.00; closed earlier in off-season.

Tel: 01320 366444 Web: www.clansmencentre.com

Fax: 01320 366444 Email: clansmen.centre@talk21.com

V21 Click Mill, Dounby (HS)

[Map: 2, C2] Off B9057, 10.5 miles NW of Kirkwall, 2 miles NE of Dounby, Click Mill, Orkney. (NGR: HY 325228 LR: 6)

The click mill, which is in working condition, is the last of its kind in Orkney.

Parking nearby.

Access at all reasonable times – access may be muddy.

Tel: 01856 841815

V22 Colbost Croft Museum

[Map: 3A, E4] On B884, 4 miles NW of Dunvegan, Colbost, Skye. (NGR: NG 215485 LR: 23)

The museum is located in a blackhouse, and contains 19th-century implements and furniture, with a peat fire burning throughout the day. There is also the replica of an illicit whisky still.

Explanatory displays. Car and coach parking. Group concessions. £.

Open Apr-Oct, daily 10.00-18.30.

Tel: 01470 521296

V23 Corrigall Farm Museum, Harray

[Map: 2, C2] Off A986, 10 miles NW of Kirkwall, Corston Road, Corrigall, Harray, Orkney. (NGR: HY 323193 LR: 6)

The museum features a late 19th-century farm with a grain-drying kiln and native livestock.

Explanatory displays. Activities. Gift shop. WC. Disabled access. Parking. £.

Open Mar-Oct, Mon-Sat 10.30-13.00 and 14.00-17.00, Sun 14.00-19.00.

Tel: 01856 771441 Web: www.orkneyheritage.com

Fax: 01856 875846 Email: steve.callaghan@orkney.gov.uk

V24 Corstorphine Doocot (HS)

[Map: 6B, E9] Dovecot Road, off Saughton Road North, near Corstorphine High Street, Edinburgh. (NGR: NT 283705 LR: 66)

Fine well-preserved round doocot, still with its nesting boxes. It was probably associated with the nearby castle, long a property of the Forresters, but no remains of which survive. **Corstorphine Old Parish Church [K7]**, also associated with the Forresters, is nearby.

Parking nearby.
Access at all reasonable times.

V25 Craig Highland Farm

[Map: 3A, F6] Off A890, 6 miles N of Kyle of Lochalsh, on shore road, between Plockton and Achmore, Craig, Ross and Cromarty, Highland. (NGR: NG 822331 LR: 24)

Located on the shore of Loch Carron, the farm has a wide range of animals and rare breeds, such as llamas, ponies, donkeys, goats and poultry, pigs and rabbits, which can be fed, as well as owls. There is also access, at low tide, to the Scottish Wildlife Island via Coral Beach Heronry.

Explanatory displays. Picnics or BBQs on beach. WC (on request). Limited disabled access. Car and coach parking. Group concessions. £.

Open Easter-Oct, daily 10.00-dusk.
Tel: 01599 544205 Email: terry.heaviside@hcs.uhi.ac.uk

V26 Cruck Cottage, Torthorwald

[Map: 6B, H9] Off A709, 4 miles E of Dumfries, Torthorwald, Dumfries and Galloway. (NGR: NY 035784 LR: 84)

The thatched cottage, which dates from the early 19th century, has been carefully restored using traditional methods and local materials.

Parking nearby.
Key from Manor Country House Hotel – arrangements are at the cottage.

V27 Dalgarven Mill Museum

[Map: 6A, F6] On A737, 5 miles N of Irvine, Dalgarven, Ayrshire. (NGR: NS 295456 LR: 63)

Dalgarven Mill is a 17th-century restored water mill, and houses exhibitions on flour production. The adjoining granaries hold the Museum of Ayrshire Countrylife and Costume collections of farming and domestic items and costumes, including Ayrshire Whitework. There are also room reconstructions of around 1880.

Costume and agricultural displays. Coffee room. Riverside walk and wild flower meadow. Parking. £.

Open all year: Easter-Oct, Tue-Sat 10.00-17.00, Sun 11.00-17.00; Nov-Easter, Tue-Sat 10.00-16.00, Sun 11.00-17.00
Tel: 01294 552448 Web: www.dalgarvenmill.org.uk
Fax: 01294 552448 Email: admin@dalgarvenmill.org.uk

Y75 Eyemouth Museum

The award-winning museum, refurbished in 1996, was opened in 1981 as a memorial to the 189 local fishermen who lost their lives in the Great Fishing Disaster of 1881. The main feature is the 15 foot by 4 foot Eyemouth Tapestry, and there are displays on local history.
See main entry Y75

V28 Fife Folk Museum, Ceres

[Map: 6B, C10] Off B939, 2.5 miles SE of Cupar, The Weigh House, High Street, Ceres, Fife. (NGR: NO 392114 LR: 59)

Overlooking the Ceres Burn, the museum is partly housed in the 17th-century tolbooth and in 18th-century cottages. The museum charts the history of Fife, and there is an outdoor display of agricultural implements, as well as a heritage trail.

Guided tours by arrangement. Explanatory displays. Gift shop. Terraced garden. Car and coach parking. Group concessions. £.

Open Easter, then May-Oct, Sat-Thu 14.00-17.00.
Tel: 01334 828180

V29 Finavon Doocot (NTS)

[Map: 4, I4] Off A94, 4.5 miles NE of Forfar, Angus. (NGR: NO 497566 LR: 54)

The doocot is the largest in Scotland with some 2400 nesting boxes, and probably dates from the 16th century. It was probably built by the Lindsay Earl of Crawford, whose castle was nearby.

Explanatory board. Car and coach parking.

Open 25 Mar-27 Oct, daily: keys from the Finavon Hotel
Tel: 01738 631296.

V30 Fochabers Folk Museum

[Map: 4, E3] On A96, High Street, Fochabers. (NGR: NJ 348587 LR: 28)

The folk museum, which is housed in a former church, charts the history of Fochabers over the last 200 years. There are displays of model engines, clocks, costumes, a village shop, and Victorian parlour. There is also a large collection of horse-drawn carts.

Explanatory displays. Gift shop. Car and coach parking.

Open all year: summer, 9.30-13.00 and 14.00-18.00; winter, closes 17.00.
Tel: 01343 821204 Fax: 01343 821291

V31 Fordyce Joiner's Workshop Visitors Centre

[Map: 4, E4] Off A98, 3 miles SW of Portsoy, Church Street, Fordyce, Banff, Aberdeenshire. (NGR: NJ 555638 LR: 29)

The visitor centre houses displays on the importance of the rural carpenter and joiner over the last 150 years. There are collections of early tools and machinery, and photographs as well as an audio-visual presentation and Victorian-style garden. There is public access to the woodwork workshop, supervised by the resident harp maker. Visitors are encouraged to try their hands at making a musical instrument. Books on Fordyce are available. Fordyce is a small picturesque village, built around the castle and an early church with canopied tombs.

Explanatory displays. Coffee and tea available. Victorian-style garden. WC. Disabled access. Parking nearby.

Open all year: summer, Thu-Mon 10.00-20.00; winter, Fri-Mon 12.00-18.00; gardens open all year.
Tel: 01261 8433222 Web: www.sixvillages.org.uk
Email: joiners.fordyce@operamail.com

V32 Foulden Tithe Barn (HS)

[Map: 6B, E12] On A6105, 5.5 miles S of Eyemouth, Foulden, Berwickshire. (NGR: NT 931558 LR: 67)

The barn, which was used to store grain for payment of the 'tithe' (or tenth) to the church, rises to two storeys and has an external stair and corbiestepped gables.

View from exterior.

V33 Fraserburgh Heritage Centre

[Map: 4, E5] Off A98, N of Fraserburgh, Banff and Buchan, Aberdeenshire. (NGR: NJ 999677 LR: 30)

The heritage centre features information on the fishing industry, the Fraser connection, other industries, **Kinnaird Head Castle [X26]** and Wine Tower, RNLI, Marconi experiments and famous 'brochers' (folk from Fraserburgh: the 'burgh' part of the town's name is pronounced *broch*).

Explanatory displays. Gift shop. Adjacent to Lighthouse Museum. Disabled access.

Open Apr-Oct, Mon-Sat 10.00-17.00, Sun 12.30-17.00; Nov-Mar, tel to confirm.

Tel: 01346 512888 Fax: 01346 512888 (phone first)

V34 Garlogie Mill Power House Museum

[Map: 4, G5] Off B9119/B9125, 9.5 miles W of Aberdeen, Garlogie, Skene, Aberdeenshire. (NGR: NJ 782054 LR: 38)

The museum is located in a restored building which houses the power sources, including a rare beam engine, for the demolished woollen mill. There are displays on the history and models of the mill, as well as an award-winning audio-visual presentation.

Explanatory displays. Audio-visual presentation. Gift shop. WC. Disabled access and WC. Car and coach parking.

Open May-Sep, Thu-Mon 12.30-17.00.

Tel: 01771 622906 Web: www.aberdeenshire.gov.uk/heritage
Fax: 01771 622884 Email: heritage@aberdeenshire.gov.uk

V35 Gearrannan Blackhouse Village

[Map: 3A, B3] Off A858, 15 miles NW of Stornoway, Gearrannan, Lewis. (NGR: NB 192442 LR: 8)

With wonderful scenery, the thatched buildings of the village, field boundaries and crofting strips are set out on gently sloping ground. The village was abandoned in 1973, but houses have been restored, and there is a museum.

Museum. Gift shop. Cafe. Live interpretation and guided tours. Parking. Groups by arrangement.

Tel to confirm.

Tel: 01851 643416 Fax: 01851 643488
Web: www.gearrannan.com Email: info@gearrannan.com

V36 Glencoe and North Lorn Folk Museum

[Map: 3B, I7] Off A82, 16 miles S of Fort William, Main Street, Glencoe, Highland. (NGR: NN 101588 LR: 41)

The museum, which is housed in two thatched cottages, features displays on the MacDonalds and the Jacobite Risings. There are also collections of domestic and farming items, dairying and slate-working equipment, and costumes and embroidery, as well as displays on geology and wildlife.

Explanatory displays. Gift area. Parking nearby. £.

Open May-Sep, Mon-Sat 10.00-17.30.

Tel: 01855 811664

V37 Glenesk Folk Museum

[Map: 4, H4] Off B966, 13 miles NW of Brechin, The Retreat, Glen Esk, Angus. (NGR: NO 507790 LR: 44)

The museum has a large collection of antiques, documents and artefacts on the history of the area, as well as records, costumes, photographs and tools. The interpretive centre has a large relief model of Glen Esk, an original stable, and displays on past and present life of the rural community.

Explanatory displays. Gift shop. Tearoom. WC. Car and coach parking. Coach parties by arrangement. Group concessions. £.

Open Easter-May, Sat-Mon 12.00-18.00; Jun-Oct, daily 12.00-18.00.

Tel: 01356 670254 Fax: 01356 670321
Email: retreat@angusglen.co.uk

V38 Greenhill Covenanters House, Biggar

[Map: 6B, F9] On A702, Burn Braes, Biggar, Lanarkshire. (NGR: NT 038378 LR: 72)

Greenhill Covenanters House, a 17th-century farmhouse formerly located at Wilston, was dismantled stone by stone and rebuilt at Biggar. It features mementoes of the turbulent Covenanting period, when folk defended the right to worship in the Covenanting or Presbyterian manner. There is the bed slept in by Donald Cargill, a noted Covenanter, who was executed in 1681, as well as other 17th-century fittings, and rare breeds of sheep and poultry.

Explanatory displays. Gift shop. Car and coach parking. Group concessions. £.

Open Easter-Sep, daily 14.00-17.00

Tel: 01899 221572 Web: www.biggar-net.co.uk
Fax: 01899 221050 Email: margaret@bmtrust.freeserve.co.uk

V39 Highland Folk Museum, Kingussie

[Map: 3B, G9] Off A9, 12 miles SW of Aviemore, Duke Street, Kingussie, Strathspey, Highland. (NGR: NH 758007 LR: 35)

The museum features a wealth of collections relating to Highland social history, displayed in realistic settings and reconstructed buildings. There is a Lewis blackhouse and a clack mill. Displays include farm machinery, country crafts, domestic life, costume and furniture.

Explanatory displays. Gift shop. Picnic area. WC. Disabled access. Car and coach parking. £.

Open all year: Easter-Aug Mon-Sat 10.30-17.30; Sept-Oct Mon-Fri 10.30-16.30; Nov-Easter, Mon-Fri guided tour only: check for details; closed Christmas and New Year.

Tel: 01540 661307 Web: www.highlandfolk.com

Fax: 01540 661004 Email: highland.folk@highland.gov.uk

V40 Highland Folk Museum, Newtonmore

[Map: 3B, G9] Off A9, Autlarie, Newtonmore, Highland. (NGR: NN 700980 LR: 42)

A fascinating glimpse into 300 years of Highland life with a reconstructed 18th-century township with costumed interpreters. There is also an early 20th-century school, clockmakers shop, and a working croft.

Gift shop. WC. Disabled access to ground floor. Parking. £.

Open May-Sep, daily.

Tel: 01540 661307 Web: www.highlandfolk.com

Fax: 01540 661631 Email: highland.folk@highland.gov.uk

V41 Inveraray Maritime Museum

[Map: 5A, C5] Off A83, The Harbour, Inveraray, Argyll. (NGR: NN 097086 LR: 53)

The museum features a fine collection of maritime displays, memorabilia and film. It is located on one of the last iron ships, *Arctic Penguin,* built in 1911. Areas in the ship include displays on emigrant and slave ships and luxury accommodation.

Guided tours by arrangement. Explanatory displays. Gift shop. WC. Play area (Davy Jones Locker). Car and coach parking. Group concessions. £.

Open all year: Apr-Sep, daily 10.00-18.00; Oct-Mar 10.00-17.00; closed Christmas and New Year's Day.

Tel: 01499 302213

V42 Islay Woollen Mill

[Map: 5A, E2] Off A846, 1 mile NE of Bridgend, Islay. (NGR: NR 352632 LR: 60)

The early-Victorian mill contains a tweed and woollen factory and produces tartan.

Guided tours. Explanatory displays. Gift shop. Picnic area. WC. Car and coach parking.

Open all year: Mon-Fri 10.00-17.00, Sat 10.00-16.00.

Tel: 01496 810563 Fax: 01496 810677 Email: islaywoollenmill@btinternet.cpm

V43 Isle of Mull Weavers

[Map: 5A, B4] On A849, 1.5 miles S of Craignure, The Steading, Torosay Castle, Mull. (NGR: NM 729353 LR: 49)

The award-winning centre has displays of traditional weaving on old dobby looms and loom-side demonstrations. The shop features a range of tweed, travel and floor rugs, and many other items made on the premises.

Guided tours. Explanatory displays. Gift shop. Disabled access. Car and coach parking.

Open Jan-Mar, Mon-Sat 9.00-17.00; Apr-Oct, daily 9.00-17.00; Nov-Dec, Mon-Sat 9.00-17.00.

Tel: 01680 812381

V44 Islesburgh Exhibition

[Map: 1, D3] Off A970, Islesburgh Community Centre, King Harald Street, Lerwick, Shetland. (NGR: HU 475415 LR: 4)

The exhibition has information on Shetland's culture and heritage, featuring knitting, music and dance demonstrations, as well as displays of crafts, knitwear, photography and a replica of a 1920s' croft house interior.

Gift shop. Cafe. WC. Disabled access. Car and coach parking. £.

Open late May-late Sep, Wed-Fri 9.00-21.30.

Tel: 01595 692114 Fax: 01595 696470

Email: islesburgh@zetnet.co.uk

V45 Kenneth MacLeod Harris Tweed Mill

[Map: 3A, B4] Off A858, 13 miles NW of Stornoway, 9 North Shawbost, Lewis. (NGR: NB 268478 LR: 8)

The mill offers guided tours, and there is a range of Harris tweed for sale.

Tel to confirm.

Tel: 01851 710251 Fax: 01851 710567

Email: enquiries@kennethmacleod.co.uk

V46 Kirbuster Museum, Birsay

[Map: 2, C2] Off A966 or A986, 10 miles N of Stromness, Kirbuster, Birsay, Orkney. (NGR: HY 283254 LR: 6)

The museum features a farmhouse, dating from the 16th century, with a traditional central hearth and stone bed. There is a Victorian garden and a putting green.

Explanatory displays. Gift shop. Gardens. WC. Disabled access. Parking. £.

Open Mar-Oct, Mon-Sat 10.30-13.00 and 14.00-17.00, Sun 14.00-19.00.

Tel: 01856 771268 Web: www.orkneyheritage.com

Fax: 01856 871560 Email: steve.callaghan@orkney.gov.uk

V47 Laidhay Croft Museum

[Map: 3B, C11] On A9, 1 mile N of Dunbeath, Laidhay, Caithness, Highland. (NGR: ND 175305 LR: 11)

The museum features a Caithness longhouse, which is thatched and dates from the 18th century, with house, byre and stable under one roof. The longhouse is furnished in 1900 style. There is a collection of early farm tools and equipment, and a cruck-framed barn.

Guided tours on request. Tearoom. Picnic area. WC. Disabled access. Group concessions. £.

Open Easter-mid Oct, daily 10.00-18.00.

Tel: 01593 731244

V48 Lewis Loom Centre

[Map: 3A, B4] Off A866, 3 Bayhead Street, Stornoway, Lewis. (NGR: NB 425325 LR: 8)

The centre provides a detailed lecture and guided tour on the history of Harris Tweed, as well as demonstrations of traditional looms, warping, waulking, hand spinning and hand carding.

Guided tours. Explanatory displays. Gift shop. WC. Disabled access. Car and coach parking. £.
Open Mon-Sat 9.00-18.00.
Tel: 01851 704500/3117/0422 Web: www.lewisloomcenter.co.uk
Fax: 01851 704500 Email: lewisloomcentre@madasafish.com

V49 Lossiemouth Fisheries and Community Museum

[Map: 4, E3] Off A941, Pitgaveny Quay, Lossiemouth, Moray. (NGR: NJ 237710 LR: 28)

The museum houses displays on the community and fishing, and there is information about Ramsay Mc-Donald, who was born in Lossiemouth, Britain's first Labour Prime Minister.

Guided tours. Explanatory displays. Gift shop. WC. Disabled access. Car and coach parking. Group concessions. £.
Open Easter-Sep, Mon-Sat 10.30-17.00.
Tel: 01343 813772 Fax: 01343 543221
Web: www.lossiemouthmuseum.fsbusiness.co.uk
Email: jsscott@nigle.fsnet.co.uk

V50 Luib Croft Museum

[Map: 3A, F5] Off A850, 7 miles NW of Broadford, Luib, Skye. (NGR: NG 565278 LR: 32)

The Luib Croft Museum displays living conditions in the early 20th century in an atmospheric blackhouse.

Explanatory displays. Gift shop. WC. Disabled access. Car and coach parking. £.
Open Apr-Oct, daily 9.00-18.00.
Tel: 01471 822427

V51 Lybster Harbour Visitor Centre

[Map: 3B, B11] Off A99, Waterlines, Lybster, Caithness, Highland. (NGR: ND 345350 LR: 11)

The visitor centre features displays charting the history of the herring industry, as well as on the bird life of the east Caithness coast and the evolution of the land from earliest times.

Explanatory displays. Coffee shop. WC. Disabled access. Boat building workshop. Yacht facilities. Parking. £ (exhibition)
Open May-Sep, daily 11.00-17.00.
Tel: 01593 721520 Fax: 01593 721325

V52 Maggie's Hoosie

[Map: 4, E6] Off B9107, 26 Shore Street, Inverallochy, E of Fraserburgh, Aberdeenshire. (NGR: NK 045653 LR: 30)

The fisher cottage has an earth floor, box bed and original furnishings.

Parking nearby.
Open Apr-Sep, Mon-Fri 10.00-12.00 and 14.00-16.30; closed Tue; Sat-Sun 14.00-16.30.
Tel: 01346 514761

V53 Mary-Ann's Cottage, Dunnet

[Map: 3B, A11] Off A836, 7 miles E of Thurso, 3 miles NE of Castletown, Dunnet, Caithness. (NGR: ND 215715 LR: 12)

The historic cottage illustrates how crofting people lived over the last 150 years.

Explanatory displays. Parking.
Open Jun-Sep, Tue-Sun 14.00-16.30.
Tel: 01847 892303 Email: rowe@zetnet.co.uk

V54 Mill of Benholm Visitor Centre

[Map: 4, H5] On A92, 6 miles E of Laurencekirk, Mill of Benholm, Kincardineshire. (NGR: NO 807693 LR: 45)

The visitor centre is housed in a working corn mill, which has been restored, and there are demonstrations of traditional corn milling.

Guided tours. Explanatory displays. Gift shop. Tearoom. WC. Woodland walk. Car and coach parking. £.
Open Easter-Oct, daily 11.00-17.00; tearoom – tel to confirm.
Tel: 01771 622906

V55 Moirlanich Longhouse (NTS)

[Map: 5B, C7] Off A827, 1 mile NW of Killin, Moirlanich, Stirlingshire (NGR: NN 557342 LR: 51)

The longhouse, which dates from the 1850s and was inhabited until 1968, is a fine example of a traditional cruck frame dwelling and byre. The longhouse has many original features.

Explanatory displays. Limited car parking. Group concessions. £.
Open (2002) 25 Mar-27 Oct, Wed and Sun 14.00-17.00.
Tel: 01567 820988

V56 Museum of Scottish Country Life, Kittochside

[Map: 6B, F7] Off A726 or A749, off Stewartfield Way, N side of East Kilbride, Glasgow. (NGR: NS 608563 LR: 64)

The museum charts the many changes in farming practice over 300 years, while the farm is worked using the techniques and equipment of the 1950s to demonstrate this late phase of the Agricultural Revolution. The farm has been held by the Reid family from the 16th century, and was presented to The National Trust for Scotland in 1992. The Georgian farmhouse and steading can also be visited.

Explanatory displays. Transport to farm. Gift shop. Cafe. WC. Parking. £.
Open all year: daily, 10.00-17.00; closed 25-26 Dec/1-2 Jan.
Tel: 01355 224181 Fax: 01355 571290
Web: www.nms.ac.uk/countrylife Email: kittochside@nms.ac.uk

V57 Nairn Fishertown Museum

[Map: 3B, E10] On A96, Laing Hall, King Street, Nairn, Highland. (NGR: NH 885565 LR: 27)

The museum charts the history and decline of the herring fishing industry in Nairn with pictures, photographs and displays. There is a reconstruction of a fisherman's house, and displays of sea charts, boat-building and fishing gear.

Explanatory displays. Guided walks available: book in advance. WC. Disabled access with assistance. Parking nearby. £.

Open Jun-Sep, Mon-Sat 10.30-12.30 & 14.30-16.30.
Tel: 01667 453331

V58 Ness Heritage Centre

[Map: 3A, A5] On A857, 26 miles N of Stornoway, Habost, Ness, Lewis. (NGR: NB 520630 LR: 8)

The heritage centre features a collection of artefacts relating to crofting life in the district of Ness, with documentary and audio-visual archives. The 10th-century cross is believed to have marked the grave of St Ronan. Dell Mill is a restored mill with a full range of equipment and machinery, together with interpretive displays on the mill and local grain production. Access to the mill is available by appointment only.

WC. Limited disabled access. Car and coach parking.

Open all year: Oct-May, Mon-Fri 9.30-17.30; Jun-Sep, Mon-Sat 9.30-17.30

Tel: 01851 810377 Fax: 01851 810488 Email:
cen.ness@virgin.net

V59 New Abbey Corn Mill (HS)

[Map: 6B, I8] Off A710, 6 miles S of Dumfries, New Abbey, Dumfries and Galloway. (NGR: NX 958663 LR: 84)

The renovated water-powered mill was used for grinding oatmeal. It is in working order, and there are regular demonstrations at 12.00 and 15.00 in summer. **Sweetheart Abbey [J32]** and **Shambellie House [Y14]** are nearby.

Audio-visual presentation 'The Miller's Tale'. Visitor centre. Gift shop. Picnic area. Joint entry ticket with Sweetheart Abbey. Parking. £. Combined ticket with Sweetheart Abbey available (££).

Open Apr-Sep, daily 9.30-18.30; Oct-Mar, Mon-Wed and Sat 9.30-16.30, Thu 9.30-12.00, Sun 2.00-16.30, closed Fri; last ticket 30 mins before closing; closed 25/26 Dec and 1/2 Jan.
Tel: 01387 850260

Y143 Newhaven Heritage Museum, Edinburgh

The museum houses exhibits about the village and people of Newhaven, covering fishing, customs and superstitions.

See main entry Y143

V60 Northfield Farm Museum

[Map: 4, E5] Off A98 or A950, 10 miles SW of Fraserburgh, New Pitsligo, Aberdeenshire. (NGR: NJ 882560 LR: 30)

The museum has a wide range of exhibits such as vintage tractors, engines, and horse-drawn farm equipment. There is also a smithy, engineer's and joiner's workshop, as well as an aviary for small birds.

Guided tours. Explanatory displays. Picnic area. WC. Disabled access. Car and coach parking. Group concessions. £.

Open May-Sep, daily 11.00-17.30.
Tel: 01771 653504

V61 Peterhead Maritime Heritage

[Map: 4, E6] Off A952, South Road, S side of Peterhead, Banff and Buchan, Aberdeenshire. (NGR: NK 123452 LR: 30)

The museum charts the history of maritime life in Peterhead, with an audio-visual display on marine life, an interactive display on fishing, whaling, navigation and the oil industry. There is also an observation box with telescope views across Peterhead Bay.

Guided tours. Explanatory displays. Gift shop. Tearoom. WC. Children's play area. Disabled access. Car and coach parking. Group concessions. £.

Open Apr-Oct, Mon-Sat 10.00-18.00, Sun 12.00-18.00; Nov-Mar, Mon-Sat 10.00-16.00, Sun 12.00-16.00. Tel to confirm.
Tel: 01779 473000 Web: www.aberdeenshire.gov.uk/ahc.htm
Email: general@abheritage.demon.co.uk.

V62 Pitmedden Garden and Museum of Farming Life (NTS)

[Map: 4, F5] On A920, 8 miles NE of Inverurie, Pitmedden, Aberdeenshire. (NGR: NJ 885281 LR: 38)

Pitmedden House is a 17th-century house, remodelled in 1853 and in 1954, and has a 17th-century five-acre walled garden, which is open to the public, and features sundials, parterre, pavilions and fountains dotted among formal flower beds. There is also the Museum of Farming Life and visitor centre, as well as a wildlife garden and woodland walk.

Museum of Farming Life. Gift shop. Tea room. WC. Disabled facilities and access. Woodland walk and wildlife garden. Car and coach parking. ££.

House not open; garden, museum and visitor centre open 1 May-1 Sep, daily 10.00-17.00; last admission 16.30; grounds open all year, daily.
Tel: 01651 843352 Fax: 01651 843188

V63 Preston Mill and Phantassie Doocot (NTS)

[Map: 6B, D11] Off A1, Preston, East Linton. (NGR: NT 590770 LR: 66)

The mill, a picturesque collection of pantiled buildings, is the oldest surviving water-driven meal mill in Scotland. It dates from the 18th century, and was last used commercially in 1957. The mill pond has many ducks. Phantassie Doocot, which is a short distance away, was built in the 16th century to house 500 birds.

Explanatory displays. Gift shop. WC. Disabled access to grounds and WC. Limited parking. £.

Open (2002) 25 Mar-27 Oct, Thu-Mon 12.00-17.00, Sun 13.00-17.00.
Tel: 01620 860426

N43 Provost Ross's House

Part of the Aberdeen Maritime Museum, which gives an insight into the maritime history of the city, including the oil industry. Unique collection of ship models, paintings, artefacts, computer interaction and set-piece exhibitions. Five star museum.

See main entry N43

Y164 Queen's View Visitor Centre

Forest walks access viewpoints, an excavated ring fort, and a reconstructed 18th-century farm village.
See main entry Y164

V64 Quendale Water Mill

[Map: 1, E3] Off A970, 3 miles NW of Sumburgh Airport, Quendale, Dunrossness, Shetland. (NGR: HU 372133 LR: 4)

The restored water mill, which dates from the 19th century, has an exhibition of old croft tools, as well as a small gift shop selling souvenirs and local crafts.
Guided tours. Video programme. Explanatory displays. Gift shop. Refreshments. WC. Disabled access. Car and coach parking. £.
Open May-Sep, daily 10.00-17.00.
Tel: 01950 460550   Web: www.quendalemill.shetland.co.uk
Email: info@quendale.shetland.co.uk

Y165 Rob Roy and Trossachs Visitor Centre, Callander

There is a Highland cottage, as well as detailed visitor information on Rob Roy and the Trossachs.
See main entry Y165

V65 Sandaig Museum, Tiree

[Map: 5A, B1] Off B8065, Thatched Cottage Museum, Sandaig, W of Tiree. (NGR: NL 939434 LR: 46)

The museum, housed in a row of traditional thatched buildings, has displays on life in the 19th century, including a byre and barn of the time.
Guided tours. Guide booklet supplied. Restaurant nearby. Disabled access with help. Car parking.
Open Jun-Sep, Mon-Fri 14.00-16.00.
Tel: 01865 311468

V66 Sandhaven Meal Mill

[Map: 4, E5] On B9031, 1.5 miles W of Fraserburgh, Sandhaven, Aberdeenshire. (NGR: NJ 963675 LR: 30)

The meal mill offers working demonstrations on how oatmeal was ground in a typical 19th-century Scottish meal mill.
Guided tours. Explanatory displays. Car and coach parking.
Open May-Sep, Sat-Sun14.00-16.30.
Tel: 01771 622906

V67 Scottish Fisheries Museum, Anstruther

[Map: 6B, C11] Off A917, St Ayles, Harbour Head, Anstruther, Fife. (NGR: NO 569035 LR: 59)

The museum, housed around a cobbled courtyard at the harbour, has fine displays on Scotland's fishing industry. The museum is in a range of 16th- to 19th-century buildings, and has extended into an old boat yard alongside. Features include boats, both real and model, and the fisherman's cottage, as well as information on all aspects of fishing.

Guided tours for groups by appt. Explanatory displays. Gift shop. Tearoom. WC. Disabled access. Car and coach parking. Group concessions. ££.
Open all year: Apr-Oct Mon-Sat 10.00-17.30, Sun 11.00-17.00; Nov-Mar Mon-Sat 10.00-16.30, Sun 14.00-16.30; closed 25/ 26 Dec & 1-2 Jan; last admission 45 mins before closing.
Tel: 01333 310268   Web: www.scottish-fisheries-museum.org
Fax: 01333 310268   Email: andrew@scottish-fisheries-museum.org

V68 Scottish Maritime Museum, Irvine

[Map: 6A, F6] Off A737, harbourside, Laird Forge, Gottries Road, Irvine, Ayrshire. (NGR: NS 315385 LR: 70)

The link house building is being developed and holds a substantial part of the museum's collection in 'open store'. The shipyard worker's flat and historic vessels can be visited during a tour.
Guided tours. Explanatory displays. Gift shop. Tearoom. WC. Disabled access to museum only (not boats). Car and coach parking. Group concessions. £.
Open Apr-Oct, daily 10.00-17.00; Nov-Mar, daily 10.00-16.00.
Tel: 01294 278283   Fax: 01294 313211

V69 Scottish Wool Centre

[Map: 5B, D7] On A821, off Main Street, Aberfoyle, Stirlingshire. (NGR: NN 523010 LR: 57)

The visitor centre features a theatre with a show telling the story of Scottish wool, as well as textile demonstrations. There is a wide range of knitwear, woollens, cottons and gifts.
Guided tours. Explanatory displays. Audiovisual presentation. Gift shop. Coffee shop. WC. Children's farm. Disabled access. Car and coach parking. Group concessions. Charge for theatre.
Open all year: Apr-Sep, Mon-Fri 9.30-17.30, Sat-Sun 9.30-18.30; Oct-Mar, Mon-Fri 10.00-17.30; closed Christmas and New Year's day; last show in theatre 15.00.
Tel: 01877 382850   Fax: 01877 382854

V70 Shawbost Crofting Museum

[Map: 3A, B4] Off A858, 13 miles NW of Stornoway, Shawbost, Lewis. (NGR: NB 255465 LR: 8)

The small museum, situated in an old church, was created under the 1970 Highland Village Competition and illustrates the old way of life in Lewis, with exhibitions of objects relating to crofting, fishing and domestic life in Lewis up to the 1950s. Nearby is the restored Norse mill, Mill of the Blacksmiths [NB 244464] and grain kiln (where the grain was dried before milling), both buildings being thatched. This is a horizontal mill which straddles the water channel for the water wheel, and was once very common throughout the Western Isles: mills and kilns like these being used until 1940.
Explanatory displays. WC. Parking nearby. Donation box.
Open Apr-Sep.
Tel: 01851 710212   Fax: 01851 710582

V71 Shetland Croft House Museum, Boddam

[Map: 1, E3] Off A970, 25 miles S of Lerwick, Southvoe, Boddam, Dunrossness, Shetland. (NGR: HU 399146 LR: 4)

The museum features a dry-stone and thatched croft, dating from the 19th century, with an inter-connected house, barn, byre, kiln and stable as well as a nearby water mill. The croft is furnished throughout with period fixtures, furniture and implements. There are box beds, sea chests, and a working water mill.

Guided tours. WC. Car and coach parking. Group concessions. £.
Open May-Sep, daily 10.00-13.00 and 14.00-17.00.
Tel: 01595 695057 Fax: 01595 696729
Web: www.shetland-museum.org.uk

V72 Shetland Textile Working Museum, Weisdale

[Map: 1, D3] On B9075, 13 miles NW of Lerwick, Weisdale, Shetland. (NGR: HU 394532 LR: 3)

The museum illustrates the history of spinning, knitting and weaving on Shetland from the earliest days to the present. There is a unique collection of Shetland textiles, and local crafts people provide demonstrations.

Explanatory displays. Cafe. WC. Disabled access. Car parking. £.
Open all year, Wed-Sat 10.30-16.30, Sun 12.00-16.30.
Tel: 01595 830419 Fax: 01595 830419

V73 Skye Museum of Island Life

[Map: 3A, E4] On A855, 5 miles N of Uig, Kilmuir, Skye. (NGR: NG 394717 LR: 23)

The museum illustrates the life of a crofting community from around the turn of the 19th century, and is housed in a group of seven thatched buildings, including a blackhouse and smithy. Displays include a wide range of agricultural implements and a house with period furniture. Flora MacDonald is buried in the nearby churchyard at Kilmuir, her grave marked by a Celtic cross.

Guided tours. Explanatory displays. Gift shop. WC. Car and coach parking. Group concessions. £.
Open Easter-Oct, Mon-Sat 9.30-17.30.
Tel: 01470 552206 Fax: 01470 552206

V74 Skyeskyns, Waternish

[Map: 3A, E4] On B886, 5 miles NE of Dunvegan, 17 Loch Bay, Waternish, Skye. (NGR: NG 270554 LR: 23)

The only traditional exhibition tannery in Scotland, showing how sheepskins are made using traditional methods. Demonstrations of rare tanning skills and hand-finishing are available, and lambs-wool rugs, leather goods and fleeces are for sale.

Guided tours. Explanatory displays. Gift shop. WC. Car and coach parking.
Open Apr-Oct, daily 10.00-18.00.
Tel: 01470 592237 Web: www.skyeskyns.demon.co.uk
Fax: 01470 592237 Email: clive@www.skyeskyns.demon.co.uk

V75 Sma' Shot Cottages

[Map: 6A, E6] Off A726 or A737, 11-17 George Place, Paisley, Renfrewshire. (NGR: NS 477640 LR: 64)

Run by the Old Paisley Society, the cottages consist of an 18th-century weaver's cottage, with accommodation and loom shop, which is linked by a garden to a 19th-century artisan's house. The cottages are fully furnished, and there is an exhibition of historic photographs and a fine collection of china and linen.

Guided tours. Gift shop. Tearoom. WC. Garden. Car parking.
Open Apr-Sep, Wed and Sat 12.00-16.00.
Tel: 0141 889 1708 Fax: 0141 889 1708
Web: www.smashot.com Email: smashot@virginnet.com

V76 Smiddy Museum, St Margaret's Hope

[Map: 2, D3] On B9043, St Margaret's Hope, South Ronaldsay, Orkney. (NGR: HY 445935 LR: 7)

The Smiddy Museum consists of a collection of horse-drawn implements and smith-made articles from the village blacksmith.
Check to confirm opening.

V77 Smithy Heritage Centre, Lochcarron

[Map: 3A, F6] On A896, 12 miles NE of Kyle of Lochalsh, 1 mile E of Lochcarron, Ribhuachan, Strathcarron, Ross-shire, Highland. (NGR: NG 926427 LR: 25)

The museum, housed in a restored smithy, has information and an audio-visual display on the history of the building and the people who worked here.

Explanatory displays. Video show. Picnic area. Wood. Disabled access. Car and coach parking.
Open Easter-Oct, Mon-Sat 10.00-17.30.
Tel: 01520 722246

V78 St Kilda (NTS)

[Map: 3A, D1] 41 miles W of Grimnish Point, North Uist, Western Isles. (NGR: NF 100994 LR: 18)

St Kilda or Hirta is a spectacular group of islands with magnificent cliffs and rising to some 1400 feet.

It was home to an isolated community for many hundreds of years. The islanders had a tough life, and survived by exploiting the thousands of seabirds. There are a large number of 'cleits', huts used for storing dried seabirds, fish, hay and turf. The islanders had a democratic administration, and decisions were taken by an island council.

The present village was set out in the 1830s, above Village Bay, but in the 1880s much of the population left for Australia, and the remaining inhabitants were finally evacuated in the 1930s because of hardship and storms, which had cut off the islands for weeks. St Kilda was bequeathed to NTS in 1957, and designated as Scotland's first World Heritage Site in 1987.

Small campsite.

The island can be visited, although it can suffer from extreme weather. Contact NTS (01631 570000) or SNH (01870 620238).

V79 St Monans Windmill

[Map: 6B, D10] Off A917, 2.5 miles W of Anstruther, St Monans, Fife. (NGR: NO 523014 LR: 59)

A late 17th-century windmill with associated salt pans. There are displays which interpret the salt industry on the Forth.

Explanatory displays. Car and coach parking in St Monans.

Open Jul-Aug, daily 12.00-16.00; Sep-Jun key available from St Monans Post Office and Spar Shop (£5 deposit).

Tel: 01334 412933   Web: museums.east@fife.gov.uk
Fax: 01334 413214   Email: museums.east@fife.gov.uk

V80 Strachur Smiddy Museum

[Map: 5A, D5] On A815, 20 miles N of Dunoon, The Clachan, Strachur, Argyll. (NGR: NN 098014 LR: 56)

The smiddy museum features a working smiddy, dating from 1790, with bellows, anvil, hammers, tongs and other tools used by the blacksmith and farrier.

Guided tours. Explanatory displays. Gift shop with modern crafts. WC. Disabled access. Car parking. Group concessions. £.

Open Easter-Sep, daily 13.30-16.30.

Tel: 01369 860565

Y187 Stromness Museum

The museum has displays on Orkney's maritime heritage: fishing, whaling, the Hudson's Bay Company, as well as the German fleet in Scapa Flow.

See main entry Y187

Y190 Tangwick Haa Museum

The museum has displays on various aspects of local life down the ages, such as agriculture, fishing, spinning and knitting.

See main entry Y190

V81 Tealing Doocot and Souterrain (HS)

[Map: 4, J3] Off A929, 5 miles N of Dundee, Tealing, Angus. (NGR: NO 412381 LR: 54)

The fine doocot dates from the 16th century. There are also the remains of an Iron Age souterrain.

Parking nearby

Access at all reasonable times.

V82 Tingwall Agricultural Museum

[Map: 1, D3] Off A971, 5 miles NW of Lerwick, Veensgarth, Gott, Shetland. (NGR: HU 428443 LR: 4)

The museum charts the history of crofting over the last 100 years, and there is a collection of agricultural implements and machinery.

Guided tours. Explanatory displays. WC. Car and limited coach parking. Group concessions. £.

Open Jun-Aug, Mon-Sat 9.00-13.00 and 14.00-17.00.

V83 Tormiston Mill

[Map: 2, C2] On A965, 9 miles W of Kirkwall, Tormiston, Orkney. (NGR: ND 319125 LR: 6)

Housed in a late 19th-century water mill with most of its original machinery, the mill has a visitor centre for the impressive tomb of **Maes Howe [B31]**. The water wheel and most of the machinery are still in place.

Explanatory displays. Gift shop. Tearoom. WC. Car and coach parking.

Open Apr-Sep, Mon-Sat 9.30-18.30, Sun 14.00-18.30; Oct-Mar, Mon-Sat 9.30-18.30, Sun 14.00-16.30, closed Thu PM and Fri.

Tel: 01856 761606

V84 Tugnet Ice House

[Map: 4, E3] Off B9104, 8 miles E of Elgin, Tugnet, Spey Bay. (NGR: NJ 349654 LR: 28)

Tugnet Ice House, the largest in Scotland and built in 1830, features displays on the history and process of commercial salmon fishing on the River Spey. There is an audio-visual programme, and information on the geography, wildlife and industries of the area.

Explanatory displays. Gift shop. WC. Disabled access. Car and coach parking.

Open May-Sep, daily 11.00-16.00.

Tel: 01309 673701   Fax: 01309 675863

V85 Ulva Heritage Centre

[Map: 5A, B3] Off B8073, 0.25 miles N of Ulva House, Ardalum House, Ulva. (NGR: NM 443398 LR: 48)

The heritage centre provides details of five waymarked walks around the fascinating island, wildlife and historical remains on Ulva. There is a faithful reconstruction of traditional thatched cottage, which was still occupied in the 1930s.

Explanatory displays. Gift shop. Tea room/Oyster Bar. WC. Limited disabled access. Waymarked walks. Charge for mountain bikes. Group concessions. ££.

Open Apr-Oct, Mon-Fri, Jun-Aug, also Sun.

Tel: 01688 500241/264   Fax: 01688 500264
Email: ulva@mull.com

V86 Unst Boat Haven

[Map: 1, A4] On A968, 10 miles NE of Belmont Ferry, Haroldswick, NE side of Unst, Shetland. (NGR: HP 638124 LR: 1)

The haven features a fine collection of wooden boats, powered by oar or sail, from Shetland, Norway and the Faroe Islands, which are up to 100 years old. There are also exhibits on fishing, boat building and preserving fish, as well as photographs and documents on the marine heritage of Shetland.

Explanatory displays. WC. Disabled access. Car and coach parking.

Open May-Sep, daily 14.00-17.00.

Web: www.unst.shetland.co.uk

V87 Warp and Weft Visitor Centre, Sandwick

[Map: 1, E3] Off A970, 12 miles S of Lerwick, Sandwick, Shetland. (NGR: HU 434238 LR: 4)

The visitor centre, which is housed in a former weaving shed, has displays of old weaving looms and radios, as well as an exhibition about local history with photographs of mining, crofting, fishing and knitting. There is a wide range of documents on the social history of Shetland.

Explanatory displays. Gift shop. Tearoom. WC. Disabled access. Car and coach parking.

Open May-Sep, Mon-Sat 10.00-17.00, Sun 12.00-17.00.

Tel: 01950 431215

V88 Weaver's Cottage (NTS)

[Map: 6A, E6] Off A737, 5 miles W of Paisley, Shuttle Street, Kilbarchan, Renfrew. (NGR: NS 402633 LR: 64)

A typical cottage of an 18th-century handloom weaver, which contains looms, weaving equipment, and domestic objects. There is a picturesque cottage garden, as well as regular weaving demonstrations.

Explanatory displays. Audio-visual programme. Sales area. Parking. £.

Open 25 Mar-27 Oct, daily 13.00-17.00; morning visits available for pre-booked groups.

Tel: 01505 705588

V89 West Highland Museum

[Map: 3B, H7] Off A82, Cameron Square, Fort William, Highland. (NGR: NN 102738 LR: 41)

The museum features displays on traditional Highland life and culture. There are many Jacobite mementoes.

Guided tours. Explanatory displays. Gift shop. WC. Disabled access. Car parking nearby (£ May-Oct). Group concessions. £.

Open all year: Jun-Sep, Mon-Sat 10.00-17.00; Jul and Aug, Sun 14.00-17.00; Oct-May, Mon-Sat 10.00-16.00.

Tel: 01397 702169 Fax: 01397 701927

V90 Westquarter Doocot (HS)

[Map: 5B, D8] Off B805, 2 miles E of Falkirk, Westquarter, Falkirk. (NGR: NS 913787 LR: 65)

The doocot, which is a fine rectangular building, has a heraldic panel over the doorway dated 1647.

Parking nearby.

Doocot: access at all reasonable times.

Y208 Wick Heritage Centre

The award-winning heritage centre, housed near the harbour in eight houses, yards and outbuildings, charts local history from prehistoric times to the herring fishing industry.

See main entry Y208

V2: Animals and Wildlife

V91 Argyll Wildlife Park

[Map: 5A, C5] On A83, 1.5 miles SW of Inveraray, Dalchenna, Argyll. (NGR: NN 082065 LR: 56)

The wildlife park, which covers some 55 acres, has many freely wandering animals, including goats, badgers, racoons, foxes, deer, buzzards, pine martens, pheasants, wild cats and wallabies, as well as a collection of owls. There are also ponds with water birds including wild swans and geese.

Guided tours. Explanatory displays. Gift shop. Tearoom. Picnic area. WC. Baby changing. Disabled access. Car and coach parking. Group concessions. ££.

Open Apr-Oct, daily 10.00-17.00.

Tel: 01499 302264/455

V92 Auchingarrich Wildlife and Highland Cattle Centre

[Map: 5B, C8] On B827, 2 miles S of Comrie, Auchingarrich, Perthshire. (NGR: NN 788195 LR: 57)

The wildlife centre, located in 100 acres of scenic countryside, has many animals including foxes, otters, meerkats, deer, Highland cows, birds of prey and wild cats. There is also a hatchery and new-born chicks can be handled.

Guided tours. Explanatory displays. Gift shop. Restaurant. Tearoom. Picnic and BBQ area. Covered walkway. Indoor play area. WC. Disabled access. Car and coach parking. Group concessions. ££.

Open all year, daily 10.00-dusk.

Tel: 01764 670486/679469 (gift shop) Fax: 01764 670486

V93 Camperdown Country Park, Dundee

[Map: 4, J3] Off A90, 3 miles NW of Dundee, Coupar Angus Road, Camperdown, Angus. (NGR: NO 365327 LR: 54)

Set in 400 acres of fine parkland with a wide variety of trees, Camperdown, a 19th-century mansion, was built for the son of Admiral Lord Duncan, who defeated the Dutch at the Battle of Camperdown in 1797. The wildlife centre has some 80 species of native and domestic animals, including brown bear, lynx, arctic foxes and pine marten. There is a network of footpaths and forest trails.

Explanatory displays. Gift shop. Picnic area. WC. Golf course. Award-winning play area. Special needs play area. Boating pond. Disabled access. Car and coach parking. Bus from Discovery Quay every hour. Group concessions. £.

Park open all year; centre open Mar-Sep, daily 10.00-16.30; Oct-Feb, daily 10.00-15.30.

Tel: 01382 434296 Fax: 01382 434778

V25 Craig Highland Farm

Located on the shore of Loch Carron, the farm has a wide range of animals and rare breeds, such as llamas, ponies, donkeys, goats and poultry, pigs and rabbits, which can be fed, as well as owls. There is also access, at low tide, to the Scottish Wildlife Island via Coral Beach Heronry.
See main entry V25

V94 Deep-Sea World

[Map: 6B, D9] Off B981, 5 miles SE of Dunfermline, North Queensferry, Fife. (NGR: NT 134804 LR: 65)
Deep-Sea World features a moving walkway through an underwater viewing tunnel. Marine life includes sharks, rays, crabs and lobsters, conger eels and Scotland's largest collection of piranhas. There is also the UK's largest collection of frogs and toads, including the world's most poisonous frog. There is also a display on an Amazonian rain forest, and new exhibits are regularly introduced.
Guided tours. Explanatory displays. Gift shop. Restaurant. Picnic area. WC. Disabled access and WC. Car and coach parking. Park and ride at busy times. Group concessions. £££.
Open Apr-Jun, daily 10.00-18.00; Jul-Aug, daily 10.00-18.30; Sep-Oct daily 10.00-18.00; Nov-Mar, daily 10.00-18.00; Sat, Sun, pub and school hols, 10.00-18.00; closed Christmas Day.
Tel: 01383 411411/0930 100300 Fax: 01383 410514
Web: www.deepseaworld.com Email: deepsea@sol.co.uk

V95 Dolphins and Seals of the Moray Firth, North Kessock

[Map: 3B, E9] Off A9, 2 miles N of Inverness, North Kessock, Inverness-shire, Highland. (NGR: NH 655479 LR: 26)
Located in the tourist information centre, there is an exhibition with an interactive computer programme about the local bottle-nosed dolphins of the Moray Firth, as well as a video display. The dolphins can be watched, as well as heard via under-water microphones.
Guided tours. Explanatory displays. Gift shop. Picnic area. WC. Disabled access. Car and coach parking. Group concessions. £.
Open daily 10.00-17.00.
Tel: 01463 731886 Email: dolphin@lineone.net

V96 Edinburgh Zoo

[Map: 6B, E9] On A8, 3 miles W west of Edinburgh city centre, Corstorphine Road, Murrayfield, Edinburgh. (NGR: NT 217733 LR: 66)
Set in 80 acres of hilly parkland, Edinburgh Zoo, founded in 1913 by the Royal Zoological Society of Scotland, is Britain's most popular wildlife attraction. There are more than 1000 animals, including threatened species. The large penguin pool has underwa-

ter viewing, and the penguin parade takes place at 14.00, March to September. Other features are the Darwin maze, based on evolution, and the African plains exhibition.
Guided tours by arrangement. Explanatory displays. Gift shop. Restaurants. Cafe (spring and summer only). Picnic area. Children's play area. WC. Disabled facilities. Car and coach parking.
Open all year: Apr-Sep, daily 9.00-18.00; Oct and Mar, daily 9.00-17.00; Nov-Feb, daily 9.00-16.30; open Christmas Day.
Tel: 0131 334 9171 Fax: 0131 316 4050
Web: www.edinburghzoo.org.uk

V97 Glasgow Zoo

[Map: 6B, E7] At M73/M74 junction, 6 miles E of Glasgow city, centre, Calderpark, Uddingston, Lanarkshire. (NGR: NS 684626 LR: 64)
The zoo has spacious enclosures in wooded parkland, with animals such as lions, tigers, rhinos, bears, monkeys, lizards and tortoises. There is a regular programme of animal displays, snake handling, and bird of prey displays, as well as a children's farm.
Explanatory displays. Gift shop. Tearoom. Picnic areas. WC. Disabled access. Car and coach parking. Group concessions. ££.
Open all year: summer, 9.30-18.00; winter, 9.30-16.00.
Tel: 0141 711 1185

V98 Glengoulandie Deer Park

[Map: 5B, B8] On B846, 8 miles NW of Aberfeldy, Comrie Farm, Keltneyburn, Perthshire. (NGR: NN 765524 LR: 52)
Glengoulandie Deer Park features native birds and animals kept in habitats as similar to those in the wild as possible. There are herds of red deer and Highland Cattle, as well as endangered species.
Gift shop. Picnic area. WC. Car and coach parking. Dogs must not be allowed out of cars. Group concessions. £££.
Open 9.00-1 hour before sunset.
Tel: 01887 830261 Fax: 01887 830261

V99 Highland Wildlife Park

[Map: 3B, G10] On B9152, 7 miles S of Aviemore, 2 miles W of Kincraig, Kingussie, Highland. (NGR: NH 804035 LR: 35)
The wildlife park features a range of wildlife in different habitats, including some now extinct in Scotland. Animals include bison, wild horse, red deer, Highland cattle, wolves, capercaillie, Arctic foxes, wildcat, pine marten, beavers, otters and owls.
Group concessions. Guided tours. Explanatory displays. Gift shop. Coffee shop. Picnic area. WC. Car and coach parking. Group concessions. £££ (reduced rates in winter).
Open Apr-Oct, daily 10.00-18.00; Jun-Aug, daily 10.00-19.00; Nov-Mar, daily 10.00-16.00 (shop closed; last entry 2 hours before closing.
Tel: 01540 651270 Fax: 01540 651236
Web: www.kincraig.com/wildlife Email: wlidlife@rzss.org.uk

V100 Highland and Rare Breeds Farm

[Map: 3B, C7] On A835, 15 miles N of Ullapool, Elphin, Sutherland, Highland. (NGR: NC 213110 LR: 15)

The farm, which covers some 15 acres of picturesque countryside, has more than 36 breeds of animals. Many of the animals can be petted or fed, and there is also a pets' corner and an organic farm.

Guided tours. Explanatory displays. Gift shop. Refreshments. Picnic area. WC. Car and coach parking.

Open May-Sep, daily 10.00-17.00.

Tel: 01854 666204 Fax: 01854 666204

V101 Jedforest Deer and Farm Park

[Map: 6B, G11] On A68, 5 miles S of Jedburgh, Mervinslaw Estate, Campdown, Borders. (NGR: NT 675135 LR: 80)

The working farm features rare breeds of animals, including sheep, cattle, pigs, poultry and waterfowl, and deer herds. Bird of prey demonstrations, and walks and other activities.

Explanatory displays. Gift shop. Cafe. WC. Play, BBQ and picnic area. Walks and activities. Car and coach parking. Group concessions. £.

Open May-Aug, daily 10.00-17.30; Sep-Oct, daily 11.00-16.30.

Tel: 01835 840364 Fax: 01835 840362

Web: www.aboutscotland.com/jedforest/

V102 Kylerhea Otter Haven

[Map: 3A, F6] On A850, 8 miles S of Broadford, Kylerhea, Skye. (NGR: NG 785205 LR: 33)

Otters can often be seen from the hide. Specially constructed paths are designed to protect the habitat and the wildlife. As well as otters, there are all sorts of wildlife in this fine setting.

Explanatory displays. Disabled access. Car parking.

Open all year.

Tel: 01320 366322 Fax: 01320 366581 Web: www.forestry.gov.uk

V103 Loch Garten Osprey Centre

[Map: 3B, G10] Off B970, 8 miles NE of Aviemore, 2 miles SE of Nethybridge, Loch Garten, Highland. (NGR: NH 974180 LR: 36)

The visitor centre features a public viewing facility from where, via CCTV, telescopes or binoculars, ospreys can be seen. There are forest walks, and the largest expanse of native Scots pine wood in Britain. There are a variety of habitats, and breeding birds such as capercaillie, crossbill, crested tit and goldeneye can also be seen here, as well as many rare northern insects. The best time to visit is from April to July for birds, plants and insects.

Visitor centre with explanatory displays. Gift shop. Disabled access to centre. Ranger service. Difficult walking away from tracks. Car and coach parking. Group concessions. £.

Open Easter-Oct, Wed-Sun 11.00-16.00.

Tel: 01479 831694 Fax: 01479 821069

V104 Moray Firth Wildlife Centre, Spey Bay

[Map: 4, E3] On B9104, 5 miles N of Fochabers, Tugnet, Spey Bay, Moray. (NGR: NJ 348655 LR: 28)

Located in a former salmon fishing station of 1768, the centre houses an exhibition about the Moray Firth dolphins and the marine environment. It is also possible to view hunting ospreys, seals, otters, many wildfowl and waders, as well as dolphins.

Explanatory displays. Gift shop. Picnic area. WC. Wildlife garden. Disabled access. Car and coach parking. Group concessions. £.

Open all year: daily 10.30-17.00; Jul-Aug, 10.30-19.30.

Tel: 01343 820339

V105 Museum and Marine Biological Station, Millport

[Map: 6A, E5] On A860, 0.5 miles E of Millport, Keppel, Great Cumbrae. (NGR: NS 175545 LR: 63)

A research centre of the Universities of Glasgow and London, founded in 1887 and extended in 1903. The recently refurbished museum and adjoining aquarium house a number of unique displays from the world of marine science.

One week courses available with accommodation and meals.

Open all year: Oct-May, Mon-Fri 9.30-12.15 & 14.00-16.45; Jun-Sep also Sat.

Tel: 01475 530581 Fax: 01475 530601

V106 North East Falconry Centre, Cairnie

[Map: 4, F4] Off A920 or A96, 3 miles NW of Huntly, Broadland, Cairnie, Huntly, Aberdeenshire. (NGR: NJ 485447 LR: 29)

The centre has around 40 birds of prey, from owls to eagles, and there are regular flying displays.

Explanatory displays. Gift shop. Tearoom. Picnic area. WC. Disabled access. Car and coach parking. Group concessions. ££.

Open Mar-Oct, daily 10.30-17.30: tel to confirm.

Tel: 01466 760328

V107 Palacerigg

[Map: 6B, E7] Off B8054 or B803, 3 miles E of Cumbernauld, Palacerigg Road, North Lanarkshire. (NGR: NS 783733 LR: 64)

The country park, which covers some 700 acres, has a visitor centre, and a Scottish and North European animal collection, with roe deer, bison, lynx, wildcat and owls.

Guided tours. Explanatory displays. Gift shop. Tearoom. Picnic areas. Nature trails. Bridle paths. Pony trekking. Golf course. Disabled access to visitor centre.

Park open all year: Apr-Sep, daily 9.00-18.00; Oct-Mar 9.30-16.30.

Tel: 01236 720047 Fax: 01236 458271

V108 Scottish Deer Centre

[Map: 6B, C9] On A91, 6 miles W of Cupar, Bow of Fife, Fife. (NGR: NO 265125 LR: 59)

The centre offers guided tours, which take about 30

minutes. Children can help bottle-feed fawns (at certain times of year), and there are indoor and outdoor adventure play areas. Other features include regular falconry displays, viewing platform, courtyard shops, and tree-top walkway.

Guided tours. Explanatory displays. Gift shop. Coffee shop. Picnic areas. Adventure playgrounds. WC. Car and coach parking. Group concessions. ££.

Open Apr-Oct, daily 9.30-18.00; Nov-Mar, daily 10.00-17.00.
Tel: 01337 810391 Fax: 01337 810447

V109 Scottish Seabird Centre

[Map: 6B, D11] Off A198, North Berwick harbour, East Lothian. (NGR: NT 553855 LR: 66)

Located in the seaside town of North Berwick, the centre features information on seabirds, some 150 000 of which, including puffins and gannets, return to the islands off the town. The **Bass Rock [G1]** is home to over 70,000 gannets, and is also associated with St Baldred. Remote cameras allow the study of birds close up and the cinema has films about the seabirds. Also see **Bass Rock [G1]**.

Explanatory displays. Audio-visual presentation. Gift shop. Cafe. WC. Disabled access. Parking nearby. £.

Open all year, summer 10.00-18.00; winter 10.00-16.00.
Tel: 01620 890202 Web: www.seabird.org
Fax: 01620 890222 Email: info@seabird.org

V110 Scottish Sealife and Marine Sanctuary, Barcaldine

[Map: 5A, B4] Off A828, 8.5 miles N of Oban, 5.5 miles N of Connel, Barcaldine, Argyll. (NGR: NM 843413 LR: 49)

Set in a picturesque location off the shore of Loch Creran, the centre features seals and other marine life. There are daily talks and feeding demonstrations. Young seals, in the seal pup nursery and hospital, can be seen in the summer before being released back into the wild.

Guided tours by appt. Explanatory displays. Gift shop. Restaurant. Coffee shop. Picnic area. Outdoor children's play area. Nature trail. WC. Car and coach parking. Group concessions. ££.

Open all year: daily 9.00-18.00; winter, 10.00-17.00: tel to confirm.
Tel: 01631 720386 Fax: 01631 720529

V111 Sea Life Centre, St Andrews

[Map: 6B, C10] Off A91, The Scores, St Andrews, Fife. (NGR: NO 510170 LR: 59)

The centre features 30 displays of sea creatures, including shrimps, starfish, sharks, conger eels, rays and seals. There is also the 'Kingdom of the Seahorse' exhibition.

Explanatory displays. Gift shop. Restaurant. Coffee shop. Picnic area. WC. Disabled access. Car and coach parking. All day re-entry ticket. Group concessions. ££ (free to wheelchair users).

Open all year, daily 10.00-18.00; tel to confirm winter hours.
Tel: 01334 474786

V112 Torridon

[Map: 3A, E6] Off A896, 9 miles SW of Kinlochewe, The Mains, Torridon, Wester Ross, Highland. (NGR: NG 905559 LR: 25)

Set amid some of Scotland's finest scenery in a 16,000 acre estate, the centre features an audio-visual presentation on local wildlife. Deer can be seen at nearby Mains, and there is also a museum on the life of the red deer.

Disabled access to visitor centre and deer museum only. Car parking. £.

Estate, deer park and deer museum open all year; visitor centre open May-late Sep, daily 10.00-18.00.
Tel: 01445 791221 Fax: 01445 791261

V113 Wildlife Park, Kirkcudbright

[Map: 6B, I7] On B727, 1 mile E of Kirkcudbright, Lochfergus Plantation, Dumfries and Galloway. (NGR: NX 769513 LR: 83)

The wildlife park features over 32 species of animals. There are guided tours, pet-handling sessions, and information on breeding and wildlife conservation of threatened species.

Guided tours Apr-Aug. Explanatory displays. Gift shop. Tearoom. Picnic areas. WC. Baby-changing facilities. Disabled access. Car and coach parking. Group concessions. £.

Open Mar and Sep-Oct, daily 10.00-16.30; Apr-Jul, daily 10.00-17.15.
Tel: 01557 331645

Top *Fordyce Joiner's Workshop*
Top right *Northfield Farm Museum*
Above *Angus Folk Museum*
Right *Barony Mills*
Below *Click Mill, Dounby*

Top *Laidhay Croft
Museum*
Above *Auchindrain
Museum*
Above left *Arnol
Blackhouse*
Left *Shetland
Croft Museum*
Below *Skye Museum
of Island Life*

W: Whisky

W1 Ardbeg Distillery

[Map: 5A, E3] On A846, 2.5 miles E of Port Ellen, Ardbeg, Islay. (NGR: NR 416462 LR: 60)

The distillery was founded in 1815 by the MacDougalls of Ardbeg, and the white-washed buildings are situated on the picturesque southern coast of Islay, near to **Laphroaig [W31]** and **Lagavulin [W30]**. The visitor centre is housed in the distillery's original kiln and malt barn, which has displays of old artefacts from the distillery and features tales from the past.

Guided tours. Gift shop. Old Kiln Coffee shop. WC. Limited disabled access. Maximum ten per group. Prebooking advisable for larger groups. Parking. £. Tour charge is redeemable on any purchase over £15.00.

Open all year, Mon-Fri 10.00-16.00, Jun-Aug also Sat & Sun 10.00-17.00; last full tour 15.30; also by appt.

Tel: 01496 302244 Fax: 01496 302040 Web: www.ardbeg.com

W2 Ben Nevis Distillery

[Map: 3B, H7] On A82, 2 miles NE of Fort William, Lochy Bridge, Highland. (NGR: NN 127757 LR: 41)

Standing by Scotland's highest mountain, the distillery was founded in 1825 by Long John MacDonald from Keppoch, whose ancestors had fought at the Battle of Culloden in 1746. There is a 30-minute tour of the distillery and an exhibition and audio-visual presentation are also available in the visitor centre. A sample of the 'Dew of Ben Nevis' is included.

Guided tours. Audio-visual and explanatory displays. Gift shop. Tearoom. WC. Car and coach parking.

Open all year Mon-Fri 9.00-17.00; Easter and weekends, Sat 10.00-16.00; Jul & Aug 9.00-19.30; last tour leaves 30 mins before closing.

Tel: 01397 700200/702476 Fax: 01397 702768

W3 Benromach Distillery

[Map: 4, E2] Off A96 (Forres bypass), Invererne Road, N of Forres, Moray. (NGR: NJ 033593 LR: 27)

The distillery and malt whisky centre reopened in 1998, and there is information on 100 years of history and tradition in whisky distilling, as well as on malt whiskies and Gordon and MacPhail. The distillery was built in 1898, and is housed in white-washed buildings with a 100-foot red-brick chimney.

Guided tours. Explanatory displays. WC. Picnic area. Disabled access to Malt Whisky Centre only. Disabled WC. Car and coach parking. Group concessions. £. Admission charge redeemable at distillery against purchase of 70cl bottle of malt whisky.

Open Apr-Sep, Mon-Sat 9.30-17.00, last tour 16.15; Jun-Aug, also Sun 12.00-16.00, last tour 15.15; Oct-Mar, Mon-Fri 10.00-16.00, last tour 15.15; closed Christmas and New Year period.

Tel: 01309 675968 Fax: 01343 540155

Web: www.benromach.com/www.gordonandmacphail.com

Email: info@gordonandmacphail.com

W4 Bladnoch Distillery

[Map: 6A, I6] On A714, 7 miles S of Newton Stewart, 1 mile SW of Wigtown, Bladnoch. (NGR: NX 420543 LR: 83)

The most southerly distillery in Scotland, Bladnoch was founded in 1817 by John and Thomas MacClelland. It has recently reopened, and a tour of the distillery, followed by a free sample of whisky, is available. There are woodland and river walks and picnic areas nearby, and a small caravan park.

Guided tours. Explanatory displays. Gift shop. Picnic and BBQ area. River woodland walks. WC. Car and coach parking. £.

Open late Mar–early Nov, Mon-Fri 9.00-17.00; Nov-Dec 11.00-15.30; other times by appt.

Tel: 01988 402605/402235 Fax: 01988 402605

Web: www.bladnoch.co.uk Email: raymond@bladnoch.co.uk

W5 Blair Athol Distillery

[Map: 5B, B9] On A924, 1 mile S of Pitlochry, Perthshire. (NGR: NN 940578 LR: 52)

Established in 1798 in the popular Perthshire town of Pitlochry, Blair Athol Distillery is one of the oldest working distilleries in Scotland. A free dram is given after the tour, and the admission charge includes a discount voucher. Children under eight years old are welcome but are not permitted to take the tour.

Guided tours. Explanatory displays. Gift shop. Coffee shop. Banqueting suite available for private parties. WC. Car and coach parking – groups should book in advance. Group concessions. £. Children under 18 free.

Open Easter-Sep, Mon-Sat 9.00-17.00; Jun-Sep, also Sun 12.00-17.00; Jul-Aug Mon-Sat 9.00-17.30; Oct, Mon-Fri 9.00-17.00; also Easter wknd and some Bank hol wknds; last tour 1 hour before closing; Nov-Easter restricted opening hours – tel for appt.

Tel: 01796 482003 Fax: 01796 482001

W6 Bowmore Distillery

[Map: 5A, E2] Off A846, School Street, Bowmore, Islay. (NGR: NR 311599 LR: 60)

Bowmore (pronounced 'beau -more') Distillery is one of the oldest in Scotland, and was licensed in 1779. The distillery uses the traditional method of producing its own floor-malted barley. The distillery offers guided tours and a video presentation explaining the process of whisky making. The shop stocks a full range of Bowmore Islay single malt Scotch whiskies. The tour includes a dram.

Guided tours. Explanatory displays. Gift shop. Visitors receive a dram of whisky. Disabled access: walkways ramped for wheelchairs & WC. Car and coach parking. Group concessions. £. Booking advisable for groups.

Open May-Sep, Mon-Fri: guided tours at 10.30, 11.30, 14.00 & 15.00, Sat 10.30, closed Sun; Oct-Apr, Mon-Fri 10.30 and 14.00.

Tel: 01496 810671 Fax: 01496 810757

Web: www.morrisonbowmore.co.uk

W7 Bunnahabhain Distillery

[Map: 5A, E3] Off A846, 3.5 miles N of Port Askaig, Bunnahabhain, Islay. (NGR: NR 418732 LR: 60)

Bunnahabhain is Gaelic for 'mouth of the river' and is pronounced 'Boon-na-ha-ven'. It is the most northerly of Islay's distilleries, in a peaceful and picturesque location on the Sound of Islay with views of Jura and to Mull. Visitors are welcome and are given a guided tour of the distillery. Individuals and groups are welcome, and the tour includes a dram of the Bunnahabhain 12-Year-Old Islay Malt Scotch Whisky.

Guided tours by arrangement. Gift shop. WC. Car and coach parking. Accommodation available in cottages.

Open all year except closed Christmas and New Year, Mon-Fri 10.00-16.00 – distillery tours by appt only.
Tel: 01496 840646 Fax: 01496 840248

W8 Caol Ila Distillery

[Map: 5A, E3] Off A846, N of Port Askaig, Caol Ila (signposted), Islay. (NGR: NR 428701 LR: 60)

Caol Ila (pronounced 'Caal-eela') distillery stands in a picturesque setting at the foot of a steep hill, with a small pier, overlooking the Sound of Islay and Paps of Jura, and local wildlife includes seals and otters. A visit involves a personal tour, and the shop has a wide range of blended whiskies and well as the Caol Ila Malt Whisky. Children under eight years of age are welcome but are not encouraged to take the tour.

Visitor centre. Guided tours by arrangement. Gift shop. WC. Car parking. £ but includes redeemable voucher.

Open all year, Mon-Fri by appt; at various times of the year the distillery is not in production although visitors are welcome and tours are provided.
Tel: 01496 840207 Fax: 01496 302763

W9 Cardhu Distillery

[Map: 4, F3] On B9102, 5 miles E of Charlestown of Aberlour, Knockando, Moray. (NGR: NJ 191430 LR: 28)

Cardhu, (pronounced 'Car-doo' and meaning 'black rock' in Gaelic) was licensed in 1824, but the origins of the distillery go back to the days of illicit whisky distilling, when crofters made their own spirit from barley and water. The visitor centre features an exhibition depicting the history of Cardhu and Johnnie Walker, and a tour includes a complimentary dram. The admission charge is redeemable in the shop against the purchase of a 70cl bottle of Cardhu single malt.

Guided tours. Explanatory displays. Gift shop. Picnic area. Disabled access. Car and coach parking. Large parties by appt only.

Open Mar-Nov, Mon-Fri, 9.30-16.30; Jul-Sep also Sat 9.30-16.30, Sun 11.00-16.00; Dec-Feb, Mon-Fri 10.00-16.00; closed Christmas and New Year.
Tel: 01340 872555/810204 Fax: 01340 872556
Email: ena.munro@udv.com

W10 Clynelish Distillery

[Map: 3B, C10] On A9, 5 miles NE of Golspie, 1 mile NW of Brora, Clynelish, Brora, Sutherland. (NGR: NC 898054 LR: 17)

Clynelish (pronounced 'Clyn-leesh') Distillery was built in 1819 by the Marquis of Stafford, later to become Duke of Sutherland, whose castle was at **Dunrobin [N23]**. A tour of the distillery is available, and the shop in the visitor centre stocks the Clynelish Malt Whisky, the exclusive Johnnie Walker 'Gold Label' 18-Year-Old Blend. Children under eight years of age are welcome but are not encouraged to take the tour.

Guided tours. Gift shop. Picnic area. Garden. WC. Disabled access. Car and coach parking. £.

Open Mar-Oct, Mon-Fri 9.30-16.00; Nov-Feb Mon-Thu 9.30-16.30; last tour 16.00; or by appt.
Tel: 01408 623000 Fax: 01408 623004
Web: www.highlandescape.com

W11 Dallas Dhu Distillery (HS)

[Map: 4, E2] Off A940, 1 mile S of Forres, Dallas Dhu, Moray. (NGR: NJ 035566 LR: 27)

A well-preserved Victorian distillery, Dallas Dhu (pronounced 'Dalla Doo') is no longer in production but was built in 1898 to supply malt whisky for Wright and Greig's 'Roderick Dhu' blend. Access is available to most areas of the distillery, and there is an audiovisual presentation, which also includes a dram.

Visitor centre. Guided tours. Explanatory displays. Audio-visual presentation. Gift shop. Picnic area. WC. Limited disabled access. Car and coach parking. £.

Open all year: Apr-Sep, daily 9.30-18.30; Oct-Mar, Mon-Wed and Sat 9.30-16.30, Thu 9.30-12.00, Sun 14.00-16.30, closed Fri; last ticket 30 mins before closing; closed 25/26 Dec and 1/2 Jan.
Tel: 01309 676548

W12 Dalwhinnie Distillery

[Map: 3B, H9] Off A9, Dalwhinnie, Highland. (NGR: NN 639854 LR: 42)

Dalwhinnie (which in Gaelic means 'the meeting place') Distillery is highest in Scotland, at over 1000 feet, and was opened in 1898. Tour guides explain the distilling process. The exhibition features the history and geography of the area; and the Classic Malts. The shop in the visitor centre has an extensive range of single malt whiskies. Children under eight years of age are welcome but are not admitted to the production areas.

Guided tours. Visitor centre with explanatory displays. Gift shop. WC. Car and coach parking. Group concessions. £. Parties of more than 12 are asked to make a reservation in advance.

Open Easter-Oct, Mon-Fri 9.30-17.00; Jun-Oct, also Sat 9.30-17.00; Jul-Aug, also Sun 12.30-17.00; last tour 1 hour before closing; Nov-Easter, restricted hours appt advisable; closed between Christmas and New Year.
Tel: 01540 672219 Fax: 01540 672228

W13 Dewar's World of Whisky

[Map: 5B, B8] Ballinluig turning off A9, on A827, 20 miles N of Perth, outskirts of Aberfeldy, Perthshire. (NGR: NN 866497 LR: 52)

Situated in magnificent Perthshire countryside, the distillery was opened in 1898 by John and Thomas Dewar, sons of John Dewar, one of the early pioneers of whisky blending. Dewar's World of Whisky features a personal audio guide with an audio-visual presentation, video wall, trivia quiz, touch screen. Guided tours illustrate the process of malt whisky distillation and maturation. All children are welcome.

Guided tours. Visitor centre. Gift shop with range of malt whiskies. Forest walk and nature trail. WC. Car and coach parking. ££.
Open Easter-Oct, Mon-Sat 10.00-18.00, Sun 12.00-16.00; Nov-Easter, Mon-Fri 10.00-16.00; last admission one hour before closing.
Tel: 01887 822010 Web: www.dewars.com/worldofwhisky
Fax: 01887 822012 Email: worldofwhisky@dewars.com

W14 Edradour Distillery

[Map: 5B, A9] Off A924, 2.5 miles E of Pitlochry, Edradour (signposted), Perthshire. (NGR: NN 960580 LR: 52)

Pronounced 'Eddra-dower' the distillery was founded in 1825 by a group of local farmers, and is Scotland's smallest distillery – and one of the most picturesque. It has remained virtually unchanged since Victorian times, and consists of solid white-washed buildings with grey-slate roofs. A dram of whisky is offered during an audio-visual show in the visitor centre in the malt barn.

Guided tours and audio-visual presentation. Explanatory displays. Gift shop. WC. Car and coach parking. Groups over 14 by appt only.
Open Mar-Oct, Mon-Sat 9.30-17.00, Sun 12.00-17.00; Nov-mid Dec, Mon-Sat 10.00-15.30; Jan-Feb, Mon-Sat 10.00-16.00 shop only; closed Christmas & New Year.
Tel: 01796 472095 Fax: 01796 472002 Web: www.edradour.co.uk

W15 Fettercairn Distillery

[Map: 4, H5] Off B966 or B974, Distillery Road, 4 miles NW of Laurencekirk, Kincardine and Deeside. (NGR: NO 645735 LR: 45)

Believed to be one of the oldest 'legal' distilleries in Scotland, Fettercairn was licensed in 1824 and was visited by Queen Victoria. The distillery visitor centre offers tours describing the processes of whisky making, and there is an audio-visual presentation, charting the Fettercairn story and history of the Mearns. A visit includes a free dram of Old Fettercairn, and the tour is free of charge.

Visitor centre. Guided tours. Explanatory displays. Gift shop. WC. Car and coach parking. Groups by appt only.
Open May-Sep, 10.00-16.30; last tour 16.00.
Tel: 01561 340205/244 Fax: 01561 340447

W16 Glen Grant Distillery

[Map: 4, F3] On A941, 3.5 miles N of Aberlour, Rothes, Moray. (NGR: NJ 283492 LR: 28)

Located in a wooded, sheltered glen on the outskirts of the Speyside village of Rothes, the distillery was founded in 1840 by two brothers, James and John Grant. Tours of the distillery are available, and feature an audio-visual presentation, and access to a restored Victorian garden, created by Major James Grant. Admission price includes a voucher redeemable against 70cl bottle of whisky, distillery tour and access to garden. Children under the age of eight years are not admitted to production areas.

Free to under-18s. Gift shop. WC. Disabled limited access and WC. Car parking. £.
Open Apr-Oct, Mon-Sat 10.00-16.00, Sun 12.30-16.00.
Tel: 01542 783318 Fax: 01542 783304 Email:
jennifer_robertson@seagram.com

W17 Glen Moray Distillery

[Map: 4, E3] Off A96, W of Elgin, Moray. (NGR: NJ 200625 LR: 28)

Situated on the banks of the River Lossie close to the ancient cathedral city and royal burgh of Elgin, the Glen Moray Distillery was developed from a brewery in 1897, and the original brewery buildings date from 1815. Glen Moray Distillery has a fine range of single malts, which are smooth, dry and light Speyside whiskies. They have been mellowed for a final period in white-wine barrels.

Open all year: Mon-Fri 9.00-17.00; tours at 9.30, 10.30, 11.30, 13.30, 14.30, 15.30; closed for two weeks over Christmas and New Year.
Tel: 01343 542577 Web: www.glenmoray.com
Fax: 01343 546195 Email: tdavidson@glenmorangieplc.co.uk

W18 Glen Ord Distillery

[Map: 3B, E9] Off A832, 10 miles W of Inverness, 3 miles N of Beauly, Muir of Ord, Highland. (NGR: NH 518509 LR: 26)

The last survivor of nine distilleries which once operated around Glen Ord, the distillery was licensed in 1838. The tour and exhibition show the history of the Black Isle and the main processes of distilling. A free dram is part of the adult admission charge,.

Visitor centre. Guided tours. Explanatory displays. Gift shop. Picnic area. WC. Disabled access. Car and coach parking. Group concessions. £.
Open all year: Mar-Oct, Mon-Fri 9.30-17.00; Jul-Sep also Sat 9.30-17.00 and Sun 12.30-17.00; Nov-Mar, restricted hours: appts advisable; closed Christmas and New Year.
Tel: 01463 872004 Fax: 01463 872008 Web: www.glenord.com

W19 Glendronach Distillery

[Map: 4, F4] At junction of B9001 and B9024, 5.5 miles NE of Huntly, Forgue, Aberdeenshire. (NGR: NJ 625438 LR: 29)

Glendronach is a traditional malt whisky distillery, established in 1825 by James Allerdes on his estate of Boynsmill. There is a reception centre with an audio-visual presentation, tastings and a gift shop. There are Highland cattle in the grounds of the distillery. The Gordon Wood was named to commemorate the Gordon Highlander regiment of the British Army.

Guided tours. Explanatory displays (audio-visual). Gift shop. Picnic areas. Woodland. WC. Car and coach parking.

Open all year, Mon-Fri: tours at 10.00 & 14.00; other times by arrangement; shop open office hours; closed Christmas and New Year.

Tel: 01466 730202   Fax: 01466 730313

W20 Glenfarclas Distillery

[Map: 4, F3] Off A95, 4.5 miles SW of Aberlour, Marypark, Ballindalloch, Moray. (NGR: NJ 211382 LR: 28)

Glenfarclas ('valley of the green grassland' in Gaelic) was founded in 1836 at Recherlich Farm by Robert Hay who died in 1865, and it was purchased by the Grant family. Since then five generations have owned, one of the few independent distilleries left in Scotland. The 'Ship's Room' in the visitor centre is a tribute to the liner, *Empress of Australia*, which was in service from 1913 until 1952. The oak panels which adorn the walls are from the ship's first-class smoking room.

Visitor centre. Guided tours. Explanatory displays. Gift shop. WC. Disabled access to centre. Car and coach parking. £. No charge for children under eighteen.

Open all year: Apr-Sep Mon-Fri 9.30-17.00; Jun-Sep also Sat 10.00-16.00, Sun 12.30-16.30; Oct-Mar, Mon-Fri 10.00-16.00; last tour 1 hour before closing; closed during Christmas and New Year.

Tel: 01807 500245/57   Web: www.Glenfarclas.co.uk
Fax: 01807 500234   Email: J&GGrant@glenfarclas.demon.co.uk

W21 Glenfiddich Distillery

[Map: 4, F3] On A941, just N of Dufftown, Moray. (NGR: NJ 324410 LR: 28)

Set close to the impressive **Balvenie Castle [53]**, the distillery was founded in 1887 by William Grant of Glenfiddich, and has remained in the Grant family ever since. Glenfiddich is the only Highland single malt Scotch whisky to be distilled, matured and bottled at its own plant. Tours cover the whisky-making process, and a free dram is included. There is an audio-visual presentation about whisky and the heritage of the Highlands – plus a Scotch whisky display.

Visitor centre. Guided tours. Explanatory displays. Gift shop. Picnic area. WC. Disabled access. Coach and car parking.

Open all year weekdays 9.30-16.30 excluding Christmas and New Year holidays. In addition open Easter-mid-Oct, Sat 9.30-16.30, Sun 12.00-16.30. Parties of more than twelve people welcome but please contact distillery.

Tel: 01340 820373   Fax: 01340 822083   Web: www.glenfiddich.com

W22 Glengoyne Distillery

[Map: 5B, D7] On A81, 2 miles S of Killearn, Dumgoyne, Stirlingshire. (NGR: NS 525826 LR: 57)

Located in the Campsie Fells, Glengoyne Distillery was first licensed in 1833, and is Scotland's most southerly Highland distillery. The distillery offers tours, and there is a shop and Heritage Room, which houses a cooperage display, and old artefacts. Admission includes a free dram.

Guided tours. Explanatory displays. Gift shop. Scenic waterfall walk. WC. Disabled access. Car and coach parking. ££. Evening functions can be booked, and parties of ten or more should make prior bookings.

Open all year: Mon-Sat 10.00-16.00, Sun 12.00-16.00; closed 25 Dec and 1 Jan.

Tel: 01360 550254   Fax: 01360 550094
Web: www.glengoyne.com   Email: hdean@edrington.co.uk

W23 Glenkinchie Distillery

[Map: 6B, E10] On A6093, 6.5 miles SW of Haddington, Glenkinchie, East Lothian. (NGR: NT 443669 LR: 66)

Set in a small glen in East Lothian, Glenkinchie is the only remaining malt whisky distillery close to Edinburgh. It was founded in 1837 by the brothers John and George Rate, who were local farmers. Visitors can see all aspects of the traditional distilling craft on a tour of the distillery. There is a unique exhibition of malt whisky production, and a scale model of a malt whisky distillery made for the British Empire Exhibition of 1924. The admission charge is redeemable in the shop.

Guided tours. Visitor centre with explanatory displays. Gift shop. Picnic area. WC. Disabled access. Car and coach parking. Group concessions. ££. Groups by appt only.

Open all year: Mar-May, Mon-Fri 9.30-16.00 (last tour); Jun-Oct, also Sun 12.00-16.00; Nov-Feb, Mon-Fri 11.00-15.00 (last tour).

Tel: 01875 342004   Fax: 01875 342007   Email: mary.f.darling@guiness.com

W24 Glenlivet Distillery

[Map: 4, F3] Off B9008, 10 miles N of Tomintoul, Glenlivet, Moray. (NGR: NJ 195290 LR: 36)

Founded in the face of opposition from illicit whisky makers and smugglers, Glenlivet Distillery was established by George Smith, a tenant of the Duke of Gordon, in 1824 at Upper Drummin Farm. The old distillery was destroyed by fire, and the plant moved to Minore in 1858. The tour of the distillery includes whisky production facilities and bonded warehouses, and features an audio-visual programme and interactive exhibition. The admission includes entry to exhibition, guided tour of distillery and free dram of whisky.

Visitor centre with audio-visual programme and exhibition. Gift shop. Cafe. Disabled access to visitor centre. Parking. £ (includes voucher for shop). Under 18s admitted free.

Open Mar-Oct, Mon-Sat 10.00-16.00, Sun 12.30-16.00. Children under age of eight are not admitted to production areas.

Tel: 01542 783220   Fax: 01542 783218
Web: www.theglenlivet.com   Email: linda_brown@seagram.com

W25 Glenmorangie Distillery

[Map: 3B, D9] On A9, 1 mile NW of Tain, Glenmorangie, Ross and Cromarty, Highland. (NGR: NH 768838 LR: 21)

Glenmorangie (which is pronounced 'Glen - MORangie' which means 'the glen of tranquillity' in Gaelic) was converted from a brewery and licensed in 1843. The visitor centre is housed in the original still-house, and features a 130-year-old working steam engine, and stories and artefacts from the distillery's past. Visitors can tour the distillery.

Guided tour. Explanatory displays. Gift shop. WC. Car and coach parking. Disabled facilities. £.

Open all year: shop Mon-Fri 9.00-17.00, Sat 10.00-16.00, Sun 12.00-16.00; tours available from 10.30; last tour 15.30; prebooking advisable: maximum fifteen per group.

Tel: 01862 892477 Web: www.glenmorangie.com
Fax: 01862 894371 Email: visitors@glenmorangieplc.co.uk

W26 Glenturret Distillery

[Map: 5B, C8] Off A85, 1 mile W of Crieff, Hosh, Perthshire. (NGR: NN 855234 LR: 59)

In a picturesque location near the town of Crieff – and formerly called Hosh – Glenturret Distillery dates from 1775 and is the oldest in Scotland. It was re-named Glenturret in 1875, and is one of Scotland's smallest distilleries. An exciting new attraction 'The Famous Grouse' has recently been opened.

Guided tours. Audio-visual presentation and exhibition in award-winning visitor centre. Gift shop. Smuggler's Restaurant and bar. Free tasting. WC. Disabled access and WC. Car and coach parking. £.

Open Feb-Dec, Mon-Sat 9.30-18.00, Sun 12.00-18.00; last tour 16.30; Jan, Mon-Fri 11.30-16.00; last tour 14.30.

Tel: 0845 0451800/01764 656565 Web: www.glenturret.com
Fax: 01764 654366 Email: glenturret@highlanddistillers.co.uk

W27 Highland Park Distillers

[Map: 2, C2] On A961, S of Kirkwall, Orkney. (NGR: HY 451096 LR: 6)

The most northerly whisky distillery in the world, Highland Park is located on a hillside with fine views over Scapa Flow. It stands on the site of an illicit still, and was founded in 1798. Tours of the distillery are available and there is a visitor centre.

Guided tours. Audio-visual and explanatory displays. Gift shop. WC. Disabled access. Car and coach parking. Group concessions. £.

Open Apr-Oct, 10.00-17.00, tours every 30 mins, last tour 16.00; Jul-Sep, Mon-Fri 10.00-17.00, Sat-Sun 12.00-17.00, last tour 16.00; Nov-Mar, tour at 14.00 only; shop open, Mon-Fri 13.00-17.00.

Tel: 01856 874619 Web: www.highlandpark.co.uk
Fax: 01856 876091 Email: lynne_grant@highlanddistillers.co.uk

W28 Isle of Arran Distillery

[Map: 6A, E4] Off A841, 14 miles N of Brodick, Lochranza, Arran. (NGR: NR 935503 LR: 69)

Set in a scenic location at Lochranza, Isle of Arran Distillery is the newest single malt whisky distillery in Scotland, having only been in production since 1995 – the first legal distillery on Arran for 150 years. The visitor centre features interactive displays and a short film illustrating whisky production on Arran over the last 150 years; and a tour concludes with a free dram. An audio-visual room is located in the mock 18th-century crofter's inn.

Visitor centre. Guided tours. Audio-visual programme and explanatory displays. Gift shop. Restaurant (tel: 01770 830328). Picnic area. Garden. WC. Disabled access. Induction loop for audio-visual programme. Car and coach parking. ££. Coach parties welcome but should tel in advance. Private functions, conference and wedding facilities.

Open all year: Apr-Oct, daily 10.00-18.00; winter hours vary: please tel to confirm; closed Christmas and New Year; for group booking contact the distillery; restaurant open 10.00-22.00; closed Mon evening; winter opening times vary: please tel for details (01770 830328).

Tel: 01770 830264 Web: www.arranwhisky.com
Fax: 01770 830364 Email: visitorcentre@arranwhisky.com

W29 Isle of Jura Distillery

[Map: 5A, E3] On A846, Craighouse, Jura. (NGR: NR 526669 LR: 61)

On the wild and picturesque island of Jura, the original distillery was built in 1810, close to where illegal distilling had occurred for 300 years.

Guided tours. Car parking.

Open by appt.

Tel: 01496 820240 Fax: 01496 820344

W30 Lagavulin Distillery

[Map: 5A, F3] On A846, 2 miles E of Port Ellen, Lagavulin, Islay. (NGR: NR 405456 LR: 60)

Near the ruins of **Dunyvaig Castle [N95]**, Lagavulin (pronounced 'Lagga-voolin') Distillery, was established in 1816 by John Johnson. Tours and tastings can be taken by appointment only.

Guided tours. Explanatory displays. Gift shop. WC. Car and coach parking. £. Children under the age of eight are welcome but are not encouraged to take the tour.

Open Apr-Oct, Mon-Fri. Tours at 10.00, 11.30 & 14.30 and are by appt only.

Tel: 01496 302400 Fax: 01496 302733

W31 Laphroaig Distillery

[Map: 5A, F3] Off A846, 1 mile E of Port Ellen, Laphroaig, Islay. (NGR: NR 387452 LR: 60)

Located in a scenic bay with otters and swans, the original distillery at Laphroaig (pronounced 'La-froyg' and meaning 'the beautiful hollow by the broad bay') was founded by Donald and Alex Johnston in 1815 and is housed in white-washed buildings. There is a shop.

Guided tours. Gift shop. WC. Disabled access. Car and coach parking.

Open all year, Mon-Fri: tours by appt only.

Tel: 01496 302418 Fax: 01496 302496
Web: www.laphroig.com Email: 106523.565@compuserve.com

W32 Miltonduff Distillery

[Map: 4, E3] Off B9010, 2 miles SW of Elgin, Miltonduff, Moray. (NGR: NJ 183602 LR: 28)

Standing in a pleasant location not far from the historic town of Elgin, the distillery was founded in 1824 and is quite near the restored **Pluscarden Abbey [J29]**. The distillery offers tours by appointment and there is a reception centre. The Black Burn is said to have been blessed by one of the abbots of Pluscarden, and thereafter the drink distilled from the burn was called 'aqua vitae' or the water of life ('uisge beatha' in Gaelic).

Open Sep-Jun – tours available by appt only.
Tel: 01343 554121 Fax: 01343 548802

W33 Oban Distillery

[Map: 5A, B4] Off A816 or A85, Stafford Street, Oban, Argyll. (NGR: NM 858300 LR: 49)

In the holiday town of Oban, the distillery was established in 1794 by the Stevenson family, who were also involved in the development of the town. There are guided tours of the distillery and there is an exhibition and audio-visual programme in the visitor centre, which charts the history of Oban. Children under eight years of age are welcome but are not permitted to tour the distillery.

Guided tours. Exhibition. Gift shop. WC. Disabled access. Guide dogs not permitted. Parking nearby. £.

Open all year, Mon-Fri 9.30-17.00; Jul-Sep, Mon-Fri 9.30-20.30; open Sat Easter-Oct 9.30-17.00; last tour leaves one hour before closing; Dec-Feb restricted hours; closed Christmas and New year period; booking advisable in winter months or when travelling any distance. Groups by appt only.
Tel: 01631 572004 Fax: 01631 572011

W34 Pulteney Distillery, Wick

[Map: 3B, B12] Off A9, Huddart Street, Wick, Caithness, Highland. (NGR: ND 365510 LR: 12)

The distillery was established in 1826 by James Henderson, and is the most northerly distillery on the British mainland. The visitor centre charts the history of Wick and its harbour, and there is information on the secrets of whisky distilling. It is possible to sample the excellent Old Pultney Scotch Whisky.

Explanatory displays. Visitor centre. Gift shop. Parking.
Open Apr-Sep, Mon-Fri 10.30-12.30 and 13.30-15.30.
Tel: 01955 602371 Web: www.inverhouse.com

W35 Royal Lochnagar Distillery

[Map: 4, G3] Off B976, 6 miles W of Ballater, Crathie, Kincardine & Deeside. (NGR: NO 267938 LR: 44)

About one mile from the Royal Family's castle at **Balmoral [R1]**, Royal Lochnagar was established in 1845 by John Begg. Lochnagar became 'Royal' after a visit by Queen Victoria and Prince Albert in 1848. In the visitor centre, converted from the old distillery farm

steading, is a whisky shop and exhibition area.

Guided tours. Explanatory displays. Whisky shop. WC. Parking nearby. £.
Open all year: Easter-Sep, Mon-Sat 10.00-17.00, Sun 12.00-16.00; Oct-Mar, Mon-Fri 10.00-17.00; closed Christmas and New Year. Children under eight years of age are not allowed in the production area.
Tel: 01339 742700 Fax: 01339 742702

W36 Scapa Distillery

[Map: 2, C2] On A964, 2 miles SW of Kirkwall, Scapa, Orkney. (NGR: HY 435090 LR: 6)

In a picturesque setting overlooking Scapa Flow, the Scapa distillery was established in 1885 by Macfarlane and Townsend.

Tours by arrangement only.
Tel: 01856 872071 Fax: 01856 876585

W37 Scotch Whisky Heritage Centre, Edinburgh

[Map: 6B, E9] Off A1, 354 Castlehill, top of Royal Mile near castle, Edinburgh. (NGR: NT 253735 LR: 66)

The Scotch Whisky Heritage centre reveals the mystery of whisky making, including how it is made, its history, and different characteristics of malts from around the country. There is an audio-visual presentation and a tour in a whisky cask. The tour takes 50 minutes, and concludes in the bar and bistro with a complimentary dram of blended whisky.

Guided tours available in eight languages: Dutch, English, French, German, Italian, Japanese, Portuguese and Spanish. Whisky Bond Bar and Bistro. Gift shop. WC. Disabled access. Corporate facilities and tutored whisky tastings also available. Group concessions. ££.
Open daily 19.30-17.00; extended hours in summer; closed 25 Dec.
Tel: 0131 220 0441 Web: www.whisky-heritage.co.uk
Fax: 0131 220 6288 Email: enquiry@whisky-heritage.co.uk

W38 Speyside Cooperage Visitor Centre

[Map: 4, F3] Off A941, 2 miles NE of Aberlour, Dufftown Road, Craigellachie, Moray. (NGR: NJ 290450 LR: 28)

An award-winning working cooperage, with a unique visitor centre, where coopers and their apprentices repair oak casks for the whisky industry. Each year the cooperage repairs around 100,000 casks – barrels, hogsheads, butts and puncheons – many of which will be used to mature different whiskies. There is also the 'Acorn to Cask' exhibition, audio-visual presentation, tasting room, and a gift shop selling a range of goods crafted from wood.

Exhibition. Audio-visual presentation. Viewing gallery. Tastings. Gift shop. Picnic area. Car and coach parking. £.
Open all year: Mon-Fri 9.30-16.00; closed Christmas & New Year. Coach parties welcome by appt.
Tel: 01340 871108 Web: www.speysidecooperage.co.uk
Fax: 01340 881437 Email: info@speyside-coopers.demon.co.uk

W39 Springbank Distillery

[Map: 5A, F4] Off A83, Campbeltown, Longrow, Kintyre, Argyll. (NGR: NR 720205 LR: 68)

In the seaside town of Campbeltown, Springbank Distillery was founded in 1828, and is owned by the Mitchell family: J & A Mitchell and Company, from 1897. Campbeltown was once the centre for whisky distilling, with 30 legal distilleries, but Springbank is the only one regularly operating. Tours are available in the summer but are strictly by appointment only.

Parking nearby. £.

Distillery tours in summer strictly by appt.
Tel: 01586 552085   Web: www.springbankwhisky.com
Fax: 01586 553232   Email: enquiries@springbankwhisky.com

W40 Strathisla Distillery

[Map: 4, E4] Off A96, Seafield Avenue, Keith, Moray. (NGR: NJ 427513 LR: 28)

Strathisla (pronounced 'Strath-eye-la') Distillery was founded in 1786 and is the oldest working distillery in the Highlands: as well as being considered the most picturesque. A visit to the distillery features coffee and shortbread in the Isla Room, a self-guided tour of the distillery and includes a free dram for those over 18, souvenir handbook and whisky nosing in the Dram Room. Children under the age of eight are not permitted in the production areas but are welcome in the visitor centre.

Self-guided tour of distillery: admission charge includes coffee and shortbread, tour of traditional warehouse, tutored nosing, sample whisky, souvenir handbook. Gift shop. ££ (includes voucher). Under 18s admitted free.

Open Apr-Oct, Mon-Sat 10.00-16.00, Sun 12.30-16.00.
Tel: 01542 783044   Web: www.chivas.com
Fax: 01542 783039   Email: jeanette_grant@seagram.com

W41 Talisker Distillery

[Map: 3A, F4] On B8009, 6 miles W of Sligachan, Carbost, Skye. (NGR: NG 378319 LR: 32)

Beneath the impressive saw-toothed Cuillin mountains of Skye, the present distillery was founded in 1830 by Hugh and Kenneth MacAskill in a scenic location on the banks of Loch Harport. The distillery offers tours, but larger parties should book in advance: the approach road is not suitable for coaches. Children under eight years of age are welcome but will not be admitted into the production area.

Guided tours. Explanatory displays. Gift shop. Picnic area. WC. Limited disabled access. Car parking. £.

Open Apr-Jun & Oct, Mon-Fri 9.00-16.30; Jul-Sep, Mon-Sat 9.00-16.30; Nov-Mar, Mon-Fri 14.00-16.30; last tour at 14.00.
Tel: 01478 640314   Fax: 01478 640401
Email: taliskerdistillery@udv.com

W42 Tamnavulin Distillery

[Map: 4, F3] On B9008, 4.5 miles NE of Tomintoul, Tomnavoulin, Moray. (NGR: NJ 213260 LR: 36)

Tamnavulin (pronounced 'Tamna-VOO -lin') Distillery was founded in 1965-6. Tours of the distillery can be made. There is a coffee and gift shop.

Gift shop. Coffee shop. Audio-visual presentation. Limited disabled access. Parking.

Open Apr-Oct, Mon-Sat 9.30-16.30; Oct, Mon-Fri 9.30-16.30; Jul & Aug, also Sun 12.30-16.30.
Tel: 01807 590442   Fax: 01807 590342

W43 Tobermory Distillery

[Map: 5A, B3] Off A848, Tobermory, Mull. (NGR: NM 505551 LR: 47)

Located in the pleasant town of Tobermory with its painted houses, the distillery was established by John Sinclair, a local merchant, in 1798. The distillery offers tours and there is a visitor centre and shop.

Guided tours. Explanatory displays. Gift shop (entrance fee discounted on certain goods). Limited disabled access. Car and coach parking. £.

Open Easter-Oct, Mon-Fri 10.00-17.00. Other times by appt.
Tel: 01688 302645   Fax: 01688 302643

W44 Tomatin Distillery

[Map: 3B, F10] Off A9, 15 miles S of Inverness, Tomatin, Highland. (NGR: NH 792294 LR: 35)

Tomatin was founded in 1897 by the Tomatin Distillery Co. There are tours of the distillery, and a free dram for visitors. The visitor centre features a fully stocked shop and an audio-visual presentation about the process and production of whisky.

Guided tours. Explanatory displays and video. Gift shop. WC. Disabled access. Car and coach parking.

Open all year, Mon-Fri 9.00-17.00; May-Oct also Sat 9.00-13.00; advance notice required for large groups.
Tel: 01808 511234   Fax: 0141 304 4589
Email: info@tomatin.co.uk

W45 Tomintoul Distillery

[Map: 4, F2] On B9136, 3.5 miles N of Tomintoul, Moray. (NGR: NJ 149254 LR: 36)

Tomintoul (pronounced 'Tom-in-towel') Distillery was founded in 1964-5, built by Tomintoul Distillery Ltd, and is one of the few independent distilleries left in Scotland. The distillery can be visited, but by appointment only.

By appt only. Group bookings limited to 10.
Tel: 01807 590274   Fax: 01807 590342

Top left *Lagavulin*
Top right *Glenlivet*
Right *Benromach*
Below *Edradour*

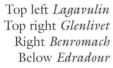

X: Industry and Transport

Museums and other sites with strong links to industry, mining, textiles transport, canals, railways and ships.

X1 Alford Valley Railway

[Map: 4, G4] On A944, 25 miles W of Aberdeen, Kingsford Road, Alford, Aberdeenshire. (NGR: NJ 580160 LR: 37)

Alford Valley Railway, a narrow-gauge passenger railway, is hauled by a steam locomotive on many weekends in the summer, and trips last for 30 minutes. The collection features an Aberdeen tram, as well as one steam and three diesel locomotives.

Explanatory displays. WC. Disabled access. Car and coach parking. £.

Open Apr, May and Sep, wknds 13.00-17.00; Jun-Aug, daily 13.00-17.00, last train 16.30.

Tel: 01975 563182   Fax: 01975 563182

X2 Aluminium Story Visitor Centre and Library

[Map: 3B, I7] Off B863, 5 miles E of Glencoe, Linnhe Road, Kinlochleven, Highland. (NGR: NN 190617 LR: 41)

The Aluminium Story tells the tale of the British Aluminium Company, with audio-visual displays and a video presentation system. The company opened a smelter and hyroelectric scheme at Kinlochleven in 1908.

Explanatory displays. Gift shop. WC. Disabled access. Car and coach parking. Group concessions. £.

Open Apr-Oct, Mon-Sat 10.00-16.00, Sat & Sun 11.30-16.30.

Tel: 01855 831663   Fax: 01855 831663
Email: cultural.leisure@highland.gov.uk

X3 Biggar Gasworks (HS)

[Map: 6B, F9] Off A702, Gas Works Road, NW of Biggar town centre, Lanarkshire. (NGR: NT 038375 LR: 72)

The only surviving small-town gas works in Scotland, dating from 1839, although there was a major reconstruction in 1914. It was closed in 1973 when North Sea gas came on-line, but the works were preserved as a museum. Managed by the Biggar Museum Trust.

Explanatory displays. WC. Car parking. £.

Open Jun-Sep, daily 14.00-17.00.

Tel: 01899 221070   Fax: 01899 221050

X4 Birkhill Clay Mine

[Map: 5B, D8] Off A706 or A904, 3 miles NW of Linlithgow, 2.5 miles SW of Bo'ness, Birkhill, West Lothian. (NGR: NS 965790 LR: 65)

The clay mine, which is set in the steep and wooded Avon Gorge, can be reached by the **Bo'ness & Kinneil Railway [X6]**. The mine, mill, clay handling buildings and haulage gear can be visited, and there are underground walks and a nature trail. There are also fossils which are more than 300 million years old.

Guided tours. Explanatory displays. Picnic area. WC. The mine can only be reached by descending 130 steps into the Avon Gorge so access for the disabled and elderly is very difficult. Car parking. Group concessions. £.

Ope Apr-mid Oct, Sat and Sun only; 2 Jul-26 Aug, daily except closed Mons; open Hol Mons.

Tel: 01506 825855   Web: www.srps.org.uk
Fax: 01506 828766   Email: srps@sol.co.uk

X5 Bonawe Iron Furnace (HS)

[Map: 5A, B5] On A85, 12 miles E of Oban, Bonawe, Taynuilt, Argyll. (NGR: NN 011319 LR: 50)

The restored remains of a charcoal furnace for iron smelting, which was established in 1753 and used until 1876. It is the most complete example of its kind, and displays illustrate how iron was made.

Explanatory displays. Kiosk. Picnic area. WC. Disabled WC. Car parking. £. Joint entry ticket for Dunstaffnage Castle available (£).

Open Apr-Sep, daily 9.30-18.30; last ticket 18.00.

Tel: 01866 822432

X6 Bo'ness and Kinneil Railway and Scottish Railway Exhibition

[Map: 5B, D9] Off A904, 6.5 miles E of Falkirk, Union Street, Bo'ness, Falkirk. (NGR: NT 004817 LR: 65)

The railway runs for 3.5 miles from Bo'ness to **Birkhill Clay Mine [X4]**, and trains are normally hauled by a steam locomotive. There are historic railway buildings, including a station and train shed. The Scottish Railway Exhibition charts the development of railways in Scotland.

Station buffet and buffet car on train. Souvenir shop. Picnic area. Disabled access. Car parking. ££ (return train fare). Entrance to the Exhibition is free. Admission to mine is extra.

Open 30 Mar-19 Oct Sat & Sun; Mon 31 Mar, all Mon May; 4 Jul-17 Aug daily except Mon; also Public Holidays – tel to check; exhibition open 11.30-17.00.

Tel: 01506 822298   Web: www.srps.org.uk
Fax: 01506 202582   Email: railway@srps.org.uk

X7 Caledonian Canal

[Map: 3B, F9] Off A862, Cana Office, Seaport Marina, Muirtown Wharf, Inverness, Highland. (NGR: NH 655460 LR: 26)

The Caledonian Canal runs between Corpach, near Fort William, to Clachnaharry at Inverness, and is used as a short-cut, avoiding having to sail around the sometimes treacherous waters of the north of Scotland. It joins the lochs of the Great Glen (Loch Lochy, Loch Oich and Loch Ness) to the sea. The canal was designed by Thomas Telford and completed in 1822, and is set in some of the finest scenery in Scotland. Pleasure cruises are available and lochs, and hotel boats also operate on the canal. The Caledonian Canal Heritage Centre is located in Fort Augustus.

Scheduled ancient monument featuring dramatic lock flights in the beautiful setting of the Great Glen.
Accessible all year – weather permitting; Caledonian Canal Heritage Centre, open Apr-Oct.
Tel: 01463 233140 Fax: 01463 710942
Web: www.scottishcanals.co.uk
Email: enquiries.caledonian@britishwaterways.co.uk

X8 Caledonian Railway

[Map: 4, I4] Off A90, The Station, 2 Park Road, Brechin, Angus. (NGR: NO 596601 LR: 44)
The Caledonian Railway runs steam trains on Sundays during the summer along the four miles of old railway line between the terminus at Brechin and the former junction at Bridge of Dun. There is a coach adapted to take wheelchairs, and a static display at the Bridge of Dun.
Guided tours by appt. Explanatory displays. Gift shop. Light refreshments. WC. Picnic area at Bridge of Dun. Baby changing facilities at Brechin. Disabled access with assistance. Disabled WC. Car and coach parking. Group concessions. ££.
Open Easter, then end May-Sep and Dec, Sun only: tel to confirm.
Tel: 01561 377760/01356 622992

X9 Castletown Flagstone Trail

[Map: 3B, A11] Off A836, 5 miles E of Thurso, Castletown, Caithness, Highland. (NGR: ND 195688 LR: 11)
This was a centre for the quarrying of flagstones in the 19th century, which were used for pavements all over Britain. There is a trail around various sites, including a ruined windmill which was used to pump water from the quarry working. There is a heritage centre in Main Street, Castletown, which has exhibits on local history.
Trail: access at all reasonable times; heritage centre: tel to confirm.
Tel: 01847 821204 (Heritage Centre)

X10 Clydebuilt, Braehead

[Map: 6B E7] King's Inch Road, Braehead, Glasgow.
Clydebuilt charts the story of Glasgow, the second city of the Empire, and the Clyde from tobacco and textiles to steel, iron and shipbuilding, and features exciting interactives, stage sets and floating exhibits. There are temporary exhibitions and ships can be visited.
Explanatory displays. Gift shop. Refreshments. WC. Disabled access. Parking. ££
Open all year: Mon-Sat 10.00-18.00, Sun 11.00-17.00.
Tel: 0141 886 1013 Fax: 0141 886 1015 Email: clydebuilt@tinyworld.co.uk

X11 Crinan Canal

[Map: 5A, D4] Off A83 or B841, the canal runs from Ardrishaig by Lochgilphead to Crinan, Argyll. (NGR: NR 840910 LR: 55)
The canal was built between 1793 and 1801 so that ships could sail between Loch Fyne and the Atlantic

without travelling around the Mull of Kintyre. The canal runs for nine miles and has 15 locks, and the associated tow path is a pleasant walk. The picturesque village of Crinan has a coffee shop, boat yard, hotel and canal basin. There is a forest walk from Crinan village [NR 783940] which has fine views of Islay, Jura, the Slate Islands and Mull.
Access to tow path at all times.
Tel: 01546 603210

X12 Cruachan Power Station

[Map: 5A, B5] On A85, 5.5 miles W of Dalmally, Ben Cruachan, Loch Awe, Argyll. (NGR: NN 077268 LR: 50)
Cruachan Power Station is located within the mountain Ben Cruachan. A short coach journey goes into the heart of the mountain, and the machine hall of this large pumped-storage system can be viewed.
Explanatory displays. Guided tours (30 mins). Gift shop. Tearoom. WC. Disabled access. Car and coach parking. £.
Open Easter-mid Nov, daily 9.30-17.00; Aug, daily 9.30-18.00.
Tel: 01866 822618 Web: www.scottishpower.plc.uk
Fax: 01866 822509 Email: visit.cruachan@scottishpower.com

X13 Discovery Point, Dundee

[Map: 4, J3] Off A92, Discovery Quay, Dundee. (NGR: NO 408302 LR: 54)
Discovery Point is the home of Royal Research Ship *Discovery*, Captain Scott's Antarctic ship, and where he and his men survived for two years frozen in the Antarctic pack ice. There are new exhibits and state-of-the-art multimedia shows about this heroic age of exploration.
Guided tours available. Explanatory displays. Gift shop. Cafe. WC. Disabled access. Car and coach parking. Group concessions. £££.
Open all year: Apr-Oct, Mon-Sat 10.00-17.00, Sun 11.00-17.00; Nov-Mar, Mon-Sat 10.00-16.00, Sun 11.00-16.00.
Tel: 01382 201245 Fax: 01382 225891
Web: www.rrsdiscovery.com Email: info@dundeeheritage.co.uk

X14 Dumfries and Galloway Aviation Museum

[Map: 6B, H8] Off A701, 2 miles NE of Dumfries, Heathhall, Dumfries and Galloway. (NGR: NY 001785 LR: 84)
The museum charts aviation from World War I, and there is a large collection of artefacts and several aircraft open for inspection. Run by volunteers.
Explanatory displays. Tearoom. WC. Baby changing facilities. Disabled access and WC. Car and coach parking. £.
Open Apr-Oct, Sat-Sun and Bank Hols 10.00-17.00; also Jul-Aug: please check with Dumfries TIC (01387 253862).
Tel: 01387 251623 Web: www.dgam.co.uk

X15 Dunaskin Experience

[Map: 6A, G6] Off A713, 9 miles SE of Ayr, Dalmellington Road, Waterside, Patna, Ayrshire. (NGR: NS 440085 LR: 70)
An open-air industrial museum, covering some 110 acres, which charts how the rural valley of Doon was

transformed into a thriving industrial complex in the 19th century. On display are many artefacts from local pits and mines, as well as Europe's best-preserved Victorian Ironworks. Chapel Row Cottage recreates an ironworks dwelling of around 1914.

Guided tours available. Audio-visual displays. Audio-tours. Gift shop. Chimneys restaurant and coffee shop. WC. Children's play area. Disabled access. Car parking. Group concessions. ££.
Open Apr-Oct, daily 10.00-17.00; winter months by appt only.
Tel: 01292 531144/5 Web: http://home.btconnect.com/dunaskin
Fax: 01292 532314 Email: dunaskin@btconnect.com

X16 Easdale Island Folk Museum

[Map: 5A, C4] Off B844, 13 miles SW of Oban, Easdale island, Easdale (Seil). (NGR: NM 740170 LR: 55)
The award-winning museum features a fine collection of photographs and objects illustrating the industrial and domestic life of the Slate Islands in the 19th century, including records of slate quarries, the volunteers, Friendly Societies, education and public health. There are fine views of the Firth of Lorn from the hilltop. A scenic walk by the remains of old gardens leads to the sea-filled slate quarries, which were devastated by the great storm of November 1881.

Explanatory displays. Puffer Bar and Restaurant nearby. WC. Car and coach parking on Seil (no cars on island). Group concessions on application. £ (museum). On-call ferry to island: check times.
Museum: open Apr-Oct, daily 10.30-17.30; island accessible at all reasonable times: check ferry times.
Tel: 01852 300370 Fax: 01852 300370 Web: www.easdale.co.uk

X17 Edinburgh Canal Centre

[Map: 6B, E9] Off A8, Bridge Inn, 27 Braid Road, Ratho, Edinburgh. (NGR: NT 135718 LR: 65)
The centre is housed in an old inn, the Bridge Inn, dating from about 1750, which stands by the side of the Union Canal. The canal was opened in 1822. The canal-boat has a restaurant, and there are sight-seeing cruises. The Union Canal has been rejoined to the Forth and Clyde Canal by the Falkirk Wheel.

Guided tours on canal cruises (Apr-Oct). Explanatory displays. Restaurant and bar on boats. WC. Garden. Play area. Wildfowl Reserve. Towpath. Disabled access to inn. Car and coach parking. Charge by facility.
Open all year: Mon-Thu 12.00-23.00, Sat 12.00-24.00, Sun 12.30-23.00; closed Christmas day except restaurant; closed 26 Dec and 1-2 Jan.
Tel: 0131 333 1320 Web: www.bridgeinn.com
Email: info@bridgeinn.com

X18 Forth Bridges Exhibition

[Map: 6B, D9] On B981, 8 miles N of Edinburgh, Queensferry Lodge Hotel, St Margaret's Head, North Queensferry, Fife. (NGR: NT 123810 LR: 65)
The exhibition features a 40 minute video presentation and tells the story of the building of the Forth Railway and Road Bridges. The bridges can be seen

from the gallery.

Explanatory displays. Gift shop. Restaurant. WC. Viewing area. Car and coach parking.
Open all year, daily 9.00-21.00; closed Christmas.
Tel: 01383 417759 Fax: 01383 417759

X19 Forth and Clyde Canal

[Map: 6B, D8] Between Glasgow at Port Dundas to the Forth at Grangemouth. (NGR: NS 907814 LR: 65)
The canal, which was opened in 1790, was built to link the industrial towns of central Scotland with the Forth at Grangemouth. The canal runs from near the centre of Glasgow through rural areas, and finally to industrial Grangemouth. The canal was closed in 1963, although it is being restored. The towpath is a fine walk, and there are boat trips from the Stables Inn, Glasgow Road, near Kirkintilloch and from Auchinstarry, near Kilsyth. The Forth and Clyde Canal has been joined to the Union Canal by the Falkirk Wheel.

Guided walks and canal events during summer months.
Access at all reasonable times.
Tel: 0141 332 6936 Fax: 0141 552 3886

X20 Galloway Hydros Visitor Centre, Tongland

[Map: 6B, I7] On A711, 2 miles N of Kirkcudbright, Tongland Power Station, Dumfries and Galloway. (NGR: NX 697535 LR: 83)
The visitor centre has displays concerning the construction of the Galloway Hydros Scheme, a hydroelectric scheme, in the 1930s. The power station can be toured and the Tongland dam and reservoir viewed. There is a reconstructed office from the 1930s.

Guided tours. Explanatory displays. Gift shop. Picnic area. WC. Disabled access. Car and coach parking. ££.
Open May-Jun, Mon-Fri 9.00-17.00; Jul-Aug, Mon-Sat 9.00-17.00.
Tel: 01557 330114 Email: visit.galloway@scottishpower.com

X21 Glenfinnan Station Museum

[Map: 3A, H6] On A830, 15 miles NW of Fort William, Station Cottage, Glenfinnan, Highland. (NGR: NM 899810 LR: 40)
The museum, which is housed in the restored station, charts the history of the West Highland Railway with displays, photographs and artefacts. **'The Jacobite [X4]**' steam train runs to the station, which is on the line between Fort William and Mallaig, in the summer. There is a restaurant in a converted railway carriage.

Explanatory displays. Gift shop. Restaurant/tearoom (open evenings in summer). WC. Disabled access. Car parking. Group concessions. £.
Open daily Jun-Sep, 9.30-16.30; winter tel for details.
Tel: 01397 722295 Fax: 01397 701292 Email: glenstat@hege-hernes.demon.co.uk

X22 Glover House, Aberdeen

[Map: 4 G5] 79 Balgownie Road, Bridge of Don, N of Aberdeen.

The family home, which has been restored to its Victorian splendour, of Thomas Blake Glover, a 19th-century Scottish industrial pioneer, who had a major influence in helping Japan develop as a naval power and modern industrial nation. There is a display of Japanese Samurai armour and swords with original Victorian furniture and kitchen.

Guided tours sometime available at extra cost in Japanese. Explanatory displays. Gift shop. WC. Garden. Limited disabled access. Parking nearby. £

Open all year by arrangement: no regular hours but usually Mon-Fri 10.30-18.30.

Tel: 01224 709303 Fax: 01224 709301

Email: info@glover-house.freeserve.co.uk

X23 Grampian Transport Museum, Alford

[Map: 4, G4] On A944, 25 miles W of Aberdeen, Alford, Aberdeenshire. (NGR: NJ 578161 LR: 37)

The museum, which is housed in a purpose-built hall, has an extensive collection of vehicles. Exhibitions are regularly changed.

Explanatory displays. Gift shop. Tea room (open Sun Apr-Oct, daily Jul and Aug). WC. Adventure playground. Disabled access. Car and coach parking. Group concessions. £

Open Apr-Oct, daily 10.00-17.00.

Tel: 01975 562292 Fax: 01975 562180 Web: www.gtm.org.uk

Y88 Grangemouth Museum

Displays include local industry, canals, shipping and shipbuilding, and the world's first practical steam ship, the *Charlotte Dundas*.

See main entry Y88

X24 Jacobite Steam Train

[Map: 3B, H7] Fort William, Highland. (NGR: NN 105743 LR: 41)

'The Jacobite' steam train runs through the picturesque scenery between Fort William and Mallaig.

Open Jun-Sep: all trains depart 10.20 – bookings only Tel: 01463 239026.

Tel: 0870 1245511 Fax: 01524 735518

X25 Keith and Dufftown Railway

[Map: 4, F3] Off A941, Dufftown Station; off A95, Keith station, Moray. (NGR: NJ 323414 LR: 28)

The line runs the 11 miles through the picturesque countryside between the two whisky-distilling towns of Keith and Dufftown. The train, called 'Spirit of Speyside', is a Class 108 diesel railcar. There are stations at Dufftown and Keith.

Explanatory displays. Gift shop. WC. Disabled access. Car parking.

Open Easter-mid Oct, Sat-Sun; contact railway for timetables.

Tel: 01340 821181 Fax: 01340 820011

Web: www.edge-of-nowhere.demon.co.uk/KDRA

X26 Kinnaird Head Castle (HS)

[Map: 4, E5] Off A98, N of Fraserburgh, Banff and Buchan, Aberdeenshire. (NGR: NJ 999675 LR: 30)

A large altered 15th-century keep, rectangular in plan, the walls of which are harled and whitewashed. It was a property of the Frasers of Philorth. A lighthouse was built into the top of the castle in 1787, and the outbuildings were built around it in 1820 by Robert Stevenson, grandfather of Robert Louis Stevenson. It now forms part of Scotland's National Lighthouse Museum. The Wine Tower, a lower tower, stands nearby. Managed by the Kinnaird Head Trust.

Visitor centre with explanatory displays and audio-visual display. Gift shop. Tearoom. WC. Disabled access to museum and toilet. Car and coach parking. Group concessions. £

Open daily all year as Lighthouse Museum, Apr-Oct , Mon-Sat 10.00-18.00, Sun 12.30-18.00; Nov-Mar, Mon-Sat 10.00-16.00, Sun 12.00-16.00; closed 25/26 Dec & 1/2 Jan – joint entry ticket.

Tel: 01346 511022 Fax: 01346 511033

X27 Kirriemuir Aviation Museum

[Map: 4 I3] Off A90, Bellie Brae, Kirriemuir, Angus.

The museum houses a collection of items associated with flight, such as radar and radio equipment, model planes, photographs, uniforms and manuals.

Guided tours. Explanatory displays. Picnic area nearby. Disabled access with assistance. Car and coach parking. Donations.

Open Apr-Sep, Mon-Thu and Sat 10.00-17.00, Fri and Sun 11.00-17.00.

Tel: 01575 573233

X28 Linlithgow Canal Centre

[Map: 6B, D8] Off A803, Canal Basin, Manse Road, Linlithgow, West Lothian. (NGR: NT 004769 LR: 65)

The small museum, which is located by the historic canal basin on the Union Canal, is housed in former stables, and there is a replica Victorian trip boat. There are also boat trips to the Avon Aqueduct. The Union Canal has been joined to the Forth and Clyde Canal by the Falkirk Wheel.

Explanatory displays. Gift shop. Tearoom. Picnic area. Disabled access to museum. WC. Parking nearby. Charge for boat trips.

Open Easter-Sep, Sat-Sun 14.00-17.00; Jul-Aug, daily 14.00-17.00.

Tel: 01506 671215 (answering machine)

Web: www.lucs.org.uk Email: info@lucs.org.uk

X29 Maud Railway Museum

[Map: 4, E5] On B9029, 12 miles W of Peterhead, Maud Railway Station, Maud, Aberdeenshire. (NGR: NJ 925479 LR: 30)

Housed in the former Maud railway station, the museum has railway memorabilia and old photographs, and exhibits on the great days of steam.

Guided tours. Picnic area. WC. Disabled access. Car and coach parking.

Open Easter-Sep, Sat-Sun and public hols 12.30-17.00.

Tel: 01771 622906 Web: www.aberdeenshire.gov.uk/ahc.htm

Fax: 01771 622884 Email: general@abheritage.demon.co.uk

Y127 McManus Galleries

There are many displays, including on the Tay Bridge Disaster.

See main entry Y127

X30 Mill Trail Visitor Centre

[Map: 5B, D8] On A91, 8 miles E of Stirling, Glentana Mill, West Stirling Street, Alva, Clackmannanshire. (NGR: NS 883970 LR: 58)

The centre charts the story of spinning and weaving in Clackmannanshire, and is told through the experiences of a 13-year-old working in the mills. There are original weaving and knitting looms, as well as a modern mill where it is possible to see jumpers being made. The shop sells local crafts, books and knitwear.

Explanatory display. Audiovisual displays. Gift shop. Coffee shop. WC. Play area. Disabled access. Car and coach parking.

Open all year: Jan-Jun and Oct-Dec, daily 10.00-17.00; Jul-Sep 9.00-18.00; closed Christmas and New Year.

Tel: 01259 769696

Y130 Mill on the Fleet

Housed in a restored 18th-century cotton mill, Mill on the Fleet has an exhibition on the history of the town with an audio-visual programme.

See main entry Y130

X31 Montrose Air Station Museum

[Map: 4, I5] Off A92, Waldron Road, Broomfield, NW of Montrose on Links, Angus. (NGR: NO 725595 LR: 54)

The airfield here was established in 1913, making it one of the oldest in the country. It was bombed by German bombers in 1940, and hangars and a mess were destroyed. The airfield was abandoned by the RAF after the war in 1957, and a museum, housed in the buildings, displays wartime memorabilia, comprising artefacts, pictures, models and uniforms relating to the site. Aircraft are also on display, including a Seahawk 131, as well as a Bofors gun.

Guided tours. Explanatory displays. Gift shop. WC. Car and coach parking. £.

Open all year, Sun 12.00-17.00; parties other times by appt.

Tel: 01674 673107/674210

X32 Moray Motor Museum

[Map: 4, E3] Off A96, Bridge Street, Elgin, Moray. (NGR: NJ 215630 LR: 28)

The museum, which is housed in an old mill, features a fine collection of cars and motor bikes.

Explanatory displays. Gift shop. WC. Disabled access. Car and coach parking. Group concessions. £.

Open Apr-Oct, daily 11.00-17.00.

Tel: 01698 267515

Y134 Motherwell Heritage Centre

There are displays on the history of Motherwell through the rise and fall of heavy industry.

See main entry Y134

X33 Motoring Heritage Centre, Alexandria

[Map: 5A, D6] Off B857, 3 miles N of Dumbarton, Main Street, Alexandria, Dunbartonshire. (NGR: NS 943413 LR: 63)

The centre, housed in a building of 1906 which was once the largest car plant in the world, charts the history of Scottish motoring with unique archive film. Other features are the once-famous Argyll marque (which was made here), a Model T Ford to sit in, and other interesting cars.

Guided tours. Video walls. Explanatory displays. Gift shop. Cafe. WC. Disabled access. Car and coach parking. Group concessions. £.

Open all year, daily 19.30-17.30; closed Xmas and New Year.

Tel: 01389 607862   Fax: 01389 607862
Web: www.motoringheritage.co.uk

X34 Mull & West Highland Narrow Gauge Railway

[Map: 5A, B4] Off A849, Old Pier Station, Craignure, Mull. (NGR: NM 725369 LR: 49)

The first passenger railway built on a Scottish island was opened in 1984, and links the Old Pier at Craignure with **Torosay Castle [S45]**. Both steam and diesel trains operate on the narrow gauge line, which is just over one mile long – a 20 minute journey. There are extensive and dramatic woodland and mountain views, and departure times normally coincide with the ferry from Craignure.

Gift shop. Disabled access: provision to carry one person seated in wheelchair on trains. Car and coach parking. Group and family concessions. £.

Open Easter-mid Oct, daily 11.00-17.00. Check timetable for departure times with TICs or tel: 01680 812494.

Tel: 01680 812494   Fax: 01680 300595
Web: www.zynet.co.uk/mull/rail

X35 Museum of Flight

[Map: 6B, D10] Off A1, 3 miles NE of Haddington, East Fortune Airfield, East Lothian. (NGR: NT 548783 LR: 66)

The museum, in a former airship base, features a range of aircraft including a Tiger Moth, Supermarine Spitfire Mk 16, De Haviland Sea Venom, Hawker Sea Hawk, Vulcan bomber, a MIG, Lightning, and Comet 4. There is an extensive display of rockets and aeroengines, an Imperial Airways office set in the Middle East, and information on Airship R34, which flew from here to New York and back in 1913.

Sales area. Cafe in Nissen hut. WC. Disabled access & WC. Parking. £.

Open Easter-Sep, daily 10.30-17.00, Jul-Aug 10.30-18.00; closed Christmas and New Year.

Tel: 01620 880308   Fax: 01620 880555
Web: www.nms.ac.uk/flight   Email: museum_of_flight@sol.co.uk

X36 Museum of Lead Mining

[Map: 6B, G8] Off B797, Wanlockhead, Dumfries and Galloway. (NGR: NS 873129 LR: 78)

The museum charts the story of lead mining over some 300 years, featuring 1.5 miles of walkways past mine heads, pumping engines, ore processing and smelting sites. Wanlockhead is the highest village in Scotland, and set among striking scenery. There are also period cottages, the well-known miners' library, displays of minerals, a gold-panning area, and an early 19th-century **Wanlockhead Beam Engine [X54]**, formerly used for draining one of the mines.

Visitor centre. Guided tours. Explanatory displays. Interactive computer presentation. Gift shop. Tearoom. WC. Car and coach parking. Group concessions. ££.

Open Easter-Oct, daily 11.00-16.30; Nov-Mar by arrangement only.

Tel: 01659 74387 Web: www.leadminingmuseum.co.uk
Fax: 01659 74481 Email: ggodfrey@goldpan.co.uk

X37 Museum of Transport

[Map: 6B, E7] Off A814, Kelvin Hall, Bunhouse Road, Glasgow. (NGR: NS 565663 LR: 64)

The museum, housed in Kelvin Hall, displays a range of Glasgow buses, a reconstruction of a 1938 Glasgow side street, and Glasgow trams. Other features include Scottish-made cars, fire engines, horse-drawn vehicles, cycles and motorcycles, and a walk-in car showroom. There are also steam locomotives, a Glasgow subway station, and a collection of model ships.

Guided tours. Explanatory displays. Gift shop. Cafe. Disabled access. Car and coach parking.

Open all year: Mon-Thu and Sun 10.00-17.00, Fri-Sat 11.00-17.00

Tel: 0141 287 2628 Fax: 0141 287 2672
Web: www.glasgow.gov.uk/cls

X38 Myreton Motor Museum

[Map: 6B, D10] Off A198, 4 miles N of Haddington, 1 mile E of Aberlady, Myreton, East Lothian. (NGR: NT 486795 LR: 66)

The museum features a wide-ranging collection of cars, motorcycles, commercial vehicles, advertising signs and automobilia from 1899 to 1969.

Explanatory displays. Gift shop. Picnic area. WC. Disabled access. Car and coach parking. Group concessions. ££.

Open all year: Easter-Sep, daily 10.30-16.30; Oct-Easter, Sat-Sun, 11.00-16.00.

Tel: 01875 870288/0794 7066666

X39 New Lanark

[Map: 6B, F8] Off A73, 1 mile S of Lanark, New Lanark, Lanarkshire. (NGR: NS 880426 LR: 71)

Surrounded by woodlands and close to the Falls of Clyde, this cotton-spinning village was founded in 1785 by David Dale, and made famous by the social pioneer Robert Owen, his son-in-law. The innovative ride in the visitor centre, the 'New Millennium Experience', features a character from the future called Harmony, on a journey to discover why New Lanark is mentioned in all the world history files. Entrance to the mills, Millworker's House, Robert Owen's School, Village Store and Robert Owen's House is also included. There is a fine walk to Falls of Clyde.

Walk from car park. Guided tours. Explanatory displays. Gift shop. Tearoom. WC. Picnic areas. Falls of Clyde Wildlife Reserve. Special needs guided tours and information. Partial disabled access and WC. Car and coach parking. Group concessions. ££ (exhibition).

Access to village at all times. Visitor centre open all year, daily 11.00-17.00 except closed Christmas Day and New Year's Day.

Tel: 01555 661345 Fax: 01555 665738
Web: www.newlanark.org (or www.robert-owen.com)
Email: visit@newlanark.org

R3 Old Royal Station, Ballater

The fine Victorian railway station has been restored, and has displays charting the 100 year history of the (dismantled) railway being used by royalty.

See main entry R3

X40 Prestongrange Museum

[Map: 6B, D10] On B1348, 8 miles E of Edinburgh, Morison's Haven, Prestongrange, East Lothian. (NGR: NT 371738 LR: 66)

One of the oldest documented coal mining sites in Britain, dating back 800 years. The museum features a Cornish beam engine, and on-site evidence of associated industries, such as brickmaking and pottery. There is a free guided tour of the site, plus a different temporary exhibition each year.

Guided tours. Visitor centre. Explanatory displays. Gift shop. Cafe. Picnic area. WC. Disabled access. Car and coach parking.

Open Apr-Oct, daily 11.00-16.00.

Tel: 0131 653 2904 Web: www.prestongrangemuseum.org
Fax: 01620 828201 Email: info@prestongrangemuseum.org

Y163 Queensferry Museum

The museum has information on the Forth Railway and Road Bridges.

See main entry Y163

X41 Robert Smail's Printing Works, Innerleithen (NTS)

[Map: 6B, F10] Off A72, 7-9 High Street, Innerleithen, Borders. (NGR: NT 333366 LR: 73)

The works is a restored Victorian printer which still has the now almost forgotten craft of hand typesetting. There is the Victorian office, with acid-etched windows, and a reconstructed waterwheel.

Guided tours. Explanatory displays. Gift shop. Disabled access to ground floor. Car and coach parking. £.

Open (2002) 25 Mar-28 Jun and 2 Sep-27 Oct, Thu-Mon 12.00-17.00, Sun 13.00-17.00; 29 Jun-1 Sep, Thu-Mon 10.00-18.00, Sun 13.00-17.00.

Tel: 01896 830206

X42 Scottish Industrial Railway Centre, Burnton

[Map: 6A, G6] Off A713, 12 miles SE of Ayr, Minnivey Colliery, Burnton, Dalmellington, Ayrshire. (NGR: NS 475069 LR: 77)

Located on the site of the former Minnivey Colliery, the centre features steam locomotives and a traditional locomotive shed. There are brake van trips, which stop at **Dunaskin [X15]**, and a museum with an extensive collection of railway memorabilia and documents.

Guided tours. Explanatory displays. Gift shop. Refreshments. WC. Disabled access. Car and coach parking. Group concessions. £.
Steam days held on the last Sun May, Jun and Sep, every Sun Jul and Aug; static display every Sat from Jun-Sep.
Tel: 01292 531144

X43 Scottish Maritime Museum – Denny Ship Model Experiment Tank

[Map: 5A, D6] Off A82, Castle Street, Dumbarton. (NGR: NS 405749 LR: 64)

The tank, which was built in 1882, was constructed to test ship design, and was restored to working order by the Scottish Maritime Museum. It retains many of its original features, and is in working order so that the original process can be demonstrated.

Explanatory displays. Gift shop. Tea room. Picnic area. WC. Group concessions. £.
Open all year, Mon-Tue, Fri-Sat 10.00-16.00; closed Christmas and New Year.
Tel: 01389 763444 Fax: 01389 743093

V68 Scottish Maritime Museum, Irvine

See main entry V68

X44 Scottish Mining Museum

[Map: 6B, E9] On A7, 10 miles S of Edinburgh, Newtongrange, Midlothian. (NGR: NT 334637 LR: 66)

Based at the historic Lady Victoria Colliery, the Scottish Mining Museum features tours led by former miners. The pithead of the surviving Victorian colliery can be visited, as well as Scotland's largest steam winding engine, and a full-scale replica of an underground coalface. An audio-visual presentation portrays underground working conditions and life in the community.

Guided tours. Explanatory displays. Audio-visual presentation. Visitor centre. Gift shop. Restaurant. Picnic area. WC. Museum fully wheelchair accessible. Car and coach parking. Group concessions. £.
Open Apr-Sep, daily 10.00-16.00; last tour 15.00.
Tel: 0131 663 7519 Web: www.scottishminingmuseum.com
Fax: 0131 654 1618 Email: enquiries@scottishminingmuseum.com

X45 Scottish Slate Islands Heritage Trust

[Map: 5A, C4] Off B844, 13 miles SW of Oban, Ellenabeich, Seil. (NGR: NM 742173 LR: 55)

The compact and fascinating heritage centre features an exhibition of photographs, models and pictures illustrating life on the Slate Islands in the 19th and 20th centuries. There is a larger museum, quarries and much more besides on **Easdale Island [X16]**.

Explanatory displays. Parking nearby. £.
Open Mar-Oct, daily 10.00-18.00.
Tel: 01852 300449 Fax: 01852 300473 Email: pwithall@sol.co.uk

X46 Scottish Vintage Bus Museum, Dunfermline

[Map: 6B, D9] On B915, 2 miles N of Dunfermline, M90 Commerce Park, Lathalmond, Fife. (NGR: NT 120898 LR: 65)

The museum features more than 100 vintage buses from the 1920s, many of them Scottish, which can be viewed during all stages of restoration.

Guided tours. Explanatory displays. Gift shop. Refreshments. WC. Disabled access (but not on vehicles). Car and coach parking. Group concessions. £.
Open Easter-early Oct, Sun 12.30-17.00.
Tel: 01383 623380 Fax: 01383 623375
Web: www.busweb.co.uk/svbm

X47 Scottish and Southern Energy Visitor Centre

[Map: 5B, A9] Off A924, Pitlochry Power Station, Pitlochry, Perthshire. (NGR: NN 935577 LR: 52)

The visitor centre has a multimedia exhibition illustrating how electricity is produced at the power station and delivered to the customer. There is a salmon ladder with a viewing chamber, as well as a walkway across the top of the dam.

Visitor centre with audiovisual displays. Gift shop. WC. Disabled access. Car parking. £ (main exhibition).
Open Apr-Oct, daily 10.00-17.30.
Tel: 01796 473152

X48 Springburn Museum

[Map: 6B, E7] Off A803, NE of city centre, Atlas Square, Ayr Street, Springburn, Glasgow. (NGR: NS 605685 LR: 64)

The museum, Glasgow's first independent community museum, covers the rise, decline and rebirth of a typical Glasgow community. Springburn was a centre for railway manufacturing, and there are photographs, models, items and graphics about the area.

Explanatory displays. Gift shop. Parking nearby.
Open all year, Tue-Fri 10.30-17.00, Sat 10.00-16.30; closed Bank hols.
Tel: 0141 557 1405 Fax: 0141 557 1405

X49 Strathspey Steam Railway

[Map: 3B, G10] Off B970, Aviemore Station, Dalfaber Road, Aviemore, Highland. (NGR: NH 898129 LR: 36)

The Strathspey Railway is Scotland's 'Steam Railway in the Highlands'. It operates from Aviemore to Boat of Garten, and there are splendid views of the Cairngorm Mountain range. Details of family fares, discounts for OAPs and booked parties, times and booking arrangements from Aviemore Station.

Gift shop. Refreshments on the trains (except Sat). WC. Disabled access. Car and coach parking. Group concessions. £££.

Open Jun-Sep, daily; limited service Easter, late May and Oct.

Tel: 01479 810725 Fax: 01479 812220

Web: www.strathspeyrailway.co.uk

X50 Summerlee Heritage Trust, Coatbridge

[Map: 6B, E8] Off A89, Heritage Way, off West Canal Street, Coatbridge, Lanarkshire. (NGR: NS 729655 LR: 64)

A major 22 acre museum of social and industrial history, on the site of the Summerlee iron works (1836). There is also the only operational electric tram in Scotland, which runs on 300 yards of track to the mine area with restored rows of miners' cottages.

Huge indoor exhibition hall with working machinery. Tramway. Underground mine. Exhibition gallery. Children's play area. Shop. Tearoom. WC. Disabled WC. Conference room. Parking.

Open all year Apr-Sep, daily 10.00-17.00; Oct-Mar, daily 10.00-16.00; closed Christmas and New Year.

Tel: 01236 431261 Fax: 01236 440429

X51 The Tall Ship at Glasgow Harbour

[Map: 6B E7] 100 Stobcross Road, Glasgow

Clyde built in 1896, the *Glenlee* features exhibitions, events and activities on Glasgow's maritime heritage, as well as a nautical souvenir shop.

Exhibitions. Events. Gift shop. Licensed restaurant. Disabled access. Car and coach parking. ££.

Open Mar-Oct, daily 10.00-17.00; Nov-Feb 11.00-16.00.

Tel: 0141 339 0631 Fax: 0141 341 0506

Web: www.thetallship.com Email: info@thetallship.com

S46 Trinity House (HS)

The fine Georgian building houses a unique collection of maritime displays. Trinity House is home to the Incorporation of Shipowners and Shipmasters, who have been closely involved in the history of Leith from the 14th century. The building stands on the site of a medieval sailors' hospital.

See main entry S46

X52 Trossachs Pier Complex

[Map: 5B, C7] On A821, 8 miles W of Callendar, Loch Katrine, Stirlingshire. (NGR: NN 495073 LR: 57)

Set in the picturesque hills of the Trossachs, the complex offers cruises on Loch Katrine on the S. S. *Sir*

Walter Scott, a steam ship first launched in 1899. There are also loch-side walks and cycle routes.

Guided tours. Explanatory boards. Gift shop. Tearoom. WC. Disabled access. Car and coach parking. £ (parking).

Open Easter-Oct, Sun-Fri 9.00-17.00, Sat 10.00-17.00.

Tel: 01877 376316 Fax: 01877 376317

X53 Verdant Works, Dundee

[Map: 4, J3] Off A92, West Henderson's Wynd, Dundee, Angus. (NGR: NO 400310 LR: 54)

The restored jute mill, dating from 1833, houses a museum about Dundee's textile industries, which employed 50,000 people in the city at its peak. Displays explain what jute is, where it came from, what it was used to make, and why Dundee came to dominate in its production. A social history gallery focuses on the lives of workers outside the mills. The wide range of exhibits include film shows, hands-on exhibits, interactive computers and historic machinery restored to working condition. Winner of the European Industrial Museum of the Year 1999.

Guided tours. Explanatory displays. Gift shop. Cafe. Disabled access. Car and coach parking. Group concessions. £££.

Open all year, daily; closed 25 Dec and 1-2 Jan.

Tel: 01382 225282 Web: www..verdantworks.com

Fax: 01382 221612 Email: info@dundeeheritage.sol.co.uk

X54 Wanlockhead Beam Engine (HS)

[Map: 6B, G8] On A797, Wanlockhead, Dumfries and Galloway. (NGR: NS 870130 LR: 78)

The beam engine, which was used for draining a lead mine, dates from the early 19th century and is a water-balance pump. There is the track of a horse engine nearby, as well as the **Museum of Lead Mining [X36]**.

Parking nearby.

Access at all reasonable times.

X55 *Waverley*, Glasgow

[Map: 6B, E7] Anderston Quay, Glasgow. (NGR: NS 540665 LR: 65)

The *Waverley* is the last sea-going paddle steamer in the world, and the last built for use on the Clyde. There are a variety of cruises available from Glasgow, Ayr and along the Clyde coast.

Bar, meals and light refreshments. Car parking.

For details of boat trips, departure points and times tel 0141 221 8152.

Tel: 0141 221 8152 Web: www.waverleyexcursions.co.uk

Fax: 0141 248 2150 Email: sharon@waverley5.freeserve.co.uk

Top left *Bonawe*
Above *Kinnaird Head*
Left *Easdale*
Below left *Forth Bridge*
Bottom left *Clydebuilt*
Below right *Alford Valley Railway*
Below right *Edinburgh Canal Centre*

Y1: Large or General Museums

Museums with large and varied collections, covering many different areas or national collections.

Y1 British Golf Museum

[Map: 6B, C10] Off A91, Bruce Embankment, St Andrews, Fife. (NGR: NO 503170 LR: 59)

The museum charts the history of golf from its origins to the present day. There are themed galleries, an audio-visual presentation, and interactive displays. *Explanatory displays. Audio-visual presentation. Gift shop. Disabled access. Guide in Braille available. Car parking.*
Open all year: Apr-Oct daily 9.30-17.30; Nov-Mar, Thu-Mon 10.00-15.00.
Tel: 01334 478880 Web: www.britishgolfmuseum.co.uk
Fax: 01334 473306 Email: hwebster@randagc.org

Y2 Burrell Collection, Glasgow

[Map: 6B, E7] 2060 Pollokshaws Road, Pollok Country Park, Glasgow. (NGR: NS 555622 LR: 64)

The Burrell Collection was amassed by Sir William Burrell over 80 years, and presented to Glasgow in 1944. It is housed in a specially designed building, which was opened in 1983. Among the 8000 items in the collection are Ancient Egyptian alabaster; Chinese ceramics, bronzes and jade; Japanese prints; Near Eastern rugs and carpets; Turkish pottery; and European medieval art, including metalwork, sculpture, illuminated manuscripts, ivories, and fine collections of stained glass and tapestries. There are also medieval doorways and windows, now set in the walls; British silver and needlework; and painting and sculptures, ranging from the 15th to the early 20th century, with work by Cranach, Bellini, Rembrandt, Millet, Degas, Manet, Cezanne and others. *Guided tours available. Explanatory displays. Gift shop. Restaurant & cafe. WC. Disabled access. Audioguides for visually impaired visitors. Parking.*
Open all year, Mon-Thu and Sat 10.00-17.00, Fri and Sun 11.00-17.00; closed 25/26 Dec &1/2 Jan.
Tel: 0141 649 7151 Fax: 0141 636 0086 Web: www.glasgow.gov.uk/cls

Y3 Coats Observatory, Paisley

[Map: 6A, E6] Off A726 or A737, 49 Oakshaw Street, Paisley, Renfrewshire. (NGR: NS 480640 LR: 64)

The observatory, which was designed by John Honeyman and first started in 1883, has an exhibition charting the history of the building, as well as displays on astronomy, meteorology and seismology. *Explanatory displays. Parking nearby.*
Open all year: Tue-Sat, Mon-Sat 10.00-17.00, Sun 14.00-17.00;
open Pub Hols 10.00-17.00; Oct-Mar, also Thu 19.00-21.30 for telescopic viewing, weather permitting.
Tel: 0141 889 2013 Web: www.renfrewshire.gov.uk
Fax: 0141 889 9240 Email: museums.els@renfrewshire.gov.uk

Y4 Hunterian Museum

[Map: 6B, E7] Off M8, University Avenue, University of Glasgow, Glasgow. (NGR: NS 597655 LR: 64)

The museum is named after Dr William Hunter, the 18th-century physician, who bequeathed his important collections of coins, medals, geological, archaeological and ethnological items to the university. There is also a major exhibition on the Romans, including distance slabs and Roman coins. The museum opened in 1807, and the collections have been added to, although the emphasis remains on geology, archaeology, coins and anthropology. *Sales area. WC. Disabled access. Lift to most levels. Parking nearby. May be charge for special exhibitions.*
Open all year, Mon-Sat 9.30-17.00; some Pub hols: tel to confirm.
Tel: 0141 330 4221 Web: www.hunterian.gla.ac.uk
Fax: 0141 330 3617 Email: reception@museum.gla.ac.uk

U11 Kelvingrove Museum
See main entry U11

Y5 Museum of Childhood

[Map: 6B, E9] 42 High Street (Royal Mile), Edinburgh. (NGR: NT 265737 LR: 66)

The Museum of Childhood, which was one of the first museums about children and childhood to open, was expanded and reorganised in 1986. It has a fine collection of toys, games, costumes, dolls and nursery equipment, and there is a programme of activities and changing exhibitions. *Explanatory displays. Gift shop. WC. Disabled access and WC. Parking nearby.*
Open all year: Mon-Sat 10.00-17.00; during Festival also Sun 14.00-17.00.
Tel: 0131 529 4142 Fax: 0131 558 3103 Web: www.cac.org.uk

Y6 Museum of Scotland

[Map: 6B, E9] Chambers Street, Edinburgh. (NGR: NT 256732 LR: 66)

This magnificent museum houses extensive collections on Scotland's history, land and people, covering the decorative arts, natural history, science and technology, working life and geology. Items of particular interest include the Monymusk Reliquary, the crosier of St Fillan, and many fine carved Pictish stones and jewellery. There is also a major display of Roman finds, including commemorative slabs, altars and the 'Traprain Treasure'. *Museum. Multi-media study room. Gift shop. Audio guides. Tearooms. Roof-top restaurant. WC. Disabled access & WC. Parking nearby.*
Open all year: Mon-Sat 10.00-17.00, Tue 10.00-20.00, Sun

Map of Areas

Scotland has been divided into nine different areas – each map is followed by a list of places to visit which appear on that map. Maps on which the tourist board areas can be found are listed opposite (page 278)
NOTE: Locations on maps are only very approximate and are for guidance only

Map 1
(page 280-1)
Shetland

Map 2
(page 280-1)
Orkney

Map 3A
(page 282-3)
Western Isles and Highlands (west)

Map 3B
(page 284-5)
Western Isles and Highlands (east)

Map 4
(page 286-7)
Aberdeen, Moray, Dundee and Angus

Map 5A
(page 288-9)
Argyll, Stirling and Perthshire (west)

Map 5B
(page 290-1)
Argyll, Stirling and Perthshire (east)

Map 6A
(page 292-3)
Southern Scotland (west)

Map 6B
(page 294-6)
Southern Scotland (east)

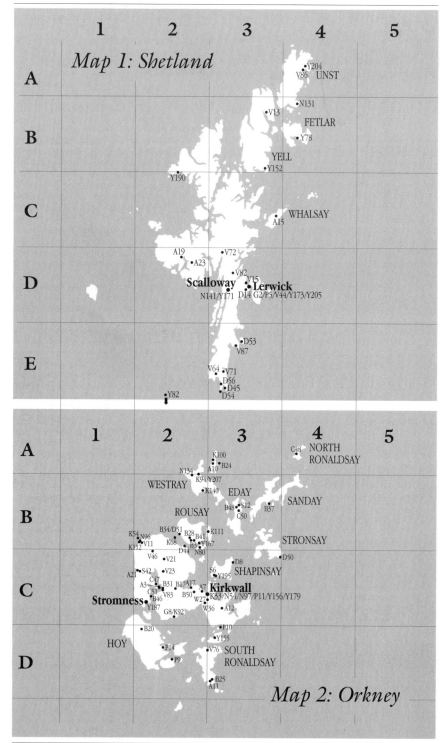

Map 1

V13 Bayanne House, Yell (B3)
V15 Bod of Gremista, Lerwick (D3)
D14 Clickhimin Broch (D3)
G2 Dim Riv Norse Longship Boat Trips, Lerwick (D3)
Y78 Fetlar Interpretive Centre (B4)
P5 Fort Charlotte (D3)
Y82 George Waterston Museum, Fair Isle (E2)
V44 Islesburgh Exhibition, Lerwick (D3)
D45 Jarlshof (E3)
D53 Mousa Broch (E3)
N131 Muness Castle (B4)
D54 Ness of Burgi Fort (E3)
Y152 Old Haa Visitor Centre (B3)
D56 Old Scatness Broch and Settlement (E3)
A15 Pettigarth's Field (C3)
V64 Quendale Water Mill (E3)
N141 Scalloway Castle (D3)
Y171 Scalloway Museum (D3)
A19 Scord of Brouster Prehistoric Settlement (D2)
V71 Shetland Croft House Museum, Boddam (E3)
Y173 Shetland Museum (D3)

V72 Shetland Textile Working Museum, Weisdale (D3)
A23 Staneydale Prehistoric Settlement (D2)
Y190 Tangwick Haa Museum (C2)
V82 Tingwall Agricultural Museum (D3)
V86 Unst Boat Haven (A4)
Y204 Unst Heritage Centre (A4)
Y205 Up Helly Aa Exhibition, Lerwick (D3)
V87 Warp and Weft Visitor Centre, Sandwick (E3)

Map 2

S6 Balfour Castle (C3)
A3 Barnhouse Prehistoric Settlement (C2)
V11 Barony Mills, Birsay (B2)
N54 Bishop's Palace, Kirkwall (C3)
B3 Blackhammer Chambered Cairn (B2)
K54 Brough of Birsay (B2)
D8 Burroughston Broch (C3)
S12 Carrick House, Eday (B3)
V21 Click Mill, Dounby (C2)
V23 Corrigall Farm Museum (C2)
N80 Cubbie Roo's Castle (B2)
B17 Cuween Hill Chambered Cairn (C2)
B20 Dwarfie Stane, Hoy (D2)
N96 Earl's Palace, Birsay (B2)
N97 Earl's Palace, Kirkwall (C3)
K68 Eynhallow Church (B2)
A7 Grain Souterrain (C2)
D44 Gurness Broch (B2)
P9 Hackness Martello Tower and Battery, Orkney (D2)
W27 Highland Park Distillers (C2)
B24 Holm of Papa Westray Chambered Cairns (A3)
B25 Isbister Chambered Cairn (Tomb of the Eagles), South Ronaldsay (D3)

P10 Italian Chapel, Orkney (D3)
V46 Kirbuster Museum, Birsay (C2)
A10 Knap of Howar Prehistoric Settlement (A3)
B28 Knowe of Yarso Chambered Cairn, Rousay (B2)
D50 Lamb Ness Broch, Stronsay (C3)
A11 Liddle Burnt Mound (D3)
B31 Maes Howe Chambered Cairn (C2)
D51 Midhowe Broch (B2)
B34 Midhowe Chambered Cairn (B2)
A12 Mine Howe, Tankerness (C3)
N134 Noltland Castle (B2)
Y155 Orkney Fossil and Vintage Centre, Burray (D2)
Y156 Orkney Museum, Kirkwall (C2)
P11 Orkney Wireless Museum, Kirkwall (C2)
G8 Orkneyinga Saga Centre, Orphir (C2)
K92 Orphir Church and Earl's Bu (C2)
K94 Pierowall Church, Westray (A2)
B37 Quoyness Chambered Cairn, Sanday (B3)
A17 Rennibister Souterrain (C2)
C47 Ring of Brodgar Circle (C2)
Y167 Rousay Heritage Centre (B2)
W36 Scapa Distillery (C2)
P14 Scapa Flow Visitor Centre, Lyness (D2)

S42 Skaill House (C2)
A21 Skara Brae Prehistoric Settlement (C2)
V76 Smiddy Museum, St Margaret's Hope (D3)
K100 St Boniface Church, Papa Westray (A3)
K33 St Magnus Cathedral, Kirkwall (C3)
Y179 St Magnus Centre, Kirkwall (C3)
K111 St Magnus Chuch, Egilsay (B3)
K112 St Magnus Church, Birsay (B2)
C48 Standing Stone, North Ronaldsay (A4)
C50 Stone of Setter, Eday (B3)
C51 Stones of Stenness (C2)
Y187 Stromness Museum (C2)
B41 Taversoe Tuick Chambered Cairn, Rousay (B2)
Y195 The Smithy, Shapinsay (C3)
V83 Tormiston Mill (C2)
B46 Unstan Chambered Cairn (C2)
B48 Vinquoy Hill Chambered Cairn, Eday (B3)
Y207 Westray Heritage Centre (B2)
K140 Westside Church (Crosskirk), Westray (B2)
B50 Wideford Hill Chambered Cairn (C2)

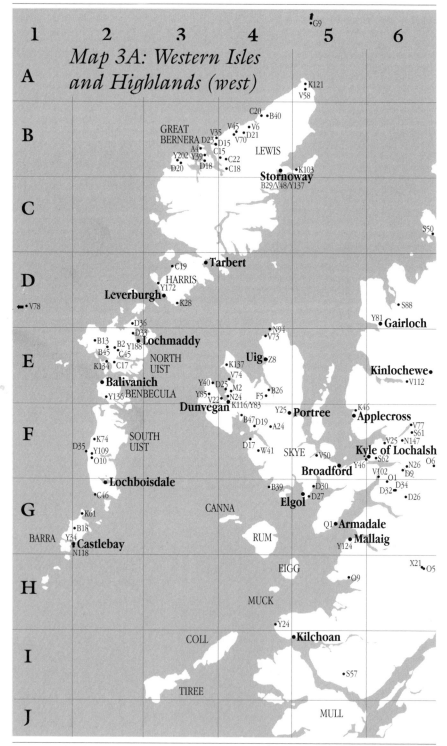

Map 3A: Western Isles and Highlands (west)

| 1 | 2 | 3 | 4 | 5 | 6 |

•G9

A · K121
V58

•C20 •B40
B GREAT •V45 •V6
BERNERA D23 V35 •V70 V21
A4• D15 LEWIS
Y202• C15•
Y39• •C22
D20• D18 •C18 STORNOWAY
•K103
B29/V48/Y137

C S50•

•C19 •Tarbert
D HARRIS
Y172
Leverburgh• •S88
•K28 Y81• •Gairloch
—•V78

•D36
•D33 •N94
•B13 B2 Y188 •Lochmaddy •V73
E B45• C45 Uig• Kinlochewe•
K134• C17 NORTH •Z8 •V112
UIST •K137
•Balivanich •V74 •K46
Y136• BENBECULA Y40• D25• M2 •B26 •Applecross
Y85• N24 F5• •V77
V22• K116/Y83 Y25 •Portree •S61
F Dunvegan B47•D19 •V25 •N147
•K74 •A24 Kyle of Lochalsh
D35• SOUTH •D17 SKYE S62• •N26 O6•
Y109• UIST •W41 •V50 Y46• V102• •D9
O10• Broadford O1•
D32• •D34
•Lochboisdale •B39 •D30 D26•
G •C46 •D27
CANNA Elgol Q1•Armadale
•K61
•B18 RUM •Mallaig
BARRA Y34• Y124•
•Castlebay X21 O5
N118 EIGG •O9

H MUCK

•Y24
COLL •Kilchoan
I
•S57

TIREE

J MULL

Map 3A

S50 Achiltibuie Hydroponicum (C6)
K46 Applecross (F5)
Y24 Ardnamurchan Point Visitor Centre (H4)
S57 Ardtornish Estate (I5)
Q1 Armadale Castle (G5)
V6 Arnol Blackhouse Museum (B4)
Y25 Aros Experience (F4)
S61 Attadale Garden (F6)
S62 Balmacara (Lochalsh Woodland Garden) (F6)
B2 Barpa Langass Chambered Cairn (E2)
Y34 Barra Heritage and Cultural Centre (G2)
O1 Bernera Barracks (G6)
Y39 Bernera Centre (B3)
Y40 Borreraig Park (E3)
A4 Bosta Prehistoric Settlement (B3)
Y46 Bright Water Visitor Centre, Kyleakin (F5)
D9 Caisteal Grugaig (F6)
C15 Callanish Standing Stones (B4)
C17 Carinish Stone Circle (E2)
C18 Ceann Hulavig Stone Circle (B4)
K61 Cille Bharra (G2)
F5 Clach Ard (E4)
C19 Clach Mhic Leoid (D3)
C20 Clach an Trushal (B4)
B13 Clettraval Chambered Cairn (E2)
C22 Cnoc Fillibhir Bheag Stone Circle (B4)
V22 Colbost Croft Museum (E4)
V25 Craig Highland Farm, Plockton (F6)
D15 Doune Broch Centre (B3)
D17 Dun Ardtreck (F4)
D18 Dun Baravat (B3)

D19 Dun Beag (F4)
B18 Dun Bharpa Chambered Cairn (G2)
D20 Dun Borranish (B3)
D21 Dun Bragar (B4)
D23 Dun Carloway (B3)
D25 Dun Fiadhairt (E4)
D27 Dun Grugaig, Elgol (G5)
D26 Dun Grugaig, Glen Elg (G6)
D30 Dun Ringill (G5)
D32 Dun Telve (G6)
D33 Dun Torcuill (E2)
D34 Dun Troddan (G6)
D35 Dun Vulan (F2)
D36 Dun an Sticar (D2)
N94 Duntulm Castle (E4)
N24 Dunvegan Castle (E4)
N26 Eilean Donan Castle (F6)
M2 Fairy Bridge (E4)
Y81 Gairloch Heritage Museum (D6)
V35 Gearrannan Blackhouse Village (B3)
Y83 Giant MacAskill Museum, Dunvegan (E4)
Y85 Glendale Toy Museum (E3)
O5 Glenfinnan Monument (H6)
X21 Glenfinnan Station Museum (H6)
O6 Glenshiel (Kintail and Morvich) (F6)
K74 Howmore Church and Chapels (F2)
S88 Inverewe Garden (D6)
Z8 Isle of Skye Brewing Company (Leann an Eilein) Ltd (E4)
V45 Kenneth MacLeod Harris Tweed Mill (B4)
B26 Kensalyre Cairns (E4)
Y109 Kildonan Museum, Cafe and Crafts (F2)
N118 Kisimul Castle (G2)
V102 Kylerhea Otter Haven (F6)
V48 Lewis Loom Centre, Stornoway (B4)
B29 Lews Castle (B4)
O9 Loch nam Uamh Cairn (H5)

V50 Luib Croft Museum (F5)
Y124 Mallaig Heritage Centre (G5)
O10 Milton (F2)
Y136 Museum nan Eilean, Lionacleit (E2)
Y137 Museum nan Eilean, Stornoway (B4)
V58 Ness Heritage Centre (A5)
C45 Pobull Fhinn Stone Circle (E2)
C46 Pollachar Standing Stone (G2)
G9 Rona (A5)
B39 Rubh' an Dunain Cairn and Dun (G4)
Y172 Seallam! Visitor Centre (D3)
V70 Shawbost Crofting Museum (B4)
V73 Skye Museum of Island Life, Kilmuir (E4)
V74 Skyeskyns, Waternish (E4)
V77 Smithy Heritage Centre, Lochcarron (F6)
K28 St Clement's Church, Rodel (D3)
K103 St Columba's Church (Ui), Aignish (B5)
V78 St Kilda (D1)
K116 St Mary's Chapel, Dunvegan (E4)
K121 St Moluag's Church, Eoropie (A5)
B40 Steinacleit Prehistoric Site (B4)
N147 Strome Castle (F6)
Y188 Taigh Chearsabhagh Museum and Art Centre (E2)
W41 Talisker Distillery (F4)
K134 Teampull na Trionaid (E2)
V112 Torridon (E6)
K137 Trumpan Church (E4)
A24 Tungadale Souterrain (F4)
Y202 Uig Heritage Centre (B3)
B45 Uneval Chambered Cairn (E2)
B47 Vatten Chambered Cairns (F4)

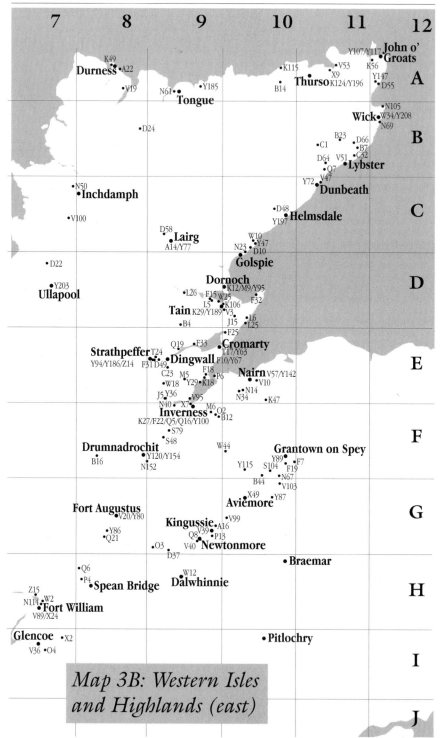

Map 3B: Western Isles
and Highlands (east)

Map 3B

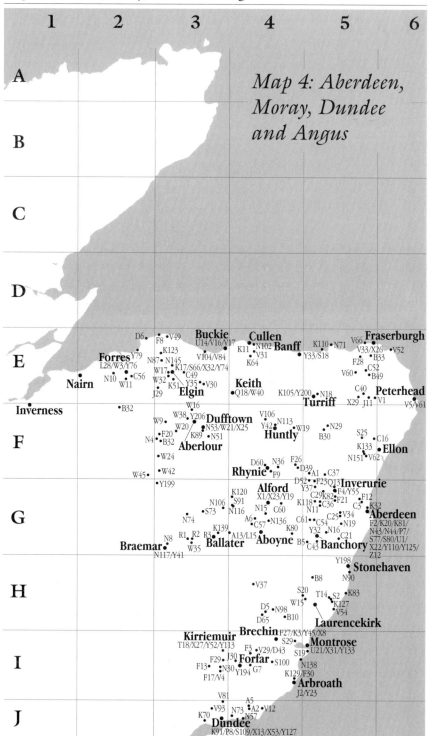

Map 4: Aberdeen, Moray, Dundee and Angus

Map 4

U1 Aberdeen Art Gallery (G5)
F2 Aberdeenshire Council Offices (G5)
V1 Aberdeenshire Farming Museum, Mintlaw (E5)
F3 Aberlemno Sculpted Stones (I4)
C3 Aikey Brae Stone Circle (G5)
Y19 Alford Heritage Centre (G4)
X1 Alford Valley Railway (G4)
V4 Angus Folk Museum (I3)
J2 Arbroath Abbey (I4)
Y23 Arbroath Museum (I4)
S2 Arbuthnott House (H5)
V5 Arbuthnott Museum and Art Gallery, Peterhead (E6)
A1 Archaeolink (F5)
A2 Ardestie Souterrain (J4)
N51 Auchindoun Castle (F3)
N4 Ballindalloch Castle (F3)
R1 Balmoral Castle (F3)
N53 Balvenie Castle (F3)
Y32 Banchory Museum (G5)
Y33 Banff Museum (E4)
V12 Barry Mill, Carnoustie (J4)
Y35 Baxters Highland Village (E3)
Y37 Bennachie Centre, Chapel of Garioch (G5)
W3 Benromach Distillery (E2)
S66 Biblical Garden, Elgin (E3)
K51 Birnie Kirk (E3)
N8 Braemar Castle (G3)
Y41 Braemar Highland Heritage Centre (G3)
Y42 Brander Museum, Huntly (F4)
F4 Brandsbutt Symbol Stone, Inverurie (G5)
K3 Brechin Cathedral (I4)
Y45 Brechin Museum (I4)
N10 Brodie Castle (E2)
N57 Broughty Castle (J4)
D5 Brown Caterthun (H4)
B5 Bucharn Cairn (G5)
V16 Buckie Drifter (E3)
V17 Buckie Fishing Heritage Museum (E3)
D6 Burghead (E2)
B8 Cairn o' Mount (H5)
X8 Caledonian Railway, Brechin (I4)
Y52 Camera Obscura, Kirriemuir (I3)
V93 Camperdown Country Park, Dundee (J3)
S73 Candacraig (G3)
C16 Candle Stone (F5)
B10 Capo Long Barrow (H4)
W9 Cardhu Distillery (F3)
A5 Carlungie Souterrain (J4)
Y55 Carnegie Museum, Inverurie (G5)
N11 Castle Fraser (G5)
N71 Castle of Troup (E5)
N73 Claypotts Castle (J4)
C21 Clune Hill Stone Circle (G5)
N74 Corgarff Castle (G3)
F8 Covesea Caves (E3)
N15 Craigievar Castle (G4)
N16 Crathes Castle (G5)
R2 Crathie Parish Church (G3)
F9 Craw Stane, Rhynie (F4)

S77 Cruickshank Botanic Garden, Aberdeen (G5)
K11 Cullen Collegiate Church (E4)
C25 Cullerlie Stone Circle (G5)
A6 Culsh Souterrain (G4)
W11 Dallas Dhu Distillery (E2)
J11 Deer Abbey (E5)
N18 Delgatie Castle (E5)
K64 Deskford Church (E4)
X13 Discovery Point, Dundee (J3)
N19 Drum Castle (G5)
S18 Duff House, Banff (E4)
N87 Duffus Castle (E3)
D39 Dunnideer (F4)
S19 Dunninald (I5)
N90 Dunnottar Castle (H5)
S80 Duthie Park Winter Gardens, Aberdeen (G5)
F12 Dyce Symbol Stones and Church (G5)
F13 Eassie Sculptured Stone (I3)
C29 Easter Aquorthies Stone Circle (G5)
N98 Edzell Castle (H4)
K17 Elgin Cathedral (E3)
Y74 Elgin Museum (E3)
Y76 Falconer Museum, Forres (E2)
S20 Fasque (H5)
W15 Fettercairn Distillery (H5)
V29 Finavon Doocot (I4)
D43 Finavon Fort (I4)
Y79 Findhorn in Time and Tide (E2)
N102 Findlater Castle (E4)
V30 Fochabers Folk Museum (E3)
V31 Fordyce Joiner's Workshop Visitors Centre (E4)
K70 Fowlis Easter Church (J3)
V33 Fraserburgh Heritage Centre (E5)
N29 Fyvie Castle (F5)
V34 Garlogie Mill Power House Museum (G5)
N30 Glamis Castle (I3)
F17 Glamis Church, Pictish Stone and Well (I3)
W16 Glen Grant Distillery (F3)
W17 Glen Moray Distillery (E3)
N106 Glenbuchat Castle (G3)
W19 Glendronach Distillery (F4)
V37 Glenesk Folk Museum (H4)
W20 Glenfarclas Distillery (F3)
W21 Glenfiddich Distillery (F3)
W24 Glenlivet Distillery (F3)
X22 Glover House, Aberdeen (G5)
P7 Gordon Highlanders Museum, Aberdeen (G5)
X23 Grampian Transport Museum, Alford (G4)
T14 Grassic Gibbon Centre, Arbuthnott (H5)
P8 H M Frigate Unicorn, Dundee (J3)
S25 Haddo House (F5)
Q13 Harlaw Monument, Inverurie (G5)
S29 House of Dun (I4)
N113 Huntly Castle (F4)
F20 Inveravon Church (F3)
T18 J. M. Barrie's Birthplace, Kirriemuir (I3)
X25 Keith and Dufftown Railway (F3)
N116 Kildrummy Castle (G4)
S91 Kildrummy Castle Gardens (G4)
K80 Kincardine O'Neil Old Parish Church (G4)

N117 Kindrochit Castle, Braemar (G3)
Y110 King's College Centre, Aberdeen (G5)
K81 King's College Chapel, Old Aberdeen (G5)
K82 Kinkell Church (G5)
X26 Kinnaird Head Castle, Fraserburgh (E5)
K83 Kinneff Old Parish Church (H5)
L15 Kinord Cross-Slab (G4)
F21 Kintore Carved Stone (G5)
K20 Kirk of St Nicholas, Aberdeen (G5)
X27 Kirriemuir Aviation Museum (I3)
Y113 Kirriemuir: Gateway to the Glens Museum (I3)
C36 Lang Stane o' Craigearn (G5)
N36 Leith Hall (F4)
C37 Loanhead of Daviot Stone Circle (F5)
B30 Logie Newton Cairns (F5)
V49 Lossiemouth Fisheries and Community Museum (E3)
C40 Loudon Hill Stone Circle (E5)
V52 Maggie's Hoosie, Inverallochy (E6)
F23 Maiden Stone, Chapel of Garioch (G5)
B32 Marionburgh Chambered Cairn (F3)
Y125 Marischal Museum, Aberdeen (G5)
X29 Maud Railway Museum (E5)
Y127 McManus Galleries, Dundee (J3)
B33 Memsie Cairn (E5)
C61 Midmar Stone Circle (G5)
V54 Mill of Benholm Visitor Centre (H5)
W32 Miltonduff Distillery (E3)
D52 Mither Tap o' Bennachie (G5)
X31 Montrose Air Station Museum (I5)
Y133 Montrose Museum and Art Gallery (I5)
V104 Moray Firth Wildlife Centre, Spey Bay (E3)
X32 Moray Motor Museum, Elgin (E3)
K89 Mortlach Parish Church (F3)
G7 Nechtansmere Memorial (I4)
A13 New and Old Kinord Prehistoric Settlement (G4)
C43 Nine Stanes Mulloch (G5)
V106 North East Falconry Centre, Cairnie (F4)
V60 Northfield Farm Museum (E5)
R3 Old Royal Station, Ballater (G3)
K91 Old Steeple, Dundee (J3)
N136 Peel Ring of Lumphanan (G4)
U14 Peter Anson Gallery, Buckie (E3)
V61 Peterhead Maritime Heritage (E6)
F26 Picardy Stone, Myreton (F4)
F27 Pictavia, Brechin (I4)
V62 Pitmedden Garden and Museum of Farming Life (F5)

S100 Pitmuies Gardens and Grounds (I4)
J29 Pluscarden Abbey (E3)
N43 Provost Ross's House, Aberdeen (G5)
N44 Provost Skene's House, Aberdeen (G5)
F28 Raven Stone, Tyrie Church (E5)
N138 Red Castle (I4)
J30 Restenneth Priory (I4)
W35 Royal Lochnagar Distillery (G3)
V66 Sandhaven Meal Mill (E5)
Z12 Satrosphere, Aberdeen (G5)
Q18 Scottish Tartans Museum, Keith (E4)
W38 Speyside Cooperage Visitor Centre (F3)
N145 Spynie Palace (E3)
K105 St Congan's Church, Turriff (E5)
K110 St John's Church, Gamrie (E5)
K32 St Machar's Cathedral, Old Aberdeen (G5)
K118 St Mary's Church, Monymusk (G5)
K120 St Mary's Kirk, Auchindour (G4)
F29 St Orland's Stone, Cossans (I3)
K123 St Peter's Church, Duffus (E3)
K127 St Ternan's Church, Arbuthnott (H5)
K129 St Vigeans Church, Arbroath (I4)
F30 St Vigeans Sculpted Stones Museum (I4)
C49 Standing Stones of Urquhart (E3)
W40 Strathisla Distillery (E4)
C52 Strichen Stone Circle (E5)
L28 Sueno's Stone, Forres (E2)
C54 Sunhoney Stone Circle (G5)
W42 Tamnavulin Distillery (F3)
D60 Tap o' Noth Fort (F4)
K133 Tarves Medieval Tomb (F5)
V81 Tealing Doocot and Souterrain (J3)
C56 Templestone Stone Setting (E2)
Y194 The Meffan, Forfar (I4)
Y198 Tolbooth Museum, Stonehaven (H5)
N151 Tolquhon Castle (F5)
W45 Tomintoul Distillery (F2)
Y199 Tomintoul Museum (G3)
C57 Tomnaverie Stone Circle (G4)
V84 Tugnet Ice House (E3)
K139 Tullich Kirk (G3)
Y200 Turriff and District Heritage Society (E5)
S109 University Botanic Garden, Dundee (J3)
X53 Verdant Works, Dundee (J3)
Y206 Village Store, Aberlour (F3)
D65 White Caterthun (H4)
B49 White Cow Wood Cairn (E5)
C60 Whitehill Stone Circle (G4)
U21 William Lamb Memorial Studio, Montrose (I5)

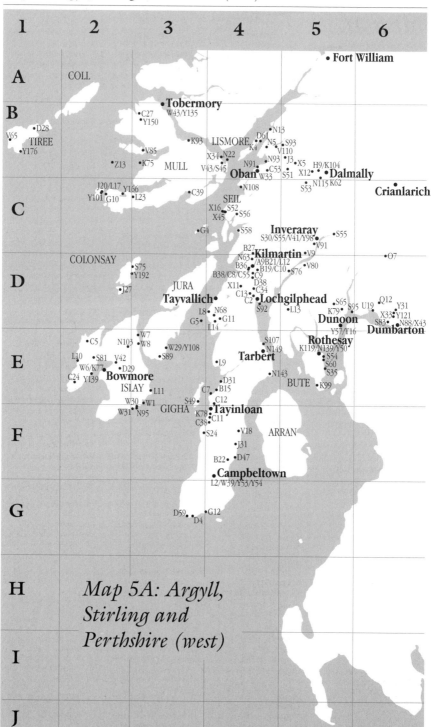

| 1 | 2 | 3 | 4 | 5 | 6 |

A

COLL

• **Fort William**

B

• C27
• Y150
W43/Y135
• **Tobermory**

V65 •
• D28
TIREE
• Y176

• K93
• N13
• D61
LISMORE
• N5
• S93
K4
• V110
• K75
• X34
• N22
V85 •
MULL
V43/S45
• N93
• J3
• X5
H9/K104
• N91
• C53
S51
• X12
• **Dalmally**
• Z13
Oban
W33
S53
• N115 K62

Crianlarich

C

J20/L17
Y166
Y101
G10
• L23
• C39
N108

SEIL

X16
• S52
X45
• S56

• G4
• S58

Inveraray
S30/S55/V41/Y98
• S55
• V91

COLONSAY
• S75
• Y192

B27
N63
• **Kilmartin**
• V9
/A9B21/L12
B36
• B19/C10
• S76
B38/C8/C55
C9
• V80
• O7

D

• J27

JURA
X11
• D38
• C34
Tayvallich
C13
Lochgilphead
C2
• L13
S92

• Q12
S65
• U19
• Y31
K79
• S95
X33
• Y121
Dunoon
S83
• N88/X43
Y57/T16
Dumbarton

L8
• N68
G5
• G11
L14

E

• C5
N103
• W7
• W8
L10 •
• S81
Y42
W6/K77
• D29
C24
• Y139
Bowmore
• W29/Y108
• S89
ISLAY
• L11
W30
• W1
GIGHA
W31
N95
• S49
C7
C12
K78
Tayinloan
C38
• C11

S107
• N149
Tarbert
• L9
• N143

Rothesay
K119/N139/Y50
• S54
• S60
• S35
BUTE
• K99

F

• S24
• V18
ARRAN
• J31

B22
• D47

Campbeltown
L2/W39/Y53/Y54

G

D59 •
• G12
D4

H

*Map 5A: Argyll,
Stirling and
Perthshire (west)*

I

J

Map 5A

S49 Achamore Gardens (E3)
C2 Achnabreck Cup and Ring Marks (D4)
S51 Achnacloich Gardens (B5)
S52 An Cala Garden, Easdale (C4)
S53 Ardanaiseig Gardens (C5)
W1 Ardbeg Distillery (E3)
J3 Ardchattan Priory (B5)
S54 Ardencraig Garden (E5)
S55 Ardkinglas Woodland Garden (C5)
S56 Ardmaddy Castle (C4)
S58 Arduaine Garden (C4)
V91 Argyll Wildlife Park, Inveraray (C5)
S60 Ascog Hall Fernery and Garden (E5)
V9 Auchindrain Township Open Air Museum (C5)
C5 Ballinaby Standing Stones (E2)
Y31 Balloch Castle (D6)
C7 Ballochroy Stone Setting (E4)
C8 Ballygowan Cup and Ring Marks (D4)
C9 Ballymeanoch Standing Stones (D4)
C10 Baluachraig Cup and Ring Marks (D4)
N5 Barcaldine Castle (B4)
C11 Beacharr Standing Stone and Chambered Cairn (F4)
S65 Benmore Botanic Garden (D5)
X5 Bonawe Iron Furnace (B5)
D4 Borgadel Dun (G3)
W6 Bowmore Distillery (E2)
C12 Braids Cup and Ring Marked Stone (E4)
W7 Bunnahabhain Distillery (E3)
Y50 Bute Museum (E5)
C13 Cairnbaan Cup and Ring Marks (D4)
L2 Campbeltown Cross (F4)
Y53 Campbeltown Heritage Centre (F4)
Y54 Campbeltown Museum (F4)
W8 Caol Ila Distillery (E3)
N63 Carnasserie Castle (D4)
V18 Carradale Heritage Centre (F4)
Y57 Castle House Museum, Dunoon (D5)
N13 Castle Stalker (B4)

N68 Castle Sween (D4)
K4 Cathedral of St Moluag and Parish Church, Lismore (B4)
S75 Colonsay House Gardens (D3)
B15 Correchrevie Cairn (E4)
C24 Coultoon Stone Circle (E2)
S76 Crarae Gardens (D5)
X11 Crinan Canal (D4)
X12 Cruachan Power Station (B5)
K62 Dalmally Church (B5)
C27 Dervaig Standing Stones (B3)
N22 Duart Castle (B4)
N88 Dumbarton Castle (D6)
D28 Dun Mor, Vaul (B1)
D29 Dun Nosebridge (E2)
D31 Dun Skeig, Clachan (E4)
D38 Dunadd (D4)
B19 Dunchraigaig Cairn (D4)
N91 Dunollie Castle (B4)
N93 Dunstaffnage Castle (B4)
N95 Dunyvaig Castle (F3)
X16 Easdale Island Folk Museum (C4)
G4 Eileach an Naoimh (C3)
G5 Eilean Mor, South Knapdale (D3)
N103 Finlaggan (E2)
S81 Foreland Walled Garden (E2)
S83 Geilston Garden (D6)
B21 Glebe Cairn, Kilmartin (D4)
Q12 Glen Fruin (D6)
S24 Glenbarr Abbey (F3)
B22 Gort na h'Uilidhe, Glen Lussa (F4)
N108 Gylen Castle (C4)
T16 Highland Mary's Statue, Dunoon (D5)
K75 Inchkenneth Chapel (B3)
S30 Inveraray Castle (C5)
Y98 Inveraray Jail (C5)
V41 Inveraray Maritime Museum (C5)
O7 Inversnaid (D6)
J20 Iona Abbey (C2)
Y101 Iona Heritage Centre (C2)
V42 Islay Woollen Mill, Bridgend (E2)
W29 Isle of Jura Distillery (E3)
V43 Isle of Mull Weavers (B4)
S89 Jura House Walled Garden (E3)
Y108 Jura Parish Church (E3)
L8 Keills Chapel (D4)
K77 Kilarrow (Bowmore) Parish Church (E2)

L9 Kilberry Sculptured Stones (E4)
L10 Kilchoman Cross (E2)
N115 Kilchurn Castle (B5)
L11 Kildalton Cross and Chapel (E3)
D47 Kildonan Dun (F4)
K78 Killean Old Parish Church (F4)
A9 Kilmartin House Museum of Ancient Culture (D4)
L12 Kilmartin Sculpted Stones and Parish Church (D4)
C34 Kilmichael Glassary Cup and Ring Marks (D4)
L13 Kilmodan Sculpted Stones (D5)
S92 Kilmory Castle Gardens (D4)
L14 Kilmory Knap Chapel (D4)
K79 Kilmun Church (D5)
S93 Kinlochlaich House Gardens (B5)
B27 Kintraw Cairns and Standing Stone (C4)
W30 Lagavulin Distillery (F3)
W31 Laphroaig Distillery (F3)
S95 Linn Botanic Gardens, Cove (D5)
H9 Loch Aweside Battle Monument (B5)
C38 Loch Clachaig Cup and Ring Marked Stone (F4)
C39 Lochbuie Stone Circle (C3)
Y121 Lomond Shores, Balloch (D6)
L17 McLean's Cross, Iona (C2)
X33 Motoring Heritage Centre, Alexandria (D6)
S35 Mount Stuart House (E5)
X34 Mull & West Highland Narrow Gauge Railway (B4)
Y135 Mull Museum, Tobermory (B3)
Y139 Museum of Islay Life, Port Charlotte (E2)
B36 Nether Largie Cairns (D4)
W33 Oban Distillery (B4)
Y150 Old Byre Heritage Centre, Dervaig (B3)
J27 Oronsay Priory (D2)
K93 Pennygown Chapel (B3)
L23 Pilgrims Way to Iona (C3)
B38 Ri Cruin Cairn, Kilmartin (D4)
Y166 Ross of Mull Historical Centre, Bunessan (C2)

N139 Rothesay Castle (E5)
J31 Saddell Abbey (F4)
V65 Sandaig Museum, Tiree (B1)
X43 Scottish Maritime Museum – Denny Ship Model Experiment Tank (D6)
V110 Scottish Sealife and Marine Sanctuary, Barcaldine (B4)
X45 Scottish Slate Islands Heritage Trust (C4)
Y176 Skerryvore Museum (B1)
N143 Skipness Castle (E4)
W39 Springbank Distillery (F4)
D59 Sron Uamha Fort (G3)
K99 St Blane's Church, Kingarth (E5)
G10 St Columba Centre, Fionnphort (C2)
G11 St Columba's Cave (D4)
G12 St Columba's Footprint, Keil (G4)
K104 St Conan's Kirk, Lochawe (B5)
K119 St Mary's Church, Rothesay (E5)
Z13 Staffa (B2)
S107 Stonefield Castle Gardens (E4)
V80 Strachur Smiddy Museum (D5)
C53 Strontoiller Cairn and Standing Stones (B4)
N149 Tarbert Castle (E4)
C55 Temple Wood Stone Circles (D4)
Y192 The Gallery, Colonsay and Oronsay Heritage Trust (D3)
U19 The Hill House (D5)
D61 Tirefour Broch (B4)
W43 Tobermory Distillery (B3)
S45 Torosay Castle (B4)
V85 Ulva Heritage Centre (B3)

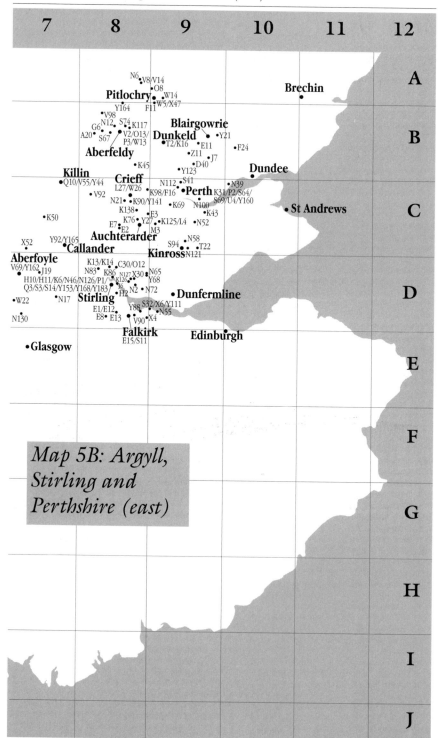

Map 5B: Argyll, Stirling and Perthshire (east)

Map 5B

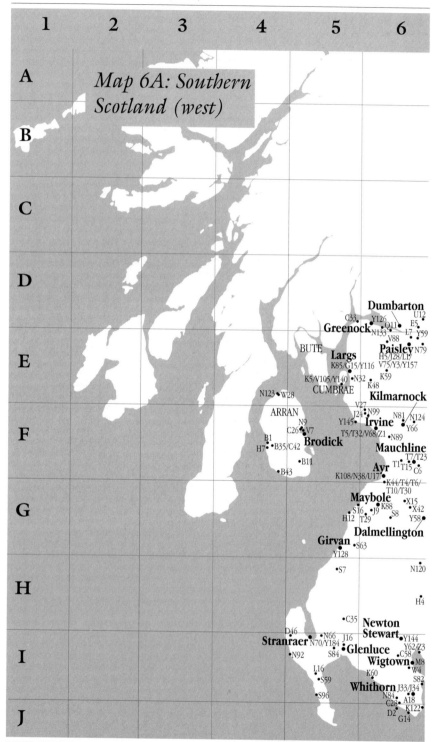

Map 6A: Southern Scotland (west)

Dumbarton

C33 Y126 U12
Greenock Q11 E5
N133 L7 Y59
V88

BUTE Paisley N79
Largs H5/J28/L17
K85/G15/Y116 V75/Y3/Y157
K5/V105/Y140 N32 K59
K48
CUMBRAE
N123 W28 Kilmarnock
V27
ARRAN J24 N99 N81 N124
N9 Y145 Irvine Y66
C26 V7 T5/T32/V68/Z1
B1 Brodick N89
H7 B35/C42
Mauchline
B11 T7/T23
Ayr T1 T15 C6
B43 K108/N38/U17 K44/T4/T6/
T10/T30
Maybole X15
S16 K88 X42
H12 T29 J9 S8 Y58
Dalmellington
Girvan S63
Y128

S7 N120

H4

C35
Newton
D46 N66 Stewart
Stranraer J16 Y144
N70/Y184 Glenluce Y62/Z3
N92 S84 C58
Wigtown M8
L16 W4
S59 K60 S82
Whithorn J33/J34
S96 N84 A18
C28 K122
D2
G14

Map 6A

K44 Alloway Old Kirk (F6)
S59 Ardwell House Gardens (I5)
V7 Arran Heritage Museum (F5)
B1 Auchagallon Cairn (F4)
K48 Auld Kirk of Kilbirnie (E6)
T1 Bachelors' Club, Tarbolton (F6)
C6 Ballochmyle Cup and Ring Marks (F6)
S7 Bardrochat (H5)
S63 Bargany Castle Gardens (G5)
L1 Barochan Cross (E6)
D2 Barsalloch Fort (J6)
E5 Bearsden Roman Bathhouse (D6)
Z1 Big Idea, Irvine (F6)
W4 Bladnoch Distillery (I6)
S8 Blairquhan (G6)
T4 Brig o' Doon, Alloway (F6)
N9 Brodick Castle (F5)
H4 Bruce's Stone, Loch Trool (H6)
T5 Burns Club and Museum, Irvine (F6)
T6 Burns Cottage and Museum, Alloway (F6)
T7 Burns House Museum, Mauchline (F6)
T10 Burns Monument and Gardens, Alloway (F6)
B11 Carn Ban, Arran (F5)
N66 Castle Kennedy (I5)
K59 Castle Semple Collegiate Church (E6)
N70 Castle of St John, Stranraer (I5)
Y58 Cathcartson Visitor Centre (G6)
K5 Cathedral of the Isles, Millport (E5)
K60 Chapel Finian (I6)
Y59 Clydebank Museum (E6)
Y3 Coats Observatory, Paisley (E6)
Y62 Creetown Exhibition Centre (I6)
Z3 Creetown Gem Rock Museum (I6)
N79 Crookston Castle (E6)
J9 Crossraguel Abbey (G6)

S16 Culzean Castle (G5)
V27 Dalgarven Mill Museum (F6)
N81 Dean Castle (F6)
C26 Deer Park Standing Stones (F5)
Y66 Dick Institute Museum and Art Galleries, Kilmarnock (F6)
N84 Druchtag Motte (I6)
C28 Drumtroddan (I6)
X15 Dunaskin Experience (G6)
N89 Dundonald Castle (F6)
N92 Dunskey Castle (I5)
N99 Eglinton Castle and Country Park (F6)
H5 Elderslie Wallace Monument (E6)
Q11 Finlaystone House (D6)
S82 Galloway House Gardens, Garlieston (I6)
J16 Glenluce Abbey (I5)
S84 Glenwhan Garden (I5)
T15 Highland Mary's Monument, Failford (F6)
L7 Inchinnan Early Christian Stones (E6)
W28 Isle of Arran Distillery (E4)
N32 Kelburn Castle (E5)
C33 Kempock Stone, Gourock (D5)
D46 Kemp's Walk Fort (I5)
J24 Kilwinning Abbey (F6)
H7 King's Cave, Drumadroon (F4)
L16 Kirkmadrine Early Christian Stones (I5)
C35 Laggangairn Standing Stones (H5)
Y116 Largs Museum (E5)
K85 Largs Old Kirk (E5)
U12 Lillie Art Gallery, Milngavie (D6)
N120 Loch Doon Castle (H6)
N123 Lochranza Castle (E4)
S96 Logan Botanic Garden (I5)
N124 Loudoun Castle (F6)
N38 Loudoun Hall, Ayr (F6)
C42 Machrie Moor Stone Circles (F4)
K88 Maybole Collegiate Church (G6)
Y126 McLean Museum and Art Gallery, Greenock (D6)

Y128 Mckechnie Institute, Girvan (G5)
B35 Moss Farm Road Cairn (F4)
V105 Museum and Marine Biological Station, Millport (E5)
Y140 Museum of the Cumbraes (E5)
T23 National Burns Memorial Tower, Mauchline (F6)
N133 Newark Castle (D6)
Y144 Newton Stewart Museum (I6)
Y145 North Ayrshire Museum, Saltcoats (F5)
J28 Paisley Abbey (E6)
Y157 Paisley Museum and Art Galleries (E6)
A18 Rispain Camp (I6)
U17 Rozelle House Galleries and Gardens, Ayr (F6)
X42 Scottish Industrial Railway Centre, Burnton (G6)
V68 Scottish Maritime Museum, Irvine (F6)
V75 Sma' Shot Cottages, Paisley (E6)
T29 Souter Johnnie's Cottage, Kirkoswald (G6)
K108 St John the Baptist's Church, Ayr (F6)
G14 St Ninian's Cave, Physgill (J6)
K122 St Ninian's Chapel, Isle of Whithorn (J6)
Y184 Stranracr Museum (I5)
T30 Tam o'Shanter Experience, Alloway (F6)
C58 Torhouse Stone Circle (I6)
B43 Torrylinn Cairn (F4)
H12 Turnberry Castle (G5)
T32 Vennel Gallery, Irvine (F6)
G15 Vikingar, Largs (E5)
V88 Weaver's Cottage, Kilbarchan (E6)
J33 Whithorn Priory (I6)
J34 Whithorn: Cradle of Christianity in Scotland (I6)
M8 Wigtown Martyrs' Monument (I6)

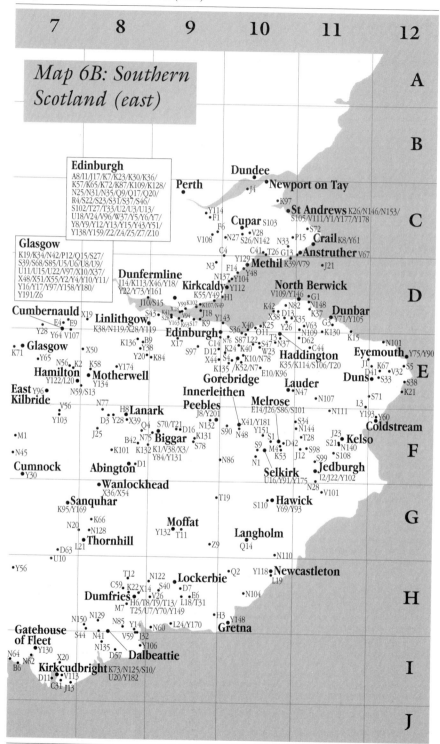

Map 6B: Southern Scotland (east)

Edinburgh
A8/I1/J17/K7/K23/K30/K36/
K57/K65/K72/K87/K109/K128/
N25/N31/N35/Q9/Q17/Q20/
R4/S22/S23/S31/S37/S46/
S102/T27/T33/U2/U3/U13/
U18/V24/V96/W37/Y5/Y6/Y7/
Y8/Y9/Y12/Y13/Y15/Y43/Y51/
Y138/Y159/Z2/Z4/Z5/Z7/Z10

Glasgow
K19/K34/N42/P12/Q15/S27/
S39/S68/S85/U5/U6/U8/U9/
U11/U15/U22/V97/X10/X37/
X48/X51/X55/Y2/Y4/Y10/Y11/
Y16/Y17/Y97/Y158/Y180/
Y191/Z6

Dundee
Perth • J4 • **Newport on Tay**
• K97
• Y114 **St Andrews** K26/N146/N153/
• F1 **Cupar** S103 S105/V111/Y1/Y177/Y178
F6 • S72
V108 • N27 V28 N33 P15 **Crail** K8/Y61
C4 S26/N142
C41 T26 G13 **Anstruther** V67
N137 Y129 F14 • **Methil** K39/V79 • J21
N3 Y48 Y104
N157 • Y112 **North Berwick**
Dunfermline **Kirkcaldy** V109/Y146 • G1
J14/K113/X46/Y18/ K55/Y49 H1 K42 • N82 N148
Y22/Y73/Y161 J10/S15 Y99 K102 K107/N49 K37 **Dunbar**
Cumbernauld X19 S43 K41 S28 J18 X38 D13 V63 Y71/Y105
• E4 • E9 Y163 K63 S17 K9 S36 X40 K25 Y26 N109 • K130
Y28 Y64 V107 **Linlithgow** Y143 X17 C14 N37 • D62 K15
• **Glasgow** K38/N119/X28/Y119 **Edinburgh** N6 S87 L22 S47 T3 • C44 • N101
K71 K136 B9 D12 K24 K40 W23 **Haddington** **Eyemouth** Y75/Y90
• Y65 N56 K2 K58 • X50 Y38 S97 X44 S4 K10/N78 K35/K114/S106/T20 J1 • K67 V32 S5
Hamilton • Y174 Y20 K84 K135 K52/N7 E10/K96 **Duns** • S33 S38
Y122/L20 • **Motherwell** • Y134 **Gorebridge** **Lauder** L3 • S71 K21
East Y96 N59/S13 **Innerleithen** N47 • N107 • S71 Y193 Y60
Kilbride • Y56 N77 **Peebles** **Melrose** N111 **Coldstream**
Y103 H8 **Lanark** J8/Y201 E14/J26/S86/S101 S34 **Kelso**
D3 Y28 • X39 Q4 S70/T21 D16 N132 X41/Y181 N144 J23
J25 B42 N75 **Biggar** K131 S90 Y151 S1 T28 S21 N140
• M1 K101 K132 K1/V38/X3/ S78 S9 M4 D42 J12 S98 S108
• N45 Y84/Y131 N86 N1 K53 **Jedburgh**
Cumnock **Abington** • D1 **Selkirk** I2/J22/Y102
• Y30 U16/Y91/Y175 N28
Wanlockhead • V101
X36/X54 • T19 • **Hawick**
• **Sanquhar** S110 Y69/Y93
K95/Y169 • K66
N20 • N128 **Moffat**
• **Thornhill** Y132 • T11 **Langholm**
• D63 L21 • Z9 Q14
• U10 • N110
• Y56
T12 N122 **Lockerbie** • Q2 Y118 • **Newcastleton**
C59 K22 X14 • S40 • D7 L19
Dumfries • V26 E6 • N104
M7 H6/T8/T9/T13/ L18/T31
T25/U7/V70/Y149
N150 N129 N85 Y14 H3 Y148
Gatehouse S44 N41 V59 J32 N60 L24/Y170 **Gretna**
of Fleet N135 • Y106
N64 • Y130 X20 D57 **Dalbeattie**
B6 N62 **Kirkcudbright** K73/N125/S10/
D11 V113 U20/Y182
C31 J13

Map 6B

Index

Index

Notes

THE **WEE GUIDE** TO SCOTLAND